*ARMY LINEAGE SERIES*

# MANEUVER AND FIREPOWER
The Evolution of Divisions and Separate Brigades

*by*
*John B. Wilson*

*CENTER OF MILITARY HISTORY*
*UNITED STATES ARMY*
*WASHINGTON, D.C., 1998*

**Library of Congress Cataloging-in-Publication Data**

Wilson, John B., 1934–
  Maneuver and firepower : the evolution of divisions and separate brigades / by John B. Wilson.
    p.  cm.
  Army lineage series
  Includes bibliographical references and index.
  1. United States. Army–Organization–History. I. Center of Military History. II. Title.
UA25.W554  1997
355.3'0973—DC20                                94–21031
                                                  CIP

CMH Pub 60–14

First Printing

---

For sale by the U.S. Government Printing Office
Superintendent of Documents, Mail Stop: SSOP, Washington, DC 20402-9328
ISBN 0-16-049571-7

# ARMY LINEAGE SERIES

Jeffrey J. Clarke, General Editor

*Advisory Committee*
(As of September 1997)

| | |
|---|---|
| Joseph T. Glatthaar<br>University of Houston | Michael J. Kurtz<br>National Archives and Records Administration |
| Raymond A. Callahan<br>University of Delaware | Brig. Gen. Fletcher M. Lamkin, Jr.<br>U.S. Military Academy |
| Maj. Gen. James J. Cravens, Jr.<br>U.S. Army Training and Doctrine Command | Carol A. Reardon<br>Pennsylvania State University |
| Carlo W. D'Este<br>New Seabury, Mass. | Col. Everett L. Roper, Jr.<br>U.S. Army War College |
| George C. Herring, Jr.<br>University of Kentucky | Mark A. Stoler<br>University of Vermont |
| Brig. Gen. Joseph R. Inge<br>U.S. Army Command and General Staff College | Lt. Gen. Frederick E. Vollrath<br>Archivist of the Army |

Gerhard L. Weinberg
University of North Carolina

*U.S. Army Center of Military History*

Brig. Gen. John W. Mountcastle, Chief of Military History

| | |
|---|---|
| Chief Historian | Jeffrey J. Clarke |
| Chief, Field Programs and Historical Services Division | John T. Greenwood |
| Editor in Chief | John W. Elsberg |

# Foreword

This work traces the evolution of two unique U.S. Army organizations—divisions and brigades—which combined combat arms, combat support, and combat service support units into well-oiled engines for war. The Army has used divisions for over two hundred and twenty years on the battlefield and for nearly eighty years has maintained them in peacetime as well. Separate combined arms brigades, a newer phenomenon, date to the 1960s. Both organizations have played a pivotal role in the American military experience, and their exploits form the core of the Army's history in the twentieth century.

The following study is a systematic account of the way these two organizations evolved, highlighting the rationales behind that evolution and the many factors that played a part in bringing those changes into reality. This book will also complement the forthcoming revised edition of *Armies, Corps, Divisions, and Separate Brigades*, a volume in the Army Lineage Series.

In this work the reader, whether military or civilian, can follow the development of two of the Army's complex organizations. Force planners today will find the challenges faced by their predecessors in making these institutions responsive to an ever-changing threat in an evolving political and technological environment highly relevant. By telling this story in a comprehensive manner, the volume makes a significant contribution to the history of the Army.

Washington, D.C.  
2 February 1998

JOHN W. MOUNTCASTLE  
Brigadier General, USA  
Chief of Military History

# The Author

John B. Wilson was born and grew up in Imperial, Pennsylvania. He is a graduate of Duquesne University, receiving a B.A. degree in history in 1963 and an M.A. degree in American history in 1966. He joined the Organizational History Branch, Center of Military History, in 1968 and served there until he retired in 1997. He compiled *Armies, Corps, Divisions, and Separate Brigades* in the Army Lineage Series and is the author of several articles on the organizations of divisions and separate brigades.

# Preface

This volume examines the evolution of divisions and separate brigades in the U.S. Army as it searched for the most effective way to fuse combat arms, combat support, and service units into combined arms teams. The Army has used divisions and brigades since the colonial era, but the national leadership did not provide for their permanency in the force until the twentieth century. When divisions became a part of the standing force, experiences on American battlefields in the eighteenth and nineteenth centuries, as well as European military practices, shaped their organization. The permanent divisions and brigades that the Army organized, however, were uniquely American.

At the beginning of the seventeenth century armies had no permanent tactical subdivisions. Administrative organizations called "regiments" were primarily designed to bring armed men to the battlefield. Upon arriving at the battle site, the men were usually grouped into battalions or squadrons, tactical organizations. King Gustavus Adolphus of Sweden established brigades during the Thirty Years War as tactical organizations, assigning several battalions to them for the duration of a campaign, an arrangement that minimized the necessity for regrouping or retraining his army before going into battle. Shortly thereafter, other nations adopted the Swedish example.

The size of armies increased by the early eighteenth century, and Frederick the Great of Prussia began dividing his army into columns, which marched as wings or lines that fell into a prearranged order on the battlefield. Such maneuvers required discipline and well-drilled troops. To overcome the Prussians, Marshal Maurice de Saxe of France reintroduced the cadence step, which had fallen into disuse, and stressed discipline to control an army on the march and in combat. By marching troops at a measured step, Maurice could judge the time required to move his army to engage an enemy. With the ability to calculate marching time, Marshal Victor F. Broglie in the mid-1700s began dividing the French Army into several permanent columns or divisions of infantry and artillery for a campaign. These divisions made an army easier to maneuver and occasionally permitted him to use part of it as an independent force. Almost two hundred years later Basil Liddell Hart described that process as making a limbless army grow arms that could grip an enemy at different points while others struck him.

During the seventeenth and eighteenth centuries European military theorists incorporated the doctrine for organizing divisions and brigades into their publications, and many of those works were known to military leaders in colonial America. The British Army also brought European methods of war to North America before the Revolutionary War, and the colonists adopted much of that practice and doctrine in developing their own divisions and brigades as command and control units.

Against this background, Chapter 1 surveys the types of brigades and divisions the Army employed in the various wars of the eighteenth and nineteenth centuries. These units and the doctrine underlying them were the basis for organizing and maintaining permanent divisions and brigades in the twentieth century. Chapters 2 through 14 trace the evolution of United States Army divisions and separate brigades from approximately 1900 to 1990. Their various reorganizations and their roles in the total Army are the grist of the study. Chapter 15 draws together some of the lessons explored in the main body of the volume. Since the manuscript was prepared seven years ago momentous changes have ocurred in the Army, and a brief look forward examines some of them.

The word "division" over the years has had many meanings within the Army, as well as within the other military services. As used in this study, the term addresses only a large, combined arms team capable of independent operations. But an integral part of the story is also the development of the "brigade," initially a command and control headquarters for two or more regiments or battalions from the same arm or branch. In the mid-twentieth century the brigade evolved into a combined arms unit smaller than a division. The combined arms brigade, although a relatively new structure, is also a subject of this study.

A few words need to be said about the charts and tables in the volume. Tables of organization and equipment (TOE) published for divisions and separate brigades and their subordinate elements served as the skeleton for the study, and the charts were derived from them. No one table, however, contains all the information that appears in each chart. Therefore, to develop each chart, I began with the largest unit, such as the division, and compiled the data for each subordinate element down to and including company, troops, battery, or detachment. The charts, nevertheless, represent only windows in time, for the organizations constantly changed. The tables listing divisions and brigades, their location, maneuver elements, and other information were also drawn from many sources. Hence, they are not attributed to any particular work or document.

Many colleagues have served as mentors in the research and writing of this manuscript. To name everyone who assisted in the work is impossible, but key supporters in the Center of Military History have been Morris J. MacGregor, Acting Chief Historian of the center in 1989–90; Dr. David Trask, former Chief Historian; and Lt. Col. Clayton R. Newell, former Chief, Historical Services Division. I am also indebted to Col. Raymond K. Bluhm, Colonel Newell's successor, who read the manuscript and offered insightful suggestions, and to Dr. John T. Greenwood, who arranged space and support for me within the center after I retired to complete the work. Janice E. McKenney, Chief, Organizational

History Branch, read, commented on, and edited numerous versions of each chapter, and Romana M. Danysh from the Organizational History Branch read and commented on the work and listened to endless hours of discussion about the scope and presentation of the material. Rebecca Robbins Raines, Donna Everett, and Edward Bedessem, all currently assigned to the Organizational History Branch, assisted in defining ideas and the relationships of arms, support, and service units to divisions and separate brigades.

Outside the branch but within the center, Dr. Edward Drea, former Chief, Historical Research and Analysis Division, offered invaluable help in clarifying the ideas presented. Maj. Glenn Hawkins and Dr. Edgar F. Raines read sections of the manuscript and forced close examination of some of its basic assumptions. Dr. Robert K. Wright, Chief, Historical Resources Branch, offered suggestions for organizing and presenting the material. Over the years the center's library staff, especially James Knight, offered indispensable help in locating books and articles and completing citations in the notes and bibliography. Geraldine Harcarik from the Historical Resources Branch cheerfully searched for countless documents in the center's archival holdings.

No serious historical work about the Army can be accomplished without drawing on holdings of the U.S. Army Military History Institute at Carlisle Barracks, Pennsylvania. The staff there was a steady source of help. In particular, John Slonaker, Dennis Vetock, and Louise Arnold-Friend always found time to stop during a busy day to respond to my requests for documents, books, and articles. They gladly shared their knowledge of Army organization, suggesting works that might not have come to my attention. Another individual in the historical community who shared his knowledge about the Army was John L. Romjue of the U.S. Army Training and Doctrine Command.

The preparation of the volume for publication has also been the result of the efforts of many people. I would like to express my appreciation to Susan Carroll, who edited the manuscript and prepared the index; Joycelyn M. Canery, who typed the final text; Beth F. MacKenzie, who designed the charts and obtained and placed the photographs; John A. Birmingham, who created the pages and designed the cover; and Sherry Dowdy who created the maps. I am particularly appreciative of the work of Catherine A. Heerin, who oversaw the editorial process, and Arthur S. Hardyman, who saw the production effort to fruition.

Many have contributed to the completion of this work by their knowledge, advice, cooperation, and encouragement—and to all of them I owe a debt of gratitude. For any and all errors of fact or interpretation, I am responsible.

Washington, D.C.  JOHN B. WILSON
2 February 1998

# Contents

| Chapter | Page |
|---|---|
| 1. EARLY EXPERIENCES | 3 |
|    *Revolutionary War* | 3 |
|    *War of 1812* | 7 |
|    *Mexican War* | 10 |
|    *Civil War* | 12 |
|    *War With Spain* | 16 |
| 2. GENESIS OF PERMANENT DIVISIONS | 23 |
|    *Reforms Following the War With Spain* | 23 |
|    *Concentration on the Mexican Border in 1911* | 29 |
|    *The Stimson Plan* | 31 |
|    *Operations on the Mexican Border, 1913–1917* | 34 |
|    *Authorization of Permanent Divisions* | 37 |
| 3. THE TEST—WORLD WAR I | 47 |
|    *First Revisions* | 47 |
|    *The Baker Board and Pershing's Staff Organizational Study* | 52 |
|    *Plans To Organize More Divisions* | 55 |
|    *Organizing the Divisions* | 58 |
|    *Expansion of the Divisional Forces* | 65 |
|    *Divisional Changes* | 67 |
| 4. THE AFTERMATH OF WORLD WAR I | 79 |
|    *Occupation and Demobilization* | 79 |
|    *The AEF Evaluates World War I Divisional Organizations* | 83 |
|    *Development of Divisions Under the 1920 National Defense Act* | 86 |
|    *Reorganization of Divisions* | 97 |
| 5 A RETURN TO THE PAST; A LOOK TO THE FUTURE | 109 |
|    *Paper Divisions* | 109 |
|    *Reserve Divisions* | 115 |
|    *More Realistic Mobilization Plans* | 117 |
|    *Motorization and Mechanization* | 120 |
|    *A New Infantry Division* | 125 |
|    *A New Cavalry Division* | 133 |

| Chapter | Page |
|---|---|
| 6. PRELUDE TO COMBAT | 143 |
|     Infantry and Cavalry Divisions Revisited | 143 |
|     Organizing Armored Divisions | 147 |
|     Mobilization of National Guard Units | 152 |
|     Expanding Divisional Forces | 154 |
|     Reorganization of the National Guard Divisions | 158 |
|     Another Reorganization | 160 |
|     Increases in the Force Structure | 169 |
| 7. THE CRUCIBLE—COMBAT | 179 |
|     Wartime Reorganization, 1943 | 179 |
|     Light Divisions | 187 |
|     Expanding Divisional Forces: Meeting the Troop Basis | 190 |
|     Deployment and More Organizational Changes | 193 |
|     Correcting Organizational Problems | 196 |
|     Redeployment | 199 |
| 8. AN INTERLUDE OF PEACE | 207 |
|     Demobilization, Occupation, and the General Reserve | 207 |
|     Reorganization of Reserve Divisions | 213 |
|     Postwar Divisional Organizations | 222 |
|     The State of Divisional Forces | 229 |
| 9. THE KOREAN WAR AND ITS AFTERMATH | 239 |
|     Deployment of Forces to Korea | 239 |
|     Rebuilding the General Reserve | 242 |
|     Organizational Trends | 247 |
|     Readjustment of Divisional Forces | 250 |
|     Improving the Reserves | 254 |
| 10. THE SEARCH FOR ATOMIC AGE DIVISIONS | 263 |
|     Exploring Alternative Divisions | 263 |
|     Pentomic Divisions | 270 |
|     Reorganization of the Divisions | 279 |
|     Evaluating ROCID and ROCAD | 281 |
| 11. A NEW DIRECTION—FLEXIBLE RESPONSE | 291 |
|     MOMAR-I | 291 |
|     The Development of ROAD | 293 |
|     ROAD Delayed | 303 |
|     The ROAD Reorganization | 308 |
|     Airmobility | 314 |
| 12. FLEXIBLE RESPONSE | 323 |
|     The Buildup of the Army | 323 |

| Chapter | Page |
|---|---|
| *Expansion of the Force* | 330 |
| *Organizational Changes to Units in Vietnam* | 333 |
| *Divisions and Brigades in Other Commands* | 336 |
| *Retrenchment* | 341 |
| 13. THE TOTAL ARMY | 353 |
| *The 21-Division, 21-Brigade Force* | 353 |
| *A New Force—Greater Integration of Regulars and Reserves* | 364 |
| 14. A NEW ASSESSMENT | 379 |
| *The Division Restructuring Study* | 379 |
| *Division-86* | 383 |
| *Elusive Light Divisions* | 390 |
| *The Army of Excellence* | 391 |
| *A New Direction* | 403 |
| 15. CONCLUSION | 413 |
| A LOOK FORWARD | 421 |
| BIBLIOGRAPHICAL NOTE | 427 |
| INDEX | 445 |

## Tables

| No. | Page |
|---|---|
| 1. National Guard Infantry Divisions, 1914 | 32 |
| 2. National Guard Infantry Divisions, 1917 | 40 |
| 3. Geographic Distribution of National Guard Divisions, World War I | 59 |
| 4. Geographic Distribution of National Army Divisions, World War I | 61 |
| 5. Expansion of Divisional Forces, 1918 | 66 |
| 6. Deployment of Divisions to France | 70 |
| 7. Demobilization of Divisions | 82 |
| 8. Distribution of Regular Army Divisions and Brigades, 1922 | 100 |
| 9. Allotment of Reserve Component Infantry Divisions, 1921 | 102 |
| 10. Allotment of Reserve Component Cavalry Divisions, 1921 | 103 |
| 11. Allotment of National Guard Cavalry Brigades, 1927 | 116 |
| 12. Divisions Active on 7 December 1941 | 157 |
| 13. Divisions Activated or Ordered Into Active Military Service in 1942 | 171 |
| 14. Divisions Activated in 1943 | 192 |

| No. | | Page |
|---|---|---|
| 15. | Deployment of Divisions to the Pacific Theater | 194 |
| 16. | Deployment of Divisions to the European Theater | 195 |
| 17. | Status of Divisions, 1 June 1946 | 209 |
| 18. | Location of National Guard Divisions, Post–World War II | 216 |
| 19. | Location of Organized Reserve Corps Divisions, Post–World War II | 220 |
| 20. | Divisions Designated as Training Centers, 1947–50 | 222 |
| 21. | Combat Divisions on Active Duty During the Korean War | 244 |
| 22. | Regular Army Training Divisions, 1950–56 | 245 |
| 23. | Operation GYROSCOPE | 253 |
| 24. | Maneuver Element Mix of Divisions: ROAD Reorganization, 30 June 1965 | 310 |
| 25. | Maneuver Element Mix of Brigades: ROAD Reorganization, 30 June 1965. | 313 |
| 26. | Divisions and Brigades: Selected Reserve Force, 1965 | 329 |
| 27. | Deployment of Divisions and Brigades to Vietnam | 333 |
| 28. | Maneuver Elements Assigned to Divisions and Brigades in Vietnam, 30 June 1969 | 336 |
| 29. | Maneuver Element Mix of Divisions and Brigades on Active Duty Outside Vietnam, 30 June 1969 | 339 |
| 30. | National Guard Divisions and Brigades, 1968 | 340 |
| 31. | Redeployment of Divisions and Brigades From Vietnam | 345 |
| 32. | The 21-Division Force, June 1974 | 362 |
| 33. | The 21-Brigade Force, June 1974 | 363 |
| 34. | Round-out Units, 1978 | 365 |
| 35. | The 24-Division Force, 1978 | 368 |
| 36. | The 24-Brigade Force, 1978 | 369 |
| 37. | Divisions, 1989 | 404 |
| 38. | Brigades, 1989 | 406 |
| 39. | Divisions and Brigades in Southwest Asia, 1990–91 | 407 |

# Charts

| No. | | Page |
|---|---|---|
| 1. | Infantry Division, 1917 | 39 |
| 2. | Cavalry Division, 1917 | 41 |
| 3. | Infantry Division, 24 May 1917 | 50 |
| 4. | Infantry Division, 8 August 1917 | 56 |
| 5. | Infantry Division, 7 October 1920 | 93 |
| 6. | Cavalry Division, 4 April 1921 | 96 |
| 7. | Cavalry Division, 1928 | 114 |

| No. | | Page |
|---|---|---|
| 8. | The Mechanized Force, 1928 | 124 |
| 9. | Proposed Infantry Division, 30 July 1936 | 128 |
| 10. | Infantry Division (Peace), 1939, Corrected to 8 January 1940 | 134 |
| 11. | Cavalry Division, 1938 | 136 |
| 12. | Infantry Division, 1 November 1940 | 146 |
| 13. | Cavalry Division, 1 November 1940 | 148 |
| 14. | Armored Division, 15 November 1940 | 151 |
| 15. | Infantry Division, 1 August 1942 | 162 |
| 16. | Armored Division, 1 March 1942 | 164 |
| 17. | Motorized Division, 1 August 1942 | 165 |
| 18. | Airborne Division, 15 October 1942 | 168 |
| 19. | Infantry Division, 15 July 1943 | 183 |
| 20. | Armored Division, 15 September 1943 | 186 |
| 21. | Light Division, 1943 | 189 |
| 22. | Airborne Division, 1944 | 197 |
| 23. | Infantry Division, 7 July 1948 | 226 |
| 24. | Armored Division, 8 October 1948 | 228 |
| 25. | Airborne Division, 1 April 1950 | 230 |
| 26. | Atomic Field Army Infantry Division, 30 September 1954 | 266 |
| 27. | Atomic Field Army Armored Division, 30 September 1954 | 268 |
| 28. | PENTANA Division | 273 |
| 29. | Airborne Division (ROTAD), 10 August 1956 | 275 |
| 30. | Infantry Division (ROCID), 21 December 1956 | 278 |
| 31. | Armored Division (ROCAD), 1956 | 280 |
| 32. | Pentomic Infantry Division, 1 February 1960 | 283 |
| 33. | Training Division, 1 April 1959 | 285 |
| 34. | Medium Division (MOMAR), 1960 | 294 |
| 35. | Heavy Division (MOMAR), 1960 | 295 |
| 36. | ROAD Division Base, 1961 | 299 |
| 37. | Airborne Division, 1961 | 301 |
| 38. | Airborne Brigade, 1961 | 302 |
| 39. | Howze Board—Air Assault Division, 1963 | 315 |
| 40. | Airmobile Division, 10 July 1965 | 317 |
| 41. | Training Division, 1966 | 342 |
| 42. | TRICAP Division | 358 |
| 43. | Training Division, 1970 | 371 |
| 44. | Heavy Division, Division Restructuring Study, 1 March 1977 | 381 |
| 45. | Heavy Division (Tank Heavy) as Briefed to General Meyer on 18 October 1979 | 385 |
| 46. | Heavy Division, 1 October 1982 | 388 |

| No. | | Page |
|---|---|---|
| 47. | Light Division, 1 October 1985 | 394 |
| 48. | Airborne Division, 1 April 1987 | 398 |
| 49. | Air Assault Division, 1 April 1987 | 399 |

## Maps

| No. | | Page |
|---|---|---|
| 1. | Corps Areas in the United States, 20 August 1920 | 88 |
| 2. | Field Armies in the United States, 1932 | 118 |
| 3. | Field Armies in the United States, Post–World War II | 218 |

## Illustrations

| | Page |
|---|---|
| *Soldiers of the American Revolution, Trenton, December 26, 1776* | 4 |
| Bvt. Lt. Gen. Winfield Scott | 8 |
| The Battle of Palo Alto | 11 |
| Camp Humphreys, Virginia, 1863 | 15 |
| Staff of the 2d Division, I Army Corps, 1898 | 17 |
| Camp Alger, Virginia, 1898 | 18 |
| The Public Views the 1904 Maneuvers, Manassas, Virginia | 26 |
| Troops Pass in Review, 1904 Manassas Maneuvers | 26 |
| Maj. Gen. Henry C. Corbin and Col. Arthur L. Wagner | 27 |
| Maj. Gen. J. Franklin Bell | 29 |
| 27th Infantry, 2d Division, Encampment, Texas City, Texas | 35 |
| 4th South Dakota Infantry, San Benito, Texas, 1916 | 36 |
| Maj. Gen. Hugh L. Scott | 48 |
| Maj. Gen. Tasker H. Bliss | 49 |
| 16th Infantry, 1st Division, Parades in Paris, 1917 | 51 |
| The Gondrecourt, France, Training Area | 51 |
| Officers of the American Expeditionary Forces and the Baker Mission | 53 |
| Draftees Drill in Civilian Clothes, Camp Upton, New York | 62 |
| Camp Meade, Maryland, 1917 | 63 |
| 165th Infantry, 42d Division, in Trenches, 1918 | 69 |
| Traffic Congestion in the Argonne, 1918 | 72 |
| American Occupation Troops Cross the Rhine at Coblenz, Germany, 1919 | 80 |
| 1st Field Artillery Brigade, 1st Division, on Occupation Duty in Germany, 1919 | 81 |
| 5th Field Artillery Troops at the 1st Division Parade, Washington, D.C., 1919 | 84 |

| | |
|---|---|
| Superior Board Members, 1919 | 86 |
| 26th Division Parade, Fort Devens, Massachusetts, 1925 | 110 |
| Maj. Gen. Charles P. Summerall | 111 |
| Officers Quarters, Fort Sam Houston, Texas, 1925 | 113 |
| 1st Cavalry Division Maneuvers, 1927 | 113 |
| Medium Armored Car of the Mechanized Force, 1931 | 123 |
| General Malin Craig | 127 |
| General George C. Marshall | 133 |
| 1st Cavalry Division Maneuvers, Toyahvale, Texas, 1938 | 135 |
| 67th Infantry (Provisional Tank Brigade) at Third Army Maneuvers, 1940 | 144 |
| 37-mm. Gun and Crew, 1941 | 145 |
| Brig. Gen. Adna R. Chaffee | 149 |
| Half-Track Personnel Car, 1941 | 152 |
| Tanks of the 68th Armored, 2d Armored Division, at the Louisiana Maneuvers, 1941 | 155 |
| Provisional Tank Destroyer Battalion, Fort Meade, Maryland, 1941 | 156 |
| Lt. Gen. Walter C. Short Reviews the Hawaiian Division, 1941 | 158 |
| Camp Shelby, Mississippi, 1941 | 160 |
| Paratroopers in a Special Demonstration, Fort Belvoir, Virginia, 1941 | 167 |
| Lt. Gen. Lesley J. McNair | 181 |
| General McNair and Maj. Gen. Elbridge G. Chapman Inspect 13th Airborne Division Troops, 1944 | 191 |
| 8th Infantry Division Arrives at Hampton Roads, Virginia, Port of Embarkation, 1945 | 200 |
| 41st Infantry Division Departs the Philippines, 1945 | 208 |
| 7th Infantry Division Band, Seoul, Korea, 1945 | 211 |
| 350th Infantry, 88th Infantry Division, Parades in Gorizia, Italy, 1945 | 221 |
| A Final Parade in Gorizia, Prior to the 88th Division's Departure, 1947 | 231 |
| 82d Airborne Division Troops at the New York City Victory Parade, 1946 | 231 |
| Elements of the 2d Infantry Division Near Wonju, Korea, 1951 | 241 |
| 40th Infantry Division Troops Prepare To Replace the 24th Division, 1952 | 246 |
| 4th Infantry Division Leaves New York for Germany, 1951 | 247 |
| 3.5-inch Rocket Launcher in Action Against the North Koreans, 1950 | 248 |
| M41 Light Tank Bound for the 705th Tank Battalion, 1954 | 249 |
| 37th Infantry Division Troops Pass in Review, 1954 | 251 |

| | |
|---|---|
| General Matthew B. Ridgway | 265 |
| General Maxwell D. Taylor | 270 |
| 101st Airborne Division Simulates an Atomic Blast During Training, 1957 | 271 |
| Honest John Rocket Launcher, 1957 | 272 |
| M60 Tank | 292 |
| M48 Tanks | 292 |
| General Clyde D. Eddleman | 296 |
| Davy Crockett Rocket Launcher | 298 |
| Little John Rocket Launcher | 300 |
| 32d Infantry Division Elements Train During the Berlin Crisis, 1961 | 304 |
| Pre-positioned Equipment in Germany During Operation BIG LIFT | 304 |
| 1st Battalion, 60th Infantry, at Fort Richardson, Alaska, 1963. | 312 |
| Elements of the 173d Airborne Brigade Arrive in Vietnam | 324 |
| 9th Infantry Division's First Base Camp in Vietnam, 1966 | 326 |
| Soldiers of the 1st Brigade, 101st Airborne Division, Fire From Viet Cong Trenches, 1966 | 327 |
| Elements of the 69th Infantry Brigade Train at Fort Riley, Kansas, 1966 | 328 |
| 3d Brigade, 25th Infantry Division, Members Engage the Viet Cong, 1966 | 331 |
| Elements of the 9th Infantry Division Departing Vietnam, 1969 | 343 |
| Tube-Launched, Optically Tracked, Wire-Guided Missile | 354 |
| General Creighton W. Abrams | 357 |
| Chaparral Surface-to-Air Missile System | 360 |
| Vulcan Air Defense System | 360 |
| General Fred C. Weyand | 380 |
| General Donn A. Starry | 384 |
| General Edward C. Meyer | 386 |
| Bradley Fighting Vehicle System | 387 |
| Multiple Launch Rocket System | 387 |
| 9th Infantry Division "Dune Buggy" | 392 |
| General John A. Wickham, Jr. | 393 |
| Winter Training, 205th Infantry Brigade, 1986 | 396 |
| Reactivation Ceremony, 29th Infantry Division, 1985 | 396 |

Illustrations courtesy of the following sources: pp. 4, 380, 386, and 393, U.S. Army Art Collection; pp. 8, 15, 17, 36, 48, 113 (*top*), 221, 247, 272, 304 (*bottom*), 324, 326, 360 (*top and bottom*), 387 (*top*), and 396 (*top*), U.S. Army Center of Military History; pp. 11, 26 (*top and bottom*), 27, and 53, Library of

Congress; pp. 18, 35, 51 (*bottom*), and 144, U.S. Army Military History Institute; p. 231 (*top*), William Gardner Bell; pp. 231 (*bottom*), 292 (*top and bottom*), 300, 304 (*top*), 328, 354, 387 (*bottom*), and 396 (*bottom*), National Guard Association; p. 298, Firestone News Service; p. 384, U.S. Army Training and Doctrine Command; and p. 392, Fort Lewis Military Museum. All other illustrations from the files of the National Archives and Records Administration.

# MANEUVER AND FIREPOWER
The Evolution of Divisions and Separate Brigades

# CHAPTER 1

# Early Experiences

*Regularity and due Subordination, being so essentially necessary, to the good Order and Government of an Army, and without it, the whole must soon become a Scene of disorder and confusion. The General finds it indispensably necessary, without waiting any longer for dispatches from the General Continental Congress, immediately to form the Army into three Grand Divisions, and of dividing each of those Grand Divisions into Brigades.*

General George Washington[1]

## *Revolutionary War*

On 22 July 1775, George Washington, General and Commander in Chief of the American revolutionary forces, ordered the army at Boston to be organized into three divisions. Each division comprised two brigades of approximately equal strength. Major generals commanded the divisions, and most brigades were commanded by brigadiers who were general officers. The division commanders had no staffs, but the brigade commanders had brigade majors to assist them. Brigade majors were officers through whom orders were issued and reports and correspondence transmitted, analogous to regimental adjutants. Initially, both divisions and brigades were administrative commands rather than tactical organizations.[2]

Divisions and brigades soon evolved into semipermanent tactical, as well as administrative, organizations. Because regiments could not maintain their authorized strengths, Washington made the brigade, consisting of several regiments, the basic tactical and administrative unit for the Continental Army. When organized in 1775 all brigades at Boston had about 2,500 men each. During the war commanders deliberately balanced the strength of the brigades for each campaign. For example, Washington employed brigades of roughly 1,400 officers and enlisted men each at Trenton in December 1776 and at Monmouth in June 1778. At Yorktown in 1781 each of his brigades had approximately 1,000 officers and enlisted men.[3]

Although the Continental Army was reorganized on several occasions, many brigades had the same regiments assigned over long periods of time. Nevertheless, Washington and other army commanders had the authority to alter regimental assignments. In 1778 he emphatically told his subordinate, Maj. Gen. Charles Lee, that he [Washington] could change it "every day if I choose to do

Soldiers of the American Revolution, Trenton, December 26, 1776,
*by H. Charles McBarron*

it." But the commander in chief also believed that frequent changes in regimental assignment without apparent cause would be ascribed to "caprice and whim" rather than "stability and judgement [*sic*]."[4]

The Continental Army employed a variety of artillery weapons, including field, siege, and garrison guns, but the use of infantry and field artillery as combined arms teams was sporadic. During some campaigns two to four field artillery guns were attached to infantry brigades, and the brigade commander in turn attached the guns to infantry battalions. Harnessing the two arms together increased firepower, provided a means to break up enemy formations, and protected infantry against bayonet charges, as well as offering a psychological advantage. A major problem for the field artillery was to keep up with the infantry on the march because of the rough, broken terrain in colonial America. The key to cross-country travel was the design of light, mobile artillery carriages, but on the battlefield guns were manhandled. Unlike European armies, colonial commanders often used field artillery for siege work because of the shortages of guns, officers, and trained gun crews.[5]

With the employment of brigades, Congress increased their staff officers. The first such officer was added in May 1777 when Congress authorized a brigade chaplain to care for the religious needs of the men. In January 1778 Washington proposed that an infantry brigade have a quartermaster, forage master, wagon master, and commissary, along with armorers, a traveling forge, and some artificers. The following May, however, Congress authorized only the brigade quartermaster. Although not provided by Congress, in June 1778 Washington introduced the position of brigade inspector, whose duties included maintaining unit rosters, regulating details (any special tasks assigned to the brigade), and caring for the formation and march of all guards and details. Furthermore, the inspector received the commander's orders and communicated them to brigade and regimental officers; thus the position incorporated duties of the brigade major. Although the brigade inspector assisted in executing brigade maneuvers, he was not in the chain of command. Congress officially authorized the position in February 1779 and made the former brigade major an aide-de-camp to the brigadier. At the same time Congress also provided a second aide for the brigadier.[6]

In early 1779 Washington directed the appointment of a conductor of military stores for each brigade. Equipped with a portable forge, an ammunition wagon, and a wagon with an arms chest for each regiment in the brigade, the conductor of military stores and his assistants (the latter being furnished by the regiments) cared for its arms. Thus, by the end of the war each infantry brigade comprised several semipermanently assigned infantry regiments and a few attached artillery pieces and their crews. The brigade commander had a staff consisting of two aides, a brigade quartermaster, an inspector, a conductor of military stores, and a chaplain. Infantry brigades were generally known by the names of their commanders, but the more permanent brigades were often known by numerical designations, such as the 1st Maryland and 2d Pennsylvania Brigades.[7]

Washington assigned infantry brigades to divisions, but the number of brigades assigned to each division varied. Divisions, nevertheless, became quasi-permanent commands, with the same brigades serving in the same divisions for extended periods of time. As this organizational relationship matured, the divisions maneuvered independently and conducted operations away from the main army.[8]

Washington occasionally expressed theories about the proper organization of divisions and brigades. In January 1777, as the army was about to be reorganized, he told Congress that three full-strength regiments, approximately 700 men each, would be sufficient for a brigade and that three brigades would be adequate for a division. The following year, during similar discussions, Washington explained that the division-brigade-regiment organization was for the sake of order, harmony, and discipline. Each brigade and division would have a general officer as its commander and would be capable of moving either jointly or separately like a "great machine" as the circumstances required. Because of shortages in personnel, at no time during the war did either divisions or brigades adhere to organizational concepts, particularly as far as the number of assigned regiments and brigades was concerned. Nevertheless, both divisions and brigades fulfilled Washington's requirement of being able to operate either jointly or separately when the need arose.[9]

The basic fighting team used during the Revolutionary War consisted of infantry and artillery, but the Continental Army also used cavalry. Cavalry units were initially mounted militia commands, but in late 1776 Congress authorized a regiment of light dragoons for the Continental Army. That act was soon followed by another, which authorized 3,000 light horsemen to be organized into four regiments. The regiments were never fully manned because of the expense of their special weapons and equipment, their horses, and their training. By 1780 the units were converted into "legionary organizations." In the mid-eighteenth century Europeans had developed small mixed units of cavalry and infantry, known as legions, to overrun or hold an area, gather information, and conduct raids away from the main army. Legions in the Continental Army were to comprise four troops of dragoons and two companies of infantry. They were not large, independent combined arms units capable of defeating the enemy such as the divisions and brigades in the Continental Army.[10]

Following the British surrender at Yorktown in 1781, the Continental Army dwindled away, and its divisions and brigades slowly disappeared. But the doctrine for their organization endured, and future leaders built upon it in the following century.

Before the new nation ratified the peace with England, Congress asked Washington for his views on the future peacetime military establishment. On 2 May 1783, recognizing his countrymen's fear of standing armies and the expense of maintaining them, he called for a military establishment consisting of a small active force organized on a regimental basis and a larger reserve based on the militia arranged by divisions. His militia division was to consist of two brigades of four infantry regiments each, with each infantry regiment organized into two four-company battalions. Furthermore, Washington recommended that two cavalry troops and two artillery companies be raised for each division. These units were not part of any combined arms concept for divisions, but merely a formula for calculating the number of cavalry and artillery units that would be needed by future armies.[11]

Eventually the legislature created a military establishment based on standing and reserve forces. In 1784 the Continental Congress set the strength of the standing army at a mere 700 men, and the Regular Army, organized on a regimental basis, grew steadily in the years that followed. In 1792 the new national Congress also provided for a reserve force based upon the state militia, which the federal government could employ under certain conditions within the United States. The militia forces were to consist of all able-bodied white male citizens between the ages of eighteen and forty-five and were to be organized into companies, battalions, regiments, brigades, and divisions. The legislation provided that each brigade consist of four two-battalion infantry regiments. A militia division could also have an artillery company and a cavalry troop, both of which were to be formed from volunteers within the brigades at the discretion of the governors. Major generals and brigadier generals were to command divisions and brigades, respectively, and the only staff officer authorized was the brigade inspector, who was also to serve as the brigade major. The strength of the brigade was to be approximately 2,500 men. Presumably divisional strength would vary, for the law prescribed no set number of brigades in a division.12

As implemented, the militia divisions and brigades were generally paper organizations. Congress provided neither federal supervision nor effective support for them. Furthermore, no provision was made for a militia force that would be available immediately to react in an emergency. Although ineffectual, the system lasted for over one hundred years. In practice, when the federal government called upon the militia, the president asked for a specific number of men from a state and the state organized them into regiments.

Shortly after Congress passed the militia law, it authorized the use of volunteers, a third category of soldiers, for national defense. Volunteers served freely, like soldiers in the Regular Army, but they were not part of any standing or reserve force. Generally, the states raised the volunteers that Congress considered necessary on a regimental basis, and the federal government used the volunteer regiments to form divisions and brigades.13

The Regular Army also experimented with the legion as a combined arms unit in the 1790s. Differing from the legions employed during the Revolutionary War, the Legion of the United States resembled the organizations described by Marshal Maurice de Saxe in 1732 and advocated in the 1780s by Maj. Gen. Frederick Wilhelm von Steuben, formerly the Inspector General of the Continental Army, and Secretary of War Henry Knox. The legion was a field army, combining infantry, cavalry, and artillery into one organization, which totaled 5,120 men. Rather than being subdivided into divisions, brigades, and regiments, the legion consisted of four sublegions, which some consider to be the forerunners of the regimental combat teams of the twentieth century. The Regular Army adopted the legion in 1792, but it was never fully manned. For the campaigns against the Miami Indians in the Northwest Territory between January 1790 and August 1795 the Army employed militia and volunteer units and the Legion of the United States. Its sublegions, however, were not employed extensively. The Army abandoned the legion in 1796 for regimental organizations. Henceforth, the regulars were scattered throughout the country, guarding its frontiers and seacoast and rarely forming organizations above the regimental level.14

## *War of 1812*

When the second war with England began in 1812, Congress raised forces by expanding the Regular Army, authorizing the use of volunteers, and calling out the militia. In raising the troops both the federal and state governments used regimental organizations, and the Army organized these regiments into ad hoc brigades and divisions, which varied widely in strength. For example, Brig. Gen. Joseph Bloomfield's New York militia brigade assigned to Maj. Gen. Henry Dearborn's force in 1813 counted 1,400 strong; Brig. Gen. Winfield Scott's Regular brigade in 1814 before the Battle of Chippewa fielded 1,300 men; and the Pennsylvania vol-

*General Scott*

unteer brigade that crossed the border into Upper Canada in 1814 numbered 413. The strength of the divisions fluctuated just as much. In 1812 the New York quota for militiamen was 13,500, which the state organized into two divisions of four brigades each. At the same time, with a quota of 2,500 men, Tennessee organized a division of two infantry regiments plus a nondivisional cavalry regiment.[15]

While assembling brigades and divisions in 1813, the question arose as to whether or not Regular Army and militia units should be "brigaded" together. Because the drill and discipline of the regulars differed greatly from that of the militia, each state prescribing its own drill, the general practice was to brigade each category of troops separately. Although Regular, militia, and volunteer brigades served at times in commands that equaled the size of a division, such organizations were frequently called "armies."[16]

Raising and maintaining troops during the War of 1812 proved to be difficult because of the opposition to the war. As a result, when divisions and brigades took to the field for the various campaigns, they were temporary organizations. Most of the units assigned to them had little training and were poorly equipped, creating largely ineffective fighting forces. One exception was Scott's Regular Army brigade. In the spring of 1814, after establishing a camp near Buffalo, New York, he used French drill regulations to train his men. When the brigade later fought at Chippewa as a well-disciplined force, it prompted the British commander to exclaim, "Those are Regulars, by God!"[17]

During the War of 1812, as in the Revolution, Army leaders discussed the organization of brigades and divisions, and their comments sometimes disagreed with the contemporary practice or with the laws then in effect. *The Register of the Army* published in 1813 stated that a brigade would consist of two regiments and a division of two brigades with but a single staff officer, the brigade major, in each. The laws in force, however, authorized a brigade staff of an inspector, subinspector, quartermaster, wagon master, and chaplain. When a brigadier general commanded a brigade, his brigade major and aides were

# EARLY EXPERIENCES

included in the staff. Major generals continued to command divisions, and their staffs consisted of a quartermaster, judge advocate, and two aides. The official handbook for infantry compiled by William Duane, the Adjutant General, in 1813 called for a brigade in the peace establishment to consist of any number of battalions, but for field service it was not to exceed 4,000 men. A division could have from two to four brigades. During congressional deliberations as to the number of major and brigadier generals needed in 1813 to conduct the war, Secretary of War John Armstrong expressed his belief that a brigade should have only two regiments because the management of 2,000 men in the field was ample duty for a brigadier general. Also, in his opinion, the direction of 4,000 men was a suitable command for a major general. But the lack of trained personnel and the short duration of campaigns in the War of 1812 resulted in ad hoc brigades and divisions that did not approach the combined arms teams of the Revolutionary War.[18]

After the War of 1812 the militia units were released from federal service, the volunteers were discharged, and the Regular Army units were eventually reduced to seven infantry and four artillery regiments. Despite the small size of the Army of the United States, Maj. Gen. Winfield Scott in 1819 secured congressional approval for the preparation of a code incorporating the laws, regulations, orders, and practices governing the Army. Having studied foreign armies, particularly the French, he thought such regulations would be useful. In them he introduced a new organization—the army corps. During the Napoleonic wars the French had decentralized their armies for greater mobility and maneuverability. French field armies had consisted of several army corps, which in turn were made up of two or three divisions of infantry or cavalry. Each division comprised two brigades. With this structure, an army could be dispersed over a wide area, but the command mechanism allowed it to concentrate quickly to destroy the enemy.[19]

Scott's *General Regulations for the United States Army*, published in 1821, thus included the new European concepts. Two regiments constituted a brigade, two brigades a division, and two divisions an army corps. Infantry and cavalry were to be brigaded separately. The only staff officer for either the brigade or the division was a "chief of staff," who acted in a manner similar to a brigade inspector or brigade major. The divisions and brigades were to be numbered according to the rank of their commanders. For ease in distinguishing each body of troops in official reports, units were to be identified by their commanders' names.[20]

Between the War of 1812 and the Mexican War these concepts meant little to the Regular Army. The periodic campaigns against the Indians, using Regular, militia, and volunteer troops, were fought with small bodies of troops, usually of regimental or smaller size. Such constabulary tactics neither influenced the formation of large units in the field nor affected the regulations that governed such organizations. The only alteration in *Army Regulations* prior to the Mexican War specified that neither the division nor the brigade was to have a fixed staff, with their size and composition varying according to the nature of their service.[21]

## Mexican War

In the fall of 1845, just before hostilities broke out between the United States and Mexico, Brevet Brig. Gen. Zachary Taylor organized the Regular Army forces that had gathered at Corpus Christi, Texas, numbering about 3,900 men, into three brigades, each consisting of two infantry regiments or their equivalent. The 2d Dragoons and Regular Army field artillery companies supported the brigades. With these forces Taylor fought and won the Battles of Palo Alto (8 May 1846) and Resaca de Palma (9 May 1846).[22]

After the declaration of war in the spring of 1846, Congress called for 50,000 volunteers. Individual states organized their volunteers into regiments, which the War Department initially planned to brigade, mixing foot and mounted infantry[23] in the same units. Two or more volunteer brigades, each consisting of three or more regiments, were to form a division. Under the wartime laws, a brigade was to be authorized at least 3,000 men and a division 6,000. Since Army Regulations called for no fixed staffs, the president was to appoint a quartermaster, commissary, and surgeon for each brigade. Each staff officer was to have an assistant. Congress further provided that the regimental officers of a brigade could employ a chaplain.[24]

In the late summer of 1846 Taylor organized his army into divisions for a campaign against Monterrey, Mexico. Using the three brigades he had organized in 1845, plus a new brigade, Taylor formed two Regular Army divisions of two brigades each. Each brigade had two infantry regiments; three brigades had a field artillery company attached; and one division had an additional field artillery company and a regiment of dragoons assigned. Because the volunteers did not deploy in any prearranged order, Taylor temporarily brigaded a portion of those who had joined him for instruction and camp service. Others he organized as a volunteer division of two brigades, each containing two 500-man infantry regiments. A regiment of mounted volunteers from Texas completed the division. With these forces Taylor captured Monterrey in September 1846.[25]

When Taylor took to the field after his victory at Monterrey, he had planned to continue to use divisional organizations. But, since the political leadership in Washington decided to shift the center of operations more directly toward Mexico City, the bulk of Taylor's troops were transferred to a new command under Maj. Gen. Winfield Scott and were replaced by green volunteers. With 5,000 mostly untrained troops, in February 1847 Taylor fought the Battle of Buena Vista, where his inexperienced troops performed well. Buena Vista was particularly a triumph for American artillery, whose mobility allowed it to counter enemy thrusts with intense firepower and close infantry support when and where needed. Infantry and artillery had formed a more effective combined arms team.[26]

Scott's command against Mexico City, a force of about 12,000 men, was initially organized into two Regular Army infantry brigades and a three-brigade volunteer division. Each brigade was supported by field artillery. After the siege of

*The Battle of Palo Alto*

Vera Cruz Scott organized the Regulars into a division, but before reaching Mexico City he had to reorganize his army anew due primarily to losses by disease and expiring enlistment terms. When more volunteers arrived, he formed his infantry into four divisions of two brigades each, with an artillery company supporting each brigade. He placed elements of three dragoon regiments in a brigade under Col. William S. Harney. Satisfied with his field dispositions, Scott attacked and then entered Mexico City on 13 September.[27]

During the course of the war both Taylor and Scott organized ad hoc divisions as combined arms teams. These underwent several reorganizations for a variety of reasons, including a lack of transportation for moving units and supplies, a need to establish and protect lines of communication, and a shortage of personnel to maintain units at some semblance of fighting strength. The war, nevertheless, brought about a new integration of infantry and field artillery within divisions, which operated as independent, maneuverable commands. The stock-trail gun carriage, adopted in 1836, was a technological breakthrough that gave U.S. field artillery in the Mexican War sufficient mobility and maneuverability for integration of the arms.[28]

The revised Army Regulations published in 1857 reflected the changes developed during the course of the war for combining the combat arms. Doctrine called for a division usually to consist of "two or three brigades, either infantry or cavalry, and troops of the other corps in the necessary proportions."[29] Each brigade was to consist of two or more regiments. "The troops of the other corps" were artillerymen and engineers, but there was no indication as to what proportion of a division they were to be. A division staff or that of a detached brigade was still minimal—artillery, engineer, and ordnance officers. The regulations changed the system for designating divisions and brigades from being numbered according to the rank of their commanders to being numbered according to their position on the line, although the names of the commanders were still to be used in reports. Finally, the regulations provided that only the War Department could authorize the formation of divisions and brigades during peacetime. In practice, such units would thus remain only wartime expedients.[30]

## *Civil War*

The Civil War brought about the first large armies in the nation's history, and both Union and Confederate leaders used brigades, divisions, and army corps as command and control units. After rebel troops fired on Fort Sumter, South Carolina, President Abraham Lincoln called for 75,000 militiamen to assist the Regular Army in quelling the rebellion. Shortly thereafter Congress began to expand the Regular Army and call for volunteers. Following the rout of the Union forces at Manassas in July 1861 Congress authorized the first large call for men, 500,000 volunteers to serve three years. To train the new Army Lincoln selected George B. McClellan, a former West Point officer and president of the Eastern Division of the Ohio and Mississippi Railroad Company.[31] McClellan later described the Union troops at Manassas, who were mostly militia, as "a collection of undisciplined, ill-officered, and uninstructed men" instead of an army. The new commander in chief had much to do.[32]

As the volunteer regiments arrived in the Washington, D.C., area, McClellan began to organize them into what became known as the Army of the Potomac. During the course of the war additional Union armies were formed and served, but the experience of the Army of the Potomac serves as the model to illustrate the difficulties faced by commanders on both sides in organizing their forces. As many of the future leaders of the Army after the war fought with the Army of the Potomac, their experiences had a profound impact on Army organization in the last half of the nineteenth century.

In the Army of the Potomac the largest unit initially was a division, which consisted of three infantry brigades, one cavalry regiment, and four artillery batteries. The division commander did not have a staff, except for his three aides and an assistant adjutant general. The brigade commander, on the other hand, had two aides, a surgeon, a commissary of subsistence, an adjutant general, and a quartermaster.[33]

McClellan planned to organize the volunteers into brigades, divisions, and army corps. Each army corps, about 25,000 men, was to consist of two or more divisions. He hesitated to implement that organization, however, until his officers gained experience as division commanders. He also delayed the organization of army corps for political reasons. Over one-half of his division commanders were Republicans who were ardent supporters of Lincoln, while McClellan, a political foe of the president, was a Democrat. In March 1862, before the Peninsula campaign began in Virginia, Lincoln, concerned about command and control in combat, directed that McClellan's forces be organized into army corps. McClellan organized the Army of the Potomac on the peninsula into four army corps of three divisions each. The Union forces on the upper Potomac were also placed into an army corps.34

Combat experience brought organizational changes to the Army of the Potomac. Cavalry assigned to divisions within army corps were generally unable to perform army-level missions. In July 1862, after the Peninsula campaign, Brig. Gen. George Stoneman, Chief of Cavalry of the Army of the Potomac, shifted cavalry units from the infantry divisions and organized two cavalry brigades for the army, but he left a cavalry squadron35 in each army corps for picket, scout, and outpost duties. Little improvement resulted from having separate cavalry brigades, which were used the same as the cavalry squadrons in the army corps.

In November 1862 Maj. Gen. Ambrose Burnside took command of the Army of the Potomac and reorganized it into three "grand divisions." He planned for each grand division to move and fight as a heavy column of two corps and a cavalry division, which removed the cavalry from army corps. The grand division commanders, however, were reluctant to use cavalry as an independent force. In February 1863 Maj. Gen. Joseph Hooker, the new commander of the Army of the Potomac, abolished the grand divisions and reverted to the army corps structure. At the same time the Union cavalry was also reorganized as a separate corps under Stoneman, with approximately 13,000 men divided into three divisions. Each division had two brigades, with each brigade having three to five regiments. Artillery was assigned to the cavalry corps headquarters. The cavalry corps operated as an independent unit thereafter, but the jest "Whoever saw a dead cavalryman?" remained within the Army of the Potomac.36 By June 1863 Union cavalry proved equal to the Confederate cavalry. At Brandy Station the Union cavalry corps excelled under the aggressive leadership of Maj. Gen. Philip H. Sheridan in 1864.37

Experience also led to the standardization of field artillery pieces and their massing within the army corps. At Manassas the Union artillery had been assigned to brigades, but when organizing the Army of the Potomac McClellan assigned it to divisions, usually one artillery battalion per division. He also approved a ratio of 2.5 artillery pieces to 1,000 infantrymen, with six artillery pieces of the same caliber, if possible, forming a battery. One of every four batteries was to be a Regular Army unit, the commander of which was to assist the division commander in organizing and training the artillery. Because of the shortage of artillery pieces in 1861, the Union's arsenals were ransacked and guns of various calibers were sent to the troops in the field, causing ammunition and supply problems. But eventually the Army of the Potomac achieved uniformity within its field artillery batteries by using 3-inch or 12-pounder "Napoleon" guns.[38]

Although standardization of weapons eased some field artillery problems, others remained. With the organization of army corps, half of each corps' divisional artillery was withdrawn to form an Army of the Potomac artillery reserve of three artillery brigades. The army corps had no artillery except that in its divisions, and division commanders were loath to lose control over their guns. By 1863 most commanders recognized that their heavy losses stemmed from frontal infantry assaults on entrenched positions. Rifles, with a maximum range of a thousand yards and an effective range of half that distance in the hands of good marksmen, plus supporting artillery fire presented formidable obstacles to mass attacks. Field artillery could break up the infantry's defensive positions, but with the guns scattered among the corps' divisions the coordination and concentration of artillery fire was difficult to orchestrate.[39]

After the Union defeat at Chancellorsville in 1863 the field artillery batteries were withdrawn from the divisions of the Army of the Potomac and concentrated in field artillery brigades directly under the corps headquarters. These brigades, with four to six batteries and their own officers and staff, rendered efficient service, which resulted in a reduction in the amount of artillery needed and in the dependence on the army's artillery reserve without any reduction in fire support. The reserve gradually became a place for recuperation and reorganization of battered batteries.[40]

To be successful, armies in the Civil War needed more than infantry, field artillery, and cavalry. As the Regular Army had few engineer units, volunteer infantry regiments often served as engineers. In the Army of the Potomac these regiments eventually formed a brigade. Army corps in other Union armies also employed infantry as engineers. As the medical, ordnance, signal, and quartermaster department lacked units, their field tasks were performed by personnel assigned to the departments or by soldiers detailed from the line regiments or by hired civilians.[41]

To coordinate all the activities within an army corps, supporting staffs grew at each level—corps, division, brigade, and regiment. Eventually an adjutant, commissaries of muster and subsistence, and a chief of ordnance comprised the divisional staff. The staff for the brigade included an adjutant, quartermaster, commissary of subsistence, and, when the brigade served as an independent command, an ordnance officer. In addition, general officers continued to have aides as their personal staff.[42]

As army corps evolved, the method by which they were designated changed. Initially each Union army corps was designated within an army—i.e., I Army Corps, Army of the Potomac—but later the practice of numbering them consecutively without any reference to the army to which they were assigned was adopted. Divisions within army corps were numbered consecutively, as were brigades within divisions.[43]

# EARLY EXPERIENCES 15

*Camp Humphreys, Virginia, headquarters of Allaback's Brigade, Pennsylvania Volunteers, 1863*

Basically the Army of the Potomac served as the model for all Union forces. In the West army corps were introduced after their organization in the Army of the Potomac. As the war ebbed and flowed commanders organized, consolidated, and discontinued army corps as needed. When regiments were reduced because of attrition, theater commanders added more regiments to the brigades to maintain their strength and that of divisions within the army corps. When the volunteer system broke down, both the Union and Confederate governments turned to draftees, substitutes (men hired to serve in draftees' places), and bounties to maintain their armies. To relieve manpower problems, the Union Army began using blacks in 1862, while the Confederate Congress authorized the enrollment of black troops in March 1865. Small numbers of Negroes had served in past wars, both in integrated and segregated units, but during the Civil War both sides organized segregated regiments. The Union eventually created the XXV Army Corps with Negro enlisted personnel from the X and XVIII Army Corps.[44]

With the Confederate Army springing from the same ancestral roots as the Union Army, it was not surprising that both armies used similar patterns of organization. At Bull Run in July 1861, the Confederates employed two provisional army corps made up of brigades without an intervening divisional-level structure. Eventually their army corps consisted of infantry brigades and divisions. Paralleling the Union armies, the field artillery batteries were organized as corps-level units, which were designated battalions rather than brigades. Confederate cavalry employed a divisional rather than a corps structure, but it functioned as an aggressive independent force earlier than Union cavalry. Unlike the Union forces, Southerners rarely numbered their brigades and divisions but used the names of commanders for identification. Army corps were numbered within their respective armies. [45]

To help control and identify units on the battlefield, armies traditionally used flags, and Union army corps and their divisions and brigades employed them during the Civil War. The national colors formed the basis of the flag system. Along with distinctive flags, Union corps badges were introduced to identify men and foster esprit de corps.[46]

Following the Civil War the War Department disbanded the field armies, along with their army corps, divisions, and brigades. Militia units returned to their states, the volunteers left service, and most of the Regular Army troops returned to scattered posts throughout the South and West. Congress in 1869 set the peacetime Regular establishment at 25 infantry, 10 cavalry, and 5 artillery regiments, but few were ever able to assemble their far-flung companies, troops, and batteries in one place until the end of the century. Field operations usually involved less than a regiment or were conducted by gathering the geographically closest elements of several regiments on a temporary basis. Army Regulations, nevertheless, continued to repeat the ideas for organizing army corps, divisions, and brigades, with the division described as "the fundamental element and basis of organization of every active army."[47]

## *War With Spain*

On 25 April 1898, Congress declared that a state of war existed between the United States and Spain. Even though the USS *Maine* had been sunk six weeks before, threatening war, the nation had taken only minimal steps toward mobilization. One of these steps, however, was congressional authorization for President William McKinley, when necessary, to organize a new army consisting of the Regular Army and the Volunteer Army of the United States. The regiments of the Volunteer Army were to be raised and officered by the states and eventually included most of their organized militia units. The regulars and volunteers were to be formed into brigades, divisions, and army corps. On 23 April the McKinley administration directed the regulars concentrated at Chickamauga National Park, Georgia, to be organized as an army corps; those at Mobile, Alabama, as an independent division; and those at New Orleans, Louisiana, as a separate brigade.[48]

After the declaration of war McKinley revised that arrangement and approved the organization of eight army corps, each of which was to consist of three or more divisions of three brigades each. Each brigade was to have approxi-

*Staff of the 2d Division, I Army Corps, 1898*

mately 3,600 officers and enlisted men organized into three regiments and, with three such brigades, each division was to total about 11,000 officers and men. Thus the division was to be about the same size as the division of 1861, but army corps were to be larger. The division staff initially was to have an adjutant general, quartermaster, commissary, surgeon, inspector general, and engineer, with an ordnance officer added later. The brigade staff was identical except that no inspector general or ordnance officer was authorized.[49]

The Commanding General of the Army, Maj. Gen. Nelson A. Miles, had planned to expand the Army in an orderly fashion by holding the volunteers in state camps for sixty days. There they would be organized, equipped, and trained for field duty. During that period the War Department was to prepare large training camps and collect the necessary stores to outfit the new army, while McKinley was to appoint the general officers who would command the new brigades, divisions, and army corps. Miles' plan soon went awry. Because of the lack of Regular Army officers to staff state camps and the need to have volunteers and regulars train together, he quickly abandoned it. In mid-May the volunteers were moved to a few large unfinished camps in the South, and when they arrived only seven instead of the eight projected army corps were organized. Two army

*Camp Alger, Virginia, 1898*

corps, the IV and V, consisted of regulars and volunteers, while the others were made up of volunteers.[50]

To facilitate command and control, corps and division commanders requested permission to use distinctive Civil War flags and badges for their units. Secretary of War Russell A. Alger, however, disapproved the request because of pressure from Civil War veterans who had been permitted by Congress to wear their distinctive unit insignia and guarded the privilege jealously. The quartermaster general, therefore, had to prepared an entirely new group of heraldic items for the recently organized army corps and their divisions and brigades.[51]

Before the new army completed its organization and training, it was thrust into combat. About two-thirds of V Army Corps, one dismounted cavalry and two infantry divisions, sailed for Cuba in June 1898. Expeditions also were mounted for Puerto Rico and the Philippine Islands in which partial army corps provided the troops. The war ended in August 1898, and less than two months later the wartime army began to fade away. The War Department disbanded the last army corps on 13 April 1900. Following the war, the Army maintained troops in the Philippines, Cuba, and Puerto Rico, but those commands did not employ army corps and divisions.[52]

# EARLY EXPERIENCES

During major conflicts of the United States prior to the twentieth century, Army leaders sought to find the best command level at which to merge infantry, cavalry, and artillery into effective, coordinated combat units. Brigades and divisions usually comprised a single arm, while the army corps was the basic combined arms unit. Within the army corps itself, little specialization existed beyond the combat arms. Usually no field units were organized for signal, medical, transportation, military police, engineers, ordnance, or other combat support services. Hired civilians or detailed soldiers provided such support in the field. By the beginning of the twentieth century, however, innovations in warfare, especially technological developments, required more sophisticated organizations, both to use the new technology and to integrate it into a larger operational and tactical framework.

## Notes

[1] George Washington, *The Writings of George Washington From the Original Manuscript Source, 1745–1799*, ed., John C. Fitzpatrick, 39 vols. (Washington, D.C.: Government Printing Office, 1931–44), 3:354–55.

[2] Ibid.; Worthington C. Ford, ed., *Journals of the Continental Congress, 1774–1789*, 34 vols. (Washington, D.C.: Government Printing Office, 1904–37), 2:103, 191 (hereafter cited as JCC); An Universal Military Dictionary (London: J. Millan, 1779; reprint, Ottawa: Museum Restoration Service, 1969), p. 36. In the initial legislation Congress made brigadiers general officers. Washington nevertheless viewed their function during the war as nothing more than regimental colonels who acted on a larger scale. Regiments of the Continental Army were authorized staff officers, which included adjutants, surgeons, quartermasters, and paymasters.

[3] Washington, *Writings*, 9:103–04, 12:60–61; Peter Force, ed., *American Archives: A Collection of Authentic Records, State Papers, and Letters and Other Notices of Public Affairs*, 9 vols. (Washington, D.C.: M. St. Clair & Peter Force, 1839–53), 2:1028; Charles H. Lesser, *The Sinews of Independence: Monthly Strength Reports of the Continental Army* (Chicago: University of Chicago Press, 1976), pp. 43, 72, 208; Robert K. Wright, Jr., *The Continental Army* (Washington, D.C.: Government Printing Office, 1983), p. 97. Infantry regiments varied in strength during the war, but were usually authorized approximately 700 officers and enlisted men each.

[4] Washington, *Writings*, 9:103–04, 12:60–61.

[5] Boyd L. Dastrup, *King of Battle: A Branch History of the U.S. Army's Field Artillery* (Fort Monroe, Va.: U.S. Army Training and Doctrine Command, 1992), pp. 12–31; Wright, *Continental Army*, pp. 54, 150; William E. Birkhimer, *Historical Sketch of the Organization, Administration, Materiel, and Tactics of the Artillery, United States Army* (Washington, D.C.: James J. Chapman, 1884), pp. 76–77, 96–97.

[6] Ford, *JCC*, 8:390–91, 11:542, 13:197–98; Washington, Writings, 10:374, 12:67, 79.

[7] Washington, Writings, 16:101. Lesser's *The Sinews of Independence* illustrates the point on brigade designations.

[8] Wright, *Continental Army*, p. 29; Washington, *Writings*, 3:354–56; James C. Scudieri, "The Continentals: Comparative Analysis of a Late Eighteenth-Century Standing Army," Ph.D. dissertation, City University of New York, 1993. Lesser's *The Sinews of Independence* illustrates the point about quasi-permanent divisions.

[9] Washington, *Writings*, 7:49, 10:363.

[10] Ford, *JCC*, 6:1025, 1045, 18:960; Mary Lee Stubbs and Stanley Russell Connor, *Armor-Cavalry, Part I: Regular Army and Army Reserve* (Washington, D.C.: Government Printing Office, 1969), pp. 3–6; Wright, *Continental Army*, pp. 105–07, 133–34, 160–61; Oliver L. Spaulding, Hoffman Nickerson, and John W. Wright, *Warfare* (Washington, D.C.: Harcourt, Brace, and Co., 1925), pp. 554–55.

[11] Washington, Writings, 27:374–98.

[12] Ford, *JCC*, 3 Jun 1784; John F. Callan, comp., *The Military Laws of the United States* (Philadelphia: G.W. Childs, 1863), pp. 95–100.

[13] Callan, *Military Laws*, pp. 122–25. This was the first law authorizing volunteers; the other laws concerning them were enacted during periods of crises. Those printed in this volume cover the period until 1863.

[14] Maurice de Saxe, *Reveries on the Art of War*, trans., Thomas R. Philipps (Harrisburg, Pa.: Military Service Publishing Co., 1944), pp. 36–38; Frederick Wilhelm von Steuben, *A Letter on the Subject of an Established Militia, and Military Arrangements. Addressed to the Inhabitants of the United States* (New York: J. McLean and Co., 1784), p. 45; Henry Knox, *A Plan for the General Arrangement of the Militia of the United States* (1786), published in *Political Pamphlets*, Jefferson Collection, Library of Congress; John K. Mahon and Romana Danysh, *Infantry, Part I: Regular Army* (Washington, D.C.: Government Printing Office, 1972), pp. 12–13; Francis B. Heitman, *Historical Register and Dictionary of the United States Army From Its Organization, September*

# EARLY EXPERIENCES

*1779 to March 2, 1903*, 2 vols. (Washington, D.C.: Government Printing Office, 1903), 1:139–41; Francis Paul Prucha, *The Sword of the Republic: The United Army on the Frontier, 1783–1846* (Bloomington: Indiana University Press, 1977), pp. 17–24.

15 Marvin A. Kreidberg and Merton G. Henry, *History of Military Mobilization in the United States Army, 1775–1945* (Washington, D.C.: Government Printing Office, 1955), pp. 44–46, hereafter cited as *Mobilization*; Benson J. Lossing, *The Pictorial Field-Book of the War of 1812* (New York: Harper and Brothers, 1869), pp. 366, 742; *American State Papers, Military Affairs*, 7 vols. (Washington, D.C.: Gales and Seaton, 1834), 1:618; Charles W. Elliott, *Winfield Scott: The Soldier and the Man* (New York: Macmillan Co., 1937), p. 151.

16 *American State Papers, Military Affairs*, 1:495.

17 Elliott, *Winfield Scott*, pp. 146–47, 162.

18 *American State Papers, Military Affairs*, 1:330, 425; William Duane, *A Hand Book for Infantry*, 9th ed. (Philadelphia: William Duane, 1814), p. 20; Callan, *Military Laws*, pp. 136, 213, 219, 228, 240.

19 *American State Papers, Military Affairs*, 1:199–200; Elliott, *Winfield Scott*, pp. 228–29.

20 *General Regulations for the United States Army*, 1821, pp. 85–89; Michael Howard, *War in European History* (Oxford: Oxford University Press, 1976), pp. 83–84.

21 *General Regulations for the Army of the United States*, 1841, p. 67.

22 Justin H. Smith, *The War With Mexico*, 2 vols. (New York: Macmillan Co., 1919), 1:143–80 passim; Kreidberg and Henry, *Mobilization*, pp. 74–75.

23 Mounted infantry men were dragoons who reached the battlefield on horse but as foot soldiers.

24 Callan, *Military Laws*, pp. 367–69, 373, 375, and 380; Kreidberg and Henry, *Mobilization*, p. 73; *Mexican War Correspondence* (Washington, D.C.: Wendell and van Benthuysen, Printers, 1848), p. 458.

25 *Mexican War Correspondence*, pp. 417–19, 498–500; Edward D. Mansfield, *The Mexican War: A History of Its Origin* (New York: A.S. Barnes and Co., 1850), p. 57.

26 *Mexican War Correspondence*, pp. 513–14; John D. Eisenhower, *So Far From God: The U.S. War with Mexico 1846–1848* (New York: Random House, 1989), pp. 178–91; Dastrup, *King of Battle*, pp. 71–78.

27 R. S. Ripley, *The War with Mexico* (New York: Harper and Brothers, 1849), pp. 17, 55–56; Mansfield, *The Mexican War*, pp. 225–27.

28 Stanley L. Falk, "Artillery for the Land Service: The Development of a System," *Military Affairs* 28 (Fall 1964): 97–110.

29 *Regulations of the Army of the United States*, 1857, p. 13.

30 Ibid., pp. 13, 71–73.

31 George B. McClellan, *McClellan's Own Story: The War of the Union* (New York: Charles L. Webster and Co., 1887), p. 2; War Department General Orders (WD GO) 49, 1861.

32 McClellan, *McClellan's Own Story*, p. 68.

33 *The War of the Rebellion: A Compilation of the Official Records of the Union and Confederate Armies*, Ser. I, 53 vols. (Washington, D.C.: Government Printing Office, 1881–98), 5:11–17, hereafter cited as OR; WD GO 49, 1861.

34 Robert M. Epstein, "The Creation and Evolution of the Army Corps in the American Civil War," *Journal of Military History* 55 (Jan 1991): 21–46; *OR*, 5:11–67 passim. Congress provided for army corps on 17 July 1862.

35 A cavalry squadron was and still is equivalent to a battalion.

36 Philip H. Sheridan, *Personal Memoirs of P.H. Sheridan, General of the United States Army*, 2 vols. (New York: Charles L. Webster & Co., 1888), 1:347.

37 Ibid.; B. W. Crowninshielf, "Cavalry in Virginia During the War of the Rebellion," *Journal of the Military Service Institution* 12 (May 1891): 527–51; Kenneth P. Williams, *Lincoln Finds a General*, 4 vols. (New York: Macmillan, 1949), 2:483, 487; OR, 25:471–72; Moses Harris, "The Union Cavalry," *Journal of the U.S. Cavalry Association* 5 (Mar 1892): 2–16.

38 Henry J. Hunt, "Our Experience in Artillery Administration," *Journal of the Military*

*Service Institution* 12 (Mar 1891): 197–224; John C. Tidball, "The Artillery Service in the War of the Rebellion, 1861–1865," *Journal of the Military Service Institution* 12 (Jul 1891): 697–733.

39 *OR*, 5:67, 471–72; Tidball, "The Artillery Service," pp. 697–733.

40 Tidball, "The Artillery Service," pp. 697–733.

41 *History and Traditions of the Corps of Engineers*, Engineer School Special Text 25–1, (Fort Belvoir, Va.: Engineer School, 1953), p. 29; OR, 15:716–17; Mary C. Gillett, *The Army Medical Department, 1818–1865* (Washington, D.C.: Government Printing Office, 1987), pp. 156–57.

42 WD GOs 12, 79, 1862; 48, 1863; and 31, 193, 1865.

43 Frederick H. Dyer, *A Compendium of the War of the Rebellion* (Des Moines, Iowa: Dyer Publishing Company, 1908), pp. 261–69.

44 See chart Civil War Army Corps based on notes from Dyer and *OR*, author's notes Civil War; OR, 15: 716–17 and 30, pt. l, pp. 211–12; George W. Williams, *A History of the Negro Troops in the War of the Rebellion, 1861–1865* (New York: Harper & Brothers, 1888; reprint, New York: Negro Universities Press, 1969), pp. 10–58 passim; James I. Robertson, Jr., *Soldiers Blue and Gray* (Columbia: University of South Carolina Press, 1988), pp. 19–40; Quartermaster General of the Army, comp., *Tabular Statements Showing the Names of Commanders of Army Corps, Divisions, and Brigades, United States Army, During the War of 1861 to 1865* (Philadelphia: Burk and McFetrigde, Printers and Lithographers, 1887), XXV Army Corps table.

45 Crowninshield, "Cavalry in Virginia," pp. 527–51; Tidball, "The Artillery Service," pp. 697–733; Richard J. Sommers, *Richmond Redeemed: The Siege at Petersburg* (New York: Doubleday and Co., Inc., 1981), pp. xii–xiii.

46 *OR*, 11, pt. 3, 33–36; John W. Wike, "The Wearing of Army Corps and Division Insignia in the Union Army," *Military Collector and Historian*, IV (June 1952): 35–38; Julia Lorrilard Butterfield, ed., *A Biographical Memorial of General Daniel Butterfield* (New York: Grafton Press, 1904), pp. 116–18.

47 WD GOs 56, 1866, and 15, 1869; *Army Regulations*, 1873, pp. 65–66; *Troops in Campaign, Regulations for the Army of the United States* (Washington, D.C.: Government Printing Office, 1892), pp. 3–4; Perry D. Jamieson, *Crossing the Deadly Ground: United States Army Tactics, 1865–1899* (Tuscaloosa: University of Alabama Press, 1994), pp. 123–27.

48 WD GOs 25 and 30, 1898; *Correspondence Relating to the War With Spain*, 2 vols. (Washington, D.C.: Government Printing Office, 1902), 1:1.

49 WD GOs 30, 36, and 96, 1898.

50 Rpt of the Maj Gen Commanding the Army, *Annual Reports of the War Department, 1898*, pp. 7–8, hereafter cited as *ARWD*; Russell A. Alger, *The Spanish-American War* (New York: Harper and Co., 1901), pp. 26–27; *Harper's Pictorial History of the War With Spain* (New York: Harper and Co., 1899), p. 187; *Correspondence Relating to the War With Spain*, 1:509, 519, 534, 539, and 547; WD GO 30 and 96, 1898.

51 Ltr, V Army Corps to The Adjutant General, U.S. Army, 28 May 1898, no subject, with five endorsements, AGO file 85411, Telegram, III Corps to the Quartermaster General (QMG), U.S. Army, 28 May 1898, no subject, AGO file 3198, Ltr, 1st Division, IV Corps, to The Adjutant General, IV Corps, 19 June 1898, no subject, Adjutant General's Office (AGO) file 114100, all in Record Group (hereafter cited as RG) 165, National Archives and Records Administration (hereafter cited as NARA); WD Cir 12, 1883; WD GO 99, 1898.

52 Rpt of the Maj Gen of the Army, *ARWD, 1898*, pp. 499–501; *Correspondence Relating to the War With Spain*, 2:705–08.

# CHAPTER 2

# Genesis of Permanent Divisions

*Officers who have never seen a corps, division, or brigade organized and on the march can not be expected to perform perfectly the duties required of them when war comes.*

Elihu Root[1]

At the opening of the twentieth century, following the hasty organization and deployment of the army corps during the War with Spain, the Army's leadership realized that it needed to create permanent combined arms units trained for war. Accordingly, senior officers worked toward that goal until the nation entered World War I. Their efforts reflected the principal mission of the Army at the time: to defend the vast continental United States and its modest insular empire in the Caribbean Sea and Pacific Ocean. During this period the infantry division replaced the army corps as the basic combined arms unit. Growing in size and firepower, it acquired combat support and service elements, along with an adequate staff, reflecting visions of a more complex battlefield environment. The cavalry division, designed to achieve mobility rather than to realize its combined arms potential, underwent changes similar to those of the infantry division. Army leaders also searched for ways to maintain permanent divisions that could take the field on short notice. That effort accomplished little, however, because of traditional American antipathy toward standing armies.

## *Reforms Following the War With Spain*

The Army began closely examining its organizations after the War with Spain. The War Department had been severely criticized for its poor leadership during the 1898 mobilization. Under the guidance of Secretary of War Elihu Root, it established a board to plan an Army war college that would "direct the instruction and intellectual exercise of the Army."[2] This concept inspired creation of the General Staff in 1903, which led to major reforms in Army organization and mobilization.[3]

Under the leadership of Maj. Gen. Adna R. Chaffee, the Chief of Staff, the new organization had a profound influence on the structure of the field army. In 1905 the War Department published *Field Service Regulations, United States Army*, in which Capt. Joseph T. Dickman, a General Staff member and future Third Army commander, drew together contemporary thought on tactics and logistics. Designed for the first level of officer training within the Army's educational system, the regulations covered such subjects as orders, combat, services of information and security (intelligence), subsistence, transportation, and organization. Under the guidance of Chaffee and other staff officers Dickman's organizational section directed the formation of provisional brigades and divisions during field exercises so that smaller permanent units could train for war.4

With these new ordinances, the Army departed from national and international practice, and the infantry division replaced the army corps, which had been used in the Civil War and the War with Spain, as the basic unit for combining arms. Since the mid-nineteenth century a typical European army corps had consisted of two or more divisions, a cavalry brigade, a field artillery regiment, and supporting units—about 30,000 men. Divisions usually included only infantry. Although they sometimes had artillery, cavalry, or engineer troops, they rarely included service units.5

In march formation (infantry in fours, cavalry in twos, guns and caissons in single file), a European army corps covered approximately fifteen miles of road, a day's march. To participate in a battle involving the vanguard, the corps' rear elements might have a day's march before engaging the enemy. Any greater distance meant that all corps elements could not work as a unit. In the continental United States an army corps actually required about thirty-five miles of road space because of the broken terrain and poor roads. Within a moving army corps, however, a division occupied only eleven miles.6

By replacing the army corps with the division, Dickman's regulation sought an organizational framework appropriate to the mission and the expected terrain. In 1905 the staff did not identify specific adversaries, but the planners believed that if war broke out a divisional organization was more appropriate for use in North America. Their assumption was that the nation would not be involved in a war overseas.7

For training, the regulations outlined a division that included three infantry brigades (two or more infantry regiments each), a cavalry regiment, an engineer battalion to facilitate movement, a signal company for communications, and four field hospitals. Nine field artillery batteries, organized as a provisional regiment, served both the division and other commands such as corps artillery. To attain a self-sufficient division, the planners added an ammunition column, a supply column, and a pack train, all to be manned by civilians. The regulations did not fix the strength of the organization, but in march formation it was estimated to use fourteen miles of road space. That distance represented a day's march, paralleling the length of a contemporary European army corps.8

In the field, divisions were both tactical and administrative units. Matters relating to courts martial, supply, money, property accountability, and administration, all normally vested in a territorial commander during peace, passed to the division commander during war. To carry out these duties, the division was to have a chief of staff, an adjutant general, an inspector general, a provost marshal, a judge advocate, a surgeon, and a quartermaster, along with commissary, engineer, signal, ordnance, and muster officers. The senior artillery officer served *ex officio* as the chief of the division artillery.9

The cavalry division, also described in the regulations, consisted of three cavalry brigades (two or three cavalry regiments each), six horse artillery batteries, mounted engineer and signal companies, and two field hospitals. Civilians were to man ammunition and supply columns. Because mounted troops were likely to be employed in small detachments, the cavalry division had no prescribed staff.10

Above the division level, the regulations only sketched corps and armies. Two or three infantry divisions made up an army corps, and several army corps, along with one or more cavalry divisions, formed an army. Specific details regarding higher command and control were omitted.11

When the *Field Service Regulations* were published, General Chaffee harnessed them to training and readiness. First, he directed the garrison schools to use them as textbooks, taking precedence over any others then in use. Second, he applied the regulations to both the Regular Army and the Organized Militia when in the field.12

Militia, or National Guard, units had dual missions. Each served its state of origin but, when called upon, also served in national emergencies. Under the Dick Act of 1903, National Guard units had five years to achieve the same organizational standards as the Regular Army units. To accomplish that goal, the federal government increased the funds for arms and equipment and annual training and provided additional Regular Army officers to assist with training.13

Having an outline for field organizations and units available to prepare for war, the Army turned its attention to training. Combined arms training—artillery, cavalry, and infantry—had been a part of the school curriculum at Fort Leavenworth, Kansas, since 1881, but Secretary Root gave such training added meaning in 1899 when he noted that officers needed to see a corps, division, or brigade organized and on the march to perform their duties in war. In 1902 some state and federal units held maneuvers at Camp Root, Kansas,14 but the first large drill took place two years later near Manassas, Virginia. At that time Guard units from eighteen states and selected Regular Army units trained together—a total of 26,000 men. Maneuvers on a lesser scale were held in 1906 and 1908. These biennial maneuvers proved beneficial to both professional and citizen soldiers. Regulars gained command experience, and guardsmen refined their military skills.15

Although periodic maneuvers had their merits, the General Staff soon realized that they fell short of preparing the Army for war. In 1906 the Regular Army was still dispersed among posts that accommodated anywhere from two companies to a regiment. To provide for more sustained training, the staff urged Secretary of War William Howard Taft to concentrate the regulars at brigade-size posts. Taft proved receptive, but most members of Congress opposed the reform, particularly if closing a post might affect their constituents adversely.16

*Public views the 1904 maneuvers, Manassas, Virginia;* below, *troops pass in review, 1904 Manassas maneuvers.*

# GENESIS OF PERMANENT DIVISIONS

*Maj. Gen. Henry C. Corbin and Colonel Wagner*

In 1909 Assistant Secretary of War Robert Shaw Oliver, a veteran with experience as a volunteer, Regular, and Guard officer, adopted another approach to readiness. Following the European example of mixing regulars and reserves in the same formation, he divided the nation into eight districts. Within each district, Oliver planned to form brigades, divisions, and corps for training Regular and Guard units. The district commander was to supervise all assigned regulars, but to exercise only nominal control over Guard units, which were to be federalized only during a national emergency or war. Nevertheless, Oliver expected the district commander to influence the citizen-soldier by manifesting an interest in the reserve forces. The plan was voluntary for the National Guard, but by early 1910 the governors of the New England states and New York had agreed to have their units participate.[17]

About the same time this agreement was reached, the Army modified its field organizations, retaining divisions but replacing the corps and army commands with a field army. Since the mid-nineteenth century military theorists had debated the need for the corps. Col. Arthur L. Wagner, a founding father of the Army school system, believed that it was a necessary echelon between division and army, but based on experience during the Civil War Maj. Gen. Andrew A. Humphreys, former Chief of Staff of the Army of the Potomac, disagreed. Humphreys wanted a strong division capable of independent operations, noting that the terrain and poor roads in the United States prevented the easy maneuver or movement of a large unit.[18]

Agreeing with Humphreys, the General Staff decided that a command made up of divisions, designated as a field army, best fit the nation's needs. As described in the *Field Service Regulations* of 1910, the field army comprised two or more infantry divisions, plus support troops, which included pioneer infantry (service troops for the forward area of the battlefield), heavy artillery, engineers, signal and medical troops, and ammunition and supply units, which could maneuver and fight independently. Cavalry might be included in the division if appropriate.[19]

To fit within the new concept, the General Staff, in conjunction with the Army School of the Line at Fort Leavenworth, made the infantry division a more powerful and self-sufficient organization. A field artillery brigade of two regiments with forty-eight guns replaced the provisional regiment. Infantry and cavalry regiments benefited from additional firepower. Based on experiments with machine guns in 1906, a provisional two-gun platoon had been added to each infantry and cavalry regiment, and with the new regulations the authorization was increased to six guns. Depending on range, one machine gun equaled the firepower of between sixteen and thirty-nine riflemen. Thus, divisional firepower grew substantially. Other changes improved communications by replacing the signal company with a two-company battalion and expanded the medical service by adding four ambulance companies. For the first time, a directive fixed the strength of a division at 19,850 men—740 officers, 18,533 enlisted, and 577 civilians, the last serving mostly in the ammunition and supply units. Transport for a division included 769 wagons and carts, 48 ambulances, and 8,265 animals.[20]

While making the division more powerful, the regulations realigned the division staff. The new staff consisted of a chief of staff, an adjutant general, an inspector general, a judge advocate, a quartermaster, a commissary officer, a surgeon, the commander's three aides, and six civilian clerks. Engineer and signal battalion commanders joined it at the discretion of the division commander. The provost marshal was eliminated, as were the ordnance, muster, and senior artillery officers, with most of these positions moving to the field army headquarters.[21]

A new nomenclature for divisions indicated their self-sufficiency. Instead of being numbered as the 1st, 2d, and 3d Divisions, I Army Corps, as during the Civil War and the War with Spain, units were to be numbered consecutively in the order of their formation. No reference to any field army appeared in divisional designations. As before, brigades were identified only as the 1st, 2d, and 3d brigades of a division.[22]

The new ordinances also included a 13,836-man cavalry division in the field army, and, as in the infantry division, internal changes affected firepower, logistics, and staff. A field artillery regiment replaced the six batteries, and each cavalry regiment fielded a provisional machine gun troop. The engineer and signal companies were expanded to battalions, and two ambulance companies were added. A pack train completed the division. For the first time, the cavalry division was given a staff similar to that in the infantry division. Designations of cavalry divisions were also to be numerical and consecutive in the order of their organization.[23]

Maj. Gen. James Franklin Bell, the Chief of Staff of the Army, established the First Field Army on 28 February 1910. Although merely a paper organization before mobilization, it consisted of three infantry divisions, each with three infantry brigades. Each infantry brigade comprised three infantry regiments, and the other divisional units included a cavalry regiment, an engineer battalion, and medical and signal units. In place of the field artillery brigade, each division had only one field artillery regiment. Because the artillery and cavalry regiments

# GENESIS OF PERMANENT DIVISIONS

were made up of both Regular Army and National Guard elements, Bell designated them as "National" regiments. The supply and ammunition trains, manned by civilians, were to be formed after mobilization.24

Within a few months the new Chief of Staff, Maj. Gen. Leonard Wood, reported to Secretary of War Jacob M. Dickinson that the First Field Army existed in name only. Noting that the Army lacked the required units and equipment to field the organization, he nevertheless believed that the War Department had taken the first step in organizing the Regular Army and the National Guard for modern war.25

Not everyone in the War Department agreed with the concept of the First Field Army. The Chief of the Division of Militia Affairs, Brig. Gen. Robert K. Evans, recommended that General Wood revoke the orders establishing the organization for two reasons. First, the field army did not fit any plan for the national defense, and, second, he believed that Regular and Guard units did not belong in the same formation. He further contended that the orders implied the existence of a field army. Events along the Mexican border soon caused the Army to abandon the organization, and eventually the secretary of war rescinded the orders.26

*General Bell*

## *Concentration on the Mexican Border in 1911*

In March 1911, during disorders resulting from the Mexican Revolution, the War Department deployed many Regular Army units of the First Field Army to the southern border. Units assembled at San Antonio, Texas, constituted the Maneuver Division and the Independent Cavalry Brigade, while others, concentrated at Galveston, Texas, and San Diego, California, made up separate infantry brigades. The division, following the *Field Service Regulations* outline, consisted of three infantry brigades, a field artillery brigade, an engineer battalion, and medical and signal units, but no trains. Thirty-six companies from the Coast Artillery Corps, organized as three provisional infantry regiments, comprised the brigade at Galveston. The brigade at San Diego had two infantry regiments and small medical, signal, and cavalry units, along with a provisional quartermaster (bakers and cooks) unit. The Galveston and San Diego brigades were intended to defend against possible attack by the Mexican Navy, while the Maneuver Division readied for offensive operations against Mexico.[27]

The Army experienced great difficulty with this assembly of troops. Scores of movement orders had to be issued, and inadequate arrangements for transportation caused innumerable delays. Upon arriving at their new stations, the units found themselves considerably under strength. The division initially had about 8,000 officers and enlisted men but, with the addition of recruits, its strength climbed to 12,809. That total represented only about two-thirds of the authorized strength outlined in the regulations for the division. Although the division impressed some American citizens, General Wood's comment was "How little."[28]

During the concentration of troops along the border, which lasted for almost five months, the Army learned many lessons about readiness. The foremost one concerned the effects of the lack of a mobilization plan, which caused delays in notifying and transporting units. Sixteen days were required to assemble the small force. By comparison, the following year the Bulgarians needed only eighteen days to mobilize 270,000 men against the Turks. After the troops arrived at the mobilization sites, the division's inspector general found many problems. No two units had the same tentage, transportation equipment, or quartermaster supplies. The large numbers of recruits overwhelmed the units and caused general confusion. Medical units performed poorly since they had been haphazardly organized.[29]

To correct these faults, the inspector general recommended that standard field equipment be issued to all units, that their peacetime strength be increased, and that permanent field hospitals and ambulance companies be maintained. Logistical problems stemmed from the lack of regulatory civilians in the ammunition and supply trains. But rather than urging the organization of those units, the inspector suggested that the Army experiment with "autotrucks."[30]

In the communications arena, the Signal Corps tested the telegraph, wireless telegraph (radio), and the airplane during tactical exercises. Cavalry employed the wireless telegraph, while infantry used telegraph wire, and both reported great success. In addition to training officers to fly, the airplane was used for reconnaissance in the division, which spurred further aeronautical development.[31]

When the Maneuver Division and the brigades were mobilized, General Wood expected that they could remain on the border for three months without asking Congress for additional money. He succeeded. The brigades at Galveston and San Diego were discontinued in June 1911, and divisional elements began returning to their home stations at the end of July. On 7 August the division headquarters passed into history.[32]

The mobilization served many purposes, not the least of which was to give impetus to General Wood's preparedness campaign. The performance of the division and the brigades illustrated the nation's unpreparedness for war.

## The Stimson Plan

After the breakup of the division and brigades, Secretary of War Henry L. Stimson requested the General Staff to review national defense policies and to develop a mobilization plan for the Army. Maj. William Lassiter, Capt. John McAuley Palmer, and Capt. George Van Horn Moseley prepared the recommendations submitted to Stimson in 1912 as the *Report on the Organization of Land Forces of the United States*.[33] Known as the Stimson Plan, it set out the need for "A regular army organized in divisions and cavalry brigades ready for immediate use as an expeditionary force or for other purposes. . . ." Behind it was to be "an army of national citizen soldiers organized in peace in complete divisions and prepared to reenforce the Regular Army in time of war." Finally, the plan called for "an army of volunteers to be organized under prearranged plans when greater forces are required than can be furnished by the Regular Army and the organized citizen soldiery."[34]

Although the Stimson Plan received support throughout the Army and the nation, changing the military establishment proved difficult. Congress balked at altering the laws governing the Army. The General Staff therefore opted to improve readiness by implementing as many of the recommendations as possible on the basis of existing legislation. After conferences with general officers, the National Guard, and concerned congressional members, sixteen divisions emerged as a mobilization force. The Regular Army was to furnish one cavalry and three infantry divisions, and the National Guard twelve infantry divisions. With these goals established, the staff developed plans to reorganize the two components.[35]

On 15 February 1913, Stimson announced his new arrangement for the Regular Army. To administer it, he divided the nation into Eastern, Central, Western, and Southern Departments and created northern and southern Atlantic coast artillery districts, along with a third for the Pacific coast. These departments and districts provided the framework for continued command and control regardless of the units assigned to them. Second, he arranged to mobilize field units into divisions and brigades. The 1st, 2d, and 3d Divisions were allotted to the Eastern, Central, and Western Departments, respectively, and the Cavalry Division (1st and 2d Cavalry Brigades) to the Southern Department. The 3d Cavalry Brigade, a nondivisional unit, was assigned to the Central Department. When necessary, two regiments in the Eastern Department were to combine to form the 4th Cavalry Brigade. The plan addressed primarily the defense of the continental United States, but also included the territory of Hawaii. The three infantry regiments stationed in the islands were to form the 1st Hawaiian Brigade.[36]

These arrangements fell short of perfection. Divisional components remained scattered until mobilization, thereby precluding continuous training. For example, the 1st Division's elements occupied fourteen posts. All divisions lacked units prescribed in the *Field Service Regulations*. Stimson, however, hoped that Congress would eventually authorize completion of the units.[37]

To organize the National Guard divisions, Stimson had to gain the cooperation of state governors who controlled the Guard units until federalized. Captain Moseley devised a system to divide the nation into twelve geographic districts, each with an infantry division. Thirty-two states accepted the scheme, two states remained noncommittal, and fifteen refused comment. Although the staff failed to gain unanimous support of its proposal, in 1914 it adopted the twelve-division force for the Guard (*Table 1*), to which was added three multidistrict cavalry divisions.[38]

Implementation of the plan moved slowly in the states. Governors hesitated to form certain units needed in the divisions, particularly expensive field artillery and medical organizations that did not support the Guard's state missions. The staff likewise moved slowly in developing procedures to instruct, supply, and mobilize the units. One bright area, the District of New York, which had maintained a division of its own design since 1908, quickly completed its part of the plan, perhaps because the state had been a pillar of support for the preparedness movement. Pennsylvania, the other state constituting a divisional district, which had supported a nonregulation division since 1879, gradually began to adjust its organization. Progress in the multistate districts, not unexpectedly, fell behind Pennsylvania.[39]

As it developed plans for the tactical reorganization of the Army, the General Staff pioneered the creation of tables of organization for all types of units. Forerunners of those used today, the tables brought together for easy comparison a mass of information about unit personnel and equipment previously buried in

## TABLE 1

### National Guard Infantry Divisions, 1914

| *Division* | *District* |
|---|---|
| 5th | Maine, New Hampshire, Massachusetts, Vermont, Rhode Island, and Connecticut |
| 6th | New York |
| 7th | Pennsylvania |
| 8th | Delaware, New Jersey, Maryland, District of Columbia, Virginia, and West Virginia |
| 9th | North Carolina, South Carolina, Florida, and Georgia |
| 10th | Alabama, Mississippi, Tennessee, and Kentucky |
| 11th | Michigan and Ohio |
| 12th | Illinois and Indiana |
| 13th | Wisconsin, Minnesota, North Dakota, South Dakota, and Iowa |
| 14th | Missouri, Kansas, Nebraska, Colorado, and Wyoming |
| 15th | Arkansas, Arizona, New Mexico, Texas, Oklahoma, and Louisiana |
| 16th | California, Oregon, Montana, Utah, Idaho, Nevada, and Washington |

various War Department publications, greatly easing the task of determining requirements for mobilizations. Although the new tables did not alter the basic combat triad structure of the infantry division, their formulation was accompanied by internal changes in the infantry regiments and the divisional support echelon. Revisions eliminated the pack train, authorized a small engineer train, and manned the engineer, supply, and ammunition trains with military personnel instead of civilians.[40]

In 1912 Congress created a service corps within the Quartermaster Corps to replace civilian employees and soldiers detailed from combat units for duty as wagonmasters, teamsters, blacksmiths, and other such laborers and artificers. Only nineteen civilians—veterinarians and clerks—remained in the division. For the first time, sources for military police and train guards were specified. Traditionally, commanders gave regiments or battalions that had suffered severely in battle the honor of serving as provost guards, especially those that had conducted themselves with distinction.[41]

In the infantry regiment, besides the provisional machine gun company provided for in 1910, provisional headquarters and supply companies were to provide mounted orderlies and regimental wagon drivers. The arrangement eliminated the need to detail men from rifle companies, a practice that had plagued unit commanders since the Revolutionary War. These and other changes raised the division's strength to 22,646 officers and enlisted men and 19 civilians.[42]

The place of possible employment continued to influence the division's basic structure. Before the tables of organization were prepared, the staff debated whether a division should have two or three infantry brigades, noting that European armies continued to use a two-division corps organization. Maj. Nathaniel F. McClure, appointed as an instructor in military art at the Army Service Schools, Fort Leavenworth, in 1913, attributed the European organization to economy in the use of personnel and to the proper use of sophisticated road networks. He concluded, however, that what the Europeans really wanted was a corps built upon multiples of three—regiments, brigades, and divisions. When preparing the Stimson Plan, the officers determined that a division with two infantry brigades limited the commander's ability to subdivide his forces for frontal and flank attacks while at the same time attempting to maintain a reserve. Along with ease of command, deployment on a road influenced the decision. Because a division containing two infantry brigades would make less economical use of road space than one of three brigades, the three-brigade division remained the Army's basis for combining arms. In march formation, it measured about fifteen miles.[43]

The revision of the cavalry division in many ways paralleled that of the infantry division. Military personnel manned ammunition and supply trains, and troopers from the cavalry regiments served as military police and train guards. Each cavalry regiment was authorized provisional headquarters and machine gun troops similar to those in the infantry regiment. The most significant change was in the division's three cavalry brigades, with each being reduced from three to two regiments since three cavalry regiments in a brigade required too much road space. The division's strength stood at 10,161, approximately 4,000 fewer men than the 1910 unit.[44]

To complement the 1914 tables of organization, Maj. James A. Logan revised the 1910 *Field Service Regulations*. The new edition emphasized the division as the basic organization for conducting offensive operations in a mobile army. Logan defined the division as "A self-contained unit made up of all necessary arms and services, and complete in itself with every requirement for independent action incident to its operations."[45] His definition became the customary description of a division.

## *Operations on the Mexican Border, 1913–1917*

The Mexican border remained a troubled area. Following the mobilization of 1911, the Army patrolled the frontier with small units, but when insurrectionists overthrew the Mexican government in 1913, President Taft decided on a show of force similar to the earlier concentration of troops. On 21 February he ordered Maj. Gen. William H. Carter, commander of the Central Department, to assemble the most fully manned of the Army's divisions, the 2d, on the Gulf coast of Texas. Unlike its mobilization of the Maneuver Division in 1911, the War Department used a mere five-line telegram to deploy the unit. Carter, who arrived with his staff in Texas within three days, established the division headquarters and its 4th and 6th Brigades at Texas City and the 5th Brigade at Galveston. The division lacked, however, some field artillery, medical, signal, and engineer elements and all its trains.[46]

Tension remained high between the United States and Mexico in 1914, and in response President Woodrow Wilson adjusted the deployment of military units to protect American interests. United States naval forces occupied Vera Cruz, Mexico, and soldiers soon relieved the sailors ashore. On 30 April the 5th Brigade, 2d Division, augmented with cavalry, field artillery, engineer, signal, bakery, and aviation units, and almost the entire divisional staff took up positions in the city. To placate uneasy United States citizens along the border, the 2d and 8th Brigades, elements of the 1st and 3d Divisions, and some smaller units moved to the southern frontier. In November the crisis at Vera Cruz ended and the 5th Brigade returned to Galveston, but activity resumed the following month when the 6th Brigade, 2d Division, deployed to Naco, Arizona. For the next few months no major changes took place in the disposition of forces. Then, in August 1915, a hurricane hit Texas City and Galveston, killing thirteen enlisted men and causing considerable damage to the 2d Division's property. Officials in Washington decided that the division was no longer needed there and ordered its units moved to other posts in the Southern Department. The divisional headquarters was demobilized on 18 October 1915.[47]

Before the Vera Cruz expedition, General Carter had evaluated the 2d

*27th Infantry, 2d Division, encampment, Texas City, Texas*

Division. Although he found no glaring deficiencies in the unit, he recommended the maintenance of permanent headquarters detachments for divisions and brigades in peacetime to ease mobilization and to prevent the breakup of regimental organizations for division details. Carter also recommended that all communications equipment be centralized in the signal unit because the training of men assigned to combat arms units to operate signal gear seemed wasteful.[48]

On 9 March 1916, trouble flared again on the southern border when Mexican bandits raided Columbus, New Mexico, killing and wounding several soldiers and civilians. The following day the Southern Department commander, Maj. Gen. Frederick Funston, ordered Brig. Gen. John J. Pershing, commander of the 8th Brigade, to apprehend the perpetrators. For his mission Pershing organized a provisional division and designated it as the Punitive Expedition, United States Army.[49]

This division differed considerably from the organizations outlined in the *Field Service Regulations*. It consisted of two provisional cavalry brigades (two cavalry regiments and a field artillery battery each) and one infantry brigade (two regiments and two engineer companies), with medical, signal, transportation, and air units as divisional troops. The design of the division followed the organizational axiom that it adapt to the terrain and roads where the enemy was located. In hostile and barren northern Mexico, Pershing planned to pursue the bandits with cavalry and to protect his communication lines with infantry.[50]

*4th South Dakota Infantry on the Mexican border, 1916*

Violence intensified along the border during the spring of 1916, causing a general mobilization. After a raid in May at Glen Springs, Texas, President Wilson called the National Guard of Arizona, New Mexico, and Texas into federal service. Following another raid on 16 June, he federalized all Guard units assigned to tactical divisions designated in the Stimson Plan.[51]

This final call exposed flaws in the nation's war plans. In some states mobilization locations were inaccessible, quartermaster supplies were insufficient, and even required forms were in short supply. Guard units were under strength and poorly trained. Some men failed to honor their enlistments, while others who were physically unfit entered the service. Besides these and other deficiencies, the need to have troops on the border meant that only two divisions, the 6th from New York and the 7th from Pennsylvania, mobilized in accordance with the Stimson Plan. On 4 August the War Department directed General Funston to organize ten divisions and six brigades provisionally from the remaining Guard units. But not all of these organizations could be formed because of the rapid shifting of units to and from the border. Although the mobilization pointed out many weaknesses in the nation's preparation for war, it provided an invaluable training opportunity for the Guard.[52]

The Punitive Expedition stayed in Mexico until February 1917. When hostile acts had abated along the border during the fall of 1916, the War Department had begun to demobilize the Guard. By the end of March most units had returned to state control. Pershing, the new Southern Department commander following

Funston's sudden death from a heart attack in February 1917, realigned the Regular Army forces. He organized provisionally a cavalry brigade and three infantry divisions, but they existed for less than three months. With the nation's entry into World War I and the need for troops in Europe, Pershing's divisions were disbanded. Smaller units, however, continued border surveillance.[53]

## *Authorization of Permanent Divisions*

While the Army concentrated most of its regulars in the United States on the Mexican border in 1915, the ongoing war in Europe prompted Secretary of War Lindley M. Garrison to reexamine national defense policies. Among other matters, he asked the General Staff to investigate the organizations and strength figures needed by the Regular Army and National Guard, the reserve forces required, and the relationship of the regulars and guardsmen to a volunteer force. Garrison held the opinion that the federal government's lack of control over the National Guard was a fundamental defect.[54]

Members of the General Staff worked for six months to answer Garrison, and the War Department published their findings as the *Statement of Proper Military Policy* in 1915. It outlined a 281,000-man Regular Army and a 500,000-man federal reserve. An additional 500,000 reserve force was to buttress the reserves. Under the new policy the National Guard was downgraded to a volunteer contingent force that would be used only during war.[55]

Proposed legislation based on the policy statement, which was dubbed the "Continental Army" plan, quickly ran into congressional opponents who were unwilling to abandon the National Guard. But the debate led eventually to the National Defense Act of 1916. The new act provided that the "Army of the United States" would consist of the Regular Army, the Volunteer Army, the Officers' Reserve Corps, the Enlisted Reserve Corps, the National Guard in the service of the United States, and such other land forces as were or might be authorized by Congress. The president was to determine both the number and type of National Guard units that each state would maintain. Both the Regular Army and the National Guard were to be organized, insofar as practicable, into permanent brigades and divisions. Command echelons above divisions reverted to army corps and armies, the traditional command system; no mention was made of independent field armies directly controlling divisions. Undoubtedly the war in Europe, which involved large armies, caused the staff to revert to that system. To resolve the long-standing question of whether Guard units could be used outside the United States, the law empowered the president to draft units into federal service under certain conditions. Men in drafted units would be discharged from state service and become federal troops subject to employment wherever needed. Congress continued to dictate regimental organizations.[56]

The War Department published new tables of organization for infantry and cavalry divisions in May 1917. The structure of the infantry division remained similar to that mandated in 1914. Internal changes dealt with firepower, another consequence of observing the pattern of the European war. Infantry regiments gained additional riflemen, and the provisional headquarters, supply, and machine gun companies were made permanent. The field artillery brigade also gained considerable firepower, with one regiment of 3.8-inch howitzers and two regiments of 3-inch guns replacing the two regiments authorized in 1914. A two-battalion engineer regiment replaced the battalion, the signal battalion grew in size, and an aero squadron equipped with twelve aircraft joined the division for reconnaissance and observation. Enlarged ammunition, supply, engineer, and sanitary trains supported the arms, and the tables provided for the trains to be either motorized or horse-drawn. The tables also called for a headquarters troop for the division and headquarters detachments for infantry and artillery brigades. These units were to furnish mess, transport, and administrative support for the division to operate on a more complex battlefield. The redesigned division for war numbered 28,256 officers and enlisted men when the trains were authorized wagons or 28,334 when they were authorized motorized equipment (*Chart 1*).[57]

The staff, in rationalizing the division, divided the road space it would use between combat and support elements. Combat elements used fourteen miles, while the support elements, depending on whether the trains were motorized or horse-drawn, used five to six miles. Although it required about twenty miles in march formation, a 25 percent increase in road space over the 1914 organization, the division was still thought to be able to move to battle on a single road.[58]

The new tables dramatically changed the structure of the cavalry division for war. Cavalry brigades reverted to three regiments each, and the nine cavalry regiments acquired permanent headquarters, supply, and machine gun troops. As in the infantry division, the cavalry division fielded an aero squadron. The tables also introduced a divisional engineer train and enlarged the ammunition, supply, and sanitary trains. The division headquarters and headquarters troop and brigade headquarters and headquarters detachments rounded out the unit. Given these changes, the size of the division rose from 10,161 to 18,164 when the trains were equipped with wagons and 18,176 when they were equipped with motorized vehicles (*Chart 2*), and it occupied approximately nineteen miles of road space on the march.[59]

To achieve the mobilization force that the *Statement of Proper Military Policy* proposed—six cavalry brigades, two cavalry divisions, and twenty infantry divisions—the Army needed more troops. In 1916 Congress increased the number of Regular Army regiments to 118 (7 engineer, 21 field artillery, 25 cavalry, and 65 infantry) and increased the size of the National Guard, 800 men for each senator and representative, to be raised over the next five years. Several developments, however, interfered with implementation of the Regular Army portion of the act, especially activities along the Mexican border, a reduction in the General Staff that prevented appropriate planning, and the nation's plunge into the European war.[60]

# CHART 1—Infantry Division, 1917

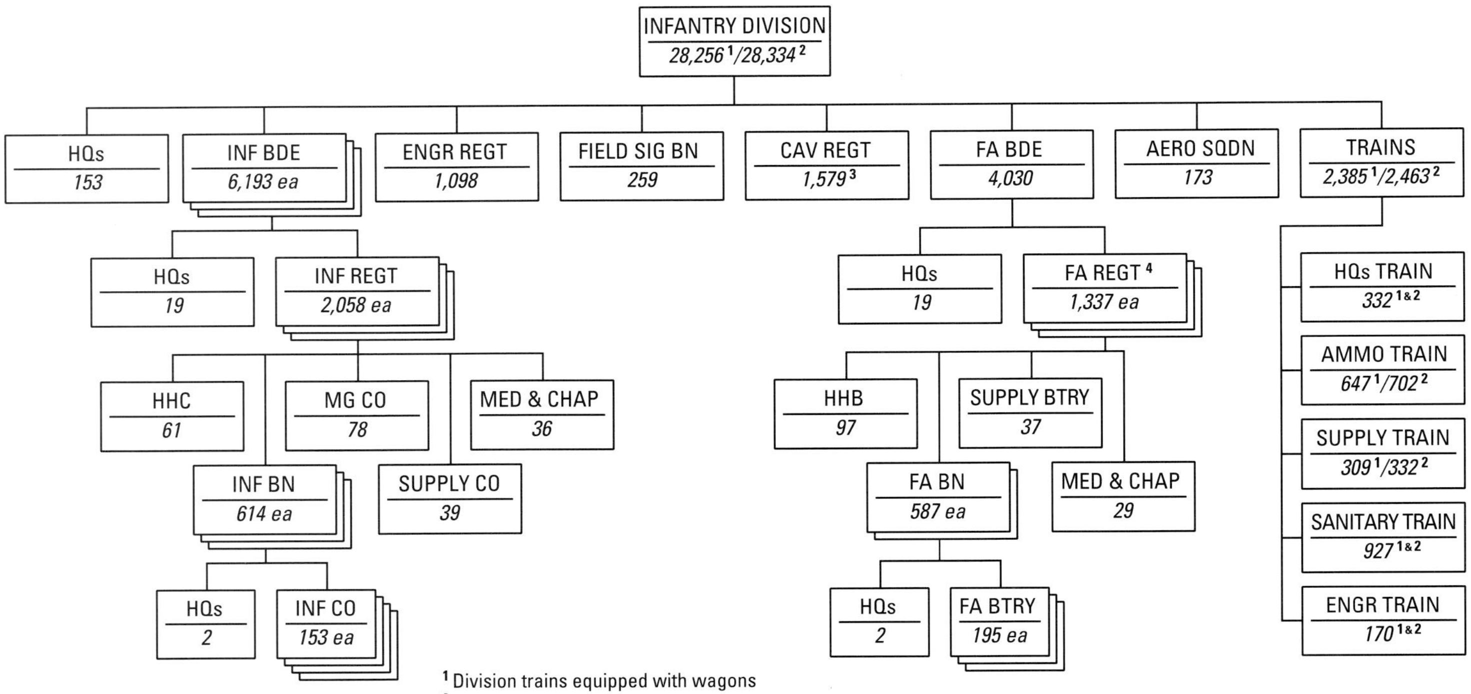

**INFANTRY DIVISION**
28,256[1] / 28,334[2]

- **INF BDE** — 6,193 ea
  - HQs — 153
  - **INF REGT** — 2,058 ea
    - HQs — 19
    - HHC — 61
    - MG CO — 78
    - SUPPLY CO — 39
    - MED & CHAP — 36
    - **INF BN** — 614 ea
      - HQs — 2
      - **INF CO** — 153 ea
- **ENGR REGT** — 1,098
- **FIELD SIG BN** — 259
- **CAV REGT** — 1,579[3]
- **FA BDE** — 4,030
  - HQs — 19
  - HHB — 97
  - **FA REGT**[4] — 1,337 ea
    - SUPPLY BTRY — 37
    - MED & CHAP — 29
    - **FA BN** — 587 ea
      - HQs — 2
      - **FA BTRY** — 195 ea
- **AERO SQDN** — 173
- **TRAINS** — 2,385[1] / 2,463[2]
  - HQs TRAIN — 332[1]
  - AMMO TRAIN — 647[1] / 702[2]
  - SUPPLY TRAIN — 309[1] / 332[2]
  - SANITARY TRAIN — 927[1 & 2]
  - ENGR TRAIN — 170[1 & 2]

[1] Division trains equipped with wagons
[2] Division trains equipped with motorized vehicles
[3] Chart 2, Cavalry Division, 1917, depicts the structure of the Cavalry Regiment
[4] Contains two 3" gun regiments and one 3.8" howitzer regiment

## TABLE 2

### National Guard Infantry Divisions, 1917

| Division | District |
|---|---|
| 5th | Maine, New Hampshire, Massachusetts, Connecticut, Vermont, and Rhode Island |
| 6th | New York |
| 7th | Pennsylvania |
| 8th | New Jersey, Delaware, District of Columbia, Maryland, and Virginia |
| 9th | North Carolina, South Carolina, and Tennessee |
| 10th | Alabama, Georgia, and Florida |
| 11th | Michigan and Wisconsin |
| 12th | Illinois |
| 13th | Iowa, Minnesota, Nebraska, North Dakota, and South Dakota |
| 14th | Kansas and Missouri |
| 15th | Oklahoma and Texas |
| 16th | Ohio and West Virginia |
| 17th | Indiana and Kentucky |
| 18th | Arkansas, Louisiana, and Mississippi |
| 19th | Arizona, California, Colorado, Nevada, New Mexico, and Utah |
| 20th | Idaho, Montana, Oregon, Washington, and Wyoming |

Meanwhile the Militia Bureau, formerly the Division of Militia Affairs, began work on new plans to organize Guard divisions. It scrapped the voluntary Stimson Plan and directed the organization of sixteen infantry and two cavalry divisions. Brig. Gen. William A. Mann, Chief of the Militia Bureau, sent the states advance copies of the new tables in January 1917 to acquaint them with the types of units they needed to maintain. Then on 5 May he forwarded the plan for organizing the divisions (*Table 2*), which gave the infantry divisions priority over the cavalry divisions. Because the Regular Army could more expeditiously organize new units for the existing emergency, Mann did not ask the states to raise any units at that time.[61]

Between the War with Spain and the United States' intervention in World War I, the Army's principal mission was to defend the national territory and its insular possessions. During this period the Army tested and adopted the infantry division as its basic combined arms unit. The underlying planning assumption was that the infantry division would fight in the United States. This meant, in turn, that one of the principal determinants of a division's size was road-marching speed. The cav-

CHART 2—Cavalry Division, 1917

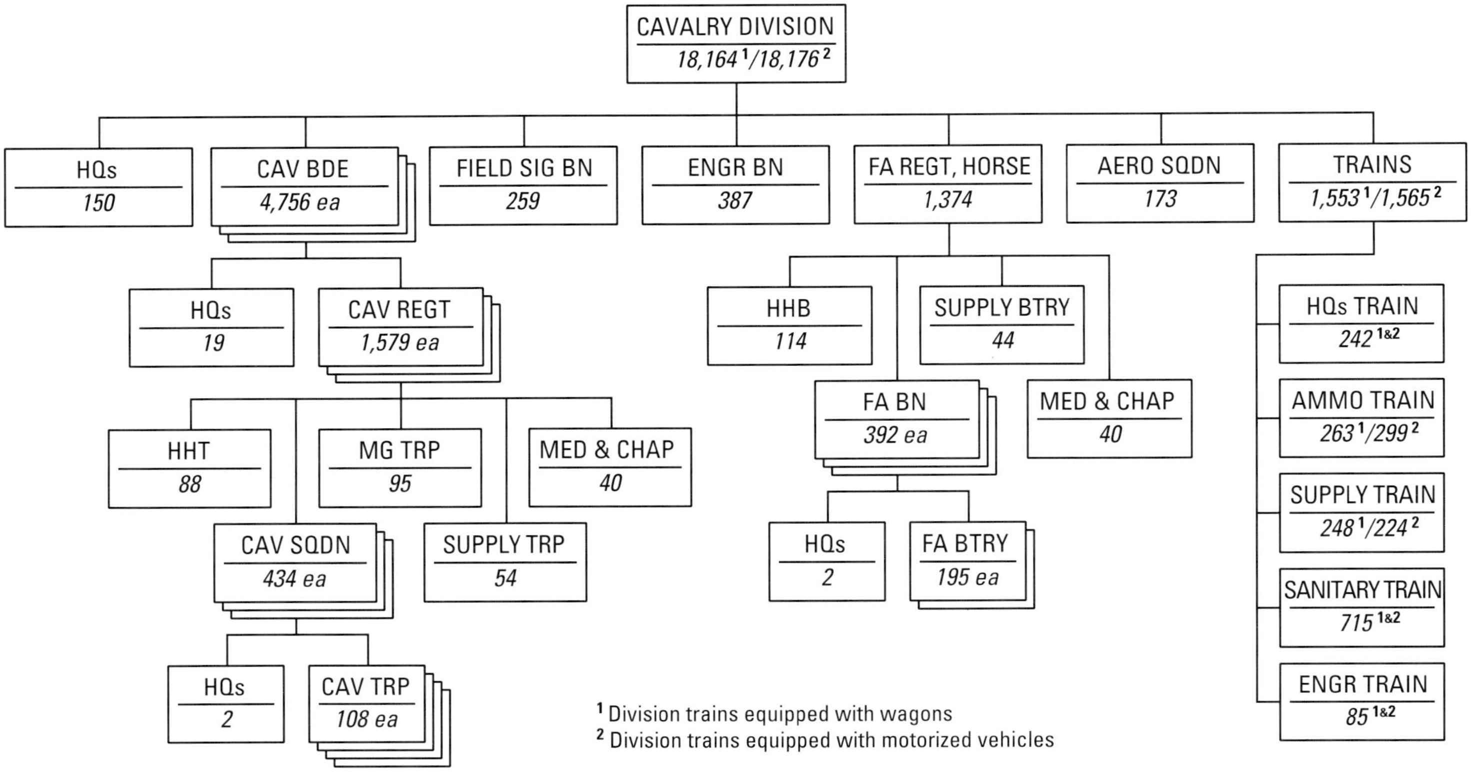

- CAVALRY DIVISION — 18,164[1]/18,176[2]
  - CAV BDE — 4,756 ea
    - HQs — 150
    - CAV REGT — 1,579 ea
      - HQs — 19
      - HHT — 88
      - MG TRP — 95
      - MED & CHAP — 40
      - SUPPLY TRP — 54
      - CAV SQDN — 434 ea
        - HQs — 2
        - CAV TRP — 108 ea
  - FIELD SIG BN — 259
  - ENGR BN — 387
  - FA REGT, HORSE — 1,374
    - HHB — 114
    - SUPPLY BTRY — 44
    - MED & CHAP — 40
    - FA BN — 392 ea
      - HQs — 2
      - FA BTRY — 195 ea
  - AERO SQDN — 173
  - TRAINS — 1,553[1]/1,565[2]
    - HQs TRAIN — 242[1&2]
    - AMMO TRAIN — 263[1]/299[2]
    - SUPPLY TRAIN — 248[1]/224[2]
    - SANITARY TRAIN — 715[1&2]
    - ENGR TRAIN — 85[1&2]

[1] Division trains equipped with wagons
[2] Division trains equipped with motorized vehicles

alry division, although not neglected, remained more or less a theoretical unit. As the Army mobilized for the Mexican border crisis and took note of trends in foreign armies during the initial campaigns of World War I, its leaders became increasingly convinced of the need to create permanent tactical divisions. Congress approved them in 1916, but the nation entered World War I before these plans had been perfected.

Events during the next two years, however, profoundly affected divisional organizations, the infantry division in particular. For the first time in the nation's experience, the United States Army mobilized a huge expeditionary force to fight overseas in Western Europe, a mission for which it was thoroughly unprepared. The day of the old constabulary army was over. Faced with threats to national security of hitherto unimagined scope emanating from the Old World, the nation had to revolutionize its army to wage war against a formidable continental opponent. The necessity for an effective combined arms organization would force extraordinary changes in its entire structure.

## Notes

1 Rpt of the Sec. of War, *ARWD, 1899*, p. 49.

2 Ibid.

3 WD GO 120, 1903.

4 Ltr, Capt Joseph. T. Dickman to Brig Gen J. Franklin Bell, 16 Sep 1904, no subject, and Ltr, Brig Gen J. Franklin Bell to Capt J. T. Dickman, 11 Nov 04, no subject, AGO file 1168, RG 393, NARA; *Field Service Regulations, United States Army, 1905*, see table of contents.

5 *Field Service Regulations, 1905* pp. 11–13; Arthur Wagner, *Organization and Tactics*, 7th ed. (Kansas City: Hudson-Kimberly Publishing Co., 1906), pp. 11–12; Paul Bronsart Van Schellendorff, *The Duties of the General Staff*, 4th ed. (London: Harrison and Sons, 1905), pp. 223–26, 235–38; William Balck, *Taktik [Tactics]*, vol. 3, *Kriegsgliederung, Nachrichten, Befehle, Marschdienst* (*Military Organization, Communications, Orders, and Marches*), 4th ed. (Berlin: R. Eisenschmidt, 1903– 07), pp. 16–17, 28–33.

6 *Field Service Regulations*, 1905, p. 44; Memo Rpt, War Plans Division to the C of S, 5 May 1905, sub: A Proper Proportion of field artillery for the mobile army of the U.S. AGO file, Journal, Reports and Related Paper of the Third Division, 1903–1910, RG 165, NARA.

7 N. F. McClure, "The Infantry Division and Its Composition," *Journal of the Military Service Institution* 50 (Jan–Feb 1912): 5–9.

8 *Field Service Regulations* 1905, p. 12, 87–88. Infantry and cavalry regiments were the largest permanent units in the peacetime Army. In 1901 Congress abolished artillery regiments (coast and field). Field artillery regiments were reestablished in 1907.

9 Field Service Regulations, 1905, pp. 25–26.

10 Ibid., p. 12.

11 Ibid.

12 WD Cirs 28, 50, and 61, 1905. In 1903 Congress revised the militia system, dividing the militia into Organized Militia and Reserve Militia classes. The Reserve Militia consisted of an unorganized manpower pool, while the Organized Militia, commonly known as the National Guard, included those units maintained by the states, territories, and District of Columbia. When discussing the National Guard, the District of Columbia is treated as a state unless otherwise noted.

13 WD GO 7, 1903.

14 Timothy K. Nenninger, *The Leavenworth Schools and the Old Army* (Westport, Conn: Greenwood Press, 1978), p. 22–23; Rpt of the Sec. of War, *ARWD, 1899*, pp. 48–49, *ARWD, 1902*, pp. 50– 52; Jamieson, *Crossing the Deadly Ground*, pp. 60–62. Camp Root, Kansas, today is Camp Whiteside, a subpost of Fort Riley.

15 *ARWD, 1904*, p. 30, *ARWD, 1906*, p. 47, *ARWD, 1908*, p. 37, *ARWD, 1909*, pp. 28–32; Rpt of the Chief of Staff, *ARWD, 1904*, p. 223.

16 Rpt of the Chief of Staff, *ARWD, 1906*, pp. 552–53; Ltr, Brig Gen J. Franklin Bell to Gen Leonard Wood, 18 Apr 12, Wood Papers, Library of Congress (hereafter cited as LC).

17 Rpt of the Sec. of War, *ARWD, 1909*, pp. 28–32; "The First Field Army, the Initial Step in the Correlation of the Regular Army with the National Guard," *The National Guard Magazine* 6 (Apr 1910): 352– 54; WD GO 35, 1910.

18 McClure, "The Infantry Division," pp. 6–9; *Field Service Regulations*, 1910, p. 13.

19 *Field Service Regulations, 1910*, p. 13.

20 *Army and Navy Journal* 46 (22 May 09): 1063; Ltr, CG, Philippine Dept, to Army C of S, 27 Jan 1914, sub: Revision of Field Service Regulations, Wood Papers, LC; *Field Service Regulations, 1910*, pp. 12–13, 15, 42–45; Edgar Raines, "MG J. Franklin Bell and Military Reform; The Chief of Staff Years, 1906–1910" (Ph.D. dissertation, University of Wisconsin, 1976), p. 470; Mahon and Danysh, *Infantry Part I*, pp. 38–40.

21 *Field Service Regulations*, 1910, p. 15–16.

22 Ibid., p. 13, 34–35; Memo for Secretary, Second Section, Army Staff, 1 Feb 1910, sub: Report of Committee of Second Section, General Staff, on proposed scheme for organizing into one

unit the mobile troops of the regular army and organized militia now stationed in New York and New England, AGO Rpt of Second Section, General Staff 1 Jan–30 Apr 1910, RG 165, NARA.

23 *Field Service Regulations*, 1910, pp. 36–37.

24 WD GO 35, 1910.

25 Rpt of the Chief of Staff, *ARWD, 1910*, p. 128.

26 Memo, Chief, Div. of Militia Affairs, to CofS, sub: Revocation of General Orders No. 35, WD 1910, 8 Jul 11, AGO file 6106–3, RG 168, NARA; *Report on Mobilization of the Organized Militia and National Guard of the United States* (Washington: D.C.: Government Printing Office, 1916), p. 48; WD GO 6, 1914.

27 Rpt of the Sec. of War, Rpt of TAG, Rpt of th QMG, *ARWD, 1911*, pp. 12–16, 238–41, 337; Memo for record, 7 Mar 11, no subject, Wood Papers, LC.

28 Rpt of the Chief of Staff and Rpt of TAG, *ARWD, 1911*, pp. 156–57, 238–42. Russell F. Weigley, *History of the United States Army* (New York: Macmillan, 1967), p. 334. The quote is from ltr, Gen Wood to Col James G. Harbord, 26 Apr 1911, Wood Papers, LC.

29 Clarence C. Clendenen, *Blood on the Border: The United States Army and the Mexican Irregulars* (New York: Macmillan, 1969), p. 148–49; WCD, "Statement for release in morning papers on Monday, Febraury 3," Wood Papers, LC.

30 Rpt of the Inspector General, *ARWD, 1911*, pp. 267–69.

31 Rpt of the Chief Signal Officer, *ARWD, 1911*, pp. 721, 739.

32 Ltr, William Howard Taft to Gen Leonard Wood, 12 Mar 1912, no subject, Wood Papers, LC: Rpt of TAG, *ARWD, 1911*, p. 242.

33 Ltr, John M. Palmer to J. F. Morrison, 22 Jan 12, John McA. Palmer Papers, LC; I. B. Holley, Jr., *General John M. Palmer, Citizen Soldiers, and the Army of a Democracy* (Westport, Conn: Greenwood Press, 1983), pp. 202–05.

34 Rpt on the Organization of Land Forces of the United States, Appendix A, *ARWD, 1912*, p. 125.

35 Rpt Sec. of War, *ARWD, 1912*, pp. 14–16; Ltr, AG, Mass. to Gen Wood, 3 Oct 1912, Wood Papers, LC (other letters from state adjutants general are in the Wood Papers; Memo for CofS, draft of Ltr to governors on the reorganization of the National Guard, 6 Nov 12, War College Division, Army Staff (hereafter cited as WCD), 7409–1, RG 168, NARA.

36 WD GO 9, 1913; WCD, "Statement for release in morning papers on Monday, February 3," 1 Feb 13, Wood Papers, LC.

37 "General Orders No. 9," *Infantry Journal* 9 (Mar–Apr 1913): 706–08.

38 George Van Horn Moseley, "One Soldier's Journey," Ms history, 3 vols., 1:103, Moseley Papers, LC; Memo 52103, C, Division of Militia Affairs, to C, WCD, sub: Organized Military Divisional Organization, 12 Jan 15, AGO file 7409–25, RG 168, NARA; WD Cir 8, 1913, and 19, 1914; "The Division Plan," *National Guard Magazine* 10 (Jan 1913): 14.

39 Rpt of the Sec. of War and Rpt of the C of S, *ARWD, 1913*, pp. 31, 174; GO 7, State of New York, 1908, printed in *Rpt of the Adjutant General, State of New York, 1908*, p. 270; GO 1, Pennsylvania National Guard, 1879, printed in *Rpt of the Adjutant General, Pennsylvania, 1879*, p. 83.

40 Memo, WCD for C of S, 21 Feb 1914, sub: *Tables of Organization, US Army, 1914*, AGO file 8371, RG 165, NARA; Tables of Organization: U.S. Army, 1914 (Washington: D.C.: Government Printing Office, 1914), p. 19 (hereafter cited as *TO, 1914*).

41 *TO, 1914*, p. 19; James A. Huston, *Sinews of War: Army Logistics* (Washington, D.C.: Government Printing Office, 1966), p. 295; Wagner, *Organization and Tactics*, pp. 19–20.

42 *TO, 1914*, pp. 12–13, 19.

43 McClure, "The Infantry Division." p. 10; *Report on the Organization of Land Forces in ARWD, 1912*, pp. 103–04.

44 *TO, 1914*, pp. 14, 23; Report on the *Organization of Land Forces*, pp. 104–05.

45 *Field Service Regulations* 1914, p. 10.

46 Rpt of the Sec. of War, *ARWD, 1912*, pp. 13–14; Rpt of the Sec. of War and Rpt of the Second Division, ARWD, 1913, pp. 9–10, 113; Thomas P Burdett, "Mobilizations of 1911 and

1913," *Military Review* 53 (Jul 1974): 72.

47 Frederic L. Huidekoper, *Military Unpreparedness of the United States* (New York: Macmillan, 1915), pp. 446–48; Rpt of the C of S, 1914, and Rpt of TAG, *ARWD, 1914*, pp. 135–36, 179; Rpt of the C of S and Rpt of TAG, *ARWD, 1915*, pp. 151–52, 211–12; Clendenen, *Blood on the Border*, p. 162; Burdett, "Mobilizations of 1911 and 1913," p. 72; Rpt of TAG, *ARWD, 1916*, p. 278.

48 Rpt of the Second Division, *ARWD, 1913*, pp. 118–19.

49 Rpt of the Chief of Staff, *ARWD, 1916*, pp. 186–89; John J. Pershing, Report of Operations of the Punitive Expedition to 30 June 1916, pp. 4–5, AGO file 2480591 RG 120, NARA; John A. Porter, "The Punitive Expedition," Quartermaster Review 12 (Jan–Feb 1933): 18–30.

50 Frederick Funston, Annual Report for FY 1916, Southern Department, p. 26, AGO file 243231, RG 120, NARA; Robert T. Thomas and Inez V. Allen, "The Mexican Punitive Expedition under Brig. Gen. John J. Pershing," Ms in the Organizational History Branch, Center of Military History, hereafter cited as DAMH-HSO, p. II–2; Porter, "The Punitive Expedition," pp. 22–23.

51 Rpt of the Chief of Staff, *ARWD, 1916*, pp. 186–89.

52 *Report on Mobilization of the Organized Militia and the National Guard of the United States, 1916*, pp. 10, 50–51; "Mobilization in Spite of War Department," *National Guard Magazine*, 13 (Aug 1916): 153+; Ltr, George Van Horn Moseley to Leonard Wood, 3 Sep 1916, no subject, Wood Papers, LC; John F. O'Ryan, *The Story of the 27th Division*, 2 vols. (New York: Wynkoop Hallenbeck Crawford Co., 1921), 1:120–25; *Pennsylvania in the World War: An Illustrated History of the Twenty-Eighth Division*, 2 vols. (Pittsburgh: States Publications Society, 1921), pp. 1:120–25.

53 Rpt of TAG, *ARWD, 1917*, p. 196–97; GO 8 and 25, Southern Department, 1917, copies in Division General files, DAMH-HSO; *Order of Battle of the United States Land Forces in the World War (1917–19), Zone of the Interior* (Washington, D.C.: Government Printing Office, 1949), pp. 602–05.

54 John P. Finnegan, *Against the Specter of a Dragon* (Westport, Connecticut: Greenwood Press, 1974), pp. 45–46; Rpt of Sec. of War, Appendix C, Statement of Proper Military Policy, ARWD, 1915, pp. 113, 126–31.

55 Statement of Proper Military Policy, pp. 126–31; Finnegan, Against the Specter of a Dragon, pp. 47–48.

56 Weigley, History of the United States Army, 344–48; WD Bull 16, 1916; Finnegan, *Against the Specter of a Dragon*, p. 44–52; "Mobilization in Spite of War Department," 153+.

57 *Table of Organization US Army, 1917* (Washington, D.C.: Government Printing Office, 1917), pp. 39–40, (hereafter cited as *TO 1917)*.

58 Ibid.

59 Ibid., pp. 57–58.

60 *Statement of Proper Military Policy*, pp. 124–26; WD Bull 16, 1916; WD GO 22 and 50, 1916.

61 Rpt of the Chief of the Militia Bureau, *ARWD, 1917*, pp. 850–52; Rpt of the Chief of the Militia Bureau, *ARWD, 1918*, p. 1102; Ltr, Chief of the Militia Bureau, to TAGs of all States, Territory of Hawaii, District of Columbia, and inspector-instructors and officers in charge of militia affairs, department headquarters, 5 May 1917, sub: Organization and entry in Federal service of National Guard, (MB) file 325.4, RG 168, NARA.

# CHAPTER 3

# The Test—World War I

*Both [French and British] commissions were anxious for an American force, no matter how small. . . . I opposed this on the ground that the small force would belittle our effort; was undignified and would give a wrong impression of our intentions. I held out for at least a division to show the quality of our troops and command respect for our flag.*

Maj. Gen. Hugh L. Scott[1]

World War I, an unprecedented conflict, forced fundamental changes in the organization of United States Army field forces. The infantry division remained the Army's primary combined arms unit, but the principles governing its organization took a new direction because of French and British experiences in trench warfare. Column length or road space no longer controlled the size and composition of the infantry division; instead, firepower, supply, and command and control became paramount. The cavalry division received scant attention as the European battlefield offered few opportunities for its use.

## *First Revisions*

Between 6 April 1917, when the nation declared war, and 12 June, when the first troops left the United States for France, the War College Division of the Army General Staff revised the structure of the infantry division extensively. British and French officers spurred the changes when they visited Washington, D.C., to discuss the nation's participation in the war. They believed the American division lacked firepower and presented command and control problems because of its many small units. But they also had their own political-military agenda. Believing that time precluded organizing and training U.S. units, they wanted the nation's immediate involvement in the war to be through a troop replacement program for their drained formations, a scheme that became known as "amalgamation."[2]

Chief of Staff Maj. Gen. Hugh L. Scott opposed Americans' serving in Allied units, believing that the U.S. division could be reorganized to overcome any French and British objections. Such a unit would prove the quality of the American soldier and ensure that the Allies did not underestimate the nation's war efforts. Scott directed the War College Division to study a divisional structure comprising two infantry brigades, each having two large infantry regiments, as a means of reducing the span of control. It was also to include light and heavy

*General Scott*

artillery, signal and engineer troops, and service units. A small division, some 13,000 infantrymen, would allow greater mobility and enhance the ability to exchange units in the line and maintain battle momentum. The French and the British had found that for each unit on line—army corps, division, brigade, regiment, battalion, or company—they needed a comparable unit prepared to relieve it without mixing organizations from various commands. The French had tried relief by army corps but had settled on relief by small divisions. Scott felt that his proposal would ease the difficulty of exchanging units on the battlefield.[3]

By 10 May 1917, Majs. John McAuley Palmer, Dan T. Moore, and Briant Wells of the War College Division outlined a division of 17,700 men, which included about 11,000 infantrymen in accordance with Scott's idea. In part it resembled the French square division. Planners eliminated 1 infantry brigade and cut the number of infantry regiments from 9 to 4, thereby reducing the number of infantry battalions from 27 to 12. But regimental firepower increased, with the rifle company swelling from 153 officers and enlisted men to 204, and the number of regimental machine guns rising dramatically from 4 to 36. To accommodate the additional machine guns, Palmer, Moore, and Wells outlined a new infantry regimental structure that consisted of headquarters and supply companies and three battalions. Each battalion had one machine gun company and three rifle companies. Given the reduction in the number of infantry units, the proportion of artillery fire support per infantry regiment increased without altering the number of artillery regiments or pieces. The new division still fielded forty-eight 3-inch guns, now twelve pieces per infantry regiment. The division was also authorized a regiment of twenty-four 6-inch howitzers for general support, and twelve trench mortars of unspecified caliber completed the division's general fire support weapons.[4]

Cavalry suffered the largest cut, from a regiment to an element with the division headquarters, a change in line with British and French recommenda-

# THE TEST—WORLD WAR I

tions. The Allies argued that trench warfare, dominated by machine guns and artillery weapons, denied cavalry the traditional missions of reconnaissance, pursuit, and shock action. Mounted troops, possibly assigned to the division's headquarters company, might serve as messengers within the division but little more. The Allies further advised that the Army should not consider sending a large cavalry force to France. Horses and fodder would occupy precious shipping space, and the French and British had an abundance of cavalry. Engineer, signal, and medical battalions and an air squadron rounded out the division.5

*General Bliss*

To conduct operations, the French advocated a functional divisional staff, that would include a chief of staff and a chief of artillery as well as intelligence, operations, and supply officers, along with French interpreters. Although small, such a body would have sufficient resources to allow the division to function as a tactical unit while a small headquarters troop would furnish work details. Adjutants alone were to comprise the staff of the infantry and artillery brigades, which had no headquarters troop for work details. The next higher headquarters, the army corps, would provide planning and administration for active operations.6

Based on the report of 10 May, War College Division officers prepared tables of organization that authorized 19,000 officers and enlisted men for the division (*Chart 3*), an increase of about 1,300. No basic structural changes took place; self-sufficiency justified the additional men. On 24 May Maj. Gen. Tasker H. Bliss, the Acting Chief of Staff,7 approved the tables, but only for the initial expeditionary force. He hoped, as did the staff, that Congress would authorize a larger infantry regiment, providing it with more firepower. Bliss also recognized that the expeditionary commander might wish to alter the division. With these factors in mind, he felt that time would permit additional changes in the divisional structure because a second division would not deploy in the near future. If a large expeditionary force was dispatched in the summer of 1917, its deployment would rest on political, not military, objectives.8

Early in May Scott alerted Maj. Gen. John J. Pershing, commander of the Southern Department, about the possibility of sending an expeditionary force to France and asked him to select one field artillery and four infantry regiments

## CHART 3—Infantry Division, 24 May 1917

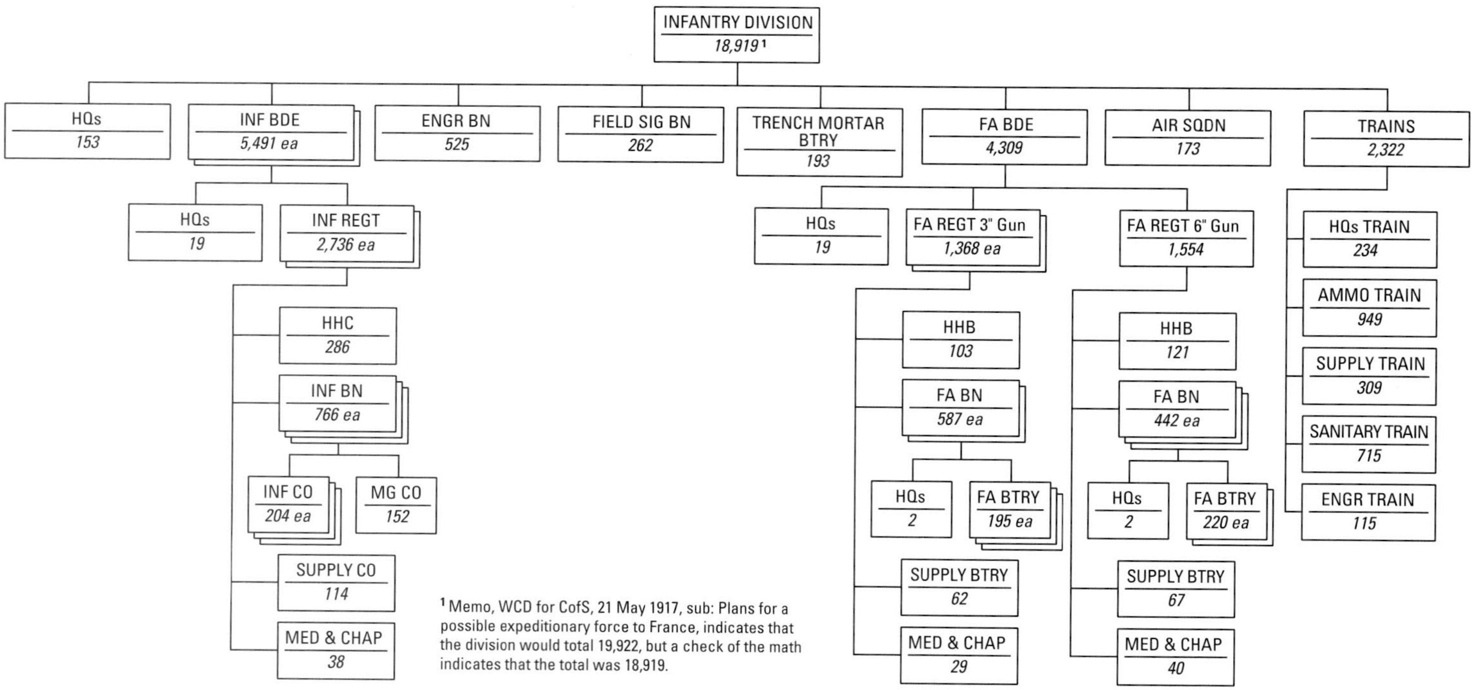

- INFANTRY DIVISION — 18,919[1]
  - INF BDE — 5,491 ea
    - HQs — 153
    - INF REGT — 2,736 ea
      - HQs — 19
      - HHC — 286
      - INF BN — 766 ea
        - INF CO — 204 ea
        - MG CO — 152
      - SUPPLY CO — 114
      - MED & CHAP — 38
  - ENGR BN — 525
  - FIELD SIG BN — 262
  - TRENCH MORTAR BTRY — 193
    - HQs — 19
  - FA BDE — 4,309
    - FA REGT 3" Gun — 1,368 ea
      - HHB — 103
      - FA BN — 587 ea
        - HQs — 2
        - FA BTRY — 195 ea
      - SUPPLY BTRY — 62
      - MED & CHAP — 29
    - FA REGT 6" Gun — 1,554
      - HHB — 121
      - FA BN — 442 ea
        - HQs — 2
        - FA BTRY — 220 ea
      - SUPPLY BTRY — 67
      - MED & CHAP — 40
  - AIR SQDN — 173
  - TRAINS — 2,322
    - HQs TRAIN — 234
    - AMMO TRAIN — 949
    - SUPPLY TRAIN — 309
    - SANITARY TRAIN — 715
    - ENGR TRAIN — 115

[1] Memo, WCD for CofS, 21 May 1917, sub: Plans for a possible expeditionary force to France, indicates that the division would total 19,922, but a check of the math indicates that the total was 18,919.

*16th Infantry, 1st Division, parades in Paris, 4 July 1917;* below, *Gondrecourt, France, training area.*

for overseas service. Pershing nominated the 6th Field Artillery and the 16th, 18th, 26th, and 28th Infantry. Following a preplanned protocol, the French requested the deployment of a division to lift Allied morale, and President Woodrow Wilson agreed.[9]

Shortly thereafter an expeditionary force was organized. The regiments picked by Pershing, filled to war strength with recruits, moved to Hoboken, New Jersey. On 8 June Brig. Gen. William L. Sibert assumed command and began organizing the 1st Expeditionary Division. Four days later its initial elements sailed for France without most of their equipment, as the French had agreed to arm them. Upon arrival in France, one divisional unit—the 2d Battalion, 16th Infantry—paraded on 4 July in Paris, where the French people enthusiastically welcomed the Americans. Following the reception, the division's unschooled recruits, except the artillerymen, underwent six months of arduous training at Gondrecourt, a training area southeast of Verdun, while the division artillery trained at a French range near Le Valdahon.[10]

## *The Baker Board and Pershing's Staff Organizational Study*

Upon completion of the Army's first World War I divisional study the 1st Expeditionary Division was deployed. Even before that investigation was finished, however, two new groups initiated additional studies. Pershing, who had been appointed commander of the American Expeditionary Forces (AEF) on 26 May, headed one group; Col. Chauncey Baker, an expert in military transportation and a West Point classmate of Pershing, headed the other. Previously Majors Palmer, Moore, and Wells had consulted Pershing as they developed their ideas about the infantry division, and he found no fault with them. Nevertheless, Pershing's staff began exploring the organization of the expeditionary forces en route to France. Lt. Col. Fox Conner, who had served as the War College Division interpreter for the French mission while in Washington; the newly promoted Lieutenant Colonel Palmer; and Majs. Alvin Barker and Hugh A. Drum assisted Pershing in this work.[11]

Independently, Secretary of War Newton D. Baker directed Colonel Baker and twelve other officers to study the British, French, and Belgian armies. After six weeks the secretary expected Baker to make recommendations that would help in organizing American forces. Colonel Baker himself met Pershing in England, and both agreed to work together after Baker conducted separate investigations in England, France, and Belgium. A single report, known as the General Organization Project, resulted from these efforts. Reflecting a consensus of the Baker and Pershing planners, it covered all aspects of the organization of the AEF except for the service of rear troops.[12]

The General Organization Project described an infantry division of about 25,000 men consisting of two infantry brigades (each with two infantry regiments and one three-company machine gun battalion), a field artillery brigade (com-

# THE TEST—WORLD WAR I

*Officers of the American Expeditionary Forces and the Baker mission*

prising one 155-mm. howitzer regiment, two 3-inch [approximately 75-mm.] gun regiments, and one trench mortar battery), an engineer regiment, a signal battalion, and trains. The trains included the division's headquarters troop and military police, ammunition, supply, ambulance, field hospital, and engineer supply units. The air squadron was omitted from the division.13

During the course of their work, Pershing and Baker reversed the rationale for the division. Instead of an organization that could easily move in and out of the trenches, the division was to field enough men to fight prolonged battles. Both planning groups sensed that the French and British wanted that type of division but lacked the resources to field it because of the extensive losses after three years of warfare. To sustain itself in combat, the division needed more, not less, combat power. The infantry regiment reverted to its prewar structure of headquarters, machine gun, and supply companies and three battalions each with four rifle companies. The rifle companies were increased to 256 officers and enlisted men, and each company fielded sixteen automatic rifles.14 Because the law specified only one machine gun company per regiment, the General Organization Project recommended the organization of six brigade and five divisional machine gun companies. These were to be organized into two battalions of three companies each and one five-company battalion. Eight of these companies augmented the four in the infantry regiments, thus providing each divisional infantry battalion with a machine gun company. The three remaining companies were assigned as the divisional reserve; two were comparable to those in the infantry regiments, and the other was an armored motorcar machine gun company labeled "tank" company.15

The major dispute between Pershing's staff and the Baker Board developed over the artillery general support weapon. The board's position, presented by future Chief of Staff Charles P. Summerall, was that one regiment should be equipped with either the British 3.8- or 4.7-inch howitzer because of their mobility, while Pershing's officers favored a regiment of French 155-mm. howitzers. The need for firepower and the possibility of obtaining 155s from the French undoubtedly influenced the staff, and its view prevailed. For high-angle fire, Baker's group proposed three trench mortar batteries in the division, but settled for one located in the field artillery brigade and six 3-inch Stokes mortars added to each infantry regiment.[16]

The report also recommended changes in cavalry and engineer divisional elements. An army corps, it suggested, needed two three-squadron cavalry regiments to support four divisions. Normally one squadron would be attached to each division, and the army corps would retain two squadrons for training and replacement units. The squadrons withdrawn from the divisions would then be reorganized and retrained. Divisional engineer forces expanded to a two-battalion regiment, which would accommodate the amount of construction work envisioned in trench warfare. Infantrymen would do the simple digging and repairing of trenches under engineer supervision, while the engineer troops would prepare machine gun and trench mortar emplacements and perform major trench work and other construction.[17]

Pershing sought a million men by the end of 1918. He envisioned five army corps, each having four combat divisions, along with a replacement and school division, a base and training division, and pioneer infantry, cavalry, field and antiaircraft artillery, engineer, signal, aviation, medical, supply, and other necessary units. The base and training division was to process incoming personnel into the theater, and the replacement and school division was to provide the army corps with fully trained and equipped soldiers. Because these support divisions did not need to be at full strength, Pershing foresaw some of the soldiers serving as replacements in combat divisions and others as cadre in processing and training units. He also anticipated that some surplus units would be attached to army corps or armies. Furthermore, Pershing wanted a seventh division for each army corps, not counted in his desired force of a million men, which was to be organized and maintained in the United States to train officers before they came to France. To assemble the first army corps, he asked the War Department to send two combat divisions, followed by the replacement and school division, the other two combat divisions, and finally the base and training division. When five army corps arrived in France, Pershing would have twenty combat divisions and ten processing and replacement divisions. Also, five more divisions were to be in training in the United States.[18]

The General Organization Project reached Washington in July, and Bliss noted the shift in divisional philosophy. Instead of a division that could move quickly in and out of trenches, Pershing wanted a unit with sufficient overhead (staff, communications, and supply units) and enough infantry and artillery to permit continuous fighting over extended periods. Because Pershing would command the divisions sent to Europe, neither Bliss nor the General Staff questioned his preference. Also, the lack of experienced divisional-level officers and staffs made a smaller number of larger divisions more practical.[19]

Using the General Organization Project, the War College Division prepared tables of organization, which the War Department published on 8 August 1917 (*Chart 4*). The tables for what became known as the "square division" included a few changes in the division's combat arms. For example, the five-company divisional machine gun battalion was reduced to four companies by eliminating the armored car machine gun unit. Pershing had decided to submit a separate tank program because he considered tanks to be assets of either army corps or field army. In the infantry regiment, the planners made the 3-inch mortars optional weapons and added three one-pounder (37-mm.) guns as antitank and anti–machine gun weapons. The supply train was motorized, and the ammunition and ambulance trains were equipped with both motor- and horse-drawn transport. The additional motorized equipment in the trains stemmed from the quartermaster general's attempt to ease an expected shipping shortage, not to enhance mobility. Crated motor vehicles occupied less space in an ocean transport than animals and fodder.[20]

The War College Division also provided a larger divisional staff than Pershing had recommended because the unit most likely would have both tactical and administrative roles. The staff comprised a chief of staff, an adjutant general, an inspector general, a judge advocate, and quartermaster, medical, ordnance, and signal officers. In addition, interpreters were attached to overcome any language barriers, particularly between the Americans and the French. As an additional duty, the commanders of the field artillery brigade and the engineer regiment held staff positions. A division headquarters troop with 109 officers and enlisted men would furnish the necessary services for efficient operations. The infantry brigade headquarters included the commander, his three aides, a brigade adjutant, and eighteen enlisted men who furnished mess, transportation, and communications services. The field artillery brigade headquarters was larger, with nine officers and forty-nine enlisted men, but had similar functions. Planners did not authorize headquarters detachments for either the infantry or field artillery brigade.[21]

## *Plans To Organize More Divisions*

While Pershing and Baker investigated the organizational requirements for the expeditionary forces, steps were taken to expand the Army at home. These measures included the formation of all 117 Regular Army regiments authorized in the National Defense Act of 1916 and the drafting of the National Guard into federal service and of 500,000 men through a selective service system. Draftees were to fill out Regular Army and National Guard units and to provide manpower for new units. Organizations formed with all selective service personnel eventually became "National Army" units. Although the War Department was unsure of either the final structure of the infantry division or the number of divisions need-

## CHART 4—Infantry Division, 8 August 1917

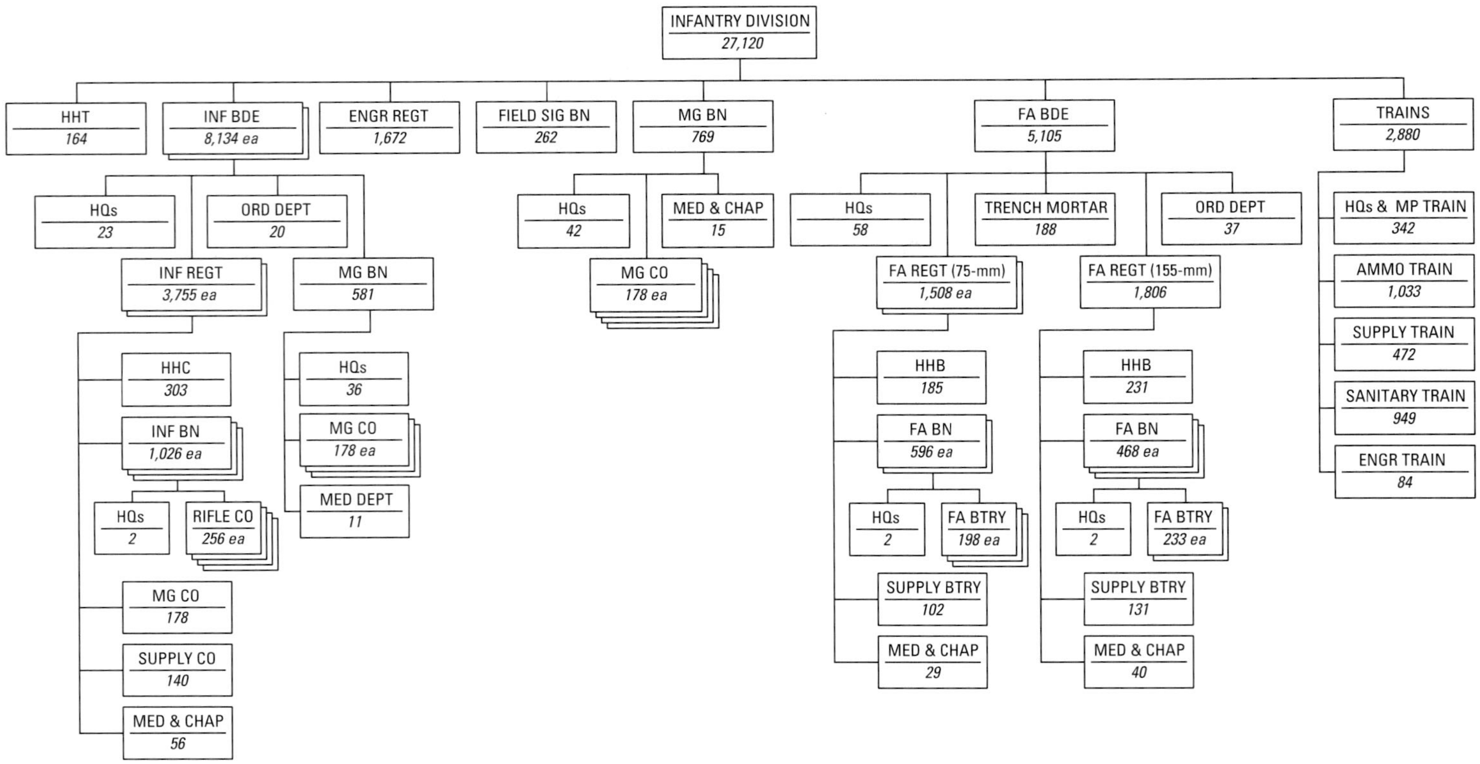

- **INFANTRY DIVISION** — 27,120
  - **INF BDE** — 8,134 ea
    - HHT — 164
    - HQs — 23
    - ORD DEPT — 20
    - INF REGT — 3,755 ea
      - HHC — 303
      - INF BN — 1,026 ea
        - HQs — 2
        - RIFLE CO — 256 ea
        - MG CO — 178
      - SUPPLY CO — 140
      - MED & CHAP — 56
    - MG BN — 581
      - HQs — 36
      - MG CO — 178 ea
      - MED DEPT — 11
  - **ENGR REGT** — 1,672
  - **FIELD SIG BN** — 262
  - **MG BN** — 769
    - HQs — 42
    - MED & CHAP — 15
    - MG CO — 178 ea
  - **FA BDE** — 5,105
    - HQs — 58
    - TRENCH MORTAR — 188
    - ORD DEPT — 37
    - FA REGT (75-mm) — 1,508 ea
      - HHB — 185
      - FA BN — 596 ea
        - HQs — 2
        - FA BTRY — 198 ea
      - SUPPLY BTRY — 102
      - MED & CHAP — 29
    - FA REGT (155-mm) — 1,806
      - HHB — 231
      - FA BN — 468 ea
        - HQs — 2
        - FA BTRY — 233 ea
      - SUPPLY BTRY — 131
      - MED & CHAP — 40
  - **TRAINS** — 2,880
    - HQs & MP TRAIN — 342
    - AMMO TRAIN — 1,033
    - SUPPLY TRAIN — 472
    - SANITARY TRAIN — 949
    - ENGR TRAIN — 84

ed, it decided to organize 32 infantry divisions immediately, 16 in the National Guard and 16 in the National Army. The Army contemplated no additional Regular Army divisions. Although existing Regular Army regiments could be shipped overseas and organized into divisions if necessary, most regulars were needed to direct and train the new army. Unlike past wars, draftees rather than volunteers would fight World War I.22

To organize National Guard and National Army divisions, the Army Staff adopted extant plans. For the Guard it used the Militia Bureau's scheme developed following the passage of the National Defense Act, and for the National Army it turned to a contingency plan drawn up in February 1917 to guide the employment of draftees. Divisions in both components had geographic bases. As far as practicable, the area that supported a Guard division coincided with a National Army divisional area.23

The thirty-two new divisions needed training areas, but the Army had only one facility large enough to train a division, Camp Funston, a subpost of Fort Riley, Kansas. Therefore, the staff instructed territorial commanders to select an additional thirty-two areas, each large enough to house and train a division. Early in the summer Secretary Baker approved leasing the sites. To save money, he decided to build tent cities for the National Guard divisions in the southern states, where winters were less severe, while camps for National Army divisions, which were to have permanent buildings, were located within the geographic areas that supported them.24

Establishing a tentative occupancy date of 1 September, the Quartermaster Corps began constructing the training areas in June. It designed each site to accommodate a three-brigade division as called for under the prewar tables of organization. When Bliss approved the square division in August, the camps had to be modified to house the larger infantry regiments. Although the changes delayed completion of the training areas, the troops' arrival date, 1 September, remained firm.25

The War College Division and the adjutant general created yet another system for designating divisions and brigades and their assigned elements. Divisions were to be numbered 1 through 25 in the Regular Army, 26 through 75 in the National Guard, and 76 and above in the National Army. Within the Regular Army numbers, mounted or dismounted cavalry divisions were to begin with the number 15. The National Defense Act of 1916 provided for sixty-five Regular Army infantry regiments, including a regiment from Puerto Rico. From those units, excluding the ones overseas, the War Department could organize thirteen infantry divisions in addition to the 1st Expeditionary Division already in France. This arrangement explains the decision to begin numbering Regular Army cavalry divisions with the digit 15. The system did not specify the procedure for numbering National Guard or National Army cavalry divisions. It reserved blocks of numbers for infantry, cavalry, and field artillery brigades, with 1 through 50 allotted to the Regular Army, 51 through 150 to the National Guard, and 151 and above to the National Army. The designation of each Guard or National Army unit, if raised by a single state, was to have that state's name in parentheses. Soldiers in National Guard and National Army units were also to wear distinctive collar insignia showing their component.[26]

As the summer of 1917 advanced, the War Department announced additional details. In July it identified specific states to support the first sixteen National Guard and the first sixteen National Army divisions and designated the camps where they would train. At that time the department announced that the designations of the National Guard's 5th through 20th Divisions were to be changed to the 26th through the 41st to conform with the new numbering system. In August the adjutant general placed the 76th through the 91st Divisions, National Army units, on the rolls of the Army and announced the appointment of commanders for both National Guard and National Army divisions. In addition to the 1st Expeditionary Division in France, the War College Division adopted plans to organize six more Regular Army divisions. No plans were made to concentrate their divisional elements for training, but they were to be brought up to strength with draftees.[27]

When the initial planning phase for more divisions closed, the mobilization program encompassed 38 divisions—16 National Guard, 16 National Army, and 6 Regular Army. With these, exclusive of the 1st Expeditionary Division in France, redesignated on 6 July as the 1st Division, the War Department met Pershing's requirement for thirty divisions. The divisions in excess of Pershing's needs were to be held in the United States as replacement units.

## *Organizing the Divisions*

Between 22 August 1917 and 5 January 1918, the Army Staff authorized one cavalry and three additional infantry divisions, for a total of forty-three divisions. But establishing these units proved a monumental task for which the Army was woefully unprepared. Besides unfinished training areas and the absence of a system for classifying new recruits as they entered service, the Army faced a shortage of equipment and officers. The quartermaster general claimed that the only items of clothing he expected to be available to outfit the National Army men were hats and cotton undershirts. Except for a handful of Regular Army officers, the National Army made do with newly minted officers fresh from twelve weeks of training.[28]

Formation of the new Army nevertheless began with the organization of the National Guard divisions. In August Guard units, which had been drafted into federal service and temporarily housed in state camps and armories, reported to their designated training camps and formed divisions in agreement with the 3 May tables. During September and October the division commanders reorganized the units to conform to the new square configuration as the 26th through 41st Divisions (*Table 3*).

# TABLE 3
## Geographic Distribution of National Guard Divisions, World War I

| Old Designation | New Designation | Geographic Area | Camp |
|---|---|---|---|
| 5th | 26th | Maine, New Hampshire, Vermont, Massachusetts, Rhode Island, and Connecticut | Greene, N.C.[1] |
| 6th | 27th | New York | Wadsworth, S.C. |
| 7th | 28th | Pennsylvania | Hancock, Ga. |
| 8th | 29th | New Jersey, Virginia, Maryland, Delaware,[2] and District of Columbia | McClellan, Ala. |
| 9th | 30th | Tennessee, North Carolina, and South Carolina | Sevier, S.C. |
| 10th | 31st | Georgia, Alabama, and Florida | Wheeler, Ga. |
| 11th | 32d | Michigan and Wisconsin | MacArthur, Tex. |
| 12th | 33d | Illinois | Logan, Tex. |
| 13th | 34th | Minnesota, Iowa, Nebraska, North Dakota, and South Dakota | Cody, N.M. |
| 14th | 35th | Missouri and Kansas | Doniphan, Okla. |
| 15th | 36th | Texas and Oklahoma | Bowie, Tex. |
| 16th | 37th | Ohio and West Virginia[3] | Sheridan, Ala. |
| 17th | 38th | Indiana and Kentucky | Shelby, Miss. |
| 18th | 39th | Louisiana, Mississippi, and Arkansas | Beauregard, Miss. |
| 19th | 40th | California, Nevada, Utah, Colorado, Arizona, and New Mexico | Kearny, Calif. |
| 20th | 41st | Washington, Oregon, Montana, and Wyoming | Fremont, Calif.[4] |

[1] Division concentrated at various locations in New England.
[2] Delaware troops relieved from the division 8 January 1918.
[3] Reassigned to the 38th Division.
[4] Camp changed from Camp Fremont, California, to Camp Greene, North Carolina.

At that time division commanders broke up many historic state regiments to meet the required organizations in the new tables, a measure that incensed the states and the units themselves.[29]

The histories of the 26th and 41st Divisions were somewhat different. Deciding to send another division to France as soon as possible, on 22 August Secretary Baker ordered Brig. Gen. Clarence E. Edwards, commander of the Northeastern Department, to organize the 26th Division in state camps and armories under the square tables. Without assembling as a unit, the 26th departed the following month for France, where it underwent training. To accelerate the formation of the 41st Division, its training site was shifted from Camp Fremont, California, which needed a sewage system, to Camp Greene, North Carolina. Maj. Gen. Hunter Liggett took over the camp on 18 September and the next day organized the 41st under the 8 August tables. In October its first increment of troops departed for France.[30]

Before the 26th Division went overseas in September, many states had wanted the honor of having their units become the first in France and pressed Baker and the War Department for that assignment. To stop the clamor, Baker proposed to Bliss that he consider sending a division to Europe representing many states. Maj. Douglas MacArthur, a General Staff officer, had earlier suggested that when Guard divisions adopted the new tables some militia units would become surplus and might be grouped as a division. MacArthur described the division as a "rainbow," covering the entire nation. After consulting Brig. Gen. William A. Mann, Chief of the Militia Bureau, the War College Division drafted a scheme to organize such a division with surplus units from twenty-six states and the District of Columbia. On 14 August the 42d Division was placed on the rolls of the Army, and six days later its units began arriving at Camp Mills, New York, eventually a transient facility for soldiers going to France. The following month Mann, who was reassigned from the Militia Bureau and appointed the division commander, organized the "Rainbow Division," which sailed for France a few weeks later.[31]

The organization of the sixteen National Army divisions also began in August when the designated division commanders, all Regular Army officers, and officer cadres reported to their respective training camps. Immediately thereafter the commanders established the 76th through the 91st Divisions and a depot brigade for each (*Table 4*).[32] On 3 September the first draftees arrived. The depot brigades processed the new draftees while the divisions began a rigorous training program. Many of these men, however, quickly became fillers for National Guard and Regular Army units going overseas, one of the reasons that National Army divisions were unready for combat for many months.[33]

One Regular Army infantry division, the 2d, was organized in France. When the first troops deployed, the U.S. Marine Corps wanted a share of the action, and Secretary Baker agreed that two Marine regiments should serve with the Army. The 5th Marines sailed with the 1st Expeditionary Division, and Pershing assigned

## TABLE 4
### Geographic Distribution of National Army Divisions
### World War I

| Designation | Geographic Area | Camp |
|---|---|---|
| 76th | Maine, New Hampshire, Vermont, Massachusetts, Rhode Island, and Connecticut | Devens, Mass. |
| 77th | Metropolitan New York City | Upton, N.Y. |
| 78th | New York and northern Pennsylvania | Dix, N.J. |
| 79th | Southern Pennsylvania | Meade, Md. |
| 80th | New Jersey, Virginia, Maryland, Delaware, and District of Columbia | Lee, Va. |
| 81st | Tennessee, North Carolina, and South Carolina | Jackson, S.C. |
| 82d | Georgia, Alabama, and Florida | Gordon, Ga. |
| 83d | Ohio and West Virginia | Sherman, Ohio |
| 84th | Indiana and Kentucky | Taylor, Ky. |
| 85th | Michigan and Wisconsin | Custer, Mich. |
| 86th | Illinois | Grant, Ill. |
| 87th | Arkansas, Louisiana, and Mississippi | Pike, Ark. |
| 88th | Minnesota, Iowa, Nebraska, North Dakota, and South Dakota | Dodge, Iowa |
| 89th | Missouri, Kansas, and Colorado | Funston, Kans. |
| 90th | Texas, Oklahoma, Arizona, and New Mexico | Travis, Tex. |
| 91st | Washington, Oregon, California, Nevada, Utah, Idaho, Montana, and Wyoming | Lewis, Wash. |

them as security detachments and labor troops in France. Shortly thereafter he advised the War Department that the marines did not fit into his organizational plans and recommended that they be converted to Army troops. The marines, however, continued to press for a combat role. Eventually the Departments of War and the Navy agreed that two Regular Army infantry regiments, initially programmed as lines of communication troops, and the two Marine regiments (one serving in France and one from the United States) should form the core of the 2d Division. The adjutant general informed Pershing of the decision, and Brig. Gen. Charles A. Doyen, U.S. Marine Corps, organized the 2d Division on 26 October 1917 at Bourmont, Haute-Marne, France. The division eventually included the 3d Infantry Brigade (the 9th and 23d Infantry and the 3d Machine Gun Battalion), the 4th Marine Brigade (the 5th and 6th Marines and the 6th Machine Gun Battalion [Marines]), the 2d Field Artillery Brigade, and support units.[34]

*Draftees drill in civilian clothes, Camp Upton, New York.*

The 3d through the 8th Divisions, Regular Army units, were organized between 21 November 1917 and 5 January 1918 in the United States. Of these divisions, only the 4th and 8th assembled and trained as units before going overseas because the Guard and National Army units occupied the divisional training areas. The 4th replaced the 41st Division at Camp Greene, and the 8th occupied Camp Fremont upon its completion. To fill the divisions, partially trained draftees were transferred from National Army units, a process that eroded the concept of the three separate components—the Regular Army, the National Guard, and the National Army.35

As the three-component idea deteriorated, Baker discussed the elimination of such distinctions altogether with Scott and Bliss. The officers opposed the action, believing it would undermine the local pride that National Guard and National Army units exhibited. General Peyton C. March, who had served as Army Chief of Staff since the spring of 1918, disagreed. He announced that the nation had but one army, the United States Army, and discontinued the distinctive names and insignia for the three components. After 7 August 1918, all soldiers, including those in divisions, wore the collar insignia of the United States Army. Nevertheless, the men still considered their divisions as belonging to the Regular Army, the National Guard, or the National Army.36

All-black units comprised a special category of troops. The draft of the

*Camp Meade, Maryland, 1917*

National Guard included some black units, and the War Department directed the organization of additional regiments if sufficient numbers of black draftees reported to National Army camps. In October 1917 Secretary Baker ordered the units at Camps Funston, Grant, Dodge, Sherman, Dix, Upton, and Meade to form the 92d Division. Brig. Gen. Charles C. Ballou organized a division headquarters at Camp Funston later that month, but the division did not assemble or train in the United States. The following June the 92d moved to France and first saw combat in the Lorraine area.[37]

After the organization of the 92d there remained the equivalent of four black infantry regiments in the United States, and the staff anticipated that their personnel would serve as replacements for the 92d or lines of communication troops in France. For administrative purposes, these black troops were organized in December 1917 as the 185th and 186th Infantry Brigades. Shortly thereafter the Headquarters, 93d Division (Provisional), a small administrative unit, was organized. Never intended to be a tactical unit, it simply exercised administrative control over the two brigades while they underwent training.[38]

Puerto Ricans comprised another segregated group in the Army, and the General Staff gave special consideration to them when organizing divisions. Initially it planned a provisional Puerto Rican division using the prewar tables that called for three infantry brigades, but that idea was soon dropped. Instead, the War Plans

Division, which had succeeded the War College Division, endorsed the creation of a Spanish-speaking square division (less the field artillery brigade), to be designated the 94th Division. Maj. Gen. William J. Snow, Chief of Field Artillery, opposed the organization of the field artillery brigade because the Army lacked Spanish-speaking instructors and an artillery training area in Puerto Rico. He believed that a brigade could be furnished from artillery units in the United States. Others opposed formation of the division on ethnic grounds, arguing that Puerto Ricans might not do well in combat. Proponents countered that good leadership would guarantee good performance in combat. The staff worked out a compromise. The divisional designation was to be withheld, but the organization of the divisional elements was to proceed. The infantry regiments were assigned numbers 373 through 376, which would have been associated with the National Army's 94th Division. During the war the Army organized only three of those regiments, with approximately 17,000 Puerto Rican draftees, but never formed the 94th Division itself.[39]

Pershing ignored French and British recommendations that cavalry divisions not be sent to France. Himself a cavalryman, the general decided that he might use such a force as a mobile reserve. After all, both Allies still hoped for a breakthrough and maintained 30,000 to 40,000 mounted troops to exploit such an opportunity. Most of the Regular Army cavalry regiments, however, had been scattered in small detachments along the Mexican border and had furnished personnel for overseas duty. The cavalry arm needed to be rebuilt. That process began when the secretary of war approved the formation of the 15th Cavalry Division. On 10 December 1917, Maj. Gen. George W. Reed organized its headquarters at Fort Bliss, Texas; the 1st Cavalry Brigade at Fort Sam Houston, Texas; the 2d Brigade at Bliss, Texas; and the 3d at Douglas, Arizona. The division had two missions: to prepare for combat in France and to patrol the Mexican border.[40]

The breakup of the 15th Cavalry Division began shortly after its formation. Responding to Pershing's request for army corps troops, the War Department detached the division's 6th and 15th Cavalry and sent them to France. Because of the paucity of cavalry units, they were not replaced in the division. In May 1918 Maj. Gen. Willard Holbrook, the Southern Department commander, informed the chief of staff of the Army that the situation on the border required the remainder of the division to remain there. Holbrook further stated that border-patrol work could be improved if the divisional organization were abandoned. On 12 May the division headquarters was demobilized, but the division's three cavalry brigades continued to serve on the border until July 1919, when their headquarters were also demobilized. With the demobilization of the division, Pershing's hope for a cavalry division died. Baker informed him that all remaining mounted troops were needed in the United States.[41]

When the first phase of the mobilization ended on 5 January 1918, the Army had 42 infantry divisions, 1 short-lived cavalry division, and 1 provisional division of 2 infantry brigades. All divisions were in various stages of training. Shortages of uniforms, weapons, and equipment remained acute.

## Expansion of the Divisional Forces

By the spring of 1918 Pershing had requested more divisions than he had outlined in the General Organization Project because the Allies' fortunes had drastically changed. Russia had been forced out of the war, and the British and French armies had begun to show the strain of manpower losses sustained since 1914. Although Germany also felt the effects of the long war, it was busy transferring troops from the now defunct Eastern Front to the West for one final offensive. Alarmed, the Allies wanted 100 U.S. Army divisions as soon as possible. Within the War Department the request caused considerable debate as to its feasibility, particularly with regard to raw materials, production, and shipping of war supplies. Only in July did President Wilson approve a plan to mount a 98-division force by the end of 1919, 80 for France and 18 in reserve in the United States.[42]

During the debate over force structure, the War Plans Division considered whether the additional divisions should be Regular Army or National Army units. Not all Regular Army infantry regiments authorized under the National Defense Act of 1916 had been assigned to divisions, thus raising the question of why those regiments should exist. The War Plans Division recommended that the Regular Army infantry regiments become the nuclei of the next group of divisions, which would be completed with National Army units. The National Army units would pass out of existence after the war.[43]

In July 1918 Secretary Baker approved the organization of twelve more divisions. Regular Army infantry regiments in the United States and from Hawaii and Panama formed the core of the 9th through 20th Divisions (*Table 5*).[44] These divisions, organized between 17 July and 1 September, occupied camps vacated by National Guard and National Army divisions that had gone to France. Conforming to Pershing's fixed army corps idea, the 11th and 17th Divisions were scheduled to be replacement and school divisions, while the 14th and 20th were programmed as base and training divisions. The only change in these divisions from the others was in their artillery. The 11th and 17th had one regiment each of 3-inch horse-drawn guns, 4.7-inch motorized howitzers, and 6-inch motorized howitzers, while the 14th and 20th each had one 3-inch gun regiment carried on trucks, one regiment of 3-inch horse-drawn guns, and one regiment of 6-inch motorized howitzers. These artillery units were to be detached from the divisions and serve as corps artillery, except the 3-inch gun regiment carried on trucks, which was to serve as part of army artillery.[45]

As the Army Staff perfected plans to organize additional Regular Army divisions, steps had been taken to assure adequate military forces in Hawaii. On 1 June 1918, the president called the two infantry regiments from the Hawaii National Guard into federal service, and they replaced units that had transferred to the United States from Schofield Barracks and Fort Shafter.[46]

The Philippine Islands also proved to be a potential source of manpower for fighting World War I. When the United States entered the conflict, the Philippine

## TABLE 5
### Expansion of Divisional Forces, 1918

| Division | Component | Camp |
|---|---|---|
| 9th | RA and NA | Sheridan, Ala. |
| 10th | RA and NA | Funston, Kans. |
| 11th | RA and NA | Meade, Md. |
| 12th | RA and NA | Devens, Mass. |
| 13th | RA and NA | Lewis, Wash. |
| 14th | RA and NA | Custer, Mich. |
| 15th | RA and NA | Logan, Tex. |
| 16th | RA and NA | Kearny, Calif. |
| 17th | RA and NA | Beauregard, La. |
| 18th | RA and NA | Travis, Tex. |
| 19th | RA and NA | Dodge, Iowa |
| 20th | RA and NA | Sevier, S.C. |
| 95th | NA | Sherman, Ohio |
| 96th | NA | Wadsworth, N.Y. |
| 97th | NA | Cody, N.M. |
| 98th | NA | McClellan, Ala. |
| 99th | NA | Wheeler, Ga. |
| 100th | NA | Bowie, Tex. |
| 101st | NA | Shelby, Miss. |
| 102d | NA | Dix, N.J. |

people offered to raise a volunteer infantry division to be a part of American forces. The offer was declined, but Congress authorized federalizing the Philippine Militia to replace U.S. Army units if necessary. Nine days after the armistice President Wilson ordered nascent militia into federal service for training, and the 1st Division, Philippine National Guard, was organized under the prewar divisional structure. The division, however, lacked many of its required units, and its headquarters was mustered out of federal service on 19 December 1918.[47]

There were also two Regular Army nondivisional infantry regiments in the Philippine Islands. In July 1918 they joined an international force for service in Siberia. To bring the regiments to war strength, 5,000 well-trained infantrymen from the 8th Division at Camp Fremont, California, joined the Siberian Expedition.[48]

In July 1918 Secretary Baker approved final expansion of divisional forces, which involved black draftees. The plan required black units to replace sixteen white pioneer infantry regiments serving in France. These white units were to be organized into eight infantry brigades and eventually be assigned to divisions partially raised in the United States. By 11 November the War Department had organized portions of the 95th through the 102d Divisions in the United States (*see Table 5*), but the brigades in France had not been organized.[49]

## *Divisional Changes*

The General Staff had approved several changes in the August 1917 structure when the Army began to organize the last group of infantry divisions for World War I. Changes included reducing the division's reserve machine gun battalion from a four-company organization to a two-company unit and increasing the infantry brigade's machine gun battalions from three to four companies. Although the total number of machine gun units remained the same, the realignment afforded better command and control within the infantry brigades. More Signal Corps men were added, and more motorized ambulances were provided for the sanitary trains. Usually each modification brought a change in the strength of the division, which by November 1918 stood at 28,105 officers and enlisted men.[50]

The demands of combat led to several changes in divisional weapons. The French agreed to replace all U.S. 3-inch guns with their 75-mm. guns in exchange for supplies of ammunition. The 3-inch Stokes mortars, optional weapons in the infantry regiment, were made permanent. To defend the division against enemy airplanes, antiaircraft machine guns were authorized in the field artillery regiments. The most significant change, however, involved machine guns and automatic rifles. In September 1918 elements of the 79th and 80th Divisions used new machine guns and automatic rifles invented by John M. Browning. The Browning water-cooled machine gun was a lighter, more reliable weapon than either the British Vickers or the French Hotchkiss, and the Browning automatic rifle (BAR) surpassed the British Lewis and French Chauchat in reliability. New Browning weapons, however, were not available in sufficient quantities for all divisions before the end of the war.[51]

Pershing formally modified the division staff during the war. In February 1918 he adopted the European functional staff, which he had been tentatively using since the summer of 1917. Under that system the staff consisted of five sections: G–1 (personnel), G–2 (intelligence), G–3 (operations), G–4 (supply), and G–5 (training). Each section coordinated all activities within its sphere and reported directly to the chief of staff, thereby relieving the commander of many routine details.[52]

Pershing and his staff also changed plans for assembling army corps to meet conditions in France. When four divisions had arrived in France, the 1st, 2d, 26th, and 42d, the American Expeditionary Forces (AEF) staff began planning a corps replacement and school division. After reviewing the readiness status of the divisions, the staff recommended that the 42d be reorganized as the replacement and school unit. Pershing disagreed. For political reasons, the "Rainbow" Division had to be a combat unit. Also, he did not agree that the army corps required a replacement and school unit at that time; he wanted a base and training division to receive and process replacements. For that job he selected the 41st Division, which had just begun to arrive in France.[53]

Shortly thereafter Pershing revised the replacement system for the AEF. Instead of relying on a replacement and school division and a base and training division for each army corps, he split the replacement function between the army corps and the "communications zone," the area immediately behind the battlefield controlled by the "Service of the Rear." In the communications zone a depot (base and training) division would process personnel into the theater, while a replacement (replacement and school) division in each army corps distributed new personnel to their units. He assigned the 41st Division to the Service of the Rear (later the Services of Supply) as a depot division, which was to receive, train, equip, and forward replacements (both officers and enlisted men) to replacement divisions of the corps, and designated the 32d Division as the I Army Corps' replacement unit. But when the German offensive began along the Somme (21 March to 6 April 1918), the 32d Division was assigned to combat duty. To channel replacements from the depot division to their assigned units, each army corps instead established a replacement battalion. The depot division processed casuals into the theater, and the replacement battalions forwarded them to the units. The 41st served as the depot division for the AEF until July 1918. No replacement division was organized during World War I.[54]

The German offensive on the Somme upset Pershing's organizational plans. He offered all American divisions to the French Army. The 1st, 2d, 26th, and 42d Divisions were sent to various quiet sectors of the line, and they and more recent arrivals did not come under Pershing's control until late in the summer of 1918. He also placed the four regiments of the black 93d Division (Provisional) at the disposal of the French with the understanding that they would be returned to his control upon request. The French quickly reorganized and equipped the regiments under their tables of organization. Although they were to be returned to Pershing's control after the crisis, they remained with French units until the end of the war. The headquarters of the provisional 93d Division was discontinued in May 1918.[55]

The Army and the nation did not have enough ships to transport forces to France, and this lack was a major obstacle to the war effort. After lengthy discussions in early 1918, the British agreed to transport infantry, machine gun, signal, and engineer units for six divisions in their ships. Upon arrival in France, these units were to train with the British. The divisional artillery and trains were to be shipped when space became available, and they were to train in American training areas. The British executed the program in the early spring of 1918, eventually moving the 4th, 27th, 28th, 30th, 33d, 35th, 77th, 78th, 80th, and 82d Divisions. By June 1918 the nation's transport capability had increased markedly. In addition, the adoption of the convoy system greatly reduced the effect of German submarines, allowing the number of divisions in France to rise rapidly (*Table 6*).[56]

As more divisions arrived, Pershing revamped his ideas about the army corps. He made it a command consisting of a headquarters, corps artillery, technical troops, and divisions. The divisions and technical troops could be varied for each specific operation. Under his system, patterned after the French, the army corps

*165th Infantry, 42d Division, in trenches, June 1918*

became a more mobile, flexible command. The concept also took advantage of the limited number of American divisions in the theater, shifting them among army corps as needed. Eventually, Pershing organized seven army corps.

To maintain them, the 39th, 40th, 41st, 76th, 83d, and 85th Divisions served as depot organizations. The 31st Division was slated to become the seventh depot division but never acted in that role, having been broken up for needed replacements. Because depot divisions needed only cadres to operate, most of the personnel, except for men in the field artillery brigades, were also distributed to combat divisions as replacements. After additional training, the field artillery brigades assigned to the 41st, 76th, 83d, and 85th Divisions saw combat primarily as army corps artillery. Those assigned to the 39th and 40th were still training when the fighting ended.[57]

When the Services of Supply reorganized the 83d and 85th Divisions as depot units, some of their elements were used as special expeditionary forces. The 332d Infantry and 331st Field Hospital, elements of the 83d Division, participated in the Vittorio Veneto campaign on the Italian front during October and November 1918. The 339th Infantry; the 1st Battalion, 310th Engineers; the 337th Ambulance Company; and the 337th Field Hospital of the 85th constituted the American contingent of the Murmansk Expedition, which served under British command in North Russia from September 1918 to July 1919.[58]

# TABLE 6
## Deployment of Divisions to France

| Division | Dates of Movement Overseas | Remarks |
|---|---|---|
| 1st | June–December 1917 | |
| 2d | September 1917–March 1918 | Organized in France |
| 3d | March–June 1918 | |
| 4th | May–June 1918 | British shipping program |
| 5th | March–June 1918 | |
| 6th | June–July 1918 | |
| 7th | July–September 1918 | |
| 8th | November 1918 | Headquarters only |
| 26th | September 1917–January 1918 | |
| 27th | May–July 1918 | British shipping program |
| 28th | April–June 1918 | British shipping program |
| 29th | June–July 1918 | |
| 30th | May–June 1918 | British shipping program |
| 31st | September–November 1918 | Skeletonized |
| 32d | January–March 1918 | |
| 33d | May–June 1918 | British shipping program |
| 34th | September–October 1918 | Skeletonized |
| 35th | April–June 1918 | British shipping program |
| 36th | July–August 1918 | |
| 37th | June–July 1918 | |
| 38th | September–October 1918 | Skeletonized |
| 39th | August–September 1918 | Depot, later skeletonized |
| 40th | July–September 1918 | Depot |
| 41st | November 1917–February 1918 | Depot |
| 42d | October–December 1917 | |
| 76th | July–August 1918 | Depot |
| 77th | March–May 1918 | British shipping program |
| 78th | May–June 1918 | British shipping program |
| 79th | July–August 1918 | |
| 80th | May–June 1918 | British shipping program |
| 81st | July–August 1918 | |
| 82d | April–July 1918 | British shipping program |
| 83d | June–August 1918 | Depot |
| 84th | August–October 1918 | Depot, later skeletonized |
| 85th | July–August 1918 | Depot |
| 86th | September–October 1918 | Skeletonized |
| 87th | June–September 1918 | Broken up for laborers |
| 88th | August–September 1918 | |
| 89th | June–July 1918 | |
| 90th | June–July 1918 | |
| 91st | June–July 1918 | |
| 92d | June–July 1918 | |
| 93d | December 1917–April 1918 | Provisional unit, discontinued May 1918 |

Heavy losses during the greatest American involvement in World War I, the Meuse-Argonne campaign that began on 26 September 1918, created a need for additional replacements. One week of combat left divisions so depleted that Pershing ordered personnel from the 84th and 86th Divisions, which had just arrived in France, to be used as replacements.[59] The arrangement was supposed to be temporary, and at first only men from infantry and machine gun units served as replacements. Eventually all divisional personnel were swallowed up, except for one enlisted man per company and one officer per regiment who maintained unit records. The manpower shortage persisted. On 17 October the 31st Division, programmed as the depot division, was skeletonized and its men used as replacements. The 34th and 38th Divisions were also stripped of their men as they arrived from the United States. Nevertheless, the high casualty rate took a toll on all combat units, and Pershing slashed the authorized strength of infantry and machine gun companies from 250 to 175 enlisted men, thereby temporarily reducing each division by 4,000 men. Smaller combat divisions, however, conducted some of the fiercest fighting of the war—attacks against the enemy's fortified positions on the hills between the Argonne Forest and the Meuse River.[60]

While scrambling for personnel, Pershing again reorganized the replacement system, trying to improve its responsiveness to the flexible army corps and army organizations. Army corps replacement battalions failed because divisions left the corps so rapidly that the battalions were unable to keep up with them. Therefore, he ordered the 40th and 85th Divisions to serve as regional replacement depots for the First and Second Armies, respectively, and the 41st and 83d as depot divisions in the Services of Supply. The other two depot divisions, the 39th and 76th, were stripped of their personnel. The replacement system, however, remained unsatisfactory to the end of the war.[61]

Divisions in France also suffered from a shortage of animals for transport. As the quartermaster general had predicted in 1917, units never had more than half the transportation authorized in their tables of organization for lack of animals. In some divisions artillerymen moved their pieces by hand. To overcome the shortage, Pershing's staff planned to motorize the 155-mm. howitzer regiments and one regiment of 75-mm. guns in each division. By November 1918, however, only eleven 155-mm. howitzer regiments had been thus equipped.[62]

Troop shortages also hit support units. During the fall of 1918 the commander of the Services of Supply, Maj. Gen. James G. Harbord, requested personnel from three combat divisions for labor units in his command. On 17 September Pershing's headquarters reassigned three divisions scheduled to arrive from the United States to Harbord. Only one of these, the 87th, reported before the end of the fighting, and it was broken up for laborers in the Services of Supply.[63]

Handicapped by the scarcity of men and animals, Pershing sought ways to make divisions more effective combat units. In October 1918 he advised new division commanders to use their personalities to increase the patriotism, morale,

*Traffic congestion in the Argonne, November 1918*

and fighting spirit of their men. One way to develop unit esprit, Pershing suggested, was for divisions to adopt distinctive cloth shoulder sleeve insignia. At that time the 81st Division had already begun using such insignia. On his return to the United States after visiting the Western Front in the fall of 1917, the division commander, Maj. Gen. Charles J. Bailey, had authorized a shoulder sleeve insignia for his unit. He instructed the men not to wear the patch until after leaving the United States. When the division arrived in France, the insignia came to Pershing's attention. Bailey explained that no official sanction existed for the emblem, but that it created comradeship among the men, helped to develop esprit, and aided in controlling small units in open warfare. Pershing apparently liked the idea for he ordered all divisions to adopt shoulder sleeve insignia. Within a short time the other divisions had their own shoulder patches, many adopting their divisional property symbols. Along with the insignia, the men began to adopt divisional nicknames, such as "Big Red One" and "Wildcat" for the 1st and 81st Divisions, respectively.[64]

Combat, particularly in the Meuse-Argonne campaign, tested the assumptions that lay behind the large square division. Designed to conduct sustained frontal attacks, not maneuver, it was thought to possess tremendous firepower and endurance. The division's firepower, however, proved ineffective. The lack of wire and the continual movement of infantry units in the offensive hindered communications between infantry and artillery. In addition, the French transportation network could handle only so many men, guns, and supplies. Traffic congestion bogged down the movement of units and also prevented communication. When divisions were on the line they suffered from the lack of food, ammunition, and other supplies. Part of the logistical problems also rested with a division's lack of combat service troops to carry rations, bury the dead, and evacuate casualties.[65]

By Armistice Day, 11 November 1918, the Army had fielded 1 cavalry division, 1 provisional infantry division, and 62 infantry divisions. Of this total, 42 infantry divisions and the provisional division deployed to Europe (*see Table 6*), with one, the 8th Division, not arriving until after the fighting had ended. On the Western Front in France, 29 divisions (7 Regular Army, 11 National Guard, and 11 National Army) fought in combat. Of the others, 7 served as depot divisions, 2 of which were skeletonized, and 5 were stripped of their personnel for replacements in combat units, laborers in rear areas, or expeditionary forces in North Russia or Italy. The provisional black division was broken up, but its four infantry regiments saw combat. Starting from a limited mobilization base, this buildup, lasting eighteen months, was a remarkable achievement.

Despite the difficulties, World War I brought about more coordination among the combat arms, combat support, and combat service organizations in the infantry division than ever before. Infantry could not advance without support from engineers and artillery; artillery could not continue to fire without a constant supply of ammunition. Transportation and signal units provided the vital materiel and command connections, while medical units administered to the needs of the wounded. This complex type of combined arms unit became possible because of advances in technology, weapons, communications, and transportation.

The adoption of the unwieldy square division, however, proved to be less than satisfactory. Pershing's staff believed that a division of 28,000 would conserve the limited supply of trained officers, maximize firepower, and sustain itself effectively in combat. In practice, the square division lacked mobility. Its deficiencies became apparent during the important Meuse-Argonne offensive, when American divisions bogged down and suffered excessive casualties. The successes and failures of the infantry division's organization set the stage for a debate that would surround it for the next twenty years.

## Notes

1 Hugh L. Scott, *Some Memories of a Soldier* (New York: Century Co., 1928), p. 552.

2 Scott, *Memories*, pp. 550–56; Frederick Palmer, Bliss, The Peacemaker: The Life and Letters of General Tasker Howard Bliss (New York: Dodd, Mead, and Co., 1934), pp. 146–56.

3 Memo, WCD for CofS, 10 May 17, sub: Plans for a Possible Expeditionary Force to France, WCD file 10050, RG 165, NARA. The WCD 10050 file is replete with background material on the development of the new division.

4 Memo, WCD, 10 May 1917, sub: Plans for a Possible Expeditionary Force to France; Draft of Memo prepared in May 1917, WCD for CofS, 7 Jul 1917, sub: The Organization of an American Army, WCD file 10050, RG 165, NARA. The French used two types of divisions in 1917, one fielding about 17,000 men based on two brigades of two infantry regiments each and the other of 14,000 organized around three infantry regiments.

5 Ibid.; Draft of Memo prepared in May 1917, WCD for CofS, 7 Jul 17, sub: The Organization of an American Army, WCD file 10050, RG 165, NARA.

6 L. Van Loan Naisawald, *The US Infantry Division: Changing Concepts in Organization 1900–39*, Project Shop, 1–ORO S–239 (Chevy Chase, Md.: Johns Hopkins University, 1952), pp. 12 and fig. 4; Memo, WCD for CofS, 21 May 17, sub: Plans for a possible expeditionary force to France, WCD file 10050, RG 165, NARA.

7 General Scott had been sent to Russia with a presidential commission to establish contact with the revolutionary government that had overthrown the czar. Scott, *Memories*, p. 570.

8 Memo, WCD for CofS, 21 May 17, sub: Plans for a possible expeditionary force to France, and Memo, CofS for WCD, 24 May 17, no subject, WCD file 10050, RG 165, NARA.

9 John J. Pershing, *My Experiences in the World War*, 2 vols. (New York: Frederick A. Stokes Co., 1921) 1:2–3; Ltr, The Adjutant General of the Army (hereafter cited as TAG) to CG, Southern Department, 23 May 17, sub: Organizations designated for foreign service, and Ltr, TAG to CG, Southern Department, 26 May 17, same subject, 1st Inf Div file, DAMH-HSO; Society of the First Division, *History of the First Division During World War 1917–1919* (Philadelphia: John C. Winston Co., 1922), p. 2.

10 Society of the First Division, *History of the First Division*, pp. 6–18; GO 1, 1st Expeditionary Division, 8 Jun 1917, 1st Inf Div file, DAMH-HSO; Forrest C. Pogue, *George C. Marshall: Education of a General* (New York: Viking Press, 1963), pp. 146–47; John Whiteclay Chambers, II, *To Raise an Army: The Draft Comes to Modern America* (New York: The Free Press, 1987), p. 147.

11 Pershing, *My Experiences*, 1:38–40, 43–44, 100–101; Ltr, TAG to Col. Chauncey B. Baker, 28 May 17, printed in *United States Army in the World War 1917–1919: Organization of the American Expeditionary Forces* (Washington, D.C.: Government Printing Office, 1948), p. 55 (hereafter cited as *Organization, AEF*); Memo, CofS for Maj Gen Pershing, 21 May 17, sub: Organizations higher than Divisions, WCD file 10050, RG 165, NARA; Memo, John McA. Palmer for Gen Pershing, 19 Oct 21, no subject, John McA. Palmer Papers, LC.

12 *Organization, AEF*, pp. 55–56, 91, 108; Ltr, Baker to Pershing, 7 Jun 17, no subject, Pershing Papers, LC. The officers who accompanied Baker were Colonels William A. Graves, Dwight E. Aultman, Mark L. Hersey, and Charles P. Summerall; Lieutenant Colonels Hanson E. Ely, Edward D. Anderson, Kirby Walker, and Sherwood A. Cheney; Majors George S. Simonds, Morris E. Lock, and Frederick A. Ellison, and Captain John J. Quakemeyer.

13 *Organization, AEF*, pp. 97–98.

14 The automatic rifle and the machine gun were viewed as similar rapid-fire infantry weapons, and the Baker Board recommended the adoption of concise descriptions for them. It proposed that the automatic rifle be defined as a weapon where recoil was sustained by the body of the firer, while recoil from the machine gun would be sustained by some sort of solid mount clamped to the weapon. (See *Organization, AEF*, p. 75).

15 *Organization, AEF*, pp. 56–89 and pp. 93–114 passim.

## THE TEST—WORLD WAR I 75

16 Ibid., pp. 109–14; Ltr, Maj Gen John J. Pershing to Maj Gen Tasker H. Bliss, 9 Jul 17, no subject, Pershing Papers, LC; James W. Rainey, "Ambivalent Warfare: The Tactical Doctrine of the AEF in World War I," *Parameters* 13 (Sep 1983): 38; Pershing, *My Experiences*, 1:106–07.

17 *Organization, AEF*, pp. 83, 99–100, 105.

18 Ibid., pp. 93–96.

19 Palmer, *Bliss*, pp. 170–71; James G. Harbord, T*he American Army in France 1917–1919* (Boston: Little Brown and Co., 1936), pp. 102–04.

20 *Organization, AEF*, p. 138; Tables of Organization (hereafter cited as T/O), Series A, Table l, Infantry Division, 1917.

21 T/O, Series A, Table 2, Headquarters, Infantry Division, Table 3, Infantry Brigade, Table 12, Field Artillery Brigade, Headquarters, 1917.

22 WD Bull 32, 1917; WD GO 88, 1917; Henry Jervey, "Mobilization of the Emergency Army," lecture at the Army War College, 3 Jan 1920, copy in DAMH Library, Washington, D.C.; Chambers, *To Raise an Army*, p. 140.

23 Memo, WCD for CofS, 20 Feb 17, sub: A plan for an expansible army of 500,000 men based on universal liability to the military service, localization of organizations, and decentralization of administration, TAG file 9433, RG 165, NARA (the memo offers the C/S three options to increase the size of the Army); Ltr, Ch of the MB, to TAGs of all States, Territory of Hawaii, District of Columbia, and inspector-instructors and officers in charge of militia affairs, department headquarters, 5 May 17, sub: Organization and entry in Federal service of National Guard, MB file 325.4, RG 168, NARA. Also see U.S. Congress, House of Representatives, Committee on Military Affairs, *The National Defense Hearings*, 69th Cong., 2d Sess., 3 May 1917, pp. 303–04.

24 Rpt of the Sec of War, *ARWD, 1917*, pp. 25–34.

25 Ibid.; Rpt of the Construction Div, *ARWD, 1918*, pp. 1283–86.

26 Memo, WCD for CofS, sub: Designation of force to compose the Army of the United States, 23 Jun 17, and Memo, WCD for CofS, sub: Designation of organizations, 23 Aug 17, WCD file 9876, RG 165, NARA; WD GOs 88 and 115, 1917; Special Regulations No. 41, Change 1, Uniform Regulations, 1917.

27 WD GOs 90, 101, 109, and 114, 1917; Army War College (hereafter cited as AWC) Statement, Proposed organization of the increased military establishment and proposed plan for providing the necessary officers, 9 Aug 17, CofS files 1917–1921, file 1080, RG 165, NARA.

28 Kreidberg and Henry, *Mobilization*, pp. 320–21; AWC Statement: Proposed organization of the increased military establishment, 9 Aug 17; *Order of Battle of the United States Land Forces in the World War (1917–19), Zone of the Interior* (Washington, D.C.: Government Printing Office, 1949), pp. 79–80.

29 *Order of Battle of the United States Land Forces in the World War, American Expeditionary Forces, Divisions* (Washington, D.C.: Government Printing Office, 1931), pp. 117–265 passim, hereafter cited as *Divisions*, and *Zone of the Interior, part 2, Directory of Troops* (Washington, D.C.: Government Printing Office, 1949), pp. 1277–78, hereafter cited as *Directory of Troops*; *Pennsylvania in the World War*, 1:131–40, 2:141; O'Ryan, *The Story of the 27th Division*, l:61–70; Frederick L. Huidekoper, *The History of the 33d Division*, A.E.F., 4 vols. (Springfield: Illinois State Historical Library, 1921) l:1–7.

30 Ltr, TAG to Brig Gen Clarence R. Edwards, sub: Preparation of the 26th Division for service abroad, 13 Aug 17, and Ltr, CG, 26th Division to TAG, sub: Organization of the 26th Division, 22 Sep 17, copies in DAMH-HSO World War I order of battle file; Harry A. Benwell, *History of the Yankee Division* (Boston, Mass.: Cornhill Co., 1919), pp. 20–21; Rpt of the Ch of the MB, *ARWD, 1918*, p. 1104; William F. Strobridge, *Golden Gate to Golden Horn* (San Mateo, Calif.: San Mateo County Historical Association, 1975), p. 3; *Divisions*, pp. 117, 256.

31 Frederick Palmer, *Newton D. Baker, American at War*, 2 vols. (New York: Dodd, Mead, and Co., 1931) l:356–57; Memo, WCD for CofS, 30 Jul 17, sub: Composition Division, National Guard for service in France, RG 165, NARA; Ltr, TAG to Dept Commanders, 1 Aug 17, same subject, TAG 322.07 ee in 42d Inf Div File, DAMH-HSO; *Divisions*, p. 275. Brig Gen William

A. Mann was the brother of James Robert Mann, who was the second ranking Republican from Illinois. His brother's appointment was a bipartisan move for World War I.

32 Secretary Baker had authorized the camp commanders, who served as division commanders, to organize depot brigades as divisional elements. The depot brigade filled two purposes: one was to train replacements for the A.E.F. since the War College Division did not agree to Pershing's seventh division for the corps; the other was to act as a receiving unit for men sent to the camps by draft boards. David F. Trask, ed., Historical Survey of US Mobilization: Eight Topical Studies of the Twentieth Century, Study 6, Terrence J. Gough, "Equipment", pp. 6–7, Ms, DAMH-HSR.

33 *Divisions*, pp. 291–421 passim; Memo, Office Chief of Staff (OCS) for TAG, 11 Aug 17, no subject, OCS 9876–59, RG 165, NARA; WD GO 101, 1917; Jervey, "Mobilization of the Emergency Army," pp. 14–15; Memo, WCD for CofS, 19 Oct 17, sub: Plan for Organization and Dispatch of Troops to Europe, WCD file 10050–119, RG 165, NARA; also see Julius O. Adler, *History of the Seventy-Seventh Division* (New York: Wynokoop Hallenbeck Crawford Co., 1919), pp. 11–18; John G. Little, Jr., *The Official History of the Eighty-Sixth Division* (Chicago: State Publication Society, 1921), pp. 1–17; and *The 88th Division in the World War of 1914–1918* (New York: Wynkoop Hallenbeck Crawford Co., 1919), pp. 27–36.

34 Memo, WCD for CofS, 21 May 17, sub: Plans for a possible expeditionary force to France, WCD file 10050–21, RG 165, NARA; Memo, WCD for CofS, sub: Organization of the 2d Division (Regular) for service overseas, approved 20 Sep 17, and Memo, TAG to multiple addresses, 21 Sep 17, Organization of 2d Division (Regular), both 2d Inf Div file, DAMH-HSO; *United States Army in the World War, 1917–1919: Policy-Forming Documents American Expeditionary Forces*, (Washington, D.C.: Government Printing Office, 1948) p. 35, hereafter cited as *Documents*; *United States Army in the World War, 1917–1919: Training and the Use of American Units with British and French*, (Washington, D.C.: Government Printing Office, 1948) pp. 491–92, hereafter cited as *Training*; Oliver L. Spaulding and John W. Wright, *The Second Division, American Expeditionary Forces in France 1917–1919* (New York: Hillman Press, Inc., 1937), pp. 6–7; Thomas Shipley, *The History of the A.E.F.* (New York: George H. Dorna Co., 1920), p. 46; Allan R. Millett, *Semper Fidelis: The History of the United States Marine Corps* (New York: Macmillan Publishing Co., Inc., 1980), pp. 289–94.

35 *Divisions*, pp. 47–109 passim.

36 Edward M. Coffman, *The Hilt of the Sword: The Career of Peyton C. March* (Madison: University of Wisconsin Press, 1966), pp. 129–30; WD GO 73, 1918.

37 Memo, WCD for TAG, 1 Aug 17, sub: Utilization of colored men drafted for the National Army, WCD file 8142–13, Memo, WCD for CofS, 21 Aug 17, same subject, Memo, OCS for TAG, 24 Oct 17, sub: Organization of the Division, Colored, WCD file 8142–24, RG 165, NARA; *Divisions*, pp. 431–35.

38 Memo, WCD for C/S, 13 Nov 17, sub: Utilization of Colored Units of the National Guard and Colored Draft, and Ltr., TAG to Brig Gen Ray Hoffman, 5 Jan 18, sub: 93d Division (Provisional), WCD file 8142, RG 165, NARA; GO 1, Provisional Division (Colored), 24 Dec 1917, 93d Inf Div file, DAMH-HSO; *Divisions*, p. 437.

39 Memo, War Plan Division (WPD) for CofS, 9 May 18, sub: Organization of Troops of the Puerto Rico Draft, WPD file 9876–191, and Memo, WPD for CofS, 27 May 18, same subject, WPD file 9876–203, RG 165, NARA; *Zone of the Interior*, p. 661–62; *Directory of Troops*, p. 1400.

40 Memo, WCD for CofS, 23 Nov 17, sub: Organization of the Cavalry Division (Regular), Memo, WCD for TAG, 27 Nov 17, same subject, WCD file 6815–32, RG 165, NARA; *Zone of the Interior*, pp. 673–74; Palmer, *Baker*, 2:18–19.

41 Memo, WPD for CofS, undated, sub: 15th Cavalry Division, and Draft Telg, WPD to CG, AEF, 10 May 18, WCD file 6815–64, RG 165, NARA; *Zone of the Interior*, p. 671–74; *Directory of Troops*, p. 1270.

42 *Zone of the Interior*, pp. 52–55; Coffman, *The Hilt of the Sword*, pp. 85–90; Edward M. Coffman, *The War To End All Wars* (New York: Oxford University Press, 1966), pp. 177–80;

THE TEST—WORLD WAR I 77

Kriedberg and Henry, *Mobilization*, pp. 302–09.

43 Memo, WPD for Dir of Operations, 31 May 18, sub: Organization of the next 23 divisions, WPD file 8481–84, RG 165, NARA.

44 Because the 15th Cavalry Division was demobilized in May 1918, the number 15 was available in July for a Regular Army infantry division without a duplication of numbers.

45 Memo, WPD for TAG, 8 Jul 18, sub: Organization of the 9th, 10th, 11th, 12th, 13th, and 14th Divisions, WPD file 8481–96, and Memo, WPD for TAG, 19 Jul 18, sub: Organization of the 15th, 16th, 17th, 18th, 19th, and 20th Divisions, WPD file 8481–97, RG 165, NARA; T/O 12, Field Artillery Brigade (Combat Division), 14 Jan 18, corrected to 26 Jun 18; *Zone of the Interior*, pp. 641–61. Motorized artillery during World War I referred to tractor-drawn field artillery.

46 *Zone of the Interior*, p. 629; *Directory of Troops*, p. 1405.

47 Rpts of the Governor General of the Philippine Islands, 1917, printed in *ARWD, 1918*, pp. 1–5, and 1918, printed in *ARWD, 1919*, p. 6; *Zone of the Interior*, pp. 674–75.

48 *Order of Battle of the United States Land Forces in the World War, American Expeditionary Forces, General Headquarters, Armies, Army Corps, Services of Supply, Separate Forces* (Washington, D.C.: Government Printing Office, 1949), p. 386, hereafter cited as *General Headquarters, Armies*.

49 Memo, CofS for TAG, 23 Jul 18, sub: Disposal of the Colored draft (Organization of new divisions), AWC file 8142–185, RG 165, NARA; *Zone of the Interior*, pp. 662–70.

50 Changes in the tables of organization and weapons can be traced through the following sources: T/O Series A, 14 January 1918, corrected to 26 June 1918 (printed in *Organization, AEF*, pp. 335–88), and tables printed in *Genesis of the American First Army* (Washington, D.C.: Government Printing Office, 1938), pp. 59–61.

51 George M. Chin, *The Machine Gun*, 3 vols. (Washington, D.C.: Government Printing Office, 1951), 1:173–86; Sevellon Brown, *The Story of Ordnance in the World War* (Washington, D.C.: James William Bryan Press, 1920), pp. 128–30.

52 AEF GO 31, 1918.

53 "Report of Assistant CofS, G–1, G.H.Q., A.E.F. and Statistics," *United States Army in World War: Reports of Commander-in-Chief, A.E.F.* (Washington, D.C., Government Printing Office, 1948), pp. 150–52, hereafter cited as *Reports of CINC*.

54 Ibid.; AEF GOs 9, 46, and 111, 1918.

55 Pershing, *My Experiences*, 1:291, 353–65; Donald Smythe, *Pershing: General of the Armies* (Bloomington: Indiana University Press, 1986), p. 72; *Divisions*, pp. 437–42.

56 Coffman, *The War To End All Wars*, pp. 168–71; Weigley, *History of the United States Army*, p. 384; *Documents, Training* contains numerous documents pertaining to the agreement and training with British and French.

57 Hunter Liggett, *AEF, Ten Years Ago in France* (New York: Dodd, Mead, and Co., 1928), p. 28 *General Headquarters, Armies*, pp. 193, 220, 237, 268, 290, 316, and 329; *Divisions*, pp. 251, 269, 293, 363–64, 379.

58 *General Headquarters, Armies*, pp. 381–83; Joel R. Moore, "The North Russian Expedition," *Infantry Journal* 29 (Jul 1926): 1–21; Richard K. Kolb, "Polar Bears vs. Bols," 78 *VFW Magazine* (Jan 1991): 16–20; *Divisions*, p. 363.

59 In addition to combat losses, the fall of 1918 witnessed one of the most severe influenza epidemics in history, which spread to over 25 percent of the Army in France (see Coffman, *The War To End All Wars*, pp. 81–84).

60 "Final Report" and "Report of Assistant CofS, G–1, G.H.Q., A.E.F., printed in *Reports of CINC*, pp. 55, 147–52; Maurice Matloff, ed., *American Military History* (Washington, D.C.: Government Printing Office, 1969), p. 401.

61 "Report of Assistant CofS, G–1, G.H.Q., A.E.F.," printed in *Reports of CINC*, pp. 147–52.

62 "Final Report of Assistant Chief of Staff (G–4)," and "Final Report of the Chief of Artillery, American Expeditionary Forces," printed in *Reports of CINC*, pp. 77, 205–06;

McKenney, "Field Artillery," p. 188.

63 John Hagood, *The Services of Supply, A Memoir of the Great War* (Boston: Houghton Mifflin Co., 1927), pp. 317–20; *Divisions*, p. 389.

64 Ltr, Pershing to Maj Gen George Bell, Jr., 24 Oct 18, no subject, Pershing Papers, LC; 1st Endorsement 323.3 (GS) Military Department and Divisions, Hq, 81st Division to CinC, AEF, 4 Oct 18, no subject, GS file 323.3, and Memo, CofS AEF for TAG, 18 Oct 18, no subject, The Institute of Heraldry (TIOH) Library, Fort Belvoir, Va.; Ken Sawitzke, "The Shoulder Patch," *Infantry* 65 (Dec 1975): 40–42.

65 Conrad H. Lanze, "The Artillery Support of the Infantry in the A.E.F," *Field Artillery Journal* 26 (Jan–Feb 1936): 67–68; Timothy Nenninger, "Tactical Dysfunction in the AEF, 1917–1918," *Military Affairs* 51 (Oct 1987): 177–81; Robert H. Fletcher, Jr., "The 35th Division in the First Phase of the Meuse Argonne Operation, September 26–October, 1918," p. 21, Ms, 35th Inf Div file, DAMH-HSO.

# CHAPTER 4

# The Aftermath of World War I

*I think that the work of this Board was undertaken so soon after the close of hostilities that the members were unduly influenced by the special situation which existed during our participation in the World War.*

General John J. Pershing[1]

The abrupt end of World War I and the immediate demand for demobilization threw the Army into disarray, but out of the disorder eventually came a new military establishment. Between the armistice in November 1918 and the summer of 1923 the Army occupied a portion of Germany, demobilized its World War I forces, helped revise the laws regulating its size and structure, and devised a mobilization plan to meet future emergencies. Amid the turmoil Army officers analyzed and debated their war experience, arguing the merits of a large, powerful infantry division designed to penetrate an enemy position with a frontal assault versus a lighter, more mobile unit that could outmaneuver an opponent. The cavalry division received a similar but less extensive examination. After close scrutiny, the Army adopted new infantry and cavalry divisions and reorganized its forces to meet postwar conditions.

## *Occupation and Demobilization*

Hostilities ended on 11 November 1918, but the Army still had many tasks to perform, including the occupation of the Coblenz bridgehead on the Rhine River. For that purpose, Maj. Gen. Joseph T. Dickman, at the direction of General Pershing, organized the Third Army on 15 November. Ten U.S. divisions eventually served with it—the 1st through 5th, 32d, 42d, 89th, and 90th in Germany and the 33d in Luxembourg—as well as the French 2d Cavalry Division. Also elements of the 6th Division began moving toward the bridgehead in later April 1919, but that movement was halted in early May. Divisional missions included the administration of civil government, the maintenance of public order, and the prevention of renewed aggression.[2]

The divisional structure proved unsatisfactory for the military government role. Its organization could not mesh with the civil government of Germany, and the Third Army lacked the time and expertise needed to mature a uniform civil affairs program. Furthermore, assigned areas for the divisional units shift-

*American occupation troops cross the Rhine at Coblenz, Germany, January 1919.*

ed rapidly as divisions departed the bridgehead for the United States. Yet, under the terms of occupation, the entire bridgehead had to remain under American supervision. By the summer of 1919 American divisions had left for home, and the military government functions moved from the tactical units to an area command, the Office of Civil Affairs. With the departure of the divisions, only brigade-size or smaller units remained in Germany, and they too departed by January 1923.[3]

As the Third Army grappled with occupation duty, officials in Washington confronted the problem of demobilizing the wartime army. On 11 November 1918 a quarter of a million draftees had been under orders to report for military duty. With the signing of the armistice the War Department immediately halted the mobilization process, but it had no plans for the Army's transition to a peacetime role.[4]

One man, Col. Casper H. Conrad of the War Plans Division, had begun to study demobilization, and he submitted his report eleven days after the armistice. From Conrad's several proposals on disbanding the forces, Chief of Staff March decided to discharge soldiers by units rather than by individuals. Because National Guard and National Army divisions originally had geographical ties, he also ruled that units returning from overseas would be demobilized at the centers nearest to where their men had entered the service.[5]

Demobilization began in November 1918. March first disbanded the partially organized divisions in the United States, making their camps available as dis-

*1st Field Artillery Brigade, 1st Division, on occupation duty in Germany, August 1919*

charge centers. In January 1919 Pershing sent home the divisions that had been skeletonized or had performed replacement functions. Combat divisions followed, beginning with the 92d, the Army's only black division. A year after the armistice the Army had demobilized fifty-five of its sixty-two divisions, including all the National Guard and National Army units (*Table 7*). Before the units left service, the War Department gave the American people the opportunity to show their appreciation to the men who had fought in the war. Boston, New York, Philadelphia, Baltimore, and Washington held divisional parades and over five hundred regiments marched through the streets of their hometowns.[6]

After November 1919 only the 1st through the 7th Divisions and a few smaller units remained active. All were Regular Army units. These divisions retained their wartime configurations, but personnel authorizations for fiscal year 1920 prevented full manning. Divisional regiments had the strengths prescribed in the prewar tables of organization issued on 3 May 1917, and the ammunition, supply, and sanitary trains had only enough men to care for their equipment. Within only a year, the mighty combat force the Army had struggled to build during 1917–18 had vanished without any plans to replace it.[7] The helter-skelter pace of demobilization and the lack of any sound transitional planning greatly undermined efforts to create an effective peacetime force. A student of demobilization, Frederic L. Paxon, characterized this situation as worse than a "madhouse in which the crazy might be incarcerated. They were at large." [8]

# TABLE 7
## Demobilization of Divisions

| Division | Returned to U.S. | Demobilized | Camp/Location |
|---|---|---|---|
| 1st | September 1919 | | Zachary Taylor, Ky. |
| 2d | August 1919 | | Travis, Tex. |
| 3d | August 1919 | | Pike, Ark. |
| 4th | August 1919 | | Dodge, Iowa |
| 5th | July 1919 | | Gordon, Ga. |
| 6th | June 1919 | | Grant, Ill. |
| 7th | June 1919 | | Funston, Kans. |
| 8th* | September 1919 | September 1919 | Dix, N.J. |
| 9th | # | February 1919 | Sheridan, Ala. |
| 10th | # | February 1919 | Funston, Kans. |
| 11th | # | February 1919 | Meade, Md. |
| 12th | # | February 1919 | Devens, Mass. |
| 13th | # | March 1919 | Lewis, Wash. |
| 14th | # | February 1919 | Custer, Mich. |
| 15th | # | February 1919 | Logan, Tex. |
| 16th | # | March 1919 | Kearny, Calif. |
| 17th | # | February 1919 | Beauregard, La. |
| 18th | # | February 1919 | Travis, Tex. |
| 19th | # | February 1919 | Dodge, Iowa |
| 20th | # | February 1919 | Sevier, S.C. |
| 26th | April 1919 | May 1919 | Devens, Mass. |
| 27th | March 1919 | April 1919 | Upton, N.Y. |
| 28th | April 1919 | May 1919 | Dix, N.J. |
| 29th | May 1919 | May 1919 | Dix, N.J. |
| 30th | April 1919 | May 1919 | Jackson, S.C. |
| 31st | December 1918 | January 1919 | Gordon, Ga. |
| 32d | May 1919 | May 1919 | Custer, Mich. |
| 33d | May 1919 | June 1919 | Grant, Ill. |
| 34th | January 1919 | February 1919 | Grant, Ill. |
| 35th | April 1919 | May 1919 | Funston, Kans. |
| 36th | June 1919 | June 1919 | Bowie, Tex. |
| 37th | April 1919 | June 1919 | Sherman, Ohio |
| 38th | December 1918 | January 1919 | Zachary Taylor, Ky. |
| 39th | December 1918 | January 1919 | Beauregard, La. |
| 40th | March 1919 | April 1919 | Kearny, Calif. |
| 41st | February 1919 | February 1919 | Dix, N.J. |
| 42d | May 1919 | May 1919 | Dix, N.J. |
| 76th | December 1918 | January 1919 | Devens, Mass. |
| 77th | April 1919 | May 1919 | Upton, N.Y. |
| 78th | June 1919 | June 1919 | Dix, N.J. |
| 79th | May 1919 | June 1919 | Dix, N.J. |
| 80th | May 1919 | June 1919 | Lee, Va. |
| 81st | June 1919 | June 1919 | Hoboken, N.J. |
| 82d | May 1919 | May 1919 | Upton, N.Y. |
| 83d | January 1919 | October 1919 | Sherman, Ohio |
| 84th | January 1919 | July 1919 | Zachary Taylor, Ky. |
| 85th | March 1919 | April 1919 | Custer, Mich. |
| 86th | January 1919 | January 1919 | Grant, Ill. |
| 87th | January 1919 | February 1919 | Dix, N.J. |
| 88th | June 1919 | June 1919 | Dodge, Iowa |

TABLE 7–*Continued*

| Division | Returned to U.S. | Demobilized | Camp/Location |
|---|---|---|---|
| 89th | May 1919 | July 1919 | Funston, Kans. |
| 90th | June 1919 | June 1919 | Bowie, Tex. |
| 91st | April 1919 | May 1919 | Presidio of San Francisco, Calif. |
| 92d | February 1919 | February 1919 | Meade, Md. |
| 93d@ | | | |
| 95th | # | December 1919 | Sherman, Ohio |
| 96th | # | January 1919 | Wadsworth, N.Y. |
| 97th | # | December 1918 | Cody, N.Mex. |
| 98th | # | November 1918 | McClellan, Ala. |
| 99th | # | November 1918 | Wheeler, Ga. |
| 100th | # | November 1918 | Bowie, Tex. |
| 101st | # | November 1918 | Shelby, Miss. |
| 102d | # | November 1918 | Dix, N.J. |

Notes: * Only part of the division overseas.
\# Did not go overseas.
@ Provisional division, headquarters demobilized in France in May 1918.

## The AEF Evaluates World War I Divisional Organizations

Although rapid demobilization destroyed the Army's combat effectiveness, military and congressional leaders wanted to avoid what they considered the major mistake made after every earlier war—the loss of well-trained, experienced, combat soldiers. Notwithstanding that World War I was to have been "the war to end all wars," perceived international realities required that the nation be prepared for war. Both Congress and the War Department had been considering changes in the National Defense Act, and Brig. Gen. Lytle Brown, Chief of the War Plans Division, suggested that March obtain the AEF's views on the new Army establishment. He suspected that division, corps, and army organizations used in the "Great War" might not meet future battlefield requirements because they were tied so closely to trench warfare, a type of warfare he thought unlikely to recur.[9]

Under War Department orders, Pershing set up boards in France to examine the AEF experiences with the arms and services and to draw appropriate lessons for the future. At his staff's suggestion, he also convened the Superior Board to review the other boards' findings. In April Pershing relieved Dickman as the commander of Third Army and appointed him and other senior officers to the review board. All its members had close professional ties to Pershing and had witnessed from various positions the "success" of the heavy infantry division during the war. The board's primary mission was an examination of that infantry division. After a two-month investigation, the Superior Board tendered its recommendation, basically endorsing the World War I square division with modifications. Changes centered on improvements in combat and service support, firepower, and command and control.[10]

*5th Field Artillery troops at the 1st Division parade, September 1919*

Changes in command and control touched all divisional echelons. The board recommended headquarters detachments for artillery and infantry brigades along with larger staffs. Because the ammunition train served primarily with the artillery brigade, it proposed making the train an organic element of that unit but serving both artillery and infantry troops. Similarly, the board members believed that the engineer train should be a part of the engineer regiment. Following the principle of placing resources under the control of those who used them, the board wanted to drop the machine gun battalion from the infantry brigade and place a machine gun company in each infantry battalion. The board members believed that only when the infantry commander had his own machine gun company could he learn to handle it properly. For training in mass machine gun fire, the board advised that the companies assemble occasionally under a brigade machine gun officer. It also advocated the retention of a divisional machine gun officer and a divisional machine gun battalion to provide a reserve for barrage or mass fire.

The board regarded the rear area division train headquarters and the accompanying military police as unnecessary. When needed, the division commander could appoint an officer to command the rear elements. The military police could become a separate company. The war had disclosed complex communication problems, particularly in the use of radios, but no uniform signal organization existed. To overcome that defect, the board advised that a closer examination of divisional signal needs be conducted with consideration given to dividing them along functional lines.

Turning to firepower, the Superior Board recommended the elimination of ineffective weapons and the addition or retention of effective ones. Based on wartime experience, the 6-inch mortar battery in the field artillery brigade was deleted and a howitzer company added to the infantry regiment. The infantry was to continue to use 37-mm. guns and 3-inch Stokes mortars temporarily, but eventually howitzers were to replace the mortars. The board found that mortars lacked mobility, accuracy, and range and were difficult to conceal and supply. The board looked upon tractor-drawn artillery pieces as a success in combat and felt that retention of motorized artillery was appropriate if future wars were fought in countries having an extensive road net like that in France. For flexibility, however, the board advised that one 75-mm. gun regiment remain horse-drawn and the other be motor-drawn, along with a motorized 155-mm. howitzer regiment. They decided that the new weapon, the tank, used during the war to break up wire entanglements and to reduce machine gun nests, belonged to the infantry, but instead of assigning tank units to the division, the officers placed them at army level. Tanks could then be parceled out to divisions according to need.

The board also addressed the combat support needs of the division. Since the division routinely employed aircraft for artillery observation, liaison, registration of fire, and reconnaissance, the board suggested the addition of an air squadron, a balloon company, a photographic section, and an intelligence officer to the division. The board endorsed the addition of a litter battalion to the sanitary train to improve medical support and the elimination of all horse-drawn transportation from that unit and from the rest of the division, except for artillery. Because engineers had often been used as infantry in combat, some board members proposed reducing the number of engineer troops. The board concluded, however, that while engineers often had been employed as infantry, this practice stemmed from a failure to understand their role. It advised the retention of the engineer regiment.

Summarizing the requirements for the future infantry division, the Superior Board recommended that it be organized to meet varying combat and terrain conditions encountered in maneuver warfare but have only those elements that it customarily needed. The army corps or army level would supply infrequently used organizations. The board's report endorsed a square division that numbered 29,000 officers and enlisted men—an organization "imbued with the divisional spirit, sense of comradeship and loyalty, that will guarantee service . . . in critical moments when the supreme effort must be made."[11]

Although Pershing had not employed a cavalry division in France, the Superior Board also examined its structure in light of Allied experiences, particularly in Italy and Palestine. The board concluded that, except for distant reconnaissance by airplanes, the missions of mounted troops—screening, shock action, and tactical reconnaissance—remained important on the postwar battlefield. To conduct such missions, the cavalry division needed to capitalize on its mobility and firepower. Finding the 1917 unit of 18,000 men too large, the board entertained two proposals for reorganizing it. One called for a division of three cavalry regiments, an artillery regiment, and appropriate combat and service support units; the other comprised two cavalry brigades, each with two cavalry regiments,

*Superior Board members.* Left to right, *Maj. Gens. Joseph T. Dickman, John L. Hines, and William Lassiter, Col. George R. Spalding, Brig. Gen. William Burtt, and Col. Parker Hitt.*

and a machine gun squadron, an artillery regiment, and auxiliary units. The board rejected the three-regiment unit because it eliminated a general officer billet, recommending instead a square cavalry division of some 13,500 men.

The Superior Board completed its work on 1 July 1919, but Pershing held the report to consider its findings. He did not forward it to the War Department until almost a year later.[12]

## Development of Divisions Under the 1920 National Defense Act

Although Pershing temporarily shelved the Superior Board Report, Congress and the War Department proceeded to explore postwar Army organization. On 3 August 1919, Secretary Baker proposed a standing army of approximately 500,000 men and universal military training for eighteen- and nineteen-year-old males. With that number the department envisaged maintaining one cavalry and twenty infantry divisions. March testified that before 1917, when the Army was stationed at small, scattered posts, officers had no occasion to command brigades or divisions or gain experience in managing large troop concentrations. Under the proposed reorganization, officers would have the opportunity to command large units and to train combined arms units, thus correcting a major weakness of past mobilizations.[13]

After much debate Congress amended the National Defense Act on 4 June 1920, providing for a new military establishment but scuttling the unpopular universal military training proposal. Instead it authorized a Regular Army of 296,000 officers and enlisted men, a National Guard of 435,000 men, and an Organized Reserve (Officers Reserve Corps and Enlisted Reserve Corps) of unrestricted size. To improve mobilization the law required that the Army, as far as practical, be organized into brigades, divisions, and army corps, with the brigades and divisions perpetuating those that had served in the war. The new law replaced the old territorial departments with corps areas, which assumed the tasks of administering and training the Army. Each corps area was to have at least one National Guard or Organized Reserve division. Corps areas were to be combined into army areas for inspection, mobilization, maneuver, and demobilization. Rather than mandating the structure of regiments as in the past, Congress authorized the number of officers and enlisted men for each arm and service and instructed the president to organize the units. To advise on National Guard and Organized Reserve matters, Congress directed the formation of committees with members from the Regular Army and both reserve components.[14]

On 1 September 1920, the War Department established the general outline of the postwar Army. It consisted of three army areas divided into nine corps areas (*Map 1*). Each army area supported one Guard and two Reserve cavalry divisions, and each corps area maintained one Regular, two Guard, and three Reserve infantry divisions, all to be sustained by combat support and combat service support units to be perfected later.[15]

Six committees of the War Plans Division developed the postwar Army. Only one, however, the Committee on Organization, dealt directly with the structure of the division through the preparation of organizational tables. Until that work was completed, no realistic calculation of future military requirements could be made. The other committees defined the roles of the National Guard and the Organized Reserves, estimated the number of Regular Army personnel required to train and administer them, established manning requirements for foreign garrisons, determined the number of regulars needed for an expeditionary force, and fixed the distribution of the Regular Army in the United States to meet strategic and training considerations.[16]

The Committee on Organization prescribed a 23,000-man square division patterned after the unit of World War I. Seeking comments from beyond the confines of the General Staff, Col. William Lassiter of the War Plans Division sent the tables to the commandants of the Infantry School at Fort Benning, Georgia; the General Service Schools at Fort Leavenworth, Kansas; and the General Staff College in Washington, D.C., as well as to General Pershing's AEF headquarters in Washington.[17]

Faced with the possibility of having a decision made without his views being considered, on 16 June Pershing finally forwarded the Superior Board report along with his comments about the infantry division, which differed substantially

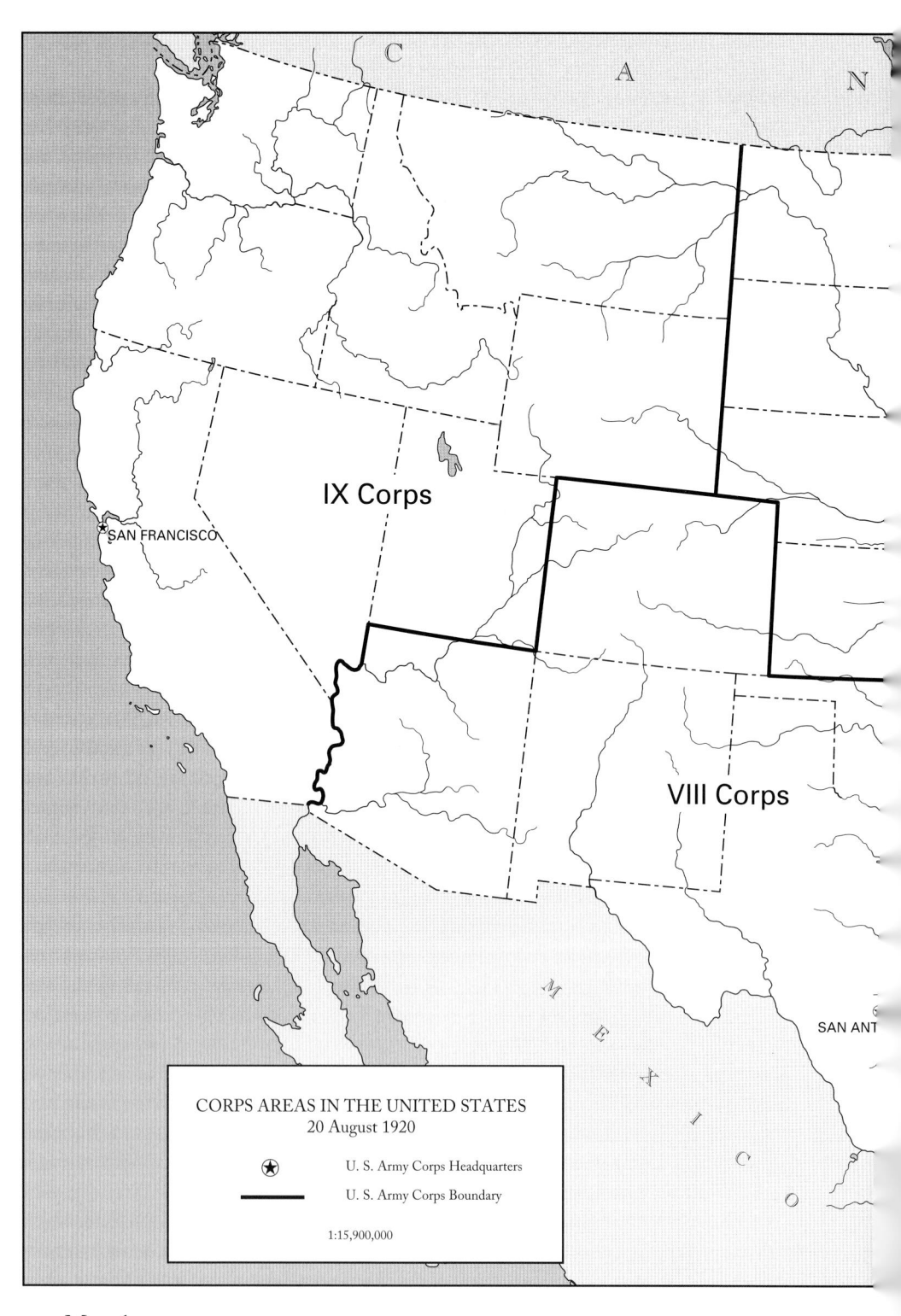

MAP 1

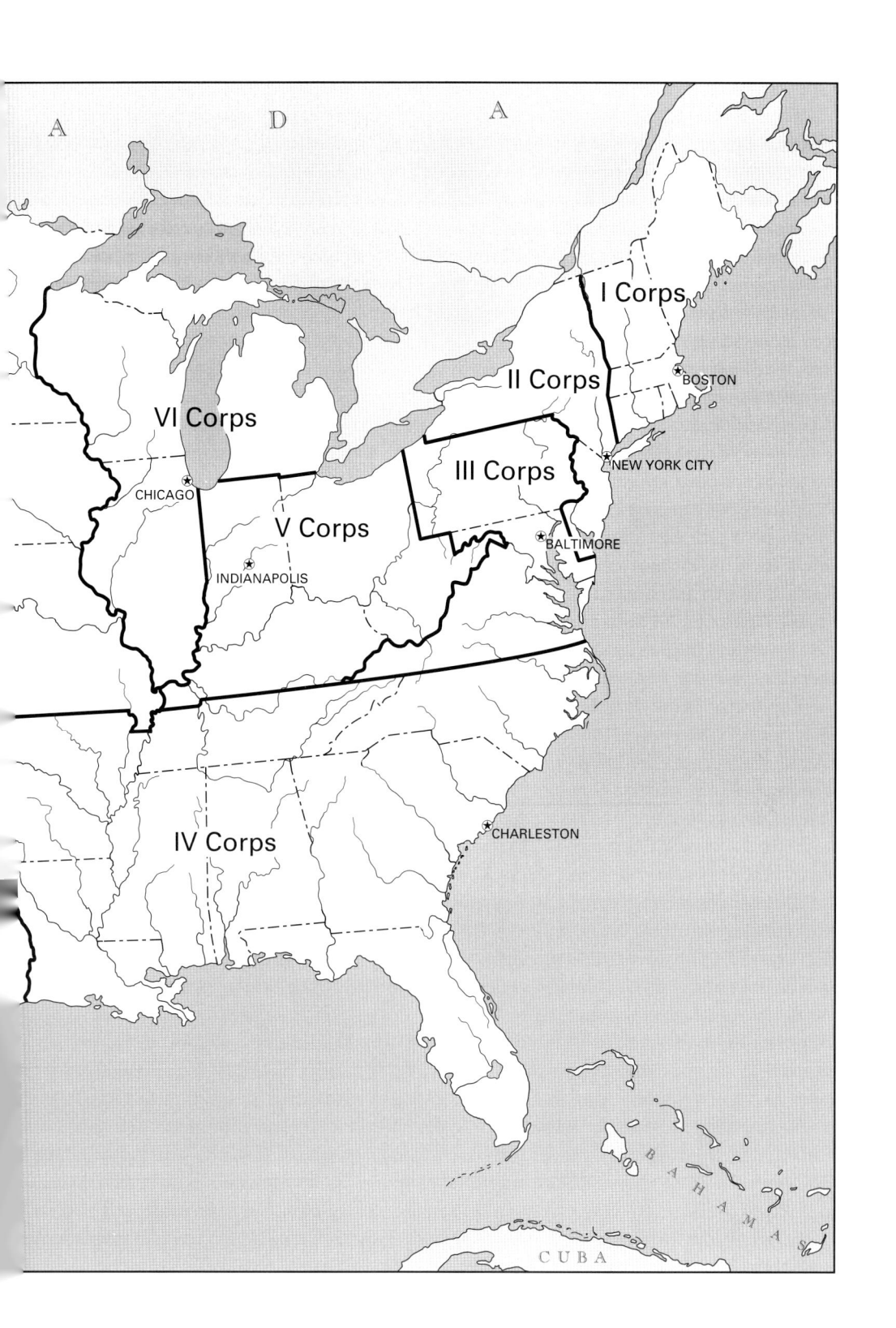

CANADA

I Corps

II Corps

BOSTON

VI Corps

III Corps

NEW YORK CITY

CHICAGO

V Corps

BALTIMORE

INDIANAPOLIS

CHARLESTON

IV Corps

BAHAMAS

CUBA

from the board's findings, to Baker. In comments prepared mostly by Col. Fox Conner, Pershing suggested a 16,875-man division having a single infantry brigade of three infantry regiments, an artillery regiment, a cavalry squadron, and combat support and combat service support units, a design that foreshadowed the triangular division the Army adopted for World War II.[18]

Pershing felt the Superior Board undertook its work too soon after the close of hostilities and that its report suffered unduly from the special circumstances on the Western Front. After examining all organizational features, he concluded that no one divisional structure was ideal for all battlefield situations. Factors such as the mobility and flexibility of the division to meet a variety of tasks, the probable theater of operations, and the road or rail network available to support the division had to be weighed. The most likely future theater of war for the Army was still considered to be North America, and he believed that the infantry divisions employed in France were too unwieldy and immobile for that region. Therefore, he recommended a small mobile division.[19]

According to Pershing, specific signposts marked the path to a smaller division, among them putting infrequently used support units at the army corps or army level, organizing the divisional staff to handle needed attached units, making a machine gun company an integral part of the infantry battalion, and providing horse- or mule-drawn vehicles throughout the division because of the poor roads in the United States. Summarizing the requirements for the infantry division, he wrote: "The division should be small enough to permit its being deployed from . . . a single road in a few hours and, when moving by rail, to permit all of its elements to be assembled on a single railroad line within twenty-four hours; this means that the division must not exceed 20,000 as maximum."[20]

On 18 June representatives from the General Staff and Pershing's headquarters conferred to iron out the differences between the two positions. The conference failed to reach agreement. Therefore, at Baker's direction, a special committee met to solve this organizational issue.[21]

Like the Superior Board, the Special Committee, commonly referred to as the Lassiter Committee, drew upon the talents of former AEF officers. From the General Staff, besides Colonel Lassiter, came Lt. Col. Briant H. Wells, Maj. John W. Gulick, and Capt. Arthur W. Lane. Majs. Stuart Heintzelman and Campbell King represented the General Staff College; Maj. Hugh A. Drum, the General Services Schools; and Col. Charles S. Farnsworth, the Infantry School. Col. Fox Conner and Capt. George C. Marshall spoke for Pershing. Except for Farnsworth, who had commanded the 37th Division during combat, all had held army corps, army, and General Headquarters staff positions where they had gained firsthand knowledge about the operation of divisions and higher commands in France. In addition, Wells had helped draft the initial proposal for the square division adopted during the war; Conner had been a French interpreter for the General Staff in 1917 when the proposal was prepared; and Heintzelman had edited General Pershing's report of operations in France.[22]

Meeting between 22 June and 8 July 1920, the committee examined three questions: Was the World War I division too large? If so, should the Army adopt a smaller division comprising three infantry regiments? Finally, if a division of four infantry regiments were retained, could it be reduced to fewer than 20,000 men, a figure acceptable to Pershing?[23]

The committee reviewed all previous divisional studies and recommendations; acquainted itself with views held by officers of the General Staff, departments, and operating services of the Army about divisions; and investigated the views about them developed at the service schools since the end of the war. Approximately seventy officers appeared before the committee, including Col. William (Billy) Mitchell of the Air Service and Brig. Gen. Samuel D. Rochenback, the former chief of the Tank Corps, who testified about two new weapon systems used in the war—the airplane and the tank.[24]

From the evidence, the committee concluded that the wartime infantry division was too large and unwieldy. In reality it had been an army corps without the proper organization. The division's size made moving the unit by road and railroad or passing through lines an extremely complex and time-consuming process. Furthermore, its size had complicated the problems of command and control of all activities in combat.[25]

The committee examined various organizational options. The argument for three (versus four) infantry regiments in the division centered on the division's probable area of employment, North America. Experts deemed another war in Europe unlikely, and they doubted that the Army would again fight on a battlefield like that seen in France. They felt technological advances in artillery, machine guns, and aviation made obsolete stabilized and highly organized lines and flanks resting on impassable obstacles, such as those encountered on the Western Front. Future enemies would most likely organize their forces in great depth; therefore, the Army had to be prepared to overcome that challenge.

Nevertheless, the committee believed a division of four infantry regiments, although lacking the flexibility of Pershing's suggested unit, would have the necessary mobility and striking power. Divisional support troops needed to be reduced, but the retention of the square division preserved the organizations for army corps and armies that had been developed during the war. Because most officers were familiar with those units, no change in doctrine was required above the division level. On a more mundane level, the retention of general officers' billets also influenced those who wanted to keep the square division. Its brigades required brigadier generals, which allowed officers to rise from second lieutenants to general officers within their specialties, while a smaller triangular division would terminate that progression at the colonel level. Concluding its examination, the committee decided a field commander could more readily modify the square division to oppose a lesser enemy than strengthen a smaller organization to fight a powerful foe.[26]

The third question remained: Could the Army reduce the size of the square division to increase mobility? Recommendations to achieve this included a reduction in the number of platoons in the infantry company from four to three and a cut in the number of companies in the battalion by a like amount, a realignment of the ratio between rifles and machine guns, elimination of the 155-mm. howitzers, and the removal of unnecessary support troops. The division could obtain additional troops from pools of combat support and service units located at the army corps or army level. The Lassiter Committee concluded that the square division could be cut in size yet retain much of its firepower.[27]

After making its report, the Lassiter Committee prepared tentative tables of organization for the division, which March approved on 31 August. When the War Department distributed the draft tables in the fall of 1920 for the division, it totaled 19,385 officers and enlisted men (*Chart 5*) and covered about thirty miles of road space in march formation. To arrive at that strength and size, each of the four infantry regiments lost 700 men. The regiment consisted of three infantry battalions and supply, howitzer, and headquarters companies. Each battalion included one machine gun company and three rifle companies. The assignment of a machine gun company to each infantry battalion simplified command and control of those weapons, and the realignment of the guns created a substantial saving in personnel. Machine gun units were eliminated from the infantry brigades, and the divisional machine gun battalion was replaced by a tank company, which was to serve as a divisional mobile reserve. The committee endorsed Pershing's suggestion of a divisional tank company but was aware that a single company could not mount an effective attack on a stabilized front; the large numbers of tanks required for that type of operation would have to come from the army level. The committee dropped the 155-mm. howitzer regiment but stipulated its return to the division when these weapons acquired the necessary mobility for use on the North American continent. The engineer regiment and train were combined and reorganized initially as a battalion because the planners thought that the division had little need for large numbers of engineers in mobile warfare, which precluded building extensive fortifications, trenches, and similar works. The chief of engineers and others, however, insisted that the regiment be retained to assure mobility, permit training of lieutenant colonels and colonels, and provide the opportunity for higher grade officers to serve at least one year in five with troops. March thus decided to retain the engineer regiment but reduced its number from 1,831 officers and enlisted men to 867. All these changes husbanded personnel spaces and increased mobility without lessening firepower.[28]

Substantial reductions also took place in divisional services. The committee cut the size of the ammunition train from 1,333 to 169 officers and enlisted men and changed its mission to serve only the field artillery brigade. Ammunition resupply for all other divisional elements shifted to the tactical units and quartermaster train. That train consisted of half motorized and half animal-drawn transportation, presuming the potential theater of operations to be the rugged North American continent. Ordnance personnel formerly

# CHART 5—Infantry Division, 7 October 1920

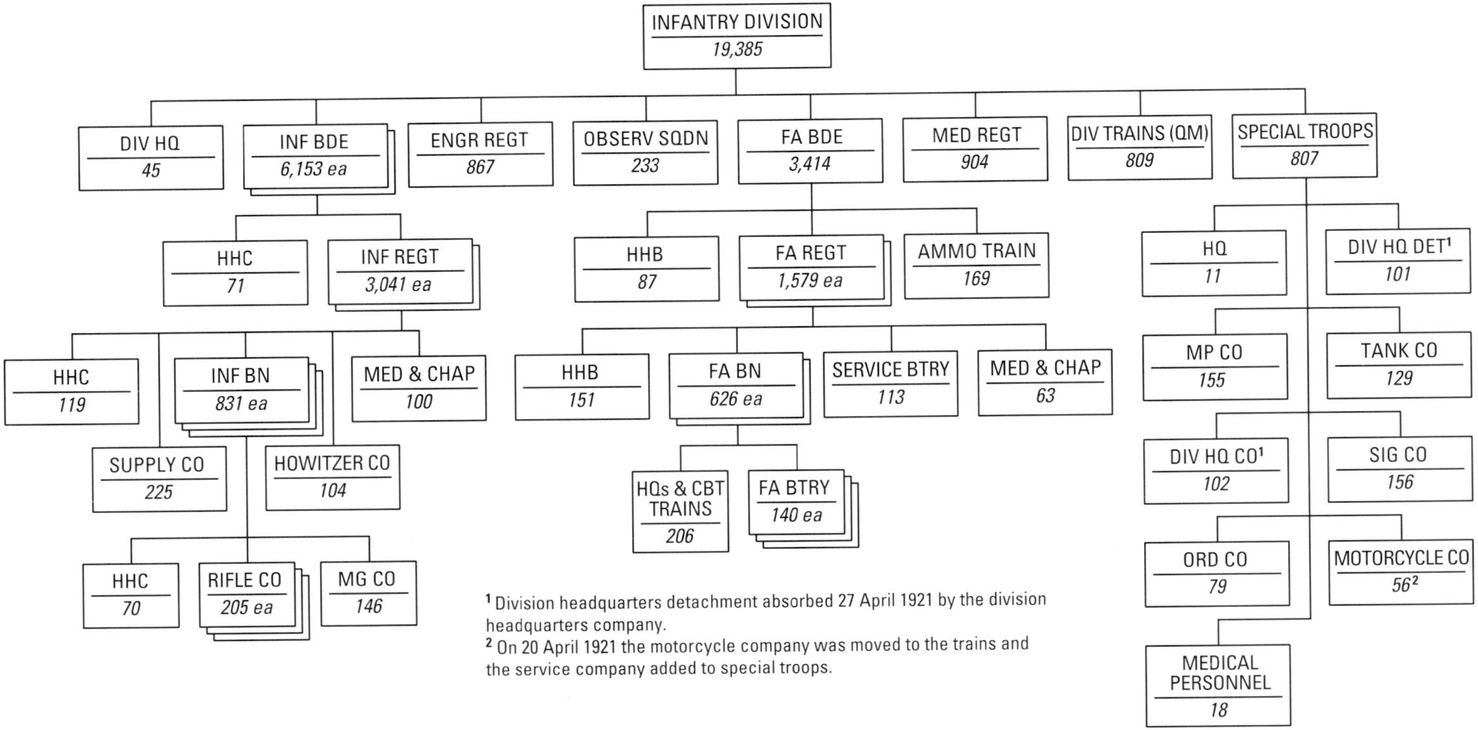

- INFANTRY DIVISION — 19,385
  - INF BDE — 6,153 ea
    - DIV HQ — 45
    - HHC — 71
    - INF REGT — 3,041 ea
      - HHC — 119
      - MED & CHAP — 100
      - SUPPLY CO — 225
      - INF BN — 831 ea
        - HHC — 70
        - HOWITZER CO — 104
        - RIFLE CO — 205 ea
        - MG CO — 146
  - ENGR REGT — 867
  - OBSERV SQDN — 233
  - FA BDE — 3,414
    - HHB — 87
    - FA REGT — 1,579 ea
      - HHB — 151
      - SERVICE BTRY — 113
      - FA BN — 626 ea
        - HQs & CBT TRAINS — 206
        - FA BTRY — 140 ea
      - AMMO TRAIN — 169
      - MED & CHAP — 63
  - MED REGT — 904
  - DIV TRAINS (QM) — 809
  - SPECIAL TROOPS — 807
    - HQ — 11
    - DIV HQ DET[1] — 101
    - MP CO — 155
    - TANK CO — 129
    - DIV HQ CO[1] — 102
    - SIG CO — 156
    - ORD CO — 79
    - MOTORCYCLE CO — 56[2]
    - MEDICAL PERSONNEL — 18

[1] Division headquarters detachment absorbed 27 April 1921 by the division headquarters company.
[2] On 20 April 1921 the motorcycle company was moved to the trains and the service company added to special troops.

attached to the various regiments and the mobile repair shop were grouped in an ordnance company, centralizing all ordnance maintenance. A signal company replaced the signal battalion, and it assumed responsibility for message traffic between division and brigade headquarters. Within the infantry and field artillery regiments, men from the combat arms were to handle all communications. The new division abandoned the train headquarters and military police organization, following the recommendation of the Superior Board, but retained a separate military police company. Given the many small separate companies in its structure (division headquarters, signal, tank, service, ordnance, and military police), the division included a new organization, headquarters, special troops, to handle their administration and discipline.

The committee substituted a medical regiment for the sanitary train and revamped health services. Three hospital companies replaced the four used during the war, and the number of ambulance companies in the regiment was similarly reduced. In addition, a sanitary (collecting) battalion comprising three companies corrected the need for litter-bearers, who had previously been taken from combat units. Veterinarians, formerly scattered throughout the division, now formed a veterinary company. A laboratory section, a supply section, and a service company completed the new regiment. Despite the innovations, the regiment fielded about the same number of men as its World War I counterpart.[29]

Attesting to the greater depth envisaged for the battlefield, an air squadron of thirteen airplanes was to serve as the reconnaissance unit for the division. As under the wartime configuration, units for ground reconnaissance were to be attached as needed.[30]

Although the committee's infantry division was larger than that contemplated in Pershing's proposal, the planners believed it had only those organic elements necessary for immediate employment under normal conditions. In an emergency, the new division could be quickly adjusted to meet an enemy armed with inferior arms and equipment. The problem the planners tried to address was how to design a division to deal with superior forces without significantly modifying it. The committee's division, nevertheless, had its opponents. Conner and Marshall of Pershing's staff still preferred the smaller triangular division for its mobility and ease of command and control. Years later Marshall recalled that if Heintzelman and King had not been such "kindly characters," the triangular division would have been adopted instead of Drum's large division.[31]

The question arises why Pershing, after becoming chief of staff on 1 July 1921, failed to replace the infantry division with one more compatible with his concept of battlefield mobility. Marshall pointed out later that the basic recommendation for retaining the square infantry division came from his own officers, the Superior Board. To disavow their advice would have been an embarrassment. Furthermore, by July 1921 the reorganization of the divisions had already begun. To undo so much work would have been unrealistic and would have implied a lack of leadership within the Army. Therefore, the square infantry division stood with the understanding that it might be modified to deal with a particular enemy.[32]

The Lassiter Committee apparently devoted little attention to the cavalry division and recorded less about its rationale for retaining the unit. Mobility and firepower dominated the new organization. The *Cavalry Journal*, the official organ for the arm, had repeatedly condemned the 1917 organization as an absurdity. Burdened with more than 18,000 men and 16,000 animals, the division was too large and cumbersome. It required a preposterous amount of road space, roughly thirty miles, and was incapable of maneuver because it lacked an efficient communication system.[33]

The postwar cavalry division, approximately two-fifths the size of its predecessor, abandoned the three-brigade structure (*Chart 6*). It included two cavalry brigades (two cavalry regiments and one machine gun squadron each), one horse artillery battalion, and combat and service support units. Each cavalry regiment consisted of two squadrons (of three troops each), a headquarters and headquarters troop and a service troop. Initially the committee desired a third squadron to train men and horses, which represented a major investment in time and money. March denied the request because the Army was to maintain training centers. Unlike the infantry, which incorporated the machine gun into the regiment, cavalry maintained separate machine gun squadrons of three troops each because of the perceived immobility of such weapons compared with other divisional arms. A headquarters for special troops was authorized, under which were placed the division headquarters troop, a signal troop, an ordnance maintenance company, and a veterinary company. All transportation was pack- or animal-drawn, except for 14 cars, 28 trucks, and 65 motorcycles scattered throughout various headquarters elements in the division. Without trains, the division measured approximately 6.5 miles if the men rode in columns of twos. The Army chief of staff approved the new cavalry division on 31 August 1920.[34]

After approving both types of divisions, March directed the preparation of final tables of organization. When published the following year, the infantry division fell just below Pershing's recommendation of 20,000, numbering 19,997 officers and enlisted men. The cavalry division totaled 7,463.[35]

As the War Plans Division prepared the new tables, it also developed tables for understrength peacetime units because the Army's leadership did not expect to be able to maintain the number of men authorized under the National Defense Act. These tables were designed so that the units could expand without having to undergo reorganization. The peacetime infantry division was thus cut to 11,000 with all elements retaining their integrity except the division headquarters and military police companies, which were combined. The peacetime cavalry division strength was set at 6,000. But severe cuts in the War Department's budget made it impossible initially even to publish the peacetime tables. Fortunately, the service journals undertook that task.[36]

## CHART 6—Cavalry Division, 4 April 1921

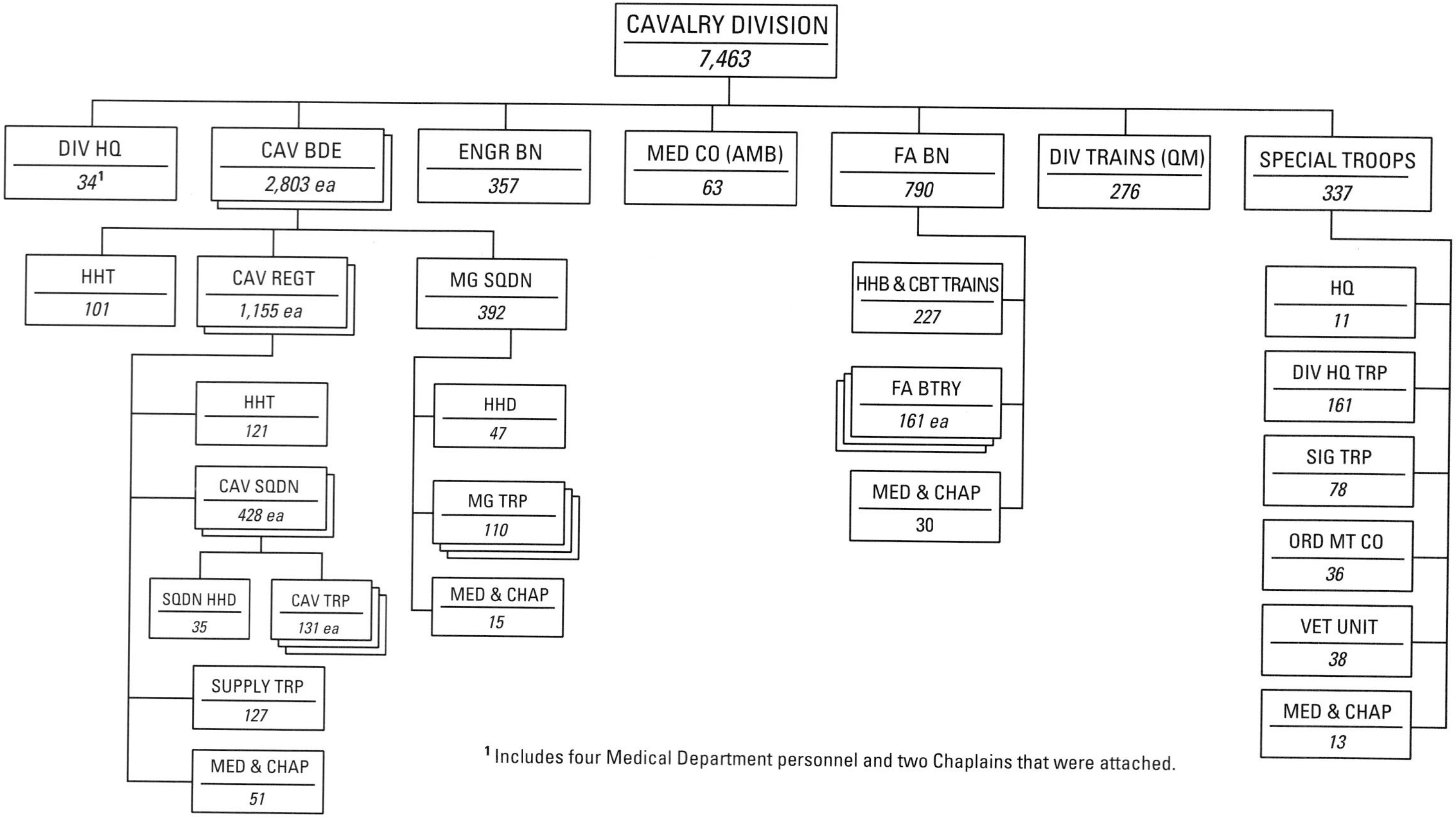

**CAVALRY DIVISION** — 7,463

- **DIV HQ** — 34[1]
- **CAV BDE** — 2,803 ea
  - **HHT** — 101
  - **CAV REGT** — 1,155 ea
    - **HHT** — 121
    - **CAV SQDN** — 428 ea
      - **SQDN HHD** — 35
      - **CAV TRP** — 131 ea
    - **SUPPLY TRP** — 127
    - **MED & CHAP** — 51
- **ENGR BN** — 357
- **MG SQDN** — 392
  - **HHD** — 47
  - **MG TRP** — 110
  - **MED & CHAP** — 15
- **MED CO (AMB)** — 63
- **FA BN** — 790
  - **HHB & CBT TRAINS** — 227
  - **FA BTRY** — 161 ea
  - **MED & CHAP** — 30
- **DIV TRAINS (QM)** — 276
- **SPECIAL TROOPS** — 337
  - **HQ** — 11
  - **DIV HQ TRP** — 161
  - **SIG TRP** — 78
  - **ORD MT CO** — 36
  - **VET UNIT** — 38
  - **MED & CHAP** — 13

[1] Includes four Medical Department personnel and two Chaplains that were attached.

## Reorganization of Divisions

March directed the War Plans Division to implement the tentative tables of organization he had approved. Planning for reorganization of the Army had been under way since 5 June 1920, when the War Plans Division had set up committees to carry out the provisions of the National Defense Act. Officers from the General Staff, the National Guard, and the Organized Reserves helped formulate the plans.[37]

One committee, originally charged with defining the missions of the National Guard and the Organized Reserves, widened its task to encompass the Regular Army. The committee delineated four missions for the regulars: form an expeditionary force in an emergency; furnish troops for foreign and coastal defense garrisons; provide personnel to develop and train the reserve components; and supply the administrative overhead of the Army. The National Guard's dual missions remained unchanged. It contributed to the federal forces during national emergencies or war and supplied the states with forces to maintain law and order and cope with local disasters. The mission of the Organized Reserves was to expand the Army during war or national emergencies. Because of the strong antiwar sentiment after World War I, the expense of maintaining large numbers of enlisted men, the lack of training facilities, and the possible adverse effect on the recruitment for the Guard, units of the Organized Reserves were to have only officers and enlisted cadres. After a declaration of war or national emergency, the remainder of the enlisted men would come from voluntary enlistments or the draft.[38]

Another committee looked into the number of divisions that could be organized and supported during peacetime. Given a Regular Army of 296,000 officers and enlisted men, the committee determined that the War Department could maintain nine infantry divisions (one per corps area), three cavalry divisions (one per army area), and one infantry brigade of black troops in the United States. Of these divisions, one cavalry and three infantry divisions were to be ready for war while the others were to be at reduced strength. This arrangement evenly distributed the expeditionary forces throughout the nation and provided an infantry division to serve as a model for the reserves within each corps area.[39]

In view of the great personnel turbulence caused by the rapid demobilization, the committee recommended that the Regular Army quickly rebuild its seven existing infantry divisions to meet the strength in the new peacetime tables and permit the units to conduct realistic training. The other two planned infantry divisions could be organized after the first seven had reached their reduced strength level, and when all nine attained that level one or more divisions could be increased to full manning for war. How the Regular cavalry divisions were to be formed remained unaddressed. With 486,000 men in the National Guard, the committee envisioned forming eighteen Guard infantry divisions, two for each corps area, and three or more Guard cavalry divisions, at least one for each army area. For the Organized Reserves, twenty-seven infantry divisions were contemplated, three per corps area, and three or more cavalry divisions, at least one for each army area.40

When March approved the structure of infantry and cavalry divisions, he also sanctioned the formation of divisions based on that report. Instead of three Regular Army cavalry divisions, he saw a need for only two. The Army's mobilization base would thus be fifty-four infantry divisions and eight or more cavalry divisions.41

Reorganization of the Regular Army began in late 1920 as the infantry elements of the 1st through 7th Divisions began to adopt the new peacetime tables. In the 2d Division a Regular Army infantry brigade, the 4th, replaced the Marine Corps unit that had been attached to the division in France. As tables for other divisional units became available, they too were put into effect.42

All this work quickly appeared somewhat premature. By the fall of 1921, cuts in Army appropriations indicated that the Regular Army could not support seven infantry divisions in the United States. Secretary of War John W. Weeks, therefore, instituted a policy allowing inactive units to remain on the "rolls" of the Army but in an inoperable status—that is, without personnel and equipment. Congressional insistence on maintaining the tactical division frameworks to ensure immediate and complete mobilization made such arrangements necessary. Judging that nothing was wrong with the mobilization plan, but recognizing the shortage of funds for the fiscal year, Weeks directed that some units be taken "out of commission" or inactivated. The policy represented a marked departure from past Army experience. Previously, when a unit could not be maintained or was not needed, it was removed from the rolls of the Army either by disbandment or consolidation with another unit. Acting otherwise threatened to obscure the Army's reduced strength through a facade of paper units.43

Nevertheless, under the new system the Army cut the divisional forces in September and October 1921 by inactivating the 4th through the 7th Divisions, except for the even numbered infantry brigade in each. These brigades—the 8th, 10th, 12th, and 14th—remained active to serve as the nuclei of their parent divisions upon mobilization. To save even more personnel, the 2d Division, programmed at wartime strength, was placed under the reduced strength tables, leaving the Army without a fully manned division in the United States.44

During the summer of 1921 the General Staff turned its attention to Regular Army cavalry divisions. On 20 August the adjutant general constituted the 1st and 2d Cavalry Divisions to meet partial mobilization requirements, and the following month the commander of the Eighth Corps Area organized the 1st Cavalry Division. The headquarters of the division and its 2d Brigade were located at Fort Bliss, Texas, and that of the 1st Cavalry Brigade at Douglas, Arizona. Resources were not available to organize a second cavalry division until World War II.45

The Regular Army divisions underwent postwar reorganization and reduction even before the War Department could determine their permanent stations. A committee established in June 1920 to make recommendations about posting units never submitted a report because of the unsettled size of the Regular Army.

# THE AFTERMATH OF WORLD WAR I

When Congress funded a Regular Army of 150,000 enlisted men for 1922, the Acting Chief of Staff, Maj. Gen. James G. Harbord, directed a new war plans group to prepare an outline for stationing these troops. If possible, he wanted units to have adequate housing and training facilities as well as to be located where the men could assist in the development of the reserve components. The recommendations called for the Second and Ninth Corps Areas each to have an infantry division, the Eighth Corps Area to have both infantry and cavalry divisions, and the remaining corps areas each to have a reinforced brigade.[46]

As the existing divisions and brigades moved to their permanent stations in 1922, the Army organized the 16th and 18th Infantry Brigades to complete the Regular Army portion of the plan (*Table 8*). To fulfill mobilization requirements for nine Regular Army infantry divisions, the adjutant general also restored the 8th and 9th Divisions to the rolls in 1923, but they remained inactive except for their 16th and 18th Infantry Brigades. The stationing plan allowed the regulars to support the reserves, but only the 2d Division was concentrated at one post—Fort Sam Houston, Texas.[47]

The last large unit recommended for the Regular Army in 1920 was a black brigade scheduled for service along the Mexican border. However, only four black regiments, two cavalry and two infantry, remained after the war, and the War Department decided that they should not be brigaded. In 1922 two of them, the 10th Cavalry and the 25th Infantry, served along the border. Of the remainder, the 9th Cavalry was stationed at Fort Riley, Kansas, the home of the Cavalry School, and the 24th Infantry was posted to Fort Benning, Georgia, where the Infantry School had been established.[48]

The post–World War I Army also maintained forces in the Philippine Islands, China, the Panama Canal Zone, Puerto Rico, Germany, and Hawaii. To assure that these areas were adequately garrisoned, the War Plans Division examined their manning needs. Based upon its findings, March approved the formation of the Panama Canal, Hawaiian, and Philippine Divisions. In 1921 the commanders of those overseas departments organized their units as best they could from available personnel and equipment. The infantry and field artillery brigades and many of the other divisional elements had numerical designations that would be associated with the 10th, 11th, and 12th Divisions. These elements, all table of organization units, could be assigned wherever needed in the force. Because the divisions themselves were not expected to serve outside of their respective territories, they had territorial designations. The division headquarters were at Quarry Heights, Canal Zone; Schofield Barracks, Hawaii; and Fort William McKinley, Philippine Islands. Personnel for the Hawaiian and Panama Canal Divisions came from the Regular Army, but the Philippine Division was filled with both regulars and Philippine Scouts, with the latter in the majority.[49]

Section V of the National Defense Act prescribed a committee to devise plans for organizing the National Guard divisions. Formed in August 1920, this group consisted of Regular Army and Guard officers who represented their embryonic

### TABLE 8

### Distribution of Regular Army Divisions and Brigades, 1922

| Corps Area | Unit | Station |
|---|---|---|
| First | 18th Infantry Brigade (9th Division) | Fort Devens, Mass. |
| Second | 1st Division | Fort Hamilton, N.Y. |
| Third | 16th Infantry Brigade (8th Division) | Fort Howard, Md. |
| Fourth | 8th Infantry Brigade (4th Division) | Fort McPherson, Ga. |
| Fifth | 10th Infantry Brigade (5th Division) | Fort Benjamin Harrison, Ind. |
| Sixth | 12th Infantry Brigade (6th Division) | Fort Sheridan, Ill. |
| Seventh | 14th Infantry Brigade (7th Division) | Fort Omaha, Neb. |
| Eighth | 2d Division | Fort Sam Houston, Tex. |
|  | 1st Cavalry Division | Fort Bliss, Tex. |
| Ninth | 3d Division | Fort Lewis, Wash. |

(Units in parentheses are the inactive parent organizations.)

corps areas. Within a short time the committee presented the states with a blueprint for eighteen infantry divisions. Corps area commanders were to resolve any divergent views or disputes among the states over the allotment of the units. The plan offered the states the 26th through the 41st Divisions, organized during World War I, and three new units, the 43d, 44th, and 45th Divisions, as Guard units. The 42d "Rainbow" Division was omitted because it lacked an association with any particular state or geographic area. All corps areas except the Fourth received two divisional designations. The states in the Fourth Corps Area, which had raised the 30th, 31st, and 39th Divisions during World War I, decided to reorganize the 30th and 39th Divisions. By the spring of 1921 the states had agreed on the allotment of most units in the infantry divisions, the War Department had furnished the new divisional tables of organization, and the states had begun to reorganize their forces accordingly. Between 1921 and 1935 the National Guard Bureau granted federal recognition to the headquarters of all eighteen Guard infantry divisions (*Table 9*). Although a few divisions lacked federally recognized headquarters until the 1930s, most of the divisional elements were granted federal recognition in the 1920s.[50]

The historical continuity of Guard units rested upon geographic areas that supported the organizations, and during the reorganization most units adopted the designations used during World War I. Some shifting of units to new geographic areas took place, resulting in some designation changes. For example, in World War I Arkansas, Louisiana, and Mississippi had raised the 39th Division, but when the 39th was reorganized in the postwar era Florida, Alabama, Mississippi, and Louisiana supported the unit. Subsequently, a joint board of Regular and Guard officers recommended that the division be renamed the 31st Division, a unit that during the war had raised troops from Florida, Alabama, and Georgia. Secretary Weeks approved the change, and on 1 July 1923 the 39th Division was replaced by the 31st Division.[51]

The allocation and organization of the Guard cavalry divisions followed the same procedure as the infantry divisions. But in order to use all existing cavalry units, a fourth cavalry division was added to the force. In 1921 the formation of the 21st through 24th Cavalry Divisions began with the First, Second, and Third Army Areas supporting the 21st, 22d, and 24th Cavalry Divisions, respectively. The 23d was the nation's at-large cavalry division, supported by all army areas (*Table 10*). In a short time the divisions had the prescribed cavalry regiments and machine gun squadrons but not the majority of their support organizations.[52]

The organization of the third component's units began in 1921 when the War Department published Special Regulations No. 46, *General Policies and Regulations for the Organized Reserves*. The regulations explained the procedures for administering, training, and mobilizing the Organized Reserves and provided a tentative outline for the corps area commanders to follow in organizing the units. Using the outline and a 6 April 1921 troop allotment for twenty-seven infantry divisions, corps area commanders set up planning boards to establish the units. In locating them, the boards considered the distribution and occupations of the population, attempting to station the units where they would be most likely to receive effective support. For example, a medical unit was not located in an area where there was no civilian medical facility. After determining the location of the units and giving the Guard some time to recruit, thus avoiding competition with it, officers began to organize the 76th through the 91st and the 94th through the 104th Divisions.[53]

Recruiting the units proved to be slow. Regular Army advisers were armed with lists of potential reservists and little else. There were not enough recruiters, office space and equipment, or funds available to accomplish the work. Furthermore, a marked apathy toward the military prevailed throughout the nation. By March 1922, however, all twenty-seven infantry divisions had skeletal headquarters (*see Table 9*).[54]

To complete the divisional forces in the Organized Reserves, the War Department added the 61st through the 66th Cavalry Divisions to the rolls of the Army on 15 October 1921. Corps area commanders followed the same procedures used previously for the infantry divisions in allotting and organizing them. Within a few months they too emerged as skeletal organizations (*see Table 10*).[55]

Thus, in early 1923 the Army had 66 divisions in the mobilization force shared among three components—11 in the Regular Army (2 cavalry and 9 infantry), 22 in the National Guard (4 cavalry and 18 infantry), and 33 in Organized Reserves (6 cavalry and 27 infantry). In addition, three understrength

# TABLE 9

## Allotment of Reserve Component Infantry Divisions, 1921

| Corps Area | Division | Component | Location |
|---|---|---|---|
| First | 26th | NG | Massachusetts |
| | 43d | NG | Connecticut, Maine, Rhode Island, and Vermont |
| | 76th | OR | Connecticut and Rhode Island |
| | 94th | OR | Massachusetts |
| | 97th | OR | Maine, New Hampshire, and Vermont |
| Second | 27th | NG | New York |
| | 44th | NG | New Jersey, New York, and Delaware |
| | 77th | OR | New York |
| | 78th | OR | New Jersey and Delaware |
| | 98th | OR | New York |
| Third | 28th | NG | Pennsylvania |
| | 29th | NG | Maryland, Virginia, and District of Columbia |
| | 79th | OR | Pennsylvania |
| | 80th | OR | Maryland, Virginia, and District of Columbia |
| | 99th | OR | Pennsylvania |
| Fourth | 30th | NG | Georgia, Tennessee, North Carolina, and South Carolina |
| | 39th | NG | Alabama, Florida, Mississippi, and Louisiana |
| | 81st | OR | North Carolina and Tennessee |
| | 82d | OR | South Carolina and Georgia |
| | 87th | OR | Louisiana, Mississippi, and Alabama |
| Fifth | 37th | NG | Ohio |
| | 38th | NG | Kentucky, Indiana, and West Virginia |
| | 83d | OR | Ohio |
| | 84th | OR | Indiana |
| | 100th | OR | Kentucky and West Virginia |
| Sixth | 32d | NG | Michigan and Wisconsin |
| | 33d | NG | Illinois |
| | 85th | OR | Michigan |
| | 86th | OR | Illinois |
| | 101st | OR | Wisconsin |
| Seventh | 34th | NG | Iowa, Minnesota, North Dakota, and South Dakota |
| | 35th | NG | Nebraska, Kansas, and Missouri |
| | 88th | OR | Minnesota, Iowa, and North Dakota |

TABLE 9—Continued

| Corps Area | Division | Component | Location |
|---|---|---|---|
|  | 89th | OR | South Dakota, Nebraska, and Kansas |
|  | 102d | OR | Missouri and Arkansas |
| Eighth | 36th | NG | Texas |
|  | 45th | NG | Oklahoma, Colorado, New Mexico, and Arizona |
|  | 90th | OR | Texas |
|  | 95th | OR | Oklahoma |
|  | 103d | OR | New Mexico, Colorado, and Arizona |
| Ninth | 40th | NG | California, Nevada, and Utah |
|  | 41st | NG | Washington, Oregon, Wyoming, Montana, and Idaho |
|  | 91st | OR | California |
|  | 96th | OR | Oregon and Washington |
|  | 104th | OR | Nevada, Utah, Wyoming, and Idaho |

# TABLE 10
## Allotment of Reserve Component Cavalry Divisions, 1921

| Division | Component | Location |
|---|---|---|
| 21st | NG | New York, Pennsylvania, Rhode Island, and New Jersey |
| 22d | NG | Georgia, Illinois, Indiana, Kentucky, Louisiana, Michigan, Ohio, West Virginia, and Wisconsin |
| 23d | NG | Alabama, Massachusetts, New Mexico, North Carolina, Tennessee, Texas, and Wisconsin |
| 24th | NG | Idaho, Iowa, Kansas, Minnesota, North Dakota, South Dakota, Utah, Washington, and Wyoming |
| 61st | OR | New York and New Jersey |
| 62d | OR | Maryland, Virginia, District of Columbia, and Pennsylvania |
| 63d | OR | Tennessee, Louisiana, Georgia, North Carolina, Texas, Oklahoma, and Colorado |
| 64th | OR | Kentucky, Massachusetts, Vermont, and New Hampshire |
| 65th | OR | Illinois, Michigan, and Wisconsin |
| 66th | OR | Nebraska, Missouri, Utah, and North Dakota |

infantry divisions were located overseas. No separate brigades existed. In almost every case, however, these divisions, which varied from inactive units to partially manned organizations, were "paper tigers."

After World War I the Army quickly demobilized its forces, but memories of the unpreparedness of 1917 caused the nation to change the way it maintained its military forces. Infantry and cavalry divisions, rather than regiments or smaller units, became the pillars that would support future mobilization. Officers examined the structure of those pillars and adopted a modified, but powerful, square infantry division designed for frontal attack and a small light cavalry division for reconnaissance. Although the lessons of war influenced the structure of these divisions, more traditional criteria regarding their local geographical employment continued to affect their organization. But with no real enemy in sight and the nation's adoption of a generally isolationist foreign policy, it is not surprising that Congress provided neither the manpower nor the materiel to equip even a caretaker force adequately.

## Notes

1 Wrapper Indorsement (Forwarding Report of A.E.F. Superior Board on Organization and Tactics), General Headquarters (GHQ), AEF, to Sec of War, 16 Jun 20, AG0 322 (4–19–19), RG 407, NARA.

2 *General Headquarters, Armies*, pp. 170–91; Henry T. Allen, *The Rhineland Occupation* (Indianapolis: Bobbs-Merrill Co., 1927), p. 13; Huidekoper, *The History of the 33rd Division*, 1: 257–95.

3 *General Headquarters, Armies*, pp. 399–404; Irwin L. Hunt, *American Military Government of Occupied Germany 1918–1920* (Washington, D.C.: Government Printing Office, 1943), pp. 76–84; Robert S. Thomas, "The United States Army 1914–1923," pt. 1, pp. XIX-48–49, Ms in Historical Resources Branch, Center of Military History, hereafter cited as DAMH-HSR.

4 *Second Report of the Provost Marshal General to the Secretary of War on the Operations of Selective Service System to December 20, 1918* (Washington, D.C.: Government Printing Office, 1919), p. 239.

5 Rpt of the CofS, *ARWD, 1919*, pp. 451–52; John W. Sparrow, *History of Personnel Demobilization of the United States* (Washington, D.C.: Government Printing Office, 1952), pp. 11–19.

6 WD Cir 77, 21 Nov 1918; Thomas, "The United States Army 1914–1923," p. XX–22; *Directory of Troops*, pp. 1310–16; Peyton C. March, *The Nation at War* (Garden City, N.Y.: Doubleday, Dorn, and Co., 1932), pp. 310–25. *The New York Times Index*, vol. 7, nos. 1, 2, and 3, provides a quick guide to the divisional parades.

7 Memo, Ch of Operations Branch to TAG, 12 Aug 19, sub: Retention of Divisional Organization, WPD file 8481–131, RG 165, NARA; WD GO 91, 1919.

8 Frederic L. Paxson, *The Great Demobilization and Other Essays* (Madison: University of Wisconsin Press, 1941), p. 7.

9 March, *The Nation at War*, pp. 330–33, 336–41; Memo, WPD for CofS, 24 Feb 19, sub: Tactical organization of the division and higher tactical units, WPD 8481–116, RG 165, NARA; John McA. Palmer, "The Military Policy of the United States as Settled by Recent Law and Executive Order," lecture at the AWC, published in WD Bull 19, 1921.

10 Memo, G–5, AEF, to General Nolon, sub: Board of Review, 16 Mar 19, RG 120, NARA; Special Orders (SO) 98, AEF, 8 Apr 19, and Rpt of the Superior Board, AEF, on Organization and Tactics, AGO 320 (6–21–20), Bulky Files, RG 407, NARA. Unless otherwise indicated, the following discussion of the infantry and cavalry divisions is based on the board report. Also see reports of the various postwar AEF boards on the arms and services, which are included in the same file. See John B. Wilson, "Mobility Versus Firepower: The Post-World War I Infantry Division," *Parameters* 13 (Sep 1983): 48, for biographical data about the board members.

11 Rpt of the Superior Board, p. 85.

12 Wrapper Indorsement (Forwarding Report of the AEF Superior Board), 16 Jun 20. Although Pershing held the report, its recommendations were widely known by the Army Staff.

13 John Dickinson, *The Building of an Army* (New York: Century Co., 1922), pp. 330–34.

14 WD Bull 25, 1920.

15 WD GO 50, 1920; Memo, WPD for Dir, WPD, 10 Jul 20, sub: Committee No. 2 Report on Army Reorganization, AWC file 52–21, Military History Institute, Carlisle Barracks, Pa, hereafter cited as MHI.

16 Memo, WPD, 5 Jun 20, sub: Committees for Working out Army Reorganization, AWC file 52–21.

17 Memo, WPD to General Staff College (hereafter cited as GSC), 14 Jun 20, sub: Army Organization, 14 Jun 20, with enclosures, Memo, WPD to GSC, 15 Jun 20, sub: Army Organization, AWC file 52–10. Pershing maintained an AEF headquarters in Washington between the time he returned from France and the time he assumed the position of Chief of Staff, Army.

[18] Wrapper Indorsement (Forwarding Report of AEF Superior Board), 16 Jun 20; Draft entitled "Notes on Organization" with Fox Conner's initials, undated, AWC file 52–21.

[19] Wrapper Indorsement (Forwarding Report of AEF Superior Board), 16 Jun 20.

[20] Ibid.

[21] Memo WPD to GSC, 15 Jun 20, sub: Army Organization, AWC file 52-10, MHI; Memo, WPD to TAG, 21 Jun 20, sub: Special Committee on Reorganization of the Army, AGO 320 (6–21–20), RG 407, NARA.

[22] Rpt of Special Committee Appointed by Dir, WPD, to Define the General Plan of Organization to be Adopted by the Army of the United States provided by the Act of 4 June 20, 8 Jul 20, AWC course material 52–51, MHI, hereafter cited as Rpt of Special Committee, WPD, 8 Jul 20; Wilson, "Mobility Versus Firepower," p. 49.

[23] Arthur W. Lane, "Tables of Organization," *Infantry Journal* 18 (May 1921): 489–91.

[24] Ibid.; Wilson, "Mobility Versus Firepower," p. 49.

[25] Lane, "Tables of Organization," pp. 489–91.

[26] Ibid.

[27] Ibid.

[28] Ibid.; App. 2 to Rpt of Special Committee, WPD, 8 Jul 20; Memo, CofS, 31 Aug 20, no subject, WPD file 6935–1, RG 165, Draft T/Os, 7 Oct 1920, WPD file 6935–8, RG 407, NARA; T/O, 15 Oct 1920, DAMH-HSO.

[29] Lane, "Tables of Organization," pp. 489–91; App. 2 to Rpt of Special Committee, WPD, 8 Jul 20; T/O 1921, Table 1 War (W), Infantry Division, 4 May 1921.

[30] T/O, 1921, Table 1 W, Infantry Division, 4 May 1921; *Field Service Regulations*, 1923, p. 18.

[31] Lane, "Tables of Organization," pp. 489–90; Ltr, George C. Marshall to Fox Conner, 17 Jan 38, and Ltr, Marshall to William M. Spencer, 18 Mar 38, Marshall Papers, George C. Marshall Research Foundation, Lexington, Va.

[32] Ltr, George C. Marshall to Walton H. Walker, 21 Dec 37, Marshall Papers.

[33] Rpt of Special Committee, WPD, 8 Jul 20; "Cavalry Organization," *Cavalry Journal* 29 (Jul 20): 116; "Cavalry Reorganization," *Cavalry Journal* 30 (Jan 21): 62–63.

[34] T/O 1921, Table 401 W, Cavalry Division, 4 Apr 21; Memo, GSC for Dir of Operations, 30 Jul 20, sub: Comments on report of Special Committee on Reorganization of the Regular Army, Memo, Ch of Cavalry for CofS, 10 Aug 20, sub: Comments on Recommendations of Special Committee on Reorganization of the Army, 11 Aug 20, CSC file 8481–136, RG 165, NARA; Memo, CofS, 31 Aug 20.

[35] T/O, Table 1 W, Infantry Division, 4 May 21; T/O, Table 401 W, Cavalry Division, 4 Apr 21.

[36] T/O, Table 1 Peace (P), Infantry Division, 1921; T/O, Table 401 P, Cavalry Division, 21; "Tables of Organization", *Cavalry Journal* 30 (Oct 1921): 422–15.

[37] Memo, CofS, 31 Aug 20; Memo, WPD, 5 Jun 20, sub: Committees for Working out Army Reorganization, AWC file 52-21.

[38] Memo, WPD for Dir, WPD, 10 Jul 20, sub: Committee Report on Army Reorganization, AWC file 52-21.

[39] Ibid.; Rpt of Committee 5, appointed by Dir, War Plans Division, June 7, 1920, 30 Jul 20, John L. Hines Papers, LC.

[40] Rpt of Committee 5, 30 Jul 20.

[41] Memo, CofS, 31 Aug 20.

[42] WD Cirs 400 and 415, 1920; GO 2, 1st Division, 1921; GO 1, 3d Division, 1921; GO 2, 4th Division, 1921; GO 10, 5th Division, 1921; GO 1, 6th Division, 1921; GO 23, 7th Division, 1921, copies of these and other divisional general orders relating to the reorganization of Regular Army units in Division General file, DAMH-HSO. Circular 400 authorized the 2d Division to be at war strength, which included its 4th Brigade.

[43] WD GO 31, 1921.

[44] WD GO 33, 1921; GO 19, 2d Division, 1921, Division General file, and 3d Ind, Historical Section, AWC to TAG, 15 Nov 21, 2d Inf Div file, both in DAMH-HSO.

45 Ltr, TAG to CG of all Corps Areas, 20 Aug 21, sub: Organization of the Cavalry, Cavalry Reorganization file, 1921-28, Historical Data Card, 1st Cavalry (Cav) Div, DAMH-HSO. By 30 June 1922 about 10,000 officers and enlisted men were available in the fourteen active cavalry regiments (see Annual Rpt, Sec of War, 1922, p. 305).

46 Memo, WPD, 5 Jun 20, sub: Committees for Working out Army Reorganization; Memo Operations and Training Division, G–3,/1575 for DCofS, 27 Dec 21, sub: Comments on Report of Board of GS officers relative to distribution, shelter, and training areas for the Army (basic report attached), AGO 320 file, 27 Dec 21, RG 407, NARA.

47 Ltr, TAG to CGs, all Corps Areas and Depts; Chief of Infantry; CG, American Forces in Germany; CG, Fort Benning, Ga.; and COs of Exempted Places concerned, sub: Organization and Redistribution of the Infantry, AGO Central file 1917–25, 320.2 (7–15–22) RG 407, NARA; WD GO 10, 1923.

48 Memo, WPD for Dir, WPD, 10 Jul 20, sub: Committee Report on Army Reorganization; "Brief History of the 24th Infantry," 27 Sep 26, Ms, 24th Infantry file, DAMH-HSO; *Historical and Pictorial Review Second Cavalry Division, United States Army* (Baton Rouge, La.: Army and Navy Publishing Co., 1941), p. 50.

49 Memo, WPD for Dir, WPD, 9 Jul 20, sub: Strength of the Foreign garrisons required and their special organization. Available troops to be considered in the connection (Report of Committee No. 3), 9 Jul 20, AWC 52-21, MHI; WD Cir 149, 1921; WD GO 15, 1921; Ltr, TAG to CG, Philippine Dept., 22 Oct 22, sub: Completion of overseas garrison, 320 (10–7–21), 12th Inf Div file, DAMH-HSO; Returns, Panama Canal, Hawaiian, and Philippine Divisions, divisional files, DAMH-HSO. The National Defense Act continued departments in the Hawaiian Islands, the Philippine Islands, and the Panama Canal Zone.

50 Memo G–3 for CofS, 14 Mar 22, sub: Basic plan for the organization of the National Guard, AGO 320 G/2253 (10–31–22) to (7–28–22), Bulky Files, RG 168, NARA; Ltr, TAG to CGs all Corps Areas, 19 Oct 20, sub: Allotment of National Guard troops, 323 (Misc. Div.); Ltr, Fourth Corps Area to TAG, 17 Nov 20, sub: Allotment of National Guard Troops; and Ltr, TAG to CG of all Corps Areas, 7 Dec 20, sub: Designation and location of units of the National Guard and the Organized Reserve, 325.344 (Misc. Div.), all Reference Files, National Guard, DAMH-HSO. The granting of federal recognition to divisional elements maybe traced through the *Official National Guard Register 1931, 1936, and 1939* and state and unit records in DAMH-HSO.

Regular Army members of the Section V committee were Col. Briant H. Wells, Lt. Col. John W. Gulick, and Maj. William Bryden; the National Guard officers were Cols. Walter E. Bare of Alabama, Greed G. Hammond of Oregon, Milton A. Reckord of Maryland, George C. Richards of Pennsylvania, Frank M. Rumbold of Missouri, and Franklin W. War of New York; Lt. Cols. Chalmer R. Wilson of Ohio and Guy M. Wilson of Michigan; and Majs. J. Ross Ives of Connecticut and J. Watt Page of Texas.

51 Ltr., TAG to CGs of all Corps Areas, 7 Dec 20, sub: Designation and location of units of the National Guard and the Organized Reserves, Reference Files, National Guard, DAMH-HSO; *Report of the Chief of the Militia Bureau, 1923*, p. 11.

52 *Rpt of the Chief of the Militia Bureau, 1922*, pp. 24–26; Memo, WPD to TAG, 15 Feb 22, sub: Normal numerical designations of units of National Guard Cavalry Divisions, WPD 9691, AGO 325.455, and Ltr, TAG to CGs all Corps Areas, 29 Nov 21, sub: Revised Tables of normal numerical designations of units National Guard Cavalry Divisions, 325–455 (11–28–21) (Misc. Div.), Reference Files, National Guard, DAMH-HSO.

53 Special Regulations No. 46, *General Policies and Regulations for the Organized Reserves, 1921*; Ltr, Maj Gen John L. Hines to John J. Pershing, 26 Dec 21, John L. Hines Papers, LC; Ltr, TAG to CGs all corps areas, 24 Jun 21, sub: Normal numerical designations of infantry divisions, AG 325.455, Reference Files, Army Reserve, DAMH-HSO.

The numbers 94, 103, and 104 were new designations, and the numbers 92 and 93 were omitted because during the war these divisions had not come from any one state or group of states. Furthermore, the 92d Division and 93d Division (Provisional) in World War I had been organized with Negro soldiers, and the department's policy was not to maintain large Negro units during peacetime.

54 *Report of the Secretary of War, 1922*, p. 18; Organized Reserves (infantry division notes), Reference Files, Army Reserve, DAMH-HSO. Also see Marken's notes on Organizational Data, ROAD Brigades, Brigade General Files, DAMH-HSO.

55 Ltr, TAG to CGs all Corps Areas, 15 Oct 21, sub: Numerical designations of Army and GHQ Reserve Troops, First, Second, and Third Field Armies, Organized Reserves, AG 320.2 Organized Reserves (10–21–21) (Misc. Div.), AG Reference files, 1921, DAMH-HSO.

CHAPTER 5

# A Return to the Past; A Look to the Future

*Nor can it be questioned that the Division as now organized and composed . . . of foot, animal, and motor elements, all with varying rates of speed, is uneconomical, unwieldy and unadapted to the demands of modern mobile warfare.*

General Malin Craig[1]

After establishing post–World War I divisions, the Army experienced a prolonged period of stagnation and deterioration. The National Defense Act of 1920 authorized a Regular Army of 296,000 men, but Congress gradually backed away from that number. As with the Regular Army, the National Guard never recruited its authorized 486,000 men, and the Organized Reserves became merely a pool of reserve officers. The root of the Army's problem was money. Congress yearly appropriated only about half the funds that the General Staff requested. Impoverished in manpower and funds, infantry and cavalry divisions dwindled to skeletal organizations.

Meanwhile, the General Staff and service schools searched for a divisional structure, particularly for the infantry, that best suited the conditions of modern warfare. Like their European counterparts, American military planners remembered, above all, the indecisiveness that had dominated the battlefield in World War I. The result had been a protracted war of hitherto unimagined devastation. The search for a sound divisional organization was part of the effort to find the means of restoring decisiveness to warfare. Otherwise, victors might suffer as much as, or even more than, the vanquished. These considerations drew attention especially to various means of improving the division's mobility and maneuverability so that the Army could avoid future wars of position that would force it to adopt the bloody strategy of attrition.

## *Paper Divisions*

Between 1923 and 1939 divisions gradually declined as fighting organizations. After Regular Army divisions moved to permanent posts, the War Department modified command relationships between divisional units and the corps areas. It placed elements of the 1st and 3d Divisions and the 8th, 10th,

*26th Division parade, Fort Devens, Massachusetts, 1925*

12th, 14th, 16th, and 18th Infantry Brigades directly under the corps area commanders, making division and brigade commanders responsible only for unit training. They were limited to two visits per year to their assigned elements—and that only if corps area commanders made funds available. Later, as a further economy move, the War Department reduced the number of command visits to one per year, a restriction that effectively destroyed the possibility of training units as combined arms teams.[2]

In July 1926 the commander of the 1st Division, Brig. Gen. Hugh A. Drum, wrote to the Second Corps Area commander, Maj. Gen. Charles P. Summerall, that "it is not an exaggeration to say that the division as a unit exists only on paper."[3] Drum requested the return of all administrative, logistical, and disciplinary functions for his divisional elements within the corps area and authority to visit each divisional regiment once a month and each brigade every three months. He also wanted to organize a proper division headquarters. Summerall concurred with Drum's request, but Chief of Staff Maj. Gen. John L. Hines denied it in the interest of economy and simplicity of administration, supply, and discipline. On 31 December 1926 Summerall, by then Chief of Staff, reversed the decision and gave Drum command of all 1st Division units in the Second Corps Area and permission to reorganize the divisional headquarters. Drum could also coordinate inspection arrangements with other corps area commanders where his units were stationed. The following July Summerall restored the same privileges to the 3d Division's commander,

*General Summerall*

Brig. Gen. Richmond P. Davis, at Fort Lewis, Washington. Brigade commanders, however, were not granted similar authority.4

While discussing the need to reconstitute the 1st Division as a combat unit, Drum stressed the importance of building esprit. Unfortunately, the few tangible symbols the Army had used to enhance morale were initially denied to divisions and brigades after the war. Regular Army soldiers returning from France were not allowed to wear divisional shoulder sleeve insignia because they "cluttered" the uniform. The men appealed to Secretary of War Newton D. Baker, who subsequently approved the use of shoulder sleeve insignia throughout the Army. When a division adopted a "patch" design, soldiers put it on their uniforms and emblazoned it on their divisional flag. The other item, the campaign streamer, representing participation in a major operation was denied to headquarters of divisions and brigades because they were command and control units rather than fighting organizations. Although the policy was contested, it was not until after the 1st and 3d Divisions reestablished effective headquarters that the War Department granted division and brigade headquarters the right to display on their flags streamers symbolizing the campaigns in which they had directed their subordinate units.5

A sharp decline in divisional readiness occurred after 1922, when Congress again cut the Regular Army's size, this time to 136,000 officers and enlisted men. The Chief of Staff, General of the Armies John J. Pershing, reduced the strength of the infantry division from 11,000 to 9,200 men, but he did not authorize the inactivation of any divisional elements. Four years later Congress expanded the Army Air Corps without a corresponding increase in the Army's total strength. Rather than cut the size of ground combat units, the War Department turned again to inactivating units. The Panama Canal Division lost an infantry regiment, the 8th Brigade an infantry battalion, and the 16th Brigade two infantry battalions. Given continuing personnel shortages, the chief of infantry complained in 1929 that not another man could be taken from his units if they were to conduct effective training. Therefore, another round of inactivations took place. The 8th, 10th, 12th, 14th, and 18th Brigades and the Philippine Division each lost a battalion. A year later the Philippine Division inactivated an infantry brigade headquarters, and in 1931 the division lost another infantry regiment.6

Infantry divisions also suffered shortages in the area of combat support. By 1930 the 1st and 2d Divisions and the Philippine Division had the only active medical regiments in the Regular Army, and they were only partially organized. During the previous year the War Department had removed the air squadron and its attached photographic section from the division. Simplicity of supply, maintenance, and coordination and better use of personnel justified the reduction. Offsetting that loss, a small aviation section was added to the division headquarters to coordinate air activities after air units were attached. In 1931, to provide quartermaster personnel for posts and stations in the United States, the quartermaster train in each active division except the 2d was reduced to two motor companies and a motor repair section. Besides these units the 2d retained one wagon company. No train headquarters remained active.7

Unlike the other organizations, in theory divisional field artillery was increased during the interwar years. Until 1929 the Army maintained two 75-mm. gun regiments for the 1st, 2d, and 3d Divisions and a battalion of 75s each for the Panama Canal Division, the Philippine Division, and the separate infantry brigades. The Hawaiian Division fielded one 155-mm. howitzer and two 75-mm. gun regiments, all motorized. During 1929 Summerall restored the 155-mm. howitzer field artillery regiment to all infantry divisions. Although the 155-mm. howitzer still lacked the mobility of the 75-mm. gun, the change made divisional artillery, in theory, commensurate with that found in foreign armies.8

Besides a shortage of personnel, the 2d Division, the only division housed on one post in the United States, lacked adequate troop quarters. Living conditions at its home, Fort Sam Houston, Texas, were deplorable for both officers and enlisted men by the mid-1920s. To remedy the situation the War Department decided to break up the division in 1927 and move its 4th Brigade to Fort D. A. Russell, Wyoming, where suitable quarters were available. That move left only the Hawaiian Division concentrated at one post, Schofield Barracks, a situation that continued until the Army began to prepare for World War II. Thus, despite the wishes of Army leaders, by 1930 the Army was again scattered throughout the country in a number of isolated bases.9

The cavalry division illustrated other aspects of the Army's dilemma between realism and idealism. In 1923 the 1st Cavalry Division held maneuvers for the first time, intending to hold them annually thereafter. However, financial constraints made that impossible. Only in 1927, through the generosity of a few ranchers who provided free land, was the division able to conduct such exercises again.10

In 1928 Maj. Gen. Herbert B. Crosby, Chief of Cavalry, faced with personnel cuts in his arm, reorganized the cavalry regiments, which in turn reduced the size of the cavalry division. Crosby's goal was to decrease overhead while maintaining or increasing firepower in the regiment. After the reorganization the cavalry regiment consisted of a headquarters and headquarters troop, a machine gun troop,

*Officers quarters, Fort Sam Houston, Texas;* below, *1st Cavalry Division maneuvers.*

CHART 7—Cavalry Division, 1928

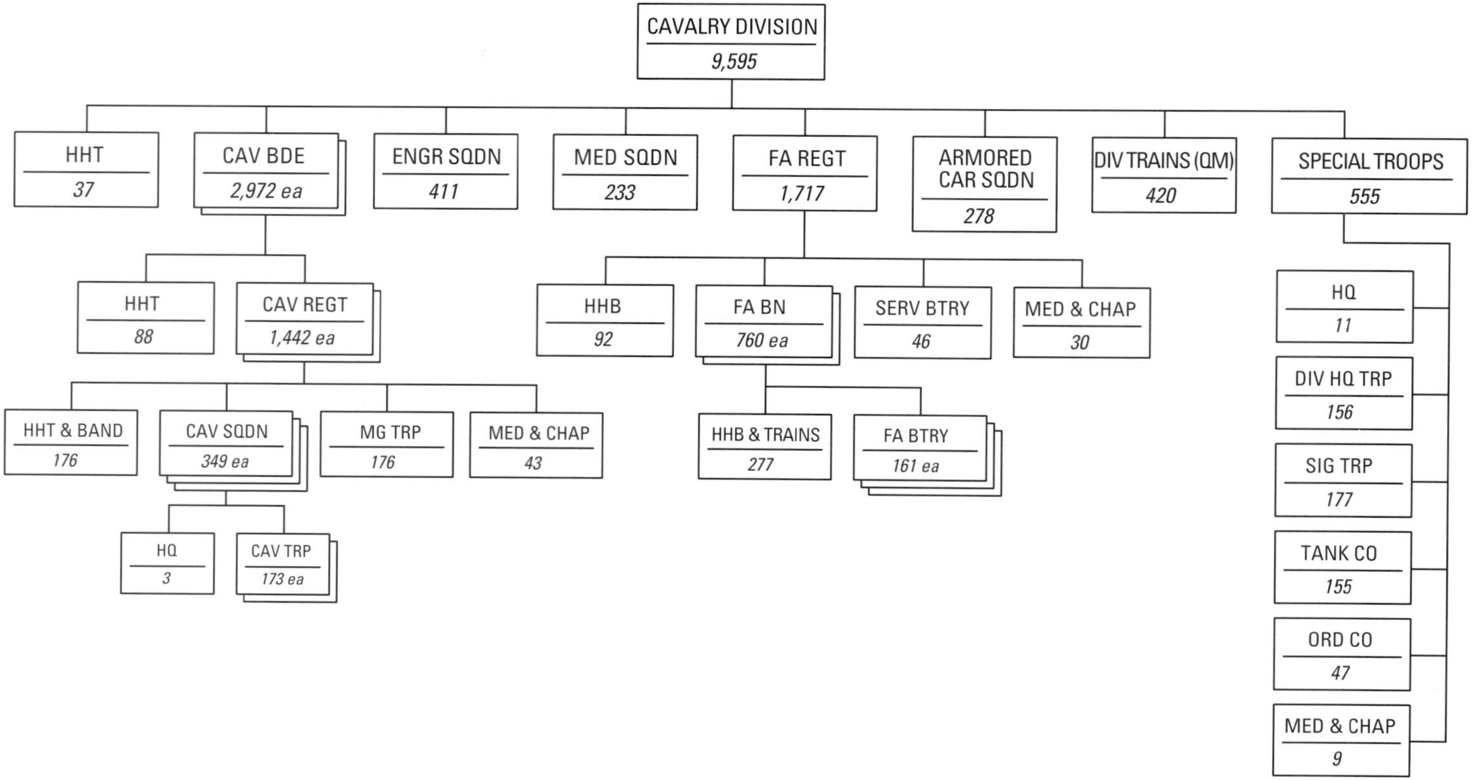

- CAVALRY DIVISION — 9,595
  - CAV BDE — 2,972 ea
    - HHT — 37
    - CAV REGT — 1,442 ea
      - HHT — 88
      - MG TRP — 176
      - MED & CHAP — 43
      - CAV SQDN — 349 ea
        - HHT & BAND — 176
        - HQ — 3
        - CAV TRP — 173 ea
  - ENGR SQDN — 411
  - MED SQDN — 233
  - FA REGT — 1,717
    - HHB — 92
    - FA BN — 760 ea
      - HHB & TRAINS — 277
      - FA BTRY — 161 ea
    - SERV BTRY — 46
    - MED & CHAP — 30
  - ARMORED CAR SQDN — 278
  - DIV TRAINS (QM) — 420
  - SPECIAL TROOPS — 555
    - HQ — 11
    - DIV HQ TRP — 156
    - SIG TRP — 177
    - TANK CO — 155
    - ORD CO — 47
    - MED & CHAP — 9

and two squadrons each with two troops. The cavalry brigades' machine gun squadrons were inactivated, while the responsibility for training and employing machine guns fell to the regimental commanders, as in the infantry.[11]

About the same time that Crosby cut the cavalry regiment, the Army Staff, seeking to increase the usefulness of the wartime cavalry division, published new tables of organization for an even larger unit. The new structure summarized changes made in the division since 1921 (*Chart 7*), which involved increasing the size of the signal troop, expanding the medical unit to a squadron, and endorsing Crosby's movement of the machine gun units from the brigades to the regiments. A divisional aviation section, an armored car squadron, and tank company were added, and the field artillery battalion was expanded to a regiment. Divisional strength rose to 9,595. Although the new tables had little impact on the peacetime cavalry structure, the 1st Cavalry Division did eventually receive one troop of an experimental armored car squadron, and a field artillery regiment replaced its field artillery battalion.[12]

Even with austere conditions, the Army did not lose sight of its tactical missions. For example, Maj. Gen. Preston Brown, commander of the Panama Canal Department, urged the replacement of the Panama Canal Division with Atlantic and Pacific command groups. Having examined the supply system, the probable tactical employment of troops, and the advantages of other command systems, he decided that a divisional structure did not represent the best solution in the Canal Zone. The War Department agreed to inactivate the division headquarters in 1932 with the understanding that special tables of organization would be kept on file to facilitate the reorganization of the division within a few hours. Such a situation, however, never occurred, and the division remained inactive.[13]

## *Reserve Divisions*

The condition of reserve divisions paralleled that of the Regular Army. In 1924, three years after the states began reorganizing the National Guard divisions, the Militia Bureau suspended federal recognition of new units because of the chronic lack of money. The suspension lasted two years, until Secretary of War Dwight F. Davis lifted it to provide additional units for the states. That decision permitted further organization of the 40th Division (California), the least developed of all the Guard infantry divisions. The repeal also allowed Minnesota and New York to organize two infantry brigade headquarters, the 92d and 93d, respectively, for nondivisional units to meet mobilization needs.[14]

Infantry divisions in the National Guard remained basically stable organizations despite being extremely under strength, and before 1940 only a few regimental changes were made. In most divisions the artillery brigade's ammunition train was not authorized because it had an exclusively wartime mission. As in the Regular Army, the 155-mm. howitzer regiment was authorized in 1930, and by mid-1937 all divisions had a federally recognized 155-mm. howitzer regiment or

## TABLE 11

### Allotment of National Guard Cavalry Brigades, 1927

| Corps Area | Unit | States Supporting a Brigade |
|---|---|---|
| First | 59th | Massachusetts and New Jersey |
| Second | 51st | New York |
| Third | 52d | Pennsylvania |
| Fourth | 55th | Louisiana, Tennessee, North Carolina, and Georgia |
| Fifth | 54th | Ohio and Kentucky |
| Sixth | 53d | Wisconsin, Illinois, and Michigan |
| Seventh | 57th | Iowa and Kansas |
| Eighth | 56th | Texas |
| Ninth | 58th | Wyoming and Idaho |

part of one. The strength of infantry divisions varied, but no division reached the 11,000 men prescribed in the peacetime National Guard tables of organization. The nadir was in 1926, following the suspension of federal recognition. By 1939 Guard infantry divisions averaged 8,300 troops each.[15]

National Guard cavalry divisions proved unsatisfactory because they were scattered over too large an area for effective training. The Militia Bureau first attacked the problem in 1927, when it realigned some divisional elements to reduce the geographic size of the divisions. Two years later the bureau limited cavalry formations to brigade-size units, assigning one brigade to each corps area (*Table 11*). The formation of the 59th Cavalry Brigade was authorized to meet the need for the additional brigade called for in the plan. At that time the bureau withdrew federal recognition from the 22d Cavalry Division headquarters, the only cavalry division to have a federally recognized headquarters. Unlike Regular Army cavalry regiments, Guard regiments retained their six line troops, except those in the 52d Cavalry Brigade, whose regiments were able to recruit and maintain sufficient personnel to support nine troops.[16]

Brigades remained the largest cavalry units in the Guard until the mid-1930s, when Congress authorized an increase in its strength. In 1936 the National Guard Bureau, formerly the Militia Bureau, returned to federally recognizing cavalry division headquarters. By mid-1940 the bureau had federally recognized headquarters for the 22d, 23d, and 24th Cavalry Divisions, but not for the 21st. At that time the 21st consisted of the 51st and 59th Cavalry Brigades, the 22d of the 52d and 54th, the 23d of the 53d and 55th Brigades, and the 24th of the 57th and 58th Cavalry Brigades; the 56th Cavalry Brigade served as a nondivisional unit.[17]

The Organized Reserves maintained infantry and cavalry divisions that were authorized a full complement of officers but only enlisted cadres. Many divisions met or exceeded their manning levels for officers, but enlisted strength fell below cadre level. In 1937 Secretary of War Harry W. Woodring held the opinion that the dearth of enlisted men kept the Organized Reserves from contributing much to mobilization. Under these conditions effective unit training was impossible.[18]

## *More Realistic Mobilization Plans*

Mobilization underpinned the maintenance of divisions, but the Army's preparedness program lacked substance. Undermanned divisions had no higher command headquarters despite ambitious plans to group all 54 infantry divisions in the United States into 18 Organized Reserve army corps and these corps into 6 Organized Reserve armies with each army also having 2 cavalry divisions. In 1927 the General Staff began to shift toward more realistic war plans. When division and corps area commanders met in Washington to discuss Army programs that year, one of the topics they examined was the status of Regular Army divisions and brigades. The senior officers believed that reinforced brigades serving as nuclei of divisions were impractical. Chief of Staff Summerall argued that to mobilize a skeletal division (a reinforced brigade) would take the same amount of time as organizing a completely new division since both would have to be filled with recruits.[19]

In August 1927 the staff released new war plans for the Regular Army that reassigned the active brigades of the 8th, 9th, and 7th Divisions to the 4th, 5th, and 6th Divisions, respectively, and the inactive brigades of the last three divisions to the first three. These were paper transactions only. In an emergency, however, the Regular Army would now be able to field the 1st through the 6th Divisions. For the 4th, 5th, and 6th, it needed only to activate divisional headquarters and support units. But with no station changes, the Army leadership lost further sight of an important World War I lesson: the need to have divisions concentrated for combined arms training.[20]

Also in 1927, for echelons above divisions in the Regular Army, the adjutant general constituted one army, one cavalry corps, and three army corps headquarters. In addition, the 3d Cavalry Division, a new Regular Army unit, was added to the rolls to complete the cavalry corps. No army corps, cavalry corps, or army headquarters was organized at that time, but moving these units in the mobilization plans from the Organized Reserve to the Regular Army theoretically made it easier to organize the units in an emergency. The Organized Reserve units, after all, were to be used to expand the Army following the mobilization of Regular Army and National Guard units.[21]

With increased tensions in the Far East and the rearmament of European nations, Chief of Staff General Douglas MacArthur scrapped existing plans for echelons above divisions and created an army group in 1932. He established General Headquarters (GHQ), United States Army, with himself as commander, and ordered the activation of four army headquarters, one each for the Atlantic and Pacific coasts and the Mexican and Canadian borders (*Map 2*). To the four

FOURTH FIELD ARMY

TH

FORT SAM
SAN ANT(

FIELD ARMIES IN THE UNITED STATES
1932

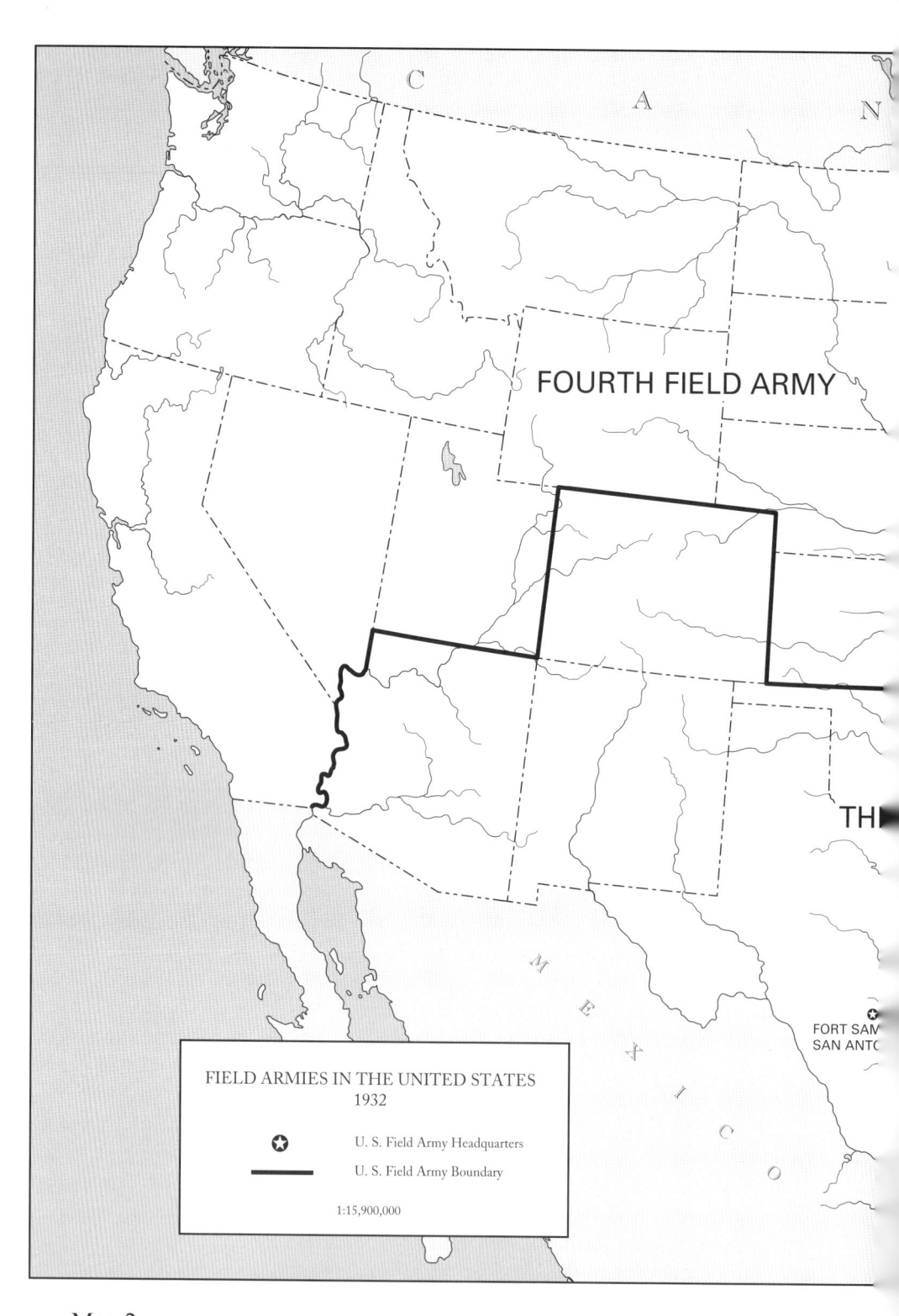

✪  U. S. Field Army Headquarters
— U. S. Field Army Boundary

1:15,900,000

MAP 2

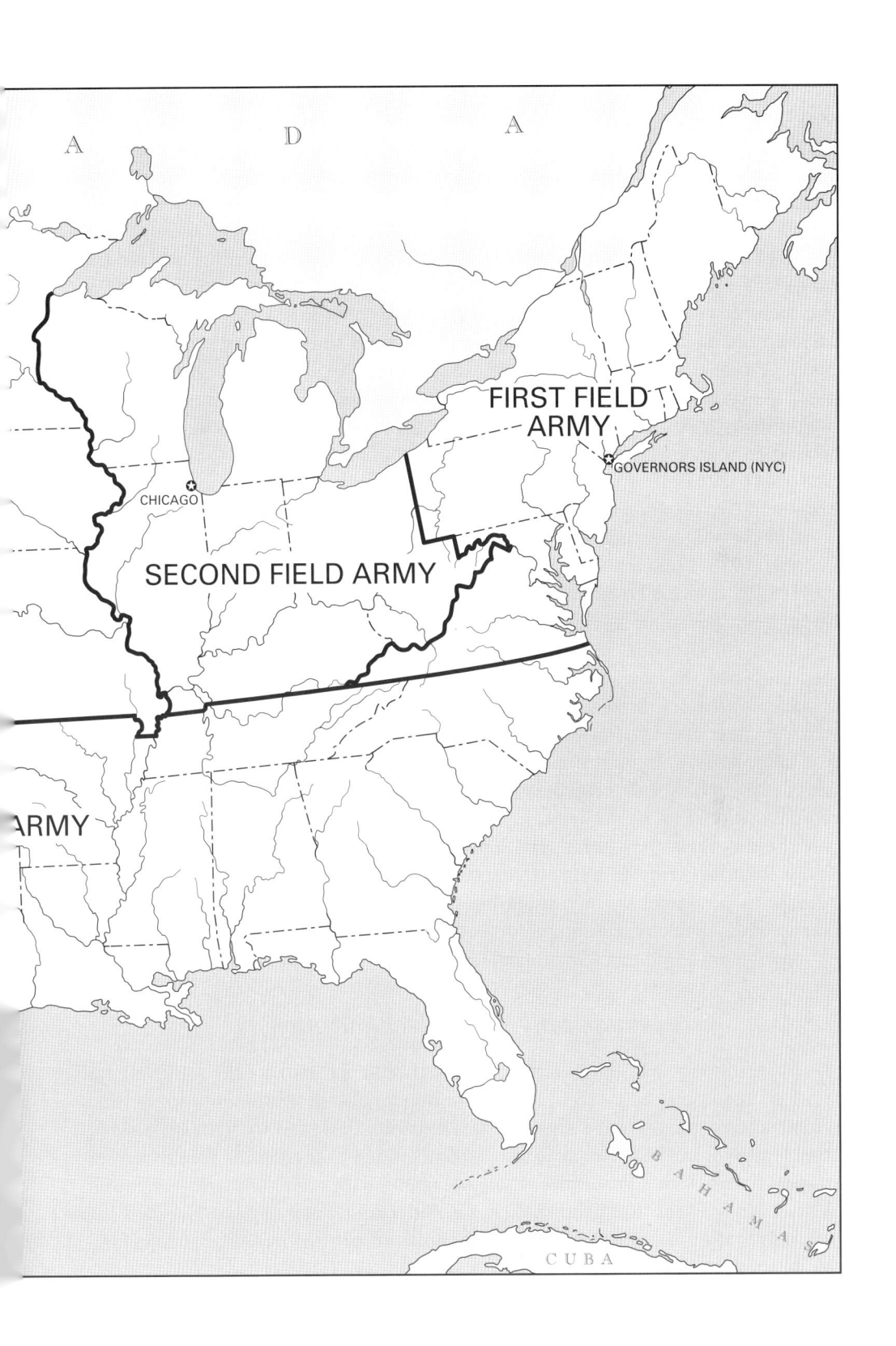

FIRST FIELD ARMY

GOVERNORS ISLAND (NYC)

CHICAGO

SECOND FIELD ARMY

army headquarters he assigned eighteen army corps headquarters, and to the corps headquarters the fifty-four infantry divisions. The Regular Army cavalry corps, which comprised the 1st, 2d, and 3d Cavalry Divisions, was assigned to the Fourth Army, and the four mounted National Guard divisions to the GHQ. Organized Reserve cavalry divisions remained in those areas where the armies were to raise units.[22]

In planning for the four armies, Brig. Gen. Charles E. Kilbourne, chief of the War Plans Division, suggested to MacArthur that he drive home to the president, the secretary of war, and the Congress exactly how the Army's strength had affected readiness. The Army could not even field four infantry divisions as a quick response force because of the lack the men to fill such a force and the bases to accommodate it. Furthermore, if such a force were concentrated, or even committed, it would be unable to support training of the reserves. Kilbourne viewed an increase in Army strength as unlikely but nevertheless recommended as a goal the maintenance of four peace-strength infantry divisions, one for each army, and five reinforced infantry brigades.[23]

The War Department established an embryonic readiness force on 1 October 1933. Divisional forces returned to their pre-1927 configuration, with the 1st, 2d, and 3d Divisions having two active infantry brigades and the 4th through 9th Divisions having only one active brigade each. In the Fourth Corps Area the 4th Division also received a third active infantry regiment, another step closer to the four-division ready force. The next year the field artillery brigades of the 1st through 4th Divisions were realigned to consist of one 155-mm. howitzer and two 75-mm. gun regiments, and each active infantry brigade was authorized a 75-mm. gun regiment. All field artillery units were partially active. No division or brigade was concentrated on a single post during the reorganization.[24]

The four-army plan introduced some realism into the arrangements for mobilizing Regular Army infantry divisions, but no true emergency force existed because of personnel shortages. During the next few years the Army revised the preparedness plans by reassigning divisions and assigning new priorities to them, but no division could meet an immediate threat.

## *Motorization and Mechanization*

Even though the status of divisions between the two world wars fell far short of readiness because of low manning levels, developments in at least organizational theory were significant. Divisions designed to fight on a static front and endure heavy casualties were no longer acceptable. World armies sought divisions that could defeat an opponent with maneuver and firepower. Writers such as the Englishmen J. F. C. Fuller and Basil Liddell Hart led the way, advocating the employment of machines to restore mobility and maneuverability to the battlefield.

Motorization, the use of machines to move men and equipment, had begun early in the twentieth century and progressively increased thereafter with technological advances. As a means of movement and transportation behind the front line in France, infantry divisions used cars, motorcycles, trucks, and motorized ambulances. Some field artillery regiments also used caterpillar tractors to move heavier artillery pieces. After World War I all divisions were authorized some motorized vehicles, but neither infantry nor cavalry divisions had enough to move all their men and equipment. *Field Service Regulations* stipulated that infantry divisions would depend upon army corps or army units to provide transportation in the field.[25]

In 1927 the 34th Infantry, an element of the 4th Division, conducted experiments using trucks to move itself, disembark, and fight. Two year later, in 1929, the Army started a program to motorize eight infantry regiments, four in the Hawaiian Division and four in the United States assigned to the 4th and 5th Divisions. To equip each of these small peacetime regiments, the staff authorized 1 passenger and 4 cross-country cars, 15 motorcycles, and 50 trucks, with most vehicles coming from obsolete World War I stocks. In 1931 Congress appropriated money for the first significant purchase of trucks since World War I, enabling the Army to motorize the supply trains of the 1st, 2d, and 3d Divisions. One wagon company in the 2d Division remained however, because of the reluctance to consign the horse and wagon to the past.[26]

By 1934 the Army had developed motorized equipment for field artillery that equaled the cross-country mobility of the horse and had sufficient endurance to conduct high-speed marches. Motorization of the Regular Army's field artillery began when Congress gave the Public Works Administration money to buy vehicles for the Army. Within five years all Regular field artillery regiments assigned to infantry divisions had truck-drawn pieces.[27]

Besides providing mobility on the battlefield, trucks helped the Army save money between World Wars I and II. In 1932 a crisis developed in the National Guard infantry divisions because they lacked a sufficient number of horses to train the field artillery. After extensive evaluation, the Guard determined that trucks were more economical than horses, and the following year it began to motorize the 75-mm. guns. By the end of 1939 all Guard divisions had truck-drawn field artillery, except for one regiment in the 44th Division.[28]

Mechanization involved employing machines on the battlefield as distinct from transporting personnel and equipment. During World War I the British and French had developed tanks to aid the infantry in the assault, and, using borrowed equipment, the AEF had organized tank brigades before the end of the war. In combat, however, tanks fought in small units, usually platoons, in infantry support roles. Their slow speed and lack of electronic communications capability made any other tactical employment impractical. After the war the tank company replaced the motorized machine gun battalion in the American infantry division. Postwar Army doctrine for tanks still prescribed that they support infantry in close combat to provide "cover invulnerable to the ordinary effects of rifle and machine gun fire, shrapnel, and shell splinters."[29] Although the British and French Armies adopted similar doctrine, continuous improvements in engines, suspension, and radios steadily increased the capabilities of such machines. In 1926 the British, responding to the prodding of Fuller, Liddell Hart, and others, tested an independent mechanized force that could make swift, deep penetrations in an enemy's rear, disorganizing and defeating an opponent before effective resistance could be mounted.[30]

The following year Secretary of War Davis observed a mechanized demonstration at Aldershot, England, and upon returning home ordered development of a similar force. On 30 December 1927, he approved an experimental brigade consisting of two light tank battalions, a medium tank platoon, an infantry battalion, an armored car troop, a field artillery battalion, an ammunition train, chemical and ordnance maintenance platoons, and a provisional motor repair section, all existing units. In July 1928 units of what was called the Experimental Mechanized Force assembled at Fort George G. Meade, Maryland, under the command of Col. Oliver Estridge. For the next three months the force, more motorized than mechanized, conducted field tests. Automobile manufacturers contributed trucks and cars, but the few available pieces of mechanized equipment were obsolete.[31]

Shortly after Davis approved the organization of the Experimental Mechanized Force, Maj. Gen. Frank Parker, Assistant Chief of Staff, G–3,[32] adopted another approach toward mechanization. He concluded that the mechanized experiment would lead nowhere because the force "would lack the fixity of tactical purpose and permanency of personnel on which to base experimental work, and its equipment will be so obsolete as to render its employment very dissimilar to that of a modernly-equipped mechanized force."[33] Parker recommended that Summerall appoint a board to prepare tables of organization and equipment for a mechanized force, establish the characteristics of its vehicles, and develop doctrine. Summerall, with Davis' concurrence, established the Mechanized Force Board on 15 May 1928.[34]

Within six months the board designed a combined arms armored force of approximately 2,000 officers and enlisted men. It consisted of a headquarters and headquarters company, a light tank battalion with an attached chemical company, a field artillery battalion, an engineer company, and two infantry battalions each consisting of two rifle and two machine gun companies (*Chart 8*). A medium tank company, an armored car troop, and a .50-caliber antiaircraft artillery detachment were to be attached to the force. Probable missions embraced spearheading an attack, serving as a counteroffensive force, penetrating enemy defenses, temporarily holding a key position, and operating in the enemy's rear area to disorganize his reserves. To carry out these missions, the officers drew up a "shopping list" for light and medium tanks, armored reconnaissance cars, semiautomatic rifles, rapid cross-country vehicles for infantry,

*Medium armored car of the Mechanized Force*

self-propelled 37-mm. antitank guns, self-propelled 75-mm. and 105-mm. howitzers, and two-way radios. The report recommended that the force begin as a small unit and build gradually to full strength. Since new mechanized equipment would not become available before fiscal year 1930, the board saw no need to assemble the unit until then. Davis endorsed the plan in November 1928.35

Two years later, just before Summerall left office, Col. Daniel Van Voorhis organized the first increment of the unit, which was designated the Mechanized Force, at Camp Eustis, Virginia. Consisting of a tank company, an armored car troop, a field artillery battery, and an engineer company, it totaled roughly 600 men. There, however, the project stopped. Because of the Great Depression, Congress never appropriated money for more new equipment, and Van Voorhis' force had to make do with World War I–vintage equipment along with horses and wagons. Of more concern, the infantry, cavalry, and other arms and services opposed the use of scarce Army funds to finance the new organization. With limited amounts of new wine available, customers wanted their old bottles filled first.36

In May 1931 the new Chief of Staff, General Douglas MacArthur, changed the direction of mechanization. He observed that recent experimental units had been based on equipment rather than on mission and that an item of equipment was not limited to one arm or service. He therefore instructed all arms or services to develop fully their mechanization and motorization potential. Under MacArthur's concept, cavalry was to continue work with combat vehicles to enhance its role in such areas as reconnaissance, flank action, and pursuit, while infantry was to explore ways to increase its striking power by using tanks. His decision spelled the end of the separate Mechanized Force, and five months later it was disbanded. Units and men assigned to the force were returned to their former assignments, except for about 175 officers and enlisted men, including Van Voorhis, who remained with mechanized cavalry. They transferred to Camp Henry Knox (later Fort Knox), Kentucky, to create a new armored cavalry unit.37

On 1 March 1932, Van Voorhis organized the 7th Cavalry Brigade to experiment with mechanization. At that time it consisted of only a headquarters, but the following January the 1st Cavalry moved from Marfa, Texas, to Fort Knox where it

CHART 8—The Mechanized Force, 1928

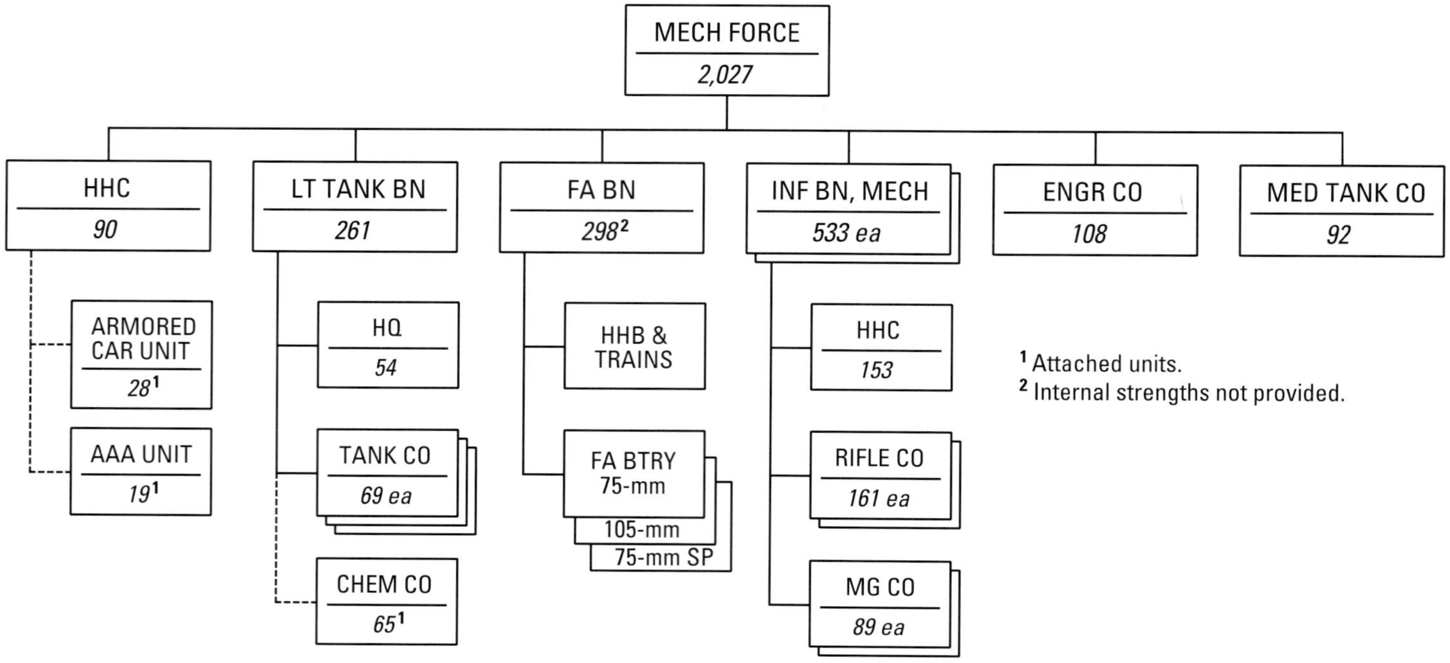

- MECH FORCE — 2,027
  - HHC — 90
    - ARMORED CAR UNIT — 28[1]
    - AAA UNIT — 19[1]
  - LT TANK BN — 261
    - HQ — 54
    - TANK CO — 69 ea
    - CHEM CO — 65[1]
  - FA BN — 298[2]
    - HHB & TRAINS
    - FA BTRY
      - 75-mm
      - 105-mm
      - 75-mm SP
  - INF BN, MECH — 533 ea
    - HHC — 153
    - RIFLE CO — 161 ea
    - MG CO — 89 ea
  - ENGR CO — 108
  - MED TANK CO — 92

[1] Attached units.
[2] Internal strengths not provided.

became part of the brigade. Shortly thereafter the regiment adopted tentative tables of organization that provided for a covering squadron, a combat car squadron, a machine gun troop, and a headquarters troop. Each squadron had two troops, and the regiment had a total of seventy-eight combat cars. That structure lasted until 1 January 1936, when the War Department outlined a new organization that consisted of a headquarters and band, two combat car squadrons of two troops each, and headquarters, service, machine gun, and armored car troops. The new tables authorized the regiment to have seventy-seven combat vehicles, all developmental items. Eventually the War Department assigned a second cavalry regiment, a field artillery battalion equipped with 75-mm. guns (mounted on self-propelled half tracks), ordnance and quartermaster companies, and an observation squadron to the brigade. The brigade became the Army's first armored unit of combined arms, contributing much to the development of mechanized theory in the interwar years. However, bureaucratic in-fighting often stifled the unit's development.[38]

Although many European theorists urged the development of independent armored forces, their armies made little progress toward the formation of such units. The British abandoned their experiments in 1927 and did not organize their first armored divisions until 1939. The French organized light armored divisions in the 1930s, but put most of their tanks in various infantry support roles. In the United States the Regular Army fielded two partially organized tank regiments as a part of the infantry arm between 1929 and 1940.[39]

Both German and Russian Armies took a different approach. Neither had employed tanks in World War I, but both saw their potential. Only after Adolph Hitler abrogated the military provisions of the Versailles Treaty in 1935, however, did the German Army develop offensive-oriented armored panzer divisions. But their interest in mechanization, especially tanks, was evident throughout the period, as witnessed by the several visits by German officers to the 7th Cavalry Brigade at Fort Knox in the mid-1930s. The Russians experimented with tanks from all industrial nations and favored the use of mass armor in the mid-thirties. On the eve of World War II, however, the Russians had shifted emphasis to small tank units in support of an infantry role.[40]

## *A New Infantry Division*

January 1929 marked the beginning of a ten-year struggle to reorganize the infantry division. The Assistant Chief of Staff, G–3, General Parker, reported that European countries were developing armies that could trigger a war of greater velocity and intensity than anything previously known. Great Britain, France, and Germany were engrossed with "machines" to increase mobility, minimize losses, and prevent stabilization of the battlefront. The British favored mechanization and the French, motorization, while the Versailles Treaty limited the Germans to ideas and dreams. Some Europeans adopted smaller, more maneuverable, triangular infantry divisions that were easier to command and control than the unwieldy square division. Since the Army planned to introduce semiautomatic rifles and light air-cooled machine guns, Parker suggested that the 2d Division conduct tests to determine the most effective combination of automatic rifles and machine guns. Summerall agreed to the proposal but extended the study to encompass the total infantry division. The study was to concentrate on approved standard infantry weapons, animal-drawn combat trains, and motorized field trains. The chief of staff placed no limit on road space, a principal determinant of divisional organization before and immediately after World War I.[41]

The Chief of Infantry, Maj. Gen. Robert H. Allen, who had responsibility for organizing and training infantry troops, agreed to the examination but objected to having the commander of the 2d Division supervise the tests, which he believed fell within the purview of his own office. Eventually Summerall agreed, and Allen assigned the job to the Infantry Board at Fort Benning, Georgia.[42]

During the investigation several proposals surfaced for a triangular infantry division, which promised greater maneuverability, better command and control, and simplified communications and supply. Nevertheless, Army leaders turned down the idea. Maj. Bradford G. Chynoweth of the Infantry Board attributed the retention of the square division, which was imminently suitable for frontal attacks, to Summerall. As a former division and army corps commander in France, Summerall saw no need for change.[43]

The question of the infantry division's organization lay dormant until October 1935, when Maj. Gen. John B. Hughes, Assistant Chief of Staff, G–3, revived it. In a memorandum for General Malin Craig, MacArthur's successor as Chief of Staff, Hughes suggested that the General Staff consider modernization of the Army's combat organizations. Although great strides had been made in weapons, equipment, transportation, and communications, organizations were still based on World War I experiences. He also noted that such organizational initiatives were the purview of the General Staff, an obvious reference to the resistance of the chief of infantry in 1929 to reexamine divisional organizations. Since the General Staff was responsible for total Army organization, Hughes thought it should conduct any such examination.[44]

In November Craig canvassed senior commanders regarding reorganization issues. He noted the infantry division in particular had foot, animal, and motor units, all with varying rates of speed, which did not meet the demands of modern warfare. Craig wondered if the division were too large, and, if so, whether or not could it be reduced in size. Possibilities for reduction included moving support and service functions to army corps or army level, cutting infantry to three regiments, and reorganizing the field artillery into a three-battalion regiment. No consensus emerged. Even the three champions of infantry—the Infantry School, the Infantry Board, and the chief of infantry—failed to agree on a suitable organization, differing especially on the continued existence of infantry and field artillery brigades as intermediate headquarters between the regiment and the division.[45]

*General Craig*

On 16 January 1936 Craig created a new body, the Modernization Board, to examine the organization of the Army. Under the supervision of Hughes, the board was to explore such areas as firepower, supply, motorization, mechanization, housing, personnel authorization, and mobilization. It was to consider recommendations from the field, the General Staff, service schools, and any earlier studies, including those concerned with foreign armies. Despite this broad charter, the board members nevertheless addressed only the infantry division, considering the total Army organization too extensive and too complex to be covered in one study. Besides, the board concluded that the formation of higher commands rested upon the structure of the infantry division.[46]

The board's report, submitted on 30 July 1936, rejected the square infantry division and endorsed a smaller triangular division (*Chart 9*), which could easily be organized into three "combat teams." Its proposal cut the infantry division from 22,000 officers and enlisted men to 13,500 and simplified the command structure. The brigade echelon for infantry and field artillery was eliminated, enabling the division commander to deal directly with the regiments. The enduring problem of where to locate the machine gun was dealt with again; one machine gun battalion was included in the infantry regiment, which also had three rifle battalions. The field artillery regiment consisted of one 105-mm. howitzer battalion and three mixed battalions of 75-mm. howitzers and 81-mm. mortars. The latter were to be attached to the infantry regiments in combat. To assist in moving, searching, and operating quickly on a broad front, cavalry returned to the division for the first time since before World War I in the form of a reconnaissance squadron, to be equipped with inexpensive unarmored or lightly armored cross-country vehicles. The anticipated rapid movement of the division minimized the need for extensive engineer work, except on roads. Therefore, an engineer battalion replaced the existing regiment. Because engineers would be primarily concerned with road conditions, they were also to provide traffic control in the divisional area. A signal company was to maintain communications between the division and regimental headquarters, and attached signal detachments were to perform these services within regiments.[47]

To increase mobility, the division's combat service support elements underwent radical changes. A battalion of trucks and a quartermaster service company of

# CHART 9—Proposed Infantry Division, 30 July 1936

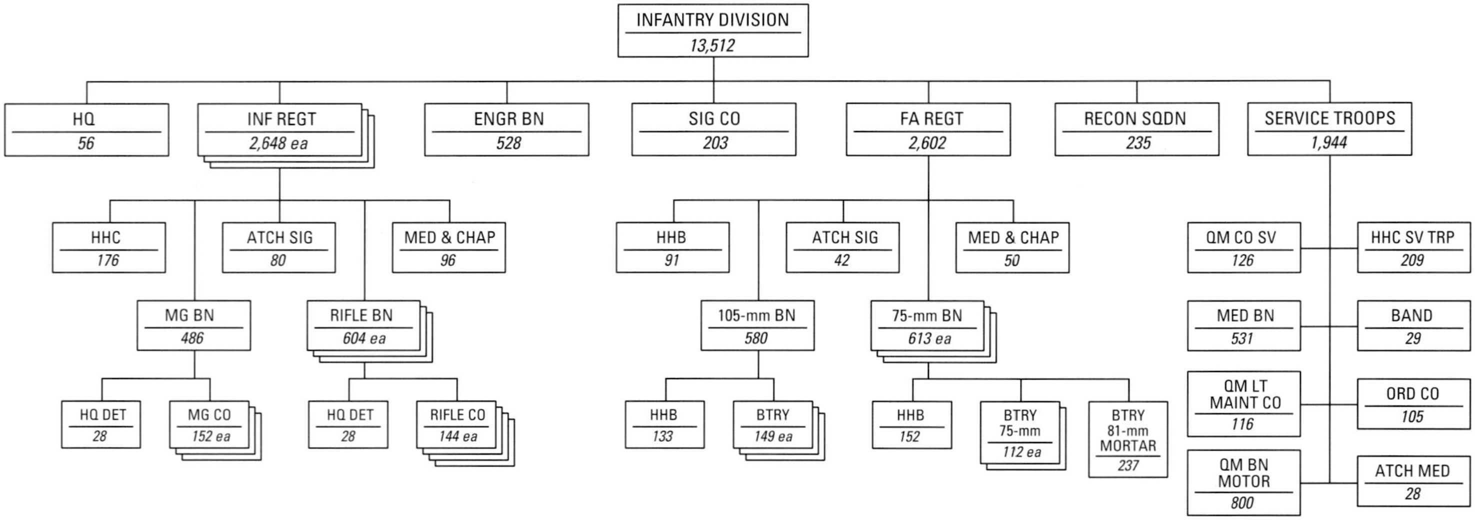

**INFANTRY DIVISION** — 13,512

## INF REGT — 2,648 ea
- HQ — 56
- HHC — 176
- ATCH SIG — 80
- MED & CHAP — 96
- MG BN — 486
  - HQ DET — 28
  - MG CO — 152 ea
- RIFLE BN — 604 ea
  - HQ DET — 28
  - RIFLE CO — 144 ea

## ENGR BN — 528

## SIG CO — 203

## FA REGT — 2,602
- HHB — 91
- ATCH SIG — 42
- MED & CHAP — 50
- 105-mm BN — 580
  - HHB — 133
  - BTRY — 149 ea
- 75-mm BN — 613 ea
  - HHB — 152
  - BTRY 75-mm — 112 ea
  - BTRY 81-mm MORTAR — 237

## RECON SQDN — 235

## SERVICE TROOPS — 1,944
- HHC SV TRP — 209
- QM CO SV — 126
- BAND — 29
- MED BN — 531
- ORD CO — 105
- QM LT MAINT CO — 116
- ATCH MED — 28
- QM BN MOTOR — 800

laborers formed the heart of a new supply system. They handled the baggage and noncombat equipment of all divisional elements. Each divisional unit was responsible for its own ammunition resupply. The new arrangement led to the elimination of the ammunition train, regimental field trains, and the quartermaster regiment. A quartermaster light maintenance company was added to service the motor equipment. The maintenance of hospitals passed to the army corps. A newly organized medical battalion collected and evacuated casualties, while infantry, field artillery, cavalry, and engineer units kept their medical detachments to provide immediate aid. All service elements were placed under a division service troops command, headed by a general officer, with a headquarters company that performed the provost marshal's duties and included the division's special staff.[48]

To comply with Craig's directive for the division to employ the latest weapons, the board recommended that its infantrymen be armed with the new semiautomatic Garand rifle, which the War Department had approved in January. For field artillery, the board wanted the even newer 105-mm. howitzer, which was not yet even in the Army's inventory.[49]

Members of the board concluded that they had given the division all the combat and service support resources needed for open warfare. Those elements not required were moved up to the army corps or army echelon. Additional units, such as heavier field artillery, antimechanized (antitank), tank, antiaircraft, aviation, motor transport, engineer, and medical units, might be required, but the board made the divisional staff large enough to coordinate the attachment of such troops. Although small, the new division was thought to have equal or greater firepower than the square division and occupied the same frontages as its predecessor.[50]

In a separate letter to Craig, Hughes summarized the advantages and disadvantages of the new infantry division. Pluses included its highly mobile nature, the ease with which infantry and field artillery could form combat teams, and the reduction in the number of command echelons and amount of administrative overhead. He also pointed to improvements in transportation, supply, and maintenance, since all animal transport was eliminated. Given such a division, he believed that the Regular Army could achieve a viable readiness force without an increase in authorized personnel. Drawbacks appeared minor. The states might not accept a reallotment of National Guard infantry divisions in peacetime. As a federal force, those divisions served only in national emergency or war, but as state forces they had been located and frequently used to cope with local emergencies and disasters. Hughes questioned splitting communication functions between the arms and the signal company and the pooling of transportation for baggage and other noncombat equipment into the service echelon. Both arrangements could generate friction because the functions would be outside the control of the user. He was also concerned about the loss of the infantry and field artillery brigades because they eliminated general officer positions. Finally, training literature would need revision and dissemination to the field.[51]

After reviewing the report, Craig decided to test the proposed division with attached antimechanized (antitank) and antiaircraft artillery battalions and an observation squadron. He selected the 2d Division, commanded by Maj. Gen. James K. Parson, to conduct the test between September and November 1937. The resulting Provisional Infantry Division (PID) included 6,000 men from the 2d Division and a similar number from other commands, which also furnished much of the equipment. The examination, the first in the history of the Army, was held in Texas, where space and terrain permitted a thorough analysis of the unit.[52]

Even before the test ended, Maj. Gen. George A. Lynch, Chief of Infantry, vetoed the proposed organization in a report to the staff in Washington. Having witnessed part of the exercise, he viewed the separation of the machine gun from the rifle battalion and the attachment of the signal detachment and mortar battery to the infantry regiment as mistakes. The first prevented teamwork in the regiment, and the second interfered with unity of command. Lynch considered the attached antitank battalion an infantry unit because it used the same antitank weapons as the infantry regiment. He objected to the commander of the service troops, contending that the presence of a general officer in this position complicated the chain of command. Furthermore, since the movement of the trains depended on the tactical situation, only the division commander could make the decision to move them. Because field, supply, and ammunition trains operated to the rear of the combat units, Lynch discerned no need for them in the division. He suggested that the Army return to the fixed army corps, in which divisions did the fighting and the corps provided the logistical support.[53]

Shortly after Lynch's negative account, the *New York Times* reported that Craig planned to appoint a special committee to design an infantry division based on the PID test. The article claimed that the committee was to include Maj. Gen. Fox Conner, Col. George C. Marshall, and a third unnamed officer. Eventually Brig. Gen. Lesley J. McNair, the Chief of Staff of the PID, was identified in private correspondence as the third member. Conner and Marshall, former members of the Lassiter Board, had supported Pershing's small division. Conner had also served as Craig's personnel representative at the PID test. Within a few days Marshall, writing from Vancouver Barracks, Washington, told a friend that such a board would look like a "stacked deck" to secure a small division. As it happened, any plans for the group fell through when Conner retired for medical reasons.[54]

The final report on the PID test, mostly the work of McNair, noted many of the divisional weaknesses identified by Lynch, but, instead of assigning the division to a fixed army corps, McNair proposed a new smaller and more powerful division. To attain it, he recommended that the infantry regiment have an antitank company and three battalions, each with one machine gun and three rifle companies. The machine gun company was to be armed with both machine guns and mortars. Inclusion of the antitank company in the regiment eliminated the need to attach such a battalion to the division. Like Lynch, he suggested eliminating signal detachments in favor of infantry, artillery, and cavalry troops. To increase firepower and range, McNair wanted to replace 75-mm. howitzers with 75-mm. guns and one battalion of 105-mm. howitzers with 155-mm. howitzers. He felt that mortars had no place in the division artillery because they could not provide close support for infantry and their rate of fire, range, and accuracy failed to meet field artillery standards. Another battery of 75-mm. guns in each direct support battalion was to replace the mortars. Because the reconnaissance squadron operated considerably in front of the division and on its flanks, he proposed that it be moved to the corps level. McNair sensed an overabundance of engineers. In a war of movement, engineers would not have the time to do extensive road work. Another responsibility, that of traffic control, could return to the military police. Therefore, the engineer battalion could be reduced to a company and a separate military police unit would combine provost marshal and traffic control missions. McNair also faulted the special command for the service troops organization and advised its elimination. He believed the ordnance company and band were unnecessary and advocated their reassignment to higher echelons. The quartermaster service company and motor battalion were to be combined as a quartermaster battalion, which was to supply the division with everything except ammunition. Each combat element was to remain responsible for its own ammunition supply. These changes produced a division of 10,275 officers and enlisted men.[55]

After analyzing all reports and comments, the Modernization Board redesigned the division, retaining three combat teams built around the infantry regiments. Each regiment consisted of a headquarters and band, a service company, and three battalions, each with one heavy weapons company armed with 81-mm. mortars and .30- and .50-caliber machine guns and three rifle companies, but no antitank unit. The .50-caliber machine guns in the heavy weapons companies and the 37-mm. guns in the regimental headquarters companies were to serve primarily as antitank weapons. The large four-battalion artillery regiment was broken up into two smaller regiments, one of three 75-mm. gun battalions and the other with a battalion of 105-mm. howitzers and a battalion of 155-mm. howitzers. Although the test had shown that the field artillery commander had no problems with the four-battalion unit, school commandants and corps area commanders questioned the quality of command and control within the regiment. Two general officers assisted the commander, one for infantry and one for field artillery, but they were not in the chain of command for passing or rewriting orders. Within the combat arms regiments, signal functions fell under the regimental commanders, while the divisional signal company operated the communication system to the regiments. The engineer battalion was retained but was reduced in size and consisted of three line companies in addition to the battalion headquarters and headquarters company. Traffic control duties moved to a new military police company that combined those activities with the provost marshal's office.[56]

The board completely reorganized the supply system. The combat arms were given responsibility for their own ammunition resupply and baggage. Therefore, the motor battalion was eliminated. A new quartermaster battalion was established, which included a truck company to transport personnel and rations, a service company to furnish laborers, and a headquarters and headquarters company. The headquarters company could do minor motor maintenance requiring less than three hours, while major motor maintenance moved to the army corps level. The quartermaster light maintenance and ordnance companies were removed from the division. Medical service within the division was based on the assumption that it would be responsible for the collection and evacuation of the sick and wounded to field hospitals established by corps or higher echelons. The former headquarters company, service troops, was incorporated into the division headquarters company.[57]

With no change expected in total Army strength, the new division had two authorized strengths, a wartime one of 11,485 officers and enlisted men and a peacetime one of 7,970. During peacetime all elements of the division were to be filled except for the division headquarters and military police companies, which were to be combined. Other divisional elements required only enlisted personnel to bring them up to wartime manning levels.[58]

After the Modernization Board redesigned the division, Craig decided to spend a year evaluating it before he determined its fate. The 2d Division, selected once more for the task, again borrowed personnel and equipment from other units to fill its ranks. Between February 1939 and Germany's invasion of Poland on 1 September, the "Provisional 2d Division" commanded by Maj. Gen. Walter Krueger tested the proposed unit. Krueger found the organization sound except for the quartermaster battalion and the need to make some minor adjustments in a few other elements. The quartermaster battalion lacked enough laborers and trucks to supply the division, and he recommended increases in both. With its many pieces of motorized equipment, the division required more maintenance personnel. Minor changes included augmentations to the divisional intelligence (G–2) and operations (G–3) staff sections, a slight increase in the signal company to handle communications for the second field artillery regiment, a complete motorization of the engineer battalion, and the replacement of the five regimental bands with one divisional band.[59]

Maj. Gen. Herbert J. Brees, Eighth Corps Area commander and the test director, concurred with most of Krueger's findings except for the engineer and quartermaster battalions. He opposed completely motorizing the engineer unit because the engineers were to be limited to the divisional area instead of a broad front. He favored an increase in the number of trucks in the quartermaster battalion but not to the extent suggested by Krueger. Brees also saw no need for infantry and artillery sections having their own general officers, because the commander could easily deal with all elements, but he recommended a staff officer, not necessarily a general officer, to coordinate field artillery fire. To make room for a second general officer in the division, he suggested that the division's chief of staff become the second-in-command with the rank of brigadier general because he would know more about the division than anyone else except for the commander.[60]

*General Marshall*

On 14 September 1939, Lt. Col. Harry Ingles of the Modernization Board summarized the evolution of the division's organization, focusing on the report of Krueger and the comments of Brees. He also recommended resolutions to the disputed points. Two days later Marshall, who had replaced Craig as Chief of Staff on 1 September, approved a new peacetime division, which included infantry and artillery sections headed by general officers in the division headquarters, a motorized engineer battalion, a divisional band within the headquarters company, and an increase in the number of trucks in the quartermaster battalion (*Chart 10*). Marshall's division was completely motorized.[61]

Still, the new organization did not totally satisfy Marshall. Having followed its development closely as chief of the War Plans Division and later as deputy chief of staff, he believed that the division should be even stronger to cope with sustained combat. In Marshall's view, however, the new organization's overwhelming advantage was that the National Guard divisions could easily adopt it. Furthermore, the onset of war in Europe added urgency because the Army could no longer delay modernization.[62]

A few days after Marshall approved the new structure he authorized the reorganization of the 1st, 2d, and 3d Divisions and the activation of the 5th and 6th Divisions, each with a strength of 7,800 officers and enlisted men. No division was concentrated because the Army did not have a post large enough to house one. Divisional elements, however, were conveniently located within corps areas to ease training. Geographically, the divisions were distributed so that one division was on each of the seaboards (Atlantic and Pacific), one near the southwest frontier, and two centrally located to move to either coast or the southwest. With the outbreak of war in Europe, Congress quickly authorized increases in the strength of the Army, and by early 1940 the infantry division stood at 9,057.[63]

## *A New Cavalry Division*

The Modernization Board took up the cavalry division in 1936. Most officers still envisioned a role for the horse because it could go places inaccessible to

CHART 10—Infantry Division (Peace), 1939
Corrected to 8 January 1940

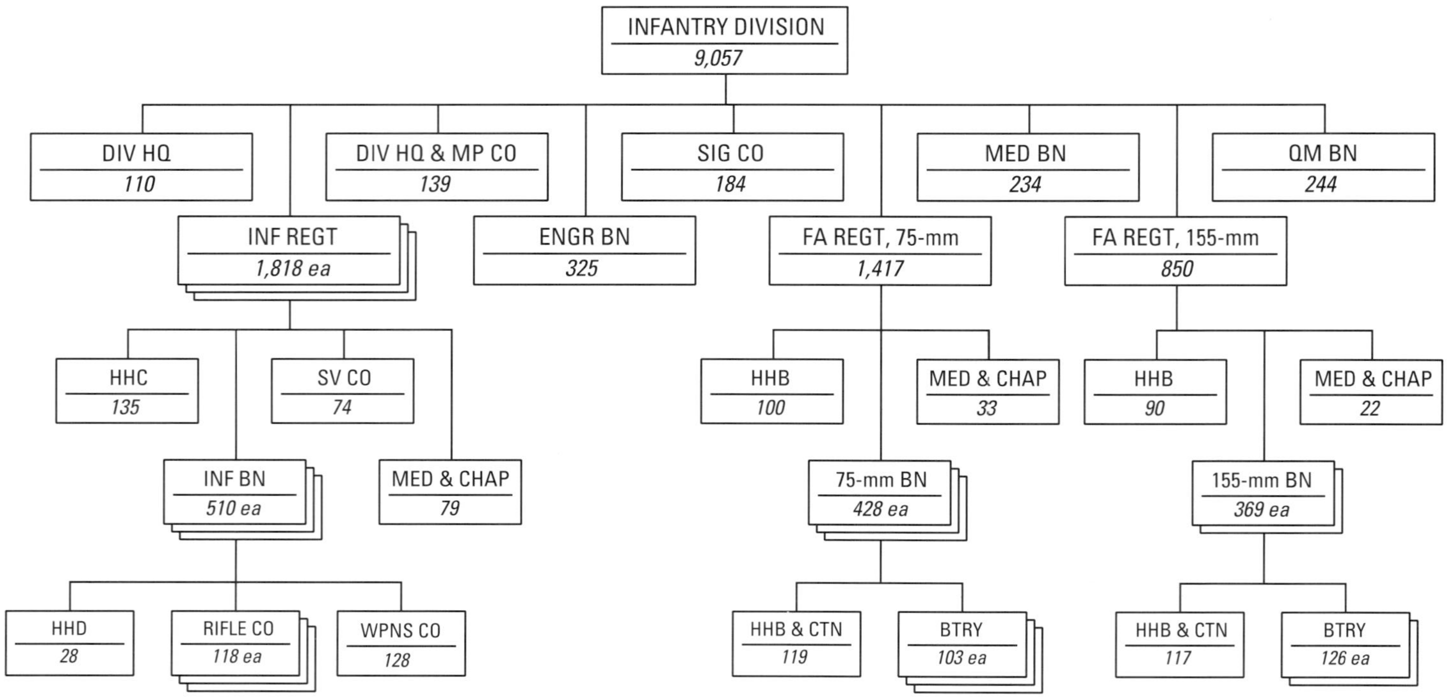

- INFANTRY DIVISION — 9,057
  - DIV HQ & MP CO — 139
    - DIV HQ — 110
  - SIG CO — 184
  - ENGR BN — 325
  - INF REGT — 1,818 ea
    - HHC — 135
    - SV CO — 74
    - MED & CHAP — 79
    - INF BN — 510 ea
      - HHD — 28
      - RIFLE CO — 118 ea
      - WPNS CO — 128
  - MED BN — 234
  - FA REGT, 75-mm — 1,417
    - HHB — 100
    - MED & CHAP — 33
    - 75-mm BN — 428 ea
      - HHB & CTN — 119
      - BTRY — 103 ea
  - QM BN — 244
  - FA REGT, 155-mm — 850
    - HHB — 90
    - MED & CHAP — 22
    - 155-mm BN — 369 ea
      - HHB & CTN — 117
      - BTRY — 126 ea

CTN = Combat Train
WPNS = Weapons
SV = Service

# A RETURN TO THE PAST; A LOOK TO THE FUTURE

*1st Cavalry Division maneuvers, Toyahvale, Texas, 1938*

motorized and mechanized equipment. Taking into account recommendations from the Eighth Corps Area, the Army War College, and the Command and General Staff School, the board developed a new smaller triangular cavalry division (*Chart 11*), which the 1st Cavalry Division evaluated during maneuvers at Toyahvale, Texas, in 1938. Like the 1937 infantry division test, the maneuvers concentrated on the divisional cavalry regiments around which all other units were to be organized.64

Following the test, a board of 1st Cavalry Division officers, headed by Brig. Gen. Kenyon A. Joyce, rejected the three-regiment division and recommended retention of the two-brigade (four-regiment) organization. The latter configuration allowed the division to deploy easily in two columns, which was accepted standard cavalry tactics. However, the board advocated reorganizing the cavalry regiment along triangular lines, which would give it a headquarters and headquarters troop, a machine gun squadron with special weapons and machine gun troops, and three rifle squadrons, each with one machine gun and three rifle troops. No significant change was made in the field artillery, but the test showed that the engineer element should remain a squadron to provide the divisional elements greater mobility on the battlefield and that the special troops idea should

CHART 11—Cavalry Division, 1938

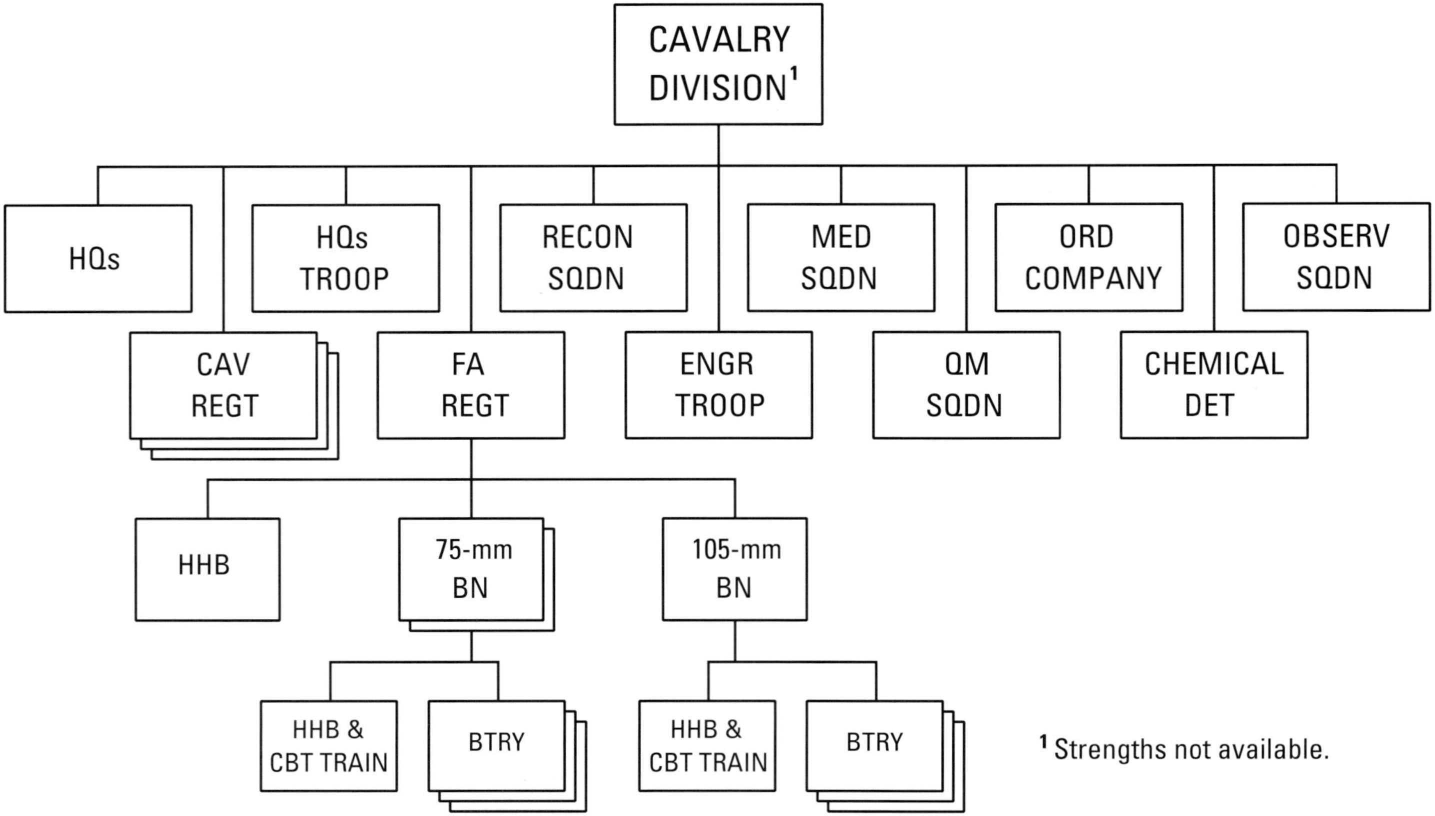

[1] Strengths not available.

be extended to include the division headquarters, signal, and ordnance troops; quartermaster, medical, engineer, reconnaissance, and observation squadrons; and a chemical warfare detachment. One headquarters would assume responsibility for the administration and disciplinary control for these forces.[65]

Although the study did not lead to a general reorganization of the cavalry division, the wartime cavalry regiment was restructured, effective 1 December 1938, to consist of a headquarters and headquarters troop, machine gun and special weapons troops, and three squadrons of three rifle troops each. The special troops remained as structured in 1928, and no observation squadron or chemical detachment found a place in the division. With the paper changes in the cavalry divisions and other minor adjustments, the strength of a wartime divisional rose to 10,680.[66]

Such paper changes characterized much of the interwar Army's work. Although planners lacked the resources to man, equip, and test functional divisions, they gave considerable thought to their organization. They developed a new concept for the infantry division, experimented with a larger cavalry division, and explored the organization of a mechanized unit. Designing the new infantry division with a projected battlefield in North America, officers took into account the span of control, the number of required command echelons, the staff, the balance between infantry and field artillery, the location of the reconnaissance element, the role of engineers, and the best way to organize the services and supply system. The triangular infantry division appeared to offer the best solution to these requirements according to the planners, who Marshall thought were among "the best in the Army."[67]

## Notes

1 Ltr, CofS to CGs all corps areas and other addresses, 5 Nov 20, sub: Reorganization of Divisions and Higher Units, AG 320.2 (11–4–35), RG 177, NARA.

2 Ltr, TAG to CGs of all corps areas, 9 Oct 22, sub: Command, AG 320.2 (10–4–22), and Memo, G–3 to CofS, 27 Aug 26, sub: Reconstitution of the 1st Division, AG 320.2 (7–19–26), RG 407, NARA.

3 Ltr, CG, 1st Division to CG, Second Corps Area, 19 Jul 26, sub: Reconstitution of the First Division, AG 320.2 (7–17–26), RG 407, NARA.

4 Ibid., with 1st Ind, CG, Second Corps Area, to TAG, 5 Aug 26, and 2d Ind, TAG to CG, Second Corps, 31 Aug 26, Memo, G–3 for CofS, sub: Reconstitution of the 1st Division, 27 Aug 26, and Ltr, TAG to CGs of all corps areas, 31 Dec 26, sub: Reconstitution of the First Division, AG 320.2 (7–19–27), RG 407, NARA; Ltr, Maj Gen Summerall to Brig Gen Richmond P. Davis, 6 Jul 27, and Ltr, Summerall to Maj Gen John L. Hines, 6 Jul 27, John L. Hines Papers, LC.

5 WD Cir 42, 1919; Memo, WPD for CofS, 16 Jan 20, sub: Recommendations of Conference of Department and Division Commanders, Memo, CofS, no subject, 23 Jan 20, Memo, Newton D. Baker to Gen March, 20 Apr 20, Memo, WPD for TAG, 28 Apr 20, sub: Shoulder Patch Insignia for Division, Corps, Services, etc., copies TIOH; Ltr, Pershing to Maj Gen Clarence R. Edwards, 27 May 20, Pershing Papers, LC; WD Cir 59, 1928.

6 Rpts of the Sec of War, *ARWD 1922*, pp. 15–16, and *ARWD 1923*, p. 125; "New Tables of Organization," *Infantry Journal* 21 (Aug 1922): 186–92 (The new tables cut the infantry regiment from 1,490 to 1,205 officers and enlisted men.); "Battalions Declared Inactive," *Infantry Journal* 30 (Jun 1927): 660; Annual Report of the Chief of Infantry, FY 1929, p. 38, RG 177, NARA; "Five Battalions of Infantry to be Made Inactive," *Infantry Journal* 32 (Sep 1929): 317; Returns, Philippine Division, 1931, RG 94, NARA; also see notes "Infantry During the Interwar Years," author's files.

7 *Army Directory*, July 1929, p. 28; Ltr, TAG to Chief of the Air Corps, 17 Jan 29, sub: Principles to be followed in assignment of Air Corps Troops to higher tactical organization, with Endorsements, AG 320.2 Air Corps (12–20–28) Pub., Microfilm A 2765, Albert F. Simpson Historical Research Center, Maxwell Air Force Base, Alabama; WD Cir 14, 1931.

8 T/O, Table 31 W, Field Artillery Brigade, Infantry Division, 18 Apr 1929; WD Cir 39, 1929; Ltr, TAG to Chiefs of all Arms and Services, and other addresses, 7 Dec 29, sub: Assignment of Troops, AG 320.2–FA (11–4–29) Misc. (Ret)-C, DAMH-HSO.

9 Memo, G–3 for CofS, 2 May 27, sub: G–3/17531-Change in Certain Regular Army Units, AG 370–5 (4–28–27), RG 94, NARA; Ltr, Summerall to Harry M. Worsback, MC, 1 Jun 27, AG 370–5 (5–21–27), Ltr, TAG to CG, Eighth Corps Area, 6 Jun 27, sub: Troop Movement, AG 370–5 (5–21–27) (Misc), RG 94, NARA; "Shifting of Infantry Units," *Infantry Journal* 31 (Jul 1927): 89.

10 Adna R. Chaffee, "The Maneuvers of the First Cavalry Division, September–October, 1923," *Cavalry Journal* 33 (Apr 1924): 133–62; George Dillman, "1st Cavalry Division Maneuvers," *Cavalry Journal* 37 (Jan 1928): 47.

11 Aubrey Lippincott, "New Regimental Organization," *Cavalry Journal* 32 (Jan 1929): 22–24.

12 T/O, Table 401 W, Cavalry Division, 10 May 1928; "Extracts from the Annual Report of the Chief of Cavalry, Major General Herbert B. Crosby," *Cavalry Journal* 37 (Jan 1928): 108; Ltr, TAG to All Corps Areas, Departments, and Exempted Stations Commanders and other addresses, 26 Oct 34, sub: Reorganization of the Field Artillery, AG 320.2 FA (12–26–33) Pub, AG Reference files, DAMH-HSO; Ltr, TAG to CG, Eighth Corps Area, 16 Oct 28, sub: Armored Car Unit, 320.2 Cavalry (10–2–28) Misc-C, and Lt Col Regnier, "History of the 91st Reconnaissance Squadron, 1st Cavalry Division," undated Ms, 91st Armored Cavalry Reconnaissance Battalion file, DAMH-HSO.

13 Ltr, Panama Canal (PC) Dept to TAG, 7 May 31, sub: Organization of troops within PC Department, Ltr, PC Dept to TAG, 5 Feb 32, sub: Reorganization of the Panama Canal Department,

with 1st Ind, TAG to CG, PC Dept, 17 Mar 32, AG 320.2 PC (5–7–31), and Returns, PC Division, all RG 407, NARA.

14 *Reports of the Chief of the Militia Bureau, 1925*, p. 13, and *1926*, pp. 17–18; Memos for Assistant Chief of Staff (ACofS), G–3, 30 Apr 26, 28 Feb 27, and 31 May 27, MB 325.4 Gen–6, War Department Mobilization Plan, 19 Mar 26, Miscellaneous files, DAMH-HSO.

15 Memos for Statistical Section, ACofS G–3, 31 Mar 27 and 2 Jan 30, MB 325.4 Gen 6, DAMH-HSO; *Report of the Chief of the Militia Bureau, 1926*, Appendix C; *Reports of the National Guard Bureau, 1936*, p. 7, and *1939*, p. 27; also see author's notes "National Guard Interwar Years."

16 *Report of the Adjutant General of New Jersey, 1927*, p. 7; *State of New York, Annual Report of the Adjutant General, 1928*, p. 21; *Reports of the Chief of the Militia Bureau, 1928*, pp. 25–26, and 1929, pp. 14, 22–23; Memos for Statistical Section, ACofS, G–3, 28 Feb 27, 31 Mar 27, and 3 Sep 29, MB 325.4 Gen–6, DAMH-HSO.

17 Memos for Statistical Section, A CofS, 1 Apr 36, 1 Nov 39, 1 Mar 40, MB 325.4 Gen, DAMH-HSO; John B. Smith, "Our First National Guard Cavalry Division," *Cavalry Journal* 46 (Sep–Oct 1936): 378–79; "Two More Cavalry Divisions Authorized," *Cavalry Journal* 48 (Jan–Feb 1939): 67; *National Guard Register* (1939), p. 15.

18 "Progress of Assignments of Infantry Reserve Officers to Infantry Division of the Organized Reserves," *U.S. Army Recruiting News* 5 (May 1922): no pagination; Comptroller's Records, US Army Divisions–Infantry and Cavalry Strength, 30 Jun 1928–1931, Reference Paper Files, Army Reserve 1916-1939, DAMH-HSO; *Rpt of the Sec of War, 1937*, p. 6.

19 War Department Mobilization Plans, 1923, 1924, and 1926, Miscellaneous files, DAMH-HSO; Proceedings of Conference of Corps Area and Division Commanders held at Washington, D.C., June 1927, p. 140, AWC course material 1927, MHI.

20 Ltr, TAG to Chiefs of all War Department Branches and other addresses, 15 Aug 27, sub: Constitution, Reconstitution, or Redesignation of Certain Units of the Regular Army and the Reorganization of Regular Army Divisions, AG Reference files, 320.2 (6–5–27) Misc (Ret), DAMH-HSO.

21 Ibid.

22 *Rpt of the Sec of War, 1932*, p. 53; Ltr, OCS to CGs of Corps Areas and Depts., 9 Aug 32, sub: Establishment of Field Armies, OCS 20696, Four Army Plan file, 1933, DAMH-HSO.

23 Memo, WPD for CofS, Sub: Four Army Organization, 27 Mar 33, WPD 3561–15, AG 320.2 (8–6–32), Section I-A, RG 407, NARA.

24 Ltr, CofS to CGs of Armies and Corps Area, 18 Aug 33, sub: Development of Four Army Organization, AG 320.2 (8–16–33) (Misc.) M-E (WPD) 3561–27, Four Army Plan file, 1933, Ltr, TAG to CGs all Corps Areas, Departments, and Exempted Stations, 26 Oct 34, sub: Reorganization of Field Artillery, AG 320.1 F.A. (12–26–33), Pub, AG Reference files, DAMH-HSO.

25 T/O, Table 1 W, Infantry Division, 1921; T/O, Table 401 W, Cavalry Division, 1921; *Field Service Regulations United States Army* (1923), p. 66.

26 *Rpt of the Sec of War, 1928*, p. 82; WD Cir 29, 1929; Erna Risch, *Quartermaster Support of the Army: A History of the Corps 1775–1939* (Washington, D.C.: Government Printing Office, 1962), pp. 717–19; WD Cir 14, 1931.

27 *Rpt of the Sec of War, 1934*, pp. 40–41, and *1935*, p. 7; Ltr, TAG to CGs all Corps Areas, Departments, and Exempted Stations, 26 Oct 34, sub: Reorganization of Field Artillery; *Army List and Directory*, 20 Oct 1939, pp. 9–10, 15.

28 John S. Shetler, "Motors for the Guard," *Quartermaster Review* 14 (Mar-Apr 1935): 47–49; *National Guard Register* (1939), pp. 1422–23.

29 Field Service Regulations (1923), p. 13.

30 J. F. C. Fuller, "Tactics and Mechanization," and "Editorial Comment: Mechanization of Military Forces," *Infantry Journal* 30 (May 1927): 457–76, 533–35. The entire issue is devoted to mechanization.

31 Timothy K. Nenninger, "The Experimental Mechanized Forces," *Armor* 78 (May–Jun 1969): 33–39; GO 16, Third Corps Area, 5 Jul 1928, 66th Armor file, DAMH-HSO; Brig Gen

Daniel Van Voorhis, lecture, "Mechanization," 13 Oct 1937, at the Army War College, AWC course material 1937–1938, MHI.

32 After World War I, the Army Staff was reorganized to consist of the Chief of Staff, Deputy Chief of Staff, and Assistant Chiefs of Staff, G–1, G–2, G–3, and G–4, and War Plans Division. The G–1 position corresponded to personnel, G–2 to intelligence, G–3 to operations, and G–4 to supply.

33 Memo, G–3 for CofS, 20 Mar 28, sub: A Mechanized Force, AWC Course material, G–3/10677, 84–17, MHI.

34 Ibid.; WD SO 110, 10 May 1928, extract printed in Rpt, Mechanized Force, 1 Oct 28, AWC course material 84–20, MHI.

35 Rpt, sub: A Mechanized Force, 1 Oct 28, Memo, Deputy CofS for CofS, 31 Oct 28, sub: A Mechanized Force, AWC course material, OCS 18500–57, 84–20, MHI. The board included Maj. Adna R. Chaffee, who would become a beacon for mechanization in the next decade.

36 Mildred Hanson Gillie, *Forging the Thunderbolt* (Harrisburg, Pa.: Military Service Publishing Co., 1947), pp. 36–40; Charles L. Scott, "Early History of Mechanization," draft Ms, Charles L. Scott Papers, LC; Nenninger, "The Experimental Mechanized Forces," pp. 33–34.

37 Nenninger, "The Experimental Mechanized Forces," p. 39; Memo, OCS, 1 May 31, sub: General Principles to Govern Mechanization and Modernization Throughout the Army, Military Intelligence Division Correspondence, 1917–1941, 2045–1192/12, RG 165, NARA; Norman Miller Cary, "The Use of Motor Vehicles in the United States Army, 1899–1939," Ph.D. dissertation, University of Georgia, 1980, p. 244; *Rpt of the Sec of War, 1931*, p. 43; Daniel Van Voorhis, "Mechanization"; Robert W. Grow, "The Ten Lean Years," Ms, Feb 1969, pp. 19–22, DAMH-HSO.

38 Ltr, TAG to CG of all Corps Areas and Depts and other addresses, 16 Jan 31, sub: Changes in Assignment of Divisional Cavalry units, AG 320.2 (12–24–31) Misc. (Ret) MC, 1st Armored Div file, DAMH-HSO; GO 2, Fifth Corps Area, 6 Feb 1932, Records of U.S. Army Continental Commands, 1920–42, RG 394, NARA; Guy V. Henry, "The Trend of Organization and Equipment of Cavalry in the Principal World Powers and Its Probable Role in Wars of the Near Future," *Cavalry Journal* 41 (Mar–Apr 1932): 5–9; T/O, Table 423 P, Cavalry Regiment (Mechanized), 1 Jan 1933; Grow, "The Ten Lean Years," pp. 22–38; T/O, Table 423 P, Cavalry Regiment (Mechanized), 14 Oct 1935; Daniel Van Voorhis, "Mechanization"; Scott, "Early History of Mechanization."

39 Corelli Barnett, *Britain and Her Army 1507–1970* (Warmondsworth, England: Allen Lane, Penguin Press, 1974), p. 469; Glenn B. Hellmich, "Charles de Gaulle: His Ideas on Mechanized Warfare and the Army of the Future and the Application of These Ideas," Master thesis, Xavier University, 1955, p. 68; Jeffery A. Gunsburg, *Divided and Conquered: The French High Command and the Defeat of the West, 1940* (Westport, Conn.: Greenwood Press, 1979), p. 9–10, 15, 41–42; Timothy K. Nenninger, "A Revised Mechanization Policy," Armor 78 (Sep–Oct 1969): 45–49.

40 Heinz Guderian, *Panzer Leader* (New York: E. P. Dutton and Co., 1952), pp. 36, 316; Gillie, Forging the Thunderbolt, p. 85–89; Richard M. Ogorkiewcz, *Armor: A History of Mechanized Forces* (New York: Frederick A. Praeger, 1960), pp. 222–28.

41 Memo, G–3 for CofS, 23 Jan 29, sub: Recent developments in organization and training in armies of England, France, Germany, and Japan, Memo, G–3 for CofS, Jan 32, sub: Prospective changes in organization based on recent developments in organization and training of foreign armies, Memo on conference, Office, Chief of Infantry (CI), 5 Jul 29, G–3 21930 and CI files, 400–112–7988, B–IV, RG 177, NARA.

42 Memo on Conference, 5 Jul 29; 1st Ind CI to G–3, 2 Feb 29, CI 320/8510-B, CI files, 400–112–7988, B–IV, RG 177, NARA.

43 Minority Report, Infantry Reorganization Project, 20 Oct 29, Division General file, DAMH-HSO; Ltr, CI to TAG, 23 Nov 29, sub: Reorganization of the Infantry Battalion, and 1st Ind, CI to TAG, 5 Dec 29, Ltr, TAG to CI, 18 Dec 29, sub: Reorganization of the Infantry Division, War, Ltr, Infantry Board to CI, 2 Apr 30, sub: Reorganization of the Infantry Division, Memo, Lt Col Bruce Magruder for General Fuqua, 7 May 31, sub: Reasons for not delaying reorganization

Project, all CI files 400–112–7899, RG 177, NARA; Ltr, Brig Gen Chynoweth to author, 30 Aug 77 author's file.

44 Memo, G–3 for CofS, 5 Oct 35, sub: Modernization of the Organization of the Army, Memo, OCS for A CofS, G–3, 28 Oct 35, sub: Modernization of the Organization of the Army, WDP G–35651, RG 165, NARA.

45 Ltr, OCS to all CGs Corps Area and other addresses, 5 Nov 35, sub: Reorganization of Divisions and Higher Units, AWC Course material, AG 320.1 (11–4–35) (Misc) F-M, 52–12, MHI; Ltr, Commandant of the Infantry School to the CI, 13 Dec 35, sub: Review of Plans for Reorganization of the Division and Higher Units submitted by the Academic Department of the Infantry School and by the Infantry Board, Ltr, CI to TAG, 31 Dec 35, sub: Reorganization of the Division and Higher Units, CI files 400–122/7988 B II, C4–1, RG 177, NARA.

46 Ltr, TAG to Brig Gen John H. Hughes, 16 Jan 36, sub: Modernization of the Organization of the Army, AG 320.1 (1–6–36) (C) Off, Memo, G–3 for CofS, 21 Dec 35, sub: Modernization of the Organization of the Army, Memo, G–3 for CofS, 30 Jul 36, sub: Initial Report of Organization Committee on "Modernization of the Organization of the Army" with special reference to the Infantry Division, G–3 35651, all RG 165, NARA; Harry C. Ingles, "The New Division," *Signal Corps Bulletin* No. 108 (Apr–Jun 1940): 15–31. The board consisted of Brig Gen John H. Hughes, Assistant Chief of Staff for Operations, as the president; Cols. Philip B. Peyton (G–1) and Fay W. Bradson (G-2), Lt Cols Gilbert R. Cook (G–3) and Leonard C. Sparks (G–4), and Maj. Harvey G. Allen, War Plans Divisions. Between 1936 and 1940 the membership on the board changed, but the G–3 remained its president and Ingles, who replaced Cook in 1936, served the longest and performed most of the work relating to the G–3.

47 Memo for CofS, 30 Jul 35, sub: Initial Report of Organization Committee.

48 Ibid.

49 Ibid.

50 Ibid.

51 Memo, G–3 for CofS, 4 Aug 36, sub: Initial Report on the Organization Committee on "Modernization of the Organization of the Army" with special reference to the Infantry Division, G–3/35641–12, RG 165, NARA.

52 Ibid.; Memo, G–3 for CofS, 5 Dec 36, sub: Tests of Proposed Infantry Division, with TAB A, Memo, Lt Col Ingles for General Hughes, 14 Jan 1937, no subject, G–3/35651–12, RG 165, NARA; Memo 2, Proposed Infantry Division (PID), 20 May 37, sub: Composition of Proposed Infantry Division and Attached units, and Memo 4, PID, 4 Jun 37, sub: Armament, AG 320–2 (1–6–36), RG 407, NARA; Herbert E. Smith, "The Proposed Infantry 'Streamlined' Division," *Recruiting News* 20 (Jan 1938): 9–11 and (Feb 1938): 8–10.

53 Ltr, CI to TAG, 26 Nov 37, sub: Report of Observation, Proposed Infantry Division Test, Vicinity of San Antonio, Texas, October 18–28, CI 400/112–7988–B II C (4–1) Inf. Div., RG 177, NARA.

54 Ltr, George C. Marshall to Walton H. Walker, 21 Dec 37, Marshall Papers; "Push Plan To Lift Mobility of Army," *New York Times*, 13 Dec 1937; Ltr, Marshall to William M. Spencer, 18 Mar 38, Marshall Papers.

55 Lesley J. McNair, High Lights of Report by CG, 2d Division of the Field Service Test of the PID including the Division Recommended, 31 Mar 1938, McNair Papers, RG 407, NARA.

56 Harry C. Ingles, "The New Division," *Infantry* 49 (Nov–Dec 1939): 521-29; Ltr, TAG to CG, Eighth Corps Area, 24 Jan 39, sub: Directive for extended field service test of new division organization, AG 320.2 (12–29–38) Misc. (Ret) M-C, 2d Infantry Division file, DAMH-HSO.

57 Ltr, TAG to CG, Eighth Corps Area, 24 Jan 39.

58 Ltr, TAG to CG, Eighth Corps Area, 15 Oct 38, sub: Reorganization of the 2d Infantry Division, AG 320.2 (9–3–38) Misc. (Ret) M-C, 2d Inf Div file, DAMH-HSO.

59 Memo, G–3 for CofS, 3 Sep 38, sub: Reorganization of the Infantry Division, G–3/35651–55, RG 165, NARA; Special Report based on Field Service Test of the Provisional 2d Division conducted by the 2d Division U.S. Army, 1939, AWC course material, MHI; Ltr, Provisional 2d Division, 7 Sep 39, sub: The test of the New Division Organization, AG 320.2 (9–7–39), RG 165, NARA.

[60] Ltr, Provisional 2d Division, 7 Sep 39, sub: The test of the New Division Organization, and 1st Ind, CG, Eighth Corps Area to TAG, Sep 1939, AG 320.2 (9–7–39) RG 165, NARA.

[61] Memo, G–3 for CofS, 14 Sep 39, sub: Reorganization of the Infantry Division, G–3/35651–55, RG 165, NARA; *Tables of Organization and Reference Data for the Infantry Division, Triangular* (Fort Leavenworth, Kansas: Command and General Staff School, 1939), pp.7-37.

[62] Ltr, Marshall to James L. Collins, 4 Oct 39, Marshall Papers.

[63] Memo, G–3 for CofS, 16 Sep 39, sub: Organization of Regular Army, First Priority (17,000 increase), 16 Sep 39, G–3/6541-Gen 697, Ltr, TAG to CI, Field Artillery, Engineers and other addresses, 8 Sep 38, sub: Preliminary measures in connection with the organization of the new Infantry Division, AG 320.2 (8–31–39) M (Ret) G-M, all Study on Triangular Divisions, 1939, DAMH-HSO.

[64] Ltr, TAG to CG, Eighth Corps Area, 12 Oct 36, sub: Organization of the Cavalry Division, AG 320.2 (10–6–36 Misc. (Ret)-C, Memo, G–3 for the Commandant, AWC, 30 Dec 36, sub: Reorganization, Cavalry Division, G–3 35651, Ltr, TAG to CG, Eighth Corps Area, 15 Feb 38, sub: 1st Cavalry Division Maneuvers, Fiscal Year 1938, 353 (1–29–38) Misc. C., Report of Board of Review, vol. I, Fort Bliss, Texas, 2 Jun 1938, all in AWC course material, MHI.

[65] Report of Board of Review, vol. I, Fort Bliss, Texas, 2 Jun 1938, AWC course material, MHI.

[66] "Revised Tables of Organization, Cavalry Regiment, Horse," *Cavalry Journal* 48 (Mar–Apr 1939): 58–63.

[67] Ltr, Marshall to Collins, 4 Oct 39, Marshall Papers.

# CHAPTER 6

# Prelude to Combat

*Military operations abroad constitute a great laboratory and proving ground for the development and testing of organization and materiel. These operations have been characterized by increasing use and importance of armored, motorized, and other specialized divisions and by concurrent effort for the development of means to counter armored (tank) divisions operating in close coordination with air and motorized units.*

General George C. Marshall[1]

The German invasion of Poland in September 1939 marked the beginning of World War II in Europe and the beginning of the gradual end of American isolationism. As the Axis threat grew ever larger, it soon became evident that paper units would no longer suffice for the nation's defense. In this new international environment, the Army began its rebuilding program. Initially an emphasis on protection of the Western Hemisphere drove mobilization, and the victories of the German Army and Navy and their possible threat to the Americas accelerated the expansion. As events in Europe unfolded, relations between the United States and Japan deteriorated, eventually culminating in the attack on Pearl Harbor on 7 December 1941. Meanwhile, the Army steadily mustered forces, gaining fresh manpower from the first peacetime draft. Army leaders and their staffs worked overtime attempting to create an effective military force from the hollowed-out interwar Army. Along with new weapons and new concepts of warfare, new divisional tactical organizations appeared, most of which underwent several transformations before seeing combat.

## *Infantry and Cavalry Divisions Revisited*

In 1939 the Army created a protective mobilization force for the defense of the Western Hemisphere. The force included the 1st, 2d, 3d, 5th, and 6th Divisions, which were organized under the new triangular configuration. These forces, however, still needed to be manned and trained for war. Congressional increases in the size of the Regular Army, which began that year, provided much of the needed manpower, while the largest peacetime maneuvers ever undertaken by the Army to date provided a taste of war in 1940.[2] Between 5 and 25 May 1940 the 1st, 2d, 5th, and 6th Infantry Divisions joined the 1st Cavalry Division, the 7th Cavalry Brigade, a provisional brigade of light and medium tanks, and other units for maneuvers near

*67th Infantry (Provisional Tank Brigade), at Third Army maneuvers, 1940*

the Louisiana and Texas border, a step envisaged at the turn of the century to train an army corps. Not surprisingly, the exercises highlighted weaknesses in most units in almost every area of concern, including organization.3

To improve the infantry division, it was again reorganized, making it more powerful and easier to command and control. A headquarters and headquarters battery, which provided a fire direction control center and a brigadier general as commander of the division artillery, replaced the field artillery section in the division headquarters. Four field artillery battalions, three direct support and one general support, replaced the two regiments. The direct support battalions were to be armed with newly approved 105-mm. howitzers, while the general support battalion fielded 155-mm. howitzers and 75-mm. guns, the latter retained primarily as antitank weapons. Each field artillery battalion also was outfitted with six 37-mm. antitank guns. To counter operations such as the German blitzkrieg, which had proven so successful in Poland, antitank resources were centralized in the infantry regiments to form regimental antitank companies outfitted with 37-mm. antitank guns. In infantry battalions the number of antitank "guns"—the .50-caliber machine guns—was doubled. For targets of opportunity, more 81-mm. mortars were added to the heavy weapons company and three 60-mm. mortars were authorized for each rifle company. A reconnaissance troop appeared in the division, reflecting the growth in its operational area on the battlefield, and the number of collecting companies in the medical battalion was increased from one to three. Finally, new tables of orga-

*37-mm. gun and crew, 1941*

nization eliminated the infantry section with its general officer in the division headquarters but provided an assistant division commander with the rank of brigadier general. These changes brought the strength of the division to 15,245 officers and enlisted men, with its combat power still focused in the three regimental combat teams (*Chart 12*).4

Despite the trend in foreign armies to replace horse cavalry with mechanized units, the Assistant Chief of Staff, G–3, Maj. Gen. Frank M. Andrews, decided to table any organizational decisions affecting the cavalry. Until a definite theater of operations could be ascertained, the Army needed to prepare general purpose forces. The horse was capable of going where a machine could not, and the cavalry division appeared to have a place in the force. Among the questions Andrews wanted answered was, again, whether the division should be built on a triangular or square configuration. He also wanted to explore if and how horse and mechanized units could operate together within a cavalry corps.5

After the 1940 maneuvers Maj. Gen. Kenyon A. Joyce, commanding the 1st Cavalry Division, recommended retention of the square cavalry division. A division with two brigades, each with two cavalry regiments, was easily split into strike and reserve forces. If the division were organized along triangular lines, the regiments would have to be enlarged to maintain their firepower, but it would make them too large for effective command and control. Joyce suggested that the cavalry regiment comprise a headquarters; headquarters and service, machine gun, and special weapons troops; and two rifle squadrons of three troops each. He

# CHART 12—Infantry Division, 1 November 1940

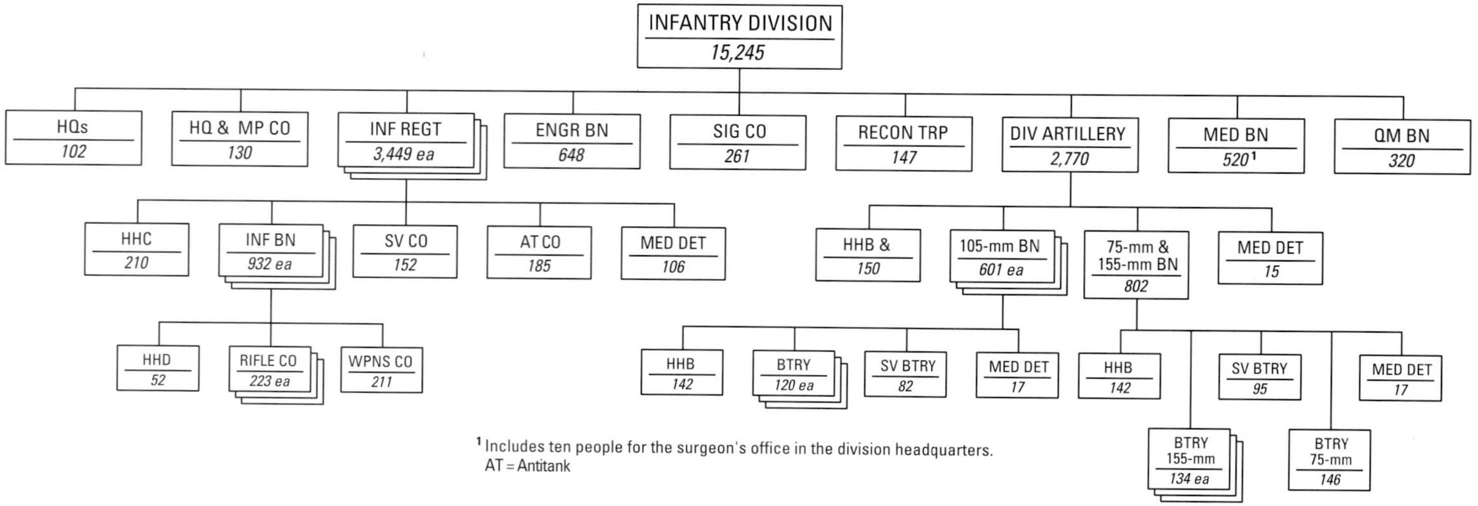

- **INFANTRY DIVISION** — 15,245
  - **HQs** — 102
  - **HQ & MP CO** — 130
  - **INF REGT** — 3,449 ea
    - **HHC** — 210
    - **SV CO** — 152
    - **INF BN** — 932 ea
      - **HHD** — 52
      - **RIFLE CO** — 223 ea
      - **WPNS CO** — 211
    - **AT CO** — 185
    - **MED DET** — 106
  - **ENGR BN** — 648
  - **SIG CO** — 261
  - **RECON TRP** — 147
  - **DIV ARTILLERY** — 2,770
    - **HHB &** — 150
    - **105-mm BN** — 601 ea
      - **HHB** — 142
      - **BTRY** — 120 ea
      - **SV BTRY** — 82
      - **MED DET** — 17
    - **75-mm & 155-mm BN** — 802
      - **HHB** — 142
      - **BTRY 155-mm** — 134 ea
      - **BTRY 75-mm** — 146
      - **SV BTRY** — 95
      - **MED DET** — 15
  - **MED BN** — 520[1]
  - **QM BN** — 320

[1] Includes ten people for the surgeon's office in the division headquarters.
AT = Antitank

wanted to strengthen the two-battalion field artillery regiment by creating batteries of six rather than four 75-mm. howitzers and adding a truck-drawn 105-mm. howitzer battalion. To improve mobility, the division needed enough trucks to move horses and equipment to the battlefield. He suggested the elimination of only one organization—headquarters, special troops—which facilitated administration in garrison, but not in the field.[6]

Joyce decided that horse and mechanized units were compatible within a cavalry corps since the 1st Cavalry Division and the 7th Cavalry Brigade (Mechanized) had successfully conducted joint operations during the maneuvers. He urged the Army to maintain a corps that included both types of units. The proportion of horse and mechanized units could vary to meet various tactical situations, but he thought the corps should be strong in artillery and engineers and contain sufficient support troops to enable it to operate with maximum speed, flexibility, and striking power.[7]

The revised cavalry division remained square and was to have 11,676 officers and enlisted men (*Chart 13*). Divisional cavalry regiments conformed to Joyce's recommendations, but instead of increasing the size of the field artillery regiment, one truck-drawn 105-mm. howitzer battalion and two 75-mm. pack howitzer battalions replaced it. As in the infantry division, the cavalry division received antitank weapons. The new wartime division tables authorized a divisional antitank troop fielding twelve 37-mm. antitank guns and a weapons troop having antitank guns and 81-mm. mortars within each brigade. The engineer, quartermaster (formerly the division train), and medical squadrons were enlarged to meet the needs of the bigger division. Draft, pack, and riding horses were limited to the cavalry brigades and the division artillery, while other elements of the division were motorized. Headquarters, special troops, was eliminated.[8]

As the 1940 Louisiana maneuvers drew to a close and the fall of France appeared imminent, the War Department authorized an increase in the number of active Regular Army infantry divisions and the adoption of the new tables. Between June and August 1940 the Army activated the 4th, 7th, 8th, and 9th Divisions.

Neither those divisions nor the other active divisions had sufficient personnel to meet the new manning levels. The 1st Cavalry Division did not adopt the revised configuration until early in 1941 when it concentrated at Fort Bliss for training.[9]

## *Organizing Armored Divisions*

During the 1940 maneuvers the Army also had tested a provisional mechanized division. After the German invasion of Poland in 1939, Brig. Gen. Adna R. Chaffee had called for "armored" divisions separate from both infantry and cavalry. Chaffee's 7th Cavalry Brigade (Mechanized), Brig. Gen. Bruce Magruder's Provisional Tank Brigade (organized in 1940 with infantry tank units), and the 6th Infantry made up the new unit. At the conclusion of the exercises, Chaffee; Magruder; Col. Alvan C. Gillem, Magruder's executive officer; Col. George S.

# CHART 13—Cavalry Division, 1 November 1940

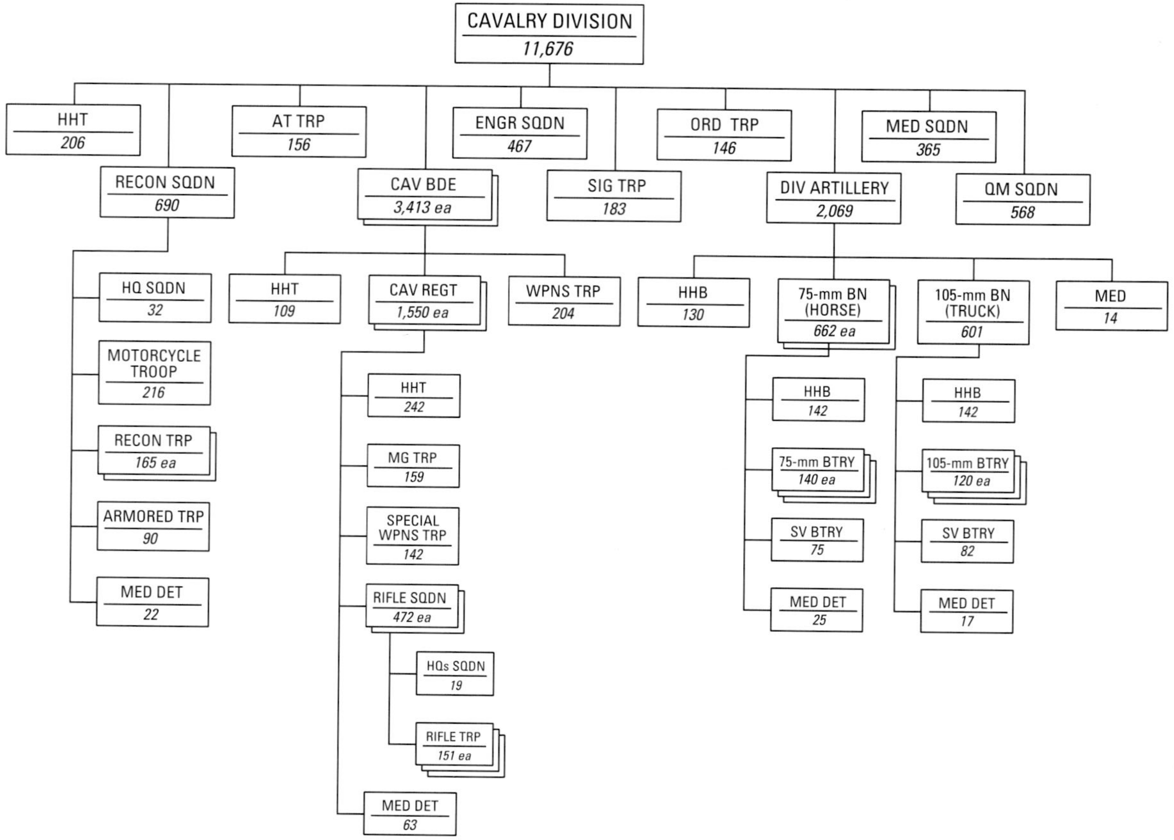

- **CAVALRY DIVISION** — 11,676
  - **HHT** — 206
  - **RECON SQDN** — 690
    - HQ SQDN — 32
    - MOTORCYCLE TROOP — 216
    - RECON TRP — 165 ea
    - ARMORED TRP — 90
    - MED DET — 22
  - **AT TRP** — 156
  - **CAV BDE** — 3,413 ea
    - HHT — 109
    - **CAV REGT** — 1,550 ea
      - HHT — 242
      - MG TRP — 159
      - SPECIAL WPNS TRP — 142
      - RIFLE SQDN — 472 ea
        - HQs SQDN — 19
        - RIFLE TRP — 151 ea
      - MED DET — 63
    - WPNS TRP — 204
  - **ENGR SQDN** — 467
  - **SIG TRP** — 183
  - **ORD TRP** — 146
  - **DIV ARTILLERY** — 2,069
    - HHB — 130
    - **75-mm BN (HORSE)** — 662 ea
      - HHB — 142
      - 75-mm BTRY — 140 ea
      - SV BTRY — 75
      - MED DET — 25
    - **105-mm BN (TRUCK)** — 601
      - HHB — 142
      - 105-mm BTRY — 120 ea
      - SV BTRY — 82
      - MED DET — 17
  - **MED SQDN** — 365
  - **QM SQDN** — 568
    - MED — 14

*General Chaffee*

Patton, commander of the 3d Cavalry at Fort Myer, Virginia; and other advocates of tank warfare met with the G–3, General Andrews, in a schoolhouse at Alexandria, Louisiana, to discuss the future of mechanization. All agreed that the Army needed to unify its efforts. The question was how. Both the chief of cavalry and the chief of infantry had attended the maneuvers, but they were excluded from the meeting because of their expected opposition to any change that might deprive their arms of personnel, equipment, or missions.10

Returning to Washington, Andrews proposed that Marshall call a conference on mechanization. The crisis in Europe had by then increased congressional willingness to support a major rearmament effort, and at the same time the success of the German panzers highlighted the need for mechanization, however costly. Andrews' initiative, made three days after the British evacuated Dunkirk, noted that the American Army had inadequate mechanized forces and that it needed to revise its policy of allowing both infantry and cavalry to develop such units separately. He suggested that the basic mechanized combined arms unit be a division of between 8,000 and 11,000 men. With the chief of cavalry planning to organize mechanized cavalry divisions, which mixed horse and tank units, such a conference seemed imperative. Marshall approved Andrews' proposal.11

From 10 to 12 June 1940 Andrews hosted a meeting in Washington centering on the organization of mechanized divisions. Along with the General Staff and the chiefs of the arms and services, Chaffee, Magruder, and other tank enthusiasts attended. Andrews disclosed that the War Department would organize an independent armored force, belonging to neither the Infantry nor Cavalry branches, in the form of "mechanized divisions." In such divisions the command and control echelon would consist of a headquarters and headquarters company and a signal company. A reconnaissance battalion with an attached aviation observation squadron would constitute the commander's "eyes," which would operate from 100 to 150 miles in advance and reconnoiter a front from 30 to 50 miles. At the heart of the division was an armored brigade made up of a headquarters and headquarters company, one medium and two light armored regiments, a field artillery regiment, and an engineer battalion. Using the two light armored regiments as the basis for two combat teams, the division was to conduct reconnaissance, screening, and pursuit missions and exploit tactical situations. An armored infantry regiment, along with armored field artillery, quartermaster, and medical battalions and an ordnance company, supported the armored brigade. Similar to the German panzer division, it was to number 9,859 officers and enlisted men.[12]

When approving the establishment of the Armored Force to oversee the organization and training of two mechanized divisions on 10 July 1940, Marshall also approved designating these units as "armored" divisions. Furthermore, he directed the chief of cavalry and the chief of infantry to make personnel who were experienced with tank and mechanized units available for assignment to the divisions. On 15 July, without approved tables of organization, Magruder organized the 1st Armored Division at Fort Knox from personnel and equipment of the 7th Cavalry Brigade and the 6th Infantry. Concurrently, Brig. Gen. Charles L. Scott, a former regimental commander in the 7th Cavalry Brigade, activated the 2d Armored Division at Fort Benning using men and materiel from the Provisional Tank Brigade. Marshall selected Chaffee to command the new Armored Force.[13]

Four months later the War Department published tables of organization for the armored division (*Chart 14*). It resembled the unit developed during the summer, except that the engineer battalion was removed from the armored brigade and assigned to the division headquarters, and the ordnance company was expanded to a battalion. To the surprise of Chaffee, who had supervised the preparation of the tables, the authorized strength of the division rose from 9,859 to 12,697, including attached personnel.

The division fielded 381 tanks and 97 scout cars when all units were at war strength.[14] Chaffee envisaged the establishment of corps-size units commanding both armored and motorized divisions, the latter essentially an infantry division with sufficient motor equipment to move all its personnel. On 15 July 1940 the War Department selected the 4th Division, which had recently been reactivated as part of the Regular Army's expansion, for this role. Collocated with the 2d Armored Division at Fort Benning, the 4th's divisional elements had earlier experimented with motorized infantry. Eventually the department published tables of organization for a motorized division that retained the triangular structure but fielded 2,700 motor vehicles including over 600 armored half-track personnel carriers.[15]

Along with the reorganization and expansion of divisional forces, the Army increased unit manning levels and concentrated units for training. A peacetime draft, adopted on 16 September 1940, provided the men, and eventually the strength of all divisions neared war level. Prior to 1940 units were scattered over 130 posts, camps, and stations in the United States, but with mobilization Congress provided funds for new facilities. The Quartermaster Corps, during the winter of 1940–41, built accommodations for 1.4 million men, including divisional posts of the type constructed in World War I.[16]

# CHART 14—Armored Division, 15 November 1940

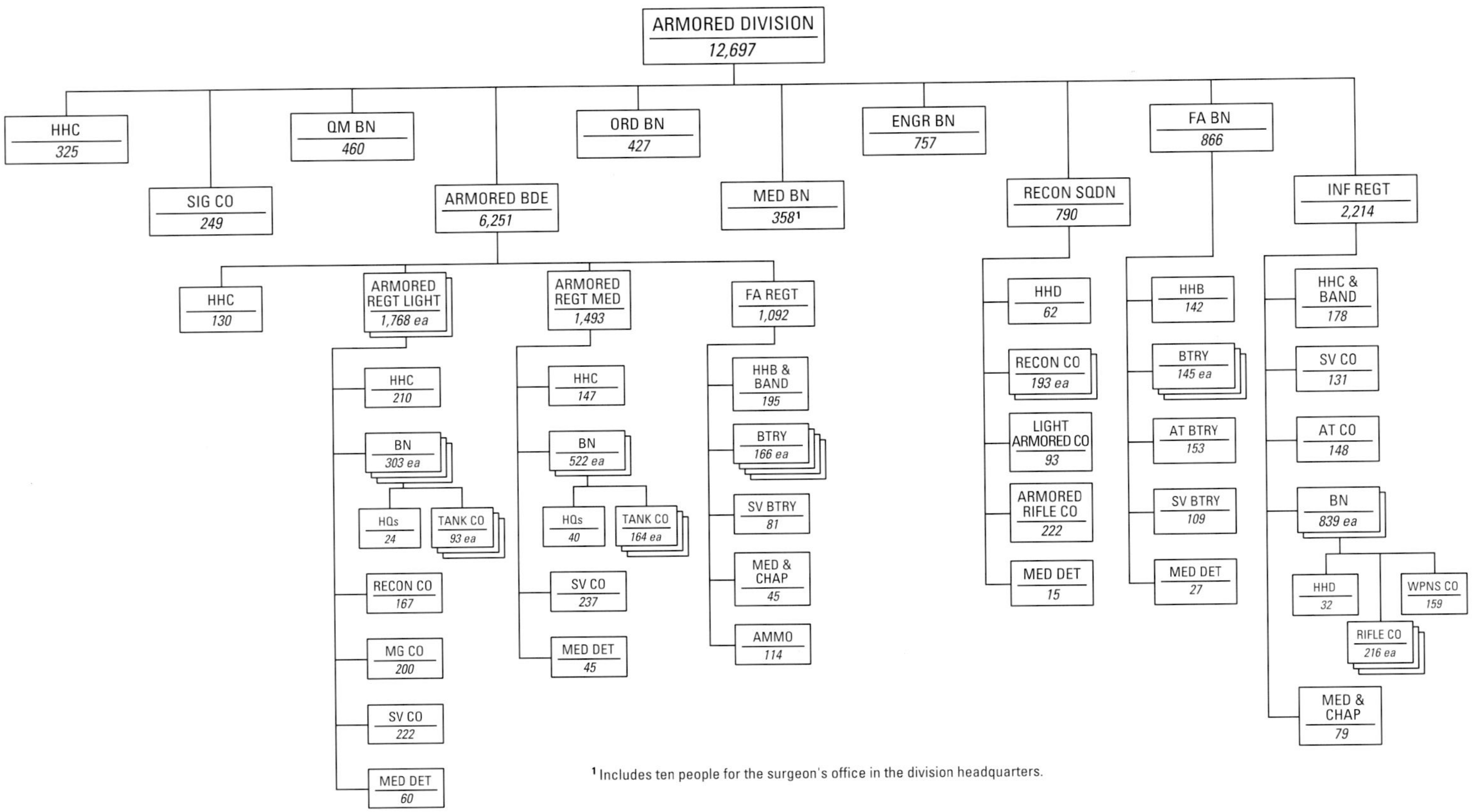

- **ARMORED DIVISION** — 12,697
  - **HHC** — 325
  - **SIG CO** — 249
  - **QM BN** — 460
  - **ARMORED BDE** — 6,251
    - **HHC** — 130
    - **ARMORED REGT LIGHT** — 1,768 ea
      - HHC — 210
      - BN — 303 ea
        - HQs — 24
        - TANK CO — 93 ea
      - RECON CO — 167
      - MG CO — 200
      - SV CO — 222
      - MED DET — 60
    - **ARMORED REGT MED** — 1,493
      - HHC — 147
      - BN — 522 ea
        - HQs — 40
        - TANK CO — 164 ea
      - SV CO — 237
      - MED DET — 45
    - **FA REGT** — 1,092
      - HHB & BAND — 195
      - BTRY — 166 ea
      - SV BTRY — 81
      - MED & CHAP — 45
      - AMMO — 114
  - **ORD BN** — 427
  - **MED BN** — 358[1]
  - **ENGR BN** — 757
  - **RECON SQDN** — 790
    - HHD — 62
    - RECON CO — 193 ea
    - LIGHT ARMORED CO — 93
    - ARMORED RIFLE CO — 222
    - MED DET — 15
  - **FA BN** — 866
    - HHB — 142
    - BTRY — 145 ea
    - AT BTRY — 153
    - SV BTRY — 109
    - MED DET — 27
  - **INF REGT** — 2,214
    - HHC & BAND — 178
    - SV CO — 131
    - AT CO — 148
    - BN — 839 ea
      - HHD — 32
      - WPNS CO — 159
      - RIFLE CO — 216 ea
    - MED & CHAP — 79

[1] Includes ten people for the surgeon's office in the division headquarters.

*Half-track personnel car, 1941*

But as in World War I, equipment shortages could not be quickly remedied and greatly inhibited preparation for war. Among other things, the Army lacked modern field artillery, rifles, tanks, and antitank and antiaircraft weapons. Although acutely aware of the shortages, Marshall believed that the Army could conduct basic training while the production of weapons caught up.[17]

## *Mobilization of National Guard Units*

As the possibility that the nation might be forced into the European war increased, some members of the War Department favored federalization of the National Guard to correct deficiencies in its training and equipment. In August 1940, after much debate, Congress approved the induction of Guard units for twelve months of training. It also authorized their use for the defense of the Western Hemisphere and the territories and possessions of the United States, including the Philippine Islands.[18]

Induction of Guard units began on Monday, 16 September, with federalization of the 30th, 41st, 44th, and 45th Divisions, less their tank and aviation units. These latter units eventually served in World War II, but not as divisional organizations. The divisions were considerably understrength, each having approximately 9,600 men, but training camps were not prepared even for that number. To bring the divisions to war level, the War Department supplied draftees, and within six months all eighteen Guard infantry divisions had entered federal service and were training at divisional posts.[19]

Federal law required Guard units to be organized under the same tables as the regulars. But the Guard divisions had not yet adopted the triangular configuration, and the General Staff hesitated to reorganize them immediately as they were in federal service only for training. Furthermore, the staff feared political repercussions when general and field grade officers were eliminated to conform to the new tables.[20]

The National Guard also maintained two separate infantry brigades, the 92d and 93d, which did not fit into any war plans of 1940. At the request of the National Guard Bureau, New York converted the 93d to the 71st Field Artillery Brigade, and Minnesota reorganized the 92d as the 101st Coast Artillery Brigade, and the units entered federal service as such.[21]

Although war plans did not call for separate infantry brigades in the United States, the War Department authorized a new 92d Infantry Brigade in the Puerto Rico National Guard to command forces there. The new headquarters came into federal service on 15 October 1940, but served less than two years without seeing combat. In July 1942 the Caribbean Defense Command inactivated the brigade and replaced it with the Puerto Rican Mobile Force.[22]

Besides infantry divisions and brigades, the National Guard maintained four partially organized cavalry divisions and one cavalry brigade. As these forces did not fit into any current war plans, the General Staff initiated a study in August 1940 to determine the Guard's requirements for horse and mechanized units. It concluded that the Guard needed both types of organizations, but not four horse cavalry divisions. At the time of the study it was rumored that the personnel from two cavalry divisions would form the nuclei of two armored divisions. The states, however, objected to the loss of cavalry regiments, and Armored Force leaders believed that armored divisions were too big and complicated for the Guard. On 1 November 1940 the National Guard Bureau withdrew the allotment of the 21st through 24th Cavalry Divisions, which in effect disbanded them. Some of their elements were used to organize mechanized cavalry regiments. After November the 56th Cavalry Brigade, a Texas unit, remained the only large unit authorized horses in the National Guard. It entered federal service before the end of the year.[23]

With 18 infantry divisions, 1 infantry brigade, and 1 cavalry brigade from the National Guard undergoing training in 1941, a crisis soon developed regarding their future. The 1940 law had authorized the federalization of the Guard for only one year, and that period was about to expire for some units. But the units were now filled with both draftees and guardsmen, and the release of the latter from federal service would completely break up these units. In the summer of 1941 the War Department thus prevailed upon Congress to extend the Guard units and men on active duty. This decision allowed Marshall to conduct the great General Headquarters Maneuvers in the summer and fall of 1941.[24]

## *Expanding Divisional Forces*

Using the protective mobilization plan, in 1941 the Army also proceeded to increase the number of cavalry, armored, and infantry divisions in response to the growing threat of war. The Regular Army organized a second cavalry division against a backdrop of domestic politics. As a result of debates over increasing the size of the Army, Congress had provided "That no Negro because of race, shall be excluded from enlistment in the Army for service with colored military units now organized and to be organized."[25] In the midst of the 1940 presidential campaign prominent black leaders complained bitterly to President Franklin D. Roosevelt about the limited number of black units. Under political pressure the Army activated the 2d Cavalry Division at Fort Riley, Kansas, on 1 April 1941, with one black and one white brigade.[26]

Armored divisions were viewed as far more essential than cavalry divisions. As early as 6 August 1940, Chaffee, commanding the Armored Force, planned more armored divisions, and he directed the 1st and 2d Armored Divisions to maintain a 25 percent overstrength as cadre for additional units. In January 1941 the War Department approved the establishment of two more armored divisions, and on 15 April the Armored Force activated the 3d and 4th at Camp Beauregard, Louisiana, and Pine Camp (later Fort Drum), New York, respectively. Shortly thereafter plans surfaced for two more armored divisions. The 5th Armored Division, added to the rolls in August, became a reality in October, and the 6th joined the force in January 1942.[27]

The European war clearly demonstrated a need to have antitank forces. Marshall had decided that all units had an antitank role, but he also recognized the requirement for specific counter-armor units. He did not want to assign them to an existing arm because their organization, tactical doctrine, and development seemed beyond the scope of any one arm. The problem struck the new Assistant Chief of Staff, G–3, Brig. Gen. Harry L. Twaddle, as similar to that of employing the machine gun during World War I. As an expedient, separate machine gun battalions had been established, although the guns were prevalent in all combat formations. Twaddle believed that antitank units, which would not be a part of any existing arm, should also be organized as an expedient to provide the strongest antitank capability possible; later the Army could sort out whether they were infantry or field artillery weapons.[28]

Twaddle's staff developed plans to provide four antitank battalions for each existing division. One battalion would serve with the division and the three others would be held at higher echelons for employment as needed. For the upcoming maneuvers the War Department authorized the formation of provisional antitank battalions in June 1941, using the antitank guns from field artillery battalions. The following December, after the maneuvers, the battalions were made permanent organizations and redesignated as tank destroyer units to indicate their offensive nature. They were not divisional elements, as recommended by First, Third,

*Tanks of the 68th Armored, 2d Armored Division, participate in the Louisiana Maneuvers, 1941.*

and Fourth Army commanders after the 1941 maneuvers, but assigned to General Headquarters (GHQ). This arrangement placed the units outside the control of the existing arms, thus creating basically a new homogeneous antitank force. The independent tank destroyer battalions would later prove an organizational error, denying division commanders a major resource that they habitually needed. It did, however, focus attention on an area that was a growing tactical concern.[29]

The possible theater of operations shifted from the Western Hemisphere to the Pacific in 1941 as relations deteriorated between the United States and Japan. To be prepared for that contingency, Lt. Gen. Walter C. Short, commanding the Hawaiian Department, requested permission to expand the square Hawaiian Division into two triangular infantry divisions with the primary mission of defending Oahu, the most populous of the islands and a major base of the U.S. Pacific Fleet. Recognizing that the Regular Army lacked the units required for the reorganization, Short proposed that Guard units complete the two divisions. The department approved Short's proposal, and on 1 October he reorganized and redesignated the Hawaiian Division as the 24th Infantry Division and activated the 25th Infantry Division. Elements of the Hawaiian Division were distributed between the two new divisions, and, as planned, each had one Hawaii National Guard and two Regular Army infantry regiments. Divisional strengths hovered around 11,000 men.[30]

*Provisional Tank Destroyer Battalion, Fort Meade, Maryland, 1941*

About the same time the Army introduced two new distinctions into its official lexicon. First, the word "infantry" was made a part of the official designation of such divisions. In the past the word infantry was understood, but, because of the expanding variety of divisions, the Army needed some way to distinguish among them. The adjutant general specified that unit designations thus include the major combat element or even the type of unit when the former was not sufficiently descriptive. Some divisions issued general orders introducing infantry as a part of the official name, and the adjutant general constituted the 25th specifically as an infantry division. The term, however, was not officially added to the tables of organization, documents that technically controlled the names of units, until 1942.[31]

The second change concerned the meaning of the term "Army of the United States." Before 1940 it had embraced the Regular Army, the National Guard while in the service of the United States, and the Organized Reserves. With the growth of the force, the term Army of the United States was broadened to encompass units that had not been a part of the mobilization plans during the interwar years. The 25th Infantry Division was the first division-size unit activated under the expanded definition.[32]

In the Pacific area, the defense of the Philippine Islands presented unique problems. They were too distant and too scattered for ground defense. Nevertheless, Marshall asked the local commander, General Douglas MacArthur, whether

# TABLE 12
## Divisions Active on 7 December 1941

| Component | Division | Date Activated or Inducted Into Federal Service | Location |
|---|---|---|---|
| RA | 1st Infantry | * | Fort Devens, Mass. |
| RA | 2d Infantry | * | Fort Sam Houston, Tex. |
| RA | 3d Infantry | * | Fort Lewis, Wash. |
| RA | 4th Infantry | 1 June 1940 | Fort Benning, Ga. |
| RA | 5th Infantry | 16 October 1939 | Fort Custer, Mich. |
| RA | 6th Infantry | 10 October 1939 | Fort Leonard Wood, Mo. |
| RA | 7th Infantry | 1 July 1940 | Fort Ord, Calif. |
| RA | 8th Infantry | 1 July 1940 | Fort Jackson, S.C. |
| RA | 9th Infantry | 1 August 1940 | Fort Bragg, N.C. |
| RA | 24th Infantry | * | Schofield Barracks, Hawaii |
| AUS | 25th Infantry | 1 October 1941 | Schofield Barracks, Hawaii |
| NG | 26th Infantry | 16 January 1941 | Camp Edwards, Mass. |
| NG | 27th Infantry | 15 October 1940 | Fort McClellan, Ala. |
| NG | 28th Infantry | 17 February 1941 | @Indiantown Gap Military Reservation, Pa. |
| NG | 29th Infantry | 3 February 1941 | @Fort George G. Meade, Md. |
| NG | 30th Infantry | 16 September 1940 | Fort Jackson, S.C. |
| NG | 31st Infantry | 25 November 1940 | Camp Blanding, Fla. |
| NG | 32d Infantry | 15 October 1940 | Camp Livingston, La. |
| NG | 33d Infantry | 5 March 1940 | Camp Forrest, Tenn. |
| NG | 34th Infantry | 10 February 1941 | Camp Claiborne, La. |
| NG | 35th Infantry | 23 December 1940 | Camp Joseph T. Robinson, Ark. |
| NG | 36th Infantry | 25 November 1940 | Camp Bowie, Tex. |
| NG | 37th Infantry | 16 October 1940 | Camp Shelby, Miss. |
| NG | 38th Infantry | 17 January 1941 | Camp Shelby, Miss. |
| NG | 40th Infantry | 3 March 1941 | Fort Lewis, Wash. |
| NG | 41st Infantry | 16 September 1940 | Fort Lewis, Wash. |
| NG | 43d Infantry | 24 February 1941 | Camp Shelby, Miss. |
| NG | 44th Infantry | 16 September 1940 | Fort Dix, N.J. |
| NG | 45th Infantry | 16 September 1940 | Camp Berkeley, Tex. |
| RA | 1st Cavalry | * | Fort Bliss, Tex. |
| RA | 2d Cavalry | 15 April 1941 | Fort Riley, Kans. |
| RA | 1st Armored | 15 July 1940 | Fort Knox, Ky. |
| RA | 2d Armored | 15 July 1940 | Fort Benning, Ga. |
| RA | 3d Armored | 15 April 1941 | Camp Beauregard, La. |
| RA | 4th Armored | 15 April 1941 | Pine Camp, N.Y. |
| RA | 5th Armored | 1 October 1941 | Camp Cooke, Calif. |

NOTES: *Active before 1 September 1939.
@En route from maneuvers, arrived at home station 9 December 1941.

*General Short reviews the Hawaiian Division, September 1941.*

he wanted a Guard division to reinforce his ground units. MacArthur instead asked for authority to reorganize the Philippine Division as a triangular unit and to fill its regimental combat teams with Regular Army personnel. Since the division's formation in 1921, most of its enlisted men were Philippine Scouts, and he wanted to use them to help organize new Philippine Army units. Marshall approved the request and initiated plans to send two infantry regiments, two field artillery battalions, a headquarters and headquarters battery for the division artillery, a reconnaissance troop, and a military police platoon to the islands. The Japanese attack on Pearl Harbor and other installations in the Pacific on 7 December 1941 aborted the plan.33

At the time of the attack the Army had thirty-six divisions, excluding the Philippine Division (*Table 12*), and two brigades on active duty. The nation was thus much better prepared for war in December 1941 than in April 1917.

## *Reorganization of the National Guard Divisions*

The Japanese attack and the ensuing American declaration of war on Japan, Germany, and Italy immediately shifted the focus of Army planning from hemispheric defense to overseas operations. The first priority was to streamline the square National Guard divisions. Even before the attack Marshall had asked Twaddle to explore that possibility, believing that the surplus units could be used overseas or to create new organizations as some divisions appeared to lend themselves to expansion. In November 1941 Twaddle took the 121st and 161st Infantry from the square 30th and 41st Divisions and reassigned them. At the time of the attack on Pearl Harbor he had replaced the 34th Infantry with the 121st Infantry in the 8th Division and had slated the 34th and the 161st for deployment to the Philippines. The day after the attack he attached one infantry regiment each from the 32d, 33d, and 36th Divisions to the Fourth Army to augment the forces protecting the West Coast. A week later the 124th Infantry from the 31st Division was assigned to the Infantry School at Fort Benning, Georgia.[34]

On 31 December 1941, Marshall asked Lt. Gen. Lesley J. McNair, Chief of Staff, GHQ, to investigate bottlenecks that had developed during attempts to ship units overseas. Six days later McNair told Marshall that the Guard divisions used to organize task forces going overseas had "overheads" (noncombat personnel) that approached the "grotesque" and recommended their immediate reorganization as triangular divisions.[35] Shortly thereafter Marshall directed the staff to prepare plans for reorganizing thirteen of the eighteen Guard divisions, omitting five because they already had orders for overseas duty. Ultimately either Marshall or his deputy approved the conversion to triangular formations of all Guard divisions except one, the 27th, which was targeted for Hawaii where that command was planning to receive a square division. Twaddle's staff prepared instructions for the reorganization, which he sent to the division commanders for comment. Units that the states had not adequately supported were to be eliminated.[36]

The reorganization began with the 32d and 37th Divisions on 1 February 1942. All infantry brigades were disbanded except the 51st, an element of the 26th Division. One infantry brigade headquarters company from each division was converted and redesignated as the division reconnaissance troop, except in the 28th and 43d Divisions. In the 43d both infantry brigade headquarters companies were disbanded, and in the 28th one brigade headquarters company became the reconnaissance troop and the other the division's military police company. The headquarters and headquarters battery of each field artillery brigade became the headquarters and headquarters battery, division artillery. Other divisional elements were reorganized, redesignated, reassigned, or disbanded. The reorganization was completed on 1 September 1942 when the 27th Division, which had arrived in Hawaii that summer, adopted the triangular configuration.[37]

In January 1942 the War Department created Task Force 6814 from surplus National Guard units to help defend New Caledonia, a French possession in the Pacific. Among these units were the 51st Infantry Brigade headquarters and the 182d Infantry from the 26th Division (Massachusetts) and the 132d Infantry from the 33d Division (Illinois). The units arrived in New Caledonia in March and others quickly followed. Eventually the Operations Division (OPD), War Department General Staff,[38] instructed Maj. Gen. Alexander M. Patch, commanding Task Force 6814, to organize a division. Because he lacked men and equipment for a

*Camp Shelby, Mississippi, home of the 37th and 38th Divisions, 1941*

complete table of organization unit, the staff decided that the division would carry a name rather than a numerical designation. Titles such as "Necal" and "Bush" surfaced, but Patch turned to the men assigned to the task force for suggestions. Pfc. David Fonesca recommended "Americal" from the phrase "American Troops on New Caledonia," and on 27 May 1942 Patch activated the Americal Division.[39]

## Another Reorganization

With the attack on Pearl Harbor on 7 December the "great laboratory" phase for developing and testing organizations, about which Marshall wrote in the summer of 1941, closed, but the War Department still had not developed ideal infantry, cavalry, armored, and motorized divisions. In 1942 it again revised the divisions based on experiences gained during the great GHQ maneuvers of the previous year. As in the past, the reorganizations ranged from minor adjustments to wholesale changes.

The Chief of Infantry, Maj. Gen. Courtney H. Hodges, proposed the principal change in the infantry division, the addition of a cannon company to the infantry regiment to provide it with artillery that could move forward as rapidly as the troops advanced on foot. The Chief of Field Artillery, Maj. Gen. Robert M. Danford, opposed the idea, contending that all cannon should be in artillery units. McNair, appointed Chief of Army Ground Forces (AGF) in March 1942 and responsible for organizing and training all ground combat units, also objected. For five years the division had been in a state of flux in an effort to make it light and therefore easier to handle. Command and control had replaced road space as the basic factor behind divisional size. Constant changes were destroying those goals. McNair advised Marshall that the division should have a maximum of 15,000 men with the arms being fixed accordingly and that it should not be increased in size at the insistence of arm-conscious chiefs. His view did not prevail. Hodges won the armament battle, and a cannon company became a part of each infantry regiment.40

The addition of regimental cannon companies was not the only change in the infantry division. To increase artillery firepower, the tables provided twelve rather than eight 155-mm. howitzers and eliminated the 75-mm. guns, which had been assigned to tank destroyer units, as antitank weapons. To protect the division from hostile aircraft, the number of .50-caliber machine guns rose from sixty to eighty-four. Improved reconnaissance capabilities were also added to the infantry division, with ten light armored cars replacing the sixteen scout cars in the reconnaissance troop. In the infantry regiments themselves, intelligence and reconnaissance platoons replaced intelligence platoons.41

The GHQ maneuvers of 1941 had also revealed a need for more trucks in the division. McNair, however, believed that the suggested number of trucks was excessive, requiring too much space on ships when sent overseas. Although the number of trucks was cut at his insistence, the division still had 315 more vehicles under the 1942 tables than those of 1940. Finally, the new tables split the division headquarters and military police company into two separate units, a headquarters company and a military police platoon. These changes together added about 270 men to the division (*Chart 15*).42

Modifications continued even after publication of the new tables of organization for the infantry division. Army Ground Forces withdrew the small ordnance maintenance platoon from the headquarters company of the quartermaster battalion and reorganized the unit as a separate ordnance light maintenance company to improve motor repair. After this change, food and gasoline supply functions became the responsibility of the regiments and separate battalions in the division, and the quartermaster battalion was reduced to a company to provide trucks for water supply and emergency rations and to augment the division's ability to move men and equipment.43

The cavalry division retained its square configuration after the 1941 maneuvers, but with modifications. The division lost its antitank troop, the brigades their weapons troops, and the regiments their machine gun and special weapons troops. These changes brought no decrease in divisional firepower, but placed most weapons within the cavalry troops. The number of .50-caliber machine guns was increased almost threefold. In the reconnaissance squadron, the motorcycle and armored car troops were eliminated, leaving the squadron with one support troop and three reconnaissance troops equipped with light tanks. These changes increased the division from 11,676 to 12,112 officers and enlisted men.44

CHART 15—Infantry Division, 1 August 1942

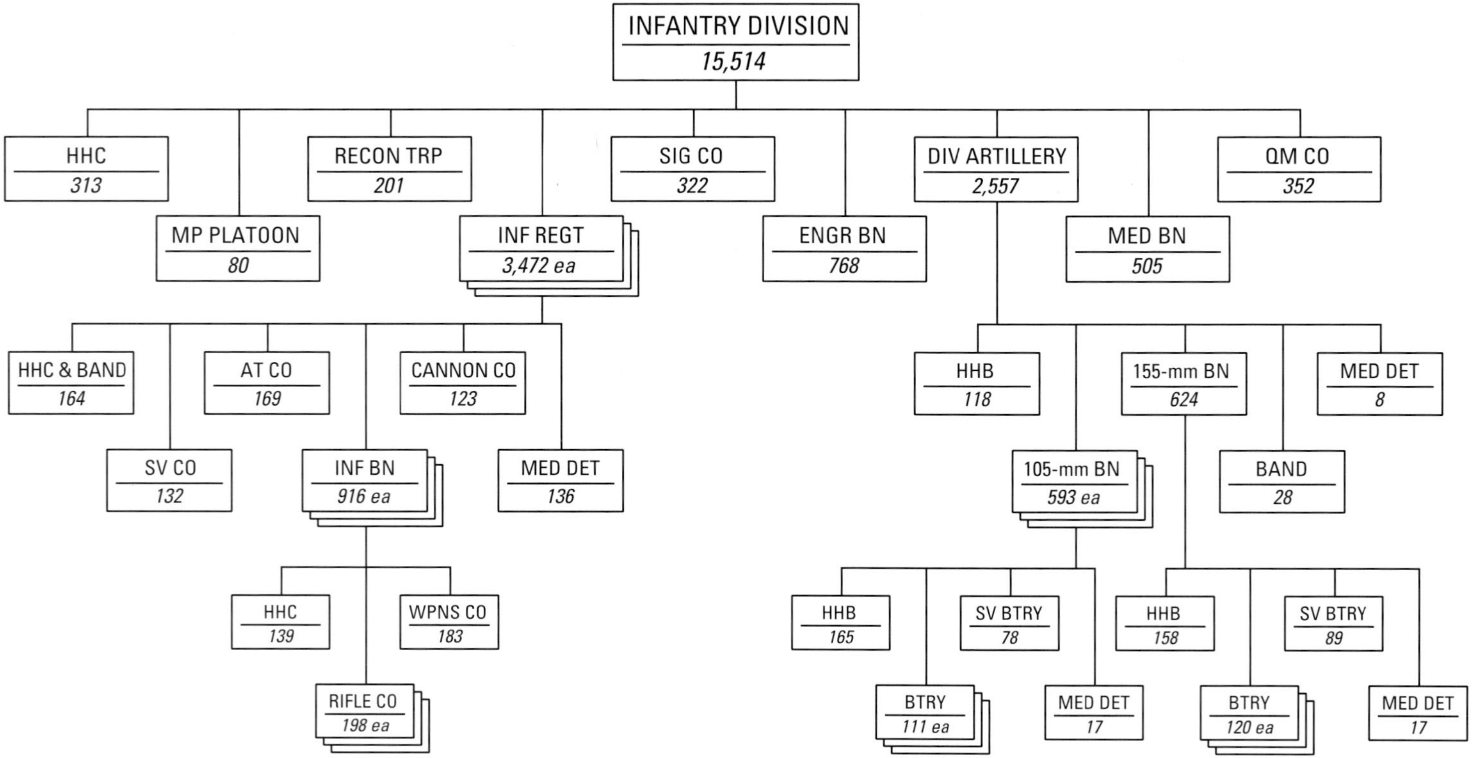

- INFANTRY DIVISION — 15,514
  - HHC — 313
  - MP PLATOON — 80
  - RECON TRP — 201
  - SIG CO — 322
  - INF REGT — 3,472 ea
    - HHC & BAND — 164
    - SV CO — 132
    - AT CO — 169
    - CANNON CO — 123
    - MED DET — 136
    - INF BN — 916 ea
      - HHC — 139
      - WPNS CO — 183
      - RIFLE CO — 198 ea
  - ENGR BN — 768
  - DIV ARTILLERY — 2,557
    - HHB — 118
    - MED BN — 505
    - MED DET — 8
    - 105-mm BN — 593 ea
      - HHB — 165
      - BTRY — 111 ea
      - SV BTRY — 78
      - MED DET — 17
    - 155-mm BN — 624
      - HHB — 158
      - BTRY — 120 ea
      - SV BTRY — 89
      - MED DET — 17
    - BAND — 28
  - QM CO — 352

The GHQ maneuvers also had a significant impact on the organization of the armored division. The exercises led to numerous situations that called for infantry, artillery, and armor to form combat teams, but the division lacked the resources to organize them. The division as organized was heavy in armor but too light in both infantry and artillery. The armored brigade complicated the command channel, while the service elements needed greater control. To correct these weaknesses, the Armored Force, under the direction of Maj. Gen. Jacob L. Devers, dramatically reorganized the division (*Chart 16*). The armored brigade headquarters and one armored regiment were eliminated, and the remaining two armored regiments were reorganized to consist of one light and two medium tank battalions each. Three self-propelled 105-mm. howitzer battalions replaced the field artillery regiment and battalion, and control of the division artillery passed to an artillery section in the division headquarters. The infantry regiment was reorganized to consist of three battalions of three companies each, and trucks replaced armored personnel carriers. The engineer battalion was authorized four, rather than three, line companies and a bridge company. Two combat command headquarters were authorized but were to have no assigned units, allowing the division commander to build fighting teams as the tactical situation dictated yet still have units in reserve. Maintenance and supply battalions replaced ordnance and quartermaster battalions, the maintenance unit taking over all motor repairs in the division. For better control of the service elements, division trains were added and placed under the command of a colonel. A service company was also added to provide transportation and supplies for the rear echelon of the division headquarters company.[45]

The 4th Division had tested the motorized structure along with attached tank, antitank, and antiaircraft artillery units during the Carolina portion of the GHQ maneuvers in the fall of 1941. At their termination, the division commander, Brig. Gen. Fred C. Wallace, reported to General Twaddle that the force was "undesirably large." Furthermore, deficiencies existed in command and control, traffic control, administrative support, rifle strength, communications, motor maintenance, ammunition supply, and engineer capabilities. Also, the attached units—tank, antitank, and antiaircraft artillery battalions—needed to be permanently assigned to the division.[46]

When the War Department published new tables of organization for the motorized division in the spring of 1942 (*Chart 17*), it differed considerably from the structure tested by Wallace. In those tables, the hand of McNair, who almost always opposed "special" units, was evident. The division closely resembled an infantry division. Motorized infantry regiments were to have an organization similar to standard infantry regiments. Gone were armored half-track personnel carriers, but the regiment was to have enough trucks to move all its men and equipment. The division headquarters and headquarters company and the artillery were identical to their counterparts in the infantry division, and the reconnaissance battalion was the same as that of the cavalry division. A reconnaissance company was added to the engineer battalion. The ordnance unit remained company size,

## CHART 16—Armored Division, 1 March 1942

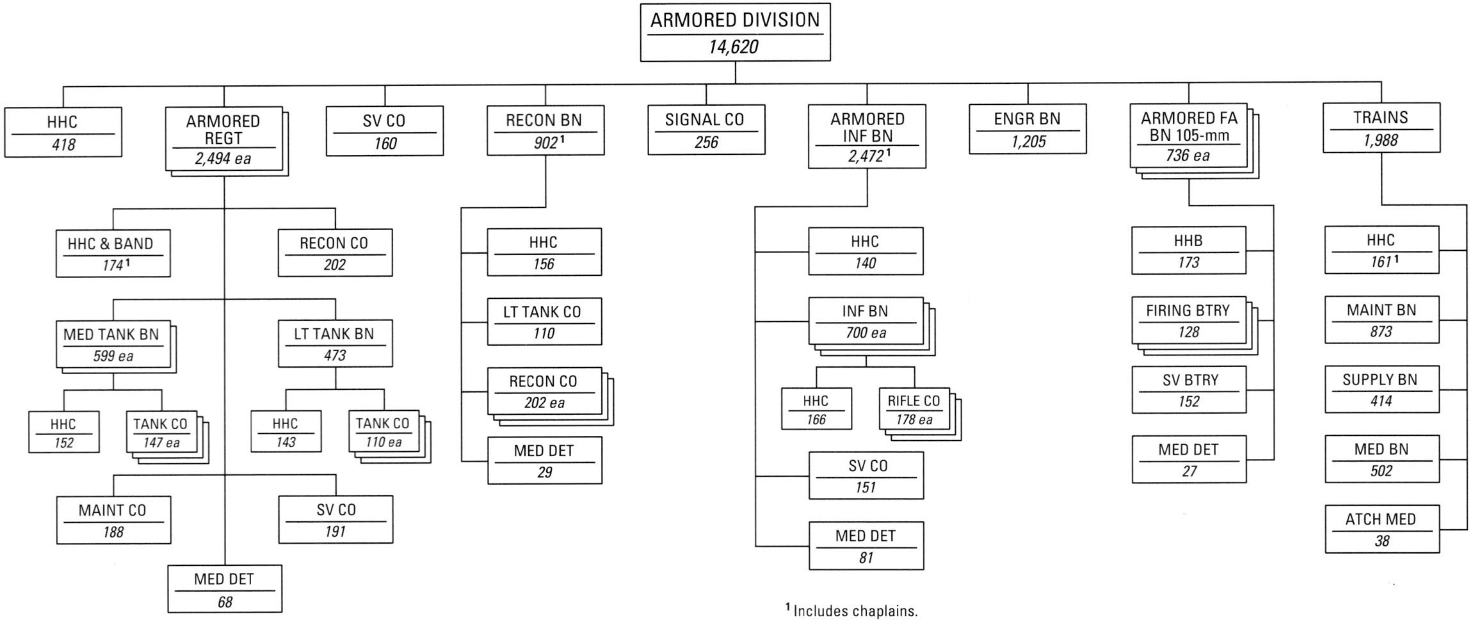

- ARMORED DIVISION — 14,620
  - HHC — 418
  - ARMORED REGT — 2,494 ea
    - HHC & BAND — 174[1]
    - MED TANK BN — 599 ea
      - HHC — 152
      - TANK CO — 147 ea
    - RECON CO — 202
    - LT TANK BN — 473
      - HHC — 143
      - TANK CO — 110 ea
    - MAINT CO — 188
    - SV CO — 191
    - MED DET — 68
  - SV CO — 160
  - RECON BN — 902[1]
    - HHC — 156
    - LT TANK CO — 110
    - RECON CO — 202 ea
    - MED DET — 29
  - SIGNAL CO — 256
  - ARMORED INF BN — 2,472[1]
    - HHC — 140
    - INF BN — 700 ea
      - HHC — 166
      - RIFLE CO — 178 ea
    - SV CO — 151
    - MED DET — 81
  - ENGR BN — 1,205
  - ARMORED FA BN 105-mm — 736 ea
    - HHB — 173
    - FIRING BTRY — 128
    - SV BTRY — 152
    - MED DET — 27
  - TRAINS — 1,988
    - HHC — 161[1]
    - MAINT BN — 873
    - SUPPLY BN — 414
    - MED BN — 502
    - ATCH MED — 38

[1] Includes chaplains.

# CHART 17—Motorized Division, 1 August 1942

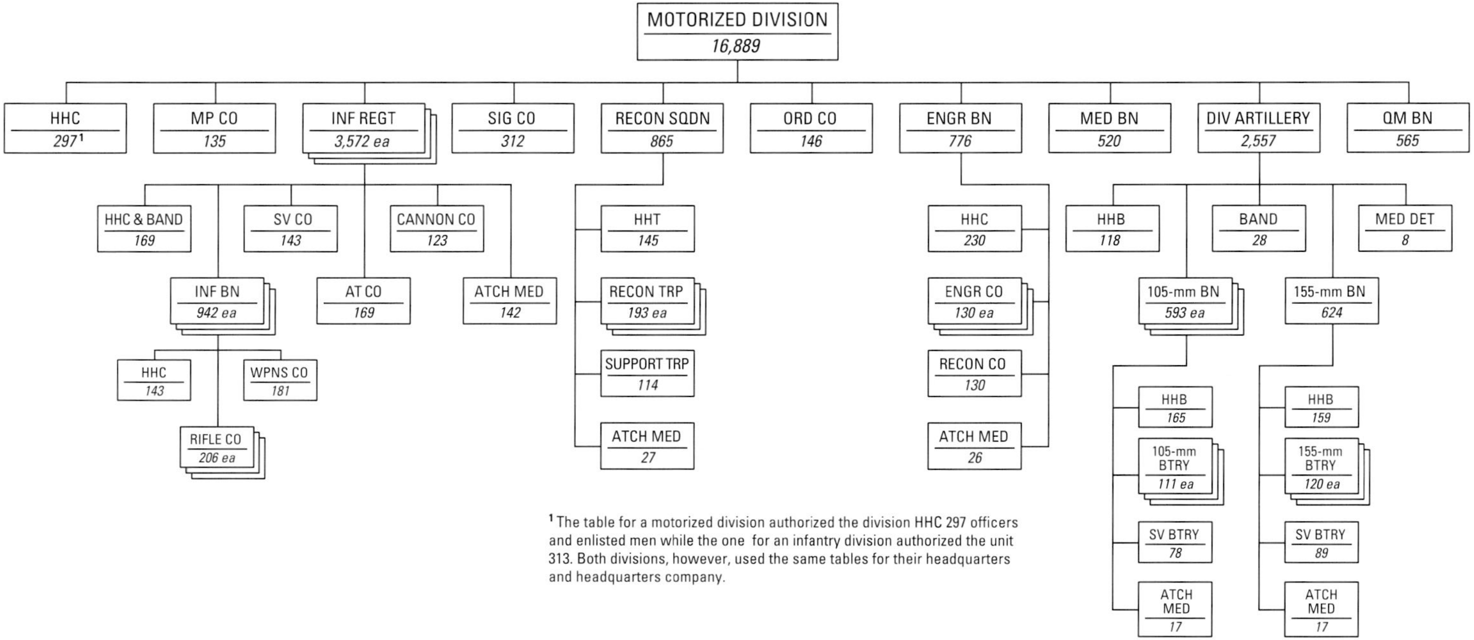

**MOTORIZED DIVISION** — 16,889

- **HHC** — 297[1]
- **MP CO** — 135
- **HHC & BAND** — 169
- **INF REGT** — 3,572 ea
  - **SV CO** — 143
  - **CANNON CO** — 123
  - **AT CO** — 169
  - **ATCH MED** — 142
  - **INF BN** — 942 ea
    - **HHC** — 143
    - **WPNS CO** — 181
    - **RIFLE CO** — 206 ea
- **SIG CO** — 312
- **RECON SQDN** — 865
  - **HHT** — 145
  - **RECON TRP** — 193 ea
  - **SUPPORT TRP** — 114
  - **ATCH MED** — 27
- **ORD CO** — 146
- **ENGR BN** — 776
  - **HHC** — 230
  - **ENGR CO** — 130 ea
  - **RECON CO** — 130
  - **ATCH MED** — 26
- **MED BN** — 520
- **DIV ARTILLERY** — 2,557
  - **HHB** — 118
  - **BAND** — 28
  - **105-mm BN** — 593 ea
    - **HHB** — 165
    - **105-mm BTRY** — 111 ea
    - **SV BTRY** — 78
    - **ATCH MED** — 17
  - **155-mm BN** — 624
    - **HHB** — 159
    - **155-mm BTRY** — 120 ea
    - **SV BTRY** — 89
    - **ATCH MED** — 17
- **MED DET** — 8
- **QM BN** — 565

[1] The table for a motorized division authorized the division HHC 297 officers and enlisted men while the one for an infantry division authorized the unit 313. Both divisions, however, used the same tables for their headquarters and headquarters company.

and a military police company was added. As redesigned, the motorized division fielded nearly 17,000 men. Following McNair's idea that a unit should have only those resources it habitually needed, the division, as other infantry divisions, lacked organic tank, tank destroyer, and antiaircraft artillery battalions.[47]

Before all the tables for the revised divisions were published in 1942, the War Department alerted the field commands about the pending reorganization of their units. Divisions were to adopt the new configurations as soon as equipment, housing, and other facilities became available. Most divisions adhered to the revised structures by the end of 1942.[48]

In the summer of 1942 the Army organized a fifth type of division. Between World Wars I and II it had experimented with transporting units in airplanes, and in 1940 the chief of infantry studied the possibility of transporting all elements of an infantry division by air. When the Germans successfully used parachutists and gliders in Holland and Belgium in 1940, the Army reacted by developing parachute units. The mass employment of parachutes and gliders on Crete in 1941 stimulated the development of glider units. Both types of units were limited to battalion size because tacticians did not envision airborne operations involving larger units. Brig. Gen. William C. Lee, commander of the U.S. Army Airborne Command, which had been established to coordinate all airborne training, visited British airborne training facilities in England in May 1942 and following that visit recommended the organization of an airborne division.[49]

At that time the British airborne division consisted of a small parachute force capable of seizing a target, such as an airfield, and a glider force to reinforce the parachutists, leaving the remainder of the division to join those forces through more conventional means. Lee reported to McNair that the British had found the movement of ordinary troops in gliders wasteful because about 30 percent of the troops suffered from air sickness and became ineffective during air-land operations. Since the British were organizing airborne divisions, in which glider personnel were to receive the same training as parachutists, Lee suggested the U.S. Army also organize them. Heeding Lee's suggestion, McNair outlined to Marshall a 9,000-man airborne division that could have a varying number of parachute or glider units in accordance with tactical circumstances.[50]

Although the General Staff accepted the proposal, it had several reservations. The division selected for the airborne role had to have completed basic training but should not be a Regular Army or National Guard unit, as many traditionalists in those components wanted nothing to do with such an experimental force. For ease of training, it also had be stationed where air facilities and flying conditions were good. The 82d Division met the criteria. It was an Organized Reserve unit, training under Maj. Gen. Matthew B. Ridgway, and located at Camp Claiborne, Louisiana. McNair recommended that it be the basis for two airborne divisions with the existing parachute infantry regiments assigned to them. For the designation of the second airborne division, the staff selected the 101st, an Organized Reserve unit that was not in active military service.[51]

*Paratroopers stage a special demonstration for members of Congress, Fort Belvoir, Virginia, 1941.*

The Third Army and the Airborne Command executed McNair's recommendation on 15 August l942. The 82d Infantry Division (less the 327th Infantry, the 321st and 907th Field Artillery Battalions, the 82d Cavalry Reconnaissance Troop, and the Military Police Platoon) plus the 504th Parachute Infantry became the 82d Airborne Division. Concurrently, the adjutant general disbanded the 101st Division in the Organized Reserve and reconstituted it in the Army of the United States, activating it as the 101st Airborne Division at Camp Claiborne, Louisiana. The 502d Parachute Infantry, the 327th Glider Infantry, and the 321st and 907th Glider Field Artillery Battalions were assigned as divisional elements. Shortly thereafter each division was authorized an antiaircraft artillery battalion, an ordnance company, and a military police platoon. The parachute infantry elements did not immediately join their divisions, but by early October 1942 all elements of both divisions assembled at Fort Bragg for training.[52]

On 15 October 1942 the War Department published the first tables of organization for the airborne division (*Chart 18*). Reflecting the light nature of the unit, the parachute infantry regiment had only .30-caliber machine guns and 60-mm. and 81-mm. mortars besides the individual weapons, and its field artillery battalions used 75-mm. pack howitzers. In the division artillery, however, a new antitank weapon was introduced, the 2.36-inch rocket launcher (the "bazooka"). Transportation equipment ranged from bicycles and handcarts to 2-1/2-ton trucks,

## CHART 18—Airborne Division, 15 October 1942

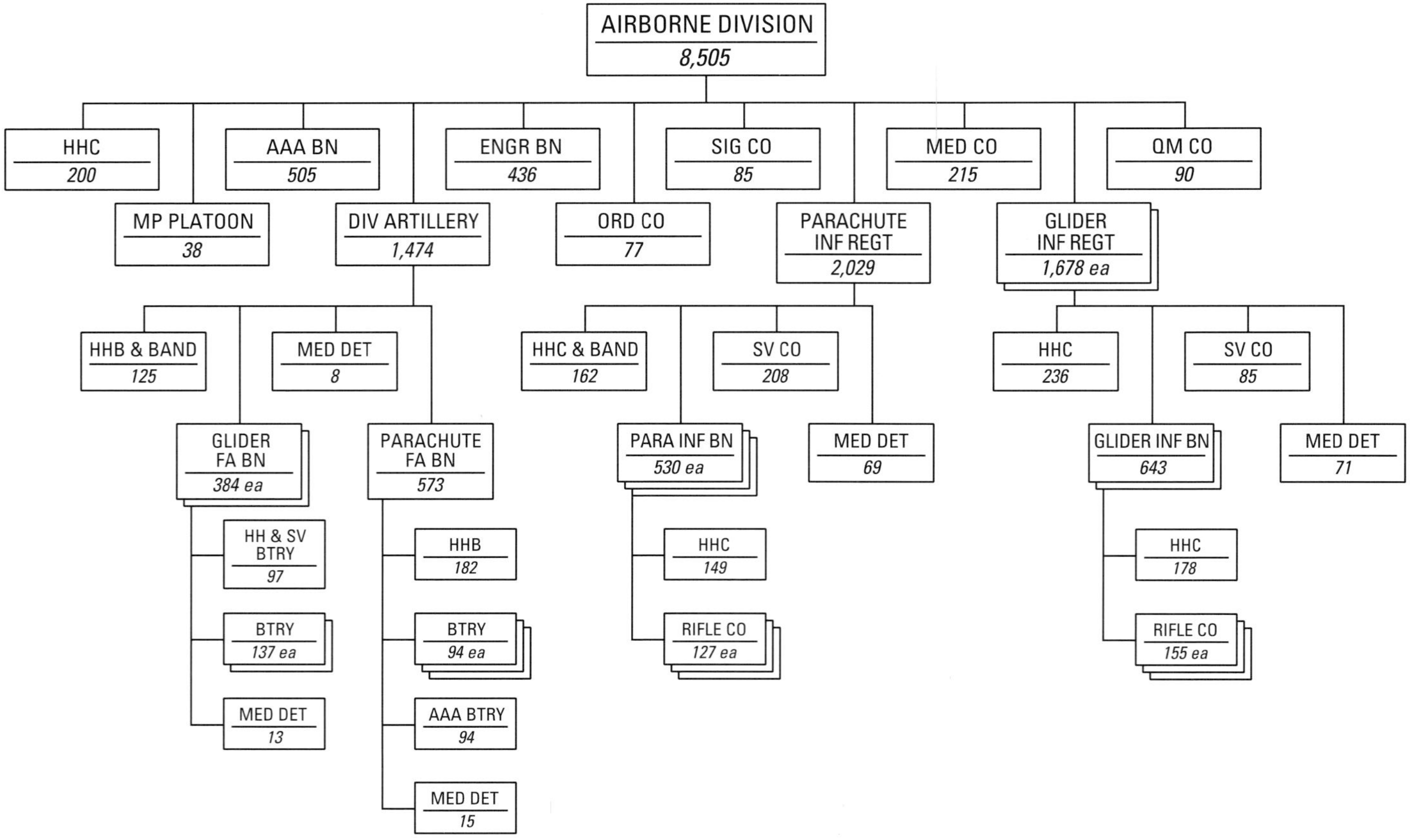

**AIRBORNE DIVISION** — 8,505

- HHC — 200
- MP PLATOON — 38
- AAA BN — 505
- ENGR BN — 436
- SIG CO — 85
- MED CO — 215
- QM CO — 90
- ORD CO — 77
- DIV ARTILLERY — 1,474
  - HHB & BAND — 125
  - MED DET — 8
  - GLIDER FA BN — 384 ea
    - HH & SV BTRY — 97
    - BTRY — 137 ea
    - MED DET — 13
  - PARACHUTE FA BN — 573
    - HHB — 182
    - BTRY — 94 ea
    - AAA BTRY — 94
    - MED DET — 15
- PARACHUTE INF REGT — 2,029
  - HHC & BAND — 162
  - SV CO — 208
  - MED DET — 69
  - PARA INF BN — 530 ea
    - HHC — 149
    - RIFLE CO — 127 ea
- GLIDER INF REGT — 1,678 ea
  - HHC — 236
  - SV CO — 85
  - MED DET — 71
  - GLIDER INF BN — 643
    - HHC — 178
    - RIFLE CO — 155 ea

but the airborne division had only 401 trucks as opposed to over 1,600 in an infantry division. The new division numbered 8,505 officers and enlisted men, of whom approximately 2,400 were parachutists.[53]

The Airborne Command also trained smaller parachute and glider units and requested the authority to organize tactical airborne brigades in 1942. The Deputy Chief of Staff, Lt. Gen. Joseph T. McNarney, turned down the request, believing that only divisions should conduct operations involving more than a regiment. The Airborne Command, nevertheless, organized the 1st Parachute Infantry Brigade, a nondeployable unit, to assist in training parachute units.[54]

## *Increases in the Force Structure*

After 7 December 1941 the General Staff also turned its attention to the future size of the Army and the number of divisions required to wage and win the war. Some officers believed that as many as 350 divisions might be needed, while others estimated considerably fewer. Outside considerations included the manpower needs of the other services and civilian industry as well as the speed at which divisions could be organized, equipped, and trained given the limited pool of experienced leaders and industrial limitations. On 24 November 1942, nearly a year after United States entered the war, the War Department published a troop basis[55] that called for a wartime force structure of 100 divisions—62 infantry, 20 armored, 10 motorized, 6 airborne, and 2 cavalry—to be organized by 1943 within a total Army force of 8,208,000 men.[56]

Meanwhile, the Army continued to expand the number of divisions. Working with tentative troop bases early in 1942, the General Staff decided to bring the Organized Reserve divisions into active military service. President Franklin D. Roosevelt signed an executive order calling units of the Organized Reserves into active military service for the duration of the war plus six months. The order was a public relations document more than anything else because most Organized Reserve personnel were already on active duty.[57]

Members of General Twaddle's staff next examined the sequence for inducting infantry divisions. They considered such factors as the number of World War I battle honors earned by units; the location and availability of training sites, particularly in the corps areas where divisions were located; and the ability of the Army to furnish divisional cadres. Based on these considerations, the staff established a tentative order, beginning with the 77th Division, which had the most combat service in World War I, and ending with the 103d, which had not been organized during World War I.[58]

Meanwhile, corps area commanders prepared the Organized Reserve units for induction early in 1942 by placing the infantry divisions under the 1940 tables of organization. Infantry and field artillery brigades were eliminated, with the headquarters and headquarters companies of the infantry brigades consolidated to form divisional reconnaissance troops. As in the National Guard divisions, the headquarters and headquarters batteries of the field artillery brigades became the headquarters and headquarters batteries of the division artillery. Other units within the division were reduced, redesignated, reassigned, or disbanded to fit the triangular configuration. The six Organized Reserve cavalry divisions were dropped from the tentative troop program and disbanded.[59]

Induction of the infantry divisions began on 25 March 1942, and by 31 December, twenty-six of the twenty-seven divisions were on active duty (*Table 13*). The 97th Infantry Division was not inducted into active military service until February 1943 because personnel were not available for its reorganization. Since none of these divisions had reserve cadre or equipment, the Army Ground Forces had to rebuild them totally. That process started when the War Department assigned a commander and selected a parent unit to provide a cadre. Approximately thirty-seven days before reorganization of the division, the commander and his staff reported to the unit's station. Officers and enlisted cadre, about 1,400 men from the parent unit, followed some seven days later, and shortly thereafter the remaining 500 officers arrived. Within five days after the arrival of all officers and cadre, a stream of about 13,500 recruits began to report. The division was considered reorganized and active fifteen days after the first fillers reached the division. Fifty-two weeks of training followed, which included seventeen weeks of basic and individual training. The divisions, after their initial fill, were to rely on replacement centers for personnel.[60]

Along with the reorganization of the Organized Reserve units, the War Department expanded the number of divisions in the Army of the United States. Reversing a post–World War I policy, the staff planned to activate some all-black divisions to accommodate the large number of black draftees. On 15 May 1942 Army Ground Forces organized the 93d Infantry Division at Fort Huachuca, Arizona. Although it had the same number as the provisional Negro unit of World War I, it had no relationship or lineal tie with the old 93d. Following its activation, the Army Staff chartered at least three more all-black infantry divisions— the 92d, 105th, and 107th. The 92d Division, the all-black unit of World War I, was to be reconstituted, but the other two were to be new units. Under the plan, the 93d Infantry Division was to furnish the cadre for the 92d, the 92d for the 105th, and the 105th for the 107th. Army Ground Forces organized the 92d on 15 October 1942, but a shortage of personnel for worldwide service units prevented the formation of the others. Eventually the 105th and 107th Divisions were dropped from the activation list.[61]

To meet the number of divisions in the troop basis, the Armored Force activated nine more armored divisions in 1942, the 6th through the 14th. In organizing them, it followed the same cadre system as the Army Ground Forces used for infantry divisions.[62]

With the increased number of armored divisions, Brig. Gen. Harold R. Bull, the G–3 on the General Staff, discerned a way to eliminate unwanted cavalry divisions. He suggested to Army Ground Forces that it consider converting the two

# TABLE 13

## Divisions Activated or Ordered Into Active Military Service in 1942[1]

| Component | Division | Date | Location |
|---|---|---|---|
| AUS | 6th Armored | 15 February | Fort Knox, Ky. |
| AUS | 7th Armored | 1 March | Camp Polk, La. |
| OR | 77th Infantry | 25 March | Fort Jackson, S.C. |
| OR | 82d Airborne | 25 March | Camp Claiborne, La. |
| OR | 90th Infantry | 25 March | Camp Berkeley, Tex. |
| AUS | 8th Armored | 1 April | Fort Knox, Ky. |
| OR | 85th Infantry | 15 May | Camp Shelby, Miss. |
| AUS | 93d Infantry | 15 May | Fort Huachuca, Ariz. |
| AUS | Americal | 27 May | New Caledonia |
| OR | 76th Infantry | 15 June | Fort George G. Meade, Md. |
| OR | 79th Infantry | 15 June | Camp Pickett, Va. |
| OR | 81st Infantry | 15 June | Camp Rucker, Ala. |
| AUS | 9th Armored | 15 July | Fort Riley, Kans. |
| AUS | 10th Armored | 15 July | Fort Benning, Ga. |
| OR | 80th Infantry | 15 July | Camp Forrest, Tenn. |
| OR | 88th Infantry | 15 July | Camp Gruber, Okla. |
| OR | 89th Infantry | 15 July | Camp Carson, Colo. |
| OR | 95th Infantry | 15 July | Camp Swift, Tex. |
| AUS | 11th Armored | 15 August | Camp Polk, La. |
| OR | 78th Infantry | 15 August | Camp Butner, N.C. |
| OR | 83d Infantry | 15 August | Camp Atterbury, Ind. |
| OR | 91st Infantry | 15 August | Camp White, Oreg. |
| OR | 96th Infantry | 15 August | Camp Adair, Oreg. |
| AUS | 101st Airborne | 15 August | Camp Claiborne, La. |
| AUS | 12th Armored | 15 September | Camp Campbell, Ky. |
| OR | 94th Infantry | 15 September | Fort Custer, Mich. |
| OR | 98th Infantry | 15 September | Camp Breckinridge, Tenn. |
| OR | 102d Infantry | 15 September | Camp Maxey, Tex. |
| OR | 104th Infantry | 15 September | Camp Adair, Oreg. |
| AUS | 13th Armored | 15 October | Camp Beale, Calif. |
| OR | 84th Infantry | 15 October | Camp Howze, Tex. |
| AUS | 92d Infantry | 15 October | Fort McClellan, Ala. |
| AUS | 14th Armored | 15 November | Camp Chaffee, Ariz. |
| OR | 99th Infantry | 15 November | Camp Van Dorn, Miss. |
| OR | 100th Infantry | 15 November | Fort Jackson, S.C. |
| OR | 103d Infantry | 15 November | Camp Claiborne, La. |
| OR | 86th Infantry | 15 December | Camp Howze, Tex. |
| OR | 87th Infantry | 15 December | Camp McCain, Miss. |

[1] Table in chronological order.

Regular Army horse divisions to mechanized cavalry because there was no foreseeable role for horse-mounted units. Maj. Gen. Mark W. Clark, Chief of Staff of Army Ground Forces, disagreed, as did Secretary of War Henry L. Stimson. The latter opposed the conversion because the war was worldwide, and he believed that horse cavalry could be useful in many places, particularly in areas where oil was scarce, a reference to the other types of divisions that required large quantities of petroleum products. He also opposed the conversion because of the time required to train new horse cavalry units. Nevertheless, because of a shortage of men in the summer of 1942, the 2d Cavalry Division was inactivated to permit organization of the 9th Armored Division. White cavalrymen were assigned to the 9th, and the all-black 4th Cavalry Brigade became a nondivisional unit. Later, when preparing troops for operations in the North African theater, the engineer and reconnaissance squadrons and the 105-mm. howitzer battalion were withdrawn from the 1st Cavalry Division and sent to North Africa.[63]

With the activation of additional armored divisions, General Twaddle decided to convert some infantry divisions to motorized divisions. He selected the 6th, 7th, and 8th Divisions for reorganization, which was accomplished by August 1942. The staff planned to form three more such divisions that year, but Army Ground Forces reorganized only the 90th because of shortages in personnel and equipment. On 9 April 1942 the adjutant general officially redesignated the 6th, 7th, and 8th Divisions as motorized. The 4th Division issued general orders adopting the "motorized" designation under an Army Ground Forces directive.[64]

From the fall of 1939 to the end of 1942 divisional designs fluctuated as the nation prepared for war. The War Department revised infantry and cavalry divisions, developed and revised armored and motorized divisions, and created airborne divisions. During this period of organizational upheaval, the Army retained the basic idea of three regimental combat teams for the infantry division and adopted the same concept for the motorized and airborne divisions. The armored division was held to two fighting teams, as was the horse cavalry division. Many officers, however, wanted to eliminate the latter because they saw no role for the horse on the modern battlefield. The trend within all types of divisions was to increase firepower and standardize divisional elements so that they could be interchanged. Organizational questions remained, however, such as the nature and location of antitank weapons or the amount of organic transportation in any tactical unit. The period proved fruitful, for the Army organized the divisions needed to pursue the war. By 31 December 1942 the Army had fielded 1 cavalry, 2 airborne, 5 motorized, 14 armored, and 51 infantry divisions, for a total of 73 active combat divisions.

# PRELUDE TO COMBAT

## Notes

1 *Rpt of the Sec of War, 1941*, p. 60.

2 Kreidberg and Henry, *Mobilization*, pp. 563–68. From the summer of 1940 to the summer of 1944 General Headquarters (GHQ) and its successor, Army Ground Forces (AGF), conducted large-scale maneuvers to provide and evaluate training at the corps level, often pitting corps against corps. Each corps fielded two or more divisions and support units, and they also came under scrutiny. Maneuver areas were at times established in New York, North and South Carolina, Tennessee, Louisiana, Texas, Oklahoma, California, Arizona, and Nevada. Over the years the Louisiana Maneuvers have received the most attention.

3 Jean R. Moenk, *A History of Large-Scale Army Maneuvers in the United States, 1935–1964* (Fort Monroe, Va.: Continental Army Command (CONARC), 1969), pp. 26–37; *History of the Third Army*, AGF Study 17 (Washington, D.C.: Historical Section, AGF, 1946), p. 7; *Army and Navy Register* 61 (14 Sep 1940): 10.

4 T/O 70, Infantry Division (Triangular), 1 Nov 1940; T/O 6–80, Division Artillery, Truck-Drawn, Infantry Division, 1 Oct 1940; T/O 7–11, Infantry Regiment, 1 Oct 1940; T/O 8–65, Medical Battalion, 1 Oct 1940; Field Manual (FM) 7–5, *Infantry, 1940*.

5 *Rpt of the Sec of War, 1941*, p. 60; Ltr, TAG to CG, 1st Cavalry Division, 24 Apr 40, sub: Report on Corps and Army Maneuvers, AGO 320.2 (4–15–40) file, RG 407, NARA.

6 Ltr, CG, 1st Cavalry Division to TAG, 9 Jul 40, sub: Report on Corps and Army Maneuvers, AGO 320.2 (4–15–40), RG 407, NARA.

7 Ibid.

8 T/O 2, Cavalry Division, 1 Nov 1940; T/O 2–11, Cavalry Regiment, Horse, 1 Nov 1940; T/O 6–110, Division Artillery, Cavalry Division, Horse, 1 Nov 1940; Ltr, TAG to Chief of all arms and services and other addresses, 13 Sep 40, sub: Cavalry Division, Horse, AG 320.2 Cav (9–11–40)P, AGO 320.2 Cavalry 8–1–40 to 4–30–41 file, RG 407, NARA; "Notes from the Chief of Cavalry," *Cavalry Journal* 49 (Sep–Oct 1940): 408–11.

9 Ltr, TAG to CG of all Corps Areas and other addresses, 22 Jun 40, sub: Organization and Movement of Units and Cadres in connection with Augmentation to the Army to 280,000, AG 320.2 (6–18–40) M (Ret) M-C, Ltr, TAG to CG of all Corps Areas and other addresses, 20 Jul 40, sub: Organization and Movement of Units and Cadres in Connection with Augmentation of the Army to 375,000, AG 320.2 (7–10–40) M (Ret) M-C, Ltr, TAG to CG of all Corps and Corps Areas, 10 Sep 40, sub: Reorganization of Triangular Divisions, AG 320.2 (8–31–40) M (Ret) M-C, Ltr, and TAG to CG of all Armies, Corps Areas, and other addresses, 13 Jan 41, sub: Constitution and Activation of Units, AG 320.2 (1–7–41) M (Ret) M-C, all AG Reference files, DAMH-HSO; Memo, G–3 for TAG, 8 Jan 41, sub: Concentration of 1st Cavalry Division at Fort Bliss, Texas and method of filling lower border posts vacated thereby with elements of the 56th Cavalry Brigade, 8 Jan 41, G–4/43327, AG 320.2 (8–26–40), RG 407, NARA; Bertram C. Wright, comp., *The 1st Cavalry Division in World War II* (Tokyo: Toppan Printing Co., 1947), p. 3; Charles E. Kirkpatrick, *An Unknown Future and a Doubtful Present: Writing the Victory Plan of 1941* (Washington, D.C.: Government Printing Office, 1989), pp. 44–47; See Historical Data Cards for 4th, 7th, 8th, and 9th Divisions, DAMH-HSO.

10 Adna R. Chaffee, "Mechanized Cavalry," AWC lecture, 29 Sep 1939, AWC course material, MHI; Gillie, *Forging the Thunderbolt*, pp. 109, 162–64; *History of the Armored Force, Command, and Center*, AGF Study 27 (Washington, D.C.: Historical Section, AGF, 1946), p. 7.

11 Memo, G–3 for CofS, 5 Jun 40, sub: Mechanization, G–3/41665, AGO 320.2 (6–5–40), RG 407, NARA. General Andrews' background was not with cavalry, infantry, or mechanized forces, but with the U.S. Army Air Corps.

12 Memo, G–3 for CofS, 5 Jun 40, sub: Mechanization; Notes on G–3 Mechanized Conference, G–4/23518–69, AGO 320.2 (6–5–40), RG 407, NARA.

13 Memo, G–3 for CofS, 23 Jun 40, sub: Mechanization, G–3/41665, AGO 320.2 (6–5–40), RG 407, NARA; Ltr, TAG to CG of all Armies, Corps Areas, and other addresses, 10 Jul 1940,

sub: Organization of the Armored Force, AG 320.2 (7–5–40) M (Ret) M-C, AG Reference files, DAMH-HSO; Historical Data Cards, 1st and 2d Armored Divisions (Armd Divs), DAMH-HSO.

[14] T/O 17, Armored Division, 15 Nov 1940; Ltr, Chaffee to Scott, 9 Sep 40, and Ltr, Scott to Chaffee, 12 Sep 40, Charles L. Scott Papers, LC.

[15] Statement of Adna R. Chaffee, 14 May 1941, Document Collection, U.S. Army Armor School Library, Fort Knox, Ky.; Ltr, Scott to Grow, 3 Sep 40, Scott Papers, LC; Ltr, TAG to CG of all Corps Areas and other addresses, 20 Jul 40, sub: Organization and Movement of Units and Cadres in Connection with Augmentation of the Army to 375,000; T/O 77, Infantry Division (Triangular, Motorized), 1 Nov 1940.

[16] *Biennial Report of the Chief of Staff, July 1, 1939 to June 30, 1941*, pp. 1–3; *Rpt of the Sec of War, 1941*, pp. 67–68.

[17] *Rpt of the Sec of War, 1941*, pp. 62, 68–70; Erna Risch and Chester L. Kieffer, 2 vols., *The Quartermaster Corps: Organization, Supply, and Services* ( Washington, D.C.: Government Printing Office, 1955), 2:293

[18] Kreidberg and Henry, *Mobilization*, pp. 575–77; WD Bull 22, 1940.

[19] *Report of the Chief of the National Guard Bureau, 1946*, pp. 24–27; Robert Bruce Sligh, *The National Guard and National Defense: The Mobilization of the Guard in World War II* (New York: Praeger, 1992), pp. 126–28.

[20] Memo, G–3 for CofS, 6 Nov 41, sub: Triangulation of National Guard Divisions, and Memo, Mobilization Branch to G–3, 12 Nov 41, same subject, G–3/41741, AGO 320.2 (8–2–40), RG 407, NARA.

[21] Memo, ACofS, G–3, 1 Aug and 1 Nov 1940, NGB 325.4 Gen.-6, DAMH-HSO; *Rpt of the Chief of National Guard Bureau, 1946*, pp. 220, 230.

[22] 92d Infantry Brigade, Organizational History From 25 August 1940 to 31 December 1941, Ms, Ltr, Puerto Rican Dept to TAG, 10 Jul 42, sub: Inactivation of unit, HHC, 92d Infantry Brigade, 320.2 Gen, and Ltr, Operations Division (OPD) to Caribbean Defense Command, 24 Jul 42, same subject, MR-OPD, all in 92d Infantry Brigade file, DAMH-HSO.

[23] *Rpt of the Chief of the National Guard Bureau, 1941*, p. 14; Ltrs, Chaffee to Scott, 5 Aug 40, and Scott to Chaffee, 8 Aug 40, Scott Papers, LC; Ltr, TAG to National Guard Bureau, 8 Nov 40, sub: Withdrawal of Certain Cavalry Units from Allotment to the National Guard, 325.4 (10–21–40) M (Ret), AG Reference file, DAMH-HSO; *Rpt of the Chief of the National Guard Bureau, 1946*, p. 217; WD Bull 26, 1940; Wright, *The 1st Cavalry Division in World War II*, p.3.

[24] Mark Skinner Watson, *Chief of Staff: Prewar Plans and Preparation,* United States Army in World War II (Washington, D.C.: Government Printing Office, 1950), pp. 214–31.

[25] WD Bull 17, 1940.

[26] Ltr, TAG to CG of All Armies and other addresses, 10 Oct 40, sub: 2d Cavalry Division, AG 320.2 (10–8–40) M (Ret) M-C, 2d Cav Div file, DAMH-HSO; Ulysses Lee, *The Employment of Negro Troops*, United States Army in World War II (Washington, D.C.: Government Printing Office, 1966), pp. 65–68, 122–28; Morris J. MacGregor, Jr., *Integration of the Armed Forces 1940–1965* (Washington, D.C.: Government Printing Office, 1981), pp. 30–31.

[27] *History of the Armored Force*, p. 50; Ltr, TAG to CG of all Armies and other addresses, 13 Jan 41, sub: Constitution and Activation of Units, AG 320.2 (1–7–41) M (Ret) M-C, Ltr, TAG to Chief, Armored Force, and other addresses, 28 Aug 41, sub: Constitution and Activation of 5th Armored Division, AG 320.2 (8–22–41) MR-M-C, and Ltr, TAG to Chief, Armored Force, and other addresses, 8 Jan 42, sub: Constitution and Activation of the 6th Armored Division, AG 320.2 (12–11–41), MR-M-C, all letters in DAMH-HSO; John B. Wilson, *Armies, Corps, Divisions, and Separate Brigades*, Army Lineage Series (Washington, D.C.: Government Printing Office, 1987), pp. 169, 187, 203, and 215.

[28] Memo, OCofS for G–3, 14 May 41, sub: Defense Against Armored Forces, G–4/21103–6, and Memo, G–3 for CofS, 18 Aug 41 sub: Organization of Antitank Units in the Army, OCS 21103–6, AG 320.2 (8–16–41), RG 407, NARA.

[29] Memo, G–3 for CofS, 18 Aug 41, sub: Organization of Antitank Units in the Army, and Ltr, TAG to CG all Armies, 24 Jun 41, sub: Organization of Provisional Division and GHQ Antitank

# PRELUDE TO COMBAT 175

Battalions for Use in Current Maneuvers, AG 320.2 (6–19–41) MR-M-C, RG 407, NARA; Ltr, TAG to CG of all Armies and other addresses, 3 Dec 1941, sub: Organization of Tank Destroyer Battalions, AG 320.2 (11–17–41) MR-M-C, Tank Destroyer File, DAMH-HSO; Christopher R. Gable, *The U.S. Army GHQ Maneuvers of 1941* (Washington, D.C.: Government Printing Office, 1992), pp. 174–76; Kent Roberts Greenfield, Robert R. Palmer, and Bell I. Wiley, *The Organization of Ground Combat Troops*, United States Army in World War II (Washington, D.C.: Government Printing Office, 1947), p. 82–84.

30 Ltr, CG, Hawaiian Dept to TAG, 26 Apr 41, sub: Reorganization of the Forces in the Hawaiian Department, AG 320.3/37, AG 320.2 (9–27–40), and Ltr, TAG to CG, Hawaiian Dept, 26 Aug 41, sub: Constitution and Reorganization of Units, Hawaiian Department, AG 320.2 (8–1–41) MR-M-C, AG 320.2 (8–1–41), RG 337, NARA; GO 53, Hawaiian Department, 1941, Hawaiian Dept, RG 338, NARA.

31 Memo, G–3 for CofS, 19 May 41, sub: Designation of Divisions, Army Corps, and Armies, G–3/45832, Division General file, DAMH-HSO; WD Cir 197, 1941; "Army Designations," *Army and Navy Register*, 9 Aug 1941; author's notes, The use of the word infantry in divisional designations; T/O 7, 1 Aug 1942.

32 "Lineage and Honors: History, Principles, and Preparation," Organizational History Branch, Office, Chief of Military History (OCMH), June 1962; Ltr, TAG to CG, Hawaiian Dept, 26 Aug 41, sub: Constitution and Reorganization of Units, Hawaiian Department, 24th Inf Div file, DAMH-HSO.

33 Louis Morton, *The Fall of the Philippines*, United States Army in World War II (Washington, D.C.: Government Printing Office, 1953), pp. 31–37.

34 Memo, G–3 for CofS, 18 Sep 41, sub: Triangularization of Square Division to Removal of Elements for Bases, G–3/41741, AGO 320.2 (8–2–40), and Memo, G–3 for TAG, 22 Nov 41, sub: Assignment of the 121st Infantry from the 30th Division to 8th Division, G–3/43726, AGO 320.2 (8–2–40), RG 407, NARA; Ltr, TAG to CG, Third and Fourth Armies, 8 Dec 41, sub: Attachment of Three Infantry Regiments, Third Army to Fourth Army, AG 370–5 (12–8–41) MC-M-C, and Ltr, TAG to CG, Third Army, 15 Dec 41, sub: Assignment of 124th Infantry, AG 352 Inf Sch (11–27–41) MR-M-C, AG Reference files, DAMH-HSO.

35 Memo, GHQ for CG, Field Forces, 6 Jan 42, sub: Triangulating Square Division, 322.13/22 (1–6–42), AGO 320.2 (1–6–42), RG 407, NARA.

36 Memo, OCS for G–3, no subject, 8 Jan 42, OCS/20117–124, RG 407, NARA. Memos pertaining to the reorganization of the National Guard divisions in 1942 are in National Guard Induction and Reorganization file, 1938–1942, DAMH-HSO.

37 Letters of instruction for reorganizing the National Guard divisions and divisional general orders implementing those instructions are in National Guard Induction and Reorganization file, 1938–1942, DAMH-HSO.

38 On 9 March 1942 the War Department's General Staff was reorganized and many of the functions of the five assistant chiefs of staff (G–1 to G–4 and the War Plans Division) were realigned. Much of the responsibility for organizing and training combat units, formerly held by the G–3, was passed to Army Ground Forces (AGF), and the Operations Division (OPD), formerly the War Plans Division, focused on the employment of units. All three, G–3, AGF, and OPD, however, would continue to deal with divisional organization during World War II.

39 Francis D. Cronin, *Under the Southern Cross, The Saga of the Americal Division* (Washington, D.C.: Combat Forces Press, 1951), pp. 4–29; Ltr, TAG to CG, U.S. Army Forces in New Caledonia, 24 May 42, sub: Constitution and Organization of AMERICAL Division, 24 May 42, AG 320.2 (5–23–42) MR-M-OPD; and GO 10, US Army Forces in New Caledonia, 1942, 23d Infantry Division file, DAMH-HSO.

40 Memo, Lesley J. McNair for CG, Field Forces, 2 Feb 42, sub: Field artillery organization, triangular division, 320.2/37 (FA)-F (2–2–42), McNair Papers; T/O 7–11, Infantry Regiment, 1942. On 9 March 1942 the chiefs of the combat arms were abolished as a part of the reorganization of the General Staff (see Hewes, *From Root to McNamara*, pp. 67–76).

41 T/O 7, Infantry Division, 1942.

⁴² Memo, CG, AGF, for Requirement Division, AGF, 4 Apr 42, sub: New Infantry regiment, 320.2 Gen-(Clear), McNair Papers; Greenfield et al., *Organization of Ground Combat Troops*, pp. 281–86; T/O 7, Infantry Division, 1 Aug 1942.

⁴³ T/O 7, Infantry Division, 1 Aug 1942; WD Cirs 245, 267, and 274, 1942; Memo, AGF for TAG, 11 Sep 42, sub: Organization of Ordnance Light Maintenance Companies, Infantry Division, 320.2/43 (Ord) (R)-GNGCT/10922 AG 320.2 (9–11–42), RG 407, NARA.

⁴⁴ T/O 2, Cavalry Division, 1 Aug 1942.

⁴⁵ Gabel, *The U.S. Army Maneuvers of 1941*, pp. 176–79; Ltr, Hqs, Armored Force to G–3, 20 Sep 41, sub: Proposed Armored Division, 20 Sep 41, and Memo, G3 for CofS, 1 Sep 41, sub: Reorganization of Armored Division, 320.2 (G3/41665, both AG 320.2 (9–20–41), RG 407, NARA; T/O 17, Armored Division, 1 Mar 1942; *History of the Armored Force*, pp. 29–32.

⁴⁶ Ltr, TAG to Third Army, 8 Jul 41, sub: Test of Motorized Division Organization, 320.2 (6–25–41) MR-M-C, 4th Infantry Division file, DAMH-HSO; Ltr, 4th Motorized Division to TAG, 9 Dec 41, sub: Test of Motorized Division Organization, 353–PMD, AG 320.2 (12–9–41), RG 407, NARA.

⁴⁷ T/O 77, Motorized Division, 1 Aug 1942.

⁴⁸ Ltr, TAG to CGs, Army Air Forces, Army Ground Forces, and other addresses, 16 Jun 42, sub: Allotments of Grades and Ratings and Authorized Strength to Tactical Units, AG 221 (6–3–42) EA-M-C, AG Reference files, and Divisional Historical Data Cards, DAMH-HSO.

⁴⁹ *The Airborne Command and Center*, AGF Study 25 (Washington, D.C.: Historical Section, AGF, 1946), pp. 1–12, 21; James A. Huston, *Out of the Blue: U.S. Army Airborne Operations in World War II* (West Lafayette, Ind.: Purdue University Studies, 1962), p. 48.

⁵⁰ Memo, AGF for CofS, 2 Jul 42, sub: Policy re Training of Airborne Troops, 320.1/26 (Inf) (GNTRG) (7–2–42), AG 320.2/3 Airborne, RG 337, NARA.

⁵¹ James M. Gavin, *On to Berlin: Battle of an Airborne Commander, 1943–1946* (New York: Viking Press, 1978), p. 3; Memo, AGF for TAG, 29 Jul 42, sub: Airborne Division, 320.2/10 (AB Cmd) (R) GNGCT/06440 (7–29–42), AG 320.2 (7–29–42), RG 407, NARA.

⁵² Ltr, AGF to CG, Third Army, 30 Jul 42, sub: Activation of 82d and 101st Airborne Divisions, 30 Jul 42, 320.2/9 AB Cmd (R)-GNGCT (7–30–42), (see amendments and revisions of this letter in the files of 82d and 101st Airborne Divisions), DAMH-HSO; *The Airborne Command and Center*, p. 21.

⁵³ T/O 71, Airborne Division, 15 Oct 1942.

⁵⁴ Ltr, AGF to CG, Airborne Command, 4 Jul 42, sub: Activation of HHC, 1st Parachute Infantry Brigade, AGF file, DAMH-HSO; Memo, AGF to CofS, 21 Nov 42, sub: Tactical Airborne Infantry Brigades, 320.2 (Airborne)(R) GNGCT (11–21–42), and Memo, G–3 for CofS, 14 Dec 42, same subject, WDCGT 320.2 Activ (11–21–42), 320.2 (11–21–42), RG 407, NARA.

⁵⁵ A troop basis was the list of military units and individuals required for the performance of a particular mission, by numbers, organization, equipment, deployment, and types of personnel.

⁵⁶ Kreidberg and Henry, *Mobilization*, pp. 625–26; Greenfield et al., *The Organization of Ground Combat Troops*, pp. 164–84.

⁵⁷ Memo, G–3 for JAG, 8 Jan 42, sub: Entry of Organized Reserves into active Federal service, G–3/6457–404, Memo, JAG for G–3, 12 Jan 42, same subject, 210.455, Military Affairs, and Memo, G–3 for CofS, 14 Jan 42, same subject, G–3/6457–404, all Reference Paper file, Army Reserve, DAMH-HSO; WD Bull 7, 1942.

⁵⁸ Memo, AWC for ACofS, G–3, 30 Dec 41, sub: Order of divisions, and Memo, G–3 for CofS, 17 Jan 42, sub: Order of activation of Reserve Divisions, G–3/6457–435, Reference Paper files, Army Reserve, DAMH-HSO.

⁵⁹ Ltr, TAG to CG, All Corps Areas and Department 30 Jan 42, sub: Reorganization of Organized Reserve (less Army Air Force units), AG–320.2 OR (1–22–42) MR-M-C; GO 15, First Corps Area, 12 Feb 42; Ltr, Second Corps Area to Executive Offices, First, Second, and Third Military Areas, 20 Feb 42; sub: Reorganization of the Organized Reserves (less Army Air Force units); GO 17, Third Corps Area, 12 Feb 42; Ltr, Fourth Corps Area to Commanding Officers all Posts and Stations, 13 Feb 42, sub: Reorganization of Units of the Army Reserves (less Army Air

Force units), Fourth Corps Area; Ltr, Fifth Corps Area to TAG, 23 Feb 42, sub: Reorganization of the Organized Reserves (less Army Air Force Units); Ltr, Sixth Corps Area to TAG, Reorganization of the Organized Reserves, 31 Mar 42, sub: Reorganization of the Organized Reserves; Ltr, Seventh Corps Area to TAG, 22 Feb 42, sub: Reorganization of the Organized Reserves (less Army Air Force Units); GO 2, First Military District, 1942, GO 27, Second Military District, 1942, GO 11, Third Military District, 1942, Eighth Corps Area; 1st Ind, Ninth Corps Area to TAG to Ltr, TAG to CG, All Corps Areas and Department, 30 Jan 42, sub: Reorganization of Organized Reserve (less Army Air Force units), all Reference Paper files, Army Reserve, DAMH-HSO.

60 Historical Data Cards, Reserve Divisions, DAMH-HSO; Robert R. Palmer, Bell I. Wiley, and William R. Keast, *The Procurement and Training of Ground Combat Troops*, United States Army in World War II (Washington, D.C.: Government Printing Office, 1948), pp. 434–41.

61 Lee, *The Employment of Negro Troops*, pp. 128, 407, 424; MacGregor, *Integration of the Armed Forces*, pp. 32–33. Also see unit files of the 92d and 93d Infantry Divisions in DAMH-HSO.

62 See unit files for the 6th through 14th Armored Divisions in DAMH-HSO.

63 Ltr, AGF to Brig Gen H. R. Bull, 5 May 42, sub: Cavalry Organization, 320.2/51 (Cav-GNTHG) (5–5–42), and Memo, SW for the Under Secretary of War, 21 Jul 42, AGF 321 Cavalry, RG 337, NARA; Ltr, AGF to CG, Second Army and Chief of the Armored Force, 3 Jun 42, sub: Activation of the 9th and 10th Armored Divisions, 320.2 (Armd Force) (R)-GNOPN (6–3–42); also AGF letters, same subject, 4 and 11 Jul 42, 9th Armd Div file, DAMH-HSO; Ltr, TAG to CG, Task Force "A," 7 Sep 42, sub: Assignment of Units to Task Force "A," AG 320.2 (9–7–42) MR-M-GN, AG Reference files, DAMH-HSO.

64 Ltr, TAG to CG, Fourth Army, 18 Nov 42, sub: Reorganization of the 7th Infantry Division, AG 320.2 (10–15–41) MR-R-C, 7th Inf Div file, DAMH-HSO; Memo, G–3 for TAG, same subject, 28 Jan 42, G–3/43930, AG 320.2 (1–28–42), RG 407, NARA; Ltr, CG, Seventh Corps Area to TAG, 24 Mar 42, sub: Designation of the 6th Infantry Division, MRD 320.2 Designation, 24 Mar 42, 6th Inf Div file, DAMH-HSO; Ltr, TAG to CGs, First, Second, and Fourth Armies, 8 Jan 42, sub: Equipment for Motorized Division, AG 320.2 (1–6–42) MR-M-C, Ltr, TAG to CGs, First and Second Armies, 27 Nov 41, sub: Motorization of Regular Army Division, AG 320.2 (11–14–41), Ltr, TAG to CGs Eastern and Western Defense Commands and Second Army, 9 Apr 42, sub: Redesignation of Infantry Divisions, AG 320.2 (4–2–42) MR-R-GN, and Ltr, AGF to CGs, Second and Third Armies, 7 Aug 42, sub: Armored and Motorized Divisions, 320.2/53 (R)-GNGCT (8–7–42), all AG Reference files, DAMH-HSO; GO 14, 4th Motorized Division, 1942, RG 407, NARA.

# CHAPTER 7

# The Crucible—Combat

*When Admiral Doenitz surrendered the German Government, every American division was in the operational theaters. All but two had seen action; one had the mission of securing the vital installations in the Hawaiian Islands; the other was an airborne division in SHAEF Reserve.*

General George C. Marshall[1]

At the end of 1942, with divisions on the offensive in North Africa and the South Pacific, World War II became the crucible in which divisions tested their combat skills. After the attack on Pearl Harbor the Army accelerated mobilization, but only a few divisions were parceled out to meet threats. For almost another year the War Department failed to decide on the ultimate number of divisions needed to fight the war in European and Pacific theaters. Force planners, however, continued to increase the size and number of divisions without regard for the domestic economy. Planners also paid little heed to logistical requirements, especially the means of moving units overseas. When logistical problems came to the fore, their solutions brought about changes in the structure of the divisions. Infantry, armored, and airborne divisions were reorganized; horse cavalry and motorized divisions were eliminated; and experiments with light divisions began. When victory came in Europe, the combat theaters fielded a total of eighty-nine divisions. These units had undergone considerable changes in less than three years.

## *Wartime Reorganization, 1943*

In the late summer and early fall of 1942, while preparing Task Force "A" to participate in Operation TORCH, the invasion of North Africa, trained soldiers were still extremely scarce. To fill the task force, the War Department deferred reorganizing and filling the 97th Infantry Division, the last of the Organized Reserve divisions to enter active military service, and reduced three partially trained divisions to less than 50 percent of their authorized strengths. To avoid stripping divisions again and disturbing their training, the War Department designated the 76th and 78th Infantry Divisions as replacement units to receive, train, and hold men until needed. The divisions served in that capacity from October 1942 to March 1943, when replacement depots took over. Both divisions, refilled, then began their combat training program anew.[2]

In late 1942 the War Department selected the 7th Motorized Division to be part of the assault forces to be used to drive the Japanese from the Aleutian Islands. In spite of growing doubts by Army Ground Forces about the usefulness of fully motorized divisions, the division was chosen because of its high state of readiness. Furthermore, it was located near Fort Ord, California, an amphibious training site, and could conveniently undergo the training required for the operation. On 1 January 1943 the 7th Motorized Division reverted to a standard infantry division.[3]

Besides the shortage of trained manpower, the nation also faced a severe shortage of ships large enough to transport divisions to the combat theaters. For this and other military and political reasons, plans for an early invasion of Europe across the English Channel were postponed. Also, the expansion and deployment of Army Service Forces and Army Air Forces units placed heavy demands on available shipping, while the success of German submarines off the Eastern Seaboard of the United States made that shortage of tonnage even more acute. Finally, the demands of the hard-pressed Pacific theaters put an unprecedented strain on shipping facilities. Therefore, from October 1942 to March 1943 no division departed the United States, and from March to November 1943 only eleven went overseas.[4]

In October 1942, acting to alleviate the growing shipping problem, Marshall directed Army Ground Forces, Army Air Forces, and Army Service Forces to eliminate unnecessary vehicles and excess noncombatants. He sought a 15 percent reduction in personnel and a 20 percent reduction in vehicles. In particular, he deemed the requirements for divisional transportation in the tables of organization and equipment to be extravagant because they represented what division commanders asked for rather than what they actually needed.[5]

To accomplish these objectives, McNair established the Army Ground Forces Reduction Board to review all units under his control. Two principles, streamlining and pooling, guided the work. The former limited a unit to what it needed on a daily basis, while the latter gathered at corps[6] or army levels resources that were believed to be only occasionally required. Pooling was derived from the assumption that a division would be usually assigned to a corps or an army.[7]

After the Reduction Board concluded its work on the infantry division in March 1943, 2,102 officers and enlisted men and 509 vehicles were stripped from the divisional tables of organization. The scalpel slashed most divisional elements. The cuts eliminated 363 men and 56 vehicles from the infantry regiment, with the cannon company deleted entirely. The regiment retained six 105-mm. towed howitzers, which required less shipping space than 75-mm. self-propelled guns, used less gasoline, and did less damage to light bridging. These were placed in the regimental headquarters company. The number of automatic rifles was pruned from 189 to 81, but the introduction of the new 2.36-inch rocket launchers (bazookas) provided powerful antitank and antipillbox resources that required no designated operator in the regiment. Reductions in medical, commu-

# THE CRUCIBLE—COMBAT

*General McNair*

nication, and service personnel accounted for most of the other regimental personnel losses.8

The board carved 475 men and 95 trucks from the division artillery. Firepower did not decline since the number of artillery pieces remained at twelve 155-mm. and thirty-six 105-mm. howitzers. The headquarters and service batteries were combined, and antitank and antiaircraft platoons were eliminated. An antitank capability remained with the addition of 166 bazookas. To save personnel spaces, the number of truck drivers, mechanics, cooks, and orderlies was reduced.9

The board provided for the return of the airplane to the infantry division, a step that reflected the expanded width and depth of the battlefield. The aero squadron had been eliminated from all divisions by 1940, but field artillery officers continued to request their own aircraft to guide counterbattery and indirect fire. In 1941 and 1942 the field artillery experimented with light planes, and on 6 June 1942 two light observation aircraft were added to each field artillery battalion and two to the headquarters of the division artillery. The board's decision formalized these additions.10

Divisional combat support and service support units were severely cut. The engineer battalion and signal company each lost about 100 men, mostly because certain bridging equipment was taken from the engineer battalion and the radio intelligence platoon was detached from the signal company. Both functions moved to army level. The quartermaster company lost about 150 men, but the number of trucks remained approximately the same. No basic changes took place in the medical battalion, ordnance company, or military police platoon.11

The board also believed that the division headquarters and its headquarters company had grown too large. To reduce the size of the headquarters company, its strength was cut almost in half by eliminating the defense platoon and some vehicles, drivers, and orderlies. The band assumed the mission of protecting the divisional headquarters as an additional duty. Divisional staff sections remained the same, but the board cut some assistant staff officers and enlisted men. Total reductions in the division represented a 13.5 percent decrease in all ranks and 23 percent in vehicles.12

Marshall tentatively approved the new division but directed that its tables of organization be sent to the theater commanders for comment. To sell the new structure, General McNair and Maj. Gen. Idwal Edwards, Assistant Chief of Staff, G–3, went to North Africa, where they found no support. The division and corps commanders in the combat zone rejected the cuts on the grounds that the division had already been reduced to the lowest acceptable minimum.13

With shipping and manpower shortages still severe, Edwards' staff prepared another set of tables for the infantry division that was a compromise between the Army Ground Forces proposal and the desires of the overseas division and corps commanders. The new division had 14,253 officers and enlisted men (*Chart 19*). Its combat support and combat service elements remained about the same as those proposed by the Reduction Board. To satisfy division and corps commanders in North Africa, cannon companies were restored to the infantry regiments and service batteries to the field artillery battalions. The 2.36-inch rocket launchers were retained as antitank weapons, but 57-mm. antitank guns replaced the 37-mm. guns. In the division headquarters company the defense platoon reappeared, as did the service platoon in the quartermaster company. Finally, Edwards' staff added a new unit—headquarters, special troops—which provided administrative support to the reconnaissance troop; to the signal, ordnance, and quartermaster companies; and to the military police platoon. As for vehicles, the new compromise organization had 2,012, almost the same as in the 1942 tables.14

In January 1943 the Reduction Board turned its attention to the motorized division concept. Several alternatives had always existed. Since the motorized and infantry divisions had similar organizations, the latter could simply be augmented as needed with 2-1/2-ton trucks, permitting the simultaneous movement of all divisional elements. Another option was to "armorize" the organization by equipping it with tanks, armored personnel carriers, and self-propelled artillery. McNair recommended to the Army Staff the reorganization of all motorized divisions as standard infantry divisions, except for the 4th, which was to be equipped with armored personnel carriers. The staff supported McNair's recommendation.15

On 12 March 1943 the Acting Chief of Staff, General Joseph T. McNarney, approved replacing motorized divisions with infantry divisions. He also approved the activation of additional truck companies organized with black soldiers to motorize the infantry division when necessary. The 4th Motorized Division, however, was to remain intact pending its possible use overseas. Also, the armored division was to be reorganized to achieve a better balance between infantry and armor elements. The following May the 6th, 8th, and 90th Motorized Divisions were reorganized as infantry divisions. Because the revised structure of the infantry division was not settled, the divisions adopted and retrained under the 1942 infantry division tables.16

After the March decision, none of the overseas commanders wanted the 4th Motorized Division because they thought it would make inordinate demands on critical shipping space and the already limited supply of tires and gasoline. The tires for a motorized division's vehicles alone required 318 tons of rubber com-

# CHART 19—Infantry Division, 15 July 1943

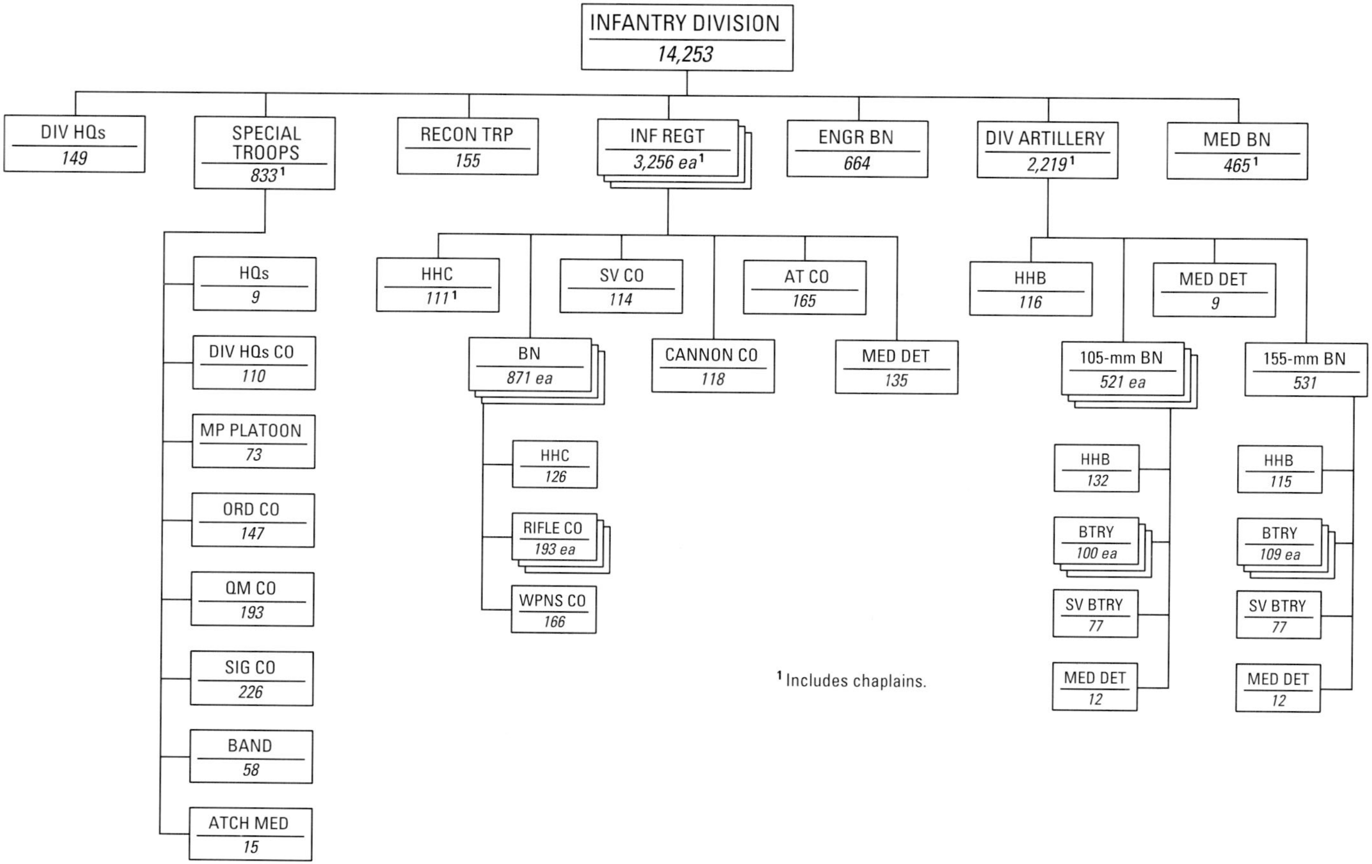

- **INFANTRY DIVISION** — 14,253
  - **DIV HQs** — 149
  - **SPECIAL TROOPS** — 833[1]
    - HQs — 9
    - DIV HQs CO — 110
    - MP PLATOON — 73
    - ORD CO — 147
    - QM CO — 193
    - SIG CO — 226
    - BAND — 58
    - ATCH MED — 15
  - **RECON TRP** — 155
  - **INF REGT** — 3,256 ea[1]
    - HHC — 111[1]
    - BN — 871 ea
      - HHC — 126
      - RIFLE CO — 193 ea
      - WPNS CO — 166
    - SV CO — 114
    - CANNON CO — 118
    - AT CO — 165
    - MED DET — 135
  - **ENGR BN** — 664
  - **DIV ARTILLERY** — 2,219[1]
    - HHB — 116
    - 105-mm BN — 521 ea
      - HHB — 132
      - BTRY — 100 ea
      - SV BTRY — 77
      - MED DET — 12
    - MED DET — 9
    - 155-mm BN — 531
      - HHB — 115
      - BTRY — 109 ea
      - SV BTRY — 77
      - MED DET — 12
  - **MED BN** — 465[1]

[1] Includes chaplains.

pared to 166 tons for those in the infantry division. Besides, the 4th was the only motorized division authorized a full complement of equipment plus additional personnel and equipment to constitute a special task force. Its potential punch in combat, however, did not appear to justify the costs of shipping and logistical support. On 1 August 1943 the 4th reverted to the standard infantry division structure.[17]

The organization of the armored division had been in question for several months because of the imbalance between armor and infantry forces. Some options existed for improvement. Lt. Gen. Jacob L. Devers, Chief of the Armored Force, wanted to obtain a better balance at corps level by having one motorized and two armored divisions in a corps and by "armorizing" the motorized division.[18] McNair believed that the armored division was "so fat there is no place to begin."[19] He wanted either to increase the infantry or reduce the armor in the existing division, changes that would result in a sweeping reorganization of the unit.[20]

Eventually McNair directed the Reduction Board to cut the divisional armor, believing the use of tanks had changed since 1940. Both the British and the Germans had successfully used a division that fielded fewer tanks than the American armored division. The armored division was not free to roam at will, as first envisioned, because of improvements in antitank weapons. McNair saw it as a unit of opportunity to exploit a breakthrough, to take part in a pursuit, or to cover a withdrawal—all former cavalry missions. Therefore, the armored division could be smaller. Furthermore, McNair saw the need for fewer armored divisions in the total force, and with fewer armored divisions more separate tank battalions, which were needed to support infantry divisions, could be organized.[21]

Combat-experienced officers in the North African theater opposed a major reorganization of the armored division. In March 1943 the Fifth Army convened a review board, chaired by Maj. Gen. Ernest N. Harmon, the commander of the 2d Armored Division. The board recommended retention of the existing division structure with the addition of more infantry and the assignment of tank destroyer and antiaircraft artillery battalions. To simplify logistical and maintenance operations, the board wanted to reduce the types of vehicles within the division, recommending that motorcycles and amphibious trucks be replaced with 1/4-ton trucks and that obsolete tanks be removed. Since the 1st Armored Division had been used in piecemeal fashion on the Tunisian front and the 2d Armored Division was the only such division to gain experience as a divisional organization, the board believed that a major reorganization of the armored division was premature.[22]

After months of study and discussion, the War Department rejected the field recommendations and on 15 September 1943 published new armored division tables of organization that followed McNair's ideas (*Chart 20*). Three tank and three armored infantry battalions replaced the armored and infantry regiments. Each tank battalion included one light and three medium tank companies, and the armored infantry battalion had three line companies. For self-sufficiency, infantry and tank battalions each had a service company that assumed many of the functions of the former regimental headquarters and service companies and rendered some maintenance. No basic change took place in the division's three field artillery battalions but, as in the infantry division, the tables provided for liaison aircraft for that arm. The results reduced the variety of vehicles. No additional organic antitank or antiaircraft artillery battalions were included, for Army Ground Forces believed that the divisions had sufficient antitank and antiaircraft resources within their infantry, armor, and field artillery units. Besides, the command felt the divisions could obtain additional antitank and antiaircraft artillery resources from pools of such units at higher echelons.23

The armored division continued to field two combat commands as task force headquarters, which were to be used to build flexible fighting teams of armor, infantry, and artillery with support appropriate for the tactical requirements. A brigadier general led one command and a colonel the other. The Reduction Board gave no explanation for this curious rank arrangement. Undoubtedly one of the billets permitted the assignment of a second general officer to the division to replace the assistant division commander, whose slot had been eliminated. The reserve command, a new organization led by an infantry colonel with a small staff, served to clarify command and control in the division's rear area. In the past the reserve commander had been the senior officer among those units.24

The tables made substantial changes in the armored division's combat support and combat service support arena. The engineer battalion lost its bridge company (higher headquarters were to supply bridging equipment) and the number of engineer line companies fell from four to three. To compensate for the removal of reconnaissance elements from tank and infantry units, the reconnaissance squadron included a troop for each of the combat commands. In addition, the squadron had two reconnaissance troops for divisional missions, an assault gun troop of four platoons (one for each reconnaissance troop), and a light tank company. The division trains comprised only medical and maintenance battalions, the supply battalion having been eliminated. Each unit was made responsible for its own resupply. Also, the divisional supply company was discarded and its functions divided between the headquarters company of the division and the headquarters company of the trains. These changes pared the division's strength from 14,630 men to 10,937, slashed the number of tanks from 360 to 263, reduced the variety of vehicles to ease repair problems, and eliminated the maintenance-prone motorcycles.25

The War Department on 16 October 1943 summarized why the reorganizing of divisions and other units was necessary in Circular 256. It cited the need to secure the maximum use of available manpower, to permit transport overseas of the maximum amount of fighting power, and to provide greater flexibility in organization in keeping with the principle of economy of force and massing of military strength at the decisive point. In addition, the reorganization was to reduce headquarters and other noncombatants in order that command function

CHART 20—Armored Division, 15 September 1943

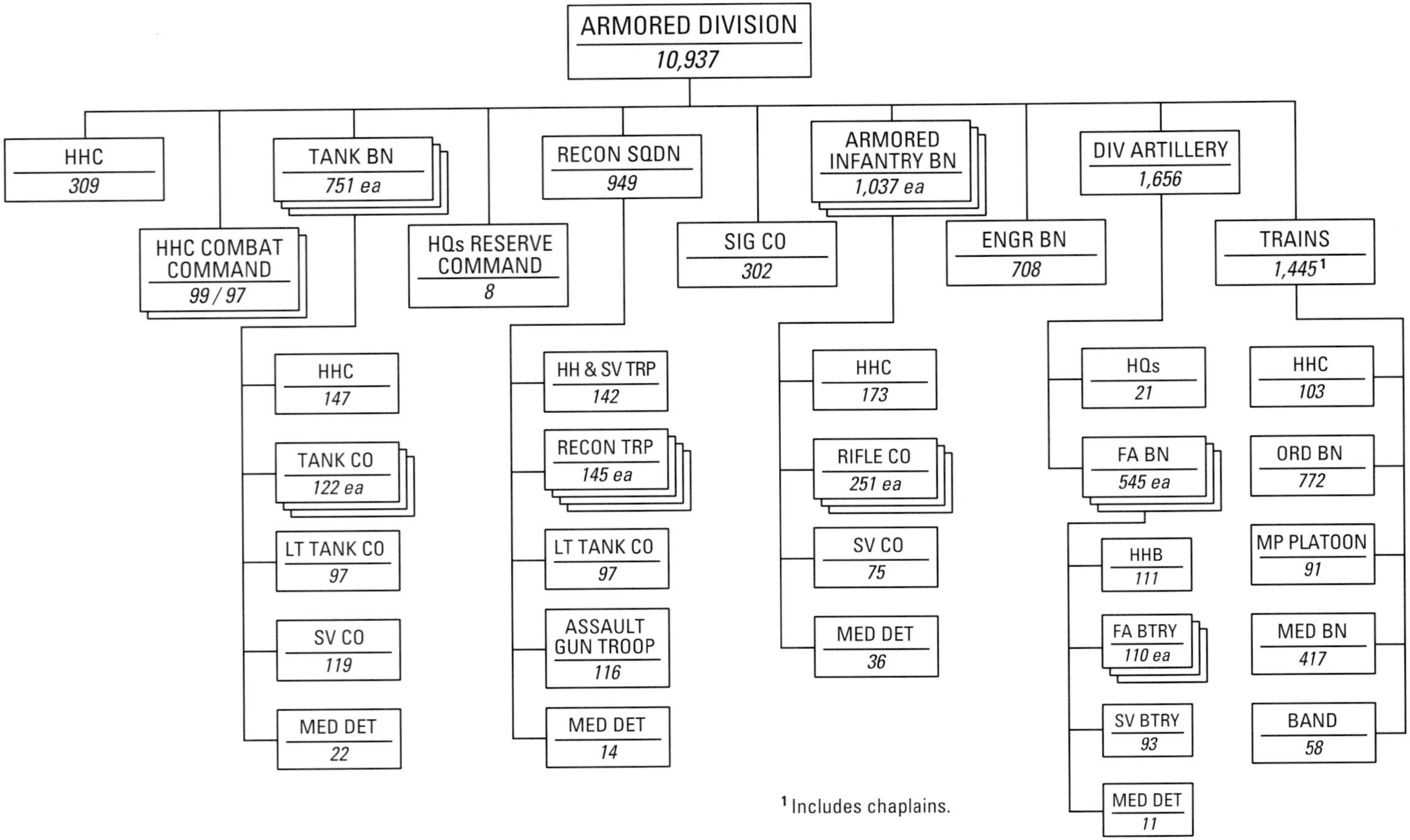

- ARMORED DIVISION — 10,937
  - HHC — 309
  - HHC COMBAT COMMAND — 99 / 97
  - TANK BN — 751 ea
    - HHC — 147
    - TANK CO — 122 ea
    - LT TANK CO — 97
    - SV CO — 119
    - MED DET — 22
  - HQs RESERVE COMMAND — 8
  - RECON SQDN — 949
    - HH & SV TRP — 142
    - RECON TRP — 145 ea
    - LT TANK CO — 97
    - ASSAULT GUN TROOP — 116
    - MED DET — 14
  - SIG CO — 302
  - ARMORED INFANTRY BN — 1,037 ea
    - HHC — 173
    - RIFLE CO — 251 ea
    - SV CO — 75
    - MED DET — 36
  - ENGR BN — 708
  - DIV ARTILLERY — 1,656
    - HQs — 21
    - FA BN — 545 ea
      - HHB — 111
      - FA BTRY — 110 ea
      - SV BTRY — 93
      - MED DET — 11
  - TRAINS — 1,445[1]
    - HHC — 103
    - ORD BN — 772
    - MP PLATOON — 91
    - MED BN — 417
    - BAND — 58

[1] Includes chaplains.

might keep pace with modern communication and transport facilities and to provide commanders with the greatest possible amount of offensive power through reduction in passive defensive elements.26

Reorganization of infantry and armored divisions began shortly after publication of the new tables. Infantry and armored divisions, including those most recently activated in the United States, adopted the new organizations between 1 August and 11 November 1943. Overseas commands reorganized their infantry divisions as soon as possible but had the authority to delay the changes if units were under alert, warning, or movement orders or if they were engaged in maneuvers or active operations against an enemy. The divisions needed time to retrain. Except for the 3d and 34th Infantry Divisions, the eight infantry divisions in the European and Mediterranean theaters were reorganized by the beginning of the new year. The 34th came under the tables immediately prior to its participation in the Anzio campaign in March 1944 and the 3d after Rome fell in June. Of the twelve infantry divisions in the Pacific theater, eight were converted by the beginning of 1944 and the remaining four by the following August.27

Reorganization of the three overseas armored divisions followed a somewhat different course. The 1st Armored Division adopted the new structure while in a rest and training area in Italy in 1944. The 2d and 3d Armored Divisions retained the 1942 configuration throughout the war. During the fall of 1943 the commander of the European Theater of Operations, General Devers, who had been a leading spokesman for the heavy armored division decided that the war was too advanced to permit changes in those units.28

When the divisions in the Pacific adopted the new tables, MacArthur restructured the Americal Division to conform to other infantry divisions. On 1 May 1943 he placed it under the tables prepared by the Reduction Board, the only division to use them, but in September it was reorganized under the 15 July structure. Because of the unit's widely acclaimed combat record, which included a Presidential Citation (Navy) for its elements' service on Guadalcanal, the War Department retained its name rather than give it a numerical designation.29

## *Light Divisions*

Early in 1943 Army Ground Forces developed a new type of unit, the light division, which the Operations Division of the Army Staff had suggested earlier as a possibility for the Pacific theater. Planners thought such a division could function in a variety of combat conditions, such as jungles and mountains, simply by varying the unit's mode of transportation. Initially, McNair, who disliked special units, opposed the idea because of the unique training it required. Given the shortage of shipping in the fall of that year, the Operations Division again put forth the proposal. By this time planners had extended the idea to include amphibious operations. When preparing for the invasion of North Africa, the Solomon Islands, and New Guinea, infantry divisions had to be reorganized, reequipped, and retrained to make assault landings. In addition, a light division structure also seemed appropriate for the airborne division.[30]

On 17 January 1943 McNair appointed Col. Michael Buckley from the Army Ground Forces G–3 section as chairman of a committee assigned the task of developing a structure for light units using pack animals or light trucks. The committee's report called for a 9,000-man triangular infantry division (*Chart 21*) with two types of field artillery and quartermaster units. The pack division had over 1,700 animals, most of which were mules for the field artillery and quartermaster units, while the truck division had only 267 1/4-ton trucks and 200 1/4-ton trailers. Both divisions were also authorized numerous handcarts.[31]

General McNarney, the Deputy Chief of Staff, decided to test these organizations and on 21 June approved the formation of three rather than two light divisions. One was to be truck, another pack, and the third a modified pack. The modified pack division's men and units were to be equipped with skis, snowshoes, toboggans, and cargo sleds. Because of the growing number of troops undergoing special winter training at Camp Hale, Colorado, Army Ground Forces suggested they be organized under a divisional structure. The adjutant general added the 10th and 71st Light Divisions to the rolls. On 15 July 1943 Brig. Gen. Robert L. Spragin, a veteran of the Guadalcanal campaign, assumed command of the 71st at Camp Carson, Colorado, and Maj. Gen. Lloyd E. Jones, former commander of the U.S. Army Forces at Amchitka, Alaska, took over the 10th at Camp Hale. The 71st was built around the 5th and 14th Infantry, regiments that had served in the jungles of Panama. The 10th was based on the 86th Infantry and other units at Camp Hale that were undergoing winter warfare training. Eventually the 87th Infantry, which had served in Alaska, joined the 10th. The 89th Infantry Division at Camp Carson supplied fillers for both divisions. On 1 August 1943 the 89th itself was reorganized and redesignated as the 89th Light (Pack) Division. Neither light amphibious nor light airborne divisions were organized because the War Department opposed any change in the existing airborne division and the Southwest Pacific Area Command lacked confidence in the light amphibious concept, preferring standard infantry divisions for amphibious operations.[32]

Army leaders quickly noted some major problems in the light divisions during their training. Neither the 71st Light (Truck) nor 89th Light (Pack) Division included adequate infantry staying power; the 1/4-ton trucks lacked suitable mobility on wet, mountainous, makeshift roads; the 75-mm. pack howitzer provided inadequate firepower; the division lacked reconnaissance resources and had insufficient engineer and medical capabilities; and the division staff was unable to operate twenty-four hours a day within the authorized assigned personnel. The divisions were not self-sustaining. Maj. Gen. John Millikin, who tested the divisions in maneuvers, recommended, "That unless a definite need for these types of divisions can be foreseen, the present Light divisions (motor and pack) [should] be returned to a standard division status."[33] No need seemed to exist for the divisions, and even the Southwest Pacific Area, the command for which they were originally designed,

# CHART 21—Light Division, 1943

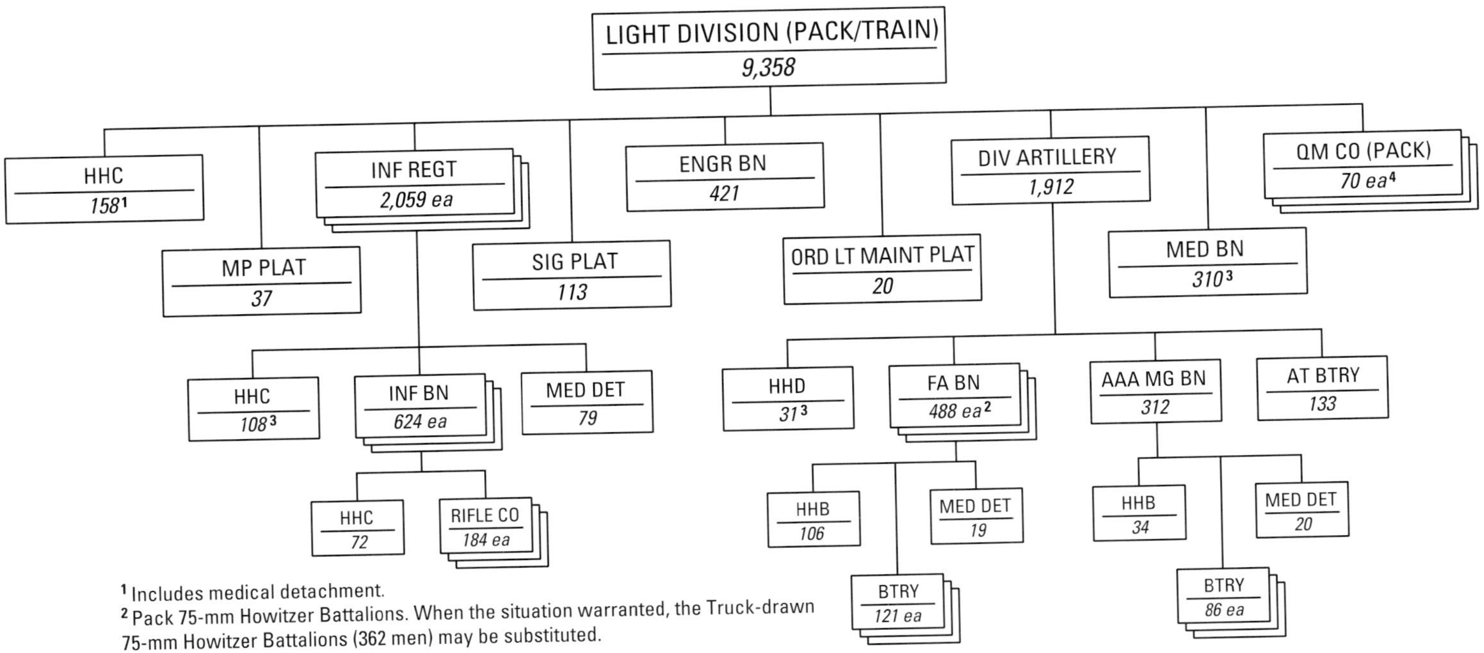

- **LIGHT DIVISION (PACK/TRAIN)** — 9,358
  - **HHC** — 158[1]
  - **MP PLAT** — 37
  - **INF REGT** — 2,059 ea
    - **HHC** — 108[3]
    - **SIG PLAT** — 113
    - **MED DET** — 79
    - **INF BN** — 624 ea
      - **HHC** — 72
      - **RIFLE CO** — 184 ea
  - **ENGR BN** — 421
  - **ORD LT MAINT PLAT** — 20
  - **DIV ARTILLERY** — 1,912
    - **HHD** — 31[3]
    - **FA BN** — 488 ea[2]
      - **HHB** — 106
      - **BTRY** — 121 ea
      - **MED DET** — 19
    - **AAA MG BN** — 312
      - **HHB** — 34
      - **BTRY** — 86 ea
    - **AT BTRY** — 133
  - **MED BN** — 310[3]
    - **MED DET** — 20
  - **QM CO (PACK)** — 70 ea[4]

[1] Includes medical detachment.
[2] Pack 75-mm Howitzer Battalions. When the situation warranted, the Truck-drawn 75-mm Howitzer Battalions (362 men) may be substituted.
[3] Includes chaplains.
[4] QM Truck Company (209 men) may be substituted for the 3 QM Pack Companies.

wanted nothing to do with them. Army Ground Forces therefore reorganized the 71st and 89th Divisions in May 1944 as standard infantry divisions.34

The 10th Light (Alpine) Division proved unsatisfactory for many of the same reasons as the truck and pack units. Marshall, however, wanted it reorganized and retained in the force because of its mountain warfare skills. Eventually Army Ground Forces recommended the addition of three weapons companies to each of the division's infantry regiments; an increase in the size of the engineer, signal, and medical elements; and the provision of mule transport for all combat elements. In November 1944 the War Department published tables of organization and equipment reflecting these changes, which gave the division 14,101 officers and enlisted men and 6,152 animals. The same month, the 10th Light Division became the 10th Mountain Division, and in December it moved to the Mediterranean theater. The division went overseas without animals, receiving them from remount stations in the theater before going into combat.35

## *Expanding Divisional Forces: Meeting the Troop Basis*

While Army Ground Forces and General Staff officers revised divisional organizations, the number of divisions expanded and a final determination was made regarding the total number needed. Army Ground Forces organized the last reserve infantry division, the 97th, in February 1943. By August 1943 it had also activated as a part of the Army of United States the 42d, 63d, 65th, 66th, 69th, 70th, 75th, and 106th Infantry Divisions; the 16th and 20th Armored Divisions; and the 11th, 13th, and 17th Airborne Divisions (*Table 14*).36

The 42d was a unique unit, for it was a reconstitution of the World War I "Rainbow Division." Except for the division headquarters, none of its earlier elements were returned, but Army Ground Forces filled its new units with personnel from every state. To emphasize the division's tie to its World War I predecessor, Maj. Gen. Harry J. Collins, the commander, activated the unit on 14 July, the eve of the twenty-fifth anniversary of the Champagne-Marne campaign in France during which the "Rainbow" had helped to stem a German drive on Paris.37

In addition to activating more airborne divisions in 1943, the War Department made changes in the airborne brigade force. To emphasize both the parachute and the glider training missions, the 1st Airborne Infantry Brigade replaced the 1st Parachute Infantry Brigade as a training unit. The Airborne Command also formed the 2d Airborne Infantry Brigade that year to help in training. The 1st Brigade existed for approximately seven months and was disbanded after most nondivisional airborne units had gone overseas. In the fall of 1943 the 2d Brigade deployed to Europe where it continued to support airborne training.38

The need for the cavalry division remained questionable. Because Secretary of War Henry L. Stimson had insisted on maintaining large horse units, Army Ground Forces replaced the organizations withdrawn from the 1st Cavalry Division for the North African campaign and reactivated the 2d Cavalry Division early in 1943 as an all-black unit split between Camp Clark, Texas, and Camp Lockett, California.[39]

Deployment of cavalry divisions, however, proved to be a thorny problem. The units remained unpopular with theater commanders because of the shipping space they required and the logistical nightmare they presented, given their horses and equipment. The need for units in the Southwest Pacific Area, however, led MacArthur to accept the 1st Cavalry Division as a dismounted unit. The division turned in its horses and associated gear in March 1943 and left for Australia in June. Many of the horses of the 1st Cavalry Division found a home in the 2d Cavalry Division.[40]

*Maj. Gen. Elbridge G. Chapman and General McNair inspect the 13th Airborne Division, 13 May 1944.*

In Australia the division was reorganized partly under infantry and partly under cavalry tables. Each cavalry squadron was allotted a heavy weapons troop similar to the weapons company in the infantry battalion. The veterinary troop in the medical squadron became a collecting troop, and the reconnaissance squadron was reduced to a troop similar to the unit in the infantry division. Some of the personnel and equipment of the reconnaissance squadron were used to create a light tank company. The addition of a 105-mm. howitzer battalion gave the artillery two 105-mm. and two 75-mm. howitzer battalions. Along with the reorganization, the adjutant general redesignated the unit as the 1st Cavalry Division, Special, because of its unique organization under infantry and cavalry tables and the desire to retain the cavalry "name" among the divisional forces. Having completed all changes by 4 December 1943, the division moved to New Guinea for combat. More organizational changes took place thereafter, particularly in the artillery, which eventually included four tractor-drawn 105-mm. howitzer battalions and an attached 155-mm. howitzer battalion.[41]

Personnel shortages dictated a different fate for the 2d Cavalry Division and the 56th Cavalry Brigade. The Mediterranean theater needed service troops, and in September 1943 the War Department decided to use the personnel of the 2d Cavalry Division in that role. Leaving the country in February 1944, the division was inactivated shortly thereafter in North Africa and its men reassigned to a variety of service units. Army Ground Forces eliminated the 56th Cavalry Brigade when no use for it developed overseas. Its headquarters troop became the

## TABLE 14
### Divisions Activated in 1943

| Component | Division | Date | Location |
|---|---|---|---|
| RA | 2d Cavalry | 25 February | Fort Clark, Tex. |
| AUS | 11th Airborne | 25 February | Camp Mackall, N.C. |
| OR | 97th Infantry | 25 February | Camp Swift, Tex. |
| AUS | 20th Armored | 15 March | Camp Campbell, Ky. |
| AUS | 106th Infantry | 15 March | Fort Jackson, S.C. |
| AUS | 17th Airborne | 15 April | Camp Mackall, N.C. |
| AUS | 66th Infantry | 15 April | Camp Blanding, Fla. |
| AUS | 75th Infantry | 15 April | Fort Leonard Wood, Mo. |
| AUS | 69th Infantry | 15 May | Camp Shelby, Miss. |
| AUS | 63d Infantry | 15 June | Camp Blanding, Fla. |
| AUS | 70th Infantry | 15 June | Camp Adair, Oreg. |
| AUS | 42d Infantry | 14 July | Camp Gruber, Okla. |
| AUS | 10th Light | 15 July | Camp Hale, Colo. |
| AUS | 16th Armored | 15 July | Camp Chaffee, Ark. |
| AUS | 71st Light | 15 July | Fort Benning, Ga. |
| AUS | 13th Airborne | 13 August | Fort Bragg, N.C. |
| AUS | 65th Infantry | 16 August | Camp Shelby, Miss. |

56th Cavalry Reconnaissance Troop, Mechanized, but did not see combat. The former brigade's cavalry regiments went on to fight in the Pacific and China-Burma-India theaters.[42]

With ongoing manpower shortages, the Army continually examined the relationship between the total military force and the manpower pool available for military service. That relationship was constantly balanced against the manpower required to maintain the productive capacity of industry, which remained vital to the overall Allied war effort. As the war progressed, staff studies suggested that the number of divisions mobilized could be cut. Soviet armies had checked the German advance, and it appeared that the Allies would gain air superiority over Europe. Therefore, shortly before the invasion of northern France in 1944, the War Department approved a troop basis that contained 90 divisions rather than 100 within a total Army strength of 7,700,000. The French were to raise ten divisions, and the United States was to equip them, which created equipment shortages. That troop basis called for 1 light, 2 cavalry, 5 airborne, 16 armored, and 66 infantry divisions. With the inactivation of the 2d Cavalry Division in May 1944, the number of divisions in the troop basis was reduced by one and the number of divisions raised during World War II remained at eighty-nine. The decision to limit the number of divisions haunted War Department planners during the remainder of the war for they feared that mobilization had not gone far enough. Marshall, however, held to the eighty-nine divisions in the troop basis.[43]

## Deployment and More Organizational Changes

Although the Army began deploying divisions shortly after the nation entered the war, the number of trained and partially trained divisions still located within the United States mounted in 1943 because of port and shipping problems. Unlike World War I, no troops were to be sent to foreign stations unless the War Department could guarantee their supply. In August 1943 sixty divisions were at various stages of readiness in the United States.[44]

Toward the end of 1943 the deployment picture brightened. With the nation's massive ship-building program and the retreat of German submarines from the western Atlantic, the War Department was able to accelerate the deployment of divisions. Most went to Europe to take part in the cross-Channel attack and the drive to strike at the German heartland. Eventually 68 divisions—47 infantry, 16 armored, 4 airborne, and 1 mountain—fought in Europe and 21 divisions—1 airborne, 1 cavalry (organized as infantry), and 19 infantry—in the Pacific area. (*Tables 15 and 16* give the date that each division moved to the port of embarkation.) No division remained in the continental United States after February 1945.[45]

Although most infantry and armored divisions had been reorganized prior to seeing combat because of the delay in moving them overseas, the Army reorganized its airborne divisions to meet specific combat needs. The first modification, involving only the 82d, took place during the preparation for the Sicilian campaign. Because of a shortage of shipping space for gliders, a crated glider being one of the largest pieces of equipment sent overseas, a parachute infantry regiment replaced one of the glider regiments, and a second parachute field artillery battalion was added. The change was in keeping with the original plan for the division, which envisioned a task force organization.[46]

After the Sicily campaign, General Ridgway, the commander of the "All American" 82d, organized a small pathfinder team to help divisional elements reach their targets. The team's mission was to jump into the assault area and guide the remainder of the division to the drop zone. After the team proved successful in Italy, other airborne divisions organized similar units.[47]

Combat operations soon demonstrated that the airborne division lacked sufficient manpower and equipment for sustained operations. In Sicily and Italy resources were not available to relieve or replace the division with either an infantry or armored division as quickly as planners had envisioned. In December 1943 Ridgway recommended changes in the airborne division to correct major deficiencies. Because it served primarily as infantry, he wanted more transportation resources; additional medical, engineer, and quartermaster support; and greater infantry and artillery firepower. Planners in Washington opposed the changes because they thought the additional equipment and personnel would prevent the division from serving as a light, mobile force, stripped to the bare essentials and easily air transportable.[48]

TABLE 15

Deployment of Divisions to the Pacific Theater

| Division | Date |
|---|---|
| 1st Cavalry | June 1943 |
| 6th Infantry | July 1943 |
| 7th Infantry | April 1943 |
| 11th Airborne | April 1944 |
| 24th Infantry | * |
| 25th Infantry | * |
| 27th Infantry | March 1942 |
| 31st Infantry | February 1944 |
| 32d Infantry | April 1942 |
| 33d Infantry | June 1943 |
| 37th Infantry | May 1942 |
| 38th Infantry | December 1943 |
| 40th Infantry | August 1942 |
| 41st Infantry | March 1942 |
| 43d Infantry | September 1942 |
| 77th Infantry | March 1944 |
| 81st Infantry | June 1944 |
| 93d Infantry | January 1944 |
| 96th Infantry | July 1944 |
| 98th Infantry | April 1944 |
| Americal | * |
| Philippine | # |

* Unit organized outside the continental United States.
#Partially organized in 1941; surrendered in April 1942.

After the assault landings by the 82d and 101st in Holland in 1944, Ridgway again attempted to revise the authorized structure of the divisions. The 82d had an additional 4,000 troops attached in the Normandy jump and over 5,000 for its operations in Holland. The 101st had also been augmented for both operations. Frustrated with the bureaucracy, Ridgway, then commanding the XVIII Airborne Corps, appealed personally to General Marshall for aid in reorganizing the divisions. Marshall directed his staff to reconsider their structure and invited Ridgway or his representative to Washington to explain his ideas. Instead of coming himself, Ridgway sent Maj. Gen. Maxwell D. Taylor, the 101st's commander. On the day the German Ardennes offensive began, the War Department published new tables of organization and equipment for the airborne division. Marshall described it to Ridgway as "in all probability wholly acceptable to you and your associates."[49]

The new airborne division consisted of one glider infantry and two parachute infantry regiments, division artillery, antiaircraft artillery and engineer battalions,

## TABLE 16
## Deployment of Divisions to the European Theater

| Division | Date | Division | Date |
|---|---|---|---|
| 1st Armored | May 1942 | 42d Infantry | November 1944 |
| 1st Infantry | June 1942 | 44th Infantry | August 1944 |
| 2d Armored | September 1942 | 45th Infantry | May 1943 |
| 2d Cavalry | February 1944 | 63d Infantry | November 1944 |
| 2d Infantry | September 1943 | 65th Infantry | December 1944 |
| 3d Armored | September 1943 | 66th Infantry | November 1944 |
| 3d Infantry | September 1942 | 69th Infantry | November 1944 |
| 4th Armored | December 1943 | 70th Infantry | November 1944 |
| 4th Infantry | January 1944 | 71st Infantry | January 1945 |
| 5th Armored | February 1944 | 75th Infantry | October 1944 |
| 5th Infantry | April 1942 | 76th Infantry | November 1944 |
| 6th Armored | February 1944 | 78th Infantry | October 1944 |
| 7th Armored | May 1944 | 79th Infantry | March 1944 |
| 8th Armored | October 1944 | 80th Infantry | June 1944 |
| 8th Infantry | November 1943 | 82d Airborne | April 1943 |
| 9th Armored | August 1944 | 83d Infantry | March 1944 |
| 9th Infantry | September 1942 | 84th Infantry | September 1944 |
| 10th Armored | September 1944 | 85th Infantry | December 1943 |
| 10th Mountain | December 1944 | 86th Infantry | February 1945 |
| 11th Armored | September 1944 | 87th Infantry | October 1944 |
| 12th Armored | September 1944 | 88th Infantry | November 1943 |
| 13th Airborne | January 1945 | 89th Infantry | January 1945 |
| 13th Armored | January 1945 | 90th Infantry | March 1944 |
| 14th Armored | October 1944 | 91st Infantry | March 1944 |
| 16th Armored | January 1945 | 92d Infantry | September 1944 |
| 17th Airborne | August 1944 | 94th Infantry | July 1944 |
| 20th Armored | January 1944 | 95th Infantry | July 1944 |
| 26th Infantry | August 1944 | 97th Infantry | February 1945 |
| 28th Infantry | September 1943 | 99th Infantry | September 1944 |
| 29th Infantry | September 1942 | 100th Infantry | September 1944 |
| 30th Infantry | January 1944 | 101st Airborne | August 1943 |
| 34th Infantry | January 1942 | 102d Infantry | September 1944 |
| 35th Infantry | May 1944 | 103d Infantry | September 1944 |
| 36th Infantry | April 1943 | 104th Infantry | August 1944 |
|  |  | 106th Infantry | October 1944 |

medical and parachute maintenance companies, and special troops, to which the division headquarters, ordnance, and quartermaster companies; military police and reconnaissance platoons; band; and medical detachment reported (*Chart 22*). The tables reversed the proportion of parachute and glider infantry regiments and considerably strengthened the units. The glider infantry regiment was authorized a third battalion and an antitank company, and both types of regiments fielded heavier weapons. In the engineer battalion the number of parachute and glider companies was also reversed. The four battalions in the division artillery, both parachute and glider units, were authorized 75-mm. pack howitzers, but a note on the tables indicated that one glider artillery battalion could be equipped with 105-mm. howitzers if more firepower was necessary. As in the other divisions, the field artillery was authorized observation and liaison aircraft. The number of trucks jumped from 400 to 1,000, and the authorized strength soared to 12,979. Approximately 50 percent of the men were parachutists.[50]

To adopt the new structure, the overseas commands were forced to rely on their own resources because the War Department made no additional men available. Existing nondivisional parachute infantry and field artillery units were assigned to the airborne divisions, and other units, including 2d Airborne Infantry Brigade headquarters, were disbanded to obtain personnel. In March 1945 the European Command reorganized the 13th, 17th, 82d, and 101st Airborne Divisions. The 11th Airborne Division in the Pacific was reorganized in July but, unlike the European divisions, the unit was authorized two 105-mm. howitzer glider battalions in place of two 75-mm. pack units, and one glider infantry regiment was converted to parachute infantry. Throughout the war Maj. Gen. Joseph Swing, the 11th's commander, had insisted upon cross-training glider and parachute troops. Only the 17th Airborne Division participated in an assault landing after the reorganization; all others served as infantry for the remainder of the war.[51]

Combat experience also led to alterations in both the infantry and armored divisions after the 1943 revision. The most significant change took place in the armored division, where the small headquarters of the division artillery command was expanded to a headquarters and headquarters battery, providing the division with a fire direction center. Because of the many minor changes, the War Department published new tables for both types of divisions in January 1945, incorporating all the changes since 1943. At that time the strength of the infantry division stood at 14,037 and the armored division at 10,700.[52]

## *Correcting Organizational Problems*

Neither infantry nor armored divisions proved to be completely satisfactory during combat because they lacked all the resources habitually needed to operate efficiently. In the European theater, when an infantry division conducted offensive operations it almost always had attached tank, tank destroyer, and antiaircraft artillery battalions. Because of the shortage of tank and tank destroyer units, these units were not available to serve regularly with the same division, resulting in considerable shuffling of attached units, which diminished effective teamwork. The cannon company in the infantry regiment was hampered by the limited cross-country ability of the 105-mm. howitzer's prime mover. Often tied to the division

# CHART 22—Airborne Division, 1944

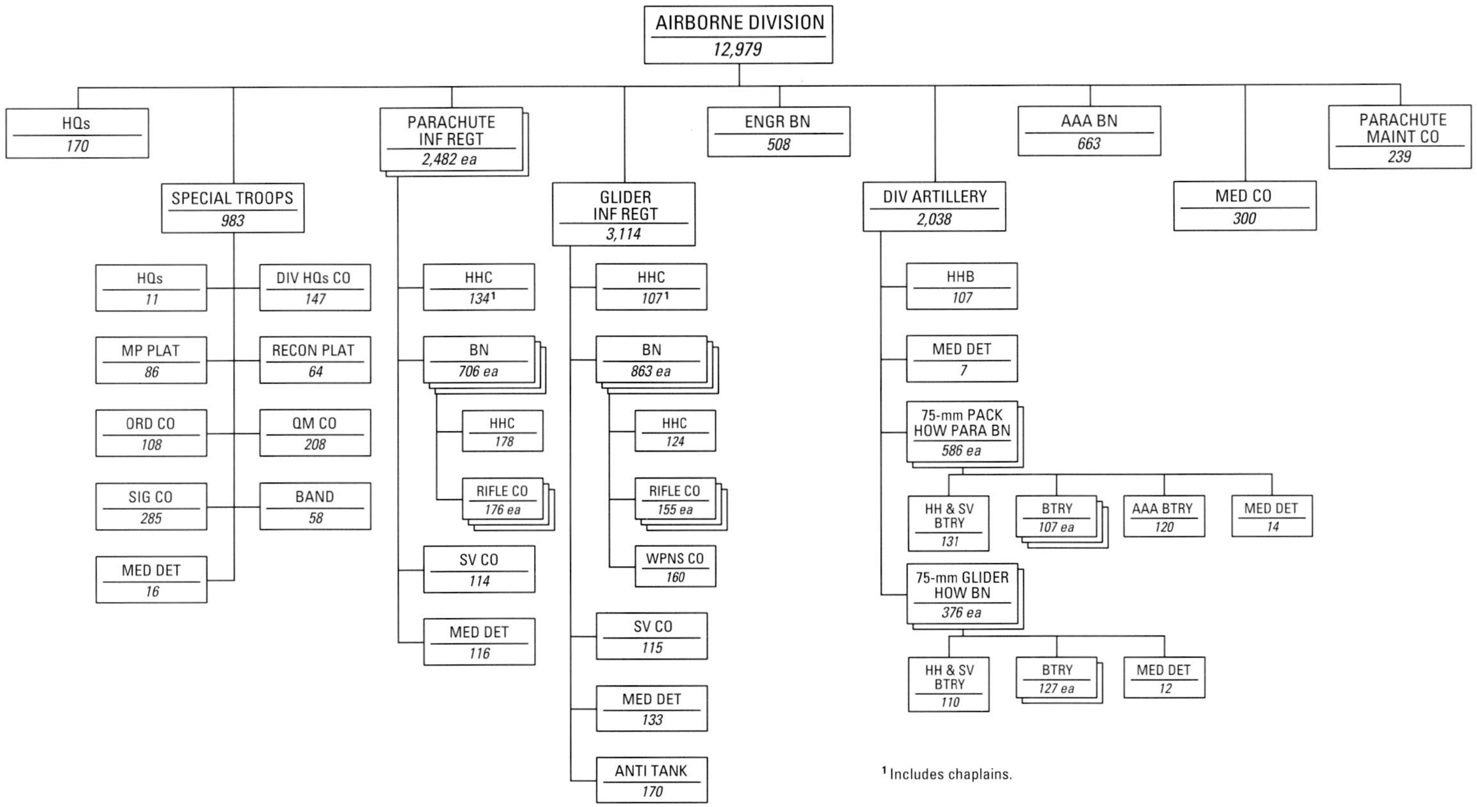

- **AIRBORNE DIVISION** — 12,979
  - HQs — 170
  - SPECIAL TROOPS — 983
    - HQs — 11
    - DIV HQs CO — 147
    - MP PLAT — 86
    - RECON PLAT — 64
    - ORD CO — 108
    - QM CO — 208
    - SIG CO — 285
    - BAND — 58
    - MED DET — 16
  - PARACHUTE INF REGT — 2,482 ea
    - HHC — 134[1]
    - BN — 706 ea
      - HHC — 178
      - RIFLE CO — 176 ea
    - SV CO — 114
    - MED DET — 116
  - GLIDER INF REGT — 3,114
    - HHC — 107
    - BN — 863 ea
      - HHC — 124
      - RIFLE CO — 155 ea
      - WPNS CO — 160
    - SV CO — 115
    - MED DET — 133
    - ANTI TANK — 170
  - ENGR BN — 508
  - DIV ARTILLERY — 2,038
    - HHB — 107
    - MED DET — 7
    - 75-mm PACK HOW PARA BN — 586 ea
      - HH & SV BTRY — 131
      - BTRY — 107 ea
    - 75-mm GLIDER HOW BN — 376 ea
      - HH & SV BTRY — 110
      - BTRY — 127 ea
    - AAA BTRY — 120
    - MED DET — 14
    - MED DET — 12
  - AAA BN — 663
  - MED CO — 300
  - PARACHUTE MAINT CO — 239

[1] Includes chaplains.

artillery, the company also created ammunition shortages for that headquarters. Divisional reconnaissance suffered because the troop lacked sufficient strength and its vehicles were too lightly armored and armed. The decision to have fewer divisions and to maintain them through a constant flow of replacements proved costly. Many recruits were killed or seriously wounded before they could be effectively worked into the fabric of frontline units.[53]

The armored division lacked sufficient infantry and medium artillery. To solve this problem, attachments took place when such units were available. Combat experience also dictated that the division have three combat teams. Under the 1942 structure the infantry regiment's headquarters in the 2d and 3d Armored Divisions was often provisionally organized as a third combat command. In the other divisions, under the 1943 configuration, an armored group headquarters and headquarters company was attached to serve as a combat command.[54] These expedients created command and control problems and complicated teamwork. The division's reconnaissance unit and replacement system suffered from the same weaknesses as in the infantry division.[55]

In January 1945, recognizing these organizational problems, the War Department began to revise the infantry division structure for units planned for redeployment from Europe, after the defeat of Germany, to the Pacific theater to aid in the conquest of Japan. The War Department cast aside its policy of rejecting changes in units because of personnel considerations and directed staff agencies to prepare tables for sound fighting teams. It ordered the elimination of dual assignments for personnel, the addition of any equipment listed earlier as special but that had been used routinely, provisions for more adequate communications in all components, and an expansion of military police resources. The infantry regiment was to receive more mobile, self-propelled howitzers and better antitank weapons. Later the War Department instructions indicated that the revised structure would not be limited to use in the war against Japan.[56]

On 1 March 1945 Army Ground Forces submitted three proposals for reorganizing the infantry division. Each specified different manning levels, but the planners recommended the one that maximized the division's size and firepower. An enlarged infantry regiment with 700 additional men provided more punch. The weapons platoon in each rifle company had two new sections, one with six 2.36-inch rocket launchers and the other with three 57-mm. recoilless rifles.[57] In the battalion's weapons company a new platoon of six 75-mm. recoilless rifles augmented the two platoons equipped with light and heavy machine guns. Because the regiment's 105-mm. howitzers lacked cross-country mobility for close support, commanders had tied the cannon company to the field artillery fire direction center to serve as an additional indirect fire battery. Army Ground Forces thus replaced the cannon company with a tank company comprising nine tanks. The tanks also replaced the 57-mm. towed guns in the antitank company, which were too lightly armored and judged to be too road-bound. The number of truck drivers, communications and postal personnel, and ammunition bearers was increased. The military police force grew from a platoon to a company and a signal battalion replaced the signal company. A tank battalion was added to the division and a fourth company to the division engineer battalion. To expand the "eyes and ears" of the division, the reconnaissance troop was increased in size and authorized two light aircraft. These changes together resulted in a proposed divisional strength of 18,285 personnel, an increase of 4,248 men over the January 1945 figure.[58]

On 5 April the Army Staff informed Army Ground Forces that because of expected personnel shortages divisions could not be reorganized according to any of the proposed changes. Instead, the staff directed the command to prepare another set of tables that would increase personnel for communications, replace the military police platoon with a company, enlarge each 105-mm. and 155-mm. howitzer battery from four to six pieces, and restructure the infantry regiment along the lines of the March proposal. Shortly after issuing these instructions, the staff told Army Ground Forces that about fifty more men could be added to the division for various service duties.[59]

On 1 June the War Department published tables for the infantry division calling for 15,838 officers and enlisted men. The division met most of the Army Staff's guidance, except for the proposed increases in the artillery batteries. The planners believed that the new organization gave the division more mobility, flexibility, and firepower, in particular for tank warfare. No unit, however, adopted the structure until October 1945.[60]

## *Redeployment*

The war ended in Europe in May 1945, and the Army had to come to grips with demobilization while still engaged in the war against Japan. Aware that the call to "bring the boys home" would eventually be irresistable, as early as 1943 Acting Secretary of War Robert P. Patterson had appointed Maj. Gen. William F. Tompkins to head the Special Plans Division (SPD), War Department Special Staff, to plan for demobilization and reorganization of the postwar Army.[61]

Tompkins began with the assumptions that the war in Europe would end first, that an occupation force would be needed there, and that those who had served the longest should be released as quickly as possible. Enough soldiers had to be retained to conclude the war in the Pacific. With these ideas in mind, the Special Plans Division and the overseas commands worked out a redeployment policy based on a point system. Under it, men received points for length of service, combat participation, military awards, and time spent overseas. Soldiers who were parents were also to receive special consideration. Out of this rating system, four categories of soldiers emerged: those to be retained for service in a command; those to be transferred to a new command; those to form new units in a command; and those to be discharged.[62]

*8th Infantry Division arrives at Hampton Roads Port of Embarkation, 1945.*

When the War Department approved the redeployment policy in the spring of 1945, planners believed the European command would need to furnish fifteen divisions to end the war in the Far East and twenty-one to the United States to reconstitute a strategic reserve, which had ceased to exist in February 1945. Following the German offensive in the Ardennes in December 1944, the last seven divisions in the ninety-division troop program had been sent to Europe. With the point system and a tentative troop basis in place, redeployment waited only for the fighting to end in Europe.[63]

On 12 May, four days after the surrender of Germany, General Dwight D. Eisenhower, the Supreme Allied Commander, set the readjustment program into motion. High and low point men switched units, and in June the 86th, 95th, 97th, and 104th Infantry Divisions left Europe for reassignment. Arriving home, the men took thirty-day leaves before undergoing training to prepare for the Pacific theater. But the successful use of atomic bombs against Hiroshima and Nagasaki in August skewed all readjustment plans toward demobilization. By September 1945, 19 divisions—1 airborne, 1 mountain, 2 armored, and 15 infantry—returned from Europe for use elsewhere. Of those units, only the 86th and 97th Infantry Divisions moved to the Far East, arriving in the Philippines and Japan after the fighting had ended.[64]

Compared to World War I, divisional organizations had rapidly adjusted to the demands of the Second World War. Initially three considerations greatly influenced the organization of the various divisions: the availability of men to field the units desired by the Army; the availability of shipping space to move them to the combat theaters; and the availability and quality of equipment. The last proved influential, continually forcing the Army to make structural changes to accommodate improved weapon systems or, in some cases, to eliminate those that proved less than successful in combat. In 1943 McNair attempted to reorganize divisional structures based on experiences acquired during the maneuvers of 1940 through 1942 and on the battlefield, where infantry, armored, and airborne divisions had to be augmented routinely, in particular to oppose tanks and airplanes. As the European war came to a close, the General Staff attempted to give infantry divisions the additional resources they habitually needed, but this effort came too late to benefit them during the conflict.

Before and during World War II the Army also sought to develop several new types of divisions and to achieve an acceptable balance between firepower and mobility. Planners tried not to sacrifice either capability to the other, seeking instead to serve both masters. This effort proved reasonably successful in the acid test of battle, especially by comparison with the performance of divisions during World War I. The accumulated experience of the twentieth century eased the task of making periodic organizational adjustments to satisfy changing requirements. Nevertheless, this evolutionary process would continue after World War II as the pace of technological developments and expanded global security roles of the United States Army forced it down roads that had never been traveled before.

## Notes

[1] *Biennial Report of the Chief of Staff of the United States Army, July 1, 1943, to June 30, 1945*, to the Secretary of War, p. 106.

[2] Memo, AGF to CofS, U.S. Army, 24 Jul 42, sub: Modification of Troop Basis, 1942, 320.2/267 (S)-GNGPS (AGF, Plans Section) (7–22–42), and 1st Ind, same subject, 8 Aug 42, AG 320.2 (7–24–42) MS-C, AG 320.2 (7–24–42), RG 407, NARA; Palmer et al., *The Procurement and Training of Ground Combat Troops*, pp. 175–79; Joseph J. Hutnik and Leonard Kobrick, eds., *We Ripened Fast, The Unofficial History of the Seventy-Sixth Infantry Division* (Frankfurt, Germany: Otto Lembeck, 1946), pp. 19–21; *Lightning: The History of the 78th Infantry Division* (Washington, D.C.: Infantry Journal Press, 1947), pp. 9–11.

[3] Stetson Conn, Rose C. Engelman, Byron Fairchild, *Guarding the United States and Its Outposts*, United States Army in World War II (Washington, D.C.: Government Printing Office, 1964), p. 277; Ltr, TAG to CGs AGF and II Armored Corps, 1 Jan 42, sub: Redesignation and Reorganization of the 7th Motorized Division, AG 320.2 (12–31–42) OB-I-GN-M (Order of Battle, Intelligence, AGF), 7th Inf Div file, DAMH-HSO.

[4] Greenfield et al., *Organization of Ground Combat Troops*, p. 286; Palmer et al., *Procurement and Training of Ground Combat Troops*, pp. 489–93,

[5] Greenfield et al., *Organization of Ground Combat Troops*, pp. 286–87.

[6] On 19 August 1942 army corps were officially redesignated as corps.

[7] Greenfield et al., *Organization of Ground Combat Troops*, pp. 288–89, 291.

[8] Ibid., pp. 274–75, 303–14; T/O 7–11, Infantry Regiment, 1 Apr 42; T/O 7–11, Infantry Regiment, 1 Mar 43. The 1942 cannon company had six 75-mm. self-propelled howitzers and two 105-mm. self-propelled howitzers.

[9] Greenfield et al., *Organization of Ground Combat Troops*, pp. 304–05.

[10] T/O 6–10, Division Artillery, Motorized, Infantry or Motorized Division, 1 Mar 43; Memo, G–3 for AGF, 6 Jun 42, sub: Organic Air Observation for Field Artillery, WDGCT (Assistant Chief of Staff, G–3, General Staff) 320.2 (2–5–42), reprinted in Richard Tierney, *The Army Aviation Story* (Northport, Ala.: Colonial Press, 1963), pp. 68–69; William E. Vance, "History of Army Aviation," *Aviation Digest* 3 (Jun 1957): 7–12.

[11] T/O 5–15, Engineer Battalion, Infantry Division, 1 Apr 42; T/O 5–15, Engineer Battalion, 1 Mar 43; T/O 11–7, Signal Company, Infantry Division, 1 Apr 42; T/O 11–7, Signal Company, Infantry Division, 1 Mar 43; T/0 10–17, Quartermaster Company, Infantry Division, 15 Sep 42; T/O 10–17, Quartermaster Company, Infantry Division, 1 Mar 43; Greenfield et al., *Organization of Ground Combat Troops*, pp. 309–11.

[12] T/O 7–1, Headquarters, Infantry or Motorized Division, 1 Jun 42; T/O 7–1, Headquarters, Infantry Division, 1 Mar 43; T/O 7–2, Headquarters Company, Infantry or Motorized Division, 1 Jun 42; T/O 7–2, Headquarters Company, Infantry Division, 1 Mar 43; Greenfield et al., *Organization of Ground Combat Troops*, pp. 311–14.

[13] Greenfield et al., *Organization of Ground Combat Troops*, pp. 314–17.

[14] Ibid., pp. 317–18; TOE 7, Infantry Division, 15 Jul 43. While preparing the 1943 tables, the War Department combined Tables of Organization and Tables of Equipment into a single document, a Table of Organization and Equipment (TOE).

[15] Memo, GNDCG (Commanding General, Army Ground Forces) for G–3, 28 Jan 43, sub: Basis of Organization of Motorized Division, 320.2/19 (Armd.F) (S)-GNDCG, Memo, Organization and Mobilization Branch, G–3, to Edwards, 18 Feb 43, sub: Conference on Motorized Division, AG 320.2 (1–28–43), and Memo, WDGCT for CofS, 24 Feb 43, sub: Reorganization of the Motorized Division, WDCGT 320 (2–24–43), AG 320.2 (2–24–43), all RG 407, NARA.

[16] Memo, WDGCT for CofS, 24 Feb 43, sub: Reorganization of the Motorized Division, and Ltr, TAG to CGs, II Armored Corps and other addresses, 7 May 43, sub: Redesignation and Reorganization of 6th, 8th, and 90th Motorized Divisions, both AG 320.2 (4–30–43) OB-I-GNGCT-M, AG Reference files, DAMH-HSO.

17 Greenfield et al., *Organization of Ground Combat Troops*, pp. 337–39; Ltr, TAG to CGs, AGF and XIII Corps, 30 Jul 43, sub: Redesignation and Reorganization of the 4th Motorized Division, AG 322 (28 Jul 43) OB-I-GNGCT-M, AG Reference files, DAMH-HSO.

18 Greenfield et al., *Organization of Ground Combat Troops*, p. 324.

19 Ibid., p. 322.

20 Memo, AGF for CofS, 7 Dec 42, sub: Organization of Armored Units, 320.2 (Armd Force) (R) (11–6–42), and Memo, WDGCT for CofS, 16 Jan 43, sub: Organizational of Armored Units, WDGCT 320 (12–7–42), both RG 407, NARA.

21 Memo, WDGCT for CofS, 16 Jan 43, sub: Organization of Armored Units; Greenfield et al., *Organization of Ground Combat Troops*, pp. 319–26.

22 Report of Proceedings of a Board of Officers, 27 Mar 1943, Memo, AGF for Requirements Section, and CG, AGF, undated, sub: Comments on Harmon Board report, both Ground AG Section, Project Decimal file 1942–1943, AGF 319.1, North African Binder, RG 337, NARA.

23 Memo, AGF for Requirements Section and CG, AGF, undated, sub: Comments on Harmon Board report; TOE 17, Armored Division, 15 Sep 43; Greenfield et al., *Organization of Ground Combat Troops*, pp. 327–31.

24 TOE 17, Armored Division, 15 Sep 43; Greenfield et al., *Organization of Ground Combat Troops*, pp. 327–31.

25 TOE 17, Armored Division, 15 Sep 43; Greenfield et al., *Organization of Ground Combat Troops*, pp. 329–35; J. M. Pittman, "Reorganization of the Armored Division," *Military Review* 24 (April 1943): 44–47.

26 WD Cir 256, 1943.

27 Ltr, TAG to CGs, AGF and other addresses, 20 Aug 43, sub: Utilization of Personnel, AG 320.2 (31 Jul 43) PE-A-M-C, Ltr, TAG to CGs, AGF and XIII Corps, 30 Jul 43, sub: Redesignation and Reorganization of 4th Motorized Division, Ltr, TAG to CGs, AGF and other addresses, 2 Aug 43, sub: Reorganization of Infantry Divisions, AG 322 (28 Jul 43) OB-I-GNGCT-M, Ltr, TAG to CGs, AGF and Third Army, 20 Sep 43, sub: Reorganization of the 38th Infantry Division, AG 322 (18 Sep 43) OB-I-GNGCT-M, Ltr, TAG to CGs, AGF and other addresses, 23 Sep 43, sub: Reorganization of the 93d Infantry Division, AG 322 (22 Sep 43) OB-I-GNGCT, Ltr, TAG to CinC, Southwest Pacific Area and other addresses, 12 Oct 43, sub: Constitution of Units, AG 322 (6 Oct 43) OB-I-GNCGT-M, Ltr, TAG to CG, North African Theater of Operations, 29 Jul 43, sub: Reorganization of the 34th Infantry Division, AG 322 (26 Jul 43) OB-I-GNGCT, Ltr, TAG to CG, South Pacific Area, 20 Sep 43, sub: Reorganization of the Americal Division, AG 322 (17 Sep 43) OB-I-GNGCT, Ltr, TAG to CG U.S. Army Forces, Central Pacific Area, sub: Reorganization of the 33d Infantry Division, AG 322 (30 Sep 43) OB-I-GNGCT-M, Ltr, TAG to AGF and other addresses, 15 Sep 43, sub: Reorganization of Armored Divisions, AG 322 (10 Sep 43) OB-I-GNGCT-M, Ltr, TAG to CGs, AGF and Third Army, 31 Aug 43, sub: Reorganization of the 4th Armored Division, AG 322 (29 Aug 43) OB-I-GNGCT-M, Ltr, TAG to CGs, AGF and Armored Command, 3 Sep 43, sub: Reorganization of the 16th Armored Division, AG 322 (1 Sep 43) OB-I-GNGCT-M, and Ltr, TAG to CGs, AGF and Armored Command, 3 Sep 43, sub: Reorganization of the 20th Armored Division, AG 322 (1 Sep 43) OB-I-GNGCT-M, all AG Reference files, DAMH-HSO; Historical Data Cards, Divisions. The sixty infantry divisions in the United States did not include the 89th Infantry Division, which was reorganized as a light division on 1 August 1943 (see below).

28 GO 118, Fifth Army, 1944, 1st Armd Div file, DAMH-HSO; Ltr, Devers to A.C. Gillem Jr., 29 Nov 43, Devers Papers, MHI.

29 Memo, AGF to TAG, 1 Apr 43, sub: Reorganization of the Americal Division, 320.2/19 (PTO) (S)-GNGCT/06414 (3–18–43), 320.2 4–1–43 (18), RG 407, NARA; Ltr, TAG to CG, South Pacific Area, 3 Apr 43, sub: Reorganization of the Americal Division, AG 320.2 (4–1–43) OB-I-GNGCT, AG Reference files, DAMH-HSO; Ltr, TAG to CG, South Pacific Area, 20 Sep 43, sub: Reorganization of Americal Division; Cronin, *Under the Southern Cross*, pp. 104, 128; Department of the Army (DA) GO 73, 1948.

30 Greenfield et al., *Organization of Ground Combat Troops*, pp. 331–43.

31 Memo, AGF for G-3, 2 Mar 43, sub: Light Division, 2 Mar 43, 322.2 (Div) (S), RG 407, NARA; TOE 72 (Trk) and (Pack), Light Division, 1 Jul 43, 89th and 71st Inf Div files, DAMH-HSO.

32 Greenfield et al., *Organization of Ground Combat Troops*, pp. 345–46; Fred Clinger, Arthur Johnson, and Vincent Masel, *History of the 71st Infantry Division* (Augsburg, Germany: E. Kieser KG, 1946), pp. 1–2; *History of the 10th Light Division*, AGF Study 28 (Washington, D.C.: Historical Section, AGF, 1946), p. 1; Maynard L. Diamond, Willard E. Simms, Edward B. Baldinger, and Meyer Siegelbaum, *89th Infantry Division, 1942-1945* (Washington, D.C.: Infantry Journal Press, 1946), pp. 47–48. Also see the 10th, 71st, and 89th Infantry Divisions files in DAMH-HSO.

33 Diamond et al., *89th Infantry Division*, p. 61.

34 Ibid., pp. 60–61; Greenfield et al., *Organization of Ground Combat Troops*, pp. 347–48; Ltr, TAG to CGs, Second Army and other addresses, 16 May 44, sub: Redesignation and Reorganization of 71st Light Division, AG 322 (12 May 44) OB-I GNGCT-M, 71st Inf Div, and Ltr, TAG to CGs, Fourth Army and other addresses, 16 May 44, sub: Redesignation and Reorganization of the 89th Light Division, AG 322 (12 May 44) OB-I-GNGCT-M, 89th Inf Div, both AG Reference files, DAMH-HSO.

35 *Training in Mountain and Winter Warfare*, AGF Study No. 23 (Washington, D.C.: Historical Section, AGF, 1946), pp. 11–12; TOE 70, Mountain Division, 4 Nov 44; Ltr, TAG to CG, Fourth Army, 1 Nov 44, sub: Reorganization and Redesignation of the 10th Light Division, AG 322 (25 Oct 44) OB-I-GNGCT, 10th Mt Div file, DAMH-HSO; Interview, author with Walter L. Galson, National Association of the 10th Mountain Division, Washington, D.C., 28 Nov 79, author's files.

36 Historical Data Cards for the 42d, 63d, 65th, 66th, 69th, 70th, 75th, and 106th Infantry Divisions; the 16th and 20th Armored Divisions; and the 11th, 13th, and 17th Airborne Divisions and unit files for each division in DAMH-HSO. In addition to the divisions listed, TAG also placed the 61st, 62d, 67th, 68th, 72d, 73d, and 74th Infantry Divisions and the 18th, 19th, 21st, and 22d Armored Divisions on the rolls, but they were never organized during the war. The 15th Airborne Division was also placed on the rolls but never organized.

37 "The 'Rainbow Division'," *National Guardsman* 3 (Aug 49): 18–19; Ltr, Harry J. Collins to George C. Marshall, 19 Jun 43, Marshall Papers.

38 Ltr, TAG to CG, Airborne Command, 1 Jul 44, sub: Organization of HHC, 1st and 2d Airborne Infantry Brigades, AG 322 (29 Jun 43) OB-I-GNGCT-M, and Ltr, TAG to CGs, AGF and Airborne Command, sub: Disbandment of HHC, 1st Airborne Infantry Brigade, 23 Nov 43, AG 322 (21 Nov 43) OB-I-GNGCT-M, both 1st Bde, 1st Inf Div, file, DAMH-HSO; Ltr, TAG to Chief, Historical Section, AWC, 21 Feb 45, sub: Organizational History, AG 314.7 OB-I, and Unit Diary, Second Airborne Infantry Brigade, 1943–1944, both 2d Bde, 1st Inf Div file, DAMH-HSO.

39 Ltr, AGF to CGs, Third Army and IX Corps, 12 Sep 42, sub: Activation of Elements of the 1st Cavalry Division, 322.13/1 (1st Cav Div) (R)-GNGNT (9–12–42), 1st Cav Div file, and Ltr, TAG to CGs, Services of Supply and other addresses, 23 Nov 42, sub: Activation of 2d Cavalry Division, AG 320.2 (11–21–42) OB-I-GN-M, 2d Cav Div file, both DAMH-HSO.

40 Greenfield et al., *Organization of Ground Combat Troops*, p. 336; Ltr, TAG to CG, Third Army, 2 Mar 43, sub: Reorganization of 1st Cavalry Division, AG 320.2 (2–28–43) OB-I-GNGCT-M, 1st Cav Div file, DAMH-HSO; James W. Hinds, *Second Cavalry Division* (no publisher, 1987), pp. 60–61.

41 Ltr, TAG to CinC, Southwest Pacific Area, 17 Sep 43, sub: Reorganization of Units in Southwest Pacific Area, AG 322 (14 Sep 43) OB-I-GNGCT-M, and Ltr, TAG to CinC, Southwest Pacific Area, 13 Nov 43, sub: Redesignation and Reorganization of 1st Cavalry Division, AG 322 (9 Nov 43) OB-I-GNGCT-M, both AG Reference files, DAMH-HSO; Wright, *The 1st Cavalry Division in World War II*, p. 240.

42 MacGregor, *Integration of the Armed Forces*, p. 33; Ltr, TAG to CGs, AGF and North

African Theater of Operations, 11 Apr 44, sub: Inactivation and Disbandment of Units, AG 322 (8 Apr 44) OB-I-GNGCT-M, AG file, DAMH-HSO; Hinds, *Second Cavalry Division*, pp. 64–67; Ltr, TAB to CGs, Fourth Army and Southern Defense Command, 24 Apr 44, sub: Assignment, Reorganization and Redesignation of Certain Cavalry Units, AG 322 (22 Apr 44) OB-I-GNGCT-M, AG Reference files, DAMH-HSO; Mary Lee Stubbs and Stanley Russell Connor, *Armor-Cavalry Part II: Army National Guard*, Army Lineage Series (Washington, D.C.: Government Printing Office, 1972), pp. 167–87.

43 Greenfield et al., *Organization of Ground Combat Troops*, table, "Ground Forces in the Army, Dec 41–Apr 45," and pp. 163–81; Maurice Matloff, "The 90-Division Gamble," *Command Decisions*, Kent R. Greenfield, ed. (Washington, D.C.: Government Printing Office, 1960), pp. 365–81.

44 Matloff, "The 90-Division Gamble," p. 374.

45 Robert W. Coakley and Richard M. Leighton, *Global Logistics and Strategy: 1943–1945*, United States Army in World War II (Washington, D.C.: Government Printing Office, 1968), p. 246–47; Palmer et al., *Procurement and Training of Ground Combat Troops*, pp. 489–92.

46 Ltr, TAG to CGs, Second Army and Airborne Command, 4 Feb 43, sub: Changes in Assignment of Units to the 82d Airborne Division and Airborne Command, AG 320.2 (2–3–43) OB-I-GN-M, 82d Abn Div file, DAMH-HSO; James E. Mrazek, *The Glider War* (London: Robert Hale and Company, 1975), p. 108.

47 James M. Gavin, *On to Berlin*, pp. 49–50.

48 Memo, AGF for CofS, 17 Dec 43, sub: Change in T/O, Airborne Division, 320.3/75 (S)-GNGCT, and Memo, G–3 for ACofS, 17 Dec 43, same subject, WDGCT 320.2, both Correspondence, Matthew Ridgway in Marshall Papers.

49 Ltr, Ridgway to Marshall, 1 Nov 44, Ltr, Ridgway to Marshall, 4 Dec 44, Summary Sheet (SS), G–3 for CofS, 8 Nov 44, sub: Reorganization of the Airborne Division, all in Matthew Ridgway, Marshall Papers; Maxwell D. Taylor, *Swords and Plowshares* (New York: W. W. Norton and Co., 1972), pp. 97–98; TOE 71, Airborne Division, 16 Dec 44; cited material from Ltr, Marshall to Ridgway, 18 Dec 44, Marshall Papers.

50 Memo, G–3 for CofS, 15 Dec 44, sub: Reorganization of the Airborne Division, WDGCT 322 (15 Dec 44), RG 407, NARA; TOE 71, Airborne Division, 16 Dec 44.

51 SS, G–3 for DCofS, 16 Dec 44, sub: Reorganization of Airborne Divisions, 322 (16 Dec 44), RG 407, NARA; Ltr, TAG to CG US Forces in the European Theater of Operations (ETO), 16 Jan 45, sub: Reorganization of the 101st Airborne Division, AG 322 (8 Jan 45) OB-I-GNGCT-M, Ltr, TAG to CG, US Forces in the ETO, 22 Feb 45, sub: Reorganization of the 13th, 17th and 82d Airborne Divisions, AG 322 (18 Feb 45) OB-I-GNGCT-M, and Ltr, TAG to CinC, USAF, Pacific, 4 Jul 45, sub: Reorganization and Redesignation of Certain Airborne Units, AG 322 (30 Jun 45), OB-I-GNGCT-M, all AG Reference files, DAMH-HSO; Edward M. Flanagan, *The Angels: A History of the 11th Airborne Division 1943-1946* (Washington, D.C.: Infantry Journal Press, 1948), pp. 1–2; also see 11th, 13th, 17th, 82d, and 101st Abn Divs files, DAMH-HSO.

52 TOE 6–160–1, Headquarters and Headquarters Battery (HHB), Division Artillery, Armored Division, 12 Feb 44; TOE 7, Infantry Division, and TOE 17, Armored Division, 24 Jan 45.

53 General Board, ETO, Report 17, Types of Divisions—Postwar Army, pp. 8–9, 1945, DAMH-Library.

54 The armored group headquarters and headquarters company was organized almost identical to the headquarters and headquarters company of a combat command in an armored division. It contained the necessary staff, communication, and transportation to enable it to function as the headquarters of a task force comparable in size to a combat command.

55 General Board, ETO, Report 17, Types of Divisions, pp. 12–13.

56 Greenfield et al., *Organization of Ground Combat Troops*, pp. 454–55.

57 Recoilless rifles had been developed during the war, and the weapons combined the effect of artillery with the mobility of hand-carried arms by using high velocity gas ports to counteract

recoil, as opposed to absorption of recoil by springs and/or oil flowing through various orifices.

58 Greenfield et al., *Organization of Ground Combat Troops*, pp. 456–75.

59 Ibid., pp. 476–77.

60 Ibid., pp. 477–83; TOE 7, Infantry Division, 1 Jun 45.

61 Hewes, *From Root to McNamara*, p. 112.

62 WD Readjustment Regulations, 1–1, 12 Feb 1945.

63 Coakley and Leighton, *Global Logistics and Strategy*, pp. 584–85.

64 "Redeployment," Ms, Occupation Forces in Europe series, pp. 82–84, 89, and Bell I. Wiley, "AGF on the Eve of Demobilization Period," Ms, History of AGF during the Demobilization Period, chart, "Arrival of Major Ground Units for Redeployment to 10 September 1945," both DAMH-HSR.

# CHAPTER 8

# An Interlude of Peace

*It seems certain that atomic, and other new weapons, which we may expect a major ruthless opponent to use in the foreseeable future, will not alter the nature of warfare to such an extent that the immediate ground combat need for versatile, mobile, and hard-hitting divisions will be diminished or altered.*

General Jacob L. Devers[1]

By the summer of 1946 the peacetime Army fielded sixteen active divisions, to be backed by an additional fifty-two in the reserve components. For the first time in its history the United States kept more than a token army in the aftermath of victory. This radical departure from tradition resulted from the international instability that characterized the postwar years and spawned the Cold War, an era of confrontation between the Soviet Union and the United States. To counter the threat of Soviet expansion, successive administrations made extensive political and military commitments around the world that matured into a foreign policy known as "containment." Associated with containment were several collective defense treaties, most notably the North Atlantic Treaty Organization (NATO), which required a significant degree of peacetime readiness on land and sea and in the air.

Shortly after establishing the postwar force, the Army leadership reorganized divisions based upon the lessons from World War II. Despite the Soviet military threat, various obstacles hindered the Army's effort to maintain readiness—the totality of the recent victory, an apathetic public, and an economy-minded Congress. One of the most critical, but widely ignored, issues facing the nation was the possible use of atomic weapons in future wars. That nuclear war did not receive extensive attention during the early postwar years was a consequence of the nation's short-lived monopoly of atomic weapons and the complexity of military decision making in a dangerous international environment.

## Demobilization, Occupation, and the General Reserve

In late 1945 the Army began to retool for new missions, which included occupying former enemy territories and establishing a General Reserve, while demobilizing the bulk of the World War II forces. The point system developed earlier, which served as an interim demobilization measure until the defeat of

*41st Infantry Division departs the Philippine Islands, July 1945.*

Japan, provided the basic methodology for execution but did not control the pace of the reduction. As after World War I, the Army failed to prepare a general demobilization plan. Demobilization thus proceeded rapidly, driven largely by public pressure and reduced resources, without the benefit of sound estimates about the size and location of the occupation forces that the Army would need or the length of time that they would have to serve overseas. The divisions that returned to the United States in 1945 and 1946 were generally administrative holding organizations without any combat capability. They were paper organizations "to bring the boys home."[2]

Within a year after the end of the war in Europe, the number of divisions on active duty dropped from 89 to 16 (*Table 17*); of these, 12 were engaged in occupation duty: 3 in Germany, 1 in Austria, 1 in Italy, 1 in the Philippine Islands, 4 in Japan, and 2 in Korea. The remaining 4 were in the United States. By the end of January 1947 three more infantry divisions overseas were inactivated: the 42d in Austria; the 9th in Germany; and the 86th in the Philippine Islands. In addition, the 3d Infantry Division was withdrawn from Germany and sent to Camp (later Fort) Campbell, Kentucky, where it replaced the 5th Division. When demobilization ended in 1947, the number of active divisions stood at twelve.[3]

# TABLE 17
## Status of Divisions, 1 June 1946

| Division | Status | Remarks |
|---|---|---|
| 1st Armored | Inactive | Inactivated 25 April 1946 |
| 1st Cavalry | Active | Japan |
| 1st Infantry | Active | Germany |
| 2d Armored | Active | Fort Hood, Texas |
| 2d Infantry | Active | Fort Lewis, Washington |
| 3d Armored | Inactive | Inactivated 10 November 1945 |
| 3d Infantry | Active | Germany |
| 4th Armored | Active | Reorganized as Constabulary |
| 4th Infantry | Inactive | Inactivated 12 March 1946 |
| 5th Armored | Inactive | Inactivated 11 October 1945 |
| 5th Infantry | Active | Camp Campbell, Kentucky |
| 6th Armored | Inactive | Inactivated 18 September 1945 |
| 6th Infantry | Active | Korea |
| 7th Armored | Inactive | Inactivated 9 October 1945 |
| 7th Infantry | Active | Korea |
| 8th Armored | Inactive | Inactivated 13 November 1945 |
| 8th Infantry | Inactive | Inactivated 20 November 1945 |
| 9th Armored | Inactive | Inactivated 13 October 1945 |
| 9th Infantry | Active | Germany |
| 10th Armored | Inactive | Inactivated 13 October 1945 |
| 10th Mountain | Inactive | Inactivated 30 November 1945 |
| 11th Airborne | Active | Japan |
| 11th Armored | Disbanded | Disbanded 31 August 1945 |
| 12th Armored | Inactive | Inactivated 3 December 1945 |
| 13th Airborne | Inactive | Inactivated 25 February 1946 |
| 13th Armored | Inactive | Inactivated 15 November 1945 |
| 14th Armored | Inactive | Inactivated 16 September 1945 |
| 16th Armored | Inactive | Inactivated 15 October 1945 |
| 17th Airborne | Inactive | Inactivated 14 September 1945 |
| 20th Armored | Inactive | Inactivated 2 April 1946 |
| 24th Infantry | Active | Japan |
| 25th Infantry | Active | Japan |
| 26th Infantry | Inactive | Inactivated 29 December 1945 |
| 27th Infantry | Inactive | Inactivated 31 December 1945 |
| 28th Infantry | Inactive | Inactivated 13 December 1945 |
| 29th Infantry | Inactive | Inactivated 17 January 1946 |
| 30th Infantry | Inactive | Inactivated 25 November 1945 |
| 31st Infantry | Inactive | Inactivated 21 December 1945 |
| 32d Infantry | Inactive | Inactivated 28 February 1946 |
| 33d Infantry | Inactive | Inactivated 5 February 1946 |
| 34th Infantry | Inactive | Inactivated 3 November 1945 |
| 35th Infantry | Inactive | Inactivated 7 December 1945 |
| 36th Infantry | Inactive | Inactivated 15 December 1945 |
| 37th Infantry | Inactive | Inactivated 18 December 1945 |
| 38th Infantry | Inactive | Inactivated 9 November 1945 |

TABLE 17—*Continued*

| Division | Status | Remarks |
|---|---|---|
| 40th Infantry | Inactive | Inactivated 7 April 1946 |
| 41st Infantry | Inactive | Inactivated 31 December 1945 |
| 42d Infantry | Active | Austria |
| 43d Infantry | Inactive | Inactivated 1 November 1945 |
| 44th Infantry | Inactive | Inactivated 30 November 1945 |
| 45th Infantry | Inactive | Inactivated 7 December 1945 |
| 63d Infantry | Inactive | Inactivated 27 September 1945 |
| 65th Infantry | Disbanded | Disbanded 31 August 1945 |
| 66th Infantry | Inactive | Inactivated 8 November 1945 |
| 69th Infantry | Inactive | Inactivated 18 September 1945 |
| 70th Infantry | Inactive | Inactivated 11 October 1945 |
| 71st Infantry | Inactive | Inactivated 11 March 1946 |
| 75th Infantry | Inactive | Inactivated 14 November 1945 |
| 76th Infantry | Disbanded | Disbanded 31 August 1945 |
| 77th Infantry | Inactive | Inactivated 15 March 1946 |
| 78th Infantry | Inactive | Inactivated 22 May 1946 |
| 79th Infantry | Inactive | Inactivated 11 December 1945 |
| 80th Infantry | Inactive | Inactivated 4 January 1946 |
| 81st Infantry | Inactive | Inactivated 20 January 1946 |
| 82d Airborne | Active | Fort Bragg, North Carolina |
| 83d Infantry | Inactive | Inactivated 27 March 1946 |
| 84th Infantry | Inactive | Inactivated 21 January 1946 |
| 85th Infantry | Disbanded | Disbanded 25 August 1945 |
| 86th Infantry | Active | Philippine Islands |
| 87th Infantry | Inactive | Inactivated 21 September 1945 |
| 88th Infantry | Active | Italy |
| 89th Infantry | Inactive | Inactivated 17 December 1945 |
| 90th Infantry | Inactive | Inactivated 27 December 1945 |
| 91st Infantry | Inactive | Inactivated 1 December 1945 |
| 92d Infantry | Inactive | Inactivated 15 October 1945 |
| 93d Infantry | Inactive | Inactivated 3 February 1946 |
| 94th Infantry | Inactive | Inactivated 7 February 1946 |
| 95th Infantry | Inactive | Inactivated 15 October 1945 |
| 96th Infantry | Inactive | Inactivated 3 February 1946 |
| 97th Infantry | Inactive | Inactivated 31 March 1946 |
| 98th Infantry | Inactive | Inactivated 16 February 1946 |
| 99th Infantry | Inactive | Inactivated 27 September 1945 |
| 100th Infantry | Inactive | Inactivated 10 January 1946 |
| 101st Airborne | Inactive | Inactivated 30 November 1945 |
| 102d Infantry | Inactive | Inactivated 12 March 1946 |
| 103d Infantry | Inactive | Inactivated 20 September 1945 |
| 104th Infantry | Inactive | Inactivated 20 December 1945 |
| 106th Infantry | Inactive | Inactivated 2 October 1945 |
| Americal | Inactive | Inactivated 12 December 1945 |

*7th Infantry Division Band on the capital grounds of Seoul, Korea, 1945*

To replace the divisions on occupation duty in Germany that were being inactivated, the U.S. European Command organized the U.S. Constabulary. Heavily armed, lightly armored, and highly mobile, the Constabulary served as an instrument of law enforcement, supporting civil authority, quelling civil disorders, and providing a covering force to engage a hostile enemy until the United States could deploy larger tactical units overseas. The 1st and 4th Armored Divisions, both experienced in mobile warfare, furnished many of the Constabulary's units.4

Although the U.S. Army saw no action in Korea during World War II, the 6th, 7th, and 40th Infantry Divisions arrived there in September and October 1945 to occupy the southern portion of the country and assist in the demobilization of the Japanese Army. An agreement with the Soviet Union had divided the former Japanese colony at the 38th Parallel. The Korean contingent for a short time remained at three divisions but soon dropped to two, the 6th and 7th Infantry Divisions. Following establishment of an independent South Korean government in 1948, the Far East Command inactivated the 6th and moved the 7th to Japan, leaving only a military advisory group in Korea.5

Demobilization and the ensuing personnel turbulence played havoc with the active divisions. During a twelve-month period the 88th Infantry Division in Italy received 29,500 officers and enlisted men and shipped out 18,500. The 1st Cavalry Division in Japan operated at one-fourth of its authorized strength during the first year on occupation duty, and most replacements were teenaged recruits. Divisions in the United States fared no better. The 3d Infantry Division was authorized approximately 65 percent of its wartime strength but fell well below that figure. Demobilization, far from being orderly, became what General George C. Marshall described as a "tidal wave" that completely disrupted the internal cohesion of the Army.6

As the nation demobilized, Congress approved, with the consent of the Philippine government, the maintenance of 50,000 Philippine Scouts (PS) as occupation forces for Japan. On 6 April 1946 Maj. Gen. Louis E. Hibbs, who had commanded the 63d Infantry Division during the war, reorganized the Philippine Division, which had surrendered on Bataan in 1942, as the 12th Infantry Division (PS). Unlike its predecessor, the 12th's enlisted personnel were exclusively Philippine Scouts.7

The War Department proposed to organize a second Philippine Scout division, the 14th, but never did so. After a short period President Harry S. Truman decided to disband all Philippine Scout units, determining that they were not needed for duty in Japan. The United States could not afford them, and he felt the Republic of the Philippines, a sovereign nation, should not furnish mercenaries for the United States. Therefore, the Far East Command inactivated the 12th Infantry Division (PS) in 1947 and eventually inactivated or disbanded all Philippine Scout units.8

Besides the requirement for occupation forces, an urgent need existed for some combat-ready divisions in the United States, where none had been maintained since February 1945. The War Department scaled back its earlier estimate for "strategic" forces and decided to maintain one airborne, one armored, and three infantry divisions, all at 80 percent strength. Initially the department designated the force as the Strategic Striking Force but soon renamed it the General Reserve, to reflect its mission more adequately. But the General Reserve quickly felt the effects of demobilization, and it was soon reduced to four divisions—the 82d Airborne, the 2d Armored, and the 2d and 3d Infantry Divisions.9

Departing from its post–World War I policy, the War Department kept divisional units in the United States concentrated on large posts to foster training and unit cohesion. However, shortages in personnel, obsolete equipment, and insufficient maintenance and training funds prevented the divisions from being combat effective. By the winter of 1947–48 the General Reserve consisted of the airborne division at Fort Bragg at near war strength, two half-strength infantry divisions, one at Fort Campbell and the other at Fort Lewis, and the armored division at Fort Hood with fewer than 2,500 men.10

As many divisions were eliminated from the active rolls, various divisional commanders jockeyed to have their units retained in the active force. By what some thought was chicanery, the 3d Infantry and 82d Airborne Divisions had replaced the 5th Infantry and the 101st Airborne Divisions on the active rolls. These changes caused considerable resentment within the ranks, and unit desig-

AN INTERLUDE OF PEACE                                                                   213

nations became a contentious issue with many active duty personnel as well as veterans. Thus, the adjutant general solicited recommendations from the commanders of Army Ground Forces and the overseas theaters for divisional numbers to be represented in the Regular Army. In the ensuing study, the adjutant general recommended the numbers 1 through 10 and 24 and 25 for infantry divisions (the 10th Mountain Division to be redesignated as the 10th Infantry Division); the numbers 1, 2, 3, and 4 for armored divisions (when elements of the 4th Armored Division serving in the Constabulary were inactivated, they were to revert to divisional units); and 82 and 101 for airborne divisions. The recommendations also included the priority for the retention of divisions on the active rolls.[11]

The study recommended that the 1st Cavalry Division be inactivated upon completion of its occupation duties and its elements retained as nondivisional units. Large horse units were not to be included in the post–World War II Army. Chief of Staff General Dwight D. Eisenhower disagreed with the elimination of the division. Therefore, the Army Staff reworked the list, designating the 1st Cavalry Division eighth on the retention list for infantry (the division had been organized partially under infantry and partially under cavalry tables during World War II) and recommending modification of the unit's designation to show its character as infantry. After examining several proposals, Eisenhower approved the name "1st Cavalry Division (Infantry)."[12]

No change in the number of divisions on active duty resulted from the study; it simply provided the nomenclature for the Regular Army's divisional forces. Eventually the 1st Cavalry Division, the 10th Mountain Division, and the Constabulary units conformed to these decisions. Also, the 101st Airborne Division and the 10th and 25th Infantry Divisions (Army of the United States units) and the 82d Airborne Division (an Organized Reserve organization) were allotted to the Regular Army.[13]

## *Reorganization of Reserve Divisions*

With the nation victorious in war and alone armed with the most awesome weapon known to man, the atomic bomb, a lasting peace appeared at hand. Some military planners believed, however, that the need for ground combat units remained unchanged. Planning for a postwar conventional force had begun in 1943, and over the next three years those plans, which included reserves, were debated in Congress and by the War Department and state officials.[14]

When Maj. Gen. Ellard A. Walsh, president of the National Guard Association, learned the staff was studying a postwar reserve structure, he pressed for consideration of reserve officers' views, petitioning Congress to ensure that the War Department establish reserve affairs committees in agreement with the provisions of the National Defense Act. In August 1944 Deputy Chief of Staff McNarney appointed a six-member committee of Regular Army and National Guard officers to prepare policies and regulations for the Guard. Then, in October, he authorized a similar committee for the Organized Reserves. He also arranged for joint meetings of the two groups where they discussed matters common to both.15

On 13 October 1945 the War Department published a postwar policy statement for the entire Army. It called for a ground military establishment consisting of the Regular Army, the National Guard of the United States, and the Organized Reserve Corps,16 which were to form a balanced force for peace and war. The Regular Army was to retain only those units required for peacetime missions, which were the same as those identified after World War I. The dual-mission Guard was to furnish units needed immediately for war and to provide the states with military resources to protect life and property and to preserve peace, order, and the public safety. The Organized Reserve Corps was to supplement the Regular Army and National Guard contributions sufficiently to meet any projected mobilization requirements.17

After the policy statement was published, the Army Staff prepared a postwar National Guard troop basis, which included twenty-four divisions. It derived that number by counting the prewar eighteen National Guard infantry and four National Guard cavalry divisions, the Americal Division (which had been largely composed of Guard units), and the 42d Infantry Division. Most soldiers considered the 42d, initially organized with state troops in 1917, as a Guard unit. The fact that the new plan allowed each of the forty-eight states to have at least one general officer also helped earn its acceptance. In the end it was necessary to approve a 27-division structure with 25 infantry divisions and 2 armored divisions to accommodate the desires of all the states. During this process New York, for example, successfully petitioned the War Department for the 42d Infantry Division. When the allotment was completed, the Guard contained the 26th through 48th and the 51st and 52d Infantry Divisions and the 49th and 50th Armored Divisions. The number 39 was used for the first time since 1923. Although a 44th Infantry Division had existed during the interwar years, the postwar 44th in Illinois was a new unit, as were the 46th, 47th, 48th, 51st, and 52d Infantry Divisions and 49th Armored Division. The 50th Armored Division replaced the 44th Infantry Division in New Jersey.18

While the states and the War Department settled troop basis issues, the National Guard Bureau changed the procedures for organizing the units. In the past states had raised companies, forming regimental headquarters only when sufficient companies existed to make a regiment. Under the new regulations, divisional and regimental headquarters were to be organized first, and they were to assist the division commander in raising the smaller units.19

During the spring of 1946 the National Guard Bureau surfaced the complex problem of how to preserve historical continuity in the Guard units. In 1942 the divisions had been reorganized from square to triangular units, which left them only vaguely resembling the formations inducted into federal service in 1940 and 1941. Furthermore, the expanded troop basis of 1946 compounded the problem by adding units that had never before existed. To keep from losing the historical link with the prewar units, some dating as far back as 1636, the bureau and the Historical Section, Army War College, reaffirmed an earlier policy validated between World Wars I and II. Units were to perpetuate organizations that had been raised in the same geographic areas, regardless of type or designation. For example, New Jersey, which had supported part of the 44th Division before the war, now supported the 50th Armored Division. Therefore most of its elements "inherited" the history of the organic units of the old 44th, and elements of the new 44th perpetuated the history and traditions of former units in Illinois.[20]

The command arrangement within the multistate divisions presented another quandary. The War Department did not rule on the question, but some states that shared a division developed and signed formal command arrangement documents. For example, Florida, Georgia, and South Carolina, states that contributed to the 48th and 51st Infantry Divisions, contracted to rotate command of the units every five years.[21]

After the state governors formally notified the National Guard Bureau that they accepted the new troop allotments (*Table 18*), the bureau authorized reorganization of the units with 100 percent of their officers and 80 percent of their enlisted personnel. The first division granted federal recognition after World War II was the 45th Infantry Division from Oklahoma on 5 September 1946. Within one year all Guard division headquarters had received federal recognition.[22]

On Veterans Day 1946, at Arlington National Cemetery, President Truman announced the return of the National Guard colors and flags of those units that had served during the war. In concurrent ceremonies in state capitals, forty-five governors received those colors and flags. The other three states obtained their standards in separate ceremonies. These actions did much to express the tie of the postwar National Guard forces to prewar units.[23]

The rebuilding of the Organized Reserve Corps divisions posed some similar problems and others that were unique to it. A tentative troop basis, prepared in March 1946 (after the National Guard organizational structure had been presented to the states), outlined 25 divisions—3 armored, 5 airborne, and 17 infantry. These divisions and all other Organized Reserve Corps units were to be maintained in one of three strength categories, labeled Class A, B, and C. Class A units were divided into two groups, one for combat and one for service, and units were to be at required table of organization strength; Class B units were to have their full complement of officers and enlisted cadre strength; and Class C were to have officers only. The troop basis listed nine divisions as Class A, nine as Class B, and seven as Class C.[24]

Maj. Gen. Milton A. Reckord, the adjutant general of Maryland, and General Walsh of the National Guard Association protested the provision for Class A divisions, whose cost, they believed, would detract greatly from funds available to the Guard. They argued that if Class A units were needed, they should be allotted to the Regular Army or the National Guard, not to the Organized Reserve Corps, because these units were augmentations to rather than essential components of

## TABLE 18
### Location of National Guard Divisions
### Post–World War II

| Division | States |
| --- | --- |
| 26th Infantry | Massachusetts |
| 27th Infantry | New York |
| 28th Infantry | Pennsylvania |
| 29th Infantry | Maryland and Virginia |
| 30th Infantry | Tennessee and North Carolina |
| 31st Infantry | Alabama and Mississippi |
| 32d Infantry | Wisconsin |
| 33d Infantry | Illinois |
| 34th Infantry | Iowa and Nebraska |
| 35th Infantry | Kansas and Missouri |
| 36th Infantry | Texas |
| 37th Infantry | Ohio |
| 38th Infantry | Indiana |
| 39th Infantry | Arkansas and Louisiana |
| 40th Infantry | California |
| 41st Infantry | Washington and Oregon |
| 42d Infantry | New York |
| 43d Infantry | Connecticut, Rhode Island, and Vermont |
| 44th Infantry | Illinois |
| 45th Infantry | Oklahoma |
| 46th Infantry | Michigan |
| 47th Infantry | Minnesota and North Dakota |
| 48th Infantry | Georgia |
| 49th Armored | Texas |
| 49th Infantry* | California |
| 50th Armored | New Jersey |
| 51st Infantry | Florida and South Carolina |
| 52d Infantry | California |

* The 52d Infantry was redesignated the 49th Infantry in 1947.

the immediate mobilization force. Maj. Gen. Ray E. Porter, director of the Special Plans Division, supported the Guard's view regarding funds and noted that facilities were not available for use by Class A divisions. Furthermore, he believed the Organized Reserve Corps divisions would compete with Guard formations for available personnel. Porter therefore proposed reclassification of all Class A divisions as Class B units. Eventually the War Department agreed and made the appropriate changes.[25]

Although the dispute over Class A units lasted several months, the War Department proceeded with the reorganization of the Organized Reserve Corps

# AN INTERLUDE OF PEACE

divisions during the summer of 1946. That all divisions were to begin as Class C (officers only) units, progressing to the other categories as men and equipment became available, undoubtedly influenced the decision. Also, the War Department wanted to take advantage of the pool of trained reserve officers and enlisted men from World War II. By that time Army Ground Forces had been reorganized as an army group headquarters that commanded six geographic armies (*Map 3*). The armies replaced the nine corps areas of the prewar era, and the army commanders were tasked to organize and train both Regular Army and Organized Reserve Corps units. The plan the army commanders received called for twenty-five Organized Reserve Corps divisions—the 19th, 21st, and 22d Armored Divisions; the 15th, 84th, 98th, 99th, and 100th Airborne Divisions; and the 76th, 77th, 79th, 81st, 83d, 85th, 87th, 89th, 90th, 91st, 94th, 95th, 96th, 97th, 102d, 103d, and 104th Infantry Divisions. Demography served as the basic tool for locating the units within the army areas, as after World War I.[26]

The twenty-five reserve divisions activated between September 1946 and November 1947 (*Table 19*) differed somewhat from the original troop basis. The First Army declined to support an airborne division, and the 98th Infantry Division replaced the 98th Airborne Division. A note on the troop list nevertheless indicated that the unit was to be reorganized and redesignated as an airborne unit upon mobilization and was to train as such. After the change, the Organized Reserve Corps had four airborne, three armored, and eighteen infantry divisions. The Second Army insisted upon the number 80 for its airborne unit because the division was to be raised in the prewar 80th Division's area, not that of the 99th. Finally, the 103d Infantry Division, organized in 1921 in New Mexico, Colorado, and Arizona, was moved to Iowa, Minnesota, South Dakota, and North Dakota in the Fifth Army area. The Seventh Army (later replaced by Third Army), allotted the 15th Airborne Division, refused the designation, and the adjutant general replaced it by constituting the 108th Airborne Division, which fell within that component's list of infantry and airborne divisional numbers.[27]

A major problem in forming divisions and other units in the Organized Reserve Corps was adequate housing. While many National Guard units owned their own armories, some dating back to the nineteenth century, the Organized Reserve Corps had no facilities for storing equipment and for training. Although the War Department requested funds for needed facilities, Congress moved slowly in response.[28]

Given a smaller Organized Reserve Corps troop basis that called for infantry, armored, and airborne divisions, six prewar infantry divisions in that component were not reactivated in the reserves. The War Department deleted the 86th, 97th, and 99th Infantry Divisions when other divisions took over their recruiting areas, and the Regular Army, as noted, retained the 82d and 101st Divisions, which had been reorganized as airborne during the war. The future of the 88th Infantry Division, still on occupation duty in Italy, remained unsettled. Within the

MAP 3

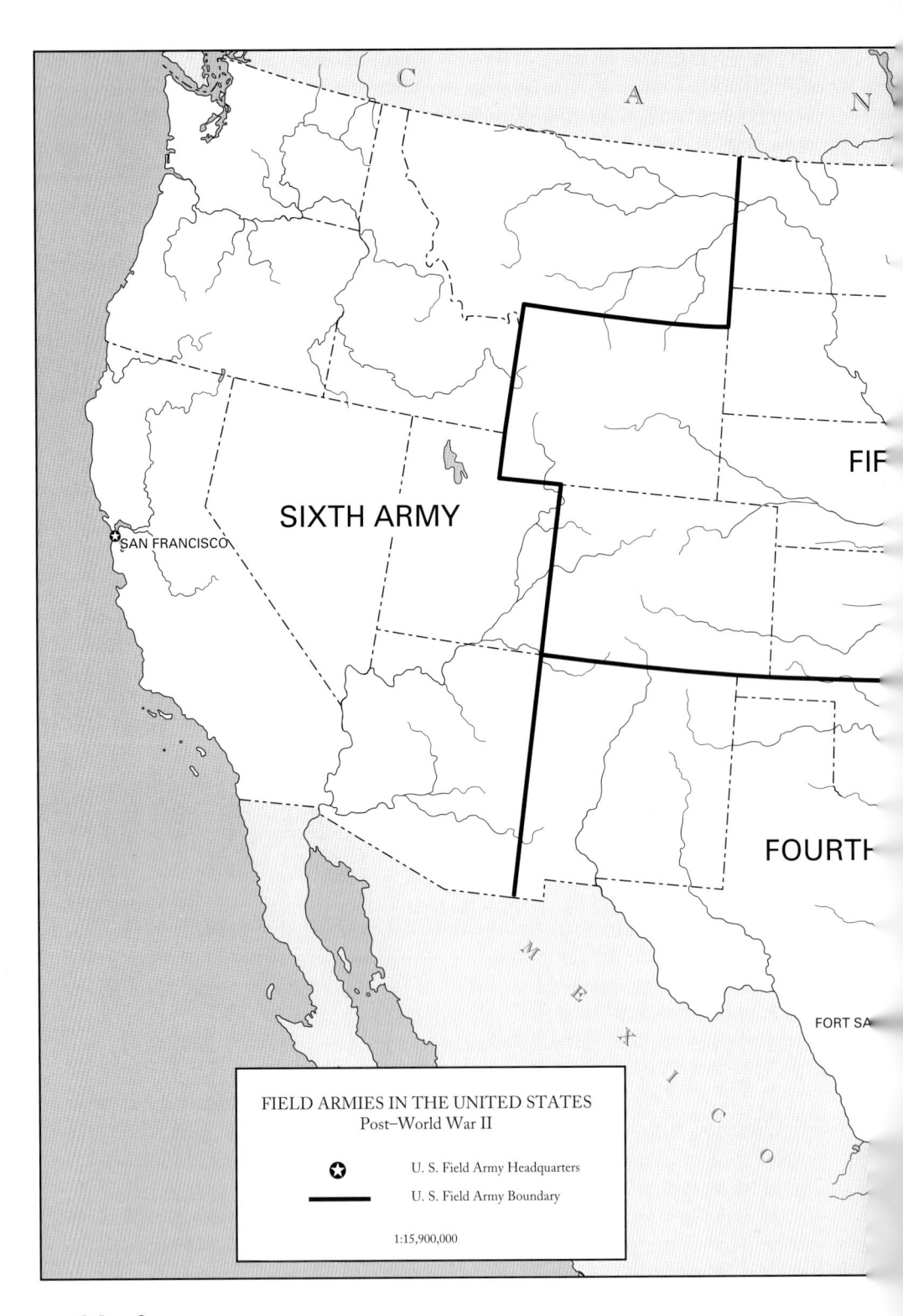

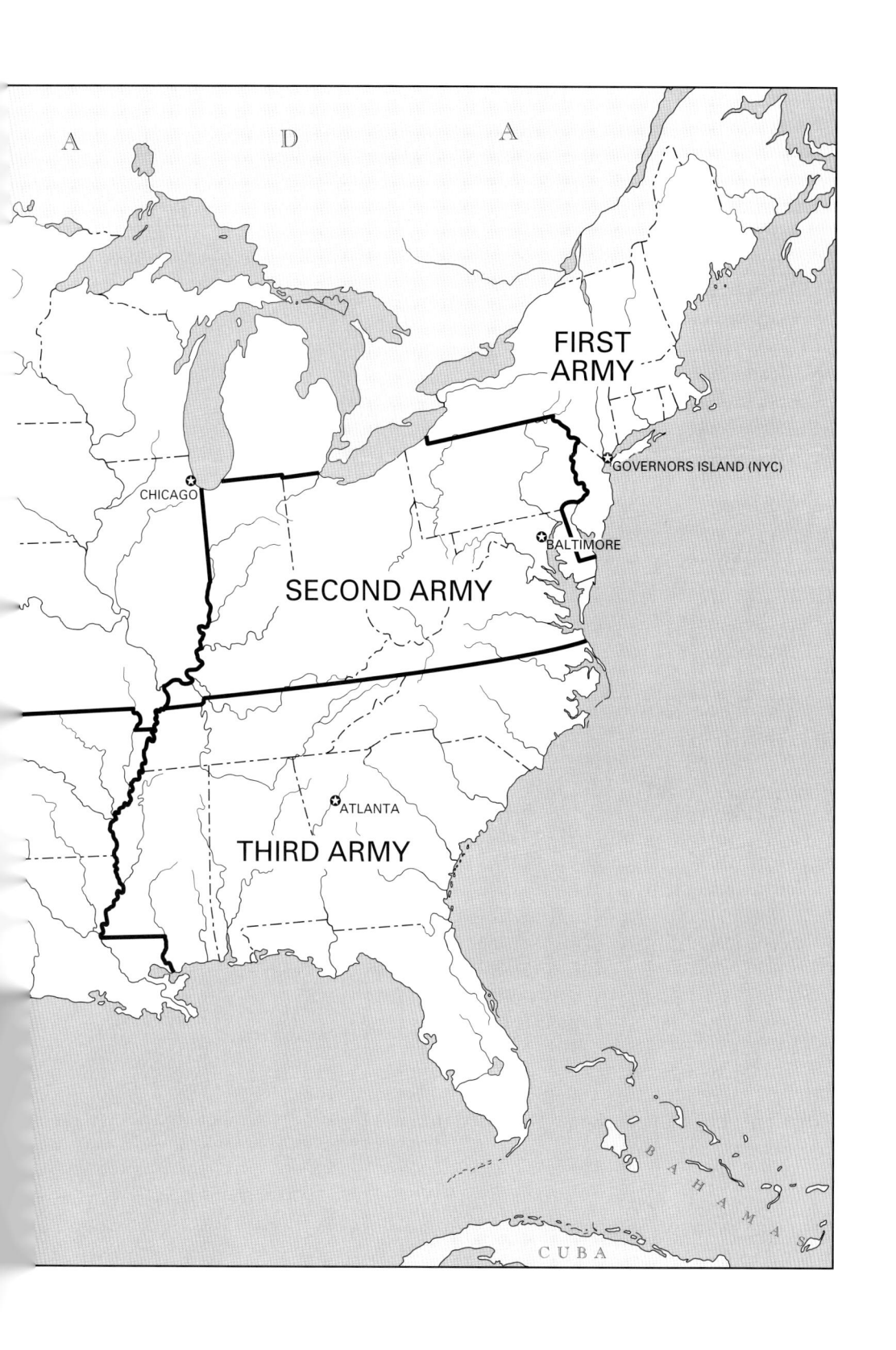

## FIRST ARMY

GOVERNORS ISLAND (NYC)

CHICAGO

BALTIMORE

## SECOND ARMY

ATLANTA

## THIRD ARMY

## TABLE 19

### Location of Organized Reserve Corps Divisions
### Post–World War II

| Division | Army Area | States |
| --- | --- | --- |
| 13th Armored* | Sixth | California, Oregon, and Arizona |
| 21st Armored | Fifth | Michigan and Illinois |
| 22d Armored | Fourth | Texas and Oklahoma |
| 76th Infantry | First | Connecticut, Rhode Island, New Hampshire, Maine, and Vermont |
| 77th Infantry | First | New York |
| 78th Infantry | First | New Jersey and Delaware |
| 79th Infantry | Second | Pennsylvania |
| 80th Airborne | Second | Maryland, Virginia, and District of Columbia |
| 81st Infantry | Third | Georgia, North Carolina, and South Carolina |
| 83d Infantry | Second | Ohio |
| 84th Airborne | Fifth | Indiana |
| 85th Infantry | Fifth | Illinois, Minnesota, South Dakota, and North Dakota |
| 87th Infantry | Third | Alabama, Tennessee, Mississippi, and Florida |
| 89th Infantry | Fifth | Kansas, Nebraska, Wyoming, and Colorado |
| 90th Infantry | Fourth | Texas |
| 91st Infantry | Sixth | California, Oregon, and Washington |
| 94th Infantry | First | Massachusetts |
| 95th Infantry | Fourth | Oklahoma, Arkansas, and Louisiana |
| 96th Infantry | Sixth | Montana, Washington, Idaho, Nevada, and Utah |
| 98th Infantry | First | New York |
| 100th Airborne | Second | Kentucky and West Virginia |
| 102d Infantry | Fifth | Missouri and Illinois |
| 103d Infantry | Fifth | Iowa, Minnesota, South Dakota, and North Dakota |
| 104th Infantry | Sixth | Washington and Oregon |
| 108th Airborne | Third | Georgia, Florida, North Carolina, and Alabama |

\* 13th Armored Division replaced the 19th Armored Division in 1947.

Organized Reserve Corps' block of numbers fell the 92d and 93d Infantry Divisions, but they were not classified as a part of that component. The War Department, however, decided not to maintain all-black divisions or use their traditional numbers in the postwar reorganization.[29]

Two changes took place shortly after the reorganization of the reserve divisions. In 1947 the 13th Armored Division replaced the 19th in the Organized Reserve Corps, and the 52d Infantry Division became the 49th in the National

*350th Infantry, 88th Infantry Division, parades in Gorizia, Italy, 1945.*

Guard. Redesignation of the 52d coincided with California's centennial celebration. The division's home area covered the region where gold had been discovered in 1849, and the state requested the name change to honor the "Forty-Niners" of that era. The 13th replaced the 19th Armored Division, also at California's bidding, because of the former unit's association with the state; the 13th had served there during and after World War II.[30]

The War Department tentatively planned to organize the 106th Infantry Division in Puerto Rico using units from all three components. The Regular Army and the National Guard were to furnish the regimental combat teams and the Organized Reserve Corps the combat support units. By early 1948 the combat elements had been organized, and the formation of most other units had been authorized, including the headquarters company of the division. The War Department determined, however, that the 106th Infantry Division was not needed and never added it to the reserve troop list. The division headquarters company was inactivated in 1950, but most other units remained active as nondivisional organizations.[31]

Manning reserve units proved to be a difficult task. Initially the Army planned that the rank and file of the units would be men who had undergone universal military training in centers operated by Regular Army divisions. With public sentiment opposed to universal military training, Congress declined to

TABLE 20

Divisions Designated as Training Centers, 1947–50

| Division | Location | Dates |
|---|---|---|
| 3d Armored | Fort Knox, Ky. | July 1947–Active |
| 4th Infantry | Fort Ord, Calif. | July 1947–Active |
| 5th Armored | Camp Chaffee, Ark. | July 1948–February 1950 |
| 5th Infantry | Fort Jackson, S.C. | July 1947–April 1950 |
| 9th Infantry | Fort Dix, N.J. | July 1947–Active |
| 10th Infantry | Fort Riley, Kans. | July 1948–Active |
| 17th Airborne | Camp Pickett, Va. | July 1948–June 1949 |
| 101st Airborne | Camp Breckinridge, Ky. | July 1948–May 1949 |

approve it. The reserves therefore relied upon volunteers who had prior service, the Reserve Officer Training Corps (ROTC), and personnel who had to complete a commitment after serving on active duty in conjunction with the draft, which was reenacted in 1948. That year to stimulate interest in the Organized Reserve Corps, Congress authorized pay for inactive duty training. With a small portion of the postwar Army dependent upon the draft, it generated few reservists for the National Guard and the Organized Reserve Corps, and those units fell considerably below full strength.[32]

Although the War Department did not use divisions as a part of a universal military training program, it decided to use divisional designations for replacement training centers in the summer of 1947. The 3d Armored Division and the 4th, 5th, and 9th Infantry Divisions were activated and their elements reorganized for that purpose. The cadres who trained the recruits responded favorably to the use of divisions as a means of building esprit since they wore the divisional shoulder sleeve insignia, and the recruits were inspired by the accomplishments of historic units. The Army authorized more training centers divisional designations in the summer of 1948 (*Table 20*). As the training load fluctuated, so did the number of "divisional" training centers, which stood at four two years later.[33]

## *Postwar Divisional Organizations*

In reorganizing the postwar divisions, the Army used World War II tables of organization and equipment, but studies of combat experience that were under way portended revisions. The U.S. European Theater of Operations established the General Board, consisting of many committees, to analyze the strategy, tactics, and administration of theater forces. A committee headed by Brig. Gen. A. Franklin Kibler, formerly the G–3, 12th Army Group, examined the requirements for various types of divisions. After weighing divisional strengths and weaknesses and considering new combinations of arms and services, the committee recommended the retention of infantry, armored, and airborne divisions. The committee concluded that a standard infantry division could accomplish missions that might require either light or mountain troops, and that therefore such special divisions were unnecessary. However, it also recommended that the Army maintain at least one horse cavalry division to guarantee that a few officers and enlisted men would continue to be trained as mounted troops. No other postwar study urged the retention of the cavalry division, and, as noted, the War Department rejected any large horse units for the future.[34]

Other General Board committees examined the requirements for each type of division. The committee for the infantry division surfaced many of the same requirements identified previously in the spring of 1945 and recommended a unit of 20,578 men. Additional men were needed in the infantry regiment to provide communications, intelligence, reconnaissance, and administration, and improved weapons were required for cannon and antitank companies. The committee proposed the development of a low silhouette 105-mm. self-propelled howitzer, but until its adoption the cannon company was to use a 105-mm. howitzer mounted on a medium tank. To arm the antitank company, the planners proposed either a self-propelled antitank gun or a medium tank, with most favoring the latter. Some committee members advocated removing the antitank company from the infantry regiment and adding a three-battalion tank regiment to the division. Because of the size and complexity of the infantry regiment, the committee urged that its commander be a brigadier general.[35]

Cavalry and field artillery arms were also expanded within the infantry division. To ensure adequate intelligence and counterreconnaissance (i.e., security), a divisional cavalry squadron replaced the troop. Because the division often lacked sufficient field artillery, the committee recommended adding a towed 155-mm. howitzer battalion for a total of two 155-mm. howitzer battalions and three self-propelled 105-mm. howitzer battalions. All fifteen artillery batteries were to have six pieces each.[36]

Divisional combat and combat service support also grew. An antiaircraft artillery battalion was added for air defense, an engineer regiment replaced the battalion, and a military police company supplanted the platoon. Given the increases in the arms and combat support elements, the division needed greater maintenance and quartermaster resources, and the committee urged expansion of these units to battalions. Finally, a new reinforcement battalion was suggested to process and forward replacements. In sum, the General Board committee preserved the division's three regimental combat teams used during the war, but added or enlarged units that had been organic or habitually attached and organizations to service them.[37]

The committee analyzing the airborne division concluded it should have the same organization and equipment as the infantry division, along with augmentations needed to perform its airborne missions. Two sets of equipment were thus recommended for the division, a lightweight set for airborne assaults and a heavy set for sustained ground combat. All divisional elements were to be trained in parachute, glider, and air transport techniques, making all divisional elements airborne units.38

The General Board's third committee on divisional organization reviewed the armored division. Examination of both the early heavy armored division and the lighter variant introduced in 1943 revealed defects that had been corrected by attaching units. Using the 1943 division as a base, the committee added a fourth 105-mm. howitzer battalion, an antiaircraft artillery battalion, and a tank destroyer battalion. During combat operations these units had been added to the division, as was an infantry battalion or regiment, when available. The committee viewed the combat command as a major weakness because it did not have assigned units, a violation of unity of command. Furthermore, both types of armored divisions had only two authorized combat commands, but in combat they normally had operated with three. To provide the third command in the heavy division, the headquarters and headquarters company of the armored infantry regiment had been organized provisionally as a combat command headquarters, and in the light division a headquarters and headquarters company of an armored group augmented the reserve command. The committee recommended that the combat commands be replaced with three regiments, each made up of one tank and two armored rifle battalions, and that brigadier generals command the regiments. Upon reflection, the committee omitted one unit previously attached to the division, the tank destroyer battalion, because of the wartime trend toward arming American tanks with high-velocity weapons capable of destroying enemy armor, an evolution that made the lightly armored tank destroyer redundant. The strength of the projected armored division rose to 19,377 officers and enlisted men, nearly double the size of light armored divisions of 1943.39

The Army Staff received the reports from the General Board and passed them along to the Army Ground Forces. In September 1945 that command began preparing new tables of organization for the postwar Army, but General Devers, commander of Army Ground Forces, refrained from making any decisions about divisional organization pending review of the board's findings and the recommendations of infantry and armored conferences being held in the spring of the following year. In July 1946 he finally forwarded proposals to the General Staff for new infantry and armored divisions that combined recommendations of the committees and of the conferences. The new tables for the infantry division were similar to those developed in 1945 when restrictions were lifted on their manning. The armored division retained its 1943 configuration with augmentations to correct organizational deficiencies. Devers believed these divisions would meet the Army's needs for versatile, mobile, hard-hitting units. Despite the availability of the atomic bomb, the nature of ground combat had not changed. The infantry division was capable of operating in jungle, arctic, desert, and mountain terrain or on plains; the armored division remained a highly mobile unit to break through a line or exploit success on the battlefield. He questioned, however, the appropriate rank for commanders of the new infantry combat teams (formerly infantry regiments) in the infantry division and combat commands in the armored division—a colonel or brigadier general.[40]

Eisenhower sent the divisional proposals to senior officers, including his own advisory group, for comment.[41] He was concerned that units were too large, possessing everything they might need under almost any condition, violating the principles of flexibility and economy of force followed during the war. He also requested the officers' views as to whether the Army should break each division into three smaller units, and if so whether the infantry regiment should be renamed an infantry combat team.[42]

The advisory group concurred with the Army Ground Forces proposals. It did not believe that divisions had too many people and too much equipment; they had only those units habitually attached during combat. The group did not fear a diminution of morale because the infantry regiment was to be known by another name. Moreover, it supported the rank of brigadier general for the commanders of infantry combat teams in the infantry division and combat commands in the armored division because it was commensurate with the assigned responsibilities.[43]

Among the other general officers who commented on the divisions, General Omar N. Bradley, head of the Veterans Administration, wanted the staff to develop a division organization that combined aspects of both infantry and armored divisions. For the time being, however, he deemed the proposed units sound. Lt. Gens. Walton H. Walker and Oscar W. Griswold, the Fifth and Seventh Army commanders, also endorsed the organizational proposals but disagreed on the appropriate rank for combat command and infantry combat team leaders. Eisenhower approved the divisions on 21 November 1946, but disapproved the change in general officer positions and the new name for infantry units. The following month Army Ground Forces prepared draft tables of organization for a 17,000-man infantry division and a 15,000-man armored division.[44]

In 1948, when the Department of the Army[45] finally published new tables for the infantry division, it authorized 18,804 officers and enlisted men (*Chart 23*). The division, however, remained basically the same as approved by Eisenhower. The ratio of combat to service troops was 4 to 1, and a 50 percent increase in firepower was attained by merely authorizing each field artillery firing battery six pieces.[46]

Some changes made between the time Eisenhower approved the division and publication of its tables, however, are noteworthy. In the medical service, a medical company replaced the attached medical detachment in each infantry regiment, and artillery, engineer, and tank battalions fielded organic medical detachments as did the division headquarters. The medical battalion was to provide only clearing and ambulance services. The reconnaissance troop was redesignated as a reconnaissance company to eliminate the term "troop" from the Army's nomenclature except for cavalry and constabulary units. At the insistence of officers who attended an Infantry conference in 1946 that discussed the status of the arm,

# CHART 23—Infantry Division, 7 July 1948

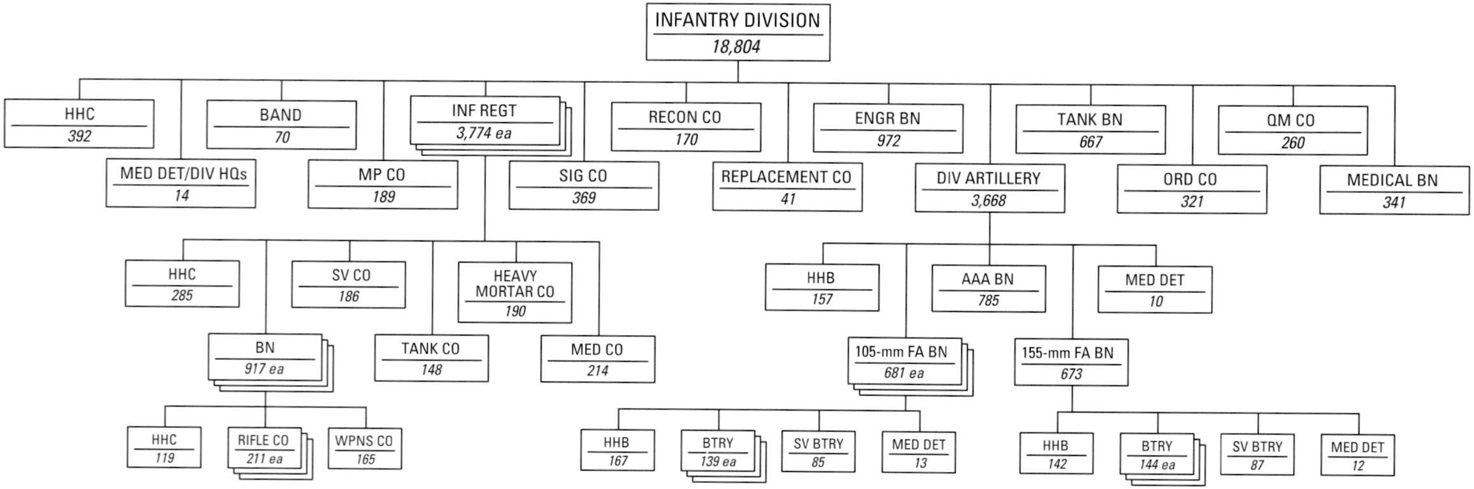

- **INFANTRY DIVISION** — 18,804
  - **HHC** — 392
  - **BAND** — 70
  - **MED DET/DIV HQs** — 14
  - **INF REGT** — 3,774 ea
    - **HHC** — 285
    - **MP CO** — 189
    - **SV CO** — 186
    - **TANK CO** — 148
    - **HEAVY MORTAR CO** — 190
    - **MED CO** — 214
    - **BN** — 917 ea
      - **HHC** — 119
      - **RIFLE CO** — 211 ea
      - **WPNS CO** — 165
  - **SIG CO** — 369
  - **RECON CO** — 170
  - **REPLACEMENT CO** — 41
  - **ENGR BN** — 972
  - **DIV ARTILLERY** — 3,668
    - **HHB** — 157
    - **AAA BN** — 785
      - **MED DET** — 10
    - **105-mm FA BN** — 681 ea
      - **HHB** — 167
      - **BTRY** — 139 ea
      - **SV BTRY** — 85
      - **MED DET** — 13
    - **155-mm FA BN** — 673
      - **HHB** — 142
      - **BTRY** — 144 ea
      - **SV BTRY** — 87
      - **MED DET** — 12
  - **TANK BN** — 667
  - **ORD CO** — 321
  - **QM CO** — 260
  - **MEDICAL BN** — 341

# AN INTERLUDE OF PEACE

Army Ground Forces added a replacement company to receive and process incoming personnel. One unit that did not survive the postwar revision was headquarters, special troops, because it was deemed unnecessary. A major general continued to command the division, and it was authorized two brigadier generals, the assistant division commander and the artillery commander. Regimental commanders remained colonels.[47]

A controversial area that affected development of the tables for the infantry division was the postwar battlefield's greater depth and breadth, which increased the difficulty of conducting reconnaissance and intelligence collection. Ten airplanes had been assigned to the division artillery in 1943 and an additional three to the infantry regiments in 1945. In 1946 Army Ground Forces proposed assigning aircraft to the division headquarters and to tank and engineer battalions. The Army Staff endorsed the additional planes but wanted them pooled in one unit, except for those in the division artillery. Opposition to that proposal came from the Army Air Forces, which argued that all air units came under their jurisdiction.[48] The Army countered that the National Security Act of 1947 authorized it to organize, train, and equip aviation resources for prompt and sustained combat incident to operations on land.[49] Nevertheless the tables provided no aviation unit, but ten planes were assigned to the division artillery and eight to the division headquarters company.[50]

The postwar armored division (*Chart 24*) retained the flexible command structure of the 1943 organization with three medium tank battalions, three armored infantry battalions, and three 105-mm. howitzer battalions, along with some significant changes. Army Ground Forces made the reserve command identical to the two existing combat commands, replaced the attached tank destroyer battalion with a heavy tank battalion, and added an antiaircraft artillery battalion, and a replacement company. Paralleling the infantry division, the military police platoon was expanded to a company and the reconnaissance squadron was redesignated as a battalion. A 155-mm. self-propelled howitzer battalion was added to give the division more general support fire, and, in the division trains, the quartermaster supply battalion, eliminated in 1943, was restored to transport fuel, provide bath and laundry facilities, and assume graves registration duties. Besides the field artillery's aircraft, ten planes were placed in the division headquarters company to serve division and combat command headquarters, the engineer battalion, and the reconnaissance battalion. The number of general officers was increased from two to three, a division commander and two combat command commanders. The commanders of the reserve command and the division artillery remained colonel billets.[51]

Infantry and armored divisions were reorganized between the fall of 1948 and the end of 1949. Most divisions, however, never attained their table of organization strengths prior to the Korean War. Only the 1st Infantry Division in Germany was authorized at full strength. Strengths in other Regular Army divisions fell between 55 and 80 percent. In the National Guard the strength of the divisional elements varied, with some units being cut by individuals, by crews

## CHART 24—Armored Division, 8 October 1948

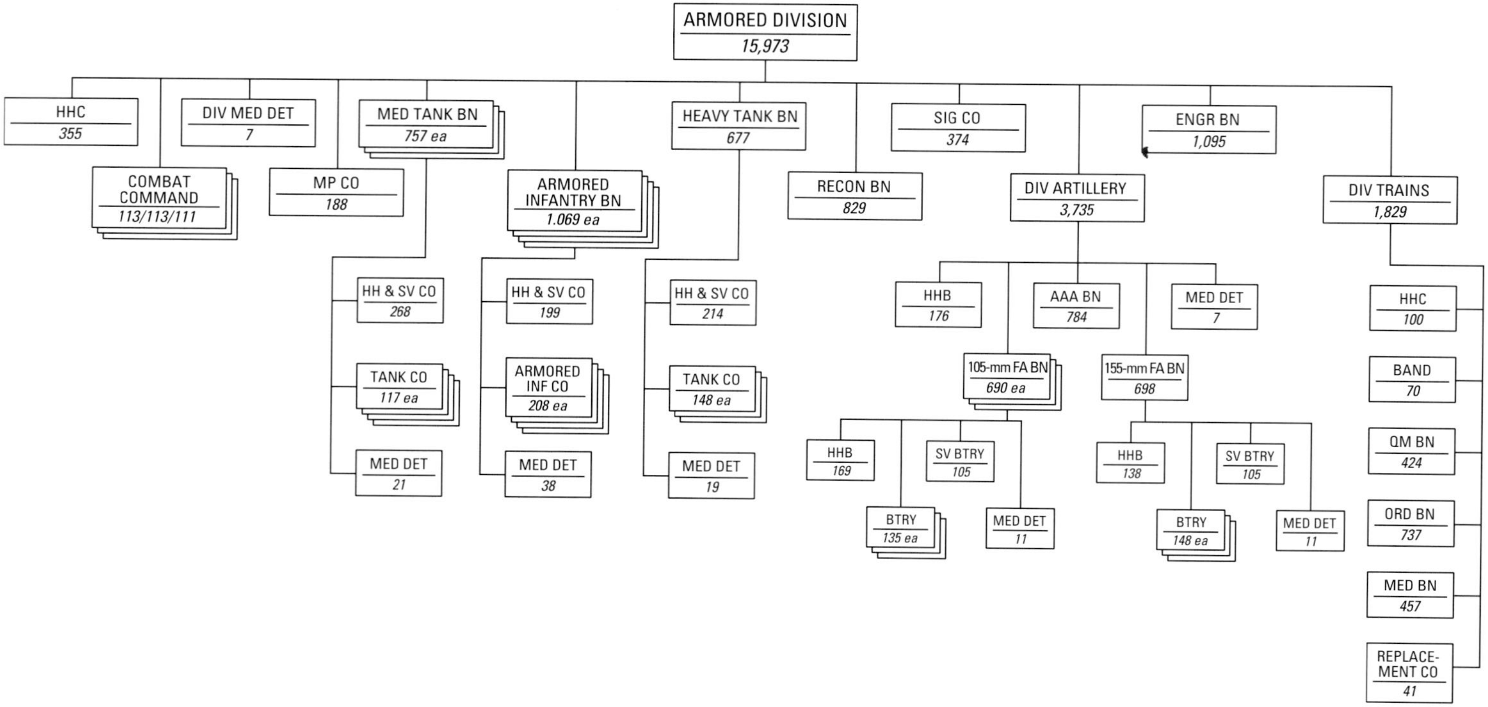

- ARMORED DIVISION — 15,973
  - HHC — 355
  - DIV MED DET — 7
  - COMBAT COMMAND — 113/113/111
  - MP CO — 188
  - MED TANK BN — 757 ea
    - HH & SV CO — 268
    - TANK CO — 117 ea
    - MED DET — 21
  - ARMORED INFANTRY BN — 1,069 ea
    - HH & SV CO — 199
    - ARMORED INF CO — 208 ea
    - MED DET — 38
  - HEAVY TANK BN — 677
    - HH & SV CO — 214
    - TANK CO — 148 ea
    - MED DET — 19
  - RECON BN — 829
  - SIG CO — 374
  - DIV ARTILLERY — 3,735
    - HHB — 176
    - 105-mm FA BN — 690 ea
      - HHB — 169
      - SV BTRY — 105
      - BTRY — 135 ea
      - MED DET — 11
    - AAA BN — 784
    - 155-mm FA BN — 698
      - HHB — 138
      - SV BTRY — 105
      - BTRY — 148 ea
      - MED DET — 11
    - MED DET — 7
  - ENGR BN — 1,095
  - DIV TRAINS — 1,829
    - HHC — 100
    - BAND — 70
    - QM BN — 424
    - ORD BN — 737
    - MED BN — 457
    - REPLACEMENT CO — 41

AN INTERLUDE OF PEACE                                                                229

(the field artillery batteries had four rather than six gun crews), or by companies (the engineer battalion had three instead of four line companies and there was no divisional replacement company). Strengths in the Guard units ranged between 5,000 and 10,500 men of all ranks. The divisions of the Organized Reserve Corps remained either Class B or Class C units.[52]

The development of the postwar airborne division took almost two years longer than infantry and armored divisions. On 16 August 1946 Army Ground Forces forwarded to the General Staff an outline for an airborne division. It was an infantry division with the addition of a pathfinder platoon and a parachute maintenance company. The division had approximately 19,000 jump-qualified officers and enlisted men and two sets of equipment, one for air assault and the other for sustained combat. Eisenhower rejected the proposal because the unit could not be air-transported. He directed Army Ground Forces to prepare an organization that could be moved by existing aircraft. Eisenhower also rejected the resulting proposal, but a third idea developed by the Organizational and Training Division of the General Staff won acceptance. The staff proposed an airborne division with two categories of units, organic elements that could be airlifted and attached ground units that were to link up with them. To make the unit air-transportable, the staff eliminated heavy mortars and tanks from infantry regiments and restricted the number of howitzers in field artillery batteries to four. The attached units included two heavy tank battalions, a 155-mm. howitzer battalion, a reconnaissance company, a medium maintenance company, and a quartermaster company, which totaled 2,580 officers and enlisted men. Those units along with the division's organic elements, which numbered 16,470, made the division's size approximately the same as the Army Ground Forces proposal.[53]

With the proposed airborne division attempting to meet two competing needs, strategic mobility and tactical sustainment, the General Staff decided to test it. The 82d Airborne Division (less one regimental combat team at Fort Benning) adopted the new structure on 1 January 1948. After the test, Army Field Forces (AFF), the successor of Army Ground Forces, recommended organizing the airborne division in the same manner as an infantry division. As organized for the test, the airborne division was not air-transportable. The Army Staff, nevertheless, still sought a large airborne unit for strategic mobility. Therefore, on 4 May 1949 the new Chief of Staff, General Omar Bradley, directed that the attached combat elements be made organic to the division and that only 11,000 of its 17,500 men be airborne qualified. The Department of the Army published new tables (*Chart 25*) mirroring these decisions on 1 April 1950. Reorganization of Regular Army and Organized Reserve Corps airborne divisions followed shortly thereafter.[54]

## *The State of Divisional Forces*

While the Army developed and reorganized its postwar divisions, it continued to maintain and redeploy its existing forces to meet changing international

# CHART 25—Airborne Division, 1 April 1950

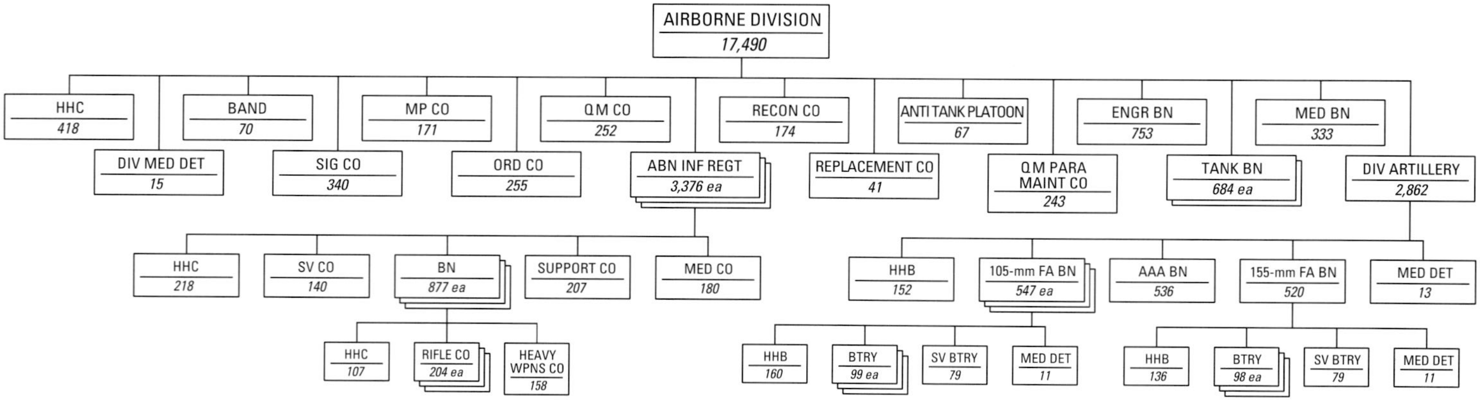

**AIRBORNE DIVISION** — 17,490

- HHC — 418
- BAND — 70
- MP CO — 171
- QM CO — 252
- RECON CO — 174
- ANTITANK PLATOON — 67
- ENGR BN — 753
- TANK BN — 684 ea
- MED BN — 333
- DIV ARTILLERY — 2,862

- DIV MED DET — 15
- SIG CO — 340
- ORD CO — 255
- ABN INF REGT — 3,376 ea
- REPLACEMENT CO — 41
- QM PARA MAINT CO — 243

ABN INF REGT:
- HHC — 218
- SV CO — 140
- SUPPORT CO — 207
- BN — 877 ea
- MED CO — 180

BN:
- HHC — 107
- RIFLE CO — 204 ea
- HEAVY WPNS CO — 158

DIV ARTILLERY:
- HHB — 152
- 105-mm FA BN — 547 ea
- AAA BN — 536
- 155-mm FA BN — 520
- MED DET — 13

105-mm FA BN:
- HHB — 160
- BTRY — 99 ea
- SV BTRY — 79
- MED DET — 11

155-mm FA BN:
- HHB — 136
- BTRY — 98 ea
- SV BTRY — 79
- MED DET — 11

*A final parade in Gorizia, before the 88th Division departs, 1947; below,* 82d Airborne Division *troops at the New York City victory parade, 1946.*

situations. With the ratification of the Italian peace treaty in the fall of 1947, the Army inactivated the 88th Infantry Division (less one infantry regiment, which remained in Trieste) and, as noted, withdrew its forces from Korea at the end of 1948. To make room in Japan for the 7th Infantry Division, the 11th Airborne Division, which had been stationed there since 1945, redeployed to Fort Campbell, Kentucky, where it was reorganized with only two of its three regimental combat teams. The reduction of forces in Korea also resulted in the inactivation of the 6th Infantry Division.[55]

Four years after the end of World War II the number of Regular Army divisions had fallen to ten. Overseas the 1st Infantry Division was scattered among installations in Germany, while the 1st Cavalry Division and the 7th, 24th, and 25th Infantry Divisions were stationed throughout Japan. In the United States the 2d Armored Division was split between Camp (later Fort) Hood, Texas, and Fort Sill, Oklahoma. The 2d Infantry Division was based at Fort Lewis, Washington; the 3d Infantry Division at Fort Benning, Georgia, and Fort Devens, Massachusetts; the 11th Airborne Division (less one inactive regimental combat team) at Fort Campbell, Kentucky; and the 82d Airborne Division at Fort Bragg, North Carolina. The twenty-five Organized Reserve Corps and twenty-seven National Guard divisions were at various levels of readiness.

Initially overwhelmed by the tidal wave of demobilization after World War II, the Army had struggled to rebuild both Regular Army and reserve divisions during the late 1940s. Its new divisional structures were based on combat experiences during the war, under the assumption that atomic weapons would not alter the nature of ground combat. Units previously attached to divisions from higher headquarters during combat were made organic to divisions, which also received additional firepower. Although the postwar divisions of the era were not fully prepared for combat because they were not properly manned and equipped, they nonetheless represented an unprecedented peacetime force in the Army of the United States, reflecting the new Soviet-American tensions.

## Notes

1 Disposition Form (DF), AGF to CofS, USA, 22 Jul 46, sub: New Infantry and Armored Divisions, App II, AGF/AG 322 Divisions, case 100, RG 337, NARA.

2 Sparrow, *History of Personnel Demobilization*, pp. 229–30.

3 William W. Epley, *America's First Cold War Army, 1945–1950* (Arlington, Va.: Institute of Land Warfare, Association of the U.S. Army, 1993), p. 4; Ltr, AGF to CG, Second Army, 31 Aug 46, sub: Inactivation of 5th Infantry Division, 322/107 (5th Inf Div) (31 Aug 46), and Ltr, TAG to U.S. Forces, European Theater, 13 Feb 47, sub: Inactivation of Units, AGAO-I 322 (13 Feb 47)-M, both AG Reference files, DAMH-HSO; Ltr, TAG to U.S. Forces, European Theater, 6 May 46, sub: Inactivation of Units, AG 322 (29 Apr 46) AO-I-E-M, 42d Inf Div file, and Ltr, TAG to CinC, Far East, 30 Dec 46, sub: Activation, Inactivation, Reorganization and Redesignation of Certain Units in the Pacific Theater, AG 322 (13 Dec 46) AO-I-WDGOT-M, 86th Inf Div file, both DAMH-HSO; *Mission Accomplished: Third United States Army Occupation of Germany, 9 May 1945–15 February 1947* (n.p., 1947), p. 23.

4 Ernest N. Harmon, "U.S. Constabulary," *Armored Cavalry Journal* 55 (Sep Oct 1946): 16; James M. Snyder, *The Establishment and Operations of the U.S. Constabulary* (Frankfurt, Germany: Historical Sub-Section, G–3, U.S. Constabulary, 1947), pp. 52–59; Ltr, TAG to CG, U.S. Forces, European Theater, 17 Jun 46, sub: Reconstitution, Redesignation, Reorganization, Activation and Assignment of Units for Constabulary Force in Europe, AG 322 (11 Jun 46) AG-I-GNGCT-M, 4th Armd Div file, DAMH-HSO.

5 James F. Schnabel, *Policy and Direction: The First Year*, United States Army in the Korean War (Washington, D.C.: Government Printing Office, 1972), pp. 6–12; Ltr, TAG to CGs, Boston, New York and other ports of embarkation, 7 Jan 46, sub: Inactivation of Certain Army Air, Ground and Service Forces Type Units, AG 322 (4 Jan 47) OB-I-SPMOU-M, 40th Inf Div file, Ltr, TAG to CinC, Far East, 24 Jan 49, sub: Inactivation of Certain Units in FECOM, AGAO-I 322 (31 Dec 48) CSGOT (Organization and Training Division, General Staff)-M, 6th Inf Div file, and AGAZ 373, Historical Data Cards, 6th, 7th, and 40th Inf Divs, all DAMH-HSO; *History of the 7th Infantry (Bayonet Division)* (Tokyo, Japan: Dai Nippon Printing Co., 1967), no pagination.

6 John P. Delaney, *The Blue Devils in Italy: A History of the 88th Infantry Division in World War II* (Washington, D.C.: Infantry Journal Press, 1947), p. 275; Wright, *The 1st Cavalry Division in World War II*, p. 206; Ltr, TAG to CG, Second Army, 26 Sep 46, sub: Reorganization of the 3d Infantry Division, AG 322 (20 Sep 46) AO-I-GNGCT-M, 3d Inf Div file, DAMH-HSO; George C. Marshall, Remarks by the Secretary of Defense at the National Preparedness Orientation Conference, 30 Nov 50, Marshall Papers.

7 WD Bull 19, 1945; Ltr, TAG to CinC, US Army Forces, Pacific, 26 Mar 46, sub: Constitution, Activation, Inactivation, Disbandment, Reorganization and Redesignation of Certain Philippine Scout Units, AG 322 (19 Mar 46) OB-I-GNGCT-M, 5th Ind, U.S. Army Forces, Western Pacific, to CinC, Army Forces, Pacific, 20 Aug 46, 12th Inf Div file, DAMH-HSO.

8 Ltr, TAG to CinC, US Army Forces, Pacific, 26 Mar 46, sub: Constitution, Activation, Inactivation, Disbandment, Reorganization and Redesignation of Certain Philippine Scout Units; *Semi-Annual Report: U.S. Army Forces Western Pacific, 1 Jan–30 Jun 46*, p. 33; Robert R. Smith, "The Status of Members of the Philippine Military Forces During World War II," Ms, pp. 45–47, Reference Paper files, Philippine Scouts, DAMH-HSO; "Philippine Scouts," *Military Review* 29 (Jul 1949): 72; Ltr, TAG to CinC, Far East, 29 Apr 47, sub: Reorganization, Assignment and Inactivation of Certain Units in the Far East Command, AGAO-I 322 (28 Mar 47) WDGOT-M, and DF, TAG to Historical Division, WD Special Staff, sub: Shoulder Sleeve Insignia, Philippine-Ryukyus Command, 27 Aug 47, AGAO-I 421.4 (30 Apr 47), both 12th Inf Div file, DAMH-HSO.

9 Joseph Rockis, "Reorganization of AGF During Demobilization," Demobilization Series, Study No. 3 (Historical Section, Army Ground Forces, 1948), pp. 36–46, DAMH-HSR.

10 Ibid.; *First Report of the Secretary of Defense, 1948*, pp. 60–63; Strength Reports of the Army, 1 Jan 1948, pp. 4–6.

11 *Mission Accomplished*, p. 23; James M. Gavin, *On to Berlin*, p. 295; SS, WDGOT to CofS, 27 Aug 46, sub: Regular Army Divisions to be Retained in the Postwar Army, 27 Aug 46, WDGOT 322 (26 Jun 46), 1st Cav Div file, DAMH-HSO.

12 Statement by the CofS, Approved WD Policies Relating to Postwar National Guard and Organized Reserve, 13 Oct 45, Reference Paper files, Army Reserve, DAMH-HSO; SS, WDGOT to CofS, sub: Regular Army Divisions to be Retained in the Postwar Army, 27 Aug 46; Memo, WDGOT for Assistant Deputy CofS, same subject, 30 Sep 46, WDGOT 322 (26 Jun 46), 1st Cav Div file, DAMH-HSO.

13 Ltr, TAG to CinC, Far East, 14 Mar 49, sub: Redesignation and Reorganization of the 1st Cavalry Division, Special, AGAO-I 322 (28 Feb 49) GCSGOT-M (General and Special Staffs, U.S. Army, Organization and Training Division), 1st Cav Div file; Ltr, TAG to CG, Armies, Zone of the Interior (ZI), 25 Jun 48, sub: Activation and Reorganization of Certain Divisions (Training), AGAO-I 322 (18 Jun 48) CSGOT-M, 10th Mt Div file; Ltr, TAGO to TAG, 27 Jun 49, sub: Designation of the 25th Infantry Division as Regular Army, AGAO-I (27 Jun 49)-M, 25th Inf Div file; and Ltr, TAGO to TAG, 15 Nov 48, sub: Designation of the 11th and 82d Airborne Divisions as Regular Army, AGAO-I 322 (15 Nov 48), 82d Abn Div file, all AG Reference files, DAMH-HSO.

14 Memo, AGF for chiefs all staff sections, 6 Mar 48, sub: Inter-relations between professional and non-professional personnel in the armed forces of a democratic state, GNGSE (AGF Secretariat) 300.6 (6 Mar 48), National Guard, Reference Paper files, DAMH-HSO.

15 Ibid.; Memo, Army Service Forces for CofS, 4 Aug 44, sub: Appointment of Committee under Section 5 of the National Defense Act of 1916, as amended, Memo, OCS for G–1, G–2, G–3, G–4, OPD, 3 Oct 44, sub: Committee to study policies affecting the Officers' Reserve Corps, the Organized Reserve Corps, and the Enlisted Reserve Corps, and Memo, OCS for CofS, 21 Sep 44, sub: Recommended War Department Policies for the Post War National Guard and Organized Reserve Corps, all National Guard Reference Paper files, DAMH-HSO.

16 The 1920 amendments to the National Defense Act designated the third component of the Army as the Organized Reserves, but in all post-World War II planning documents the term Organized Reserve Corps was used and it was officially adopted in 1948. Therefore, to be consistent with the planning documents, the term Organized Reserve Corps is used hereafter.

17 Statement, Approved WD Policies Relating to Postwar National Guard and Organized Reserve, 13 Oct 45.

18 Memo, WDGCT for CofS, 2 Nov 45, sub: National Guard Troop Basis, WDGCT 320 Troop Basis (2 Nov 45), National Guard, Reference Paper files, DAMH-HSO; *Report of the Chief of the National Guard Bureau, 1946*, pp. 324–76; National Guard Troop Basis and Troop Allotments, 1 Sep 46, National Guard, Reference Paper files, DAMH-HSO; Ltr, Sec of War to W. G. Andrews, House of Representatives, 13 May 46, and DF, Chief, NGB, to TAG, 26 Jun 46, sub: Numerical Designation, 325.4–42 Div 3, AG 322 file, RG 407, NARA; Ltr, TAG to CG, AGF, and Chief, NGB, 17 Sep 46, sub: Allotment of 42d Infantry Division to the National Guard, AG 322 (17 Sep 46) AG-I-WDSNG-M (National Guard Bureau, WD Special Staff), 42d Inf Div file, DAMH-HSO.

19 *Report of the Chief of the National Guard Bureau, 1946*, pp. 110–11.

20 Memo, NGB for Chief, Historical Section, AWC, 18 Apr 46, sub: Continuity of History of the National Guard Units, WDNGR (National Guard Register, WD) 314.7 Gen.-23 (18 Apr 46), NGB Cir 9, 1932, and Memo, Historical Section, AWC, for Col. E. Colby, National Guard Bureau, 19 Apr 46, all National Guard, Policy and Precedence files, DAMH-HSO.

21 Draft agreement between the States of Georgia, South Carolina, and Florida, undated, and Ltr, Florida National Guard (FNG) to Chief, NGB, 25 Feb 59, sub: Reorganization of 48th Armored Division, FNG–10, both 48th Armd Div file, DAMH-HSO.

22 Ltr, AGF to CGs First, Second, Fourth, Fifth, Sixth, and Seventh Armies and other addresses, 6 Jun 46, sub: Training and Administration of the Civilian Components, Incl 1, AGF plan for the National Guard of the U.S., 6 Jun 46, 326/215 (6 Jun 46) GNGCT–11, AGF Pt. 1, RG 319, NARA; see National Guard Federal Recognition Reports, 1946–47, National Guard General files, DAMH-HSO; *Report of the Chief the of National Guard Bureau, 1947*, p. 73.

23 *Report of the Chief of the National Guard Bureau, 1947*, pp. 8–10.

24 Statement, Approved WD Policies Relating to the Postwar NG and ORC, 13 Oct 45; Ltr, AGF to CGs, First, Second, Fourth, Fifth, Sixth, and Seventh Armies and other addresses, 6 Jun 46, sub: Training and Administration of the Civilian Components, Incl 3, AGF Plan for the Organized Reserve Corps; Richard B. Crossland and James T. Currie, *Twice the Citizen: A History of the United States Army Reserve, 1908–1983* (Washington, D.C.: Government Printing Office, 1984), p. 86.

25 Memo, WDSSP (Special Planning Division, General and Special Staffs), for ACofS, G–3, 14 Mar 46, sub: Class A Units, Organized Reserve Corps, and Memo, WD Gen Staff, Organization and Training Division, for all WD Agencies, 20 Dec 46, sub: Clarification of WD Policies Pertaining to the National Guard and the Organized Reserve Corps, WDGOT 325 (9 Oct 46), both Army Reserve, Reference Paper files, DAMH-HSO.

26 Ltr, AGF to CGs, First and Second Armies, and other addresses, 6 Jun 46, sub: Training and Administration of Civilian Components, Incl 3, AGF Plan for the Organized Reserve Corps; WD Cir 138, 1946; C. T. Tench, "The New Organization," *Infantry Journal* 59 (Jul 46): 18–22.

27 Ltr, AGF to CGs, First and Second Armies, and other addresses, 6 Jun 46, sub: Training and Administration of Civilian Components, Incl 3, Plan for the Organized Reserve Corps; see author's notes for activation dates of ORC divisions, which are based on unit divisional files in DAMH-HSO.

28 "Our Floundering Army Reserve Program," *Reserve Officer* 25 (Jul 1948): 4–6ff.

29 AGF map showing location of division headquarters and states to which division have been allotted, 27 Apr 47, Army Reserve Reference Paper files, DAMH-HSO; WD Cir 124, 1946.

30 Ltr, TAG to CG, Sixth Army, 8 Aug 47, sub: Inactivation and Assignment of 19th Armored Division and Assignment and Activation of 13th Armored Division, AGAO-I 322 (31 Jul 47) GNGCT-M, 13th Armd Div file, DAMH-HSO; Assembly Joint Resolution No. 38 Relative to the perpetuation of the 13th Armored Division to this State, *Ch. 191, 57th Sess, California State Legislature*, 13th Armd Div file, DAMH-HSO; *Biennial Report of the Adjutant General, California, 1947–1948*, p. 11, and GO 56, Adjutant General of California, 1947, reprinted in the report, pp. 72–73.

31 Ltr, Michael S. Davison to author, 13 Feb 78; Ltr, TAG to CG, U.S. Army Caribbean, 25 Mar 48, sub: Activation of Units of the Organized Reserves, AGAO-322 Org Res (8 Feb 48) GSCOT-M, Ltr, CG, U.S. Army Caribbean to TAG, 21 Aug 50, sub: Inactivation of ORC TOE Units not included in the New ORC troop Program, AG 326 (CG), and Ltr, TAG to CG, U.S. Army Caribbean, 27 Sep 50, sub: Inactivation of Units of the Organized Reserve, AGAO-I Org Res (21 Aug 50) G–3–M, all 106th Inf Div file, DAMH-HSO.

32 *Annual Report of the Secretary of the Army, 1948*, pp. 34–35; Joint Army and Air Force Bull No. 9, 1948 (in 1948 and 1949 the Departments of the Army and Air Force jointly published bulletins).

33 Ltr, TAG to CGs, First, Second, Third, and Sixth Armies, 8 Jul 47, sub: Discontinuance of Replacement Training Centers and Activation of the 3d Armored and the 4th, 5th, and 9th Infantry Divisions, AGAO-I 322 (10 Jun 47), GNGCT-M, 3d Armd Div file, DAMH-HSO; C. D. Dunlap, Jr., "The Third Armored Training Division," *Armored Cavalry Journal* 57 (Jul–Aug 48): 26–29; Ltr, TAG to CG, Armies, ZI, 25 Jun 48, sub: Activation and Reorganization of Certain Division (Training), AGAO-I 322 (18 Jun 48) CSGOT-M, 3d Armd Div file, DAMH-HSO; also see the unit files of 3d and 5th Armored, the 4th, 5th, 9th, and 10th Inf, and the 17th and 101st Abn Divs in DAMH-HSO.

34 General Board, "Types of Divisions Postwar Army," Rpt 17, U.S. Forces, ETO.

35 General Board, "The Infantry Division," Rpt 15, U.S. Forces, ETO.

36 Ibid.

37 Ibid.

38 General Board, "Organization, Equipment, and Tactical Employment of the Airborne Division," Rpt 16, U.S. Forces, ETO.

39 General Board, "Organization, Equipment, and Tactical Employment of the Armored Division," Rpt 48, U.S. Forces, ETO.

40 DF, AGF to CofS, 22 Jul 46, sub: New Infantry and Armored Divisions, Appendix II.

41 The Chief of Staff's Advisory Group, established in May 1946, consisted of senior officers who advised him on matters pertaining to the Army's long-range program. Lt Gen Wade H. Haislip; Maj Gens Gilbert Cook (who had written the 1935 memorandum to General Craig advocating the studies that resulted in the triangular division), Alexander D. Surles, and Howard M. Snyder; and Brig Gen William E. Hall made up the group. Memo, OCS for CGs, AAF, AGF, ASF, and other addresses, 8 May 46, OCS (1946) 334 "A," RG 165, NARA.

42 Memo, DCofS for CofS's Advisory Group, 10 Sep 46, no subject, WDCSA 322 (6 Aug 46), OCS (1946) 334 "A," RG 165, NARA.

43 Memo, Lt Gen Haislip to DCofS, 13 Sep 46, no subject, OCS (1946) 334 "A," RG 165, NARA.

44 Memo, Acting CofS for Generals Stilwell, Bradley, Walker, Eddy, and Griswold, 24 Sep 46, no subject, Memo, Omar N. Bradley to Gen Thomas T. Handy, 6 Nov 46, sub: Comments on proposed divisional organization for Infantry and Armored Divisions, Memo, Lt Gen Walton H. Walker to Gen Handy, 29 Oct 46, no subject, Ltr, Lt Gen O. W. Griswold to General Handy, 3 Oct 46, no subject, Memo, Maj Gen Louis A. Craig for Army Commander, 27 Sep 46, no subject, WDCSA 332 file, and Ltr, C. P. Hall to CG, AGF, 22 Nov 46, sub: Types of Divisions in the Postwar Army (Armored and Infantry), WDGOT 370.01 (22 Nov 46), G–3 (1946) 370.01, vol. 3, all RG 165, NARA.

45 In 1947 Congress established the Department of Defense comprising the Departments of the Army, Navy, and Air Force. The War Department was perpetuated by the Department of the Army.

46 TOE 7 N, Infantry Division, 1948.

47 Ibid.; Ltr, AGF to CGs, First, Second, Fourth, Fifth, Sixth, and Seventh Armies and other addresses, 28 Feb 47, sub: Charts for New Infantry Division, 322/101 (Divs) (28 Feb 47) GNGCT-71/4365, Division General file, DAMH-HSO; DA Cir 47, 1947; "The Division Replacement Company," *Infantry School Quarterly* 33 (Oct 48): 67–74.

48 Ltr, AGF to Dir of Organization and Training, WDGS, 16 Jun 47, sub: Headquarters and Headquarters Company New Divisions (Infantry and Armored), with 1st, 2d, and 3d Inds, 322 (Divs) (16 Jun 47) GNGCT–71–5066, and Memo, Organization and Training Division, General Staff, for Brig Gen Benjamin F. Caffey, 31 Oct 47, sub: Liaison Aircraft in New Divisions TOEs, with Bolte's hand written comments, 3 Nov 47, AFG/AG 322 Divisions, case 100, RG 337, NARA; Wilson B. Powell, "Army Ground Force During the Demobilization Period," Demobilization Series, Study 4 (Historical Section, Army Ground Forces, undated), p. 149, DAMH-HSR.

49 Kenneth W. Condit, *The Joint Chiefs of Staff and National Policy, 1955–1956*, vol. 6, History of the Joint Chiefs of Staff (Washington, D.C.: Government Printing Office, 1992), p.72.

50 TOE 7 N, Infantry Division, 1948.

51 Ltr, AGF to CGs, First, Second, Fourth, Fifth, Sixth, and Seventh Armies and other addresses, 13 Mar 47, sub: Charts for New Armored Division, 322/101 (Divs) (13 Mar 47) GNGCT–71–4556, Division General file, DAMH-HSO; TOE 17, Armored Division, 1948; James I. King and Melvin A. Goers, "Modern Armored Cavalry Organization," *Armored Cavalry Journal* 57 (Jul–Aug 1948): 47–50.

52 See AG letters of instruction, "Reorganization of Regular Army Divisions, 1948–1949," and "Reorganization of ORC Divisions, 1949," author's files; also see division files, DAMH-HSO; "The New T/O—Greater Firepower, Greater Strength," National Guardsman 2 (Nov 48): 25; *Report of the Chief of the National Guard Bureau, 1949*, pp. 3, 29, and 109; Program Review and Analysis Division, Comptroller of the Army, *The Troop Program and Troop List: Part III, Army Reserve Establishment*, 1 Jun 50, CMH Library.

53 DF, WD Dir Organization and Training, to CG AGF, 26 Aug 46, sub: Organization of the Airborne Division, 322 (Div) (26 Aug 46– GNGPS, AGF/AG 322 Div, Case 100, RG 337, NARA; Donald T. Kellett and William Friedman, "Airborne On Paper Wings," Part I, *Infantry Journal* 62 (May 1948): 9–14, Part II (Jun 1948): 30–33; Powell, "AGF During the Demobilization Period," p. 150; Ltr, AGF to CGs First, Second, Third, Fourth, Fifth, and Sixth Armies and other addresses, 16

# AN INTERLUDE OF PEACE

Oct 47, sub: Charts for New Airborne Division, 322/101 (Divs) (16 Oct 47) GNGCT–71–5521, Division General file, DAMH-HSO.

54 Annual History, Office, Chief of Army Field Forces (OCAFF), 1 Jan 1949–31 Dec 1949, Ch. 8, pp. 4–6, Manuscript Collection, DAMH-HSR; TOE 71, Airborne Division, 1 Apr 1950; Ltr, TAG to CGs, ZI, 19 May 50, sub: Reorganization of Organized Reserve Airborne Divisions, AGAO-I-322 (OR Res) (24 Mar 50) G–3–M, Ltr, TAG to CG, Second Army, 14 Jun 50, sub: Reorganization of the 11th Airborne Division, AGAO-I 322 11th Abn Div (31 May) G–1–M, and Ltr, TAG to CG, Third Army, 12 Jun 50, sub: Reorganization of the 82d Airborne Division, AGAO-I 322 82d Abn Div (25 May 50) G–1–M, all AG Reference files and airborne divisions files, DAMH-HSO.

55 Ltr, TAG to CG, USAF in the Mediterranean Theater of Operations, 12 Nov 47, sub: Inactivation of Units, AGAO-I 322 (12 Nov 47)–M, Ltr, TAG to CG, Second Army, 10 Mar 49, sub: Reorganization of the 11th Airborne Division, AGAO-I 322 11th Abn Div (12 Feb 49) CSGOT-M, Ltr, TAG to CinC, Far East, 24 Jan 49, sub: Inactivation of Certain Units in FECOM, AGAO-I 322 (31 Dec 48) CSGOT-M, and Ltr, TAG to CinC, Far East, 22 Jul 49, sub: Reorganization of Certain Infantry Divisions, AGAO-I 322 (22 Jul 49)–M, all AG Reference files, and AGAZ 373 Historical Data Cards, 6th, 7th, and 88th Infantry Divisions and 11th Airborne Division, division files, all DAMH-HSO.

CHAPTER 9

# The Korean War and Its Aftermath

*It is apparent that the United States is required to increase its military strength and preparedness not only to deal with the aggression in Korea but also to increase our common defense, with other free nations, against further aggression.*

President Harry S. Truman[1]

In June 1950, when a Soviet trained and armed North Korean army attacked South Korea, the Cold War turned hot. The U.S. Army was forced to adopt emergency expedients during the first months of the war, but the maintenance of a significant military sustaining base after World War II, a response to Soviet-American tensions, allowed the nation to mobilize more quickly and easily than in the past. Within a year and a half the number of Army combat divisions on active duty went from ten to twenty. The Army, reacting to changing political, strategic, and operational requirements worldwide, for the first time in its history reassessed its reserve forces during a major war. Nevertheless, the end of the fighting in Korea brought new reductions, which resulted in fewer Army divisions by the end of the decade than during the war.

## *Deployment of Forces to Korea*

The invasion of South Korea on 25 June 1950 exposed a hollow Army. Divisions in Japan were completing a reorganization that reflected greatly reduced manning and equipment levels. The 1st Cavalry Division and the 7th, 24th, and 25th Infantry Divisions all lacked reconnaissance, military police, and replacement companies, medical detachments, and bands. Their infantry regiments were each short one battalion and the tank company, and the 105-mm. howitzer battalions had only two firing batteries. Only one company or battery was filled in the tank and antiaircraft artillery battalions. Tank companies were equipped with the M24 light tank because the Far East Command had feared that heavier tanks would damage Japanese roads and bridges. The one exception was the 25th Infantry Division, which fielded a black regimental combat team built around the 24th Infantry. In that team the infantry regiment and the field artillery battalion had all their elements, but at reduced levels. The authorized strengths of the divisions ranged between 12,500 and 13,650 officers and enlisted men.[2]

Although the divisions fell well below war levels, President Harry S. Truman responded to the United Nations resolution to stop aggression in South Korea by ordering troops to Korea on 30 June. The next day Task Force Smith, elements of the 24th Infantry Division, the closest to Korea at Kobura, Japan, deployed to Suwon, South Korea, by air. The rest of the division quickly followed by sea. Shortly after the 24th's departure, the Far East Command brought the 25th Infantry Division and the 1st Cavalry Division to some semblance of effective fighting strength by stripping the 7th Infantry Division. By the end of July both divisions had joined in the fight, with the almost totally gutted 7th Division remaining in Japan.[3]

As the three understrength divisions fought in Korea, the Army Staff set about to bring them to full strength, along with the 7th Infantry Division in Japan. Personnel were involuntarily extended, and the length of their overseas tours was increased. Other commands were cannibalized for units, personnel, and equipment. Particularly scarce in the Far East Command were tanks and antiaircraft artillery. Because all the divisional tank and antiaircraft artillery battalions there had been reduced to a company or battery, replacement units had to come from the United States. With the divisions in Korea taking heavy casualties and the replacement system on the verge of bankruptcy, several months elapsed before the units neared war levels.[4]

Heavy losses and the amount of time required for units and personnel to reach the Orient resulted in an agreement on 15 August between the Far East Command and the South Korean government for the temporary assignment of Korean nationals to U.S. Army units. Under the Korean Augmentation to the United States Army (KATUSA) program, approximately 8,600 Koreans were to serve in each American division as soldiers. Various barriers—language, cultural differences, inadequate training, and unfamiliarity with Army organization, weapons, and tactics—hindered the program from achieving its goal. A few months after the plan's inception, the command curtailed it because of improvements in the replacement system and the desire to concentrate on rebuilding the Republic of Korea Army. Although U.S. divisions continued to receive some Korean recruits, no division received the 8,600 initially envisaged.[5]

With United Nations troops being overwhelmed in South Korea, General Douglas MacArthur, the United Nations Forces commander, requested immediate reinforcements from the United States. In July he asked for the 2d Infantry Division, stationed at Fort Lewis; a regimental combat team from the 82d Airborne Division at Fort Bragg; and some smaller units. Army Chief of Staff General J. Lawton Collins refused to send a regimental combat team from the 82d Airborne Division, preferring to keep the division intact for other contingencies. Instead, he favored dispatching a team from the 11th Airborne Division at Fort Campbell built around the 187th Airborne Infantry. The Joint Chiefs of Staff obtained President Truman's approval for the moves on 9 July, but many units in the United States had to be stripped to fill the 2d Division before it could deploy.

*2d Infantry Division elements move through a mountain pass south of Wonju, Korea, 1951.*

Elements of the 2d arrived in Korea on 31 July, and the division entered combat in late August. The 187th did not arrive until October.[6]

The arrival of the 2d Infantry Division in Korea allowed Lt. Gen. Walton H. Walker, commanding the Eighth Army there, to withdraw the 24th Infantry Division from combat along the Naktong River. Due to the heavy losses sustained by the division, Walker decided to transfer all personnel and equipment from the 34th Infantry and the 63d Field Artillery Battalion to other units in the division, replacing them with the 5th Regimental Combat Team (organized around the 5th Infantry), which had recently arrived from Hawaii. With the infusion, the division was ready for combat again by the end of August. Subsequently the 34th Infantry and 63d Field Artillery Battalion returned to Japan, where they were reorganized to train replacements.[7]

In August 1950 MacArthur planned an amphibious assault at Inchon, Korea, that would include the 7th Infantry Division, the only U.S. Army division left in Japan. To replace it in his reserve, he requested deployment of the 3d Infantry Division, the last Regular Army infantry division in the United States. After much debate in Washington, Truman sanctioned its deployment. Since a large portion of its personnel and equipment had been withdrawn earlier to meet other demands in Korea, the 3d Division had fewer than 5,000 men. To address the personnel problem, the division commander reassigned the personnel from one of its regimental combat teams and one general support field artillery battalion elsewhere in the division. At the same time, the Army Staff assigned two field artillery battalions and attached the 65th Infantry, the Puerto Rican regiment, to the division. The 3d Infantry Division arrived in Japan on 15 September, except for the 65th Infantry, which had moved directly to Korea from Camp Losey, Puerto Rico. In Japan the division received a Korean augmentation and began to train for combat. As elements of the 3d arrived in Japan, elements of the 7th Infantry Division landed at Inchon. Following the Chinese intervention in the war during the fall of 1950, the 3d Infantry Division also moved to Korea where the 65th Infantry joined it.[8]

The attachment of the 65th Infantry to the 3d Infantry Division marked a departure in the Army's segregation policies. In the past native Puerto Ricans were assigned exclusively to Puerto Rican units. In September 1951 the only units in which Puerto Ricans could serve outside the Caribbean area were elements of the 65th Regimental Combat Team in Korea. However, since more Puerto Ricans had entered the Army than were needed for these segregated Spanish-speaking units, the Army removed all restrictions on the assignments of Puerto Ricans who spoke English.[9]

The first few months of the war the Army relied on stopgap measures to field its six undermanned divisions in Korea but was still able to evolve a strategy for conducting the war. Under MacArthur, a strategy of attrition was quickly replaced by a strategy of annihilation. When the Chinese entered the war in the fall of 1950 the United Nations reverted to an attrition strategy, but one which depended on firepower rather than manpower. No major reinforcements would be provided to the forces in Korea. Although limited manpower mobilization in the United States solved many personnel problems in the Far East Command, divisions continued to lack trained infantry and artillery troops. After the United Nations spring counteroffensive, which ended on 8 July 1951, negotiations began for an armistice, with the number of Army divisions in Korea remaining fixed at six until the summer of 1953.[10]

## *Rebuilding the General Reserve*

To field the divisions destined for Korea, the Army stripped the General Reserve of its resources. After the summer of 1950 its divisional units consisted of only the understrength 2d Armored Division, the partially organized 11th Airborne Division, and, closest to its wartime authorized strength, the 82d Airborne Division. The reserve had to be quickly rebuilt for other contingencies, particularly for Western Europe, where many national leaders feared a major challenge from the Soviet Union. In July defense officials began discussing the means for enlarging the Army, but many months passed before they

# THE KOREAN WAR AND ITS AFTERMATH 243

decided upon a program. In the meantime, the Army expanded piecemeal. Secretary of Defense Louis Johnson approved the activation of another infantry division on 14 July 1950, but it was not until October that the 4th Infantry Division, which had been serving as a training division at Fort Ord, moved to Fort Benning to be reorganized as a combat unit. The Army Staff expected the division to be trained by the late spring of 1951.[11]

Because it would have taken too much time to organize new Regular Army divisions and Class B Organized Reserve Corps divisions (officers and enlisted cadre), the Army's leadership decided to recommend bringing some understrength National Guard divisions into federal service. On 10 August the president approved inducting four Guard infantry divisions. To accommodate them, the Army reactivated four World War II camps, and early in September the 28th (Pennsylvania), 40th (California), 43d (Connecticut, Rhode Island, and Vermont), and 45th (Oklahoma) Infantry Divisions entered active federal service. Army Field Forces and the Army Staff selected those units because of their geographic distribution, the status of their equipment, and their strength, which ranged from 8,000 to 9,500 officers and enlisted men each. The Army Staff immediately began working to bring the divisions up to their full table of organization and equipment strength.[12]

Initially individual reservists recalled to active duty filled Regular and Guard divisions, but to maintain them and other divisions, as well as organize new units, the Army Staff relied on volunteers and draftees who were schooled in existing or reactivated training centers. To operate the centers, Army Field Forces activated five Regular Army divisions, the 8th Infantry at Fort Jackson, South Carolina; the 101st Airborne at Camp Breckinridge, Kentucky; the 5th Armored at Camp Chaffee, Arkansas; the 6th Armored at Fort Leonard Wood, Missouri; and the 7th Armored at Camp Roberts, California, between August and November 1950. The 6th Infantry Division was also reactivated to replace the 4th at Fort Ord.[13]

The Chinese intervention in the fall of 1950 stimulated broader mobilization measures. After considerable debate, President Truman declared a national emergency, which required additional military forces to meet the Soviet threat in Europe as well as to fight the war in Korea. The mobilization plan called for eighteen combat divisions to be on active duty by June 1952. To obtain the additional divisions, the president approved the induction of the National Guard's 31st (Alabama and Mississippi) and 47th (Minnesota and North Dakota) Infantry Divisions into federal service in January 1951. These were reorganized under reduced tables that called for approximately 14,500 officers and enlisted men. For the eighteenth division, the Army reactivated the Regular Army's 1st Armored Division in March. This last unit improved the balance in the active force among infantry, armored, and airborne divisions, which stood at 2 armored, 2 airborne, and 14 infantry.[14]

In the fall of 1951 the Joint Chiefs of Staff reevaluated the mobilization program and set a new goal of twenty-one active duty combat divisions by 31 December 1955. From the National Guard, the 37th (Ohio) and 44th (Illinois)

TABLE 21

Combat Divisions on Active Duty During the Korean War

| Division | Component |
| --- | --- |
| 1st Armored | Regular Army |
| 1st Cavalry | Regular Army |
| 1st Infantry | Regular Army |
| 2d Armored | Regular Army |
| 2d Infantry | Regular Army |
| 3d Infantry | Regular Army |
| 4th Infantry | Regular Army |
| 7th Infantry | Regular Army |
| 11th Airborne | Regular Army |
| 24th Infantry | Regular Army |
| 25th Infantry | Regular Army |
| 28th Infantry | National Guard |
| 31st Infantry | National Guard |
| 37th Infantry | National Guard |
| 40th Infantry | National Guard |
| 43d Infantry | National Guard |
| 44th Infantry | National Guard |
| 45th Infantry | National Guard |
| 47th Infantry | National Guard |
| 82d Airborne | Regular Army |

Infantry Divisions were brought into federal service in early 1952, but the twenty-first division was not federalized or activated because of budgetary limitations. Thus the Korean War and the Cold War mobilization peaked at twenty divisions (*Table 21*).[15]

Personnel policies for manning divisions during the Korean War differed from those used in World Wars I and II. Prior to 1951, when soldiers went overseas to fight, their tour was usually for the duration of the war. With far-flung commitments throughout Europe and Asia, Army leaders adopted a personnel rotation policy during the second year of the Korean War. They hoped such a system would avoid alienating the general public and maintain the morale of the soldiers themselves. To accommodate the additional personnel needed to implement the rotation, the training base was further expanded in the spring of 1951. The 5th Infantry Division was activated at Indiantown Gap Military Reservation, Pennsylvania, increasing the number of training divisions to ten, the maximum number during the Korean War (*Table 22*). General Reserve divisions were also tasked to train recruits.[16]

By April 1951 the Army was able to provide additional forces to improve the security of Japan, where no divisional reserve had existed since the Chinese inter-

## TABLE 22
### Regular Army Training Divisions, 1950–56

| Division | Location | Remarks |
| --- | --- | --- |
| 3d Armored[1] | Fort Knox, Ky. | Reorganized as a combat division in 1955 |
| 4th Infantry[1] | Fort Ord, Calif. | Reorganized as a combat division in 1950 |
| 5th Armored | Camp Chaffee, Ark. | Activated in 1950; inactivated in 1956 |
| 5th Infantry | Indiantown Gap Military Reservation, Pa. | Activated in 1951; inactivated in 1953 |
| 6th Armored | Fort Leonard Wood, Mo. | Activated in 1950; inactivated in 1956 |
| 6th Infantry[2] | Fort Ord, Calif. | Activated in 1950; inactivated in 1956 |
| 7th Armored | Camp Roberts, Calif. | Activated in 1950; inactivated in 1953 |
| 8th Infantry | Fort Jackson, S.C. | Activated in 1950; reorganized as a combat division in 1954 |
| 9th Infantry[1] | Fort Dix, N.J. | Reorganized as a combat division in 1954 |
| 10th Infantry[1] | Fort Riley, Kans. | Reorganized as a combat division in 1954 |
| 69th Infantry[3] | Fort Dix, N.J. | Activated in 1954 |
| 101st Airborne | Camp Breckinridge, Ky. | Activated in 1950; inactivated in 1953; activated in 1954; reorganized as a combat division in 1956 |

[1] Activated before 1950.
[2] Replaced the 4th Infantry Division.
[3] Replaced the 9th Infantry Division.

vention in the Korean War. The 40th and 45th Infantry Divisions moved to Japan, where they completed their training. Congress insisted, however, that the National Guard divisions have an opportunity to fight, and in the winter of 1951–52 the 40th and 45th Divisions replaced the 1st Cavalry and 24th Infantry Divisions in Korea. The method of exchange revived a technique that had been developed during World War II. Ships that carried the 40th and 45th Infantry Divisions to Korea brought the 1st Cavalry Division and 24th Infantry Division back to Japan. The

*40th Infantry Division troops prepare to replace the 24th Infantry Division, January 1952.*

units swapped all heavy equipment and supplies while the men carried only their personal arms and equipment with them. Thus the units experienced only a limited decline in combat efficiency. The two seasoned divisions returned to Japan to serve as a reserve. Until July 1953 the 2d, 3d, 7th, 25th, 40th, and 45th Infantry Divisions carried the fight in Korea. During the waning days of the conflict, immediately before the armistice on 25 July, the 24th Infantry Division returned to Korea as a rear area force to bolster the security of prisoner-of-war camps.17

In 1952 Congress authorized what were in effect eight more divisions for the National Guard to replace the units in federal service. These organizations gave some areas of the country military forces where none had existed since units were federalized two years earlier for the Korean War. Under the new law the federal government could retain National Guard units (exclusive of personnel) for five years, but the states could organize replacements for the units in federal service. The new local units were to have the same designations as the units in federal service, with the additional identification NGUS (National Guard of the United States). Furthermore, the legislation required that when the Guard units in federal service were returned to the states, they were to be consolidated with their sister organizations. States began organizing NGUS units in 1952, and by the end of the Korean War on 23 July 1953, six out of the eight Guard divisions in federal service had local counterparts. Of the remaining two, the 37th Infantry Division (NGUS) received federal recognition on 15 January 1954, but the 44th never had an NGUS counterpart. The governor of Illinois, as an economy move, declined to organize it and requested the state's troop allotment be amended to delete the 44th Infantry Division. The division was removed from the force when it was released from federal service in December 1954.18

In addition to fighting the war in Korea in the early 1950s, the nation committed forces to the North Atlantic Treaty Organization (NATO). Since 1947 only the 1st Infantry Division had been stationed in Europe, but with the establishment of NATO President Truman announced a substantial increase in forces there. Between May and November 1951 the 2d Armored Division and the 4th, 28th,

# THE KOREAN WAR AND ITS AFTERMATH

*4th Infantry Division leaves New York en route to Germany, 1951.*

and 43d Infantry Divisions joined the 1st Infantry Division in Germany. The commitment of these forces and similar actions by the NATO partners demonstrated a new reliance on collective security to deter aggression.[19]

## *Organizational Trends*

During the Korean War the Army modified some aspects of its divisional organizations, but the basic triangular structures adopted during World War II and revised in the immediate postwar period for infantry, armored, and airborne divisions remained intact. In 1952 a divisional ordnance battalion replaced the ordnance company, which increased self-sufficiency in each type of division. The trend in most organizations, however, was to save personnel and increase firepower. Chief of Staff Collins estimated that the changes in the infantry division enhanced its firepower by 68 percent compared to its World War II counterpart with only a 20 percent increase in personnel.[20]

Firepower in the infantry regiment was increased through a series of changes. A 105-mm. recoilless rifle found a place within the regiment, as did the more powerful 3.5-inch "bazooka," a rocket fired from a shoulder position. In the first engagements of the Korean War, the 2.36-inch bazooka had proved inadequate against the Soviet T–34 tanks supplied to the North Koreans. To meet the Far East Command's requirement for an improved antitank weapon, 3.5-inch rocket launchers were rushed to the theater. On 20 July 1950 elements of the 24th Infantry Division used

*3.5-inch rocket launcher in action against the North Koreans*

them to knock out several Russian-built tanks, and thereafter the weapon received wide use. Infantry used new models of the 81-mm. and 4.2-inch mortars, and the number of automatic rifles was increased in the regiment.[21]

Improved aircraft technology provided all three types of divisions with new resources. The helicopter, boasting both vertical lift and hover capability, became a practical tactical and transport asset, playing a key role in supply and medical evacuation in Korea. Infantry and airborne divisions were authorized sixteen traditional fixed-wing aircraft and ten helicopters, while each armored division fielded eighteen aircraft and ten helicopters. The debate again surfaced as to whether all divisional aviation should be located in one unit since they usually used the same airfield. No separate aviation unit won approval, and technically the aircraft remained dispersed to the various units throughout the divisions. Divisions in combat, however, centralized their aircraft under divisional aviation officers who organized provisional aviation companies.[22]

The Army made more significant changes in the armored division. Although large armored formations were considered unsuitable for the rugged terrain in Korea, the Army still faced a massive Soviet armored threat in Europe. In response, the armored division fielded the first new family of tanks since World War II. The M103 (T43) tank armed with a 120-mm. gun was authorized for the heavy tank battalion. Weighing about sixty tons, it was the largest and most powerful American combat vehicle adopted to date. The new medium tank, the M47, had an improved fire control system and a high-velocity 90-mm. gun, which enhanced its lethality, but it did not become available in any quantity until 1953. For the reconnaissance squadron the tables provided for the new M41 light tank, nicknamed the "Walker Bulldog" for General Walker, who had been killed in a jeep accident in Korea. In all, the armored division fielded 343 tanks.23

The divisions deployed in Korea, Japan, and Germany usually adopted changes shortly after they were announced, in contrast to those in the United States. The latter, except for the 82d Airborne Division, served in a training capacity, mostly providing replacements for the overseas forces. As noted, training centers failed to meet the demand for replacements, but the political decision to limit mobilization precluded expanding the existing training centers or opening others, forcing the Army to use combat divisions to perform that function.24

*An M41 light tank (Walker Bulldog) destined for the 705th Tank Battalion, 102d Infantry Division*

The Korean War brought about a major social change that touched all units throughout the Army. The Army had maintained all-black units since the Civil War, but military efficiency tests showed that blacks fought and performed better in integrated units than in segregated ones. Also, post–World War II social attitudes increased the demand for integration. In 1948 President Truman had directed desegregation of the armed forces, but the Army was slow, as were the other services, to respond. By May 1951, however, 61 percent of the line infantry companies in Korea had both white and black soldiers because little consideration was given to replacement by race. On 1 July of that year the Army authorized the new Far East commander, General Matthew B. Ridgway (Truman had relieved MacArthur the previous April) to integrate all units under his control, except for the 40th and 45th Infantry Divisions. These units, which had recently arrived from the United States, were exempt from the order because they were National Guard organizations. The Army feared political repercussions from the states if their units were racially mixed. Nevertheless, despite the initial hesitation, the 40th and 45th were integrated shortly after they entered combat in Korea.25

The Far East Command usually integrated units through normal administrative processes. For example, the 3d Battalion, 9th Infantry, and the 3d Battalion, 15th Infantry, elements of the 2d and 3d Infantry Divisions that had been filled with black soldiers, were desegregated by simply reassigning them. The 25th Infantry Division had the 24th Infantry, the only all-black regiment in the Regular

Army, and Ridgway approved inactivating the regiment to disassociate all divisional elements with segregation. The Army Staff transferred the 14th Infantry, less its personnel and equipment, from the United States to the Far East Command, and on 1 August 1951 the regiment replaced the 24th in the division. Most of the 24th's black soldiers were dispersed throughout the command, while white soldiers to fill the 14th were drawn from the 34th Infantry in Japan. Units in the other regional commands integrated soon thereafter.[26]

## Readjustment of Divisional Forces

Hostilities ended in Korea on 23 July 1953 when the United Nations and North Korea signed an armistice, but demobilization, like mobilization, did not follow a preplanned course. A threat still hung over Korea, and the defense of Western Europe remained of paramount concern. The size of the Army depended on the new president, Dwight D. Eisenhower, inaugurated in January 1953, who was committed to reducing military expenditures. Between 1 July 1953 and 1 July 1956, the Congress, at the president's request, cut the active Army from 1.5 to 1 million men, a reduction that required major adjustments in divisional forces.[27]

By that time the annual load in the training centers had stabilized at a lower peacetime level, and the Army Staff had turned its attention to improving the General Reserve, particularly as a reenforcement force for Europe. In October 1953 the staff designated the 1st Armored Division and 44th Infantry Division as 30-day reinforcement units for NATO and named the 82d Airborne Division as the Western Hemisphere's contingency force. To bring these and other divisions in the General Reserve up to war levels, the 5th Infantry, 7th Armored, and 101st Airborne Divisions, which had been operating training centers, were inactivated and their personnel reassigned. The training center operated by the 10th Infantry Division was also closed, and a new mission was planned for the division.[28]

In December 1953 Eisenhower, who had hesitated to reduce forces in Korea because of the precarious armistice, announced that two of the seven U.S. Army divisions there were to return home, a step permitted by improved capabilities of the South Korean Army. United States Army Forces, Far East, selected the 40th and 45th Infantry Divisions for return to the United States, and they departed Korea in the spring of 1954 with only a token personnel complement. Shortly thereafter the divisions were released from active federal service and reverted to state control. Concerned about the effects of demobilization because of events in Southeast Asia (the French were on the verge of withdrawing from that area), Secretary of Defense Charles E. Wilson suspended further reductions in the Far East Command on 7 April 1954.[29]

Although the Army could retain National Guard designations for five years, Secretary Wilson decided to release the 28th, 31st, 37th, and 43d Infantry Divisions to state control in June 1954. This decision was primarily an adminis-

# THE KOREAN WAR AND ITS AFTERMATH

*37th Infantry Division passes 10th Infantry Division in review before leaving Fort Riley.*

trative action and did not affect the actual number of combat or training divisions in active service. In Europe the 9th and 5th Infantry Divisions replaced the 28th and 43d Infantry Divisions, while the 8th and 10th Infantry Divisions in the United States replaced the 31st and 37th at Fort Carson and Fort Riley. The 69th Infantry Division and the 101st Airborne Division were reactivated to fill the gaps left by the 5th and 9th in the training base.[30]

By the summer of 1954 the Mutual Defense Treaty with the Republic of Korea and the expansion of its army to twenty divisions permitted additional American reductions in Korea and allowed the Department of Defense to release all reserve units from active duty. In October the 25th Infantry Division with its personnel and equipment moved from Korea to Hawaii, where it became part of the Pacific area reserve. Shortly thereafter the 2d and 3d Infantry Divisions, reduced to near zero strength in Korea, replaced the National Guard 44th and 47th Infantry Divisions at Forts Lewis and Benning. The Guard divisions returned to state control, thus ending the involvement of the reserve divisions in the Korean War. When those divisions left federal service, only their designations reverted to the states since the guardsmen themselves had been released earlier. The states reorganized the units, except for the 44th, which Illinois did not want, by using the NGUS divisions as the nuclei, as planned.[31]

After many revisions of the blueprints for a residual force in Korea, the Department of Defense instructed the services to plan for three divisions, one Army, one Marine, and one United Nations, plus combat support and combat service support units to remain there. In December 1954 Secretary Wilson decided that the Marine unit would return to the United States, leaving two Army divisions in Korea. As a result, the 24th Infantry Division, in the midst of moving to Japan, reversed its course and rejoined the 7th Infantry Division in Korea.[32]

To improve the balance within Regular Army divisional forces after the Korean War, General Ridgway, who had become Army Chief of Staff in 1953, decided to revise the ratios among infantry, armored, and airborne units. In June 1954 the Fourth Army activated the 4th Armored Division, the first division to be equipped with the new M48 90-mm. tank. Ridgway planned to organize another armored division, raising the Regular Army total to four, but tank production lagged, preventing its formation until 1955. The 3d Armored Division was then converted from a training to a combat unit.33

Although total Army strength declined and the reserves were released, the Army remained committed to an active force of twenty divisions. The Department of Defense, therefore, authorized the activation of the 23d and 71st Infantry Divisions. Those units, dubbed "Wilson Divisions" after Secretary of Defense Wilson, who approved their activation while cutting the strength of the Army, made use of existing regimental combat teams. The 23d Infantry Division, the former Americal Division of World War II fame, controlled units stationed in the Canal Zone, Puerto Rico, and the southeastern United States from its headquarters at Fort Amador, Panama Canal Zone. The 71st, with its headquarters at Fort Richardson, Alaska, included units in Alaska and the northwestern United States. Because of their scattered divisional elements, the Army Staff labeled the divisions "static units," indicating that they were not capable of early deployment.34

With further cuts on the horizon for the Regular Army, the Army Staff had to economize on manpower if it was to maintain twenty divisions. A review of all divisional tables of organization resulted in slightly smaller divisions. For example, without a change in structure, the infantry division dropped from 18,212 men of all ranks to 17,452. In addition, the tables provided for a reduced peacetime strength division, with some 2,700 fewer men for each division in the General Reserve. Before its divisions were sent into combat, they would, of course, need sufficient time and personnel to be brought to war strength as required for sustained operations. The lessons of Task Force Smith and the deployment of other units to Korea in the summer of 1950 thus appeared to be already lost. General Reserve divisions adopted the new tables in the summer of 1955. In addition, because of the Army's severe manpower shortages divisions in Europe were also reorganized under the reduced tables that same summer, and the tables were applied to the 25th Infantry Division, posted at Schofield Barracks, the following year.35

Besides looking at the organizational tables for possible personnel cuts, the Army examined the individual replacement system. The system traditionally required the Army to maintain a large manpower overhead as a substantial percentage of its soldiers were always in transit. Lt. Gen. John E. Dahlquist, Chief of Army Field Forces, and Maj. Gen. Robert N. Young, the Army Staff's Deputy Chief of Staff for Personnel (G–1), believed that a unit replacement system would be more economical, improve esprit de corps, and provide more efficient units. In response, the Army Staff developed the GYROSCOPE program, which paired a division in the United States with an overseas division. Personnel from the paired divisions were to exchange places every three years. In addition, the divisions in the United States were to conduct basic and advanced individual training, cutting the training base and providing each soldier with a home throughout most of his career. It also theoretically made it possible to replace an entire division if it were destroyed in a nuclear attack.[36]

Beginning in 1955 fourteen divisions participated in the GYROSCOPE program (*Table 23*). To meet the changing needs of the Army, however, some deviation occurred during the duration of the program. For example, the 11th Airborne Division from Fort Campbell replaced the 5th Infantry Division in Germany in 1956, but the 5th's new station was Fort Ord, a former training center. Several benefits resulted: the European command received an airborne division, a unit it had wanted for some time; the U.S. Continental Army Command (CONARC), successor to the Army Field Forces, gained a post, Fort Campbell, and equipment to test a new divisional structure for the airborne division; and the number of divisions remained unchanged.[37]

As the divisions rotated, the U.S. Army, Europe, and Seventh Army closely monitored their activities and readiness to determine the effect of the moves on the units. They found that divisional combat efficiency declined for a number of weeks before and after rotation, and Lt. Gen. Bruce C. Clarke, Seventh Army commander, recommended limiting GYROSCOPE to units smaller than divisions. In 1958 the last divisional exchange took place when the 3d Infantry Division from Fort Benning replaced the 10th Infantry Division. Thereafter the program involved only smaller-size units. On 1 September 1959 the Army terminated GYROSCOPE, following the recommendations of General Clyde D. Eddleman, Commander, U.S. Army, Europe, who believed that other replacement systems worked better with less disruption. GYROSCOPE helped to sustain morale, but the scheme did not save money or improve combat readiness.[38]

## TABLE 23

### Operation GYROSCOPE

| Year | CONUS Division | Station | OCONUS Division | Station |
|---|---|---|---|---|
| 1955 | 10th Infantry | Fort Riley, Kans. | 1st Infantry | Germany |
| 1956 | 11th Airborne | Fort Campbell, Ky. | 5th Infantry[1] | Germany |
| 1956 | 3d Armored | Fort Knox, Ky. | 4th Infantry[2] | Germany |
| 1956 | 2d Infantry | Fort Lewis, Wash. | 71st Infantry[3] | Alaska |
| 1956 | 8th Infantry | Fort Carson, Colo. | 9th Infantry | Germany |
| 1958 | 4th Armored | Fort Hood, Tex. | 2d Armored | Germany |
| 1958 | 3d Infantry | Fort Benning, Ga. | 10th Infantry | Germany |

[1] The 5th Infantry Division's new station was Fort Ord, California.
[2] The 4th Infantry Division was reduced to zero strength.
[3] The 71st Infantry Division was inactivated, and the 4th Infantry Division replaced it.

With divisions in the GYROSCOPE program conducting individual training, the Department of the Army reduced the number of training centers. By 1 July 1955 only seven major training centers remained, of which five were operated by divisions. The continued use of divisional names for the centers, however, was being questioned. Lt. Gen. Walter L. Weibir, the G–1, wanted to change the centers' names to reflect their missions more accurately. For some time the divisional designations had confused the general public, government officials, and the trainees. In the spring of 1956 the Army thus inactivated the 6th and 69th Infantry Divisions and 5th and 6th Armored Divisions and reassigned the 101st Airborne Division as a test unit. Branch replacement centers replaced the training divisions. For example, the organization at Fort Chaffee, Arkansas, became the U.S. Army Training Center, Field Artillery.[39]

The savings that resulted from the revised tables of organization, modifications in the replacement system, and a reduction in the training base did not equal the required cuts in Army strength. The Army was therefore unable to maintain twenty Regular Army divisions. Further reductions required the commanders of United States Army, Caribbean, and Sixth Army to inactivate the 23d and 71st Infantry Divisions in 1956. Some of their elements, however, continued to serve in the active force.[40]

## *Improving the Reserves*

The structure of the reserve components came under close scrutiny during the Korean War. By then military leaders had decided the large undermanned force of fifty-two divisions developed after World War II was unrealistic. On 24 October 1950 the chief of staff directed a committee to reevaluate the reserve structure and develop plans to meet both limited and major mobilizations. Six months later, before the decision to mobilize 20 divisions due to the Korean War, the committee reported that the Army needed 18 divisions on active duty—12 Regular Army and 6 National Guard—and 33 reserve divisions to back them up. The latter divisions fell into two categories for mobilization, an early ready force of 9 divisions from the National Guard and a late ready force of 24 divisions with 12 from the Guard and 12 from the Organized Reserve Corps. The units in the National Guard were to be maintained at 100 percent officer and 50 percent enlisted strength, while those in the Organized Reserve Corps were to have 100 percent of their officers but only an enlisted cadre. The committee decided that the remaining thirteen Organized Reserve Corps divisions were unnecessary and recommended their immediate inactivation.[41]

During the summer and fall of 1951 the six army commanders in the United States, staff agencies, and the Section V Committee, created after World War I for the reserve components to have a voice in their affairs, evaluated the plan. The army commanders urged that all divisions in the Organized Reserve Corps be infantry divisions because they believed that the reserves could not adequately

THE KOREAN WAR AND ITS AFTERMATH                                         255

support armored and airborne training. They thought thirteen, rather than twelve, reserve divisions should be maintained to provide a better geographic distribution of the units. The Section V Committee opposed the reduction of the Organized Reserve Corps from twenty-five to thirteen divisions because it feared unfavorable publicity, particularly with the nation at war. On 20 December the Vice Chief of Staff, General John E. Hull, delayed reduction in the number of Reserve Corps divisions until 31 December 1952 but directed the reorganization and redesignation of airborne and armored divisions as infantry as soon as practicable. In March 1952 the 80th, 84th, 100th, and 108th Airborne Divisions were reorganized and redesignated as infantry divisions, and the 63d, 70th, and 75th Infantry Divisions replaced the 13th, 21st, and 22d Armored Divisions. The Army made no other divisional changes in the reserve troop basis at that time.[42]

Along with the reorganization of the Organized Reserve Corps divisions, the Army published new regulations formalizing a "Ready Reserve" concept. Under the new rules the Ready Reserve comprised Early and Late Ready Forces, categories which replaced the old Class A, B, and C units. The Early Ready Force was to have 110 percent officer and 100 percent enlisted strength, while the Late Ready Force, which included all Organized Reserve Corps divisions, was to have 100 percent officer and 5 percent enlisted strength. In July 1952 Congress passed new legislation that redesignated the Organized Reserve Corps as the Army Reserve and gave legal status to the concept of the Ready Reserve.[43]

Before the dust had settled on the reforms, the Army realized that it had failed to improve unit manning or meet reasonable mobilization requirements. In the fall of 1952 Army leaders thus proposed that the personnel from the thirteen inactivated Army Reserve divisions be assigned to strengthen the remaining twelve divisions. A new reserve troop basis resulted, this time calling for 37 divisions, 27 in the National Guard and 10 in the Army Reserve. To keep the unneeded fifteen Army Reserve divisions active, they were to be reorganized as training divisions to staff training centers upon mobilization or man maneuver area commands for training troops. The continental army commanders implemented the new Army Reserve troop basis in 1955 piecemeal. They reorganized, without approved tables of organization, the 70th, 76th, 78th, 80th, 84th, 85th, 89th, 91st, 95th, 98th, 100th, and 108th Infantry Divisions as cadre for replacement training centers and organized the 75th "Maneuver Area Commands" using the resources of the 75th Infantry Division. Two years later the 75th Infantry Division was inactivated along with 87th Infantry Division. Assets of the 87th were used to organize a maneuver area command; thus one unneeded division remained in the troop basis.[44]

To prepare for challenges in Western Europe, the new troop basis authorized the conversion of four National Guard infantry divisions to armored divisions. New York, California, Georgia, and Florida agreed to convert the 27th, 40th, and 48th Infantry Divisions. For the fourth armored division, the Army planned to use the slot temporarily occupied by the 44th Infantry Division, which Illinois no longer wanted. Eventually Tennessee and North Carolina, which shared the 30th Infantry

Division, each agreed to maintain a division; Tennessee organized the 30th Armored Division, while North Carolina organized the 30th Infantry Division.[45]

In 1955 Congress again legislated measures to improve the reserves. Among the amendments to the 1952 law was a provision that allowed young men eighteen and a half years old to enlist in the Army Reserve for eight years. Not less than three and not more than six months of that obligation was to be spent on active duty for basic training. The law also provided that reservists who did not perform satisfactorily after basic training might be ordered, without their consent, to active duty not to exceed forty-five days. Although the Army Reserve hoped these provisions would help to meet manning problems, the measure failed. Most young men were uninterested in military service, and for the few who were the active Army lacked the resources to provide basic training and the National Guard proved more attractive than the Army Reserve.[46]

At the beginning of 1957 the Army thus had 56 combat divisions and 12 training divisions. Of these, the Regular Army fielded 18 combat divisions, many not fully manned; the National Guard 27; and the Army Reserve 11. Of the 56 divisions, 3 were airborne, 10 were armored, and the remainder were infantry.

Between 1950 and 1957 Army divisions fought a war in Korea and deterred the Soviet challenge in Western Europe. At the height of the Korean War the active Army had eight divisions in the Far East, five in Germany, and a seven-division General Reserve in the United States. Divisions retained their World War II structure with modifications while gaining additional firepower. As the United States assumed leadership of the Western democracies, a ready force, backed by fully manned and equipped reserves, took on added significance. Nevertheless, the Regular Army, National Guard, and Army Reserve divisions all suffered from a lack of personnel. After the Korean War budgetary constraints exacerbated the manning conditions, while the general reliance of the Eisenhower administration on nuclear deterrence put the fiscal emphasis on weapons systems rather than on the combat divisions.

## Notes

1 *Public Papers of the Presidents of the United States: Harry S. Truman, January 1, 1950 to December 1950* (Washington, D.C.: Government Printing Office, 1965), p. 532.

2 Ltr, TAG to CinC, Far East, 12 Jun 50, sub: Activation, Inactivation, Redesignation, and Reorganization of Certain Units in the Far East Command, AGAO-I 322 (10 Apr 50) G–1–M, AG Reference files, DAMH-HSO; Schnabel, *Policy and Direction*, pp. 86–87, 90–94; Stubbs and Connor, *Armor-Cavalry*, p. 77.

3 Schnabel, Policy and Direction, pp. 80–88.

4 Ltr, TAG to CinC, Far East, 26 Jul 50, sub: Reorganization of Certain Units in the Far East Command, AGAO-I 322 (21 Jul 50) G–1 M, AG Reference files, DAMH-HSO; Elva Stillwaugh, "Personnel Policies in the Korean Conflict," ch. l, pp. 32–40, Ms, DAMH-HSR.

5 Roy E. Appleman, *South to the Naktong, North to the Yalu*, United States Army in the Korean War (Washington, D.C.: Government Printing Office, 1961), pp. 385–89; Charles G. Cleaver, "History of the Korean War," vol. 3, pt. 2, Personnel Problems, pp. 7–12, Ms, DAMH-HSR; David Curtis Skaggs, "The KATUSA Experiment: The Integration of Korean Nationals into the U.S. Army, 1950–1965," *Military Affairs* 38 (Apr 1974): 53–58.

6 Schnabel, Policy and Direction, pp. 92–96, 168–71.

7 Appleman, *South to the Naktong*, pp. 389–90; T.R. Fehrenback, *This Kind of War: A Study in Unpreparedness* (New York: Macmillan Company, 1963), p. 202; Ltr, Henry P. Carrington to Edgar M. Howell, 18 Nov 50, 63d Field Artillery Battalion file, DAMH-HSO; Military History Section, "A Brief History of the 34th Infantry Regiment" (United States Army Forces, Far East, Nov 1954), 34th Infantry file, DAMH-HSO.

8 Schnabel, *Policy and Direction*, pp. 131–34; Max W. Dolcater, *3d Infantry Division in Korea* (Tokyo: Toppan Printing Co., 1953), pp. 57–65; Ltr, TAG to CGs, Third and Second Armies, 25 Aug 50, sub: Organization and Reorganization of Certain Units, AGAO-I 322 (17 Aug 50) G–1–M, Ltr, TAG to CinC, Far East, 6 Oct 50, sub: Changes of Certain Units in the Far East Command, AGAO-I 322 (4 Sep 50), G–1–M, and Ltr TAG to CG, Third Army, 19 Mar 51, sub: Change in Status of Certain Units, AGAO-I 322 (2 Mar 51) G–1–M, all 3d Inf Div file, DAMH-HSO.

9 Stillwaugh, "Personnel Policies," ch. 6, pp. 1–4.

10 Billy C. Mossman, *Ebb and Flow, November 1950–July 1951*, United States Army in the Korean War (Washington, D.C.: Government Printing Office, 1990), pp. 237, 247, 503; Walter G. Hermes, *Truce Tent and Fighting Front*, United States Army in the Korean War (Washington, D.C.: Government Printing Office, 1966), p. 472.

11 Schnabel, *Policy and Direction*, pp. 117–20; Stillwaugh, "Personnel Policies," ch. 1, pp. 9–12; Ltr, TAG to CGs, Third, Fourth, and Sixth Armies, 16 Oct 50, sub: Change in Status of Certain Units, AGAO-I 322 (29 Aug 50), G–1–M, 4th Inf Div file, DAMH-HSO.

12 Schnabel, *Policy and Direction*, pp. 122–25, 294; National Guard Bureau, "Induction and Release of Army National Guard Units," pp. 21–24, National Guard Induction, Korean War, Reference Paper files, DAMH-HSO; OCAFF Diary, "Action in Support of FECOM 3 July 1950– 30 September 1950," Ms, DAMH-HSR; Ltr, TAG to CGs, First, Second, Third, Fourth, Fifth, and Sixth Armies, 6 Sep 50, sub: Reorganization of Certain Units Called to Active Duty from Civilian Components, AGAO-I 322 Gen Res (23 Aug 50) G–1–M, AG Reference files, DAMH-HSO.

13 Crossland and Currie, *Twice a Citizen*, pp. 96–97; Ltr, TAG to CG, Third Army, 10 Aug 50, sub: Activation of the 8th Infantry Division (Training), AGAO-I 322 (7 Aug 50) G–1–M, 8th Inf Div file, GO 51, Fort Jackson, South Carolina, 1950, Ltr, TAG to CG, Second Army, 10 Aug 50, sub: Activation of the 101st Airborne Division (Training), AGAO-I 322 (7 Aug 50) G–1–M, 101st Abn Div file, Ltr, TAG to CG, Fourth Army, 21 Aug 50, sub: Activation of the 5th Armored Division, 21 Aug 50, AGAO-I 322 Training Div (15 Aug 50) G–1–M, 5th Armd Div file, Ltr, TAG to CG, Fifth Army, 21 Aug 50, sub: Activation of the 6th Armored Division,

AGAO-I 322 Training Div (15 Aug 50) G–1–M, 6th Armd Div file, Ltr, TAG to CG, Sixth Army, 10 Nov 50, sub: Activation of the 7th Armored Division, AGAO-I 322 (11 Oct 50) G–1–M, 7th Armd Div file, Ltr, TAG to CGs, Third, Fourth, and Sixth Armies, 16 Oct 50, sub: Change in Status of Certain Units, AGAO-I 322 (29 Aug 50), 4th Inf Div file, and Divisional Historical Data Cards, all DAMH-HSO.

[14] Schnabel, *Policy and Direction*, pp. 298–300; Truman, *Papers of the President*, 1950, pp. 746–47; "Induction and Release of Army National Guard Units," pp. 39–41; Ltr, TAG to CGs, Third and Fourth Armies, 26 Apr 51, sub: Reorganization of Certain General Reserve Units, AGAO-I 322 Gen Res (2 Apr 51) G–1–M, AG Reference files, Ltr, TAG to CGs, Third and Fourth Armies, 1 Mar 51, sub: Activation of the 1st Armored Division, AGAO-I 322 (24 Feb 51) G–1–M, 1st Armd Div file, DAMH-HSO.

[15] Stillwaugh, "Personnel Policies," ch. 1, pp. 51–60; "Induction and Release of Army National Guard Units," pp. 48–58.

[16] Stillwaugh, "Personnel Policies," ch. 3, p. 1; Ltr, TAG to CG, Second Army, 21 Feb 51, sub: Activation of the 5th Infantry Division (Training), AGAO-I 322 (2 Feb 51) G–1–M, 5th Inf Div file, and Historical Data Card 5th Inf Div, DAMH-HSO; Robert W. Coakley, Karl E. Cocke, Daniel P. Griffin, "Demobilization Following the Korean War," OCMH Study 29, pp. 71–73, Ms, DAMH-HSR.

[17] Hermes, *Truce Tent and Fighting Front*, pp. 202–04. Prior to the redeployment of 24th Infantry Division to Korea in summer of 1953, elements of the 1st Cavalry Division and 24th Infantry Division had served there as security forces on a rotation basis since October 1952.

[18] DA Bull 15, 1952; *Annual Report of the Chief of the National Guard Bureau, 1953*, pp. 2–3, 1954, p. 15; see notes based on NG-AROTO (National Guard Bureau-Organization and Training Branch) 325.4 letters, 1952–54, author's files; "Illinois Declines Allotment to Reorganize 44th Division," *Army Times*, 9 Jan 54; "Protests Rip Illinois Guard; Generals Urge Boyle's Removal," *Army Times*, 16 Jan 54; Ltr, NGB to AG, Illinois, 17 Feb 54, sub: Withdrawal of Federal Recognition, National Guard Units, NG-AROTO 325.4–Ill, 44th Inf Div file, DAMH-HSO.

[19] Truman, *Papers of the President*, 1950, p. 626; Dean Acheson, *Present at the Creation: My Years in the State Department* (New York: W. W. Norton and Co., 1969), pp. 437–40; Historical Data Cards for the 4th, 28th, and 43d Inf Divs and the 2d Armd Div, DAMH-HSO.

[20] TOE 7, Infantry Division, 15 May 1952; TOE 17, Armored Division, 29 Dec 1952; TOE 57, Airborne Division, 1 Jan 1952; Lloyd Norman, "The New Look Strategy," *Combat Forces Journal* 4 (Feb 1954): 15–20.

[21] TOE 7–11, Infantry Regiment, 15 May 1952; "Tools for the Fighting Man: Small Arms," *Armed Forces Talk* (18 Jan 1952) pp. 1–15; Walter H. Ramsey, "The Big Bazooka: Russian Tanks Were No Match for Our 3.5-Inch Weapon," *Ordnance* 35 (May–Jun 1951): 638–40.

[22] TOE 7, Infantry Division, 15 May 1952; TOE 17, Armored Division, 29 Dec 1952; TOE 57, Airborne Division, 1 Jan 1952; James C. Smith, "Centralized Operations," *Army Aviation Digest* 1 (Mar 1955): 19–25; Joseph Bonanno, "The Helicopter in Combat," *Ordnance* 37 (Mar–Apr 1954): 868–72; Donald F. Harrison, "A History of Army Aviation," ch. V, pp. 11–20, 25–27, Ms, DAMH-HSR.

[23] TOE 17, Armored Division, 29 Dec 1952; Stubbs and Connor, *Armor-Cavalry*, pp. 77–78; "The T43 Heavy Tank," *Armor* 63 (May–Jun 1954): 32–33; "Army's New M48 Medium Tank Ready for Distribution to Armor Troops," *Armor* 61 (May–Jun 1952): 30–31.

[24] Ltr, TAG to CinC, U.S. Army, Europe, 6 Feb 53, sub: Change in Status of Certain Units, AGAO-I (M) (28 Jan 53) G–1, and Ltr, TAG to CG, U.S. Army Forces, Far East (Main), 9 Feb 53, sub: Change in Status of Certain Units, AGAO-I (M) 322 (4 Feb 53) G–1, both AG Reference files, DAMH-HSO; OCAFF, "Summary of Major Events and Problems, FY 1953," ch. 9, pp. 1–18.

[25] DA Bull 23, 1948; Morris J. MacGregor, *Integration of the Armed Forces*, pp. 428–59 passim.

[26] MacGregor, *Integration of the Armed Forces*, pp. 442–45; Bernard C. Nalty and Morris J.

MacGregor, *Blacks in the Military: Essential Documents* (Wilmington, Del.: Scholarly Resources Inc., 1981), pp. 309–11; Ltr, TAG to CGs, Third and Fifth Armies, 9 Aug 51, sub: Change in Status of Certain General Reserve Units, AGAO-I 322 (26 Jul 51) G–1–M, 14th Inf file, DAMH-HSO; "FE Racial Integration Means New Names for 2 Regiments," *Army Times*, 4 Aug 52.

27 *Public Papers of the Presidents of the United States, Dwight D. Eisenhower, 1954* (Washington, D.C.: Government Printing Office, 1960), pp. 121–25; Coakley et al., "Demobilization," pp. 8–9.

28 Coakley et al., "Demobilization," pp. 69–72, 85–87.

29 Eisenhower, *Papers of the Presidents, 1953*, pp. 860–61; Coakley et al., "Demobilization," pp. 28–29; "Induction and Release of Army National Guard Units," pp. 21–24. In 1952 General Mark W. Clark reorganized the Far East Command as a unified command with U.S. Army Forces, Far East, as the Army's element.

30 Ltr, TAG to CinC, U.S. Army, Europe, and CG, First Army, 7 Apr 54, sub: Change in Status of Certain Divisions, AGAO-I (M) 322 (2 Apr 54) G–1, 9th Inf Div file, Ltr, TAG to CGs, Third and Fifth Armies, 27 Apr 54, sub: Change in Status of Certain Divisions, AGAO-I (M) 322 (22 Apr 54) G–1, 8th Inf Div file, Ltr, TAG to CG, Fifth Army, 27 Apr 54, sub: Reorganization of the 10th Infantry Division, AGAO-I (M) 322 (22 Apr 54) G–1, 10th Inf Div file, Ltr, TAG to CG, First Army, 23 Apr 54, sub: Activation of the 69th Infantry Division (Training), AGAO-I (M) 322 (22 Apr 54) G–1, 69th Inf Div file, and Historical Data Cards for the 5th, 8th, 9th, 28th, 31st, 43d, and 69th Inf Divs and the 101st Abn Div, all DAMH-HSO.

31 *Semiannal Report of the Secretary of Defense, 1954*, pp. 56–57; Coakley et al., "Demobilization," pp. 39–43; Ltr, TAG to CG, Sixth Army, 27 Sep 54, sub: Reorganization of the 2d Infantry Division, AGAO-I (M) 322 (16 Sep 54) G–1, 2d Inf Div file, and Ltr, TAG to CG, Third Army, 27 Oct 54, sub: Reorganization of the 3d Infantry Division, AGAO-I (M) 322 (19 Oct 54) G–1, 3d Inf Div file, both DAMH-HSO; "Schofield Ready to Welcome 25th Division," *Army Times*, 18 Sep 54; "Induction and Release of Army National Guard Units," pp. 48–58; *Report of the Chief of the National Guard Bureau, 1955*, pp. 14–15.

32 Coakley et al., "Demobilization," pp. 29–38.

33 Summary of Major Events and Problems, FY 1954, OCAFF, ch. 14, pp. 1–4; Ltr, TAG to CG, Fourth Army, 28 May 54, sub: Activation of the 4th Armored Division, AGAO-I (M) 322 (26 May 54) G–1, 4th Armd Div file, and Ltr, TAG to CGs, Second Army and Continental Army Command (CONARC), 9 Mar 55, sub: Change in Status of 3d Armored Division, AGAO-I (M) 322 3d Armd Div (8 Mar 55) G–1, 3d Armd Div file, both DAMH-HSO; "4th Armored Reactivated at Ft. Hood," *Army Times*, 26 Jun 54; "4th Armd Build-Up Underway," *Army Times*, 3 Jul 54; William R. Rock, *3d Armored Division (Spearhead), A History of the 3d Armored Division* (Darmstadt, Germany: Stars and Stripes, 1957), pp. 45–46.

34 Ltr, TAG to CGs, U.S. Army, Caribbean, and Third Army, 2 Dec 54, sub: Organization of the 23d Infantry Division, AGAO-I (M) 322 (17 Nov 54) G– , 23d Inf Div file, and Ltr, CGs, U.S. Army, Alaska, and Sixth Army, 27 Oct 54, sub: Organization of the 71st Infantry Division, AGAO-I (M) 322 71st Inf Div (12 Oct 54) G–1, 71st Inf Div file, both DAMH-HSO; *Semiannual Report of the Secretary of the Army, 1 Jul–Dec 54*, p. 20; "Scattered from Here to Yon, Two `Wilson Divisions' Formed," *Army Times*, 20 Nov 54.

35 Coakley et al., "Demobilization," pp. 88–89; TOE 7R, Infantry Division, 1955; TOE 17R, Armored Division, 1955; TOE 57, Airborne Division, 1955; Ltr, TAG to CGs, CONARC, and Second and Fourth Armies, 23 May 55, sub: Reorganization of 1st, 3d, and 4th Armored Divisions, AGAO-I (M) 322 (18 May 55) G–1, Ltr, TAG to CGs, CONARC, and Third, Fifth, and Sixth Armies, 23 May 55, sub: Reorganization of Certain Infantry Divisions, AGAO-I (M) 322 (19 May 55) G–1, Ltr, TAG to CGs, CONARC, and Third Army, 1 Aug 55, sub: Reorganization of the 11th Airborne Division, AGAO-I (M) 322 (20 Jul 55) G–1, Ltr, TAG to CGs, CONARC and Third Army, 26 May 1955, sub: Reorganization of 82d Airborne Division, AGAO-I (M) 322 (24 May 55) G–1, Ltr, TAG to CinC, U.S. Army, Europe, 9 Sep 55, sub: Confirmation of Reorganization of Certain Units, AGAO-O (M) 322 (16 Aug 55) G–1, and Ltr,

TAG to CG, U.S. Army, Pacific, 5 Mar 56, sub: Change in Status of Certain Units, AGAO-O-322 (27 Feb 56) DCSPER (Deputy Chief of Staff for Personnel), all AG Reference files, DAMH-HSO; Historical Data Cards for divisions, DAMH-HSO.

36 Memo for Record, sub: Unit Rotation Plan, 23 Feb 54, and Ltr, John E. Dahlquist to Matthew B. Ridgway, 7 Apr 54, Records of the Army Staff, G–1, 210.21 Feb–Mar 54, RG 319, NARA; "World-wide Unit Rotation," *Army Combat Forces Journal* 5 (Nov 1954): 37; Robert N. Young, "Operation GYROSCOPE, Rotation Plus Stability," *Army Information Digest* 10 (Mar 1955): 2–6; Historical Division, U.S. Army Europe (USAREUR), *Operation GYROSCOPE in the US Army Europe, 1957*, pp. 1–2 (Secret, material used unclassified), DAMH-HSR.

37 Historical Section, USAREUR, *Operation GYROSCOPE in the US Army Europe*, pp. 26–40; SS, G–1 for CofS, sub: Training Center Designations, Tab A, 15 Dec 55, G–1 S 323.3, Division General file, DAMH-HSO.

38 Historical Section, USAREUR, "The Replacement and Augmentation System in Europe (1945–1963)," pp. 47–48, Ms, DAMH-HSR.

39 Coakley et al., "Demobilization," pp. 72–80; U.S. Congress, Senate, *Eleventh Report of the Preparedness Subcommittee of the Committee on Armed Services of the United States Senate under the Authority of S.Res. 18*, 82d Cong., 1st Sess., Apr 1951; SS, G–1 for CofS, sub: Training Center Designations, 15 Dec 55, SS, DCSPER for CofS, same subject, 27 Jan 56, DCSPER S 323, and DOD News Release No. 152–56, sub: Army to Stop Using Division Designations to Identify Training Divisions, 23 Feb 56, all Division General file, DAMH-HSO; also see unit files of the 101st Abn, 6th and 9th Inf, and 5th and 6th Armd Divs, DAMH-HSO.

40 Ltr, TAG to CG, U.S. Army, Caribbean, 1 Mar 56, sub: Change in Status of Certain Units, AGAO-O (M) 322 (10 Feb 56) DCSPER, 23d Inf Div file, and Ltr, TAG to CGs, CONARC and Sixth Army, 6 Sep 56, same subject, AGAO-O 322 (9 Aug 56) DCSPER, 71st Inf Div file, DAMH-HSO.

41 Memo, G–1 for G–3, 24 Oct 50, sub: Development of Army's Position in a Complete Review of Civilian Components Structure, G–1 326 (24 Oct 50), and SS, G–3 for CofS, 5 Apr 51, sub: Development of Army Position in a Complete Review of Civilian Components Structure, G–3 326 (24 Oct 50), both Army Reserve file, DAMH-HSO.

42 SS, G–3 for CofS, 18 Dec 51, sub: Implementation of the Approved Outline Plan, Army Reserve Forces, 326 (5 Dec 51), Army Reserve Forces Conference, Department of the Army, Army Field Forces, Continental Armies, Fort Monroe, Virginia, 5–9 Nov 1951, Memo for Record, OCofS, 20 Dec 51, sub: Implementation of the Army Reserve Force Reserve Divisional Reorganization, GS 326 (19 Nov 51), and DA Army Reserve Forces Program Summary, 1 Mar 52, all Army Reserve Reference files, Ltr, TAG to CG, Second Army, 18 Apr 52, sub: Change in Status of Certain Army Reserve Divisions, AGAO-I 322 Army Res (6 Mar 52) G–3–M, Ltr, TAG to CG, Third Army, 23 Feb 52, same subject, AGAO-I 322 Army Res (28 Jan 52), Ltr, TAG to CG, Fourth Army, 21 Feb 52, same subject, AGAO-I 322 Army Res (30 Jan 52) G–3–M, Ltr, TAG to CG, Fifth Army, 13 Feb 52, same subject, AGAO-I 326 (25 Jan 52) G–3–M, Ltr, TAG to CG, Sixth Army, 22 Feb 52, same subject, AGAO-I 322 Army Res (29 Jan 52), all AG Reference files, and Historical Data Cards, Army Reserve divisions, all DAMH-HSO. The Section Five Committee, established in 1920, was the vehicle for reserve officers to provide input about reserve affairs.

43 AR 140–305, 1 Feb 1952; DA Bull 7, 1952.

44 Karl Cocke, "The Reserve Components," OCMH Study 130, pp. V–38–49, VI–1–45 passim, Ms, DAMH-RAD; "General Staff Study Leading to the Preparation of Reserve Components Mobilization Preparedness Objectives Plan I," 1 Jul 53, DAMH-HSR; Ltr, TAG to CG, First Army, 15 Mar 55, sub: Designation and Organization of Certain Divisions of the Army Reserve, AGAO-I (M) 322 (21 Feb 55) Army Res, Ltr, TAG to CG, Second Army, 19 May 55, same subject, AGAO-I (M) 322 Army Res (21 Mar 55) Army Res, Ltr, TAG to CG, Third Army, 15 Feb 55, sub: Designation and Organization of 108th Infantry Division (Replacement Training), AGAO-I (M) 322 (9 Feb 55) Army Res, Ltr, TAG to Fourth Army, 25 Jan 55, sub: Designation and Organization of the 95th Infantry Division, AGAO-I (M) 322 95th Inf Div (18 Jan 55) Army

Res, and Ltr, TAG to CG, Fifth Army, 23 May 55, sub: Designation and Organization of Certain Divisions of the Army Reserve, AGAO-I (M) 322 Army Res (11 May 55) Army Res, all AG Reference file, DAMH-HSO; GO 152, Sixth Army, 1955; Ltr, TAG to CG, Fourth Army, 11 Mar 55, sub: Change in Status of Certain Army Reserve Units, AGAO-I (M) 322 Army Res (17 Feb 55) RES, and Ltr, TAG to CGs, CONARC, and Third and Fourth Armies, 10 Jan 57, sub: Change in Status of Certain Units of the Army Reserve, both AG Reference files, DAMH-HSO.

[45] Ltr, NGB to AG, California, 15 Jun 54, sub: Organization, Conversion, Reorganization, and Redesignation of National Guard Units (40th Division), NG-AROTO 325.4-Calif (4 Jun 54), 40th Inf Div file, Ltr, NGB to CofS, Div of Military and Naval Affairs, New York, 15 Dec 54, sub: Organization, Reorganization, Conversion, and Redesignation, National Guard Units of the 27th Infantry Division to be the 27th Armored Division, NG-AROTO 325.4-NY (13 Dec 54), 27th Inf Bde file, Ltr, NGB to AG, Georgia, 17 Oct 55, sub: Allotment, Conversion, Redesignation, Organization, Reorganization and Withdrawal of Federal Recognition, Army National Guard Units, NG-AROTO 325.4 (30 Sep 55) GA, GA NG file, Ltr, NGB to AG, Florida, 17 Oct 55, sub: Allotment, Conversion, Redesignation, Organization, Reorganization and Withdrawal of Federal Recognition, Army National Guard Units, NG-AROTO 325.4-Fla, FL NG file, Ltr, NGB to AG, Tennessee, 20 Oct 54, sub: National Guard Troop Allotment (Tennessee), 20 Oct 54, NG-AROTO 325.4-Tenn, TN NG file, and GO 33, North Carolina National Guard, 18 Oct 54, NC state file, DAMH-HSO; *Report of the Chief, National Guard Bureau, 1955*, p. 15, and 1956, p. 21.

[46] DA Bull 12, 1955; Crossland and Currie, *Twice the Citizen*, pp. 120–27.

# CHAPTER 10

# The Search for Atomic Age Divisions

*Since we cannot equal our potential enemies on a man for man basis, we must give our soldiers the means of increasing their effective firepower and we must create an organization to control it.*

Col. Stanley N. Lonning[1]

After the Korean War the Eisenhower administration adopted a military posture that emphasized nuclear capability through air power rather than ground combat. Three considerations dictated this change: limited resources, a worldwide commitment to contain communism, and the desire to reduce defense spending. Given the declining number of ground combat troops, the Army fielded fewer divisions, but because the possibility of nuclear war remained, Army leaders wanted to devise units that could fight and survive on a nuclear as well as on a conventional battlefield. The divisions developed by the Army for the two combat environments were smaller than in the past, and they were authorized weapons and equipment still under development and not yet in the inventory. The newly designed divisions, however, staked out a role for the Army on the atomic battlefield, which justified appeals for funds to develop new weapons.

## *Exploring Alternative Divisions*

Some Army planners thought a general war would be too costly to wage by conventional means because the Communist bloc could field more men and resources than the United States and its allies. Firepower appeared to be the answer for overcoming the enemy. Ever since the United States dropped the first atomic bomb in 1945, American military planners had pondered the use of nuclear weapons on the battlefield. The Army, however, was hampered in its effort to understand the effects of tactical nuclear weapons by the lack of data. Studies suggested that nuclear weapons could be used much like conventional artillery. To achieve the aim of increased firepower with decreased manpower, the Army began to take a closer look at that proposition in the early 1950s.[2]

As had happened between World Wars I and II, the new divisional studies began with the infantry regiment. Army Field Forces initiated the studies in 1952, when it asked the Infantry School to examine both infantry and airborne infantry regiments. Four goals were to guide the effort: elimination of nonfighters; expansion and more effective use of firepower; simplification and improved organization and control; and a reduction in the size of the regiment. Army Field Forces dropped the last goal when it decided austerity should begin in service and support units before being applied to infantry and airborne infantry regiments. Both regiments were to be alike except for the number of antitank weapons.[3]

The infantry regiment recommended by the Infantry School consisted of three rifle battalions, a headquarters and headquarters company, a service company, an antitank company, and a weapons company armed with .50-caliber machine guns. Removed from the regiment were the medical, heavy mortar, and tank companies. Assets of the tank company were transferred to the division and those of the heavy mortar company to the division artillery; instead of the medical company, medical personnel were assigned directly to the infantry battalions. The study proposed merging the heavy weapons company of each infantry battalion with the battalion headquarters company, except for the heavy .50-caliber machine guns, which were to be integrated into each battalion's three rifle companies. Additional automatic rifles were placed in the battalions, and more communication personnel were assigned throughout the regiment.[4]

Maj. Gen. Robert N. Young, Commandant of the Infantry School, had many reservations about the proposed changes and believed that thorough field testing was needed to evaluate them. As a result, an underequipped and understrength 325th Infantry, an element of the 82d Airborne Division, began testing the organization in May 1953 and completed the evaluation in September. The results indicated that the proposed regimental organization was less effective than the one then being used in Korea.[5]

In the meantime, the Tactical Department of the Infantry School had also begun work on a new type of infantry division. The redesign effort also sought to eliminate nonfighters and to increase firepower as well as to simplify the organization and improve control at the divisional level by using task force organizations similar to those in the armored division. A fixed organization such as an infantry regiment, the studies noted, forced the commander to base his operational plans on the organization rather than on the mission. Task force structures would permit him to organize his forces to accomplish a broader variety of missions. The division that evolved consisted of three brigade headquarters, nine infantry battalions, two armored battalions, division artillery, and combat and combat service support. The brigade headquarters elements had no permanently assigned combat or support units. No reduction resulted in the size of the division, which totaled 18,762 officers and enlisted men.[6]

In April 1954 Army Chief of Staff Ridgway shifted the emphasis of divisional studies. Under pressure from the Defense Department for smaller units, he noted that divisions had increased firepower and capabilities but were larger and less mobile than their World War II counterparts. The possibility existed, he

# THE SEARCH FOR ATOMIC AGE DIVISIONS

*General Ridgway*

believed, to make divisions more mobile, more flexible, and less vulnerable to atomic attack. To achieve such goals he directed Army Field Forces to explore the following seven objectives: (1) greater combat manpower ratios; (2) greater combat to support unit ratios; (3) greater flexibility and greater mobility in combat units; (4) maximum use of technological improvements; (5) improvements in the Army's capability to sustain land combat; (6) development of tactical doctrine to support the changes; and (7) reorganization of the units by 1 January 1956.[7]

Although Army Field Forces became the executive agent for the study, the Command and General Staff College at Fort Leavenworth did much of the work required to meet the tight schedule. The study centered on infantry and armored divisions because of the similarity between infantry and airborne divisions. Changes in the infantry division would automatically apply to major aspects of the airborne division. By the fall of 1954 Army Field Forces had developed the Atomic Field Army, or "ATFA–1," which it believed could be organized in 1956.[8]

Under ATFA–1 infantry and armored divisions were as similar as possible (*Chart 26*). The infantry division included a separate headquarters battalion; signal, engineer, and tank battalions; seven infantry battalions; division artillery; and a support command. Within the division headquarters battalion were aviation and reconnaissance companies, and within its headquarters and service company were three combat command headquarters along with the divisional staff. One 4.2-inch mortar and two 105-mm. howitzer battalions made up the division artillery. The support command, a new organization, comprised a battalion, which included medical, maintenance, supply and transport, and personnel service companies. Divisional elements lost all administrative functions except those needed to maintain unit efficiency. Personnel for administration, mess, and maintenance functions were concentrated in battalion headquarters companies throughout. All staffs were minimal; the divisional G–1 and G–4 functions were reduced to policy, planning, and coordinating activities. Routine administrative and logistical matters were moved to the support command. Infantry divisions, similar to armored divisions, were to use task force organizations as situations required. Combat command headquarters, the combat arms battalions, and the support units were the building

CHART 26—Atomic Field Army Infantry Division, 30 September 1954

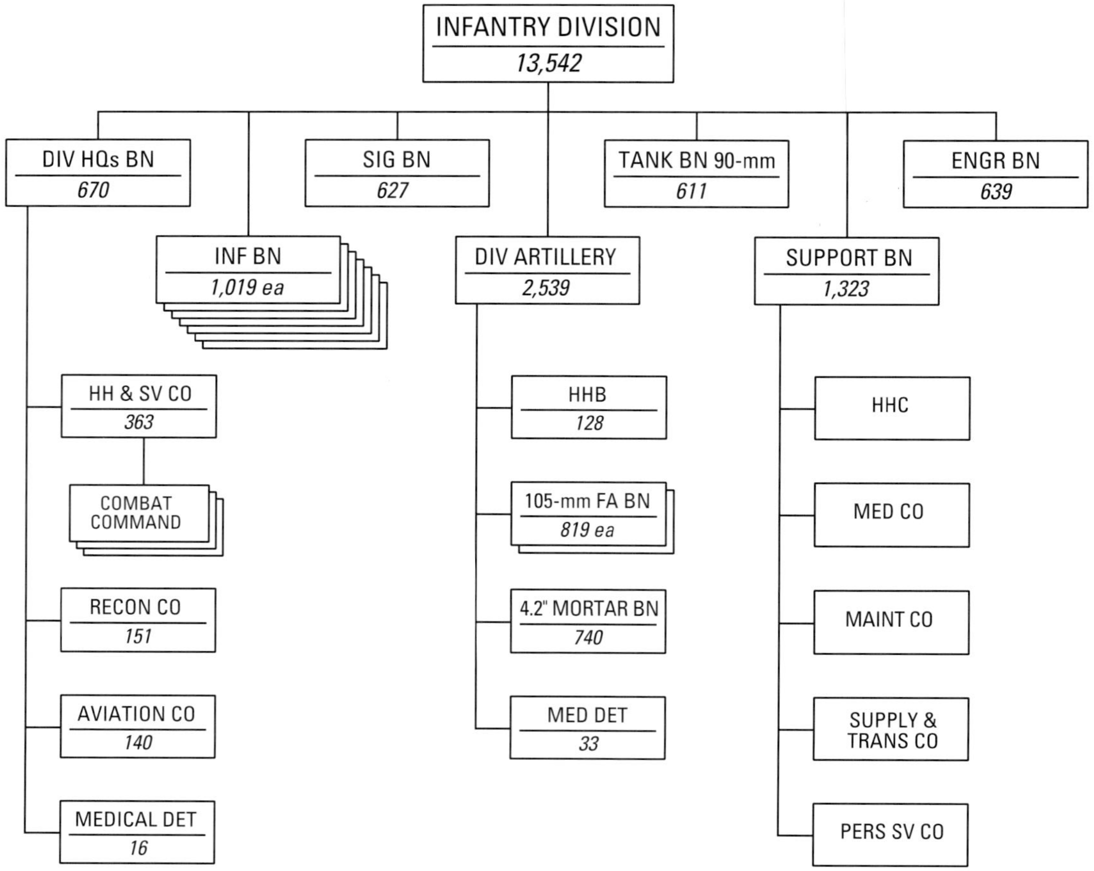

- INFANTRY DIVISION — 13,542
  - DIV HQs BN — 670
    - HH & SV CO — 363
    - COMBAT COMMAND
    - RECON CO — 151
    - AVIATION CO — 140
    - MEDICAL DET — 16
  - INF BN — 1,019 ea
  - SIG BN — 627
  - DIV ARTILLERY — 2,539
    - HHB — 128
    - 105-mm FA BN — 819 ea
    - 4.2" MORTAR BN — 740
    - MED DET — 33
  - TANK BN 90-mm — 611
  - SUPPORT BN — 1,323
    - HHC
    - MED CO
    - MAINT CO
    - SUPPLY & TRANS CO
    - PERS SV CO
  - ENGR BN — 639

blocks. The strength of the division stood at approximately 13,500 officers and enlisted men, a cut of nearly 4,000 from the 1953 division.9

The armored division (*Chart 27*) retained its task force structure. It consisted of headquarters, signal, engineer, and reconnaissance battalions; three medium and three heavy tank battalions; three armored infantry battalions; division artillery; and a support command. The headquarters battalion was the same as in the infantry division except for the reconnaissance unit, which was a separate battalion. The artillery was also similar to that in the infantry division, but the 105-mm. howitzers were self-propelled rather than towed. A maintenance battalion and a supply and transport battalion were assigned to the support command, but the division had no separate medical or personnel service units, those functions being integrated into the support battalion. The strength of the division was approximately 12,000 officers and enlisted men, a drop of almost 2,700 soldiers.10

Within both divisions the designers of the Atomic Field Army–1 introduced some significant changes. All aircraft were gathered into an aviation company in the headquarters battalion. The signal battalion, rather than maintaining communications along various axes, provided a grid system that encompassed the entire division area. New FM (frequency modulation) radios permitted that change. Antiaircraft guns were placed in the field artillery battalions, and the military police functions were split between the personnel service and the supply and transport units in the support commands. Separate antiaircraft artillery battalions and military police companies disappeared from both divisions. Neither division fielded nuclear weapons, which were instead located at the field army level.11

In February 1955 the 3d Infantry Division in Exercise FOLLOW ME and the 1st Armored Division in Exercise BLUE BOLT tried out these new organizations. The results of the infantry division test showed that independent infantry battalions and the combat commands added flexibility and that the support command provided an acceptable base from which to improve logistical functions. Generally, however, the division lacked the capability to wage sustained combat operations. It needed more on-the-ground strength to execute normal battlefield missions during an atomic war and larger reconnaissance forces to cover the extended frontages and depths envisaged for the nuclear battlefield. Additional antitank and artillery weapons were also required. Staffs at division, combat command, and battalion levels were too small to be fully effective. BLUE BOLT neither proved nor disproved that the 1st Armored Division possessed less vulnerability to atomic attacks. But the use of the same command posts for combat command headquarters and tank battalions increased the division's vulnerability to air attacks, as did the omission of the antiaircraft artillery battalion.12

Following the exercises Army Field Forces revised the two organizations, and the 3d Infantry Division and 1st Armored Division again tested them, this time in Operation SAGEBRUSH, a joint Army and Air Force exercise. Both divisions retained combat commands, but their staffs were increased to allow them to conduct operations from separate command posts. The infantry division had two tank

CHART 27—Atomic Field Army Armored Division, 30 September 1954

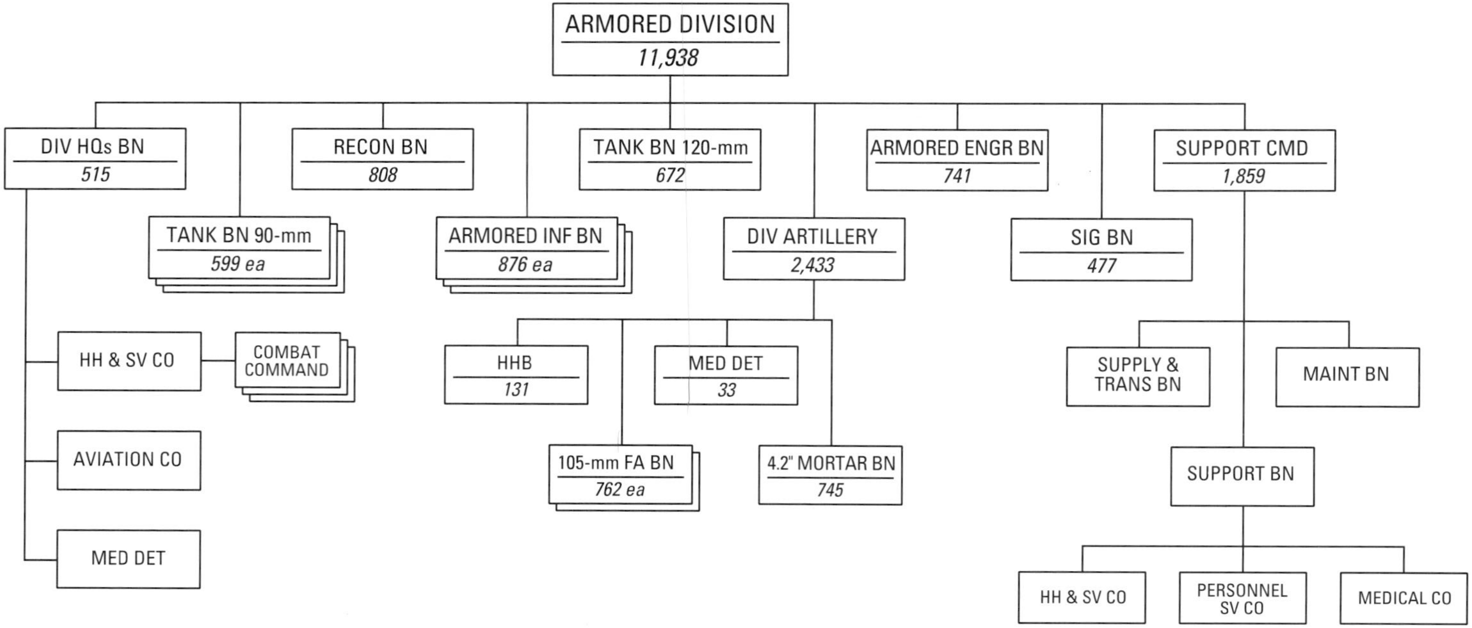

- ARMORED DIVISION — 11,938
  - DIV HQs BN — 515
  - RECON BN — 808
  - TANK BN 90-mm — 599 ea
  - ARMORED INF BN — 876 ea
  - TANK BN 120-mm — 672
  - DIV ARTILLERY — 2,433
    - HHB — 131
    - 105-mm FA BN — 762 ea
    - MED DET — 33
    - 4.2" MORTAR BN — 745
  - ARMORED ENGR BN — 741
  - SIG BN — 477
  - SUPPORT CMD — 1,859
    - MAINT BN
    - SUPPLY & TRANS BN
    - SUPPORT BN
      - MEDICAL CO
      - PERSONNEL SV CO
      - HH & SV CO
  - COMBAT COMMAND
  - HH & SV CO
  - AVIATION CO
  - MED DET

battalions and eight four-company infantry battalions, while the armored division had one heavy and three medium tank battalions and four infantry battalions of four companies each. To improve command and control, separate division headquarters, aviation, and administration companies replaced the headquarters battalion. The division's artillery reverted to its traditional structure of a headquarters and headquarters battery, a medical detachment, and one 155-mm. and three 105-mm. howitzer battalions with an antiaircraft artillery battery in each battalion. A reconnaissance battalion, identical to the one in the armored division, improved the "eyes and ears" of the infantry division. Engineer resources were increased in both divisions, and a bridge company was restored to the armored division. The support commands in both organizations were restructured to consist of a headquarters and headquarters company, a band, military police and medical companies, a maintenance battalion, and a supply and transport unit. In the infantry division the supply and transport unit remained a company, while in the tank division it was a battalion. The signal battalion in both divisions continued to furnish an area system of communications. These changes increased the strength of the infantry division from 13,542 to 17,027 troops and the armored division from 11,930 to 13,971.[13]

Maj. Gen. George E. Lynch, the "Marne" Division commander, and Maj. Gen. Robert L. Howze, commanding "Old Ironsides," reached different conclusions about the revised divisions. Lynch found that the infantry division operated in much the same manner as a conventional division with an improved logistical system. He nevertheless concluded that the Army should return to the traditional division organization with three regimental combat teams, which, he believed, were as flexible as combat commands. Furthermore, Lynch thought regimental organization fostered morale; encouraged teamwork between subordinate and superior commanders, as well as their staffs; provided knowledge about capabilities and weaknesses of units and their leaders; and stimulated cooperative working methods. Lynch's proposed changes raised the divisional strength to 21,678 officers and enlisted men. Howze, on the other hand, found the armored division generally acceptable. He suggested returning all mess and second-echelon maintenance to the company level, converting the medical unit to a battalion, forming headquarters and service companies or batteries for battalions in all the arms, concentrating antiaircraft resources into one battalion, and augmenting maintenance throughout the division. Howze did not specify the strength of his proposed division, but Lt. Gen. John H. Collier, Fourth Army commander, in whose area the operation was conducted, reported on the test and recommended 15,819 of all ranks.[14]

In 1956 the U.S. Continental Army Command, which had replaced Army Field Forces, distributed revised tables of organization for Atomic Field Army divisions throughout the Army for review and comment. While controversies persisted, the command noted that gains had been made in the infantry division's ability to carry out a variety of missions and to protect itself against atomic attack. The Atomic Field Army studies refrained from making any revolutionary changes in the armored division. Recommended changes incorporated such desirable features as the area system of communications, the administrative services company as a home for special staffs and the replacement section, an aviation company for more flexibility in the use of aircraft, and the new support command for better logistical support.15

At this point Chief of Staff General Maxwell D. Taylor called a halt. On 10 April 1956, he decided the Army would not adopt the recommendations of the Atomic Field Army studies. They were not achieving more austere divisions, but, in fact, were recommending units that were larger than the post–World War II ones. He directed the Continental Army Command to terminate all initiatives concerning the Atomic Field Army but to complete reports for future reference.16

*General Taylor*

The Army's search for austere units that could survive on both conventional and nuclear battlefields thus appeared to have gone nowhere. Those who had tested or commented on the Atomic Field Army divisions either disagreed with or had misunderstood the overall objectives of Ridgway and the Army Staff. Maj. Gen. Garrison H. Davidson, Commandant of the Command and General Staff College, opposed a "lean" division because he thought it would sacrifice training between the combat arms and services. He also thought that such a division was inappropriate for use as a mobilization base. The college, he noted, preferred "a very flexible outfit, which could be beefed up or skinned down as necessary on deployment."17

Furthermore, those who evaluated the divisions paid little heed to use of tactical atomic weapons. Over 250 simulated tests had been conducted in the SAGEBRUSH exercise. Taylor concluded after the exercises that "we in the Army have a long way to go before we understand the problems of using these weapons," noting that "we would have probably destroyed ourselves and all our friends had we tossed atomic weapons about a real battlefield in the way we did in this maneuver."18

## *Pentomic Divisions*

In response to Ridgway's directive in November 1954, the Army War College had begun work on a study entitled "Doctrinal and Organizational Concepts for Atomic-Nonatomic Army During the Period 1960–1970," which had the short title

THE SEARCH FOR ATOMIC AGE DIVISIONS 271

*101st Airborne Division simulates an atomic bomb blast, Fort Campbell, Kentucky, 1957.*

of PENTANA. Ridgway wanted the study to outline broad doctrinal and organizational concepts applicable to sustained ground combat on the Eurasian land mass during the period 1960–70. While the study was to make use of the maximum technological developments, including nuclear weapons of all types, Ridgway also desired that the Army retain a capability for conventional warfare.[19]

Completed in December 1955, the Army War College study called for a completely air transportable 8,600-man division to replace infantry, airborne, and armored divisions. The new division was to be built around five small, self-sufficient "battle groups" that would include their own artillery. The battle groups were to meet the tactical requirements for dispersion of forces, operations in depth, and increased flexibility and mobility on the atomic battlefield. Organic division artillery, although meager, included the Honest John, a surface-to-surface rocket with a nuclear warhead. The division had minimal logistical and administrative support and lacked tanks, antiaircraft artillery, engineer, and reconnaissance units (*Chart 28*).[20]

Not surprisingly, many Army leaders found the PENTANA division unacceptable. When General John E. Dahlquist, commander of the Continental Army Command, forwarded the study to Washington, he noted that the reaction of the arms and services to the division was directly related to the impact of the proposal on their strengths and missions. Those who perceived an increase in responsibility endorsed the idea, those who saw no change acquiesced, and those who discerned a diminution of strengths and responsibilities violently opposed it. The Armor School objected to the lack of divisional tanks, the Artillery School desired more conventional artillery, and the Command and General Staff College questioned the division's staying power. The most damning comment came from Chief of Engineers Lt. Gen. Samuel D. Sturgis, Jr., who considered the concept "completely unacceptable intellectually and scientifically."[21]

Nevertheless, Chief of Staff Taylor approved the PENTANA study on 1 June 1956 as a goal for future research and development of new weapons, equipment, and organizations. It was not an entirely new idea for him. As the commander of the Eighth Army he had experimented with a division having five subordinate elements in the Korean Army. In the meantime, the Army was to fill the gap

*Honest John rocket launcher*

between what it had and what it wanted by adopting modified versions of the concept, using new weapons and equipment as they became available. He believed that until the goal of a PENTANA division could be reached, the Army would continue to need infantry, airborne, and armored divisions.[22]

Before Taylor approved the PENTANA study, he had directed the reorganization of the airborne division using a modification of the concept. He judged the existing airborne division incapable of functioning effectively either in an airborne role or in sustained ground combat. It could neither be divided into balanced task forces nor be airlifted. Taylor suggested a division of 10,000 or 12,000 men organized into five battle groups that fielded nuclear weapons. Including such arms in the division, he believed, would both stimulate their development and assist in developing doctrine for their use.[23]

On 15 December 1955, the Continental Army Command submitted a proposal for an airborne division that incorporated features of both the PENTANA and ATFA studies. Each one of its five battle groups would consist of four infantry companies; a 4.2-inch mortar battery; and a headquarters and service company comprising engineer, signal, supply, maintenance, reconnaissance, assault weapons, and medical resources. A divisional support group made up of a maintenance battalion and administrative, medical, and supply and transport companies provided logistical services. The divisional command and control battalion assets included the division headquarters, a headquarters and service company, an aviation company, and a reconnaissance troop. A signal battalion furnished a grid communication system, and a small engineer battalion provided the resources needed to construct an airstrip within forty-eight hours. The artillery fielded three

CHART 28—PENTANA Division

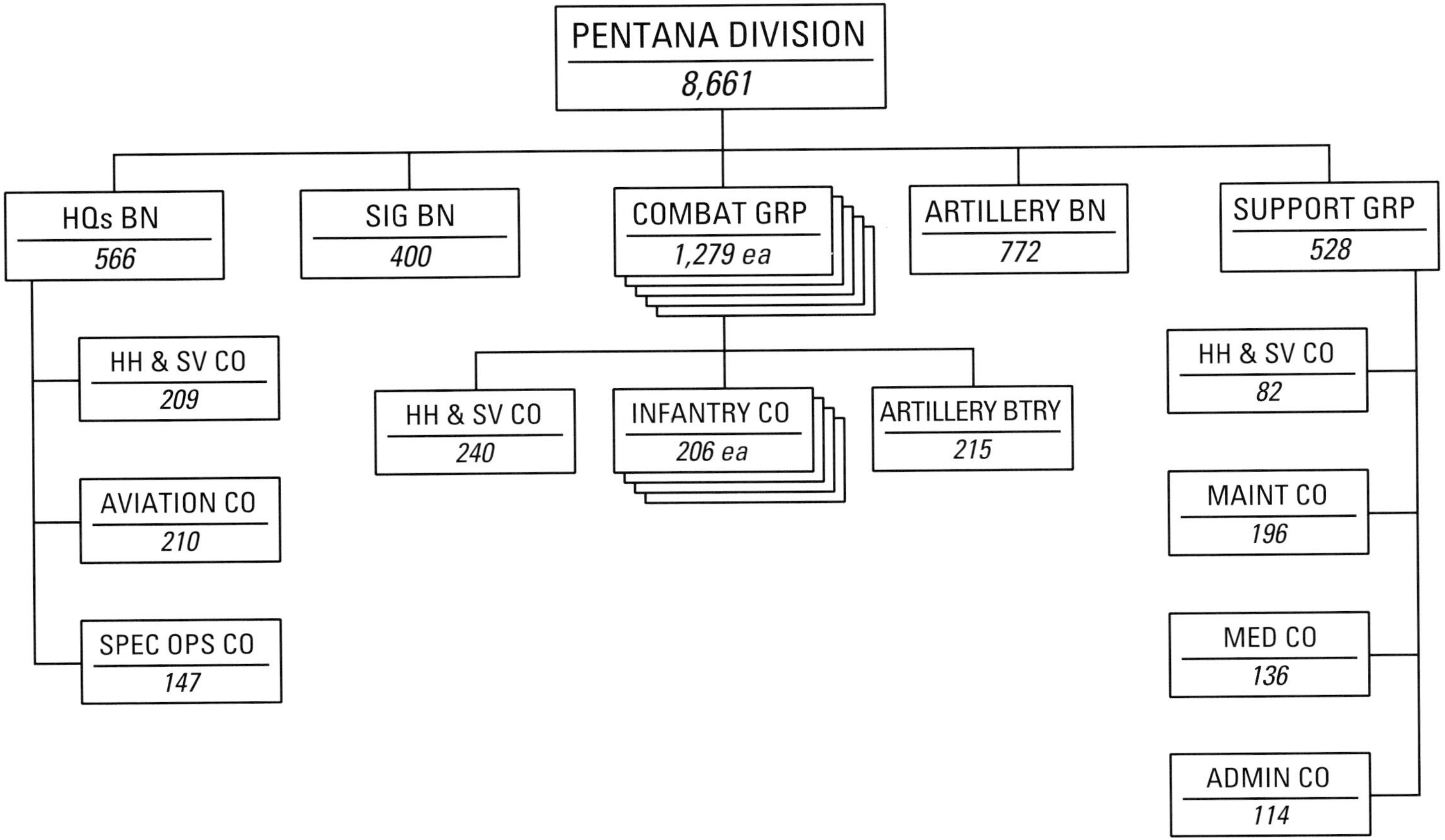

- PENTANA DIVISION — 8,661
  - HQs BN — 566
    - HH & SV CO — 209
    - AVIATION CO — 210
    - SPEC OPS CO — 147
  - SIG BN — 400
  - COMBAT GRP — 1,279 ea
    - HH & SV CO — 240
    - INFANTRY CO — 206 ea
    - ARTILLERY BTRY — 215
  - ARTILLERY BN — 772
  - SUPPORT GRP — 528
    - HH & SV CO — 82
    - MAINT CO — 196
    - MED CO — 136
    - ADMIN CO — 114

105-mm. howitzer batteries (eight pieces each) for direct support and one nuclear weapons battery, equipped with two cumbersome 762-mm. Honest John rockets, for general support. Planners sacrificed the range of the 155-mm. howitzers to gain the air deliverability of the 105-mm. howitzers and their prime movers. No command level intervened between the division headquarters and the battle groups or between the battle groups and company-size units, speeding response time. Staffs for all units were minimal. Because of the lean nature of the division, mess facilities were eliminated except in the medical company and the headquarters company of the support group. Instead, the Continental Army Command recommended the attachment of a food service company in garrison.[24]

Taylor approved the concept in February 1956 with the following modifications: the addition of a fifth infantry company to each battle group, an increase in the number of 105-mm. howitzer batteries from three to five (while reducing the number of pieces from eight to five), inclusion of a band, and the elimination of the attached food service company. He also wanted the administration company moved from the support group to the command and control battalion and the artillery group redesignated as division artillery.[25]

Following Taylor's guidance, the command published tables of organization and equipment on 10 August 1956 known as ROTAD (Reorganization of the Airborne Division). The division had 11,486 officers and enlisted men (*Chart 29*), and, for the first time in its history, all men and equipment, except for the Honest Johns, could be carried on existing aircraft. The designers of the new division thought that it was capable of operating from three to five days independently, but it would need to be reinforced for operations that lasted for a longer period.[26]

To test what Taylor called the new "pentomic"[27] division, he selected his former unit, the 101st Airborne Division, then serving as a training division at Fort Jackson. On 31 April 1956, the division moved without its personnel and equipment to Fort Campbell, Kentucky, where it was reorganized, acquiring personnel from the 187th and 508th Regimental Combat Teams and equipment from the 11th Airborne Division that had been left at Fort Campbell after the unit had participated in the GYROSCOPE program.[28]

The "Screaming Eagles" conducted a series of individual unit evaluations rather than one divisional exercise. Lt. Gen. Thomas F. Hickey, the test director, judged the new division suitable for short-duration airborne assaults, with improved prospects for survival and success during either an atomic or a conventional war. However, he noted major deficiencies in the direct support artillery—its short range and lack of lethality; in logistical resources, which were less effective than in the triangular division; and in the total strength of the division. The division was so austere that it could not undertake garrison duties and maintain combat readiness.[29]

To remedy these weaknesses, Hickey recommended replacing the 105-mm. howitzers with 155-mm. pieces except for parachute assaults. Instead of five howitzer batteries, he proposed four. The larger howitzer would give the direct support artillery the range he believed that the division required. Also, since the fifth battle

CHART 29—Airborne Division (ROTAD), 10 August 1956

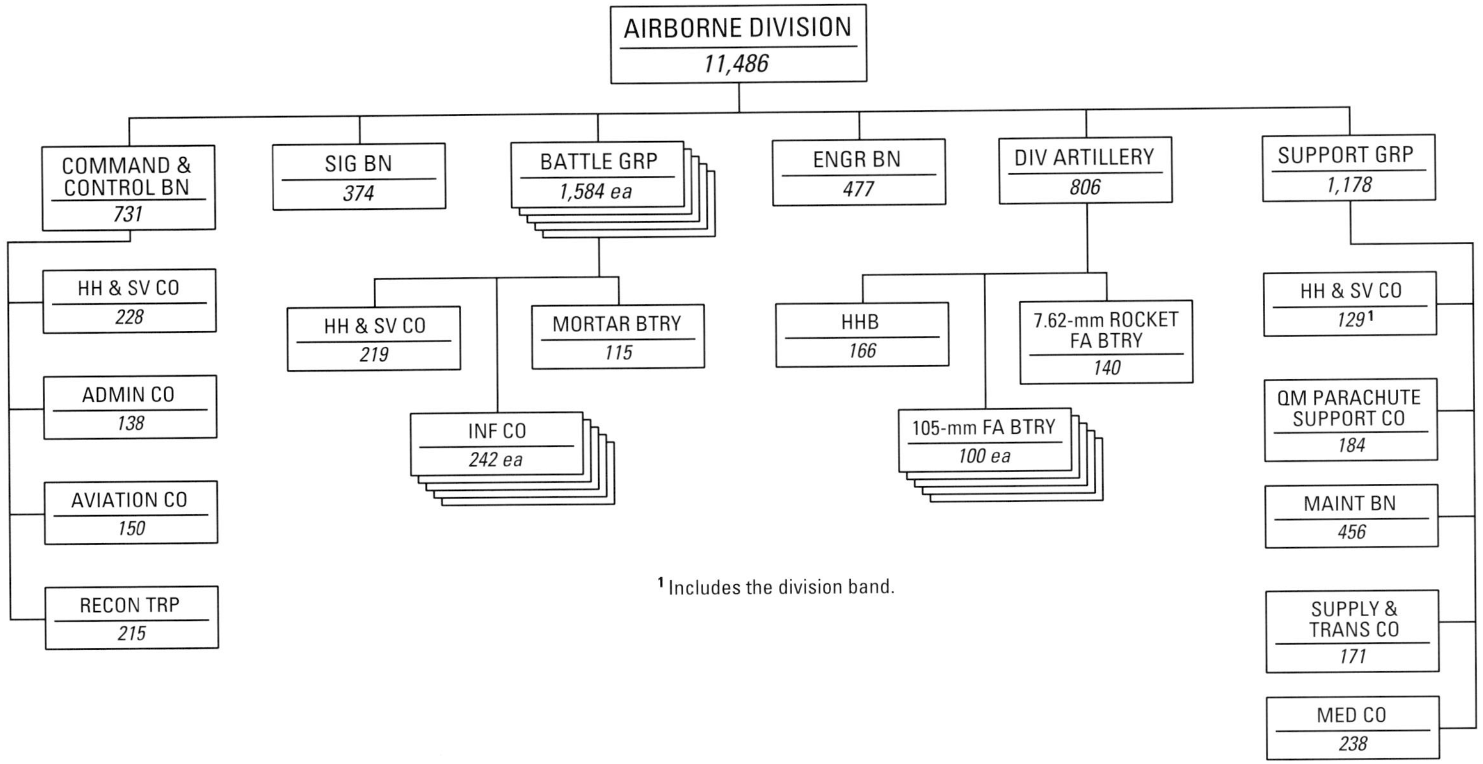

- AIRBORNE DIVISION — 11,486
  - COMMAND & CONTROL BN — 731
    - HH & SV CO — 228
    - ADMIN CO — 138
    - AVIATION CO — 150
    - RECON TRP — 215
  - SIG BN — 374
  - BATTLE GRP — 1,584 ea
    - HH & SV CO — 219
    - MORTAR BTRY — 115
    - INF CO — 242 ea
  - ENGR BN — 477
  - DIV ARTILLERY — 806
    - HHB — 166
    - 7.62-mm ROCKET FA BTRY — 140
    - 105-mm FA BTRY — 100 ea
  - SUPPORT GRP — 1,178
    - HH & SV CO — 129[1]
    - QM PARACHUTE SUPPORT CO — 184
    - MAINT BN — 456
    - SUPPLY & TRANS CO — 171
    - MED CO — 238

[1] Includes the division band.

group in the division was to be held in reserve, he proposed deleting its direct support artillery battery. Other recommendations included eliminating the support group and reorganizing the logistical resources, except for maintenance organized along functional lines, in a pre–Atomic Field Army configuration. A 10 percent increase in divisional strength was suggested, as well as an enlarged garrison complement wherever a pentomic division was stationed. Hickey wished to move the administration company to the rear because its functions did not require the unit's presence in the forward area; he thought the infantry platoon should be eliminated from the reconnaissance troop because it lacked the mobility of the troop's other elements; and he wanted a military intelligence detachment added to the division's headquarters battalion to help with order of battle, photographic interpretation, and other G–2 duties. Finally, he advocated an increase in the grades of the commanders of the rifle companies, mortar batteries, and howitzer batteries to make their rank commensurate with the responsibilities associated with independent actions required on the "pentomic battlefield."[30]

The test findings and Hickey's recommendations worked their way through the Continental Army Command. Dahlquist agreed with most of Hickey's proposals except for the artillery and support group. He believed that 105-mm. howitzers should be retained as direct support weapons because they could be airlifted in two helicopter loads or towed by 3/4-ton trucks. Rather than decreasing the number of artillery batteries, he wanted the division to retain five, each with six pieces. He opposed changes in the support group because its structure had not been fully tested, and he felt that Hickey's recommendation to eliminate it was premature.[31]

The Army Staff agreed with Dahlquist's views regarding the number of artillery batteries but not on increasing the number of pieces in each battery. No change in the support group won approval, and the staff opposed the elimination of the infantry platoon from the reconnaissance troop, the addition of the military intelligence detachment, and alterations in the rank of company and battery commanders. The Continental Army Command published tables of organization for the pentomic airborne division reflecting the views of the Army Staff in June 1958 without a change in unit's overall strength. Both the 82d and 101st Airborne Divisions adopted them by December.[32]

Shortly after the 101st Airborne Division began testing ROTAD, Taylor directed the Continental Army Command to develop a new infantry division along similar pentagonal lines. It was to have five battle groups (a headquarters and service company, one mortar battery, and four infantry companies each); conventional and nuclear artillery; tank, signal, and engineer battalions; a reconnaissance squadron with ground and air capabilities; and trains. The trains, who commander was responsible for the activities of the service troops in the rear area, were to include a transportation battalion, an aviation company, and an administration company. The transportation battalion was to have sufficient armored personnel carriers to move an entire battle group at one time, and the aviation company was to be placed in the trains for better supervision of its maintenance. Taylor wanted to optimize the span of control in the division by giving each commander the maximum number of subordinate elements that could be controlled effectively. He believed such a division could be organized with 13,500 men of all ranks, a reduction of nearly 4,000 from the 1955 infantry division.33

On 15 October 1956 the Continental Army Command forwarded manning charts (*Chart 30*) for "ROCID" (Reorganization of the Current Infantry Division) to Washington. The planners followed Taylor's general guidance but recommended a division slightly larger than expected. They provided the tank and engineer battalions with five companies each and the division artillery with two battalions—five batteries of 105-mm. howitzers in one and an Honest John rocket, one 8-inch howitzer, and two 155-mm. howitzer batteries in the other. Each 105-mm. howitzer battery fielded six pieces and boasted of its own fire direction center, and each mortar battery in the battle group had assigned liaison, fire direction, forward air controller, and forward observer personnel. In addition to headquarters and headquarters detachment and band, the division trains included medical, ordnance, and transportation battalions and aviation, administrative, and quartermaster companies. 34

Taylor hesitated to adopt the pentagonal structure for the armored division because he feared that such a change would make the organization too large. Nevertheless, Lt. Gen. Clyde Eddleman, the Deputy Chief of Staff for Military Operations, instructed the Continental Army Command to modernize the division by adding atomic weapons, increasing target acquisition capabilities, and reducing the number of vehicles. To carry out his wishes, the command added a reconnaissance and surveillance platoon to the reconnaissance battalion, provided aircraft in the aviation company to support it, and replaced the 155-mm. howitzers in one battery of the general support battalion with 8-inch howitzers that could fire nuclear rounds. No significant reduction in the number of vehicles took place because the atomic and conventional battlefields required more transportation resources than authorized in the existing division. A command and control battalion that included administration and aviation companies was added. To offset increases in the divisional elements, the command eliminated the antiaircraft artillery battalion.35

On 5 November 1956 the Army Staff approved the pentomic armored division with some exceptions. The staff directed the formation of separate divisional headquarters, aviation, and administrative companies in place of the suggested command and control battalion and moved the administration company to the trains. The former 155-mm. howitzer battalion was reorganized as a composite unit comprising an Honest John, an 8-inch howitzer, and two 155-mm. howitzer batteries. The Army published the "ROCAD" (Reorganization of the Current Armored Division) tables reflecting these changes in December 1956. They called for a division of 14,617 officers and enlisted men (*Chart 31*), 34 fewer than included in the 1955 tables. The tank count stood at 360, of which 54 were armed with 75-mm. guns and 306 with 90-mm. guns. All the medium tanks were in four tank battalions.36

## CHART 30—Infantry Division (ROCID), 21 December 1956

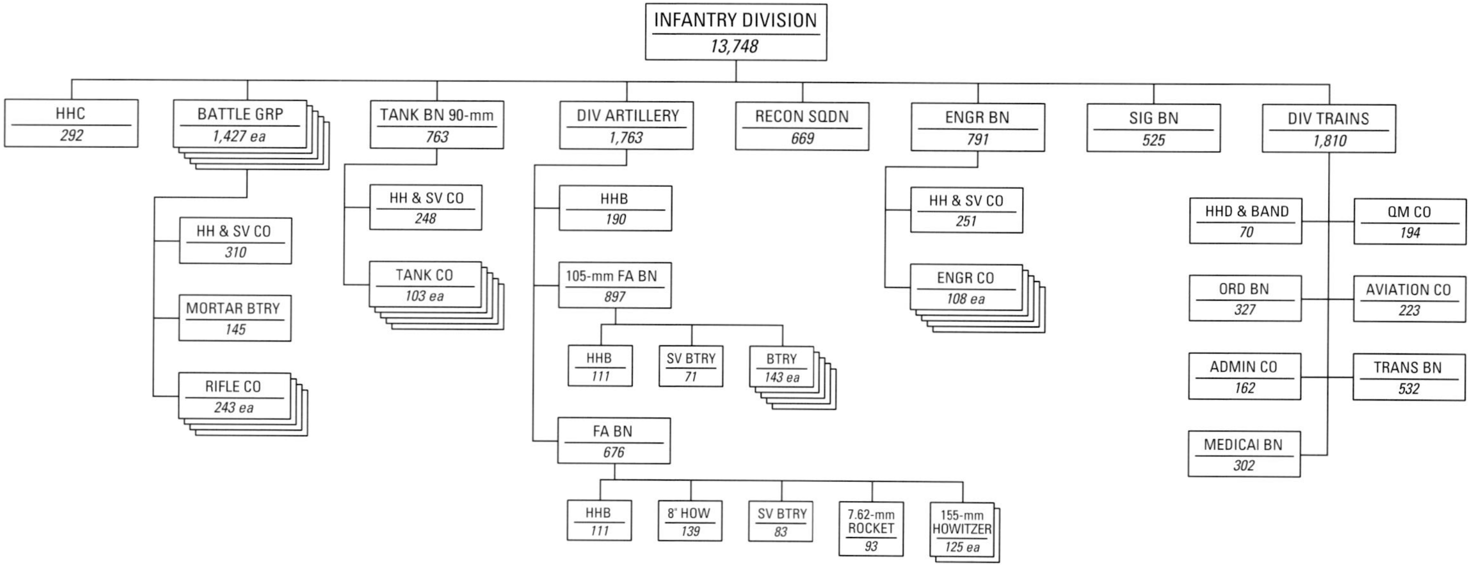

**INFANTRY DIVISION** — 13,748

- **HHC** — 292
- **BATTLE GRP** — 1,427 ea
  - HH & SV CO — 310
  - MORTAR BTRY — 145
  - RIFLE CO — 243 ea
- **TANK BN 90-mm** — 763
  - HH & SV CO — 248
  - TANK CO — 103 ea
- **DIV ARTILLERY** — 1,763
  - HHB — 190
  - 105-mm FA BN — 897
    - HHB — 111
    - SV BTRY — 71
    - BTRY — 143 ea
  - FA BN — 676
    - HHB — 111
    - 8" HOW — 139
    - SV BTRY — 83
    - 7.62-mm ROCKET — 93
    - 155-mm HOWITZER — 125 ea
- **RECON SQDN** — 669
- **ENGR BN** — 791
  - HH & SV CO — 251
  - ENGR CO — 108 ea
- **SIG BN** — 525
- **DIV TRAINS** — 1,810
  - HHD & BAND — 70
  - QM CO — 194
  - ORD BN — 327
  - AVIATION CO — 223
  - ADMIN CO — 162
  - TRANS BN — 532
  - MEDICAL BN — 302

## *Reorganization of the Divisions*

After the Continental Army Command completed the tables of organization for infantry and armored divisions, Taylor met with Army school commandants on 28 February 1957 to sell them on the pentomic reorganization of the Army. He noted that the doctrine of massive retaliation ruled out nuclear war, but that the chance existed that war might stem from unchecked local aggression or error. The Army had to be prepared to prevent or stop a small war as well as conduct a nuclear conflict. He believed that the new divisions, although controversial, could meet both challenges.[37]

More important was what Taylor did not say about the pentomic divisions and why the Army was adopting them. The Army's budget called for unglamorous weapons and equipment such as rifles, machine guns, and trucks, which had little appeal for Congress or the nation. Secretary of Defense Charles E. Wilson earlier had returned the Army's budget to Taylor, directing him to substitute "newfangled" equipment that Congress would support.

The Army's literature soon reported on such ideas as "convertiplanes," which combined the advantages of rotary-wing and fixed-wing aircraft; one-man "flying platforms"; and the adoption of pentomic divisions, which fielded nuclear weapons. Later Taylor wrote, "nuclear weapons were the going thing and, by including some in the division armament, the Army staked out its claim to a share of the nuclear arsenal."[38]

When reorganizing Regular Army infantry and armored divisions in 1957 under the pentomic structure, several major changes were made in the force to accommodate a cut of 100,000 men and changing world conditions. In the Far East, the United States agreed to withdraw all ground combat troops from Japan. Subsequently the 1st Cavalry Division moved to Korea, where it replaced the 24th Infantry Division. While the 7th Infantry Division remained in Korea, the 24th was eventually reorganized in Germany to replace the 11th Airborne Division. Also in Germany, the 3d Infantry Division replaced the 10th Infantry Division, which was returned to Fort Benning as part of Gyroscope. With these changes U.S. Army, Europe, still fielded five divisions, the 3d and 4th Armored Divisions and the 3d, 8th, and 24th Infantry Divisions. The European command also retained an airborne capability by reorganizing two battle groups in the 24th Infantry Division as airborne units. At Fort Benning, Georgia, the 2d Infantry Division, which earlier had been reduced to zero strength, replaced the 10th Infantry Division, which was inactivated. The 5th Infantry Division was also inactivated at Fort Ord; the 1st Armored Division, less its Combat Command A, was reduced to zero strength; and the 25th Infantry Division was cut one battle group. When the game of musical chairs with divisions was over, the Regular Army consisted of fifteen divisions. In most cases only the division names and flags moved, not the personnel and equipment. These changes in the divisional designations reflected the desire of Army leaders to keep divisions with outstand-

## CHART 31—Armored Division (ROCAD), 1956

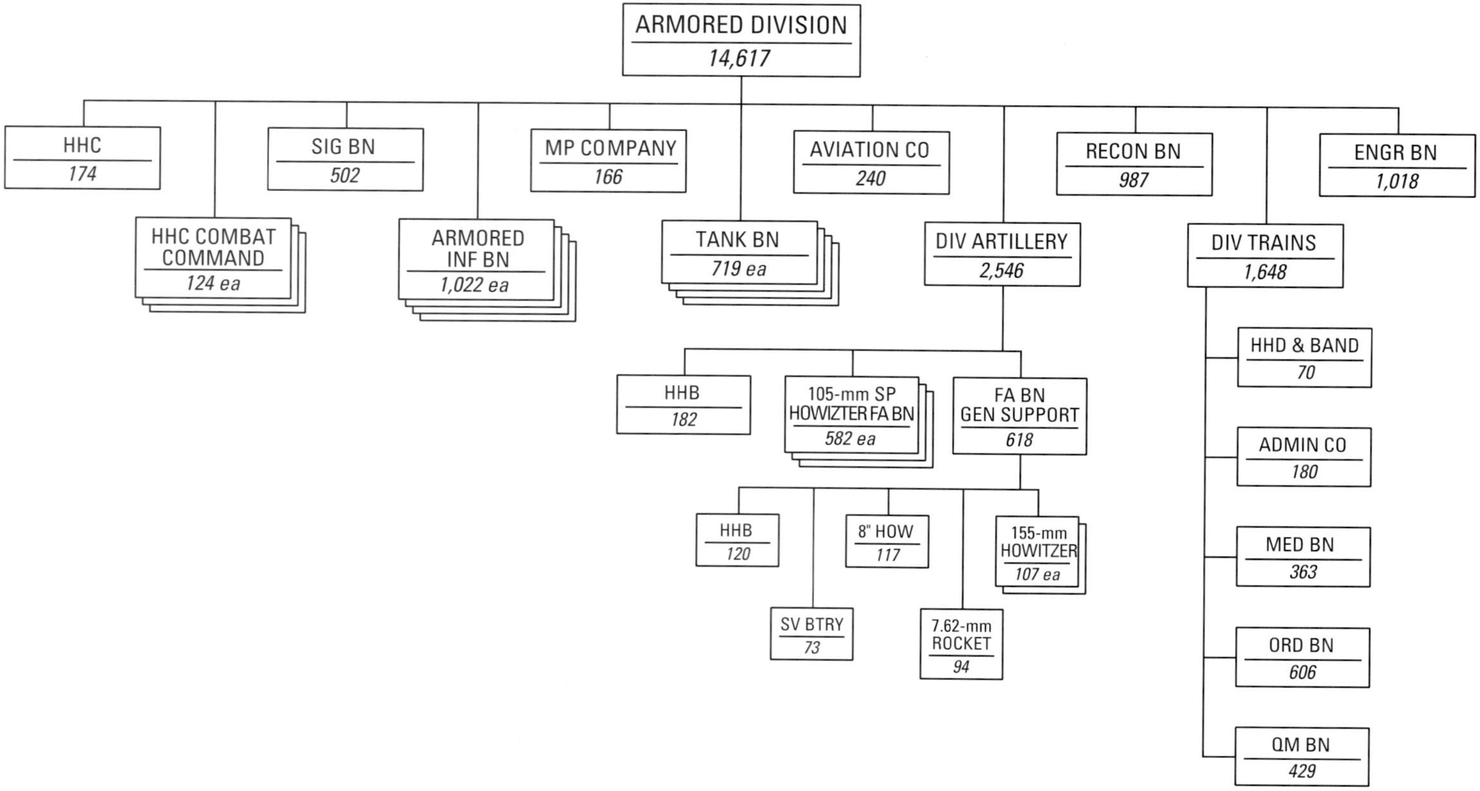

- **ARMORED DIVISION** — 14,617
  - HHC — 174
  - HHC COMBAT COMMAND — 124 ea
  - SIG BN — 502
  - ARMORED INF BN — 1,022 ea
  - MP COMPANY — 166
  - TANK BN — 719 ea
  - AVIATION CO — 240
  - DIV ARTILLERY — 2,546
    - HHB — 182
    - 105-mm SP HOWITZER FA BN — 582 ea
    - FA BN GEN SUPPORT — 618
      - HHB — 120
      - SV BTRY — 73
      - 8" HOW — 117
      - 7.62-mm ROCKET — 94
      - 155-mm HOWITZER — 107 ea
  - RECON BN — 987
  - DIV TRAINS — 1,648
    - HHD & BAND — 70
    - ADMIN CO — 180
    - MED BN — 363
    - ORD BN — 606
    - QM BN — 429
  - ENGR BN — 1,018

ing histories on the active rolls. Most soldiers, however, did not understand the rationale, and unit morale suffered.39

As the Army reorganized and shuffled divisions around the world, it adopted the Combat Arms Regimental System (CARS) for infantry, artillery, cavalry, and armor. During the ATFA and PENTANA studies a debate arose regarding unit designations. Traditionally regiments were the basic branch element, especially for the infantry, and their long histories had produced deep traditions considered essential to unit esprit de corps. The new divisional structure, replacing infantry regiments with anonymous battle groups, threatened to destroy all these traditions. Secretary of the Army Wilber M. Brucker settled the question on 24 January 1957 when he approved the Combat Arms Regimental System. Although regiments would no longer exist as tactical units except for armored cavalry, certain distinguished regiments were to become "parent" organizations for the combat arms. Under the new concept, the Department of the Army assumed control of regimental headquarters, the repository for a unit's lineage, honors, and traditions, and used elements of the regiments to organize battle groups, battalions, squadrons, companies, batteries, and troops, which shared in the history and honors of their parent units.40

When infantry regiments were eliminated in divisions as tactical units, they were also eliminated as nondivisional organizations. The Army replaced the nondivisional regimental combat teams with separate, flexible combined arms "brigades," shifting the concept of a brigade. Instead of being composed of two or more regiments or battalions of the same arm or service, the concept encompassed a combined arms unit equivalent to a reinforced regiment. Initially only two brigades were formed. First was the 2d Infantry Brigade, activated at Fort Devens on 14 February 1958 to replace the 4th Regimental Combat Team. No tables of organization existed for the unit, which at the time consisted of a headquarters, two battle groups, one artillery battalion, a reconnaissance troop, two engineer and two armor companies, and trains. The last element was an adaptation of the trains of an infantry division and consisted of a headquarters element and administration, ordnance, quartermaster, and medical companies. A miniature division, the 2d Brigade had 4,188 officers and enlisted men commanded by a brigadier general. To support the Infantry School at Fort Benning, the Third United States Army organized the 1st Infantry Brigade on 25 July 1958. It contained two battle groups; one artillery battalion (one Honest John, one 155-mm. howitzer, and two 105-mm. howitzer batteries); armor, transportation, and engineer companies; and signal and chemical platoons, but no trains. A colonel commanded the 3,600 officers and enlisted men assigned to the unit.41

## *Evaluating ROCID and ROCAD*

After completing the pentomic reorganization in the Regular Army, the Continental Army Command conducted further tests of the new organizations. In general, such efforts elicited favorable reports, finding the divisions to be adequate for atomic and conventional warfare. In particular, the command noted the new infantry division's flexibility, unity of command, mobility, and decisive combat power in terms of nuclear firepower. The infantry division, however, suffered from deficiencies in four areas—staying power, ground surveillance, artillery support, and staff organization. To correct these problems, the command made several recommendations: adding a fifth rifle company and a radar section to each battle group; eliminating the 4.2-inch mortar as an artillery weapon (but retaining some in the headquarters company of the battle group); reorganizing the artillery into one divisional composite battalion (one Honest John and two 8-inch howitzer batteries) and five 105/155-mm. howitzer battalions (two self-propelled and three towed); and bolstering the aviation company with an aircraft field maintenance element, an avionics repair team, and approach control teams. More staff officers were essential, particularly for the G–3 operation sections. The transportation battalion's truck company was found to be inadequate, and officers in the field suggested that all companies in the battalion be equipped with armored personnel carriers.[42]

As in the development of the pentomic airborne division, rank structures also came under scrutiny. Because of the increased command responsibility, the Continental Army Command recommended that the commander of the headquarters company of the battle group be raised from a captain to a major and that commanders of the smaller artillery battalions be reduced from lieutenant colonels to majors. Compared to an infantry regiment, the new battle group lacked billets for majors, a circumstance that would adversely affect the career pattern of infantry officers.[43]

On 29 December 1958 Deputy Chief of Staff for Military Operations Lt. Gen. James E. Moore approved the recommendations for reorganizing the infantry division with some changes. He rejected changes in the grades of the commanders of artillery battalions and the headquarters company of the battle groups and vetoed additional armored personnel carriers for the transportation battalion. He dropped an 8-inch howitzer battery from the composite artillery battalion, leaving it with only one 8-inch howitzer battery and one Honest John battery, and split the headquarters company of the battle group into two organizations, a headquarters company and a combat support company. All tactical support, including the radar section and the reconnaissance, heavy mortar, and assault weapons platoons, were to be contained in the battle group's combat support company to achieve improved command and control. A separate transportation detachment was added to provide third-echelon aircraft maintenance. With this guidance in hand, the Continental Army Command published new tables of organization for the division, without a change in its overall strength—13,748 of all ranks *(Chart 32)*.[44]

For the armored division, further tests led to a number of minor adjustments. These included moving the reconnaissance and surveillance platoon in the recon-

CHART 32—Pentomic Infantry Division, 1 February 1960

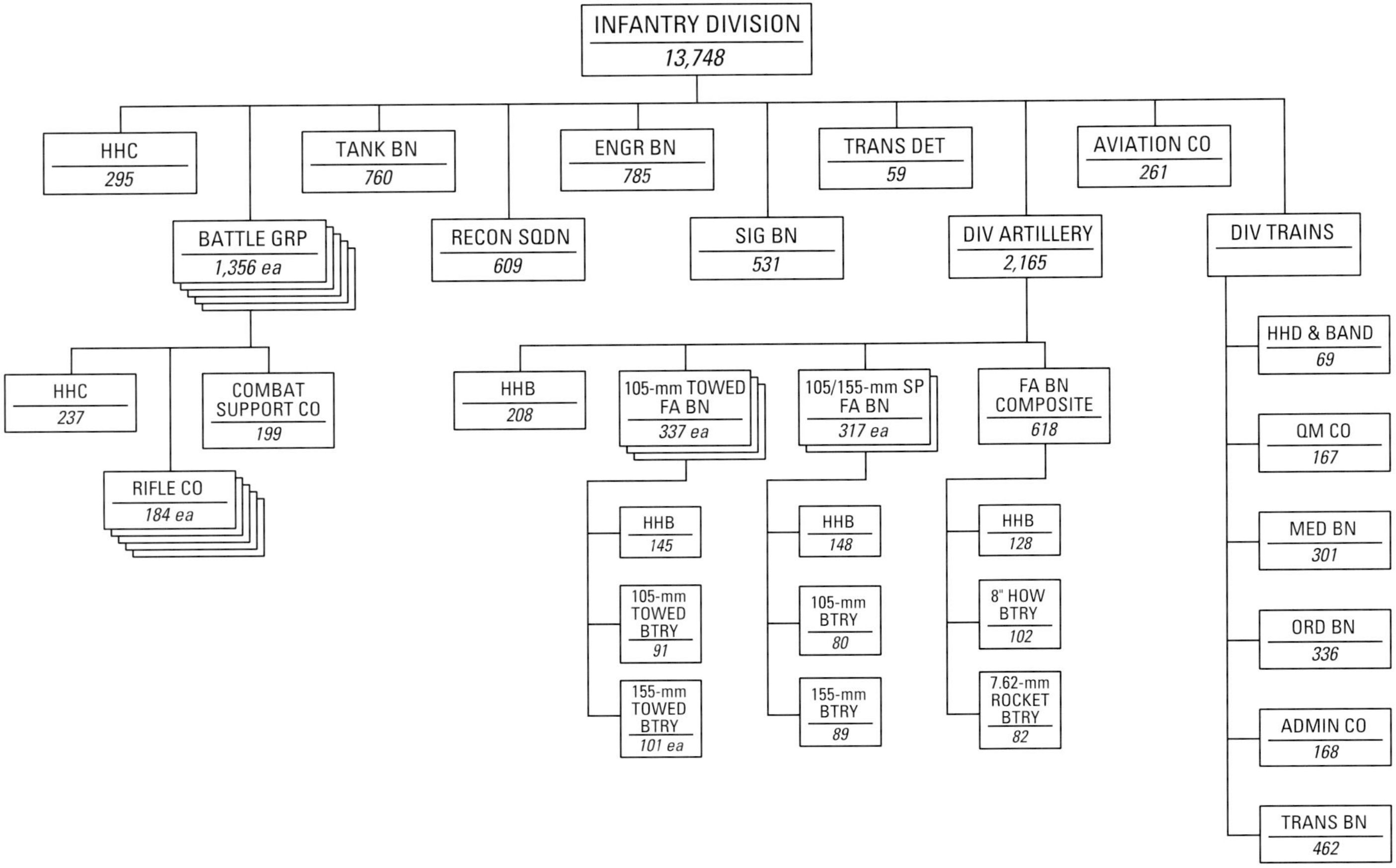

- INFANTRY DIVISION — 13,748
  - HHC — 295
  - TANK BN — 760
  - BATTLE GRP — 1,356 ea
    - HHC — 237
    - COMBAT SUPPORT CO — 199
    - RIFLE CO — 184 ea
  - RECON SQDN — 609
  - ENGR BN — 785
  - SIG BN — 531
  - TRANS DET — 59
  - DIV ARTILLERY — 2,165
    - HHB — 208
    - 105-mm TOWED FA BN — 337 ea
      - HHB — 145
      - 105-mm TOWED BTRY — 91
      - 155-mm TOWED BTRY — 101 ea
    - 105/155-mm SP FA BN — 317 ea
      - HHB — 148
      - 105-mm BTRY — 80
      - 155-mm BTRY — 89
    - FA BN COMPOSITE — 618
      - HHB — 128
      - 8" HOW BTRY — 102
      - 7.62-mm ROCKET BTRY — 82
  - AVIATION CO — 261
  - DIV TRAINS
    - HHD & BAND — 69
    - QM CO — 167
    - MED BN — 301
    - ORD BN — 336
    - ADMIN CO — 168
    - TRANS BN — 462

naissance squadron to the aviation company, providing a transportation aircraft maintenance detachment to support the aviation company, and reorganizing the reconnaissance squadron as in the infantry division. Observers also saw the need for an alternate, or backup, divisional command post, a larger staff for the artillery coordination center, and the establishment of a radiological center to detect radioactive contaminates. Minor alterations were also to be made in the service units to support these new alignments. All changes in the armored division were made without increasing its strength of 14,617.[45]

In 1959 and 1960 the Army placed Regular Army infantry and armored divisions under the revised tables that resulted from the field tests. Also, to meet a Department of Defense manpower ceiling of 870,000, the Army Staff decided to eliminate the 9th Infantry Division at Fort Carson, Colorado. The Fifth United States Army reduced the division to zero strength and later inactivated it, cutting the number of active Regular Army divisions to fourteen. In Korea the Army continued to resort to the Korean Argumentation to U.S. Army (KATUSA) program, begun during the Korean War, to keep the 1st Cavalry Division and the 7th Infantry Division at full strength; each division was assigned about 4,000 South Koreans.[46]

The Army Staff had delayed reorganization of the reserves, but in 1959 it decided to realign National Guard and Army Reserve divisions under pentomic structures. A controversy immediately surfaced over the required number of reserve divisions. Secretary of Defense Neil H. McElroy decided on 37 divisions, 27 National Guard and 10 Army Reserve. By 1 September 1959 the twenty-one infantry and six armored divisions in the Guard had reorganized, and one month later ten Army Reserve infantry divisions completed their transition, but at a reduced strength. The eleventh combat division, the 104th, in the Army Reserve was converted to training, for a total of thirteen training divisions, all of which were in the Army Reserve.[47]

Following the pattern established by the regulars, the states eliminated nondivisional regimental combat teams from the Guard and replaced them with separate combined arms brigades. Hawaii, Puerto Rico, and Arizona organized the 29th, 92d, and 258th Infantry Brigades, respectively. These units had varying numbers of combat arms elements but lacked trains needed to support independent operations.[48]

When reserve units began to adopt pentomic configurations, the Continental Army Command developed separate organizational tables for training divisions. These tables permitted the Army Reserve to retain the existing authorization of three general officers—the commander and two assistant commanders—and ensured standardization of these noncombat divisions. Each training division consisted of a headquarters and headquarters company, five regiments (an advanced individual, a common specialist, and three basic combat training regiments),[49] a receiving company, and a band (*Chart 33*). Each division in reserve status had about 3,100 of all ranks and on mobilization would run a replacement training center capable of training 12,000 men. The continental armies reorganized the

# CHART 33—Training Division, 1 April 1959

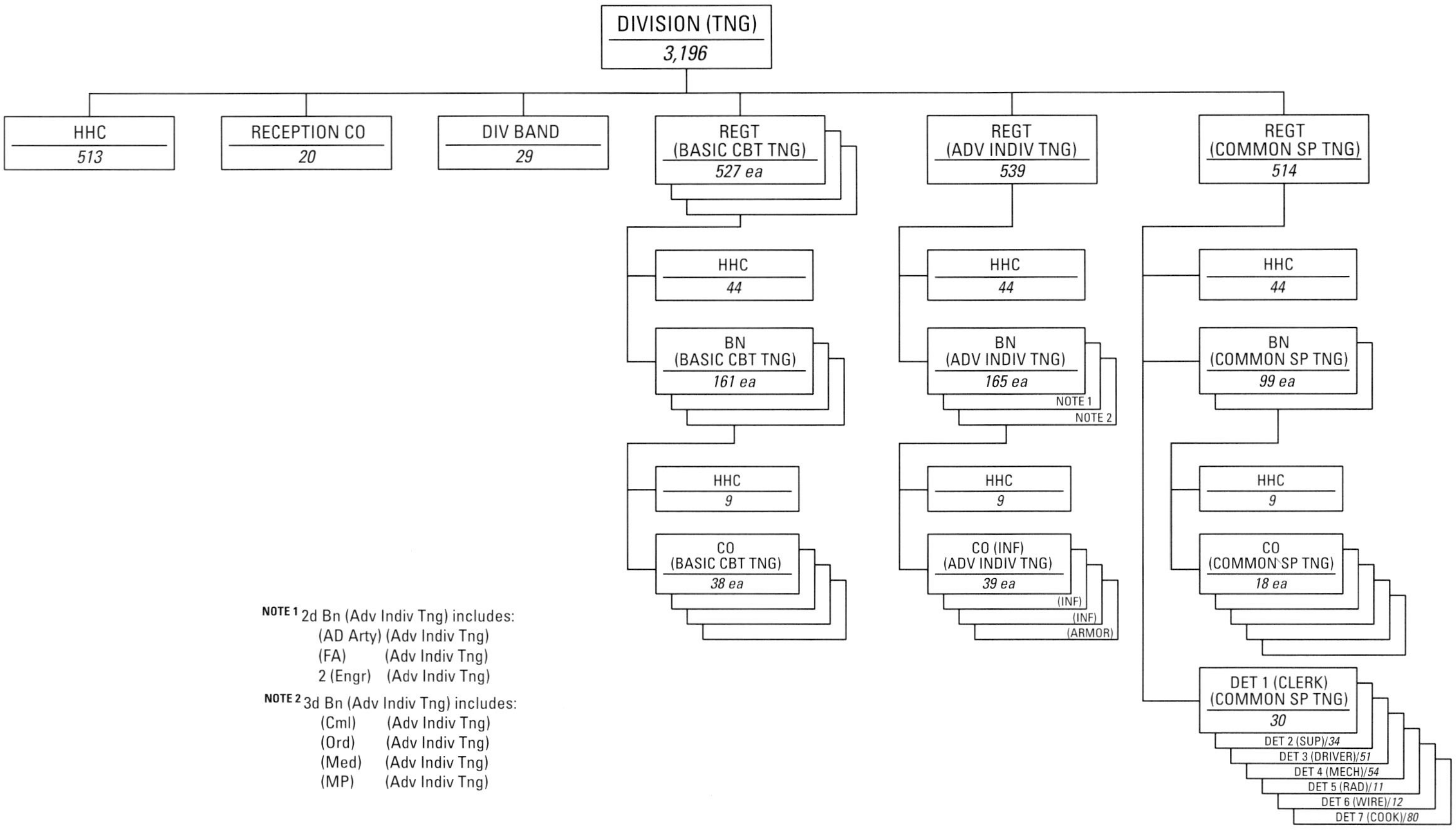

**DIVISION (TNG)** — 3,196

- HHC — 513
- RECEPTION CO — 20
- DIV BAND — 29
- **REGT (BASIC CBT TNG)** — 527 ea
  - HHC — 44
  - BN (BASIC CBT TNG) — 161 ea
    - HHC — 9
    - CO (BASIC CBT TNG) — 38 ea
- **REGT (ADV INDIV TNG)** — 539
  - HHC — 44
  - BN (ADV INDIV TNG) — 165 ea  NOTE 1, NOTE 2
    - HHC — 9
    - CO (INF) (ADV INDIV TNG) — 39 ea  (INF) (ARMOR)
- **REGT (COMMON SP TNG)** — 514
  - HHC — 44
  - BN (COMMON SP TNG) — 99 ea
    - HHC — 9
    - CO (COMMON SP TNG) — 18 ea
    - DET 1 (CLERK) (COMMON SP TNG) — 30
      - DET 2 (SUP)/34
      - DET 3 (DRIVER)/51
      - DET 4 (MECH)/54
      - DET 5 (RAD)/11
      - DET 6 (WIRE)/12
      - DET 7 (COOK)/80

NOTE 1: 2d Bn (Adv Indiv Tng) includes:
(AD Arty) (Adv Indiv Tng)
(FA) (Adv Indiv Tng)
2 (Engr) (Adv Indiv Tng)

NOTE 2: 3d Bn (Adv Indiv Tng) includes:
(Cml) (Adv Indiv Tng)
(Ord) (Adv Indiv Tng)
(Med) (Adv Indiv Tng)
(MP) (Adv Indiv Tng)

training divisions in 1959, and the adjutant general officially redesignated them as "divisions (training)."[50]

One of the objectives of the pentomic reorganization was to enable the units to absorb new equipment. The M14 rifle, a 7.62-caliber rifle that could fire in semiautomatic or automatic modes, replaced the vintage M1 rifle, the carbine, the submachine gun, and the Browning automatic rifle; the 7.62-caliber M60 machine gun replaced the heavy water-cooled and light air-cooled Browning .30-caliber machine guns. These new weapons simplified production; reduced spare parts, maintenance, and training time; and used standard NATO cartridges, permitting greater compatibility with Western European weapons. The diesel-powered M60 tank, armed with a 105-mm. gun, and the low silhouette, air-transportable M113 armored personnel carrier also entered the Army's inventory. Work began on new antiaircraft weapons, recoilless rifles, and 4.2-inch mortars, but most did not become available for several more years.[51]

When the Army completed the pentomic reorganization in 1960, it had 51 combat divisions in its three components (14 in the Regular Army, 10 in the Army Reserve, and 27 in the National Guard), 5 infantry brigades (2 in the Regular Army and 3 in the Guard), and 1 Regular Army armored combat command. Although divisions were organized for nuclear warfare, only a few were actually ready for combat. Some Regular Army divisions continued to conduct their own basic training courses to reduce costs and personnel, and Korean nationals served in the divisions in Korea. Guard units ranged between 55 and 71 percent of their authorized strengths, while Army Reserve organizations varied from 45 to 80 percent.[52]

In sum, as the Eisenhower administration reduced the Army's budget from $16 billion to $9.3 billion between 1953 and 1960, the total force dropped to the lowest number of divisions since the beginning of the Korean War. On the surface, changing concepts of warfare during this period led the Army to adopt pentomic divisions, structures that fell outside traditional organizational practices. But whatever the concerns of Army leaders for operating on a nuclear battlefield, Taylor, the primary force behind the new divisions, clearly was using the pentomic concepts to get increases in the military budget from political leaders who were less interested in supporting more conventional military systems. Nevertheless, the fertile ideas of this period resulted in new organizational concepts and new equipment and weapon systems, all of which were to see further development in the next two decades.

## Notes

1 Col Stanley N. Lonning to Acting Assistant Commandant, The Infantry School (TIS), 23 Apr 53, sub: Proposed Reorganization of the Infantry and Airborne Divisions, UA 27.51 I5 (4/23/53), Infantry School Library (ISL), Fort Benning, Ga.

2 John J. Midgley, *Deadly Illusions: Army Policy for the Nuclear Battlefield* (Boulder, Colo.: Westview Press, 1986), pp. 2–5.

3 Ltr, OCAFF to CG, Infantry Center, 28 Apr 52, sub: Organization of the Infantry Regiment, 28 Apr 52, ATTNG (Deputy Chief of Staff, G–3-Training)-23 322/6 (Regt) (28 Apr 52), ISL.

4 Report of Board of Officers, to CG, Infantry Center, 11 Aug 52, sub: Report of Board of Officers, ISL.

5 1st Ind, TIS to OCAFF, 11 Aug 52, sub: Report of Board of Officers, GNKEAD-R 320 (11 Aug 52), and Ltr, Infantry School Representatives, XVIII Airborne Corps, to CG, XVIII Airborne Corps, 25 Sep 53, sub: Report of Evaluation, Phase III, Operation FALCON, Infantry School Representatives, ABCGC (Airborne Corps General Correspondence) 353 Opn FALCON, ISL; OCAFF, "Summary of Major Events and Problems, FY 1953," ch. 8, pp. 1–12, DAMH-HSR.

6 Ltr, Attack Group, Tactical Department, TIS, 28 Jul 52, sub: Proposed Reorganization of Infantry Units, ISL; Col Lonning to Acting Assistant Commandant, TIS, 23 Apr 53, sub: Proposed Reorganization of the Infantry and Airborne Divisions.

7 Matthew B. Ridgway, *Soldier: The Memoirs of Matthew B. Ridgway* (New York: Harper and Brothers, 1956), pp. 286–87; Ltr, OCofS to OCAFF, 19 Apr 54, sub: Organizational Studies to Improve the Army Combat Potential-to-Manpower Ratio, RG 337, Army Field Forces, NARA.

8 Midgley, *Deadly Illusions*, pp. 44–45; Ltr, OCofS to OCAFF, 19 Apr 54, sub: Organizational Studies to Improve the Army Combat Potential-to-Manpower Ratio, Ltr, OCAFF to Chief of Information, Department of the Army (CINFO), 13 Sep 54, sub: Fact Sheet, Project ATFA-1 (hereafter cited as Fact Sheet, Project ATFA-1, 13 Sep 54), both ATTIS (OCAFF, Information Section) 320, RG 337, NARA.

9 Fact Sheet, Project ATFA-1, 13 Sep 54; TOE 7 ATFA, Infantry Division, 30 Sep 1954.

10 Fact Sheet, Project ATFA-1, 13 Sep 54; TOE 17 ATFA, Armored Division, 30 Sep 1954.

11 Fact Sheet, Project ATFA-1, 13 Sep 54.

12 Ltr, CONARC to TAG and other addresses, 25 Apr 56, sub: Concept and Technical Review of the Tentative 1956 ATFA Infantry Division, ATTNG-D&R (Office of the CofS, G–3-Research and Development, 322/50 (Div) (25 Apr 56), and Ltr, CONARC to TAG and other addresses, 23 May 56, sub: Concept and Technical Review of the Tentative 1956 ATFA Armored Division, ATTNG-D&R 322/16 (Div) (23 May 56), both Division General file, DAMH-HSO; Midgley, *Deadly Illusions*, p. 49.

13 Moenk, *Large-Scale Army Maneuvers*, pp. 205–20; TOE 7, ATFA Infantry Division, 30 Jun 1955; TOE 17, ATFA Armored Division, 30 Jun 1955.

14 3d Infantry Division, Final Evaluation Report on the ATFA Infantry Division (TOE 7T), 15 Jan 56, Command and General Staff College (CGSC) Library, Fort Leavenworth, Kans.; Ltr, CONARC to TAG and other addresses, 25 Apr 56, sub: Concept and Technical Review of the Tentative 1956 ATFA Infantry Division, ATTNG-D&R 322/50 (Div) (25 Apr 56), RG 337, NARA; Ltr, 1st Armd Div to CG, Fourth Army, 1 Jan 56, sub: Final Report on Exercise BLUE BOLT II, AKDHD-CG 354.2, and Ltr, Fourth Army to CG, CONARC, 13 Feb 56, Final Report, Exercise BLUE BOLT II, AKADC-M-BEG 354.2, both CGSC Library; Ltr, CONARC to TAG and other addresses, 23 May 56, sub: Concept and Technical Review of the Tentative 1956 ATFA Armored Division, ATTNG-D&R 322/16 (Div) (23 May 56), RG 337, NARA.

15 Ltr, CONARC to TAG and other addresses, 23 May 56, sub: Concept and Technical Review of the Tentative 1956 ATFA Armored Division, and Ltr, CONARC to TAG and other addresses, 25 Apr 56, sub: Concept and Technical Review of the Tentative 1956 ATFA Infantry Division.

16 Ltr, TAG to CG, CONARC, 6 Jun 56, sub: The 1956 Army Reorganization, AGAM-P

(Office of the Adjutant General, Publications Branch) 320 (5 Jun 56) DCSOPS, Division General file, DAMH-HSO.

17 Ltr, Garrison H. Davidson to Willard G. Wyman, 21 Feb 56, CGSC Library.

18 Moenk, *Large-Scale Army Maneuvers*, p. 212; Transcript of Address by General Maxwell D. Taylor, Chief of Staff, United States Army, Before the Army School Commandants, Room 2E-715A, The Pentagon, Washington, D.C., Thursday, 28 Feb 57, CS 322 (1 Feb 57), RG 319, NARA.

19 Ltr, G–3 to CG, CONARC, 17 Nov 54, sub: Organization of the Army During the Period FY 1960–1970, RG 319, NARA; Midgley, *Deadly Illusions*, pp. 58–59.

20 Ltr, CONARC to TAG and other addresses, 28 Oct 55, sub: PENTANA Army (U), ATSWD (Combat Developments)-G–322/4 (Army) (28 Oct 55), 322/4 (Army), RG 319, NARA.

21 Ltr, John E. Dahlquist to Maxwell D. Taylor, 12 Dec 55, 322/19/Army 6–10 Aug 56, RG 319, NARA.

22 Taylor, *Swords and Plowshares*, pp. 152–53; John M. Taylor, *General Maxwell Taylor: The Sword and the Pen* (New York: Doubleday, 1989), pp. 198–99; Ltr, Maxwell D. Taylor to CG, CONARC, sub: Army Organization, 1 Jun 56, Division General file, DAMH-HSO.

23 Ltr, CofS to CG, CONARC, sub: Reorganization of the Airborne Division and the Development of Special Airborne Reconnaissance Units, 20 Sep 55, RG 319, NARA.

24 Ltr, CONARC to CofS, 15 Dec 55, sub: Reorganization of the Airborne Division (S), ATSWD 322/31 (Div) (15 Dec 55), 101st Abn Div file, DAMH-HSO. During the planning for the pentomic reorganization the Army returned to use troop and squadron for cavalry reconnaissance units.

25 Ltr, DCofS for Military Operations to CG, CONARC, 20 Feb 56, sub: Reorganization of the Airborne Division, OPS OT DC 2, 101st Abn Div file, DAMH-HSO.

26 TOE 57T, ROTAD, Airborne Division, 1956; CONARC, "Summary of Major Events and Problems, 1956," vol. 1, Doctrine and Requirements Division, G3 Section, 1 Jan–30 Jun 56, Reorganization and Test of the Airborne Division (Project ROTAD), pp. 1–4, DAMH-HSR.

27 Taylor coined the Madison Avenue term "pentomic" to describe units organized with pentagonal structures and atomic capabilities. See Taylor, *Swords and Plowshares*, p. 171.

28 DOD News Release No. 1205–55, 14 Dec 55, Ltr, TAG to CG, Third Army, 4 Jun 56, sub: Reorganization of the 101st Airborne Division, AGAO-O (M) 322 (23 May 56) DCSPER, and Wilber Brucker, Address before AMVETS National Convention, 1 Sep 56, all 101st Abn Div file, DAMH-HSO; "Run Down on the 101," *Army* 7 (Oct 1956): 51–53.

29 CONARC, "Summary of Major Events and Problems, 1 Jul 56–30 Jun 57," vol. 1, ch. 2, pp. 1–5.

30 Ibid., p. 6–12.

31 Ibid.

32 Ibid., p. 13; CONARC, "Summary of Major Events and Problems, 1 Jul 57–30 Jun 58," vol. 3, Organization and Equipment Division, pp. 1–4, DAMH-HSR; TOE 57D, Airborne Division, 1958; Ltr, TAG to CG, Third Army, 19 Nov 58, sub: Reorganization of the 82nd and 101st Airborne Divisions, AGAO-O (M) 322 (20 Oct 58) DCSPER, 101st Abn Div file, DAMH-HSO; "The Army's Month," *Army* 8 (Apr 1958): 20.

33 Ltr, CofS to CONARC, 23 Aug 56, sub: Reorganization of Current Infantry Division, Division General file, DAMH-HSO.

34 Ltr, CONARC to DCofS for Military Operations and other addresses, 15 Oct 56, sub: Reorganization of Current Infantry Division, ATTNG-D&R 322/53 (Div) (15 Oct 56), and Ltr, CG, CONARC, to CofS, 21 Dec 56, sub: Basic Doctrinal Guidance in Connection with New (ROCID) Division Organization, ATCG (CG, CONARC), both Division General file, DAMH-HSO.

35 Taylor's address, 28 Feb 57; CONARC, "Major Events and Problems, 1 Jul 56–30 Jun 57," vol. 1, Doctrine and Requirements Division, G3 Section, 1 Jan–30 Jun 57, pp. 20–23.

36 CONARC, "Major Events and Problems, 1 Jul 56–30 Jun 57," vol. 3, Organization and Equipment, G3 Section, pp. 3–7; TOE 17T ROCAD, Armored Division, 1956.

37 Taylor's address, 28 Feb 57.

38 Taylor, *Swords and Plowshares*, p. 171; Glenn Hawkins, "United States Force Structure

and Force Design Initiatives, 1939–1989," Ms, pp. 35–36, DAMH-RAD; "Infantry of Tomorrow," Army, 6 (Sep 1955): 47–48; "Let's All Fly on Platforms," *Army* 6 (Dec 1955): 25.

39 DF, Office, Deputy Chief of Staff for Operations (ODCSOPS) to Sec of the General Staff and other addresses, sub: Reorganization of Divisions, 2 May 57, OPS OT OR 1, Pentomic Divisions, Division General file, Ltr, TAG to CinC, U.S. Army, Pacific (USARPAC), and other addresses, 22 Aug 57, sub: Transfer of the 24th Infantry Division and Reorganization of the 1st Cavalry Division, AGAO-O (M) 322 (16 Aug 57) DCSPER, Ltr, TAG to CinC, USARPAC, and other addresses, 29 Aug 57, same subject, AGAO-O (M) 322 (27 Aug 57) DCSPER, Ltr, TAG to CinC, U.S. Army Europe (USAREUR), and other addresses, 8 Feb 57, sub: Reorganization of the 1st Infantry Division, AGAO-O (M) 322 (5 Feb 57) DCSPER, Ltr, TAG to CinC, USAREUR, 21 Jun 57, sub: Reorganization of the 2d Armored Division, AGAO-O (M) 322 (13 Jun 57) DCSPER, Ltr, TAG to CGs, CONARC, and Third U.S. Army, 17 Mar 58, sub: Change in Status of the 2d and 10th Infantry Divisions, AGAO-O (M) (5 Feb 58) DCSPER, Ltr, TAG to CinC, USAREUR, and other addresses, 30 Aug 57, sub: Reorganization of the 3d Armored Division, AGAO-O (M) 322 (26 Aug 57) DCSPER, Ltr, TAG to CinC, USAREUR, 26 Dec 57, sub: Change in Status of Certain Units, 26 Dec 57, AGAO-O (M) 322 (13 Dec 57) DCSPER, Ltr, TAG to CinC, USAREUR, and other addresses, 12 Mar 57, sub: Reorganization of the 4th Armored Division, AGAO-O (M) 322 (6 Feb 57) DCSPER, Ltr, TAG to CG, CONARC, and other addresses, 27 Mar 57, sub: Reorganization of the 4th Infantry Division, AGAO-O (M) 322 (25 Mar 57) DCSPER, Ltr, TAG to CG, U.S. Army Far East, and other addresses, 31 May 57, sub: Reorganization of the 7th Infantry Division, AGAO-O (M) 322 (24 May 57) DCSPER, Ltr, TAG to CinC, USAREUR, 16 Jul 57, sub: Reorganization of the 8th Infantry Division, AGAO-O (M) 322 (10 Jul 57) DCSPER, Ltr, TAG to CinC, USAREUR, and other addresses, 13 Nov 57, sub: Reorganization of the 9th Infantry Division, AGAO-O (M) 322 9th Inf Div (8 Oct 57) DCSPER, Ltr, CinC, USAREUR, and other addresses, 14 Jun 47, sub: Reorganization of the 10th Infantry Division, AGAO-O (M) 322 (31 May 57) DCSPER, Ltr, TAG to CinC, USAREUR, 20 Feb 57, sub: Reorganization of the 11th Airborne Division, AGAO-O (M) 322 (19 Feb 57) DCSPER, Draft letter, undated, sub: Organization of the 24th Infantry Division, Ltr, TAG to CinC, USAREUR, 11 Feb 57, sub: Reorganization of the 1st Armored Division, AGAO-O (M) 322 (5 Feb 57) DCSPER, Ltr, TAG to CGs, CONARC and Fourth U.S. Army, 5 Dec 57, sub: Change in Status of Certain Units, AGAO-O (M) 322 (13 Nov 57) DCSPER, and Ltr, CGs, CONARC and Sixth U.S. Army, 27 May 57, sub: Inactivation of the 5th Infantry Division, AGAO-O (M) 322 (24 May 57) DCSPER, all AG Reference files; and Historical Data Cards, Divisions, DAMH-HSO.

40 Memo, Sec of Army for Sec of Defense, 31 Jan 57, sub: Combat Arms Regimental System (CARS), and Fact Sheet, undated, sub: Combat Arms Regimental System, both CARS files, and News Release, Historic Traditions of Regiments to be Preserved in Pentomic Army, 7 Feb 57, Division General file, all DAMH-HSO.

41 CONARC, "Summary of Major Events and Problems, 1 Jul 56–30 Jun 57," vol. 4, Doctrine and Requirements Division, G3 Section, 1 Jan–30 Jun 57, pp. 18–19; Information Paper: Separate Combined Arms Brigades in the Reserve Components, 30 Apr 58, Brigade General file, Ltr, TAG to CGs, CONARC and First U.S. Army, 12 Feb 58, sub: Organization of the 2d Infantry Brigade, AGAO-O (M) 322 (5 Feb 58) DCSPER, and Ltr, TAG to CG, Third Army, 8 Jul 58, sub: Change in Status of 1st Infantry Brigade and other units, AGAO-O (M) 322 (11 Jun 58), DCSPER, all AG Reference files; and Historical Data Cards, all DAMH-HSO.

42 Ltr, CONARC to DCofS for Military Operations, 28 Aug 58, sub: Evaluation of ROCID, ATTNG-D&R 322/17 (Div) (28 Aug 58), Division General file, DAMH-HSO.

43 Ibid.

44 1st Ind, ODCSOPS to CG, CONARC, 29 Dec 58, sub: Evaluation of ROCID, OPS OT OR 2, Division General file, DAMH-HSO; TOE 7D, Infantry Division, 1960.

45 John A. Beall, "Revisions of ROCAD," Armor 68 (Mar–Apr 1959): 48–51; TOE 17D, Armored Division, 1960.

46 Ltr, TAG to CG, Fifth U.S. Army, 14 Jul 60, sub: Reorganization of the 9th Infantry

Division, AGAO-O (M) 322 (27 Jun 60) DCSPER, and Ltr, TAG to CG, Fifth U.S. Army, 30 Jan 62, sub: Inactivation of 9th Infantry Division and 9th Military Intelligence Detachment, AGAO-0 (M) 322 (23 Jan 62) DCSPER, 9th Inf Div file, DAMH-HSO; Historical Data Cards for the 1st, 2d, 3d, 4th, 7th, 8th, 9th, 24th, and 25th Inf Divs, the 2d, 3d, and 4th Armd Divs, and 1st Cav Div, DAMH-HSO; *United States Defense Policies in 1959* (Washington, D.C.: Government Printing Office, 1964), p. 32; *Annual Report of the Secretary of the Army, July 1, 1959, to June 30, 1960*, p. 143; Skaggs, "The KATUSA Experiment," p. 55.

[47] John W. Bowen, "Reorganizing the Reserve Components," *Army Information Digest* 13 (Nov 1959): 11–15; *Annual Report of the Chief, National Guard Bureau, FY 1960*, p. 33; Fact Sheet on Department of the Army Revised Plan for Reorganization of the United States Army Reserve, undated, Army Reserve file; Ltr, TAG to CG, Sixth U.S. Army, 31 Mar 59, sub: Reorganization of the 63d Infantry Division, AGAO-O (M) 322 (16 Mar 59) RES, Ltr, TAG to CG, First U.S. Army, 7 Apr 59, sub: Reorganization of the 77th Infantry Division, AGAO-O 322 (20 Mar 59) RES, Ltr, TAG to CG, Second U.S. Army, 17 Mar 59, sub: Reorganization of the 79th Infantry Division, AGAO-O (M) 322 (2 Mar 59) RES, Ltr, TAG to CG, Third U.S. Army, 10 Apr 59, sub: Reorganization of the 81st Infantry Division, AGAO-O (M) 322 (26 Mar 59) RES, Ltr, TAG to CG, Second U.S. Army, 19 Mar 59, sub: Reorganization of the 83d Infantry Division, AGAO-O (M) 322 (2 Mar 59) RES, Ltr, TAG to CG, Fourth U.S. Army, 19 Mar 59, sub: Reorganization of the 90th Infantry Division, AGAO-O (M) 322 (3 Mar 59) RES, Ltr, TAG to CG, First U.S. Army, 6 Apr 59, sub: Reorganization of the 94th Infantry Division, AGAO-O (M) 322 (16 Mar 59) RES, Ltr, TAG to CG, Sixth U.S. Army, 29 Apr 59, sub: Reorganization of the 96th Infantry Division, AGAO-O (M) 322 (10 Apr 59) RES, Ltr, TAG to CG, Fifth U.S. Army, 11 May 59, sub: Reorganization of the 102d Infantry Division, AGAO-O (M) 322 (1 May 59) RES, Ltr, TAG to CG, Fifth U.S. Army, 20 Apr 59, sub: Reorganization of the 103d Infantry Division, AGAO-O (M) 322 (10 Apr 59) RES, Ltr, TAG to CG, Sixth U.S. Army, 30 Apr 59, sub: Redesignation and Reorganization of the 104th Infantry Division, AGAO-O (M) 322 (24 Apr 59) RES, all DAMH-HSO.

[48] Information Paper, Separate Combined Arms Brigades in the Reserve Components, 30 Apr 85; Ltr, NGB to AG, Hawaii, 23 Jan 59, sub: Troop Allotment, Consolidation, Conversion, Redesignation, and Reorganization, Army NG Units, NG-AROTO, Ltr, NGB to AG, Arizona, 4 Feb 59, sub: Reorganization of Army NG 1958–60, NG-AROTO 325.4 Arizona, Ltr, NGB to AG, Puerto Rico, 6 Feb 59, sub: Reorganization of the Army NG 1958–60, NG-AROTO 325.4-Puerto Rico, all National Guard state files, DAMH-HSO.

[49] Regiments in training divisions were not tactical units, therefore fell outside the Combat Arms Regimental System.

[50] TOE 29–7T, Division Training, 1959; Fact Sheet, Department of the Army Revised Plans for Reorganization of the United States Army Reserve; see notes, Historical Data Cards for the 70th, 76th, 78th, 80th, 84th, 85th, 89th, 91st, 95th, 98th, 100th, 104th, and 108th Divs (Training), DAMH-HSO.

[51] *Annual Report of the Secretary of Defense, 1959*, pp. 169–81.

[52] DCSPER, The Troop Program of the Army, Annex I, Troop Bases Data, Current Actions Strength, 30 Jun 60, pp. 29–35, ACofS Reserve Components, Reserve Components Control Program of the Army, FY 1960, pp. 53–96, Office, Chief of Army Reserve and Reserve Officer Training Corps, "Summary of Major Events and Problems, 1 Jul 60–30 Jun 61," p. 14, all DAMH-HSR; *Annual Report of the Chief, National Guard Bureau, Fiscal Year 1960*, p. 33; Donald McGowan, "Army National Guard Today," *Army Information Digest* 15 (Mar 1960): 17.

# CHAPTER 11

# A New Direction—Flexible Response

*I am directing the Secretary of Defense to undertake a reorganization and modernization of the Army's divisional structure, to increase its non-nuclear firepower, to improve its tactical mobility in any environment, to insure its flexibility to meet any direct or indirect threat, to facilitate its coordination with our major allies, and to provide more modern mechanized divisions in Europe and bring their equipment up to date, and [to provide] new airborne brigades in both the Pacific and Europe.*

President John F. Kennedy[1]

President John F. Kennedy ushered in the era of "flexible response" in 1961, deciding that the threat of a general nuclear war had become remote, but that the possibility of brush-fire wars had increased. To meet the varied challenges of the era, the Army soon abandoned pentomic structures and struck out in new directions. Eventually divisions with a standard divisional base and interchangeable maneuver elements—infantry, mechanized infantry, airborne infantry, and armor battalions—emerged as a means of tailoring units for service in diverse environments. The idea theoretically resulted in more flexible forces and divisions that took full advantage of new equipment, in particular new tanks, armored personnel carriers, and helicopters. International events delayed immediate reorganization, and when the Army was able to act, constraints on personnel and funds forced the adoption of many compromises in the structure of the divisions that emerged.

## *MOMAR-I*

To move beyond the unrealistic PENTANA concept of a universal division, General Bruce C. Clarke, commander of the Continental Army Command, put his staff to work in early 1959 on a new organizational model, the "Modern Mobile Army 1965 (MOMAR-I)." Clarke, who had served as General Maxwell D. Taylor's deputy in Korea, believed the Army of the future had to be capable of operating effectively on both nuclear and nonnuclear battlefields anywhere in the world against a variety of threats. Its units had to be capable of fighting independently or semi-independently under a diverse set of geographical and climatic conditions. Furthermore, he believed that conventional firepower had to be increased and tactical mobility and maneuverability improved, primarily by using armor-protected vehicles and aircraft.[2]

*The M60 and,* below, *M48 tanks*

When completed, MOMAR-I called for heavy and medium divisions (*Charts 34 and 35*). Both types had five combat commands, but within the commands were three task force headquarters to which commanders could assign tank and infantry companies and elements of a train (support) company and "moritzer" battery. The proposed moritzer was to be a cross between a mortar and howitzer. Thus, the new models retained the flexible command structure of the armored division and foreshadowed the idea of "building blocks" around which to organize forces. Every man and every piece of equipment in both divisions was to be carried or mounted on vehicles.3

War games indicated that medium and heavy MOMAR-I divisions could not meet the Army's needs in many potential trouble spots throughout the world, and they were never field tested. In December 1960 the Vice Chief of Staff, General Clyde Eddleman, rejected the concept entirely. He noted that MOMAR-I divisions lacked the simplicity, homogeneity, versatility, and flexibility that the Army needed to fulfill its worldwide responsibility in the coming decade.4

## *The Development of ROAD*

General Eddleman set the Army on a new organizational course on 16 December 1960 when he directed General Herbert B. Powell, who had replaced Clarke as commander of the Continental Army Command, to develop divisions for the period 1961–65. The vice chief wanted the command to consider infantry, armored, and mechanized divisions. The heart of his mechanized division was to be armored infantry units that had the mobility and the survivability needed for the nuclear battlefield. But all divisions were to have both nuclear and conventional weapons, as well as any other new weapons or equipment that might become available by 1965. Because of the many areas for potential employment throughout the world, Eddleman suggested that divisions be tailored for different environments. However, since he still wanted to make the types of divisions as similar as possible, Eddleman instructed the planners to weigh the retention of battle groups or their replacement with infantry battalions in both infantry and airborne divisions. He questioned whether those divisions should have a combat command or a regimental command level between the division commander and the battalions as in the armored division. Furthermore, preliminary evidence suggested the possibility of interchanging battalion-size armor, mechanized infantry, infantry, and artillery units within the divisions. No set strengths were established for divisions, but Eddleman expected none to exceed 15,000 men.5

Eddleman's instructions reflected many of the organizational ideas he had developed after leaving the position of deputy chief of staff for military operations in May 1958 and before returning to Washington as the vice chief of staff in November 1960. In the intervening period he served as commander of U.S. Army, Europe, and Seventh Army, becoming involved with the establishment of the West German Army. That army, unlike those of some NATO countries that had adopted

## CHART 34—Medium Division (MOMAR), 1960

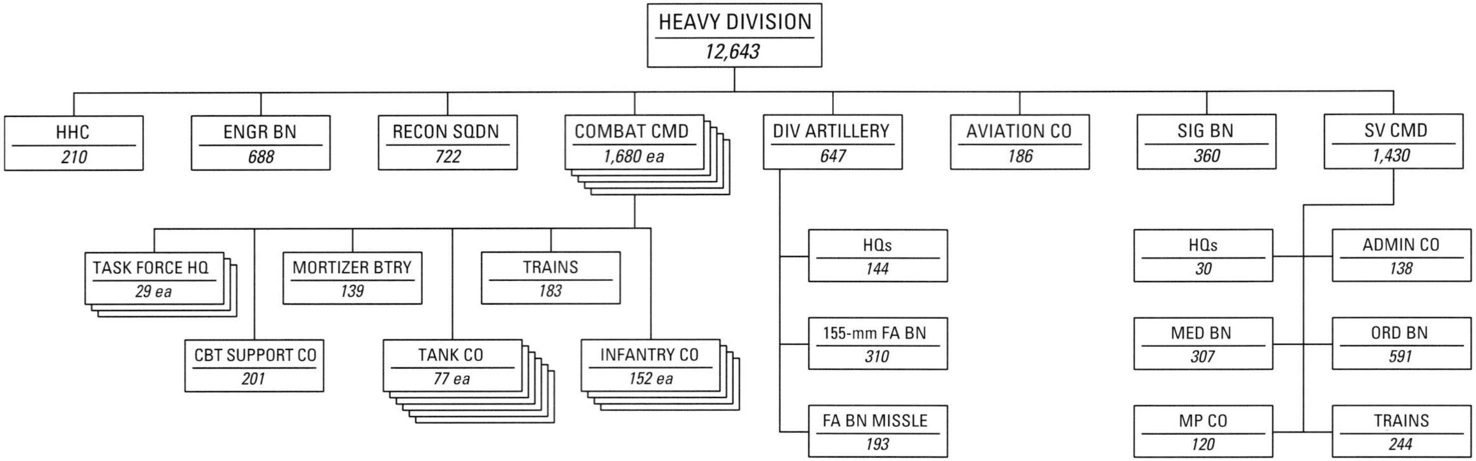

- HEAVY DIVISION — 12,643
  - HHC — 210
  - ENGR BN — 688
  - RECON SQDN — 722
  - COMBAT CMD — 1,680 ea
    - TASK FORCE HQ — 29 ea
    - CBT SUPPORT CO — 201
    - MORTIZER BTRY — 139
    - TRAINS — 183
    - TANK CO — 77 ea
    - INFANTRY CO — 152 ea
  - DIV ARTILLERY — 647
    - HQs — 144
    - 155-mm FA BN — 310
    - FA BN MISSLE — 193
  - AVIATION CO — 186
  - SIG BN — 360
  - SV CMD — 1,430
    - ADMIN CO — 138
    - HQs — 30
    - ORD BN — 591
    - MED BN — 307
    - TRAINS — 244
    - MP CO — 120

# CHART 35–Heavy Division (MOMAR), 1960

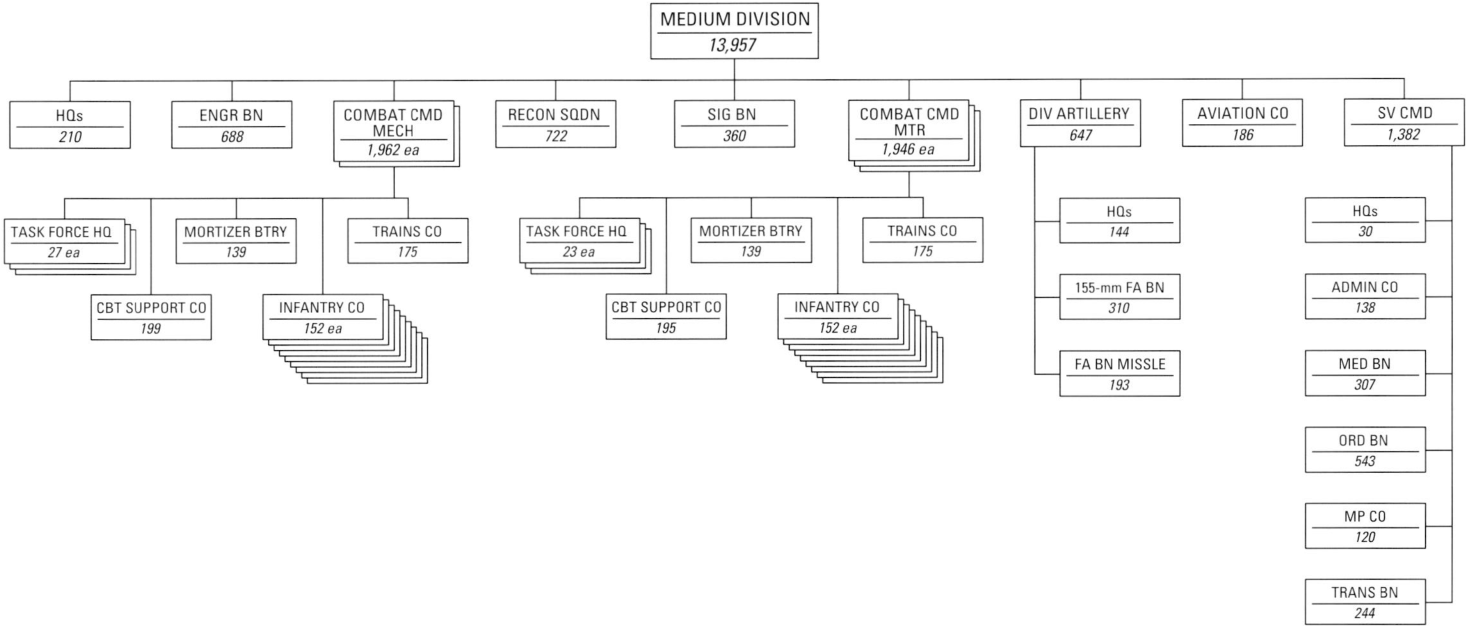

**MEDIUM DIVISION** — 13,957

- **HQs** — 210
- **ENGR BN** — 688
- **COMBAT CMD MECH** — 1,962 ea
  - **TASK FORCE HQ** — 27 ea
    - **MORTIZER BTRY** — 139
    - **INFANTRY CO** — 152 ea
    - **CBT SUPPORT CO** — 199
  - **TRAINS CO** — 175
- **RECON SQDN** — 722
- **SIG BN** — 360
- **COMBAT CMD MTR** — 1,946 ea
  - **TASK FORCE HQ** — 23 ea
    - **MORTIZER BTRY** — 139
    - **INFANTRY CO** — 152 ea
    - **CBT SUPPORT CO** — 195
  - **TRAINS CO** — 175
- **DIV ARTILLERY** — 647
  - **HQs** — 144
  - **155-mm FA BN** — 310
  - **FA BN MISSLE** — 193
- **AVIATION CO** — 186
- **SV CMD** — 1,382
  - **HQs** — 30
  - **ADMIN CO** — 138
  - **MED BN** — 307
  - **ORD BN** — 543
  - **MP CO** — 120
  - **TRANS BN** — 244

*General Eddleman*

pentagonal divisions, employed a building-block approach to organization. Rather than establishing permanent infantry and armored divisions, the Germans relied on infantry and armored brigades that would be formed into divisions tailored for specific missions. The German brigades, although fixed organizations, could also control additional battalions. To increase flexibility, elements of armor and mechanized infantry battalions could be interchanged to form combat teams heavy in infantry or armor.[6]

In less than three months Powell submitted a study entitled "Reorganization Objective Army Divisions (1961–1965)," usually called ROAD, to the Army Chief of Staff, General George H. Decker. Unlike the PENTANA and MOMAR-I studies, ROAD did not address the general reorganization of the Army; it dealt only with infantry, mechanized infantry, and armored divisions. Using the armored division as a model, the study called for all three to have a common base to which commanders could assign varying numbers of "maneuver" (i.e., ground combat) elements—infantry, mechanized infantry, and tank battalions. The predominant maneuver element determined whether the division was classified as infantry, mechanized infantry, or armor.[7]

The base for every ROAD division would consist of a headquarters element, which included the division commander and two assistant division commanders; three brigade headquarters; a military police company; aviation, engineer, and signal battalions; a reconnaissance squadron with an air and three ground troops; division artillery; and a support command. The division artillery included three 105-mm. howitzer battalions, an Honest John rocket battalion, and a composite battalion (one 8-inch and three 155-mm. howitzer batteries). All artillery was self-propelled. The division artillery commander, however, was reduced from a brigadier general to a colonel. The support command embodied a headquarters and headquarters company, an administration company, a band, and medical, supply and transport, and maintenance battalions. Although structured alike in all divisions, the supply and transport and the maintenance battalions varied in strength and equipment to accommodate the missions of the divisions. The commander of the support command assumed responsibility for all divisional supply, maintenance, and medical services and the rear area activities, including security. Supply and maintenance functions were to be provided at one-stop service points. Elements of the support command were designed so that they could be detached and sent to support task forces in independent or semi-independent operations. The brigade headquarters, like the combat commands in the existing armored division, were not to have permanently assigned units and were not to enter the administrative chain of command; instead, they were to function exclusively as command and control headquarters, supervising from two to five maneuver elements in tactical operations.[8]

Responding to Eddleman's wishes, the designers of ROAD determined that an infantry battalion was more appropriate than a battle group as the main building block of the infantry division. Benefits of a battalion included a better span of control, simpler training procedures, greater dispersion on the battlefield, and more career opportunities for infantry officers. In the battle group, the commander's effective span of control was too great. He had so many diverse elements to supervise (infantry, artillery, engineer, medical, signal, reconnaissance, supply, and maintenance) that he found it difficult to manage the unit. A return to the infantry battalion would simplify command and control, logistics and maintenance, and also training. Given the need for dispersion on the battlefield, the study noted that 20 percent of the pentomic infantry division's combat strength was in each battle group. The loss of a single battle group in combat would be significant. With nine infantry battalions, the new division would lose only 11 percent of its battle strength if one of its battalions were hit by nuclear fire. In addition, many situations in combat required a greater variety of responses than the battle group could easily provide. Some tasks were too large for a company but too small for a battle group; others called for a force larger than one battle group but smaller than two. The smaller-size infantry battalions appeared to answer those needs. Finally, the battle group provided little opportunity for infantry officers to gain command experience. If the battle group were retained, only 5 percent of the Army's infantry lieutenant colonels would receive command assignments and only 4 percent of the majors would serve as second-in-command. Weighing all these aspects, the planners recommended that infantry battalions replace battle groups.[9]

In an effort to provide maximum homogeneity, simplicity, and flexibility, the maneuver battalions were kept as similar as possible consistent with their individual roles. Each infantry, mechanized infantry, and armor battalion comprised a headquarters, three line companies, and a headquarters and service company. Similarity among the maneuver battalions extended to the reconnaissance platoons, which were the same in all battalions, and to the platoons in the reconnaissance squadrons. Given battalions of this nature, companies and platoons could be used to build task forces for specific operations with a minimum of turbulence. Taking advantage of the latest weapons, all infantry battalions and reconnaissance squadrons had two Davy Crocketts, low-yield nuclear weapons that were considered the "Sunday punch" of the ROAD divisions. Infantry and mechanized infantry battalions also had the new ENgin-Teleguide Anti-Char (ENTAC) missile, a French-designed antitank weapon.[10]

*Davy Crockett rocket launcher*

With fixed bases and varying numbers and types of maneuver battalions, planners envisaged that divisions could be tailored in three ways. The first, "strategic tailoring," gave the Army Staff the opportunity to design units for a particular environment; the second, "internal tactical tailoring," allowed the division commander to build combat teams for specific missions; and the third, "external tactical tailoring," permitted army or corps commanders to alter divisions according to the circumstances. In the past, divisions had been adapted in all three ways, but ROAD made such tailoring easier at all levels.[11]

On 4 April 1961 officers from the Continental Army Command and the Army Staff briefed Decker on the concept, and he approved it nine days later. He told Powell, however, that divisions were to be largely fixed organizations because the Army lacked the resources to maintain a pool of nondivisional maneuver battalions for intra- or intertheater tailoring. In Decker's opinion, the interchangeable characteristics of the battalions were sufficient to provide tailoring within and among divisions without keeping extra units. He asked Powell only to consider substituting towed artillery for self-propelled artillery, eliminating the 155-mm. howitzers, and reorganizing the rocket battalion so that it would include both an Honest John rocket and two 8-inch howitzer batteries. The amount of organic transportation in the infantry battalion also seemed excessive, and Decker wanted reductions if possible. The study provided only two Davy Crocketts for each infantry battalion and reconnaissance squadron; Decker suggested adding a third, making one available for each line company or troop in those units. As a priority, Decker wanted doctrine and training literature to be quickly developed, particularly for the support command. Doctrine for the employment of nuclear weapons remained unclear.[12]

Within a few months the Continental Army Command published draft tables for ROAD infantry, mechanized infantry, and armored divisions (*Chart 36*). They called for 105-mm. howitzers in the infantry division to be towed and a 30 percent reduction in the organic transportation of the infantry battalions. The 155-mm./8-inch howitzer battalion remained as planned, but a new rocket battalion was designed consisting of a headquarters and service element and two Honest John batteries. Each infantry battalion and reconnaissance squadron had three, instead of two, Davy Crocketts.[13]

Before briefing Chief of Staff Decker on ROAD, Eddleman asked Powell's Continental Army Command to have available a concept for reorganizing the airborne division along similar lines. The vice chief of staff believed that ROAD could be modified to incorporate lighter equipment for such forces. For

# CHART 36—ROAD Division Base, 1961

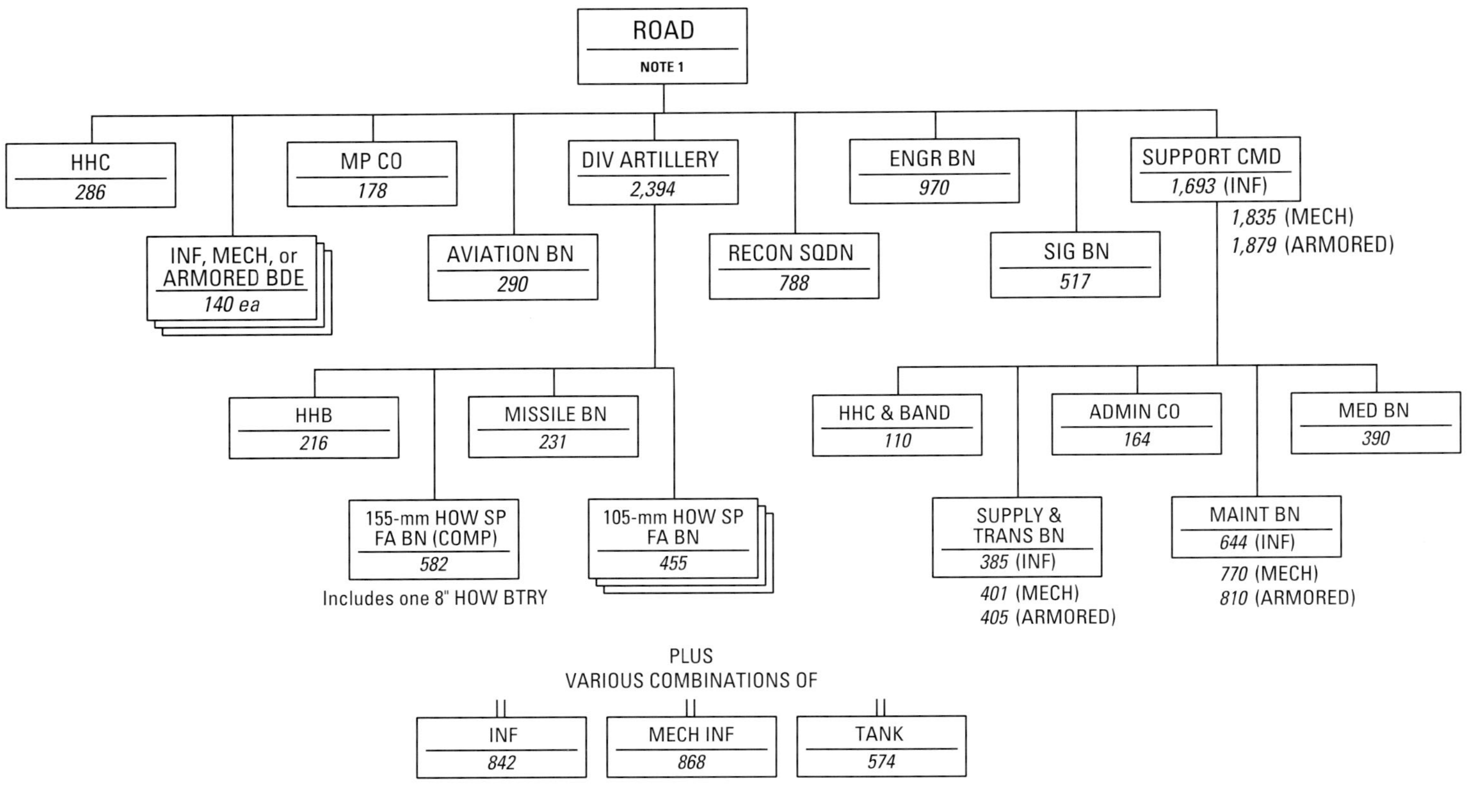

- **ROAD** (NOTE 1)
  - **HHC** — 286
  - **INF, MECH, or ARMORED BDE** — 140 ea
  - **MP CO** — 178
  - **AVIATION BN** — 290
  - **DIV ARTILLERY** — 2,394
    - **HHB** — 216
    - **MISSILE BN** — 231
    - **155-mm HOW SP FA BN (COMP)** — 582 (Includes one 8" HOW BTRY)
    - **105-mm HOW SP FA BN** — 455
  - **RECON SQDN** — 788
  - **ENGR BN** — 970
  - **SIG BN** — 517
  - **SUPPORT CMD** — 1,693 (INF) / 1,835 (MECH) / 1,879 (ARMORED)
    - **HHC & BAND** — 110
    - **ADMIN CO** — 164
    - **MED BN** — 390
    - **SUPPLY & TRANS BN** — 385 (INF) / 401 (MECH) / 405 (ARMORED)
    - **MAINT BN** — 644 (INF) / 770 (MECH) / 810 (ARMORED)

PLUS VARIOUS COMBINATIONS OF

- **INF** — 842
- **MECH INF** — 868
- **TANK** — 574

**NOTE 1** Strength will vary depending on the combination of maneuver elements assigned.

*Little John rocket launcher*

example, the airborne division would not need as many infantry or tank battalions as other units, towed artillery could be substituted for self-propelled, the 8-inch howitzer battery could be eliminated, and a lighter rocket could be used in place of the Honest John.[14]

After the approval of ROAD, the Continental Army Command quickly applied the concept to the airborne division. Its airborne study called for a division base similar to ROAD units. For the artillery, the 318-mm. Little John rocket replaced the larger Honest John, and two batteries of Little Johns along with a battery of 155-mm. howitzers formed a composite artillery battalion. They recommended deleting the bridge company from the ROAD engineer battalion and reducing the airborne division's reconnaissance squadron by one ground troop. The light tank battalion was to be equipped with new M551 Sheridans, armored reconnaissance airborne assault vehicles, but, pending their availability, the unit would employ 106-mm. recoilless rifles mounted on 1/4-ton trucks.[15]

In September 1961 the Army Staff approved the concept in principle with minor modifications. The new 90-mm. self-propelled antitank guns (M56 SPATs) would replace the recoilless rifles, and the number of vehicles was cut throughout the division. When the tables (*Chart 37*) were published, the airborne division also lacked the composite artillery battalion because the 155-mm. howitzer was not air-transportable. Instead, the Little John rockets were organized into a two-battery battalion.[16]

The doctrine of flexible response required combined arms units smaller than divisions, and the Continental Army Command responded by developing an air-

CHART 37—Airborne Division, 1961

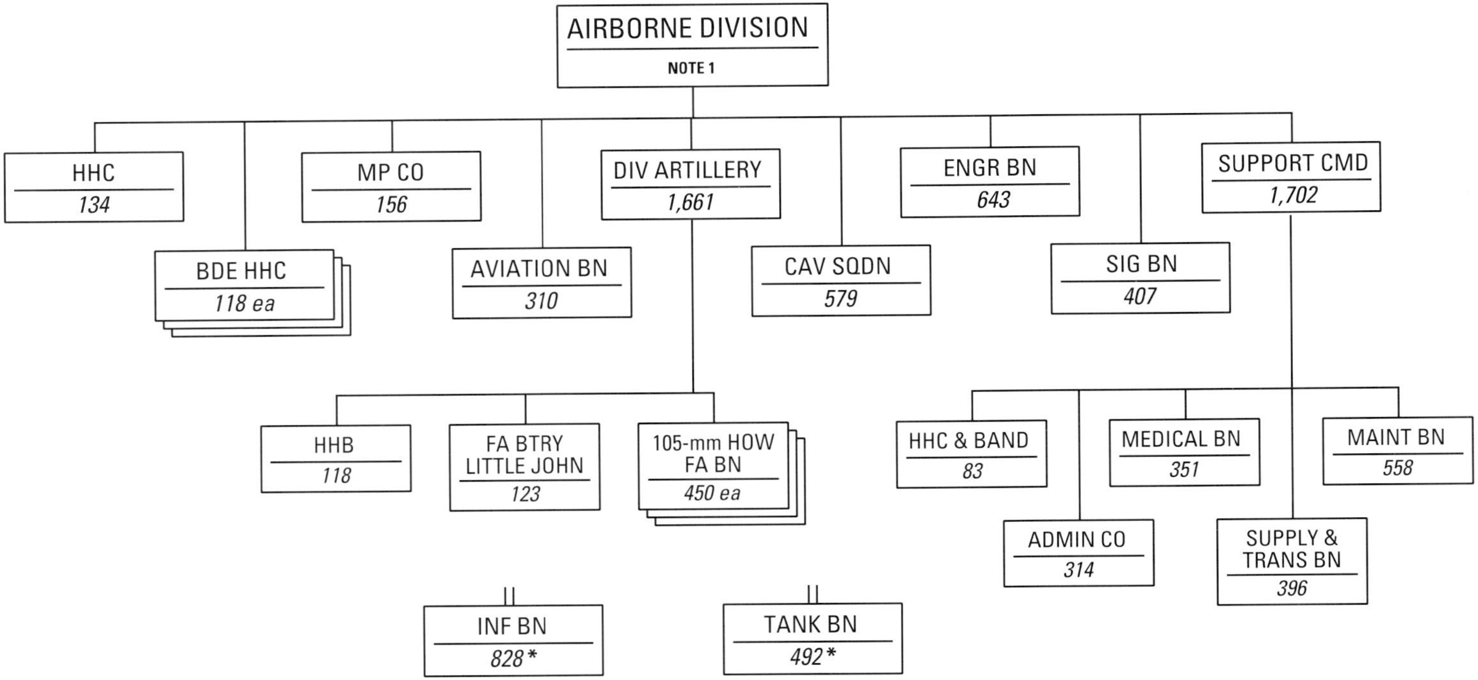

- AIRBORNE DIVISION (NOTE 1)
  - HHC — 134
  - BDE HHC — 118 ea
  - MP CO — 156
  - AVIATION BN — 310
  - DIV ARTILLERY — 1,661
    - HHB — 118
    - CAV SQDN — 579
    - FA BTRY LITTLE JOHN — 123
    - 105-mm HOW FA BN — 450 ea
  - ENGR BN — 643
  - SIG BN — 407
  - SUPPORT CMD — 1,702
    - HHC & BAND — 83
    - ADMIN CO — 314
    - MEDICAL BN — 351
    - MAINT BN — 558
    - SUPPLY & TRANS BN — 396

- INF BN — 828*
- TANK BN — 492*

*Number and type of maneuver battalions may vary.

NOTE 1 Strength will vary depending on the number and type of manuever elements assigned.

CHART 38—Airborne Brigade, 1961

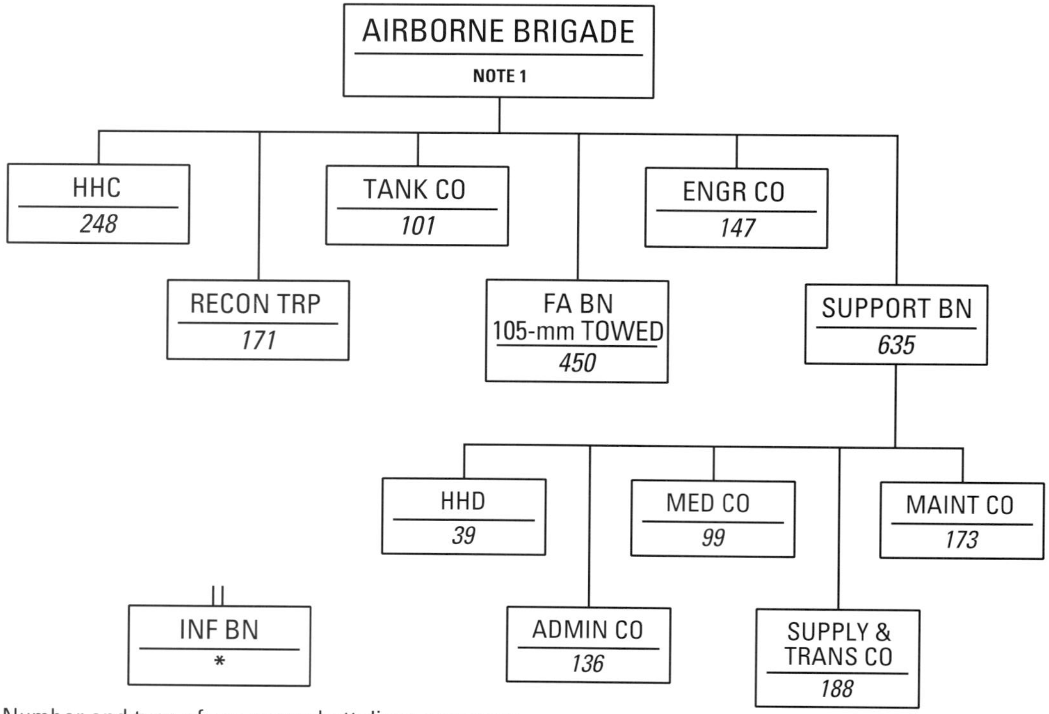

```
                            AIRBORNE BRIGADE
                                 NOTE 1
                                    |
   ┌──────────┬────────────┬────────────┬────────────┬────────────┐
  HHC      RECON TRP    TANK CO      FA BN        ENGR CO     SUPPORT BN
  248        171          101     105-mm TOWED      147           635
                                     450                           |
                                                    ┌──────────┬───┴──────┬──────────────┐
                                                   HHD       MED CO    MAINT CO     SUPPLY &
                                                   39         99         173        TRANS CO
                                                                                      188
                                                    |
                                                 ADMIN CO
                                                   136

                        ‖
                      INF BN
                         *
```

*Number and type of maneuver battalions may vary.

**NOTE 1** Strength will vary depending on the combination of manuever elements assigned.

borne brigade. Like divisions, the brigade had no fixed structure but consisted of a base, which could command and control from two to five maneuver battalions. The brigade base consisted of a headquarters company; a reconnaissance troop; light tank and engineer companies; a 105-mm. howitzer battalion; and a support battalion (*Chart 38*). Within the latter organization were administrative, medical, supply, transport, and maintenance resources that allowed the brigade to conduct independent operations. The brigade, however, had limitations, including inadequate air defense artillery and airlift resources. Its mobility on land was restricted by its limited number of organic vehicles. Nevertheless, the brigade met most of the Army's requirements for a small airborne combat team. At the Army Staff's direction, the idea was extended to armor, infantry, and mechanized infantry brigades. Since such units could operate independently or reinforce divisions, they promised to greatly increase the overall flexibility of the field army.[17]

Powell suggested to Eddlemen during the early development of ROAD that if it were approved the Army should have a comprehensive information plan explaining the rationale for such a major reorganization. Both the military and the general public had to be reminded that organizations evolved in response to past experience and new equipment. Furthermore, political implications had to be considered. General Taylor, the primary advocate of pentomic divisions, then serving on the White House staff, might question the radical shift. Also, the reserve community might object to the turbulence so soon after completing the pentomic reorganization.[18]

Powell's desire for a publicity plan received a boost when the new Kennedy administration, reacting to the worldwide struggle with communism, decided to improve the readiness of the nation's military forces. On 25 May 1961, President John F. Kennedy announced to a joint session of Congress that the Army's divisional forces would be modernized to increase conventional firepower, improve tactical mobility in any environment, and ensure flexibility. In addition, separate brigades would be organized to help meet direct or indirect threats throughout the world.[19]

## *ROAD Delayed*

Kennedy's statement implied an immediate reorganization, but international events delayed changes. During the summer of 1961 relations between the Soviet Union and the United States deteriorated, particularly over the status of Berlin, and on 25 July the president asked Congress for funds to fill existing pentomic divisions and modernize their equipment. He also sought authority to order the reserves to a year of active duty. Congress agreed, and the Army postponed the ROAD reorganization.[20]

To answer Soviet initiatives in Berlin, Secretary of Defense Robert S. McNamara directed that the five divisions in Europe be brought to full table of organization strength and that the 3d, 8th, and 24th Infantry Divisions each be

*Elements of the 32d Infantry Division train at Fort Lewis, Washington, during the Berlin crisis;* below, *pre-positioned equipment in Germany awaits the arrival of the 4th Armored Division in Operation BIG LIFT.*

authorized an additional 1,000 troops. The troop increase permitted the complete mechanization of the divisions with additional armored personnel carriers. The readiness of the Strategic Army Force was increased in the United States and the training base was expanded, eliminating the basic training mission in combat divisions.[21]

In the summer of 1961 Congress also authorized the Defense Department to order 250,000 reservists (individuals as well as those in units) to active duty for twelve months. The subsequent closing of the Berlin border on 13 August 1961 sparked another series of mobilization measures. In October the Army Reserve's 100th Division (Training) was ordered to active military duty to open the training center at Fort Chaffee, Arkansas. That same month the Kennedy administration approved the deployment of two additional combat divisions to the European command. Two National Guard divisions were federalized in October to replace the divisions programmed to be deployed from the strategic force, bringing the total number of divisions on active duty to sixteen. The 32d Infantry Division (Wisconsin) was sent to Fort Polk, Louisiana, and the 49th Armored Division (Texas) reported to Fort Hood, Texas. In all, 113,254 officers and enlisted men of the Army National Guard and Army Reserve were ordered into active military service.[22]

During the crisis no division deployed to Germany, but during the next few months the Army took other steps to strengthen its forces in Europe. Measures included equipping the troops with new M14 rifles and M60 machine guns and accelerating production of M60 main battle tanks and M113 armored personnel carriers, actions that permitted the Army to field those systems earlier than planned. To shorten the time required to move units to Europe, the Army positioned sufficient materiel in Germany to equip one armored division, one infantry division, and several nondivisional battalions. To maintain the equipment, personnel from the 2d Armored and 4th Infantry Divisions moved to Germany, but eventually permanent caretaker units replaced these men. Shortly after the equipment was placed in Germany, the Army launched Operation BIG LIFT, with units from the United States traveling to Europe and conducting exercises with the stockpiled equipment, a precursor of similar exercises that were soon to become a regular fixture in the Army.[23]

The Army also increased combat readiness in other commands. It replaced the cumbersome Honest Johns with Little Johns in the 82d and 101st Airborne Divisions and 4th and 25th Infantry Divisions, a step directed toward improving the ability to move these units by air. The 25th Infantry Division was brought to full strength in Hawaii, and the reinforced airborne battle group that had been sent to Okinawa in June 1960 was relieved from assignment to the division but remained in Okinawa. In Korea the strength of two divisions was also increased.[24]

Following the call-up of the reserves for the Berlin crisis, Congress authorized a modest permanent increase in the strength of the Regular Army, and in January 1962 Secretary McNamara approved the activation of the first two

ROAD divisions, which were eventually to replace the two National Guard units in the strategic force. On 3 February the Fourth U.S. Army reorganized the 1st Armored Division, using its Combat Command A as its nucleus, at Fort Hood. The division became a mechanized infantry unit having four armor and six mechanized infantry battalions. Sixteen days later the Fifth U.S. Army reactivated the 5th Infantry Division (less its 2d Brigade and a tank battalion) at Fort Carson, Colorado, by absorbing the personnel of the training center there. The 2d Brigade, 5th Infantry Division, was activated at Fort Devens, Massachusetts, using the resources of the 2d Infantry Brigade, which was inactivated. The brigade continued to support reserve training in the First U.S. Army area, while one of the 5th Division's tank battalions stationed at Fort Irwin, California, supported the Combat Developments Command's test and evaluation programs. Stretched from coast to coast, the 5th Infantry Division had three infantry battalions at Fort Devens, one armor and six infantry battalions at Fort Carson, and one tank battalion at Fort Irwin.[25]

When McNamara approved the activation of the two Regular Army divisions in early 1962, he decided to delay reorganization of the remainder of the Army until fiscal year 1964 because of the Berlin crisis. But events soon overtook that decision. For example, during the spring of 1962 Powell directed that all instruction at the Infantry School after 1 July reflect ROAD doctrine. Therefore, the Infantry School asked for permission to reorganize the 1st Infantry Brigade under a ROAD structure. Instead, the Army Staff decided to inactivate the pentomic-structured brigade and replace it with a new ROAD unit, the 197th Infantry Brigade, which resolved a unit designation issue.[26]

The ROAD reorganization once again brought up the matter of unit designations. Divisional brigades had not appeared in the Army force structure since the demise of the old square division. Army leaders decided that two out of the three new brigade headquarters in each infantry division would inherit disbanded or inactivated infantry brigade headquarters associated with the former square divisions. With the designation 1st Infantry Brigade slated to return to the 1st Infantry Division when it converted to ROAD, the existing unit at Fort Benning required a new name. For it and other separate brigades, the staff selected infantry brigade numbers that had been associated with Organized Reserve divisions that were no longer in the force. For the new ROAD brigade at Fort Benning, Georgia, for example, the adjutant general on 1 August 1962 restored elements of the 99th Reconnaissance Troop, which thirty years earlier had been organized by consolidating infantry brigade headquarters and headquarters companies of the 99th Infantry Division, as Headquarters and Headquarters Companies, 197th and 198th Infantry Brigades. The following month the 197th Infantry Brigade was activated at Fort Benning. For the third brigade in each infantry division, the staff redesignated the division headquarters company, which had been disbanded during the pentomic reorganization, as a brigade headquarters. For example, the 3d Brigade, 5th Infantry Division, perpetuated Headquarters Company, 5th Infantry Division, which had been inactivated in 1957. In the armored division, Combat Commands A, B, and C were redesignated as the 1st, 2d, and 3d Brigades.[27]

When the Third U.S. Army activated the 197th Infantry Brigade at Fort Benning to support training at the Infantry Center, it consisted of a composite artillery battalion (105-mm. and 155-mm. howitzers and Honest Johns), an armor battalion, a mechanized infantry battalion, two infantry battalions, an engineer company, and a chemical platoon, but no support battalion. The strength of the brigade was approximately 3,500 men.[28]

After the aborted Bay of Pigs invasion and rumors of Soviet assistance to Cuba, McNamara decided to bolster available Army forces in the Caribbean area. The Army replaced the battle group in the Canal Zone with the 193d Infantry Brigade, which was activated on 8 August 1962. Initially it consisted of only one infantry battalion and one airborne infantry battalion, but shortly after activation an artillery battery and an engineer company were added.[29]

By mid-August 1962 the 1st Armored and 5th Infantry Divisions attained the approved readiness status for the strategic force, and the Army readjusted its divisions by releasing the reserve units three months early. Subsequently the National Guard's 32d Infantry Division and 49th Armored Division left federal service and reverted to state control, and the 100th Division (Training) also reverted to reserve status, closing the training center at Fort Chaffee.[30]

In October 1962, less than three months after the 1st Armored Division had become part of the strategic force, the Army used it as part of an emergency assault force being assembled to counter the buildup of Soviet missiles in Cuba. For more immediate access to port facilities, the division moved from Fort Hood to Fort Stewart, Georgia, where it conducted a series of amphibious exercises. As tensions eased during the late fall, "Old Ironsides" returned to Fort Hood without conducting any active operations against Cuba.[31]

When the Army put off reorganizing the remainder of the Regular Army divisions under ROAD until January 1963, the delay permitted the 1st Armored and 5th Infantry Divisions to evaluate the concept. General Decker reported to Secretary of the Army Cyrus R. Vance that "ROAD provides substantial improvements in command structure, organization flexibility, capability for sustained combat, tactical mobility (ground and air), balanced firepower (nuclear and nonnuclear), logistical support, and compatibility with Allied forces (particularly NATO)."[32] The chief of staff added that commanders of the 1st Armored and 5th Infantry Divisions had not identified any major problems that would require changes in the general concept.[33]

Decker saw advantages and disadvantages in the pending ROAD reorganization. A comparison between the ROAD infantry and mechanized infantry divisions with the augmented pentomic infantry division showed some significant gains for the new organization. With only a 2 percent increase in manpower strength, the ROAD organization exhibited a profound growth in combat power, which in some weapons systems was over 200 percent. But the new divisions were going to be costly and the full implementation of ROAD would have to await the arrival of new equipment. Until then fixed-wing aircraft would have to be used in place of helicopters, and infantry battalions would substitute for mechanized infantry battalions until armored personnel carriers were available. Furthermore, because of insufficient personnel, the divisions would be maintained at less than ideal strength.[34]

## *The ROAD Reorganization*

The Army Staff began planning for the ROAD reorganization during the summer of 1962. It set the combination of maneuver elements as follows: for the armored division, six tank and five mechanized infantry battalions; for the mechanized infantry division, three tank and seven mechanized infantry battalions; for the infantry division, two tank and eight infantry battalions; and for the airborne division, one assault gun (tank) and eight airborne infantry battalions. The planners anticipated difficulty in finding the men to fill the units because the authorized strength of the Regular Army was only 960,000. Decker recommended that Secretary of the Army Cyrus Vance seek Department of Defense approval for an increase in Army strength as well as the retention of 3,000 KATUSA personnel in both the 1st Cavalry and 7th Infantry Divisions stationed in Korea. If no increase could be obtained, then Decker recommended that divisions in the United States and Korea have fewer maneuver battalions than outlined in the plan.[35]

Reorganization of the remaining divisions took place between January 1963 and May 1964 (*Table 24*). But, as feared, the Department of Defense decided not to seek an increase in the size of the Army, and the reorganization left the Army's divisions at reduced strength except for the units in Europe. Infantry, mechanized infantry, and armored divisions ranged between 14,000 and 16,000 men each, except for the 1st Cavalry and 7th Infantry Divisions, which were authorized about 12,000 men each plus their KATUSA personnel. In the airborne divisions, nine airborne infantry battalions and a tank battalion replaced the eight airborne infantry battalions and assault gun (tank) battalion, but the airborne tank battalion was allotted only experimental equipment. The 82d and 101st Airborne Divisions fielded about 13,500 men each. In Germany the airborne capability was moved from the 24th Infantry Division at Augsburg to the 8th Infantry Division at Bad Kreuznach, with one brigade containing all the airborne assets.[36]

As the Regular Army completed the ROAD reorganization, the Army made further revisions in the division organizations. Headquarters and service batteries in all artillery battalions except for the Honest John unit were combined to save personnel. More important, the Davy Crocketts were restricted to infantry battalions, and the weapons were to be issued only in response to specific instructions. The Army had debated the appropriate level at which to control nuclear weapons since their introduction. Like its predecessors, the Kennedy administration continued to stress political control of such weapons.[37]

Departing from past practice, the Defense Department decided to reorganize the reserve divisions concurrently with the Regular Army's conversion to ROAD. Immediately the old question arose about the number of divisions needed in the reserves to meet mobilization requirements. Studies after the pentomic reorganization suggested that the Army needed forty-three divisions, including twenty-nine in the reserves. The new numbers gave the Army a surplus of eight reserve divisions, but Army leaders also wanted more separate brigades to add flexibility to the force. Late in 1962 the Defense Department approved reorganizing reserve units under ROAD.[38]

Following the Defense Department's guidance, the Army Staff decided to retain one Army Reserve division in each of the six Army areas and to eliminate four divisions. Army commanders selected the 63d, 77th, 81st, 83d, 90th, and 102d Infantry Divisions for retention and reorganized them under ROAD by the end of April 1963. Each division had two tank and six infantry battalions. With the elimination of the 79th, 94th, 96th, and 103d Infantry Divisions, the Army decided to retain their headquarters as a way to preserve spaces for general and field grade officers. It reorganized the units as operational headquarters (subsequently called command headquarters [division]) and directed them to supervise the training of combat and support units located in the former divisional areas and to provide for their administrative support. If an extensive mobilization were to occur, the staff believed that these units could become the nuclei for new divisions.[39]

In December 1962 Secretary Vance asked the states and territories to accept a new National Guard troop allotment containing 23 divisions (6 armored and 17 infantry). The Army Staff initially planned to mechanize two of the seventeen infantry divisions, but shortages of equipment forced their retention as standard infantry organizations. Somewhat reluctantly, the governors accepted the new troop basis. By 1 May 1963 the states completed the reorganization, a month ahead of schedule, with the infantry divisions having two tank and six infantry battalions and the armored divisions controlling five tank and four mechanized infantry battalions.[40]

Because of equipment shortages each National Guard infantry division lacked its full ROAD base. The states were allowed to omit two company-size units in each division base from the following menu: an airmobile company in the aviation battalion, an air cavalry troop in the reconnaissance squadron, or the Honest John battery in the composite artillery battalion. They chose not to organize a total of 16 air cavalry troops, 13 airmobile companies, and 5 Honest John batteries.[41]

In planning the ROAD reorganization, the Army Staff determined that the Regular Army needed one airborne and five infantry brigades for unique missions not appropriate for a division. The airborne brigade was to replace the battle group on Okinawa, thus significantly increasing the forces there, and the infantry brigades were to serve in Berlin, Alaska, the Canal Zone, and the United States. No fixed combination of maneuver elements was established for the brigades, which were, instead, to be tailored for their special missions.[42]

TABLE 24

Maneuver Element Mix of Divisions
ROAD Reorganization, 30 June 1965

| Division | Location of Headquarters | Date | Inf | Mech | Abn | Ar | Amb | Total |
|---|---|---|---|---|---|---|---|---|
| *Regular Army* | | | | | | | | |
| 1st Armored | Ft. Hood, Tex. | Feb 62 | 5 | 4 | | 2 | | 9 |
| 1st Cavalry | Ft. Benning, Ga. | Jul 63 | 5 | 2 | | 2 | (8b) | 9 |
| 1st Infantry | Ft. Riley, Kans. | Jan 64 | 5 | 2 | | 2 | | 9 |
| 2d Armored | Ft. Hood, Tex. | Jul 63 | | 4 | | 5 | | 9 |
| 2d Infantry | Ft. Benning, Ga. | Apr 64 | 5 | 2 | | 2 | | 9 |
| 3d Armored | Germany | Oct 63 | | 5 | | 6 | | 11 |
| 3d Infantry | Germany | Aug 63 | | 7 | | 3 | | 10 |
| 4th Armored | Germany | Aug 63 | | 5 | | 6 | | 11 |
| 4th Infantry | Ft. Lewis, Wash. | Oct 63 | 5 | 2 | | 2 | | 9 |
| 5th Infantry | Ft. Carson, Colo. | Feb 62 | 8 | | | 2 | | 10 |
| 7th Infantry | Korea | Jul 63 | 5 | 2 | | 2 | | 9 |
| 8th Infantry | Germany | Apr 63 | 4 | | 3 | 3 | | 10 |
| 24th Infantry | Germany | Feb 63 | | 7 | | 3 | | 10 |
| 25th Infantry | Hawaii | Aug 63 | 6 | 1 | | 1 | | 8 |
| 82d Airborne | Ft. Bragg, N.C. | May 64 | | | 9 | 1a | | 10 |
| 101st Airborne | Ft. Campbell, Ky. | Feb 64 | | | 9 | 1a | | 10 |
| *National Guard* | | | | | | | | |
| 26th Infantry | Boston, Mass. | Mar 63 | 6 | | | 2 | | 8 |
| 27th Armored | Syracuse, N.Y. | Apr 63 | | 4 | | 5 | | 9 |
| 28th Infantry | Harrisburg, Pa. | Apr 63 | 6 | | | 2 | | 8 |
| 29th Infantry | Baltimore, Md. and Staunton, Va. | Mar 63 | 6 | | | 2 | | 8 |
| 30th Infantry | Raleigh, N.C. | Mar 63 | 6 | | | 2 | | 8 |
| 31st Infantry | Birmingham, Ala. and Jackson, Miss. | Apr/May 63 | 6 | | | 2 | | 8 |

TABLE 24—Continued

| Division | Location of Headquarters | Date | Inf | Mech | Abn | Ar | Amb | Total |
|---|---|---|---|---|---|---|---|---|
| *National Guard* (cont.) | | | | | | | | |
| 32d Infantry | Milwaukee, Wisc. | Apr 63 | 6 | | | 2 | | 8 |
| 33d Infantry | Urbana, Ill. | Apr 63 | 6 | | | 2 | | 8 |
| 36th Infantry | Austin, Tex. | Mar 63 | 6 | | | 2 | | 8 |
| 37th Infantry | Columbus, Ohio | Apr 63 | 6 | | | 2 | | 8 |
| 38th Infantry | Indianapolis, Ind. | Mar 63 | 6 | | | 2 | | 8 |
| 39th Infantry | New Orleans, La. and Little Rock, Ark. | May 63 | 6 | | | 2 | | 8 |
| 40th Armored | Los Angeles, Calif. | Mar 63 | | 4 | | 6 | | 9 |
| 41st Infantry | Portland, Ore. and Seattle, Wash. | Mar 63 | 6 | | | 2 | | 8 |
| 42d Infantry | New York, N.Y. | Apr 63 | 6 | | | 2 | | 8 |
| 45th Infantry | Oklahoma City, Okla. | Apr 63 | 6 | | | 2 | | 8 |
| 46th Infantry | Lansing, Mich. | Mar 63 | 6 | | | 2 | | 8 |
| 47th Infantry | St. Paul, Minn. | Apr 63 | 6 | | | 2 | | 8 |
| 48th Armored | Macon, Ga. | Apr 63 | | 4 | | 5 | | 9 |
| 49th Armored | Dallas, Tex. | Mar 63 | | 4 | | 5 | | 9 |
| 49th Infantry | Alameda, Calif. | Mar 63 | 6 | | | 2 | | 8 |
| 50th Armored | East Orange, N.J. | Jan 63 | | 4 | | 5 | | 9 |
| *Army Reserve* | | | | | | | | |
| 63d Infantry | Bell, Calif. | Apr 63 | 6 | | | 2 | | 8 |
| 77th Infantry | New York, N.Y. | Mar 63 | 6 | | | 2 | | 8 |
| 81st Infantry | Atlanta, Ga. | Apr 63 | 6 | | | 2 | | 8 |
| 83d Infantry | Cleveland, Ohio | Apr 63 | 6 | | | 2 | | 8 |
| 90th Infantry | Austin, Tex. | Mar 63 | 6 | | | 2 | | 8 |
| 102d Infantry | St. Louis, Mo. | Apr 63 | 6 | | | 2 | | 8 |

[a] Equipment only.
[b] Reorganized as an airmobile division 30 June 1965.

*1st Battalion, 60th Infantry, at Fort Richardson, Alaska*

Eventually four more Regular Army brigades were organized in addition to the 193d and 197th Infantry Brigades (*Table 25*). To test new materiel at Fort Ord, California, the Combat Developments Command formed the 194th Armored Brigade, which assumed the mission of the 5th Infantry Division element. United States Army, Alaska, organized the 171st and 172d Infantry Brigades at Forts Wainwright and Richardson, and U.S. Army, Pacific, organized the 173d Airborne Brigade in March 1963 on Okinawa. The 2d Battle Group, 503d Infantry, stationed there since 1960, and the 1st Battle Group, 503d Infantry, deployed from Fort Bragg, formed the nucleus of that brigade. Shortly thereafter the 173d's battle groups were reorganized as airborne infantry battalions. Berlin, however, did not receive a table of organization infantry brigade but retained the Berlin Brigade organized in 1961 under a mission-oriented table of distribution and allowances.[43]

In the Army Reserve some former divisional units assigned to the 79th, 94th, 96th, and 103d Infantry Divisions were used to organize four brigades, which added flexibility to the force as well as provided four general officer reserve billets. In January and February 1963 the 157th, 187th, 191st, and 205th Infantry Brigades were organized with headquarters in Pennsylvania, Massachusetts, Montana, and Minnesota, respectively (*see Table 25*). As with the Regular Army brigades, the number and type of maneuver elements in each Army Reserve brigade varied.[44]

The 34th, 35th, 43d, and 51st Infantry Divisions, multistate National Guard units, dropped out of the force during the reorganization, and in part were replaced by the 67th (Nebraska and Iowa), 69th (Kansas and Missouri), 86th (Vermont and Connecticut), and 53d (Florida and South Carolina) Infantry Brigades. Each brigade fielded five maneuver elements. In addition, the governors also agreed to maintain the 34th (Iowa), 35th (Missouri), 43d (Connecticut), 51st (South Carolina), and 55th (Florida) Command Headquarters to supervise the training of combat and support units located in the former divisional areas. The states also reorganized the 29th, 92d, and 258th Infantry Brigades, which had been formed in 1959.[45]

TABLE 25

Maneuver Element Mix of Brigades
ROAD Reorganization, 30 June 1965

| Component | Brigade | Location of Headquarters | Date Reorganized | Inf | Mech | Abn | Ar | Total |
|---|---|---|---|---|---|---|---|---|
| NG | 29th Infantry | Honolulu, Hawaii | Apr 63 | 3 | | | | 3 |
| NG | 53d Armored | Tampa, Fla. | Feb 63 | | 2 | | 3 | 5 |
| NG | 67th Infantry | Lincoln, Neb. | Apr 63 | | | 3 | 2 | 5 |
| NG | 69th Infantry | Topeka, Kans. | Apr 63 | 2 | | | | 2 |
| NG | 86th Armored | Montpelier, Vt. | Apr 63 | | | 2 | 2 | 4 |
| NG | 92d Infantry | San Juan, Puerto Rico | May 64 | 4 | | | 1 | 5 |
| AR | 157th Infantry | Upper Darby, Pa. | Jan 63 | 1 | 1 | | 2 | 4 |
| RA | 171st Infantry | Ft. Wainwright, Alaska | Jul 63 | 1 | 1 | | 1a | 3 |
| RA | 172d Infantry | Ft. Richardson, Alaska | Jul 63 | 1 | 1 | | 1a | 3 |
| RA | 173d Airborne | Okinawa | Mar 63 | | | 2 | 1a | 2 |
| AR | 187th Infantry | Boston, Mass | Jan 63 | 3 | | | 1 | 4 |
| AR | 191st Infantry | Helena, Mont. | Feb 63 | 1 | 1 | | 2 | 4 |
| RA | 193d Infantry | Ft. Kobbe, Canal Zone | Aug 62 | 1 | 1 | 1 | | 3 |
| RA | 194th Armored | Ft. Ord, Calif. | Dec 62 | | | | 1 | 2 |
| RA | 197th Infantry | Ft. Benning, Ga. | Sep 62 | 2 | 1 | | 1 | 4 |
| AR | 205th Infantry | Ft. Snelling, Minn. | Feb 63 | 3 | 1 | | 1 | 5 |
| NG | 258th Infantry | Phoenix, Ariz. | Mar 63 | 3 | | | 1 | 4 |

a Company-size unit

The following year, to increase further flexibility in the reserves, the National Guard's 53d and 86th Infantry Brigades were converted to armored brigades, and the 67th Infantry Brigade was reorganized as mechanized infantry. The 53d and 67th retained their five maneuver elements, but the 86th lost one battalion. The 1964 reorganization also provided the 258th Infantry Brigade in Arizona with an armor battalion from Missouri and a field artillery battalion from far-away Virginia.[46]

## *Airmobility*

The ROAD reorganization sought flexible forces to meet worldwide commitments on various battlefields, but by April 1962 McNamara had become concerned about unit mobility. He believed that firepower had been favored over maneuverability and that more aircraft could achieve a better balance. The Army's earlier explorations had focused primarily on the number of aircraft, airplanes and helicopters, needed for observation and transportation, but some championed a tactical role for the latter. McNamara wanted the Army to take a new look at the employment of aircraft in land warfare, particularly the helicopter.[47]

In the spring of 1962 the Continental Army Command appointed the Mobility Requirements Board, often referred to as the Howze Board after its president, Lt. Gen. Hamilton H. Howze, to study the matter. After three months of frantic work, including field exercises, the board came to the general conclusion that the adoption of airmobility, the capability of a unit to deploy and receive support from aircraft under the control of a ground commander, was necessary and desirable. In some ways, the transition seemed as inevitable as that from animal to motor transport.[48]

The Howze Board recommended sweeping changes in the use of aircraft, including the organization of air assault divisions. Although combat support elements were not identified, these divisions were to resemble ROAD organizations (*Chart 39*) and were to have sufficient aircraft to lift one-third of the divisional combat elements at one time. The division had some fixed-wing aircraft, but most were to be in an air transport brigade, a nondivisional unit, which was to reinforce the transport capabilities of the division. To keep the division as light as possible, the board suggested the use of new, lighter 105-mm. howitzers, Little John rockets, and air-to-ground rockets mounted on helicopters as replacements for the 155-mm. howitzers. In addition, infantry was to be relieved of all burdens except for those associated with combat. The board's estimates for divisional aircraft ranged between 400 and 600, but ground vehicle requirements fell from 3,400 to 1,100. Air assault divisions were to replace airborne divisions, and the board recommended assigning airborne-qualified personnel to the new units. Air cavalry combat brigades (ACCB) were endorsed for classic cavalry missions—screening, reconnoitering, and delaying actions. Such brigades were to be strictly air units, and they were to employ attack helicopters in antitank roles. The board also rec-

CHART 39—Howze Board—Air Assault Division, 1963

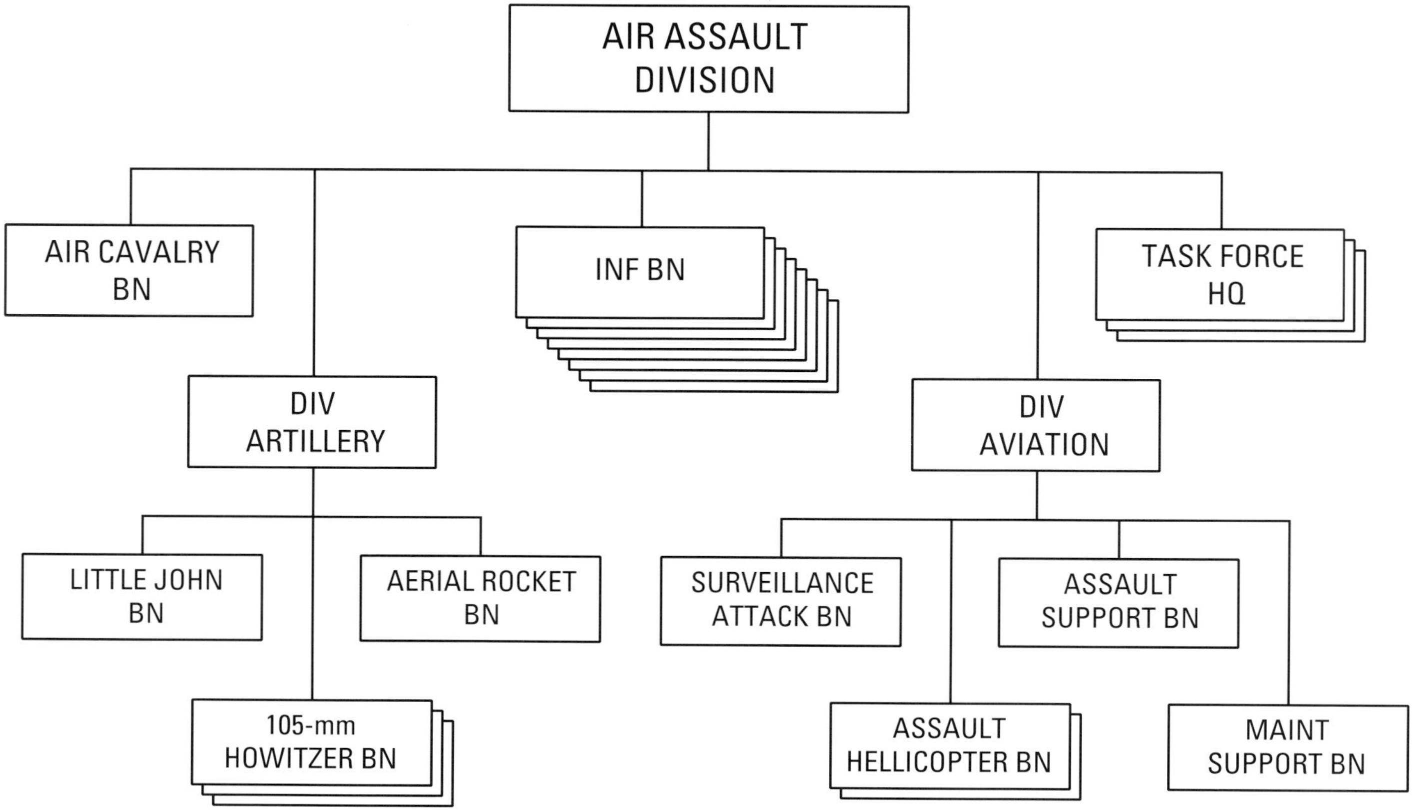

```
                           AIR ASSAULT
                            DIVISION
    ┌───────────────┬───────────────┬───────────────┐
AIR CAVALRY      DIV            INF BN         TASK FORCE
   BN          ARTILLERY                           HQ
           ┌──────┬──────┐                ┌────────┴────────┐
      LITTLE   AERIAL   105-mm         DIV AVIATION
       JOHN   ROCKET   HOWITZER
        BN      BN        BN
                    ┌──────────┬──────────┬──────────┐
              SURVEILLANCE  ASSAULT    ASSAULT    MAINT
                ATTACK     HELICOPTER  SUPPORT   SUPPORT
                  BN          BN         BN        BN
```

ommended more aircraft for infantry, mechanized infantry, and armored divisions; and the formation of aviation units for corps, army, and special warfare units.[49]

The Continental Army Command developed tables of organization for a ROAD-type air assault division, which the Department of the Army decided to test. The first step was the activation of the 11th Air Assault Division (the former 11th Airborne Division) on 1 February 1963, along with the 10th Air Transport Brigade, at Fort Benning, Georgia. As proposed by the Howze Board, the air transport brigade was not organic to the division, but was to serve as a lines of communications unit for hauling men, equipment, and supplies in the field. In October and November 1964 the experimental division, including 3,250 soldiers from the 2d Infantry Division, and the transport brigade conducted full-scale tests of assault tactics. At the conclusion of the test the director, Lt. Gen. Charles W. G. Rich, recommended the addition of both units to the permanent force structure. He reported that the integration of Army aircraft into the ground units provided the crucial maneuver capability for light mobile forces to close with and destroy the enemy. Operating with other divisions, airmobile units offered a balance of mobility and increased Army combat readiness on a theater level.[50]

The recommendation to organize an airmobile division set off a debate within the Joint Chiefs of Staff. The U.S. Air Force had been watching the development and growth of Army aviation for years with increasing concern. Each divisional reorganization after World War II resulted in more aircraft being added to these units. The chief of staff, U.S. Air Force, believed activation of the division premature and judged it too specialized to be cost effective. Although not stated, the Air Force felt that airmobility infringed on its ground support mission. Earlier in the 1960s the Air Force had conducted tests to enhance the mobility and combat effectiveness of divisions by improving troop lift, aerial resupply, close air support, and aerial fire support, but found most of the Army's equipment too large for its aircraft. At the time the Air Force had recommended that the Army develop equipment in the infantry division that was more compatible with existing Air Force planes. McNamara now disagreed. He and the Defense Department staff had been pushing for greater Army involvement in aviation since 1962. The Army's proposal met his approval, and he directed the formation of an airmobile division as part of the permanent force. The air transport brigade, however, did not win a place in the force.[51]

The Army Staff selected the 1st Cavalry Division to become the Army's first airmobile division. Since that unit was serving in Korea, this resulted in a massive paper shuffle, with men and materiel remaining in place and unit designations moving back and forth. In the end the Korean-based 1st Cavalry Division was replaced by the 2d Infantry Division while the assets of the 2d Infantry Division and 11th Air Assault Division at Fort Benning were used to reorganize the 1st Cavalry Division (Airmobile).[52]

The 1st Cavalry Division's configuration differed from the test unit (*Chart 40*). It had no Little John rocket battalion or attack helicopter battalion because the Air

CHART 40—Airmobile Division, 10 July 1965

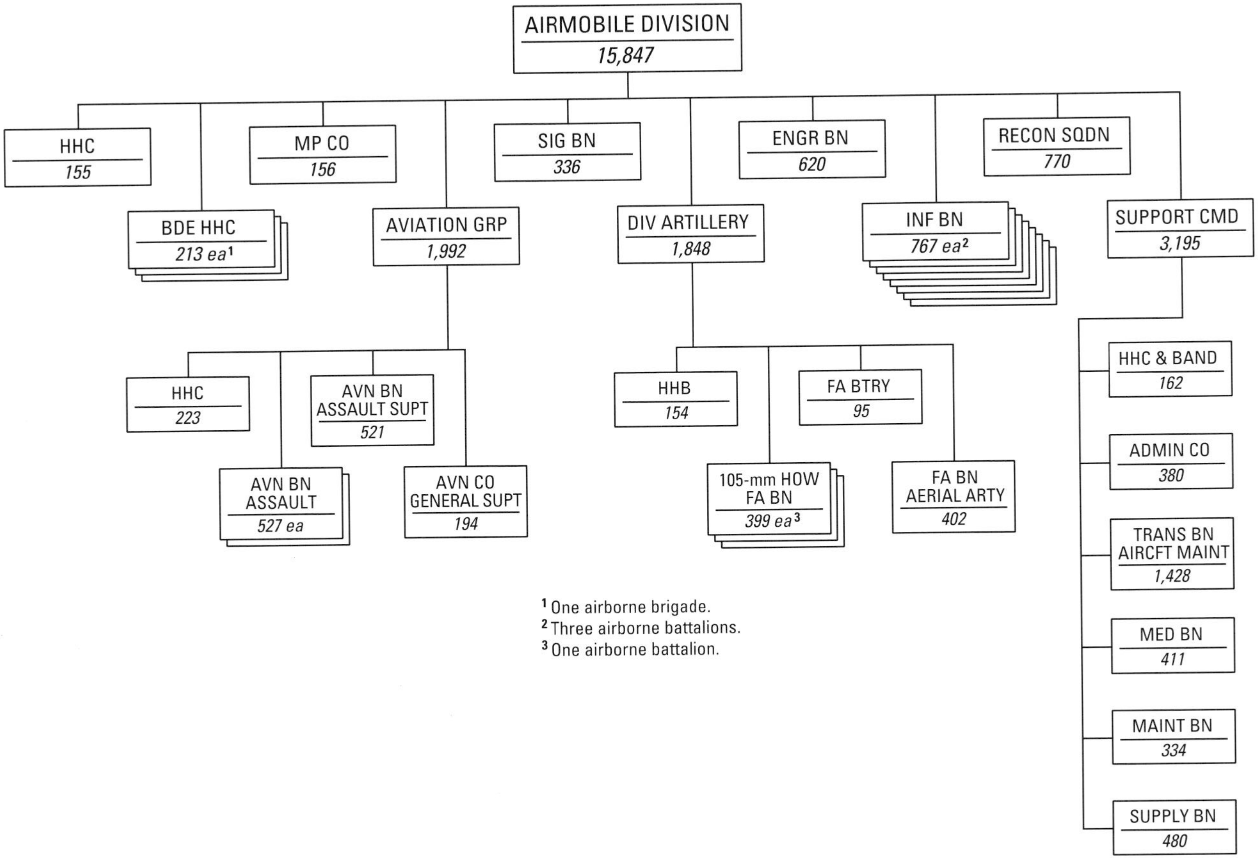

- AIRMOBILE DIVISION — 15,847
  - HHC — 155
  - BDE HHC — 213 ea[1]
  - MP CO — 156
  - AVIATION GRP — 1,992
    - HHC — 223
    - AVN BN ASSAULT — 527 ea
    - AVN BN ASSAULT SUPT — 521
    - AVN CO GENERAL SUPT — 194
  - SIG BN — 336
  - DIV ARTILLERY — 1,848
    - HHB — 154
    - 105-mm HOW FA BN — 399 ea[3]
    - FA BTRY — 95
    - FA BN AERIAL ARTY — 402
  - ENGR BN — 620
  - INF BN — 767 ea[2]
  - RECON SQDN — 770
  - SUPPORT CMD — 3,195
    - HHC & BAND — 162
    - ADMIN CO — 380
    - TRANS BN AIRCFT MAINT — 1,428
    - MED BN — 411
    - MAINT BN — 334
    - SUPPLY BN — 480

[1] One airborne brigade.
[2] Three airborne battalions.
[3] One airborne battalion.

Force or other organic divisional weapons assumed the nuclear fire support mission of the rockets. The division fielded an aviation group (a general aviation support company and one assault support and two assault aviation battalions). Divisional helicopters numbered 335. Although the Howze Board believed the number of ground vehicles could be cut by two-thirds, the division was authorized 1,500, or approximately half the number in the other types of ROAD divisions. The vehicles moved supplies, artillery, and antitank weapons and helped in ground reconnaissance. The airmobile infantry battalion had one combat support company (reconnaissance, mortar, and antitank resources) and three rifle companies. Although the battalion lacked ENTACs, 4.2-inch mortars, and .50-caliber machine guns, the infantrymen had a number of new weapons. The M14 rifle was superseded by the lighter MX16E1 (M16), which put out more firepower and was supplemented by the M79 40-mm. grenade launcher with a dedicated grenadier.[53]

The question as to whether the airmobile division should replace the airborne division had not been resolved. Planners decided that one brigade—three infantry battalions and one artillery battalion—was to be authorized airborne-qualified personnel as an interim measure.[54]

In summary, the ROAD reorganization ensured the Army's ability to offer flexible responses to changing world conditions. On 1 July 1965, the Army's division and brigade forces consisted of 45 divisions (16 in the Regular Army, 23 in the National Guard, and 6 in the Army Reserve) and 17 brigades (6 in the Regular Army, 7 in the National Guard, and 4 in the Army Reserve). Of the Regular Army divisions, eight served outside the continental United States and eight within. Divisions and brigades in the three components had more flexibility than ever before. As in the past, personnel problems prevented the Army from fielding divisions at their ideal strength, but ROAD's inherent capability for interchanging battalions meant that, if necessary, some units could be brought to wartime standards quickly. The divisions, however, still awaited their true test—combat.

From the Army's point of view the Kennedy era had produced measurable organizational gains. The budget-driven pentomic divisions had been adopted primarily for political purposes and had never been popular within the Army. While Army leaders were enamored of the new airmobile concept backed by McNamara and others, the ROAD divisions were more popular, providing the Army with solid standard divisional bases and the ability to tailor brigade-size task forces within the division using a variable mix of combat battalions. And with Kennedy's support for expanding the ground components and technological capabilities, the future of the Army seemed more secure in the budget-driven defense community.

## Notes

1 *Public Papers of the Presidents of the United States: John F. Kennedy, 1961* (Washington, D.C.: Government Printing Office, 1962), p. 401.

2 Robert A. Doughty, *The Evaluation of US Army Tactical Doctrine, 1946–76: Leavenworth Papers* (Fort Leavenworth, Kans.: Combat Studies Institute, 1979), p. 19.

3 Modern Mobile Army 1965–1970 (U) (Short Title: MOMAR I), (Fort Monroe, Va.: Continental Army Command, 1960), DAMH-HSO; Gordon B. Roger, "Ground Mobility," *Armor* 69 (Sep–Oct 1960): 24–26.

4 Ltr, OCofS to CG, CONARC, 16 Dec 60, sub: Reorganization of Infantry and Armored Divisions and Creation of a Mechanized Division, Division General file, DAMH-HSO.

5 Ibid.; Interview, author with Col George Sedberry, 19 Jun 78, DAMH-HSO; Memo, George Donmis for General Starry, sub: Historical Background of Three Versus Four Companies, 16 May 69, Historical Office, U.S. Army Training and Doctrine Command (TRADOC).

6 Interview, author with Eddleman, 18 Sep 74, DAMH-HSO; J. Perret-Gential, "Divisions—Three or Five Elements?" *Military Review* 41 (Feb 1961): 16–25.

7 Ltr, CG, CONARC, to CofS, 1 Mar 61, sub: Reorganization Objective Army Divisions 1961–1965, ATCG 322 (Div), Division General file, DAMH-HSO; Reorganization Objective Army Divisions 1965 (hereafter cited as ROAD 65) (Fort Monroe, Va.: U.S. Army Continental Army Command, 1960). Some speculate that the ROAD concept was worked out at the Army War College before Eddleman instructed the command to undertake the study. (See Memo, Donmis to Starry, sub: Historical Background on Three Versus Four Companies.)

8 ROAD 65, Annex E.

9 Ibid., Annex A.

10 Ibid., Annex E, Annex F.

11 Ibid., Annex B.

12 Ltr, G–3, CONARC, to DCofS for Military Operations, DA, 10 Apr 61, sub: Preparation of TOE for ROAD-65 Concept, ATTNG-O&E 320.3, and Ltr, CofS to CG, CONARC, 13 Apr 61, sub: Reorganization of Army Divisions, both Division General file, DAMH-HSO.

13 TOE 7E (Draft), Infantry Division, undated; TOE 17E (Draft), Armored Division, undated; and TOE 37E (Draft), Mechanized Infantry Division, undated.

14 Memo for Record, CONARC, Combat Developments Plans Division, 23 Mar 61, sub: DCSOPS Preliminary Report to the Vice Chief of Staff on "Reorganization Objective Army Division 1965 (ROAD-65)," ATSWD-P 322 (Army), Division General file, DAMH-HSO.

15 Reorganization Objective Army Divisions 1965 (ROAD-65) Airborne Division (Fort Monroe, Va.: Continental Army Command, 1961), DAMH-HSO.

16 CONARC, "Summary of Major Events and Problems, FY 1962," vol. 3, pp. 3–7, DAMH-HSR; TOE 57E, Airborne Division, 15 Aug 1963.

17 Ltr, CONARC to DCofS for Military Operations, 31 May 61, sub: ROAD-65 Type Brigade (Separate, Airborne), ATSND-P 322 (Div), and Ltr, CONARC to Commandant, U.S. Armor School, 28 Sep 61, sub: Separate Brigade Organizations Under ROAD, ATTNG-D&R (Div), both Brigade General file, DAMH-HSO.

18 Ltr, Powell to Eddleman, 23 Feb 61, Division General file, DAMH-HSO.

19 Kennedy, *Papers of the Presidents*, 1961, p. 401.

20 Ibid., pp. 533–36; DA Bull 5, 1961.

21 Robert W. Coakley, Walter G. Hermes, James F. Schnabel, and Earl F. Ziemke, "U.S. Army Expansion and Readiness, 1961–1962," Ms, ch. II, DAMH-HSR. The Strategic Army Force (STRAF) was comprised of units to provide a mobilization expansion base, a source of trained units and replacements to support forces deployed overseas, and a combat-ready element designed to serve as a readily available force for use wherever needed.

22 Ibid.; Executive Order 10957, DA Bull 5, 1961; Department of the Army, *Forces in Depth, "One Army" in Action, 1961–1962* (Washington, D.C.: n.p., 1962) (hereafter cited as

*"One Army" in Action*).

23 Forrest K. Kleinman, "Front and Center: The Changing Army," *Army* 12 (Feb 1962): 16; *Department of Defense Annual Report, FY 1962*, pp. 100, 110, 113; Public Affairs Division, *Big Lift 1963* (U.S. Army, Europe, 1963).

24 Kleinman, "Front and Center," pp. 17–18; Ltr, TAG to CGs, Third and Sixth Armies, and Chief of Engineers, 28 Nov 61, sub: Reorganization of Units, AGAO-O (M) 322 (6 Nov 61) DCSPER, Ltr, TAG to CG, Third U.S. Army, 27 Feb 62, sub: Reorganization of the 82d Airborne Division, AGAO (M) 322 (16 Feb 62) DCSPER, Ltr, TAG to CinC, USARPAC, 14 Jun 61, sub: Change in Status of Units, AGAO-O (M) 322 (2 Jun 61) DCSPER, Ltr, TAG to CinC, USARPAC, 27 Mar 62, sub: Change in Status of Units, AGAO-O (M) 322 (14 Mar 62) DCSPER, and Ltr, TAG to CG, Sixth U.S. Army, 15 Feb 62, sub: Reorganization of the 4th Infantry Division, AGAO-O (M) 322 (15 Feb 62) DCSPER, all AG Reference files, Historical Data Cards, Divisions, DAMH-HSO.

25 Coakley et al., "Army Expansion, 1961–62," pp. 124–57 passim; Memo, Deputy Sec of Defense to Sec of Defense, sub: Plan for Activation of Two Additional Active Army Divisions, 18 Jan 62, Division General file, and Ltr, TAG to CGs, CONARC, and other addresses, 22 Jan 62, sub: Change in Status of Units, 22 Jan 62, AGAO-O (M) 322 (22 Jan 62) DCSPER, and Ltr, TAG to CGs, CONARC, and other addresses, 26 Jan 62, same subject, AGAO-O (M) 322 (26 Jan 62) DCSPER, both AG Reference files, all DAMH-HSO.

26 Ltr, CofS, U.S. Army Infantry Center, to CGs, CONARC and Third U.S. Army, 12 Mar 62, sub: Reorganization of 1st Brigade under ROAD, AGICT (Adjutant General, Infantry Center), Ltr, CONARC to CG, U.S. Army Infantry Center, same subject, 13 Jun 62; ATUR-P&O (Unit Training and Readiness-Plans and Operation Branch, DF, DCofS/Unit Training and Readiness), CONARC, to DCG and CofS, CONARC, same subject, 23 May 62, and Ltr, TAG to CG, Third U.S. Army, 20 Sep 62, sub: Change in Status of 1st and 197th Infantry Brigade, AGAO-O (M) 322 (5 Sep 62) DCSPER, all 1st Brigade, 1st Inf Div, DAMH-HSO.

27 John W. Wike, "173d Airborne Brigade," Fact Sheet for DOD Hearings, 30 Apr 63, 173d Airborne Brigade file, DAMH-HSO; Ltr, TAG to CG, Third U.S. Army, 20 Sep 62, sub: Change in Status of 1st and 197th Infantry Brigade.

28 Ltr, TAG to CG, Third U.S. Army, 20 Sep 62, sub: Change in Status of 1st and 197th Infantry Brigade.

29 Matloff, *American Military History*, pp. 594–95; Memo, CofS for SA, 15 Aug 62, sub: Schedule for Conversion of Army Divisions to ROAD, 320 (15 Aug 62), Division General file, DAMH-HSO; Ltr, OTAG to TAG, 27 Aug 62, sub: Change in Status of Unit, AGAO-O (M) 322 (15 Aug 62), GO 69, U.S. Army Caribbean, 1962, and Ltr, TAG to CG, U.S. Army Caribbean, 11 Feb 63, sub: Change in Status of Units, all 193d Inf Bde file, DAMH-HSO.

30 *Department of Defense Annual Report, FY 1963*, p. 109; Army News Service, Release No. 46, 19 Jul 62, SA Sends Message to Army National Guardsmen and Reservists, Berlin Crisis 1961–1962, Reference Paper files, DAMH-HSO; *"One Army" in Action*.

31 *Department of Defense Annual Report, FY 1963*, pp. 111–14; Joseph R. Wisnack, "Old Ironsides' Response to the Cuban Crisis,"*Army* 13 (Apr 1963): 26–30; Ltr, 1st Armored Division to CG, III Corps, 20 Apr 63, Incl, sub: Historical Narrative of the 1st Armored Division in the Cuban Crisis, 1962, AKDFA-CG, 1st Armd Div file, DAMH-HSO.

32 Memo, CofS to SA, 15 Aug 62, sub: Schedule for Conversion of Army Divisions to ROAD.

33 Ibid.

34 Ibid.

35 Ibid.; Fact Sheet on Reorganization of Army Division (ROAD), 10 Jan 63, Division General file, DAMH-HSO.

36 Ltr, TAG to CG, Fourth U.S. Army, and other addresses, 31 May 63, sub: Reorganization of the 2d Armored Division Under ROAD, AGAO-O (M) (10 May 63) DCSPER, Ltr, TAG to CinC, USAREUR, 21 Jun 63, sub: Reorganization of 3d Armored Division Under ROAD TOE, AGAO-O (M) (22 May 63) DCSPER, Ltr, TAG to CinC, USAREUR, 19 Jun 63, sub: Reorganization of the 4th Armored Division Under ROAD TOE, AGAO-O (M) (22 May 63) DCSPER, Ltr, TAG to CinC,

USARPAC, and CG, CONARC, 15 Jul 63, sub: Reorganization of the 1st Cavalry Division, AGAO-O (M) (14 Jun 63) DCSPER, Ltr, TAG to CG, Fifth U.S. Army, 23 Oct 63, sub: Reorganization of the 1st Infantry Division, AGAO-O (M) (30 Sep 63), DCSPER, Ltr, TAG to CinC, USAREUR, and other addresses, 25 Jan 63, sub: Change in Status of Units, AGAO-O (M) (22 Jan 63) DCSPER, Ltr, TAG to CINCs, USAREUR and USARPAC, 23 May 63, sub: Reorganization of 3d Infantry Division, AGAO-O (M) (18 Apr 63) DCSPER, Ltr, TAG to CGs, CONARC and Sixth U.S. Army, 21 Aug 63, sub: Reorganization of the 4th Infantry Division Under ROAD, AGAO-O (M) (29 Jul 63) DCSPER, Ltr, TAG to CinC, USARPAC, and CG, CONARC, 7 Jun 63, sub: Reorganization of the 7th Infantry Division, AGAO-O (M) (31 May 63) DCSPER, Ltr, OTAG to TAG, 20 Sep 63, sub: Change in Status of Units, 20 Sep 63, AGAO-O (M) (13 Sep 63), Ltr, TAG to CinC, USAREUR, 8 May 63, sub: Reorganization of the 24th Infantry Division (Mechanized), AGAO-O (10 Apr 63) DCSPER, Ltr, TAG to CinC, USARPAC, and CG, CONARC, 17 Jul 63, sub: Reorganization of the 25th Infantry Division, AGAO-O (M) (24 Jun 63) DCSPER, Ltr, TAG to CG, Third U.S. Army, 21 Jan 64, sub: Reorganization of STRAF Units, No. 18, FY 64, AGAO-O (M) (31 Dec 63) DCSPER, Ltr, TAG to CG, Third U.S. Army, 6 Mar 64, sub: Reorganization of STRAF Units, No. 58, FY 64, AGAO-O (19 Feb 64) DCSPER, all AG Reference files, Historical Data Cards, Divisions, DAMH-HSO; "8th Infantry Division," *Soldiers* 39 (Jan 1985): 13–14.

37 TOE 7E, Infantry Division, 1963; TOE 17E, Armored Division, 1963, TOE 37E, Mechanized Infantry Division, 1963, and TOE 57E, Airborne Division, 1963, and subordinate TOEs for each division; Midgley, *Deadly Illusions*, p. 116.

38 Army News Service, "Reorganization of Army Forces," Release No. 4, 9 Jan 63, Division General file, DAMH-HSO; Memo, OCofS for DCofS and other addresses, 9 Sep 61, sub: Review of Plan to Reorganize and Realign the Reserve Components of the Army, 326 (9 Sep 61), Memo, ACofS for Reserve Components (ACSRC) for CofS, 13 Dec 61, sub: White House Briefing, ACSRC-OT-M&P (Organization and Training-Mobilization and Personnel), Ltr, Under SA to F. Edward Hebert, 20 Jun 62, no subject, all Army Reserve file, DAMH-HSO.

39 Army News Service, "Army Announces Plans for Reorganization of Reserve Components," Release Number 29, 5 Apr 62, and Msg 922374, Chief of Information, DA to, CG, CONARC, and other addresses, 040007Z Dec 62, no subject, both Army Reserve file, DAMH-HSO; Ltr, TAG to CGs, CONARC, and First U.S. Army, 25 Mar 63, sub: Reorganization of the 77th Infantry Division Under ROAD, AGAO-O (M) (18 Mar 63) OCAR, Ltr, TAG to CGs, CONARC, and Second U.S. Army, 27 Mar 63, sub: Reorganization of the 83d Infantry Division Under ROAD, AGAO-O (M) (18 Mar 63) OCAR, Ltr, TAG to CGs, CONARC, and Third U.S. Army, 26 Mar 93, sub: Reorganization of 81st Infantry Division Under ROAD, AGAO-O (M) (18 Mar 63) OCAR, Ltr, TAG to CGs, CONARC, and other addresses, 22 Mar 63, sub: Reorganization of the 90th Infantry Division Under ROAD, AGAO-O (M) (18 Mar 63) OCAR, Ltr, TAG to CGs, CONARC, and Fifth U.S. Army, 26 Mar 63, sub: Reorganization of the 102d Infantry Division Under ROAD, AGAO-O (M) (18 Mar 63) OCAR, Ltr, TAG to CGs, CONARC, and Sixth U.S. Army, 27 Mar 63, sub: Reorganization of 63d Infantry Division Under ROAD, AGAO-O (M) (18 Mar 63) OCAR, all AG Reference files, DAMH-HSO; "DA Publishes Details on Reorganization of the Army Reserve," *Army Reservist* 9 (Mar 1963): 6–10; TOE 29–701T, Command Headquarters, Divisional, 1963; Wilson, *Armies, Corps, Divisions, and Separate Brigades*, pp. 436, 523, 534; GO 1, XIV U.S. Army Corps, 1963, 103d Inf Div file, DAMH-HSO; "'Cross of Lorraine Division' 79th Command HQ (Div)," Army Reserve Magazine 11 (Nov 1965): 4–5.

40 "The Guard Goes ROAD," *National Guardsman* 17 (Feb 1963): 2–4; News Release No. 665–63, "Army Reserve Components Complete Reorganization," 10 May 63, Army Reserve file, DAMH-HSO; *Annual Report of the Chief, National Guard Bureau, FY 1963*, p. 27.

41 "The Guard Goes ROAD," pp. 2–4; see notes based on NG letters, 1963, copies in author files.

42 Memo, CofS for SA, 15 Aug 62, sub: Schedule for Conversion of Army Divisions to ROAD, 15 Aug 62, Army News Service, ROAD Reorganization of Army Forces, 9 Jan 63, Army News Service, Reorganization of Army Divisions Begins this Month at Fort Benning, Release No. 8, 22 Jan 63, all Division General file, DAMH-HSO.

43 Ltr, TAG to CG, U.S. Army Combat Developments Command, 4 Dec 62, sub: Change in Status of Units, AGAO-O (M) (26 Nov 62) DCSPER, 194th Armd Bde file, Ltr, TAG to CG, U.S. Army, Alaska, 20 May 63, sub: Change in Status of Units, AGAO-O (M) (1 May 63) DCSPER, 171st Inf Bde file, Ltr, TAG to CinC, USARPAC, 2 May 63, sub: Activation of 173d Airborne Brigade, AGAO-O (M) (26 Mar 63) DCSPER, 173d Abn Bde file, and Ltr, TAG to CinC, USARPAC, 31 Jul 63, sub: Reorganization of the 173d Airborne Brigade, AGAO-O (M) (28 Jun 63) DCSPER, 173d Abn Bde file, all DAMH-HSO. As a Table of Distribution and Allowance unit, the Berlin Brigade was not counted as a part of division and brigade forces.

44 "Reorganization of Army Reserve," *Army Reservist*, p. 7; "157th Infantry Brigade," *Army Reserve Magazine,* 12 (Jul–Aug 66): 4-5; Historical Data Card, 187th Inf Bde, GO 1, Sixth U.S. Army, 1962, 191st Inf Bde file, GO 1, XIV U.S. Army Corps, 1963, 205th Inf Bde file, all DAMH-HSO. The designation of each brigade was derived from the lowest numbered infantry brigade associated with the division under the square structure.

45 *Annual Report of the Chief, National Guard Bureau Report, FY 1963*, p. 27; see notes based on NG letters, 1963, copies in author's files.

46 *Annual Report of the Chief, National Guard Bureau, 1965*, p. 29; Reserve Component Program of the Army, FY 1965, Annex II, Army National Guard Unit Program, pp. 144–53.

47 Barbara A. Sorrill and Constance J. Suwalsky, *The Origins, Deliberations, and Recommendations of the U.S. Army Tactical Mobility Requirements Board (Howze Board)* (Fort Leavenworth, Kans.: U.S. Army Combat Developments Command, 1969), pp. 10–11.

48 U.S. Army Tactical Mobility Requirements Board (Howze Board), Final Report, 20 Aug 62, p. 95, DAMH-HSR; Hamilton H. Howze, *Memoirs of a Twentieth-Century Army General: A Cavalryman's Story* (Washington, D.C.: Smithsonian Institution Press, 1996), pp. 233–57.

49 Howze Board, pp. 19, 34–50 passim and Incl 5; Howze, *A Cavalryman's Story*, p. 251; Christopher C.S. Cheng, *Air Mobility: The Development of a Doctrine* (Westport, Conn.: Praeger, 1994), pp. 179-80.

50 John J. Tolson, *Airmobility, 1961–1971* (Washington, D.C.: Government Printing Office, 1973), pp. 50–57.

51 Richard Fryklund, "Soldiers of the Sky," National Guardsman 18 (March 1964): 3-7+; SS, ACSFOR (Assistant Chief of Staff for Force Development) to the CofS, 25 Feb 65, sub: Plan for Introduction for an Air Mobile Division in the Active Army, and Memo, SD to SA and Chairman, JCS, 15 Jun 65, sub: Organization of Airmobile Division, both 1st Cav Div file, DAMH-HSO.

52 SS, ACSFOR for CofS, 25 Feb 65, sub: Plan for Introduction of an Air Mobile Division, Ltr, TAG to CGs, Third U.S. Army, and other addresses, 22 Jul 65, sub: Reorganization of 1st Cavalry Division (Amb) STRAF, No. FY 66, AGAO-O (M) (8 Jul 65) DCSPER, and GO 185, Third U.S. Army, 1965, all 1st Cav Div file, DAMH-HSO.

53 SS, ACSFOR for CofS, 25 Feb 65, sub: Plan for Introduction of an Air Mobile Division; TOE 67T, Airmobile Division, 1965; Walter G. Hermes, Vietnam Buildup, ch. 5, p. 30, undated Ms, DAMH-HD.

54 TOE 67T, Airmobile Division, 1965.

# CHAPTER 12

# Flexible Response

*General Westmoreland has the authority to use the American forces that are now in Viet-Nam in the way which he considers most effective to resist the Communist aggression and the terror that is taking place. . . . I have ordered . . . American troops ashore in order to give protection to hundreds of Americans who are still in the Dominican Republic. . . . Over the past 15 months the North Koreans have pursued a stepped-up campaign of violence against South Korean and the American troops. . . . We are taking certain precautionary measures to make sure that our military forces are prepared for any contingency that might arise.*

President Lyndon B. Johnson[1]

President Lyndon B. Johnson ordered the first American combat units to the Republic of Vietnam in 1965. After the French abandoned Indochina, the 1954 Geneva Accords created two Vietnams, South and North, using the 17th Parallel as the demarcation line. Almost immediately the Army began advising the South Vietnamese Army, and over the next decade the armed conflict between North and South Vietnam slowly escalated, finally leading to the direct participation of U.S. Army divisions and brigades and the use of the tailoring principles embodied in ROAD. In addition, Army divisions continued to stand vigilant in Europe and Korea against Communist aggression and restored order in the Dominican Republic following a period of political unrest.

## *The Buildup of the Army*

In May 1965 President Johnson committed Regular Army combat units to South Vietnam to halt North Vietnamese incursions and suppress National Liberation Front insurgents. The 173d Airborne Brigade from Okinawa was the Army's first combined arms unit to arrive in Southeast Asia. In July the 2d Brigade, 1st Infantry Division, and the 1st Brigade, 101st Airborne Division, also deployed from the United States. The brigade from the 101st was originally planned to replace the 173d Airborne Brigade but, with the need for additional combat units, both brigades remained in Vietnam. Two months later the 1st Cavalry Division, recently reorganized as an airmobile unit, reported in country, and the remainder of the 1st Infantry Division arrived in October.[2]

As the Army responded to its new mission, divisions were reorganized using ROAD's tailoring concepts. Before the 1st Infantry Division deployed, it had field-

*Elements of the 173d Airborne Brigade arrive in Vietnam, May 1965.*

ed five infantry, two mechanized infantry, and two armor battalions. With the change in assignment from NATO reinforcement to counterinsurgency in Vietnam, the division was restructured. Honest Johns and Davy Crocketts disappeared while requirements for infantry rose. As no pool of unassigned maneuver battalions existed, two infantry battalions from the 2d Brigade, 5th Infantry Division, at Fort Devens, Massachusetts, were relieved and assigned to "The Big Red One." The 1st Division also reorganized two of its mechanized infantry battalions as standard infantry, bringing the number of infantry battalions in the division to nine.[3]

The commander of the 1st Infantry Division, Maj. Gen. Jonathan O. Seaman, wanted to take a tank battalion to Vietnam, but General Harold K. Johnson, Chief of Staff since July 1964, overruled him. Tanks were too vulnerable to mines, and no major enemy armor threat existed. Furthermore, Johnson thought that the tempo of the battlefield might be slowed by the limitations of the tank, whose presence might foster a conventional war mentality rather than the light, fast-moving, unconventional approach needed. General William C. Westmoreland, commander of U.S. Army, Vietnam, agreed, reporting that few places existed in Vietnam where tanks could be employed. Johnson, however, granted Seaman permission to take the reconnaissance squadron's M48A3 tanks to test the effectiveness of armor units.[4]

The decision to commit divisions and separate brigades to Vietnam triggered a debate within the administration about the means of expanding the Army to maintain the strategic force. Proposals ranged from calling up the reserves to increasing the draft. On 28 July, however, President Johnson rejected use of the reserves and announced that the Army would base its expansion on volunteers and draftees. Shortly thereafter, Secretary of Defense McNamara disclosed that one infantry division and three infantry brigades would be added to the Regular Army in fiscal year 1966 (between 1 July 1965 and 30 June 1966).[5]

Expansion of the Army began in September 1965, when the First U.S. Army organized the 196th Infantry Brigade. The 2d Brigade, 5th Infantry Division, less its personnel, moved to Fort Carson, Colorado, where it was refilled, and the remaining men at Fort Devens became the cadre for the 196th Infantry Brigade. The 196th eventually consisted of three infantry battalions and the brigade base, a reconnaissance troop, an engineer company, a support battalion, and a field artillery battalion. Recruits were assigned to the brigade under a "train and retain" program, which lessened the impact of limited mobilization on the training base.[6]

The brigade's infantry battalions used a new light structure designed for counterinsurgency warfare. Each battalion consisted of a headquarters and headquarters company, three rifle companies, and a combat support company. The latter organization, similar to that in the airmobile infantry battalion, had mortar, reconnaissance, and antitank platoons. These light battalions fielded about half the number of vehicles assigned to a standard infantry battalion, and the riflemen carried M14 rifles.[7]

The Fifth U.S. Army activated the 9th Infantry Division, the second unit in the expansion program, at Fort Riley, Kansas, on 1 February 1966, also employing the "train and retain" concept. Filled in three increments, the division included one mechanized infantry battalion and eight infantry battalions. By the end of July the division had graduated the last cycle of basic trainees, and it was expected to be combat ready by the end of the year.[8]

While organizing the 9th Infantry Division, the Army decided to use it as a part of the Mobile Afloat (Riverine) Force in Vietnam. Brig. Gen. William E. DePuy, who was serving on Westmoreland's staff, had developed the idea of a joint Army-Navy force for use in Vietnam's Mekong River Delta. Army units were to include a brigade-size element that would live and move on ships and work with two brigade-size shore contingents. Learning of the riverine mission, Maj. Gen. George S. Eckhardt, the 9th Division's commander, requested permission to mechanize one infantry battalion, which would allow him to have one brigade (three infantry battalions) aboard naval ships and two brigades (one mechanized infantry and two infantry battalions each) operating from land bases. The Army Staff in Washington agreed, and Eckhardt organized the second mechanized infantry battalion in October. To take advantage of the dry season in Vietnam, the division began departing Fort Riley at the end of 1966 and by February 1967 elements of the "Old Reliables" took part in the first U.S. Army-Navy riverine operation of the war.[9]

*9th Infantry Division's first base camp in Vietnam, 1966*

Shortly thereafter, the Army's buildup plan went awry. Army Chief of Staff General Johnson had requested his staff to consider forming a divisional-type brigade (i.e., without the supporting units common to a separate brigade) to replace the 25th Infantry Division at Schofield Barracks, Hawaii, which was programmed for deployment to Vietnam in early 1966. Resources scheduled for one of the remaining brigade authorizations could then be used for the Hawaiian unit. Another proposal, calling for organizing both the remaining brigades in McNamara's expansion program in Hawaii, was presented to the Army Staff. However, the Army had activated the 199th Infantry Brigade at Fort Benning, Georgia, on 1 June 1966 in response to a request from Westmoreland for a brigade to protect the Long Binh–Saigon area. Units in Europe were tasked to furnish the cadre for the brigade, which fielded three light infantry battalions. In less than six months it deployed to Vietnam.[10]

Having authority to organize only one more brigade, the Army activated the 11th Infantry Brigade, a pre–World War II element of the 6th Infantry Division, in Hawaii on 1 July 1966. Behind the selection of the 11th was the assumption that the 6th would be the next division to be activated. The 11th consisted of three infantry battalions, a support battalion, a reconnaissance troop, and a military police company. Because of a shortage of personnel and equipment, the brigade lacked its field artillery battalion, engineer company, and signal platoon authorized for an independent brigade. But despite their absence, training began and the missing units were eventually organized. Rather than remaining in Hawaii as planned, the 11th Infantry Brigade deployed to South Vietnam in December 1967 in answer to an ever-growing need for forces there.[11]

As the Army's involvement in Southeast Asia deepened, more units moved to Vietnam. As noted, the 25th Infantry Division was alerted for deployment in December 1965, and at that time General Johnson, Army chief of staff, directed that two new infantry battalions be added to it. However, almost immediately after their organization began, the battalions were inactivated and replaced with two existing battalions from Alaska, a means of speeding the departure of the division. When the division deployed in the spring of 1966 it fielded one mecha-

*Men of the 1st Brigade, 101st Airborne Division, fire from old Viet Cong trenches.*

nized infantry battalion and eight infantry battalions. In addition, the commander, Maj. Gen. Frederick C. Weyand, insisted on taking the divisional tank battalion.[12]

The 4th Infantry Division, the last Regular Army infantry division available in the United States in 1965 for service in Vietnam, experienced similar turbulence. The Sixth U.S. Army relieved one tank battalion from the division, equipped the other with M48 tanks, reorganized one mechanized infantry battalion as standard infantry, and added two more infantry battalions, giving the division the same maneuver mix (1–1–8) as the 25th Infantry Division. Shortly after the 4th completed its reorganization in November 1965, the division received 6,000 recruits to bring all units up to full strength. From June through August 1966 the 4th also assisted forty-seven nondivisional units in preparing for duty in Vietnam and helped activate the training center at Fort Lewis, Washington. Nevertheless, the "Ivy Division" deployed to Vietnam between August and October 1966.[13]

As the conflict in Vietnam intensified, Westmoreland requested additional infantry for the 173d Airborne Brigade and the 1st Cavalry Division. When the 173d Airborne Brigade arrived in Vietnam, it had only two airborne battalions and was augmented with an Australian battalion, while the 1st Cavalry Division had only eight airmobile infantry battalions, which left one of its brigades short a

*Elements of 69th Infantry Brigade, part of the Selected Reserve Force, train at Fort Riley, Kansas, 1966.*

maneuver element. After considerable deliberation, the Continental Army Command activated one airborne battalion and one airmobile battalion, using personnel drawn from the 101st Airborne Division and the 5th Infantry Division. Both battalions deployed to Vietnam in the summer of 1966 to join the 173d Airborne Brigade and the 1st Cavalry Division, respectively.[14]

With the departure of units for Vietnam, the reserves took on a more significant role. The nation needed a reserve contingent that could report to mobilization stations on a seven-day notice. The Army, therefore, created the Selected Reserve Force in the Army National Guard that included three infantry divisions and six infantry brigades, one of which was mechanized. To assure the force's equitable geographical distribution so that one section of the nation would not be asked to bear the burden of a partial mobilization, each division consisted of the division base and one brigade in one state, while the other two brigades were divisional units from adjacent states (*Table 26*). The Army selected the 28th, 38th, and 47th Infantry Divisions for the force. For the separate brigades, the states organized three new units, and again their geographic distribution played a role. Elements from the 36th, 41st, and 49th Infantry Divisions were withdrawn to form the 36th, 41st, and 49th Infantry Brigades. The divisions themselves remained active, but each lacked a brigade. The force's other three brigades were the 29th, 67th, and 69th Infantry Brigades, which had been organized earlier.[15]

To improve the readiness of the Selected Reserve Force, the Army authorized its units to be fully manned, increased their number of drill days, and raised their priority for receiving new equipment. Because of shortages in personnel and equipment, McNamara achieved a long-standing controversial goal of the Defense Department, a reduction of the reserve troop basis. Those reserve units that were

## TABLE 26
### Divisions and Brigades
### Selected Reserve Force, 1965

| Unit | State |
| --- | --- |
| 28th Infantry Division | Pennsylvania |
|    3d Brigade, 28th Infantry Division | Pennsylvania |
|    3d Brigade, 29th Infantry Division | Maryland |
|    3d Brigade, 37th Infantry Division | Ohio |
| 38th Infantry Division | Indiana |
|    76th Brigade, 38th Infantry Division | Indiana |
|    2d Brigade, 46th Infantry Division | Michigan |
|    3d Brigade, 33d Infantry Division | Illinois |
| 47th Infantry Division | Minnesota |
|    2d Brigade, 47th Infantry Division | Minnesota |
|    1st Brigade, 32d Infantry Division | Wisconsin |
|    3d Brigade, 45th Infantry Division | Oklahoma |
| 29th Infantry Brigade | Hawaii and California |
| 36th Infantry Brigade | Texas |
| 41st Infantry Brigade | Washington and Oregon |
| 49th Infantry Brigade | California |
| 67th Infantry Brigade (Mechanized) | Iowa and Nebraska |
| 69th Infantry Brigade | Kansas and Missouri |

judged unnecessary and others that were undermanned and underequipped could now be deleted with minimum controversy and their assets used to field contingency forces. Among the units inactivated were the last six combat divisions in the Army Reserve—the 63d, 77th, 81st, 83d, 90th, and 102d Infantry Divisions—and the 79th, 94th, and 96th Command Headquarters (Division). The 103d Command Headquarters (Division) was converted to a support brigade headquarters.[16]

In the spring of 1965 the Army also responded to a crisis in the Caribbean area. To help restore political stability and protect United States citizens and property, President Johnson sent the 82d Airborne Division and other forces to the Dominican Republic. Subsequently, the Inter-American Peace Force was organized there, and by the autumn the only United States combat force left was one brigade of three battalions from the 82d Division. The Joint Chiefs of Staff asked that the brigade be returned to the United States so that the 82d could resume its place in the strategic force as a full-strength unit. In response, the Army selected the 196th Infantry Brigade to replace the divisional brigade in June 1966. But by the time the 196th had completed its training, stability had returned to the Dominican Republic, and the president withdrew all United States forces from the country.[17]

To meet Westmoreland's continuing demand for more troops in Vietnam, President Johnson then approved the transfer of the 196th Infantry Brigade to Southeast Asia. As the unit had been trained for street fighting and riot control, the 196th had to undergo additional training for combat in Southeast Asia. Also, support units normally attached to separate brigades in Vietnam had to be organized, including signal and military police platoons and chemical, military intelligence, Army Security Agency, military history, and public information detachments. The training process began in June, and by August 1966 the 196th had deployed to Vietnam.[18]

## *Expansion of the Force*

After July 1966 no further increase took place in the number of divisions and brigades until the spring of 1967. In March of that year, responding to Westmoreland's request for additional forces, the Army Staff considered organizing either an infantry or a mechanized infantry brigade for service along the demilitarized zone between North Vietnam and South Vietnam. The original request called for a mechanized infantry brigade with personnel drawn mostly from the 1st and 2d Armored Divisions at Fort Hood. Before the unit could be activated, Westmoreland decided that he needed a standard separate infantry brigade. On 10 May the 198th Infantry Brigade was activated using personnel from the 1st and 2d Armored Divisions. Two days later, at the insistence of General Ralph E. Haines, Vice Chief of Staff and former commander of the 1st Armored Division, the brigade's three infantry battalions and artillery battalion were inactivated and replaced with units taken from regiments assigned to the 1st and 2d Armored Divisions. In turn, new battalions from those regiments were activated to replace the units taken from the two divisions.[19]

Westmoreland's plan to use the 198th along the demilitarized zone between the two Vietnams went astray. Unable to wait for the brigade to arrive, he established a blocking force in April 1967 with units already in the theater. Designated "Task Force Oregon,"[20] it included the 196th Infantry Brigade; the 3d Brigade, 25th Infantry Division; and the 1st Brigade, 101st Airborne Division.[21]

In August 1967 a complex organizational exchange took place in Vietnam due in large part to the awkward location of units in relation to their parent divisions. Both the 4th and the 25th Infantry Divisions had "orphan" brigades that operated outside their parent division's areas. To correct the problem, Headquarters and Headquarters Company, 3d Brigade, 4th Infantry Division, and the brigade's non–color-bearing elements were transferred (less personnel and equipment) from Tay Ninh to Task Force Oregon at Chu Lai; Headquarters and Headquarters Company, 3d Brigade, 25th Infantry Division, and its non–color-bearing units (less personnel and equipment) concurrently joined the 25th Infantry Division at Tay Ninh. The color-bearing units (infantry and artillery battalions) attached to the brigades were relieved from the divisions in place and reassigned. These administrative actions gave the commander of the 25th Infantry Division operational control of his 3d Brigade for the first time in Vietnam. The 3d Brigade, 4th Infantry Division, however, remained under the operational control of Task Force Oregon.[22]

*3d Brigade, 25th Infantry Division, engages the Viet Cong between Ban Me Thuot and Pleiku.*

Soon after forming Task Force Oregon, Westmoreland decided to replace it with a division. For the unit's designation, he selected the Americal Division because it was to be organized under circumstances similar to those in which that division first had been formed during World War II with National Guard units from Task Force 6814 in New Caledonia. Westmoreland had originally planned to assign the 11th and 198th Infantry Brigades, then preparing to deploy, and the 196th Infantry Brigade, already in Vietnam, to the division. The Army Staff agreed but insisted that the unit's official designation be the 23d Infantry Division rather than "Americal" (the Americal Division had been redesignated as the 23d Infantry Division in 1954). On 25 September 1967 the division was activated to control the 196th Infantry Brigade; the 1st Brigade, 101st Airborne Division; and the 3d Brigade, 4th Infantry Division. The division base was to be activated as requirements were identified.[23]

In December 1967 the 23d Infantry Division received its planned brigades. In addition to the 196th Infantry Brigade, the 11th and 198th Infantry Brigades, reorganized as light infantry units, had arrived in Vietnam and replaced the brigades of the 4th Infantry and 101st Airborne Divisions, which returned to their parent units.[24]

To strengthen the forces in Vietnam, Westmoreland had requested the remainder of the 101st Airborne Division by February 1968. Because of ominous intelligence reports about the enemy's activities, Westmoreland pressured Washington to advance the division's arrival date. Thus, by 13 December 1967, following the longest troop movement by air in history, the "Screaming Eagles" arrived in Vietnam. The division fielded ten airborne infantry battalions, the three that had deployed with the 1st Brigade in 1965 and the seven that arrived in 1967.[25]

To replace the 101st Airborne Division and the 11th Infantry Brigade in the Army strategic contingency forces, the Army activated the 6th Infantry Division, with nine infantry battalions, on 24 November 1967. Initially all units of the division were to be organized at Fort Campbell, Kentucky, but U.S. Army, Pacific, requested that one brigade be transferred to Hawaii to take over the property and nondeployable personnel of the 11th Infantry Brigade. Accordingly, the 6th Infantry Division was split between Fort Campbell (the division base and two brigades) and Schofield Barracks (one brigade), Hawaii.[26]

With the attachment of the 11th Infantry Brigade, originally a component of the 6th Infantry Division, to the 23d Infantry Division in Vietnam, a new designation was needed for the 6th Infantry Division's third brigade headquarters. The staff, in an unprecedented move, decided to use the designation 4th Brigade, 6th Infantry Division, until the 11th could be returned to the division.

January 1968 turned into a month of crises for the nation. On 23 January, after a series of incidents in Korea, the North Koreans seized the intelligence ship *Pueblo* in the Sea of Japan and incarcerated the crew. This resulted in the strengthening of United States air and naval forces there and the authorization of hazardous duty pay for elements of the 2d Infantry Division in Korea. Shortly thereafter the North Vietnamese began their expected offensive during the Tet holiday in Vietnam, shocking both Westmoreland and the nation with its intensity. President Johnson ordered additional forces to Vietnam, including the 3d Brigade (three airborne infantry battalions) of the 82d Airborne Division and a Marine Corps unit. Those units arrived in February, and eventually the 82d's 3d Brigade, organized as a separate brigade, became a part of the standing forces in Vietnam.[27]

Because of other contingency plans the Marine unit had to return to the United States, and Westmoreland asked for a mechanized infantry brigade to replace it. Army Chief of Staff Johnson approved the 1st Brigade, 5th Infantry Division, as the replacement. The unit, reorganized as a separate brigade fielding one battalion each of infantry, mechanized infantry, and armor, arrived in Vietnam in July 1968 and was the last large Army unit to be sent to Southeast Asia (*Table 27*).[28]

The seizure of the *Pueblo*, the Tet offensive, and the need to maintain the strategic force prompted the president to call a limited number of National Guard and Army Reserve units to active duty in the spring of 1968. The call included two brigades from the National Guard, the 29th Infantry Brigade (Hawaii), which reported to Schofield Barracks on 13 May, and the 69th Infantry Brigade (Mechanized) (Kansas), which took up station at Fort Carson. To ease the burden of mobilization, the brigades acquired elements not previously associated with them. The 29th got the 100th Battalion, 442d Infantry, from the Army Reserve, and the 69th included the 2d Battalion, 133d Infantry, from the Iowa National Guard.[29]

Following the Tet offensive and the limited reserve mobilization, the Department of Defense ended the buildup of divisional and brigade units in the

## TABLE 27
### Deployment of Divisions and Brigades to Vietnam

| Unit | Date Arrived in Vietnam |
|---|---|
| 1st Cavalry Division | September 1965 |
| 1st Infantry Division | October 1965 |
|     2d Brigade* | July 1965 |
| 4th Infantry Division | October 1965 |
|     2d Brigade* | August 1966 |
| 1st Brigade, 5th Infantry Division | June 1968 |
| 9th Infantry Division | December 1966 |
|     2d Brigade* | January 1967 |
| 23d Infantry Division | September 1967 |
|     11th Infantry Brigade* | December 1967 |
|     196th Infantry Brigade* | August 1966 |
|     198th Infantry Brigade* | October 1967 |
| 25th Infantry Division | April 1966 |
|     2d Brigade* | January 1966 |
|     3d Brigade* | December 1965 |
| 3d Brigade, 82d Airborne Division | February 1968 |
| 101st Airborne Division | December 1967 |
|     1st Brigade* | July 1965 |
| 173d Airborne Brigade | May 1965 |
| 199th Infantry Brigade | December 1966 |

\* Arrived separately.

active Army. At peak strength the Army had 19 divisions (counting the 3 brigades attached to the 23d as 1 division), with 7 divisions serving in Vietnam, 2 in Korea, 5 in Europe, and 5 in the United States, and 11 brigades, of which 4 were in Vietnam, 2 in Alaska, 1 in the Canal Zone, and 4 in the continental United States.

## *Organizational Changes to Units in Vietnam*

Airmobility gave commanders the ability to concentrate men and their firepower on the Vietnamese battlefield quickly, and the Army planned to organize a second airmobile division as early as 1966. These plans foundered until 1968 because of the aviation needs of other combat units in Vietnam and the general shortage of aviation equipment. But after the 101st Airborne Division arrived in Southeast Asia, U.S. Army, Vietnam, began a phased reorganization of the division into an airmobile configuration, which took over a year to complete.[30]

During the conversion of the 101st, the Army adopted a decentralized approach to aircraft maintenance. Initially the 101st, like the 1st Cavalry Division, was to have a large aircraft maintenance battalion, but the need of company-, battery-, and troop-size aviation units for their own maintenance organizations resulted in a cellular maintenance structure. In the 1st Cavalry Division and 101st Airborne Division an aircraft maintenance detachment was activated to support each company-size aviation unit.[31]

When the 101st was reorganized as an airmobile unit, confusion and contention reigned over its designation. Instructions from Washington renamed the division the 101st Infantry Division (Airmobile) because the designation was thought to accurately describe its mission. Officers in Vietnam opposed the change, and after much discussion the Army Staff sent new instructions redesignating both the 101st Airborne Division and the 1st Cavalry Division as "air cavalry." In July 1968 Westmoreland replaced Harold K. Johnson as Army Chief of Staff, and Westmoreland directed that the divisions retain their historic designations.[32]

Ever conscious of ways to save personnel, U.S. Army, Vietnam, requested permission in September 1968 to reorganize the 23d Infantry Division (the Americal) along the lines of other infantry divisions to save over 500 personnel spaces. The request proposed that the 11th, 196th, and 198th Infantry Brigades be redesignated as the 1st, 2d, and 3d Brigades, 23d Infantry Division, and that a complete division base be organized. Westmoreland, as chief of staff, approved the reorganization of the division but not the numerical redesignation of the brigades. He directed that the brigades be attached rather than assigned as organic elements of the division. His reasons for retaining the separate brigade designations included the complexity of the units' histories and the desire not to change the designations of units serving in Vietnam. On 15 February 1969, the 23d was thus reorganized with a division base resembling that in other infantry divisions, except for the attached brigade headquarters and the omission of the organic cavalry squadron. The 1st Squadron, 1st Cavalry, an element of the 1st Armored Division, had been serving with the "Americal" because General Haines, the former 1st Armored Division commander, had wanted the squadron to represent "Old Ironsides" in Vietnam. The staff chose not to tamper with this arrangement.[33]

To increase firepower, some divisions and brigades received an additional battalion or battalions of infantry without upsetting their structure. As noted above, the 1st Cavalry Division and the 173d Airborne Brigade each had an additional infantry battalion assigned in 1966. The following year the 173d was assigned a fourth infantry battalion, and after the 1968 Tet offensive the 9th Infantry Division and the 11th, 198th, and 199th Infantry Brigades each gained an additional infantry battalion. At the peak of the buildup the combined arms teams in Vietnam fielded eighty-three infantry and armor battalions.[34]

Divisions and brigades deployed to Vietnam with infantry, light infantry, airborne infantry, and airmobile infantry battalions but, responding to the demands of the conflict, U.S. Army, Vietnam, reorganized most of them under modified light infantry tables of organization. Each of these battalions consisted of a headquarters and headquarters company, four rifle companies, and a combat support company. The fourth rifle company provided a unit for base defense and allowed the battalion to operate with three companies outside the base camp.35

Combat brought about several changes in the infantryman's weapons. The light M16 rifle became the standard individual weapon, and a one-man light antitank weapon (LAW) often replaced the heavy and awkward 90-mm. recoilless rifle. Because of the nature of the fighting, heavier infantry weapons, such as the ENTAC, 4.2-inch mortar, and 106-mm. recoilless rifle, saw little service. When used, both the 81-mm. and 4.2-inch mortars were usually "slaved" to fire direction centers at American fire bases. Units did not suffer a loss of effective firepower because their mobility allowed them to concentrate their remaining weapons, while improved field radio communications aided in putting tremendous amounts of supporting fire at their disposal. Given organic, attached, and supporting aviation and signal units, all divisions and brigades had extensive airmobile and communications capabilities.36

Although only one armor company, equipped with 90-mm. self-propelled antitank guns, assigned to a brigade and three divisional armor battalions, equipped with M48A3 tanks, served in Vietnam, divisions and brigades there had considerable armor. Each divisional reconnaissance squadron, except for the two in the airmobile divisions, had tanks and reconnaissance vehicles. The latter carried additional machine guns and gun shields, permitting the reconnaissance squadrons to function as armor. Also, the eight mechanized infantry battalions in Vietnam frequently performed as light armor units, using modified armored personnel carriers. By 1969 some reconnaissance and mechanized infantry units employed Sheridans, the M551 armored reconnaissance assault vehicles, in place of the light tank and armored personnel carriers. The Sheridan filled the need for a light tracked vehicle with greater firepower than the M113 armored personnel carrier.37

Artillery, the third combat arm assigned to divisions and brigades, also underwent modifications in Vietnam. In the two airmobile divisions, a 155-mm. howitzer battalion was permanently attached after the 1st Cavalry Division demonstrated that the heavy howitzer could be moved by helicopter. Because of the large operational areas of divisions and separate brigades, their direct support artillery battalions often had four firing batteries, which were created in various ways. In the 173d Airborne Brigade, a fourth battery was authorized; in the 23d Infantry Division, each direct support battalion consisted of two five-gun and two four-gun batteries; and in the 1st Infantry Division, one or two 4.2-inch mortar platoons were attached to direct support artillery battalions as Batteries D and E.38

By mid-1969 the seven divisions and four separate brigades in Vietnam reached their final configuration (*Table 28*). The ROAD building-block concept worked well, particularly in a war that was fought by brigades with divisions serving in a corps-like role. The Army, however, had difficulty meeting the demands of commanders for more tactical maneuver units because there was no pool of separate battalions to draw upon when needed for additional support.

TABLE 28

Maneuver Elements Assigned to Divisions and Brigades in Vietnam
30 June 1969

| Division/Brigade | Inf | Mech Inf | Mod Inf | Armor | Total |
|---|---|---|---|---|---|
| 1st Cavalry Division | | | 9 | | 9 |
| 1st Infantry Division | | 2 | 7 | | 9 |
| 4th Infantry Division | | 1 | 8 | 1 | 10 |
| 1st Brigade, 5th Infantry Division | | 1 | 1 | 1 | 3 |
| 9th Infantry Division | 2 | 1 | 7 | | 10 |
| 23d Infantry Division | | | 11 | | 11 |
| 25th Infantry Division | | 3 | 6 | 1 | 10 |
| 1st Brigade, 82d Airborne Division | | | 3 | | 3 |
| 101st Airborne Division | | | 10 | | 10 |
| 173d Airborne Brigade | | | 4 | * | 4 |
| 199th Infantry Brigade | | | 4 | | 4 |
| Total | 2 | 8 | 70 | 3 | 83 |

* A company.

## *Divisions and Brigades in Other Commands*

The Army directed its major effort in the mid- and late- 1960s toward Vietnam, and divisions and brigades in other commands supported that endeavor. All active duty divisions and brigades in the United States furnished units or men for service in Vietnam, and as a result most fell below combat-ready status. Ultimately the maneuver element mix in the 1st and 2d Armored Divisions was reduced to four tank and four mechanized infantry battalions, which was considerably below the prototype of six tank and five infantry battalions. To maintain them as fully manned armored divisions, the Army designated one mechanized infantry and two armor battalions from the National Guard as "round-out" units for each. Round-out units maintained a close association with their designated divisions, even taking annual field training with them, but were not on active federal service.[39]

Although the Army did not withdraw any divisions from Europe for service in Vietnam, U.S. Army, Europe, also contributed to the combat effort. As already noted, the cadre for the 199th Infantry Brigade had come from Europe. Beginning in February 1966 the Army levied the command in Europe for officers and enlisted personnel with specific skills, particularly junior grade and noncommissioned officers. Within a year 1,800 soldiers a month were departing for duty in Vietnam to meet the levy. This drain on the European forces severely affected unit leadership and the readiness of the remaining forces.[40]

# FLEXIBLE RESPONSE 337

In the armored and mechanized infantry divisions designed to fight in Europe, aviation battalions were eliminated after a study on the use of aircraft rationalized that heavy divisions did not need extensive air lines of communications. Fifty-seven helicopters remained in each division, spread throughout the reconnaissance squadron, maintenance battalion, division artillery, and division and brigade headquarters companies. The operation of the divisional airfield passed to a new transportation detachment attached to the supply and transport battalion. Although not stated, the forty aircraft removed from each armored and mechanized infantry division were needed in Vietnam.[41]

Notwithstanding personnel and equipment problems in Europe, divisions still had to be prepared to counter Soviet mechanized forces, primarily through increased firepower. In the 3d, 8th, and 24th Infantry Divisions an armor battalion replaced a mechanized infantry battalion in 1966. (Armor battalions required fewer people than mechanized infantry battalions but had more firepower.) The change gave the divisions a maneuver mix of four armor and six mechanized infantry battalions. In those battalions, as well as in the reconnaissance squadron and the artillery battalions, an air defense section that used the new shoulder-fired, low-altitude, Redeye guided missile was introduced. In the artillery of both the armored and mechanized infantry divisions, self-propelled 155-mm. howitzers replaced 105-mm. pieces because the larger howitzers could fire both conventional and nuclear warheads and had a longer range. The capability of firing nuclear rounds from conventional artillery tubes also eliminated the need for the jeep-mounted Davy Crocketts.[42]

Although the military and political leadership still perceived a Soviet threat in Western Europe, the first reduction in the number of Army divisions stationed in Europe since the beginning of NATO took place during the Vietnam conflict. The desire of the United Kingdom, the Federal Republic of Germany, and the United States to realign their balance of payments precipitated the reduction. By mutual agreement one division (less one brigade) and some smaller units in Germany were to return to the United States but were to remain under the operational control of the commander in Europe and return periodically to Germany for training exercises. The divisional brigade that remained in Germany was to be replaced by one from the United States during each training exercise. The staff named the plan REFORGER, "Return of Forces to Germany." During the first half of 1968 the 24th Infantry Division, without its 3d Brigade, moved to Fort Riley.[43]

The following December the Department of Defense announced that the first REFORGER exercise would take place in early 1969 but, to prevent personnel turbulence, no rotation of brigades would occur. Since the Warsaw Pact countries had invaded Czechoslovakia the previous August, the timing of the exercise, between 5 January and 23 March 1969, demonstrated to NATO that the United States would honor its commitments.[44]

Special mission brigades throughout the world also contributed to the forces in Vietnam. In late 1965 an infantry battalion of the 197th Infantry Brigade, which supported the Infantry School, was inactivated at Fort Benning to provide personnel for expanding the Army in Vietnam. In a personnel-saving action, the Combat Developments Command's 194th Armored Brigade at Fort Ord was replaced by a battalion-size combat team and reorganized at Fort Knox to support the Armor School in place of the 16th Armor Group. Under the new configuration the brigade included one mechanized infantry and two armored battalions. The 171st and 172d Infantry Brigades in Alaska each lost their aviation company, and in the 193d Infantry Brigade in the Canal Zone, the airborne battalion was replaced with a standard infantry battalion. (*Table 29* shows the composition of divisions and brigades outside Vietnam in 1969.)[45]

In 1968 Secretary of Defense Clark Clifford decided to reduce forces in the continental United States to four divisions because the budget did not permit filling and maintaining five divisions. He directed the inactivation of the 6th Infantry Division, the activation of a brigade to replace the 82d's 3d Brigade in Vietnam, and higher manning levels for the 69th Infantry Brigade attached to the 5th Infantry Division at Fort Carson and the 29th Infantry Brigade at Schofield Barracks. The 6th Division was inactivated on 25 July 1968, and the rest of Clifford's proposals were accomplished by early 1969.[46]

Four weeks after the 6th Infantry Division was inactivated, the Vice Chief of Staff, General Bruce Palmer, Jr., considered reactivating the division in response to the invasion of Czechoslovakia by the Warsaw Pact armies. Lacking men to organize the unit, the staff considered the division's reactivation a "show the flag" action. The plan was eventually dropped because it was an empty gesture. Thus, the strategic reserve forces in the United States stood at four divisions in September 1968 and remained at that level until the close of the Vietnam era.[47]

During the 1960s the Department of Defense continued to scrutinize the reserve forces and to question the number of divisions and brigades as well as the redundancy of maintaining two reserve components, the National Guard and the Army Reserve. In 1967 Secretary of Defense McNamara decided that 15 combat divisions in the Army National Guard were unnecessary and cut the number to 8 divisions (1 mechanized infantry, 2 armored, and 5 infantry), but increased the number of brigades from 7 to 18 (1 airborne, 1 armored, 2 mechanized infantry, and 14 infantry). The loss of the divisions did not set well with the states. Their objections included the inadequate maneuver element mix for those that remained and the end to the practice of rotating divisional commands among the states that supported them. Under the proposal, the remaining division commanders were to reside in the state of the division base. No reduction, however, in total Army National Guard strength was to take place, which convinced the governors to accept the plan.[48]

The states reorganized their forces accordingly between 1 December 1967 and 1 May 1968. All remaining divisions were shared by two or more states (*Table 30*). Divisional brigades located in states without the division base consist-

## TABLE 29

### Maneuver Element Mix of Divisions and Brigades on Active Duty Outside Vietnam, 30 June 1969

| Unit | Location | Inf | Mech Inf | Abn Inf | Armor | Total |
|---|---|---|---|---|---|---|
| 1st Armored Division | Fort Hood, Tex. | | 4 | | 4 | 8 |
| 2d Armored Division | Fort Hood, Tex. | | 4 | | 4 | 8 |
| 2d Infantry Division | Korea | 5 | 2 | | 2 | 9 |
| 3d Armored Division | Germany | | 5 | | 6 | 11 |
| 3d Infantry Division | Germany | | 6 | | 4 | 10 |
| 4th Armored Division | Germany | | 5 | | 6 | 11 |
| 5th Infantry Division | Fort Carson,[1] Colo. | | 8 | | 2 | 10 |
| 7th Infantry Division | Korea | 5 | 2 | | 2 | 9 |
| 8th Infantry Division | Germany | | 6 | | 4 | 10 |
| 24th Infantry Division | Fort Riley,[2] Kans. | | 6 | | 3 | 9 |
| 82d Airborne Division | Fort Bragg,[3] N.C. | | | 9 | | 9 |
| 29th Infantry Brigade | Hawaii | 3 | | | | 3 |
| 171st Infantry Brigade | Alaska | | 2 | | | 2 |
| 172d Infantry Brigade | Alaska | | 2 | | | 2 |
| 193d Infantry Brigade | Canal Zone | 3 | | | | 3 |
| 194th Armored Brigade | Fort Knox, Ky. | 1 | | | 2 | 3 |
| TOTAL | | 17 | 52 | 9 | 39 | 117 |

[1] Does not include the 1st Brigade in Vietnam, but does include the 69th Infantry Brigade.
[2] One brigade in Germany.
[3] Does not include the 1st Brigade in Vietnam, but does include the 4th Brigade, 82d Airborne Division.

## TABLE 30
## National Guard Divisions and Brigades, 1968

| Unit | Location |
| --- | --- |
| 26th Infantry Division | Massachusetts and Connecticut |
| 28th Infantry Division | Pennsylvania, Maryland, and Virginia |
| 30th Armored Division | Alabama, Mississippi, and Tennessee |
| 30th Infantry Division (M)* | North Carolina, South Carolina, and Georgia |
| 38th Infantry Division | Indiana, Michigan, and Ohio |
| 42d Infantry Division | New York and Pennsylvania |
| 47th Infantry Division | Illinois, Iowa, and Minnesota |
| 50th Armored Division | New Jersey, New York, and Vermont |
| 29th Infantry Brigade | Hawaii and California |
| 32d Infantry Brigade | Wisconsin |
| 33d Infantry Brigade | Illinois |
| 36th Infantry Brigade | Texas |
| 39th Infantry Brigade | Arkansas |
| 40th Armored Brigade | California |
| 40th Infantry Brigade | California |
| 41st Infantry Brigade | Oregon |
| 45th Infantry Brigade | Oklahoma |
| 49th Infantry Brigade | California |
| 53d Infantry Brigade | Florida |
| 67th Infantry Brigade (M)* | Nebraska |
| 69th Infantry Brigade | Kansas |
| 71st Airborne Brigade | Texas |
| 72d Infantry Brigade (M)* | Texas |
| 81st Infantry Brigade | Washington |
| 92d Infantry Brigade | Puerto Rico |
| 256th Infantry Brigade | Louisiana |

*Mechanized.

ed of the maneuver elements, an artillery battalion, an engineer company, a medical company, a forward support maintenance company, and an administrative section. The remainder of each division was located in the state with the division base. Infantry divisions had ten maneuver battalions, as did the mechanized infantry divisions, except the 47th, which had eleven. The 30th and 50th Armored Divisions had ten and eleven maneuver battalions, respectively. A single state maintained each of the eighteen separate brigades, except for the 29th (Hawaii), which had elements in the continental United States.[49]

The Army Reserve brigades also felt McNamara's axe. Initially the Defense Department planned no combat forces for the Army Reserve, but congressional opposition saved the 157th (Pennsylvania), 187th (Massachusetts), and 205th (Minnesota and Iowa) Infantry Brigades. All their expensive armor and mechanized infantry battalions, however, were eliminated, leaving each brigade with only three standard infantry battalions. In the western part of the country, the poorly manned 191st Infantry Brigade fell out of the force, with its headquarters being inactivated in February 1968 at Helena, Montana. The following June an armor battalion was restored to the 157th Infantry Brigade to increase its capabilities.[50]

Concurrent with reorganizing the reserves, Secretary of the Army Stanley Resor authorized a new Selected Reserve Force in 1967 to lessen the heavy burden of the accelerated training program. All units in the original force retained their equipment but lost their priority for new equipment. The new "selected reserve" force, designed specifically to reinforce the Army in Southeast Asia, consisted of the 26th and 42d Infantry Divisions and the 39th, 40th, 157th, and 256th Infantry Brigades. But two years later the secretary abolished the force, seeking to bring all National Guard and Army Reserve units to the same readiness level.[51]

The Defense Department did not question the number of training divisions in the Army Reserve, but they were reorganized to conform to Regular Army training centers. In 1966 the Continental Army Command developed new tables of organization that eliminated regiments in training divisions and replaced them with brigades (*Chart 41*). The division fielded two basic combat training brigades, each consisting of four battalions with five training companies each; an advanced individual training brigade, three battalions with three to six companies or batteries of field artillery, armor, infantry, and engineers each; and a combat support training brigade, two battalions of five companies each, and a committee directorate. All basic training instructors were concentrated in a committee group. Along with the division headquarters and headquarters company, the division had support and special training companies and a noncommissioned officer/drill sergeant academy. These changes enhanced the training division's ability for self-sustainment in both reserve and active duty status, but it could not train as many men under the new structure. All thirteen divisions were organized under the new tables by 1968.[52]

## *Retrenchment*

On 8 June 1969, President Richard Nixon announced that 25,000 men would be withdrawn from Vietnam as part of a "Vietnamization" effort, which involved transferring increased responsibility for conducting all aspects of the war to the Republic of Vietnam. An underlying cause was the disillusionment of the American people with a war that seemed permanently stalemated. Popular sentiment favored the return of U.S. forces from Vietnam and a retrenchment of U.S. involvement in world affairs, particularly in Asia.[53]

# CHART 41—Training Division, 1966

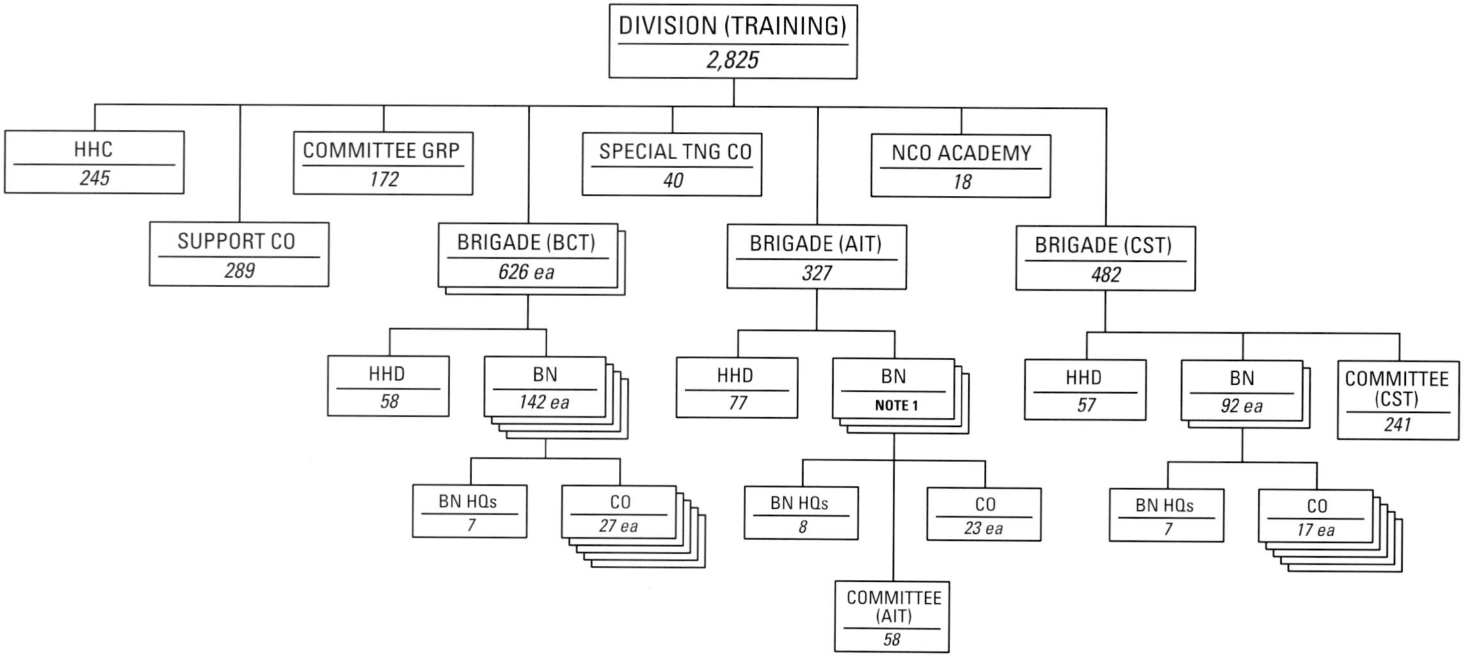

DIVISION (TRAINING) — 2,825

- HHC — 245
- SUPPORT CO — 289
- COMMITTEE GRP — 172
- BRIGADE (BCT) — 626 ea
  - HHD — 58
  - BN — 142 ea
    - BN HQs — 7
    - CO — 27 ea
- SPECIAL TNG CO — 40
- BRIGADE (AIT) — 327
  - HHD — 77
  - BN — NOTE 1
    - BN HQs — 8
    - CO — 23 ea
  - COMMITTEE (AIT) — 58
- NCO ACADEMY — 18
- BRIGADE (CST) — 482
  - HHD — 57
  - BN — 92 ea
    - BN HQs — 7
    - CO — 17 ea
  - COMMITTEE (CST) — 241

[1] Each battalion will contain 3-6 of any of the following types of companies/batteries (AIT): Infantry, Field Artillery, Armor, or Engineer.

*Elements of the 9th Infantry Division begin departing Vietnam, July 1969.*

General Creighton Abrams, commander of U.S. Army, Vietnam, designated two brigades of the 9th Infantry Division serving in the Mekong Delta to be the first combined arms units to leave. In July 1969 the 2d Brigade, 9th Infantry Division, departed Vietnam and was inactivated at Fort Riley. The following month the division base and the 1st Brigade moved to Hawaii to become a part of the Pacific reserve. The 3d Brigade, 9th Infantry Division, was reorganized as a separate brigade and continued to serve in Vietnam.[54]

The incremental redeployments from Vietnam between 1969 and 1972 caused considerable confusion, but less than in previous conflicts where demobilization had to be accomplished rapidly. Shortly after the withdrawal began, Acting Secretary of the Army Thaddeus R. Beal announced a reduction in total Army forces for economic reasons. One result was the immediate inactivation of the 9th Infantry Division, except for its brigade in Vietnam. To replace the 29th Infantry Brigade in Hawaii, which was to be released from federal service along with other reserve units in December 1969, the U.S. Army, Pacific, activated the 4th Brigade, 25th Infantry Division, on 6 December and returned the 29th Infantry Brigade to state control on 13 December. When disclosing the formation of the new brigade, Secretary of Defense Clifford stressed that the 25th Infantry Division was not returning from Vietnam, explaining that the designation was selected only as a tribute to the division's service in Vietnam. Nevertheless, the announcement caused some rumors that the 25th would soon be home.[55]

Meanwhile, in September 1969 President Nixon announced another troop withdrawal. The only large unit in that increment was the 3d Brigade, 82d Airborne Division, which returned to Fort Bragg in December to replace the division's 4th Brigade. As noted, the Army released the reserve units in December, including the 69th Infantry Brigade. To maintain a full division at Fort Carson, the Fifth U.S. Army activated the 4th Brigade, 5th Infantry Division, a Regular Army unit.[56]

A pattern of redeployment soon emerged.[57] As one group of units left Vietnam the president announced another reduction. Under redeployment policies, selected units ceased to receive replacements sixty days before leaving the command; their equipment was turned in for storage or redistribution; and personnel were generally reassigned elsewhere in Vietnam. Usually each returning unit had only a small detachment to safeguard its colors or flags and essential records. Few soldiers had opportunity to participate in any welcome-home ceremonies. Unneeded company-size or smaller units were inactivated in Vietnam, while battalion-size and larger units, including divisions and brigades, returned to the United States for retention or inactivation. The Army generally followed these policies over the next two and one-half years as divisions and brigades left Vietnam (*Table 31*).[58]

To accommodate some redeploying units, the Army rearranged the location of divisional designations in the Regular Army. In 1970 the 1st Infantry Division replaced the 24th Infantry Division at Fort Riley and in Germany, and the 4th Infantry Division succeeded the 5th Infantry Division at Fort Carson. The 1st Brigade, 25th Infantry Division, replaced the 4th Brigade, 25th Infantry Division, in Hawaii. The 1st and 4th Infantry Divisions simultaneously became mechanized infantry units, adapting to a NATO reinforcement role. In the 1st, the maneuver elements consisted of 4 armor and 6 mechanized infantry battalions, while the 4th included 1 infantry, 2 armor, and 7 mechanized infantry battalions.[59]

Another complex exchange of divisions took place in 1971 when the 1st Cavalry Division returned to the United States. At that time the Army planned to test a new air cavalry combat brigade in conjunction with airmobile and armor units. The staff had programmed the 1st Armored Division at Fort Hood as the test unit, but when the 1st Cavalry Division returned from Southeast Asia it replaced the armored division, which was to be inactivated. Protests by former members of "Old Ironsides" against taking the unit designation out of the active force led Westmoreland, now Army chief of staff, to retain the division on the active rolls by transferring it to Germany where it replaced the 4th Armored Division. The 1st Cavalry Division, less its 3d Brigade, which remained in Vietnam, was reorganized at Fort Hood.[60]

The 173d Airborne Brigade posed a problem for redeployment planners because it had been the first large unit sent to Vietnam. They wanted to retain it in the force, but the brigade was no longer needed in Okinawa as negotiations were under way to return the island to Japan. Westmoreland decided to station the brigade at Fort Campbell until the 101st Airborne Division returned and to use the unit or some of its elements later to reorganize the 101st. The 173d

TABLE 31

Redeployment of Divisions and Brigades From Vietnam

| Unit | Date Redeployed | Remarks |
|---|---|---|
| 1st Cavalry Division (less 3d Brigade) | April 1971 | Replaced the 1st Armored Division at Fort Hood, Texas |
| 3d Brigade | June 1972 | Replaced the 4th Brigade, 1st Cavalry Division |
| 1st Infantry Division | April 1970 | Replaced the 24th Infantry Division at Fort Riley, Kansas, and in Germany |
| 4th Infantry Division (less 3d Brigade) | December 1970 | Replaced the 5th Infantry Division at Fort Carson, Colorado |
| 3d Brigade | April 1970 | Replaced the 4th Brigade, 5th Infantry Division, at Fort Carson, Colorado |
| 1st Brigade, 5th Infantry Division | August 1971 | Inactivated |
| 9th Infantry Division (less 3d Brigade) | July 1969 | Inactivated |
| 3d Brigade | October 1970 | Inactivated |
| 23d Infantry Division | November 1971 | Inactivated |
| 11th Infantry Brigade | November 1971 | Inactivated |
| 198th Infantry Brigade | November 1971 | Inactivated |
| 25th Infantry Division (less 2d Brigade) | December 1970 | 1st Brigade replaced the 4th Brigade, 25th Infantry Division, at Schofield Barracks, Hawaii; concurrently division headquarters and 3d Brigade reduced to zero strength |
| 2d Brigade | April 1971 | Reduced to zero strength |
| 3d Brigade, 82d Airborne Division | December 1969 | Replaced the 4th Brigade, 82d Airborne Division at Fort Bragg, North Carolina |
| 101st Airborne Division (less 1st, 2d, and 3d Brigades) | March 1972 | Returned to Fort Campbell, Kentucky |
| 1st Brigade | January 1972 | Returned to Fort Campbell, Kentucky |
| 2d Brigade | February 1972 | Returned to Fort Campbell, Kentucky |
| 3d Brigade | December 1971 | Returned to Fort Campbell, Kentucky |
| 173d Airborne Brigade | August 1971 | Inactivated at Fort Campbell, 1972 |
| 196th Infantry Brigade | June 1972 | Inactivated |

arrived at its new post in September 1971, and the following January the brigade headquarters was inactivated while some of the brigade's elements were reassigned to the 101st.[61]

In June 1972 the last two U.S. combat brigades, the 3d Brigade, 1st Cavalry Division, and the 196th Infantry Brigade, left Vietnam. The cavalry brigade rejoined its parent unit at Fort Hood, replacing the 4th Brigade, 1st Cavalry Division, while the 196th was inactivated at Oakland, California. The last brigade element, the 3d Battalion, 21st Infantry, departed Vietnam in August 1972, marking the end of U.S. Army divisions' and separate brigades' direct participation in the war in Vietnam.[62]

Shortly after the withdrawal of troops from Vietnam had begun in 1969, President Nixon adopted a new doctrine for military involvement in world affairs. He based the "Nixon Doctrine" on several principles: the United States would honor all treaty commitments; it would provide a shield if a nuclear power threatened one of its allies or a nation whose survival was considered vital to U.S. national interest; and it would offer military and economic assistance to its allies when requested. But the United States expected a nation directly threatened to assume primary responsibility for its own defense. Following these principles, Nixon directed a 20,000-man reduction of Army forces in Korea by 30 June 1971. To accomplish that goal, the 7th Infantry Division concluded its 21-year stay in Korea and returned to Fort Lewis, where it was inactivated on 2 April. Its departure left only the 2d Infantry Division, now reorganized to consist of two armor and six infantry battalions, augmented by Korean forces.[63]

With a smaller Army the nation could no longer maintain two brigades in Alaska, and Westmoreland decided to eliminate one. In September 1969 both brigades had been reorganized from mechanized to light infantry as modernization and cost-saving measures. U.S. Army, Alaska, chose to inactivate the 171st Infantry Brigade and reorganize the 172d. Under the new alignment a light infantry battalion and the reconnaissance troop were stationed at Fort Wainwright, while two light infantry battalions and the remainder of the brigade base were at Fort Richardson. The reduction of forces in Alaska was completed by November 1972.[64]

By May 1972 post-Vietnam retrenchment had cut the active forces by about 650,000 men from its peak wartime figure of 1.5 million. The number of Regular Army divisions fell to twelve, and only four special-mission brigades remained. The divisions, particularly those in the United States, were far from being effective fighting teams. The vicissitudes of the war in Vietnam and the reductions in the size of the Army combined to erode combat effectiveness. The decline in unit capabilities had been less abrupt than in 1919 or 1945–46 but just as alarming.

The years between 1965 and 1972 had been tumultuous for both the Army and the nation. Organizationally, however, the ROAD concept had proved sound. The active Army increased more than 66 percent during this period, and divisions and brigades had been tailored for various missions within various regional commands. Light units campaigned effectively in Vietnam, heavy units continued to meet NATO commitments in Europe, and Army forces in the United States covered contingencies for all commands. The major problem for the Army was the acquisition of personnel and equipment. All divisions and brigades, except for those in Vietnam, suffered a decline in readiness, the price of meeting the demands of the conflict. Soldiers were withdrawn from Vietnam as individuals, and most units returned to the United States as paper organizations. The Army appeared to have solved its organizational problems associated with flexible response, but it had not come to grips with its perennial difficulty, shortages of human and materiel resources.

## Notes

1 *Public Papers of the Presidents of the United States, Lyndon B. Johnson, 1965* (Washington, D.C.: Government Printing Office, 1966), pp. 461, 736; 1969, p. 77.

2 Johnson, *Public Papers, 1965*, p. 495; U. S. G. Sharp and W. C. Westmoreland, *Report on the War in Vietnam: 1964–1968* (Washington, D.C.: Government Printing Office, 1969), pp. 275–76; Hermes, "Vietnam Buildup," ch. 5, pp. 34–38.

3 Richard P. Weinert, *The Role of USCONARC in the Army Buildup, FY 1966* (Fort Monroe, Va.: U.S. Continental Army Command, 1967), pp. 113–18; Ltr, TAG to CGs, First and Fifth U.S. Armies, 30 Sep 65, sub: Reorganization of the 1st Infantry Division, AGAO-O (M) (20 Sep 65) DCSPER, 1st Inf Div file, DAMH-HSO.

4 Donn A. Starry, *Mounted Combat in Vietnam* (Washington, D.C.: Government Printing Office, 1978), pp. 54–58.

5 Johnson, *Public Papers, 1965*, p. 795; Hermes, "Vietnam Buildup," ch. 5, pp. 2–11; "Army Units Plan Swift Activation," *Washington Post*, 6 Aug 1965.

6 Weinert, *Army Buildup, 1966*, pp. 82–84; TOE 77–100T, Separate Light Infantry Brigade, 1965; Ltr, TAG to CG, First U.S. Army, 7 Oct 65, sub: Change in Status of STRAF Units, AGAO-O (M) (21 Sep 65) DCSPER, and Fact Sheet (OSD 1078), ACSFOR for White House, The 196th Infantry Brigade has achieved a Combat Ready Posture, 20 Jun 66, both 196th Inf Bde file, DAMH-HSO.

7 TOE 7–175T, Infantry Battalion, Light Infantry Division or Light Infantry Brigade, 1965.

8 Msg, DCSPER to CG, CONARC, DA 748172, 22 Jan 66, sub: Activation of the 9th Infantry Division, Msg, ACSFOR to CG, CONARC, DA 748332, 24 Jan 66, same subject, Msg, CG, Fifth U.S. Army, to CG, CONARC, 161806Z Feb 66, same subject, Ltr, TAG to CG, Fifth U.S. Army, 18 Feb 66, same subject, all 9th Inf Div file, DAMH-HSO; Richard P. Weinert, *The Role USCONARC in the Army Buildup, FY 1967* (Fort Monroe, Va.: U.S. Continental Army Command, 1968), p. 73–76.

9 William F. Fulton, *Riverine Operations, 1966–1969* (Washington, D.C.: Government Printing Office, 1973), pp. 26–41, 51–60; Ltr, TAG to CG, Fifth Army, and CinC, USARPAC, 21 Mar 67, sub: Reorganization of Elements of the 9th Infantry Division, AGSD-C (M) (21 Oct 66) ACSFOR, 2d Bn, 47th Inf, file, DAMH-HSO.

10 Weinert, *Army Buildup, 1966*, pp. 97–99; Hermes, "Vietnam Buildup," ch. 13, pp. 34–38; Ltr, TAG to CG, Third U.S. Army, 17 Jun 66, sub: Activation of the 199th Infantry Brigade, AGSD-C (M) (3 Jun 66) ACSFOR, and The 199th Light Infantry Brigade (Sep) "Redcatcher," undated, Ms, both 199th Inf Bde file, DAMH-HSO; Sharp and Westmoreland, *Report of the War in Vietnam*, p. 129.

11 Ltr, TAG to CinC, USARPAC, 21 Jul 66, sub: Activation of the 11th Infantry Brigade, AGSD-C (M) (21 Jul 66) ACSFOR, and Joe F. Galle, "A History of the 11th Infantry Brigade, 1 July 1966–1 May 1970" (3d Military History Detachment, 1970?), p. 9, Ms, both 11th Inf Bde file, DAMH-HSO; SS, ACSFOR for CofS, 1 Apr 66, sub: Brigade Activations, FOR PP TP, Memo, ACSFOR for VCofS, 16 Oct 67, sub: Activation of the 6th Infantry Division, Incl 1, FOR PP TP, and Memo for Record, OCMH, 29 Sep 67, same subject, all 6th Inf Div file, DAMH-HSO.

12 Starry, *Mounted Combat*, p. 58; Ltr, TAG to CinC, USARPAC, 26 Jan 66, sub: Reorganization of the 25th Infantry Division, AGAO-O (M) (26 Jan 66) ACSFOR, and Ltr, TAG to CinC, USARPAC, 10 Mar 66, sub: Reorganization of Elements of the 25th Infantry Division, AGSD-C (M) (10 Mar 66) ACSFOR, both 25th Inf Div file, DAMH-HSO; Ltr, TAG to CG, U.S. Army, Alaska, 10 Jan 66, sub: Activation of Units, AGAO-O (M) (10 Jan 66), AG Reference files, DAMH-HSO; Hermes, "Vietnam Buildup," ch. 13, pp. 1–13.

13 Ltr, TAG to CG, Sixth U.S. Army, 29 Dec 65, sub: Reorganization of the 4th Infantry Division, AGAO-O (M) (12 Nov 65) DCSPER, 4th Inf Div file, DAMH-HSO; Weinert, *Army Buildup*, 1966, pp. 122–25; Hermes, "Vietnam Buildup," ch. 13, pp. 27–34.

14 Weinert, *Army Buildup, 1966*, pp. 99–101; Hermes, "Vietnam Buildup," ch. 13, pp. 14–18; Ltr, TAG to CGs, Third and Fifth U.S. Armies, 20 Apr 66, sub: Activation of Aviation Units, AGSD-

C (M) (13 Apr 66) ACSFOR, 5th Bn, 7th Cav file, DAMH-HSO. The subject of the letter is the activation of aviation units, but it pertains to the activation of infantry and cavalry units.

15 Ltr, TAG to Chief, NGB, and other addresses, 9 Oct 65, sub: Increased Readiness of the Selected Reserve Component Force, AGAM-P (M) (8 Oct 65) ORC (Office of Reserve Components) -OPT (Organization, Plans and Training)-OF, Selected Reserve Force file, DAMH-HSO; "Reserve Units In Selected Reserve Force," *Army Reserve Magazine* 11 (Dec 1965): 4–6; Ltr, NGB to AG, California, 1 Nov 65, sub: Reorganization of California ARNG, 1965, to Include SRF Units, NG-AROTO 1002-California, Ltr, NGB to AG, Texas, 24 Jan 66, sub: Reorganization of Texas ARNG to Include SRF units, NG-AROTO 1002-01-Texas, Ltr, NGB to AG, Washington, 28 Oct 65, sub: Reorganization of the Washington ARNG, 1965, to Include SRF Units, NG-AROTO 1002-01-Washington, and Ltr, NGB to AG, Oregon, 28 Oct 65, sub: Reorganization of the Oregon ARNG, 1965, to Include SRF Units, NG-AROTO 1002-01-Oregon, all NGB Reference files, DAMH-HSO.

16 Ltr, TAG to Chief, Organized Reserve Components, 13 Nov 65, sub: Inactivation of USAR Reinforcing Reserve Units, AGAM (M), Selected Reserve Force file, DAMH-HSO.

17 "Stability Operations Dominican Republic," pt. I, vol. 1, ch. II, p. 1, Ms, DAMH-HSR; Hermes, "Vietnam Buildup," ch. 2, pp. 34–36, ch. 15, pp. 1–4.

18 Weinert, *Army Buildup, 1966*, pp. 85–88; *Department of Defense Annual Report, 1967*, p. 144.

19 Weinert, *Army Buildup, 1967*, pp. 97–101; Telephone information request sheets, sub: Composition of the 198th Infantry Brigade, 2 and 5 May 1967, Msg DA 813926 to CG, CONARC, 9 May 67, sub: Organization of the 198th Inf Bde, and Memo for Record, undated, sub: Evolution of 198th Inf Bde, all 198th Inf Bde file, DAMH-HSO.

20 Task Force Oregon was named for the home state of its commander, Maj Gen William E. Rosson.

21 William C. Westmoreland, *A Soldier Reports* (Garden City, N.J.: Doubleday and Co., 1976), p. 201.

22 Msg, USARV to USARPAC, 181303 May 67, sub: 3d Brigades, 4th and 25th Infantry Division, Msg, ACSFOR to CinC, USARPAC, DA 824266, 192355Z Jul 67, same subject, GO 144, USARPAC, 1967, Ltr, TAG to CinC, USARPAC, 12 Sep 67, sub: Change in Status of USARPAC Units, AGSD-C (M) (1 Sep 67) ACSFOR, all 3d Bde, 25th Inf Div file, DAMH-HSO.

23 SS, ACSFOR for CofS, 7 Sep 67, sub: Americal Division, FOR PP TP, Memo for Record, 29 Sep 67, sub: Organization and Activation of the 23d Infantry Division, and GO 175, USARPAC, 20 Sep 1967, all 23d Inf Div file, DAMH-HSO.

24 Ltr, TAG to CinC, USARPAC, 29 Sep 67, sub: Change in Status of Units, AGSD-C (20 Sep 67) ACSFOR, Ltr, TAG to CG, CONARC, 28 Sep 67, sub: Reorganization of the 198th Infantry Brigade, AGSD-C (M) (21 Sep 67) ACSFOR, both AG Reference files, DAMH-HSO; "For Freedom Under the Southern Cross," *Americal* 1 (May 1968): 2–6.

25 Sharp and Westmoreland, *Report on the War in Vietnam*, p. 156; News Release, 1170–67, Arrival of 101st Airborne Division in Vietnam, 13 Dec 67, and Ltr, TAG to CG, Third U.S. Army, 30 Nov 67, sub: Reorganization of Elements of the 101st Airborne Division, AGSD-C (M) (15 Nov 67) ACSFOR, both 101st Abn Div file, DAMH-HSO.

26 SS, ACSFOR for CofS, 18 Oct 67, sub: Activation of the 6th Infantry Division, FOR PP TP, Msg, DA ACSFOR for CG, CONARC, and CinC, USARPAC, 837848, 261426Z Oct 67, same subject, Msg, CinC, USARPAC, to ACSFOR, 062056 Nov 67, same subject, and GO 358, Third U.S. Army, 1967, all 6th Inf Div file, DAMH-HSO.

27 W. W. Rostow, *The Diffusion of Power* (New York: Macmillan Co., 1972), p. 410; Report by the J–1 to the JCofStaff on Special Pay for Duty subject to Hostile fire in Korea, 21 Feb 68, JCS 2478/130, Korea, Special Pay for Hostile Fire file, DAMH-HSO; Sharp and Westmoreland, *Report of the War In Vietnam*, pp. 157–62, 183–84.

28 Ltr, TAG to CG, Fifth U.S. Army, 13 May 68, sub: Change in Status of Units, AGSD-C (M) (2 May 68) ACSFOR, 5th Inf Div file, DAMH-HSO; Msg, DA to CG, CONARC, and other addresses, 866004, 28 May 68, sub: Final Movement Directive 68–56, 1st Bde, 5th Inf Div, file, DAMH-HSO; Unit History of the 1st Infantry Brigade, 5th Infantry Division (Mechanized), 1917–1971, Ms, MHI.

[29] Lyndon Baines Johnson, *The Vantage Point* (New York: Holt, Rinehard, and Winston, 1971), pp. 385–415 passim; Msg, ACSFOR, DA, to JCS, and other addresses, 859314, 11 Apr 68, sub: Mobilization Order, Msg, ACSFOR, DA, to JCS, and other addresses, 860342, 18 Apr 68, sub: Mobilization Station Change, 18 Apr 68, and ORC-OPT, Fact Sheet, sub: 12 Apr 68, Selection of Reserve Components for Mobilization, all Vietnam, Reserve Component file, DAMH-HSO.

[30] Tolson, *Airmobility*, pp. 195–98; Msg, ACSFOR, DA, to CinC, USARPAC, 866236, 28 May 68, sub: Second Airmobile Division, 101st Abn Div file, DAMH-HSO.

[31] Tolson, *Airmobility*, p. 197; Msg, ACSFOR, DA, to CinC, USARPAC, 907931, 6 May 69, sub: Activation/Inactivation/ Reorganization of Units in RVN, and GO 577, USARPAC, 1969, both 1st Cav Div file, DAMH-HSO.

[32] Draft SS, ACSFOR for CofS, undated, sub: Redesignation of 101st Air Cavalry Division, FOR PP FP, and Msg, ACSFOR, DA, to CinC, USARPAC, 877510, 26 Aug 68, sub: Redesignation of Airmobile Division, 101st Abn Div file, DAMH-HSO.

[33] Cover Sheet (OPS 28) ACSFOR, 15 Nov 68, sub: Reorganization of the 23d Infantry Division (Americal), FOR OT OR PO, and GO USARV 113, 69, both 23d Inf Div file, DAMH-HSO.

[34] Richard P. Weinert, *The Role of USCONARC in the Army Buildup, FY 1968* (Fort Monroe, Va.: U.S. Continental Army Command, 1969), p.71; Ltr, TAG to CG, CONARC, and other addresses, 7 Mar 67, sub: Activation of STARF Units, 7 Mar 67, AGSD-C (M) (14 Mar 67) ACSFOR, Ltr, TAG to CG, CONARC, 20 Oct 67, sub: Activation of STRAF Units, AGSD-C (M) (16 Oct 67) ACSFOR, and Ltr, TAG to CinC, USARPAC, 2 Oct 67, sub: Activation of Units, AGSD-C (M) (22 Sep 67) ACSFOR, all AG Reference files, DAMH-HSO. In addition to the infantry battalions assigned to divisions and brigades, one nondivisional infantry unit served in Vietnam in a military police role.

[35] Mahon and Danysh, *Infantry*, pp. 115–16; Westmoreland, *A Soldier Reports*, p. 283.

[36] Mahon and Danysh, *Infantry*, p. 115; George E. Dexter, "Search and Destroy in Vietnam," *Infantry* 56 (Jul–Aug 1966): 36–42.

[37] Starry, *Mounted Combat*, pp. 142, 234–37; John H. Hay, Jr., *Tactical and Materiel Innovations* (Washington, D.C.: Government Printing Office, 1974), pp. 111–16; Army Concept Team in Vietnam, Final Report: Optimum Mix of Armored Vehicles for Use in Stability Operations, p. H–20, CGSC Library, Fort Leavenworth, Kans. Although nine mechanized infantry battalions served in Vietnam, only eight served there at any given time. The assets of the 5th Battalion, 60th Infantry, an element of the 9th Infantry Division, were used to organize the 1st Battalion, 16th Infantry, an element of the 1st Infantry Division, in 1968.

[38] David Ewing Ott, *Field Artillery 1964–1973* (Washington, D.C.: Government Printing Office, 1972), pp. 168–73.

[39] USCONARC/ARSTRIKE (Army Strike) "Annual Historical Summary, FY 1969," p. 87.

[40] Andrew P. O'Meara, "Drawdown for Vietnam: How USAREUR Makes Do," *Army* 16 (Oct 1966): 73–75+; James H. Polk, "A Changing US Army Europe: Building Combat Capability for Tomorrow," *Army* 17 (Oct 1967): 65–66+.

[41] Aviation Requirements for Combat Structures of the Army, Annex II, 1965; TOE 17G, Armored Division, 1966; TOE 37G, Infantry Division (Mechanized), 1966; TOE 1–87G, Division Aviation Support Detachment, 1966.

[42] Msg, ACSFOR to CinC, USAREUR, DA 737567, 22 Oct 65, sub: Reorganization of USAREUR Division, Division General file, Ltr, TAG to CinC, USAREUR, 12 Apr 66, sub: Change in Status of Units, AGSD-C (M) (12 Apr 66) ACSFOR, both (26 Sep 66), Ltr, TAG to CinC, USAREUR, 3 Oct 66, sub: Activation of US Army Europe Units, AGSD-C-C (M)(26 Sep 66) ACSFOR, AG Reference files, Msg, ACSFOR to CinC, USAREUR, and CG, CONARC, 112158Z Feb 66, sub: Transfer of the 5th Bn 32d Armor, DA 750634, 5th Bn, 32d Armor, file, all DAMH-HSO; TOE 17G, Armored Division, 1966; TOE 37G, Mechanized Infantry Division, 31 Mar 1966; TOE 7–45G, Mechanized Infantry Battalion, 1966; TOE 17–35G, Tank Battalion, 31 Mar 1966; John S. Yakshe, "REDEYE Ground to Air," *Infantry* 56 (Jul–Aug 1966): 22–23.

[43] "US, UK, and Germany Conclude Trilateral Talks," *Department of State Bulletin* 56 (22 Nov 67): 788–89; Richard P. Weinert, *USCONARC and Redeployment of Forces from Europe* (REFORGER) (Fort Monroe, Va.: U.S. Continental Army Command, 1969).

## FLEXIBLE RESPONSE
## 351

44 Msg, DA to CG, CONARC, 889661, 6 Dec 68, sub: Public Announcement-Reforger I, and Ltr, TAG to CG, CONARC, and other addresses, 28 May 69, sub: After Action Report, Exercise Reforger I, AGAM-P (23 May 69) FOR OT UT 69E001, both Reforger file, DAMH-HSO.

45 Ltr, TAG to CG, Third U.S. Army, 23 May 66, sub: Inactivation of the 2d Battalion, 29th Infantry, AGSD-C (M) (3 May 66), 197th Inf Bde file, DAMH-HSO; Telephone or Verbal Conversation Record, Mrs Stubbs and Lt Col Derhay, 11 Jun 67, sub: An Armored Brigade for Ft Knox, and Ltr, TAG to CG, U.S. Army Combat Developments Command, 24 Jan 68, sub: Reorganization of Unit, AGSD-C (M) ACSFOR, both 194th Armd Bde file, Ltr, TAG to CG, US Army, Alaska, 10 Jul 67, ADSD-C (M) (3 Jul 67) ACSFOR, 171st Inf Bde file, and GO 70, U.S. Forces Southern Command, 1968, 3d Bn, 5th Inf file, all DAMH-HSO.

46 Msg, OCINFO DA to CG, CONARC, and CinC, USARPAC 870873, 3 Jul 68, sub: Decision by the Secretary of Defense not to Activate the 6th Infantry Division, and Ltr, TAG to CG, CONARC, and CinC, USARPAC, 18 Nov 68, sub: Change in Status of Units, AGSD-C (M) (31 Jul 68) ACSFOR, both 6th Inf Div file, DAMH-HSO; Ltr, TAG to CG, CONARC, 7 Nov 68, sub: Change in Status of Units, AGSD-C (M) (10 Oct 68) ACSFOR, 4th Bde, 82d Abn Div, file, and Ed Gerhardt, Unit History of the 69th Infantry Brigade (Mechanized) 1963–1978, 15 Feb 79, Ms, pp. 10–21, 69th Bde, 35th Inf Div, file.

47 Memo for Record, Sec of the General Staff, sub: Meeting with VCSA on Re-examination of Reduction of Forces in Europe and Reconstitution of the 6th Division (2 Brigades), 23 Aug 68, and OPS Form 28, ACSFOR to CofS, 30 Sep 67, sub: Activation of Division Headquarters and a Brigade size Force of the 6th Infantry Division (Show the Flag Concept), FOR PP FP, 6th Inf Div file, DAMH-HSO.

48 Chief of Information, DA, *Why Merge* (Washington, D.C.: Government Printing Office, 1965); Ltr, TAG to CinC, USAREUR, and other addresses, 14 Jun 67, sub: Reserve Component Reorganization, AGAM-P (M) (13 Jun 67) ORC-OPT-OP, Ltr, TAG to CinC, USAREUR, and other addresses, 20 Jul 67, same subject, AGAM-P (M) (20 Jul 67) ORC-OPT-OP, and News Release, 27 Nov 67, Army Reserve Components Will Commence Reorganization, all Army Reserve file, DAMH-HSO; "The President Reports to the 89th General Conference," *National Guardsman*, 21 (Oct 1967): inside front cover and pp. 36–39; "Division Command Rotation Plan Set Aside," *National Guardsman*, 22 (Mar 1968): 16; James F. Cantwell, "A Salute to the `Lost' Divisions," *National Guardsman*, 22 (Feb 1968): inside front cover. The Guard wanted the maneuver element mix for mechanized infantry and armored divisions to be the same as the prototype divisions under the 1966 tables of organization, but for infantry divisions it desired eight infantry, two mechanized infantry, and two armor battalions; thus the infantry division would have been larger than Regular Army divisions.

49 *Report of the Chief, National Guard Bureau, 1968*, pp. 33–34; Keith E. McWilliams, "Divisions or Brigades for the National Guard," *Military Review* 51 (Jan 1971): 37; also NG-AROTO 1002–1 letters 1967–1968, copies in CMH.

50 Office of Reserve Components, "Annual Historical Summary, 1 Jul 67–30 Jun 68," p. 4, DAMH-HSR; Historical Data Cards, 157th, 187th, 191st, and 205th Inf Bdes, DAMH-HSO.

51 Ltr, TAG to CinC, USAREUR, 25 Apr 68, sub, SRF II Troop List, AGAM-P (M) (16 Nov 67) ORC-OPT-OP, Army Reserve file, DAMH-HSO; "CONARC Report on US Army Reserve 68," *Army Reserve Magazine* 25 (Mar 1968): 4–5; "SRF Born 27 September 1965; Died September 1969," *National Guardsman* 23 (Sep 1969): 12–16; *Department of the Army Historical Summary, 1970*, p. 70.

52 TOE 29–7T–3, Division (Training), 1966; "Things to Come: CONARC Present Plans for the New Year," *Army Reserve Magazine* 13 (Dec 1967): 8–9; Notes, "Training Division Reorganization, 1967–1968," Division General files, DAMH-HSO.

53 *Public Papers of the Presidents of the United States, Richard Nixon, 1969* (Washington, D.C.: Government Printing Office, 1971), p. 443.

54 Westmoreland, *A Soldier Reports*, p. 381; GO 236, Fifth US Army, 23 Jul 1969; Ltr, TAG to CinC, USARPAC, and other addresses, undated, sub: Letter of Instruction for Redeployment of US Army Forces from RVN (U), AGAM-P (21 Jul 69) OPS OD FE, Vietnam Redeployment file, Msg,

CINFO, DA, to CG, USARPAC and other addresses, 919410, 8 Aug 69, sub: Inactivation of 9th Infantry Division, 9th Inf Div file, GO 2434, USARV, 6 Jul 69, 3d Bde, 9th Inf Div, file, all DAMH-HSO.

55 Msg, CINFO, DA, to CG, USARPAC and other addresses, 919410, 8 Aug 69, sub: Inactivation of 9th Infantry Division; Ltr, TAG to CinC, USAREUR and Seventh Army and other addresses, 18 Dec 69, sub: Plan for Release of Units and Individuals ordered to Active Duty under the Reserve Forces Mobilization, May 68, AGAM-P (M) (13 Dec 68) DCSPER-PLD, Vietnam, Reserve Component, file, DAMH-HSO; Msg, DCSOPS, DA, 922222, 2 Sep 69, sub: Demobilization of the 29th Inf Bde, 29th Inf Bde file, DAMH-HSO; Ltr, NGB to AG, Hawaii, 12 Nov 69, sub: Reestablishment and Reorganization of the 29th Infantry Brigade, NG-AROTO 1002-01-Hawaii 29th Inf Bde, DAMH-HSO; GO 645, USARPAC, 26 Aug 1969; Msg, SECDEF to CinC, Pacific Area Command, 6 Nov 69, sub: Public Affairs Guidance for Activation of Units in Hawaii, 4th Bde, 25th Inf Div, file, DAMH-HSO.

56 Nixon, *Public Papers*, 1969, p. 718; Msg, CG, U.S. Army, Vietnam (USARV), to CG, 3d Bde, 82d Abn Div, 134411 140847Z Oct 69, sub: Implementing Instructions to USARPAC Advance Movement Directive 13–69, and Ltr, TAG to CG, CONARC, 9 Jan 70, sub: Approval of MTOE, AGAO-D (M) (17 Dec 69) ACSFOR, both 3d Bde, 82d Abn Div, file, DAMH-HSO; Ltr, NGB to AG, Kansas, 2 Dec 59, sub: Reestablishment of 69th Inf Bde and 995th Maint Co in Kansas ARNG, NG-AROTO-01, Kansas, Kansas NG file, DAMH-HSO.

57 Redeployment had a broader meaning than just transferring units from one command to another. It included the inactivation of units in Vietnam, the transfer of units to other commands for retention in the force, and the return of units to the United States for inactivation.

58 Msg, CinC, USARPAC, to DCSPER, 12134Z Dec 1969, sub: Personnel Policies to Support Subsequent Redeployment from RVN, as amended, Vietnam Redeployment file, DAMH-HSO.

59 Msg, ACSFOR to CinC, USARPAC, 940715 9 Feb 70, sub: Inactivation/reorganization/activation, ACSFOR MF CRA, and Ltr, TAG to CinC, USARPAC, and other addresses, 14 Nov 70, sub: Letter of Instruction for the Fifth Increment Redeployment of US Army Forces from RVN, AGDA (M) (14 Nov 70) OPS OD TR, both Vietnam Redeployment file, DAMH-HSO.

60 Ltr, TAG to CinC, USARPAC, and other addresses, 17 Feb 71, sub: Letter of Instruction for the Sixth Increment Redeployment of US Army Forces from RVN, AGPA-A (M) (12 Feb 71) OPS OD TR, Vietnam Redeployment file, DAMH-HSO; Ltr, TAG to CinC, USARPAC, 15 Apr 71, sub: Letter of Instruction for the Reorganization/Inactivation of the 1st/4th Armored Division, AGDA-A (M) (8 Apr 71) OP OD TR, GO 147, III Corps and Fort Hood, 1971, and Ltr, 1st Armd Div to U.S. Army Institute of Heraldry, 25 May 71, sub: Request for Information, AETSKA, OPS 28 Form, ACSFOR, sub: Redesignation of the 1st Armored Division, DAFD-MFP-T, 22 Sep 72; all 1st Armd Div file, DAMH-HSO; Ltr, Bruce Clark to Westmoreland, 26 Mar 71, and Ltr, Hal Pattison, Chief of Military History to Clark, 31 Mar 71, both 4th Armd Div file, DAMH-HSO.

61 Memo for Record, Vincent M Russo, Asst Sec of the Gen Staff, 22 Jun 71, sub: Stationing of the 173d Airborne Brigade, and Msg, ACSFOR to CG, CONARC, 172206Z Dec 71 sub: Organization of 101st Abn Div (Ambl) in CONUS, both 173d Abn Bde file, DAMH-HSO.

62 Ltr, TAG to CinC, USARPAC, and other addresses, 5 Jun 72, sub: Letter of Instruction for the Twelfth Incremental Redeployment of US Army Forces from RVN, DAAG-PAP-A (M) (24 May 72) DAMO-ODT, and Ltr, TAG to CinC, USARPAC, and other addresses, 10 Aug 72, sub: Letter of Instruction for the Thirteenth Incremental Redeployment of US Army Forces from RVN, DAAG-PAP-A (M) (2 Aug 72), DAMO-ODT, both Vietnam Redeployment file, DAMH-HSO.

63 Nixon, *Public Papers, 1969*, pp. 905–06; Ltr, TAG to CinC, USARPAC, and other addresses, 22 Jun 71, sub: Letter of Instruction for Redeployment of US Army Forces from the Republic of Korea, ADGA-A (M) (8 Jun 71) OPS OD TR, Korea, Redeployment of Units 1971–1972 file, DAMH-HSO; GO 162, Sixth US Army, 1971, 7th Inf Div file, DAMH-HSO.

64 US Army Alaska, "Annual Historical Summary, 1 Jul 68–30 Jun 69," p. 14, 1 Jul 69–30 Jun 70, p. 17, DAMH-HSR; *Department of the Army Historical Summary, 1972*, p. 10; GO 657, US Army Alaska, 1972, 171st Inf Bde file, DAMH-HSO.

# CHAPTER 13

# The Total Army

*The United States must continue to maintain adequate strength to meet its responsibilities. . . . The capabilities of our active forces must be improved substantially through modernization and improved readiness. At the same time, we are placing increased emphasis on our National Guard and Reserve components so that we may obtain maximum defense capabilities from the limited resources available. The strengthening of the National Guard and Reserve Forces . . . is an integral part of the total force planning.*

Secretary of Defense Melvin R. Laird[1]

Disillusioned with the experience in Vietnam, the nation questioned and reexamined the role of the United States in world affairs. The Army turned to a smaller, all-volunteer force for the first time since the end of World War II. A smaller Army, however, required more conventional firepower to provide a credible deterrent against Soviet aggression. A reexamination of division and brigade organizations began, resulting in the incorporation of new, sophisticated weapons and equipment. To meet the nation's needs with fewer resources, planners relied upon the concept of "One Army" or "Total Army," depending upon the jargon in vogue, which stressed the integration of the Regular Army, Army National Guard, and Army Reserve. Although the three components had served the nation together in the past, they had always remained separate and distinct from one another in many ways.

## *The 21-Division, 21-Brigade Force*

The Nixon doctrine and smaller budgets drove Secretary of Defense Melvin R. Laird to set an Army goal of 21 divisions, 13 in the Regular Army and 8 in the National Guard, by 1973. Structured and equipped primarily to defend Western Europe, the divisions were designed for conventional warfare against the Soviet Union's heavy armor forces. To complement the divisions, the Army maintained 21 separate combined arms brigades, 18 in the Army National Guard and 3 in the Army Reserve. In addition, the Regular Army continued to employ special mission brigades as theater defense forces.[2]

In October 1969 the Army Staff suspended all new work on revised tables of organization and equipment for armored, infantry, and mechanized infantry divisions because the proposed changes required too many men to field them. Instead, it directed the Combat Developments Command to develop divisions of fewer than

17,000 men. The project, entitled AIM (armored, infantry, and mechanized infantry divisions), would occupy Army planners' attention for the next several years and focus primarily on the European battlefield.3

In their final form the new AIM tables neither altered the overall ROAD doctrine nor radically modified divisional structures but addressed ways to counter various types of Soviet threats. To defend against low-altitude hostile aircraft and surface targets, the tables provided each division with an air defense artillery battalion equipped with Chaparral missiles and Vulcan guns, weapons that had been under development since 1964. The new battalion gave divisions the first dedicated antiaircraft artillery unit since pentomic reorganization. Aviation companies reappeared in mechanized infantry and armored divisions to enhance air support. In the divisional support command, adjutant general and finance companies replaced the administration company to improve personnel services, and automatic data processing equipment was added to provide centralized control of personnel and logistics. Eventually automatic data processing led to the introduction of a materiel (supply and maintenance) management center in each division.4

*TOW (tube-launched, optically tracked, wire-guided) missile*

In infantry, mechanized infantry, and armor battalions, the tables concentrated combat support (scouts, mortars, air defense and antitank weapons, ground surveillance equipment, and maintenance resources) into a combat support company. Tube-launched, Optically tracked, Wire-guided missiles (TOWs) replaced ENTACs and 106-mm. recoilless rifles as antitank weapons in the infantry and mechanized infantry battalions. Since the TOW was only just emerging from its developmental stage, the tables approved the retention of the 106-mm. recoilless rifle as a temporary measure.5

Modernization of armored, infantry, and mechanized infantry divisions became an ongoing process primarily to due to shortages of equipment. Because of the need for antiaircraft weapons in the divisional area, the Air Defense Artillery School at Fort Bliss, Texas, inaugurated a program in the spring of 1969 to activate and train Chaparral-Vulcan battalions, which were assigned to divisions upon completion of training. After the new divisional tables were published in

1970, the Honest John rocket battalions were eliminated as divisional units, and new Lance missile units replaced them at corps level. The adjutant general and finance companies were introduced in 1971, the aviation companies returned in 1972, the materiel management center appeared in 1973, and new combat intelligence companies were assigned beginning in 1974 (replacing the combat intelligence unit, which had been regularly attached to every division since the pentomic reorganization of 1957). The company provided a battlefield information coordination center to plan and manage the collection of intelligence and consolidated ground surveillance radar and remote sensors under one commander.[6]

The standard maneuver element mix of the mechanized infantry division was also adjusted for the European battlefield. An additional armor battalion was added to the model division, making the mix five armor and six mechanized infantry battalions. Subsequently the Army activated additional armor battalions for the 3d and 8th Infantry Divisions stationed in Germany in 1972. That same year the Continental Army Command replaced a mechanized infantry battalion with an armor battalion in the 4th Infantry Division at Fort Carson, Colorado, and in 1973 made a similar change, giving the division a maneuver element mix of four armor and six infantry battalions. In the armored division the maneuver mix remained at five mechanized infantry and six armor battalions. Infantry divisions fielded one armor, one mechanized infantry, and eight "foot" infantry battalions.[7]

To have thirteen Regular Army divisions, the Army Staff directed the 25th Infantry Division, which fielded only one brigade after leaving Vietnam, to be reorganized at Schofield Barracks in the spring of 1972. Because of environmental issues surrounding the use of Schofield Barracks at that time, the division had only two brigades (six infantry battalions), with the Hawaii Army National Guard agreeing to "round out" the 25th with the 29th Infantry Brigade. Since the brigade included the 100th Battalion, 442d Infantry, from the Army Reserve, the division was truly representative of the "Total Army."[8]

For the thirteenth Regular Army division in the force, the Continental Army Command reactivated the 9th Infantry Division at Fort Lewis on 21 April 1972. Over the next few months the division organized one armor, one mechanized infantry, and seven infantry battalions, which was one less infantry unit than the standard for an infantry division. The division base had all its authorized elements except for the Honest John battalion, then under consideration for elimination in all divisions. Two years later the Army Staff directed the 9th to establish one brigade as an armored unit to support contingency plans, and when it became evident that the active Army was unable to field an additional tank battalion, the Washington Army National Guard agreed to furnish a tank battalion as a round-out unit.[9]

While organizing the thirteen-division force, the Continental Army Command determined that the 197th Infantry Brigade, assigned to the Infantry School at Fort Benning, Georgia, was overmanned for its training support mission in the post-Vietnam Army. To provide personnel needed for the school, the command directed that the school support troops be reorganized and the 197th be restructured as a unit in the Strategic Army Force. On 21 March 1973 the brigade officially joined the strategic force, fielding one battalion each of infantry, mechanized infantry, and armor.[10]

The Regular Army also maintained three other brigades with special missions in the early 1970s. The 172d and 193d Infantry Brigades served in Alaska and the Canal Zone, respectively, as theater defense units. At Fort Knox, Kentucky, the 194th Armored Brigade was a brigade in name only. It had been reduced to a headquarters, and its infantry, armor, and field artillery units had been assigned directly to the Armor School. The 194th, however, remained at Fort Knox as a command and control organization for various units ranging in size from a finance section to a supply and service battalion.[11]

In late 1972 the Army approved the reorganization of the 101st Airborne Division using new airmobile divisional tables. Since returning from Vietnam, the 101st had comprised two airmobile brigades and one airborne brigade, with the airborne brigade separately deployable. Defense planners had insisted that the division serve as a quick reaction force until the thirteen-division force was combat ready. The existing division employed a conglomeration of old, new, and test tables of organization and equipment, which created organizational problems in the division's combat and support units, particularly in signal resources and medium-range field artillery. After extensive study Army Chief of Staff Creighton Abrams approved the reorganization of the division under new tables, which continued to provide two airmobile brigades and one airborne brigade, with its supporting elements parachute qualified. Signal, engineer, maintenance, and aviation resources were increased; and an air defense artillery battalion, adjutant general and finance companies, and a materiel management center added. A 155-mm. howitzer battalion, which had been used in Vietnam by the division, was made an organic element in the tables, but in fielding the new structure, Abrams directed that the 155-mm. towed howitzer battalion be temporarily eliminated as a way to reduce personnel requirements.[12]

By early 1974 the thirteen-division Regular Army force was deemed combat ready, and contingency plans no longer required an airborne brigade in the 101st. United States Army Forces Command, which in part replaced the United States Continental Army Command in 1973, reorganized the division as a completely airmobile organization. The reorganization also eliminated internal rivalries between the higher paid paratroopers (soldiers on "jump status") and the regular airmobile soldiers. To compensate for its loss of airborne status in recruiting, Maj. Gen. Sidney B. Berry, the commander of the 101st, decided to capitalize on the division's air assault training, requesting that the division's parenthetical designation be changed from "airmobile" to "air assault" and that the personnel who completed air assault training be authorized to wear a special badge. The Army Staff approved the change in designation and eventually authorized the air assault badge.[13]

*General Abrams*

The airborne division was the last type of division to be modernized. As in other divisions, the new tables provided an air defense artillery battalion, adjutant general and finance companies, and a materiel management center. The structure also continued to include a much debated light armor battalion, equipped with reconnaissance airborne assault vehicles, which had been assigned to the division in 1969. The most significant change, however, was the replacement of the supply company with a supply and service battalion, which provided the division with over 500 additional service personnel. The one remaining active airborne division, the 82d, with nine airborne infantry battalions and an armor battalion, adopted the new structure by the fall of 1974.[14]

After returning from Vietnam the 1st Cavalry Division had been given two primary missions: evaluate the interaction of armor, mechanized infantry, airmobile infantry, and air cavalry (armed helicopters); and fill the role of an armored division in the strategic reserve force. To cover the second mission, the division continued to use National Guard round-out units, which had originally been designated for the 1st Armored Division—the unit that the 1st Cavalry Division replaced at Fort Hood in 1971. To evaluate the interaction of armor, air cavalry, and mechanized and airmobile infantry, the "First Team" was organized under new tables (*Chart 42*) that included resources for an air cavalry combat brigade (ACCB). This was not to be the type of brigade the Howze Board had suggested in 1962, which was to be a completely air-fighting unit, but one that troops in Vietnam and Europe had been testing under limited conditions as a combined arms assault unit. With the division combining armor, infantry, and air cavalry in one organization, Westmoreland coined the term "TRICAP" (triple capability) to describe it.[15]

During the evaluation of TRICAP two views emerged about the structure of an air cavalry combat brigade. Some planners saw it primarily as a separate antiarmor brigade with infantry and air cavalry integrated into attack helicopter squadrons without organic support. Others desired the brigade to be a strong, well-balanced, versatile organization with attack helicopter, infantry, reconnaissance, artillery, and combat support units that could perform a variety of missions, including an antitank role. During the summer of 1972 Vice Chief of Staff

# CHART 42—TRICAP Division

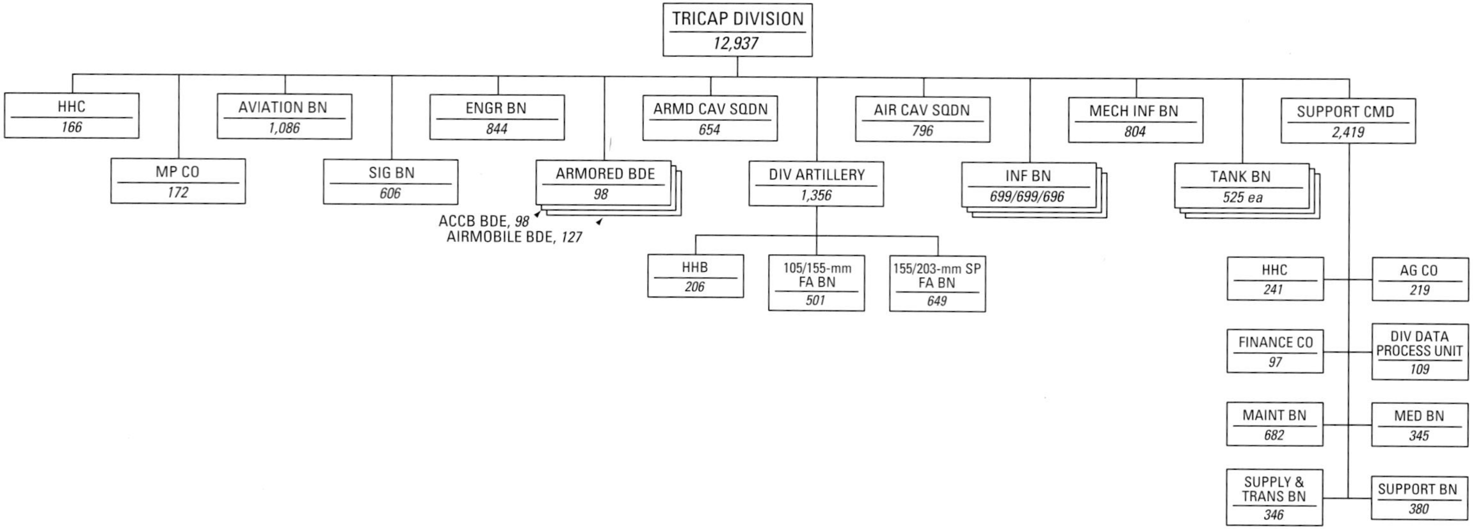

- TRICAP DIVISION — 12,937
  - HHC — 166
  - MP CO — 172
  - AVIATION BN — 1,086
  - SIG BN — 606
  - ENGR BN — 844
  - ARMORED BDE — 98 (ACCB BDE, 98; AIRMOBILE BDE, 127)
  - ARMD CAV SQDN — 654
  - DIV ARTILLERY — 1,356
    - HHB — 206
    - 105/155-mm FA BN — 501
    - 155/203-mm SP FA BN — 649
  - AIR CAV SQDN — 796
  - INF BN — 699/699/696
  - MECH INF BN — 804
  - TANK BN — 525 ea
  - SUPPORT CMD — 2,419
    - HHC — 241
    - AG CO — 219
    - FINANCE CO — 97
    - DIV DATA PROCESS UNIT — 109
    - MAINT BN — 682
    - MED BN — 345
    - SUPPLY & TRANS BN — 346
    - SUPPORT BN — 380

Bruce Palmer noted that a brigade consisting of only attack helicopter squadrons was an expensive organization. (The table for such a proposed squadron called for 88 (45 attack, 27 observation, and 16 utility) helicopters. Therefore he did not envision it as an independent strike force. Nevertheless, he directed further development of an attack helicopter squadron because of concerns voiced by General Michael S. Davison, the commander of U.S. Army, Europe, and Seventh Army. In Europe Soviet armor forces greatly outnumbered their NATO counterparts, and Davison needed some sort of long-range capability that could destroy, disrupt, or at least delay enemy mechanized units behind the main battlefield. Following the development of the squadron, Palmer believed that the planners could sort out the matter of whether the brigade should be assigned to a division or a corps.[16]

By the end of 1972 the course of the TRICAP/ACCB studies appeared set. The Combat Developments Command recommended reorganizing the 1st Cavalry Division to consist of two armored brigades (with two mechanized infantry and four armor battalions divided between them) and one air cavalry combat brigade. The latter, to be employed as a part of the division or independently, was to consist of an airmobile infantry battalion and two attack helicopter squadrons. The brigade was to have no organic support battalion. Round-out battalions continued to be assigned to the 1st Cavalry Division so that it could deploy as a full armored division along with the air cavalry combat brigade.[17]

Before the ink dried on the new instructions, Abrams decided to reorganize the air cavalry combat brigade as a separate unit for employment at corps level and to make the division exclusively an armored unit. With one organic brigade organized as air cavalry, the 1st Cavalry Division with only two mechanized infantry and four armor battalions lacked the necessary ground-gaining and holding ability of a normal armored division. On 21 February 1975 the Army thus organized the 6th Cavalry Brigade (Air Combat) at Fort Hood, Texas. The first of its type, the brigade consisted of a headquarters and headquarters troop, an air cavalry squadron (without the armored cavalry troop), two attack helicopter battalions, a support battalion, and a signal company. Strictly an air unit, the brigade's mission was to locate, disrupt, and destroy enemy armored and mechanized units by aerial combat power. In the summer of that year the 1st Cavalry Division was reorganized wholly as an armored division with four armor and four mechanized infantry battalions in the Regular Army. One mechanized infantry and two armor battalions in the National Guard continued to round out the division.[18]

Although the 21-division, 21-brigade force did not alter the number of reserve divisions and brigades, the reserve components underwent numerous changes after the Army withdrew from Vietnam. Like the Regular Army, the Guard began increasing its heavy forces in 1971 with the 32d (Wisconsin) and 81st (Washington) Infantry Brigades being converted to mechanized infantry. In 1972 the states began modernizing their divisions and brigades using the recently published tables, but they lacked the materiel to complete the process.

*The Chaparral short-range air defense surface-to-air missile system;* below, *the Vulcan air defense system.*

# THE TOTAL ARMY

To field air defense artillery battalions, Guard units used "Dusters," M42 tracked vehicles with dual-mounted 40-mm. antiaircraft guns, rather than Chaparrals and Vulcans. As only limited numbers of M60 tanks, M551 assault vehicles (Sheridans), and AH–1 helicopters (Cobras) were available, the Guard continued to use vintage equipment.[19]

Shortly after the National Guard reorganized its divisions, a controversy arose over the command of the 30th Armored Division, a multistate unit supported by Tennessee, Mississippi, and Alabama. Tennessee was about to appoint a new divisional commander, and the governors of Mississippi and Alabama threatened to withdraw their units from the division unless their officers had the opportunity to be the divisional commander. Governor Winfield Dunn of Tennessee objected to rotation of the commander's position, and Secretary of the Army Robert F. Froehlke supported him. Abrams therefore directed Maj. Gen. Francis S. Greenlief, Chief of the National Guard Bureau, to review such command arrangements in all Guard divisions.[20]

Before Greenlief could propose a solution, other events made the question moot. The Department of Defense directed the Army to convert six reserve brigades from infantry to armored or mechanized infantry as reinforcements for Europe. In the meantime, Mississippi Governor William L. Waller decided to withdraw his units from the 30th Armored Division. Given the requirement to convert some brigades, the Army Staff decided to have Tennessee, Mississippi, and Alabama each organize an armored brigade and to move the allotment of the armored division to Texas, which could support the necessary units itself. After much negotiating, Tennessee, Alabama, and Mississippi agreed to organize the 30th, 31st, and 155th Armored Brigades, and Texas took on the 49th Armored Division in 1973. For the other three brigades, the Army replaced the 30th Infantry Division, another tri-state division, with the 30th (North Carolina), 48th (Georgia), and 218th (Louisiana) Infantry Brigades and reorganized the 40th Infantry Division in California. All were mechanized infantry. The reorganization did not change the total number of reserve divisions or brigades, and the National Guard continued to field 8 divisions (1 mechanized infantry, 2 armored, and 5 standard infantry) and 18 brigades (3 armored, 6 mechanized infantry, and 9 standard infantry), while the Army Reserve supported 3 brigades (1 mechanized infantry and 2 infantry).[21]

By 30 June 1974, the Army had attained the 21-division, 21-brigade force (*Tables 32 and 33*). The 25th Infantry Division at Schofield Barracks, with two brigades, and the 197th Infantry Brigade at Fort Benning were regarded as equivalent to one division in the Regular Army. Some Regular Army divisions in the continental United States, however, had round-out battalions from the reserves to meet mobilization missions. More serious was the fact that reserve divisions and brigades continued to experience readiness problems. Recruitment lagged because of the end of the draft, and equipment shortages continued due to the lack of money. The "total force" thus exhibited significant weaknesses.[22]

## TABLE 32
### The 21-Division Force, June 1974

| Division | Component | Location of Headquarters | Inf | Mech | Ar | Abn | AAST |
|---|---|---|---|---|---|---|---|
| 1st Armored | RA | Ansbach, Germany | | 5 | 6 | | |
| 1st Cavalry[1],[3] | RA | Fort Hood, Tex | | 2 | 4 | | |
| 1st Infantry[2] | RA | Fort Riley, Kans. | | 5 | 5 | | |
| 2d Armored[3] | RA | Fort Hood, Tex. | | 4 | 4 | | |
| 2d Infantry | RA | Camp Casey, Korea | 4 | 2 | 2 | | |
| 3d Armored | RA | Frankfurt, Germany | | 5 | 6 | | |
| 3d Infantry | RA | Wuerzburg, Germany | | 6 | 5 | | |
| 4th Infantry | RA | Fort Carson, Colo. | | 6 | 4 | | |
| 8th Infantry | RA | Bad Kreuznach, Germany | | 6 | 5 | | |
| 9th Infantry | RA | Fort Lewis, Wash. | 7 | 1 | 1 | | |
| 25th Infantry[3] | RA | Schofield Barracks, Hawaii | 6 | | | | |
| 26th Infantry | NG | Boston, Mass. | 8 | 1 | 1 | | |
| 28th Infantry | NG | Harrisburg, Pa. | 8 | 1 | 1 | | |
| 38th Infantry | NG | Indianapolis, Ind. | 8 | 1 | 1 | | |
| 40th Infantry | NG | California | | 6 | 4 | | |
| 42d Infantry | NG | New York, N.Y. | 8 | 1 | 1 | | |
| 47th Infantry | NG | St. Paul, Mich. | 8 | 1 | 1 | | |
| 49th Armored | NG | Austin, Tex. | | 5 | 6 | | |
| 50th Armored | NG | East Orange, N.J. | | | 5 | 6 | |
| 82d Airborne | RA | Fort Bragg, N.C. | | | 1 | 9 | |
| 101st Airborne | RA | Fort Campbell, Ky. | | | | | 9 |

[1] Does not include the 6th Cavalry Brigade units.
[2] One brigade deployed forward in Germany.
[3] Less round-out unit or units assigned.

TABLE 33

The 21-Brigade Force, June 1974

| Brigade | Location of Component | Headquarters | Inf | Mech | Ar | Lt Inf |
|---|---|---|---|---|---|---|
| 29th Infantry | NG and AR | Honolulu, Hawaii | | 2 | | |
| 30th Armored | NG | Jackson, Tenn. | | 1 | 2 | |
| 30th Infantry (M)[1] | NG | Clinton, N.C. | | 2 | 1 | |
| 31st Armored | NG | Tuscaloosa, Ala. | | 2 | 1 | |
| 32d Infantry (M)[1] | NG | Milwaukee, Wisc. | | 2 | 1 | |
| 33d Infantry | NG | Chicago, Ill. | 3 | | | |
| 39th Infantry | NG | Little Rock, Ark. | 3 | | | |
| 41st Infantry | NG | Portland, Oreg. | 3 | | | |
| 45th Infantry | NG | Edmond, Okla. | 3 | | | |
| 48th Infantry (M)[1] | NG | Macon, Ga. | | 2 | 1 | |
| 53d Infantry | NG | Tampa, Fla. | 3 | | | |
| 67th Infantry (M)[1] | NG | Lincoln, Neb. | | 2 | 1 | |
| 69th Infantry | NG | Topeka, Kans. | 3 | | | |
| 81st Infantry (M)[1] | NG | Seattle, Wash. | | 2 | 1 | |
| 92d Infantry | NG | San Juan, Puerto Rico | 3 | | | |
| 155th Armored | NG | Tupelo, Miss. | | 1 | 2 | |
| 157th Infantry (M)[1] | AR | Horsham, Pa. | | 2 | 1 | |
| 172d Infantry[2] | RA | Fort Richardson, Alaska | | | | 3 |
| 187th Infantry | AR | Wollaston, Mass. | 3 | | | |
| 193d Infantry[2] | RA | Fort Kobbe, Canal Zone | 2 | 1 | | |
| 194th Armored | RA | Fort Knox, Ky. | No assigned battalions | | | |
| 197th Infantry[3] | RA | Fort Benning, Ga. | 1 | 1 | 1 | |
| 205th Infantry | AR | Fort Snelling, Minn. | 3 | | | |
| 218th Infantry (M)[1] | NG | Newberry, S.C. | | 2 | 1 | |
| 256th Infantry | NG | Lafayette, La. | 3 | | | |

[1] Mechanized unit.
[2] Special mission brigade.
[3] The brigade and the 25th Infantry Division with two active brigades counted as a divisional equivalent.

## A New Force—Greater Integration of Regulars and Reserves

As the Army struggled to meet the 21-division, 21-brigade force, General Abrams turned his attention to the nation's ability to execute its military strategy without resorting to nuclear weapons and to the task of providing the resources needed to deal with a variety of world situations. In testimony before congressional committees in 1974, he characterized the Regular Army's portion of the 21-division force as a high-risk, "no room for error" force.23 He further testified that through more efficient management, cuts in nonessential support activities, and reorganization of various headquarters throughout the Army, a 785,000-man Regular Army could support sixteen divisions. Congress gave no opposition, and the Department of Defense lent its support. Therefore, Abrams directed his staff to plan for three additional Regular Army divisions by 1980.24

Although some officers on Abrams' staff were thunderstruck at the directive, since a 785,000-man force had not been sufficient in the past to maintain 16 Regular Army divisions, the Army Staff eventually developed plans involving both regulars and reserves to raise a 24-division force. A mechanized infantry division and two infantry divisions were to be phased into the force over the next few years. The first increment was to include activating three new divisional brigades, reorganizing the 1st Cavalry Division as an armored division (as decided earlier), and adjusting the number of maneuver elements in other divisions in the United States. Phase two was to provide the base and an additional brigade for each of the three new divisions. Phase three was vague, but the divisions were to be completed using reserve round-out units.25

During the summer of 1974 Forces Command began to implement the 24-division force. To provide some of the resources, various headquarters throughout the Army were reorganized, cuts were made in nonessential support activities, and the 1st and 4th Infantry Divisions each saw one of their Regular Army maneuver battalions inactivated and replaced by a National Guard round-out unit. On 21 October the command activated the 7th Infantry Division headquarters and the 1st Brigades of the 5th, 7th, and 24th Infantry Divisions at Forts Polk, Ord, and Stewart, respectively. The 7th and 24th were standard, or "foot," infantry divisions, and the 5th was mechanized infantry. Because Fort Polk, in Louisiana, lacked adequate housing facilities, the brigade of the 5th fielded only two maneuver battalions. The larger facilities at Fort Ord, California, allowed the 7th to support four maneuver battalions, and the brigade of the 24th at Fort Stewart, Georgia, fielded three. As noted above, Forces Command organized the 6th Cavalry Brigade (Air Combat) as a separate corps-level aviation unit and reorganized the 1st Cavalry Division as an armored division consisting of four armor and four mechanized infantry battalions in the Regular Army and three round-out battalions from the National Guard.26

Phase two of the program required organizing the base and a second brigade for each division. For the 5th and 24th Infantry Divisions elements of the 194th Armored Brigade and the 197th Infantry Brigade were to be used, but all ele-

TABLE 34

Round-out Units, 1978

| Division | Unit | Component |
|---|---|---|
| 1st Cavalry | 2d Battalion, 120th Infantry | N.C. NG |
| | 2d Battalion, 252d Armor | N.C. NG |
| | 1st Battalion, 263d Armor | S.C. NG |
| 1st Infantry | 2d Battalion, 136th Infantry | Minn. NG |
| 2d Armored | 3d Battalion, 149th Infantry | Ky. NG |
| | 1st Battalion, 123d Armor | Ky. NG |
| | 2d Battalion, 123d Armor | Ky. NG |
| 4th Infantry | 1st Battalion, 117th Infantry | Tenn. NG |
| 5th Infantry | 256th Infantry Brigade | La. NG |
| 7th Infantry | 41st Infantry Brigade | Wash. NG |
| | 8th Battalion, 40th Armor | Army Reserve |
| 9th Infantry | 1st Battalion, 803d Armor | Wash. NG |
| 24th Infantry | 48th Infantry Brigade | Ga. NG |
| 25th Infantry | 29th Infantry Brigade | Hawaii NG and Army Reserve |

ments of the second brigade in the 7th Infantry Division were to be newly organized. On 28 August 1975, however, the Army canceled the plans to use the 194th Armored and 197th Infantry Brigades because of congressional pressure to improve the ratio of combat to support troops. All units in phase two were to be formed new in the Regular Army.[27]

Forces Command began activating phase two units in the fall of 1975, organizing all required Regular Army units within two years. While the Regular Army units were being activated, Louisiana, Washington, and Georgia agreed that the 256th, 41st, and 48th Infantry Brigades would be assigned to round out the 5th, 7th, and 24th Infantry Divisions, respectively. Because the 7th needed an armor battalion, the 8th Battalion, 40th Armor, an Army Reserve unit, was assigned to it. Hence, in order to raise the 24-division force, the round-out concept was extended to all divisions except those forward deployed in Germany and Korea and the airborne and airmobile units (*Table 34*).[28]

Although Forces Command did not use the 194th Armored and 197th Infantry Brigades to organize the new divisions, both brigades were assigned strategic missions after 21 October 1975. Responding to General Abrams' congressional testimony to provide a better balance of combat to support units, the Army Staff converted 4,000 general support spaces to combat positions in the continental United States, and the command used some of them to reorganize the 194th as a strategic reserve unit. The brigade eventually included one mechanized infantry battalion and two tank battalions. In addition, it continued to support the Armor School at Fort Knox.[29]

In 1974 congressional dissatisfaction led Senator Sam Nunn of Georgia to sponsor an amendment requiring the Army to reduce the number of support forces in Europe by 18,000 officers and enlisted personnel but permitting those spaces to be used to organize combat units there. The new units could include battalions or smaller units of infantry, armor, field and air defense artillery, cavalry, engineers, special forces, and aviation, which were to improve the visibility of the nation's combat power in Europe.[30]

To execute the Nunn amendment U.S. Army Forces Command and U.S. Army, Europe, and Seventh Army agreed to a plan for organizing a mechanized infantry brigade and an armored brigade for Europe, which were known as Brigade-75 and Brigade-76. Under the plan the headquarters and a support battalion for each brigade were to be stationed in Germany while the infantry, armor, and field artillery battalions, engineer companies, and cavalry troops from the United States were to rotate every six months. No provisions were made for dependents to accompany the soldiers since they were to be away from home on temporary duty for only 179 days. The short duration of the assignment was to be a cost-saving measure, which indirectly also attacked the balance of payment problem between the United States and its allies, and a morale booster. To support the rotation of Brigade-75, the first unit in the program, the Army selected the 2d Armored Division, at Fort Hood, Texas. Between March and June 1975 the 3d Brigade, 2d Armored Division, deployed to Germany, with its headquarters at Grafenwoehr and its elements scattered at various training areas. A few weeks before each unit departed Fort Hood, Forces Command activated a similar unit, including Headquarters and Headquarters Company, 4th Brigade, 2d Armored Division, to maintain the three-brigade structure of the division in the continental United States. During the deployment the Army Staff approved a request from Forces Command to use a battalion from the 1st Cavalry Division, rather than have all elements from the 2d Armored Division, in order to reduce personnel turbulence in the 2d. Because of the shortage of tank crews, the Army changed Brigade-75 from an armored to a mechanized infantry unit. Another factor in the decision to deploy a mechanized brigade was the shortage of tanks resulting from U.S. replacement of tanks the Israelis had lost in their 1973 war against the Arabs. In September 1975 the first rotation of brigade elements between Germany and Fort Hood began.[31]

Forces Command selected the 4th Infantry Division to support Brigade-76 and in December 1975 activated the 4th Brigade, 4th Infantry Division, at Fort Carson, Colorado. The following year the brigade moved to Germany. To lighten the burden of the 4th Infantry Division at Fort Carson, a mechanized infantry battalion from the 1st Infantry Division at Fort Riley was included in the rotation scheme. Following the procedure used to send Brigade-75 to Europe, new organizations were activated in the 1st and 4th Infantry Divisions to maintain their divisional integrity.[32]

As elements of the 3d Brigade, 2d Armored Division, and the 4th Brigade, 4th Infantry Division, rotated, the Army monitored the effect on the budget, readiness,

# THE TOTAL ARMY

and morale. Evidence soon suggested that the rotation of the brigades improved neither cost effectiveness nor readiness. Therefore, the Army decided that the brigades would be assigned permanently to U.S. Army, Europe, and Seventh Army. The reassignment of the 4th Brigade, 4th Infantry Division, took place in the fall of 1976. At that time the 3d Battalion, 28th Infantry, the element of the 1st Infantry Division supporting the brigade, was reassigned to the 4th Infantry Division. To improve the alignment of Allied forces in Europe, Army leaders decided to station Brigade-75 (the 3d Brigade, 2d Armored Division) in northern Germany, where no American combat unit had served since the end of World War II. Such problems as the lack of housing, particularly for dependents, and opposition from German nationals over the impact of the troops on the environment, caused the elements of the brigade to continue to rotate until the questions could be resolved. Two years later, after building a new military complex at Garlstedt, the 3d Brigade, 2d Armored Division, became a permanent part of the European forces. At Fort Hood the 4th Brigade, 2d Armored Division, and the battalion of the 1st Cavalry Division that supported the brigade were inactivated. A new battalion was assigned to the 2d Armored Division from its traditional regiments to replace the 1st Cavalry Division unit inactivated in Germany. The net result of the Nunn amendment on divisional forces was two more brigades forward deployed in Germany but a reduction of one brigade in the 2d Armored Division in the United States.[33]

Readiness became the watchword for the seventies. Although some Army leaders believed that the first battle of any future war might be the last and final ground battle, a high state of readiness served as a deterrent against aggression. Improving readiness in the Army's 24-division force thus became the primary objective of Army Chief of Staff Fred C. Weyand, who was appointed after Abrams died in office in September 1974. Weyand requested the National Guard Bureau to explore the consolidation of the 50th Armored and the 26th, 28th, 38th, 42d, and 47th Infantry Divisions into single or bi-state configurations and to consider the possibility of forming five more brigades. The latter were to be organized only with the secretary of defense's approval. In 1975 and 1976 the 50th Armored Division was reorganized in New Jersey and Vermont, the 28th Infantry Division in Pennsylvania, and the 42d Infantry Division in New York. Former elements of the 28th from Maryland and Virginia supported the new 58th and 116th Infantry Brigades, respectively. In 1977 Ohio dropped out of the 38th Infantry Division, leaving Indiana and Michigan to maintain it. Ohio organized the 73d Infantry Brigade. The only divisional element not concentrated within each division's new recruiting area was the air defense artillery battalions. With these changes, the Army reached the 24-division, 24-brigade force (*Tables 35 and 36*). Also, the 36th Airborne Brigade and 149th Armored Brigade headquarters were organized and federally recognized in the National Guard, but they were headquarters only, without assigned elements.[34]

The Army Reserve continued to maintain three brigades within the total force. These brigades were the least combat ready units in the Army. Without the draft, the

TABLE 35

The 24-Division Force, 1978

| Division | Component | Location of Headquarters | Inf | Mech | Ar | Abn | AAst | Remarks |
|---|---|---|---|---|---|---|---|---|
| 1st Armored | RA | Ansbach, Germany | | 5 | 6 | | | |
| 1st Cavalry[1] | RA | Fort Hood, Tex. | | 4 | 5 | | | See Table 34 |
| 1st Infantry[2] | RA | Fort Riley, Kans. | | 5 | 4 | | | See Table 34 |
| 2d Armored[3] | RA | Fort Hood, Tex. | | 6 | 5 | | | See Table 34 |
| 2d Infantry | RA | Camp Casey, Korea | 4 | 2 | 2 | | | |
| 3d Armored | RA | Frankfurt, Germany | | 5 | 6 | | | |
| 3d Infantry | RA | Wuerzburg, Germany | | 6 | 5 | | | |
| 4th Infantry[4] | RA | Fort Carson, Colo. | | 7 | 5 | | | See Table 34 |
| 5th Infantry (−) | RA | Fort Polk, La. | | 3 | 3 | | | See Table 34 |
| 7th Infantry (−) | RA | Fort Ord, Calif. | 6 | | | | | See Table 34 |
| 8th Infantry | RA | Bad Kreuznach, Germany | | 6 | 5 | | | |
| 9th Infantry (−) | RA | Fort Lewis, Wash. | | 7 | 1 | 1 | | See Table 34 |
| 24th Infantry (−) | RA | Fort Stewart, Ga. | | 4 | 2 | | | |
| 25th Infantry (−) | RA | Schofield Barracks, Hawaii | 6 | | | | | See Table 34 |
| 26th Infantry | NG | Boston, Mass. | 8 | 1 | 1 | | | |
| 28th Infantry | NG | Harrisburg, Pa. | 8 | 1 | 1 | | | |
| 38th Infantry | NG | Indianapolis, Ind. | 8 | 1 | 1 | | | |
| 40th Infantry | NG | Long Beach, Calif. | | 6 | 5 | | | |
| 42d Infantry | NG | New York, N.Y. | 8 | 1 | 1 | | | |
| 47th Infantry | NG | St. Paul, Mich. | 8 | 1 | 1 | | | |
| 49th Armored | NG | Austin, Tex. | | 5 | 6 | | | |
| 50th Armored | NG | Somerset, N.J. | | 5 | 6 | | | |
| 82d Airborne | RA | Fort Bragg, N.C. | | | 1 | 9 | | |
| 101st Airborne | RA | Fort Campbell, Ky. | | | | | 9 | |

[1] One battalion supported the 3d Brigade, 2d Armored Division (Brigade-75).
[2] The 1st Infantry Division Forward was in Germany.
[3] Supported 3d Brigade, 2d Armored Division (Brigade-75) in Germany.
[4] Supported 4th Brigade, 4th Infantry Division (Brigade-76) in Germany.

TABLE 36

The 24-Brigade Force, 1978

| Brigade | Component | Location of Headquarters | Inf | Mech | Ar | Lt Inf | Remarks |
|---|---|---|---|---|---|---|---|
| 29th Infantry (RO) | NG & AR | Honolulu, Hawaii | 3 | | | | |
| 30th Armored | NG | Jackson, Tenn. | | 1 | 2 | | |
| 30th Infantry | NG | Clinton, S.C. | | 2 | 1 | | |
| 31st Armored | NG | Northport, Ala. | | 1 | 2 | | |
| 32d Infantry (M) | NG | Milwaukee, Wisc. | | 2 | 1 | | |
| 33d Infantry | NG | Chicago, Ill. | 3 | | | | |
| 36th Airborne | NG | Houston, Tex. | No assigned battalions | | | | |
| 39th Infantry | NG | Little Rock, Ark. | 3 | | | | |
| 41st Infantry (RO) | NG | Portland, Oreg. | 3 | | | | |
| 45th Infantry | NG | Edmond, Okla. | 3 | | | | |
| 48th Infantry (M) (RO) | NG | Macon, Ga. | | 2 | 1 | | |
| 53d Infantry | NG | Tampa, Fla. | 3 | | | | |
| 58th Infantry | NG | Pikesville, Md. | 3 | | | | |
| 67th Infantry (M) | NG | Lincoln, Neb. | | 2 | 1 | | |
| 69th Infantry | NG | Topeka, Kans. | | 2 | 1 | | |
| 73d Infantry | NG | Columbus, Ohio | 3 | | | | |
| 81st Infantry (M) | NG | Seattle, Wash. | | 2 | 1 | | |
| 92d Infantry | NG | San Juan, Puerto Rico | 4 | | | | |
| 116th Infantry | NG | Staunton, Va. | 3 | | | | |
| 149th Armored | NG | Bowling Green, Ky. | No assigned battalions | | | | |
| 155th Armored | NG | Tupelo, Miss. | 1 | 2 | | | |
| 157th Infantry (M) | AR | Horsham, Pa. | 2 | 1 | | | |
| 172d Infantry | RA | Fort Richardson, Alaska | 1 | 1 | 1 | | Special Mission |
| 187th Infantry | AR | Fort Devens, Mass. | 3 | | | | |
| 193d Infantry | RA | Fort Kobbe, Canal Zone | | | | | Special Mission |
| 194th Armored | RA | Fort Knox, Ky. | | 2 | 1 | | |
| 197th Infantry | RA | Fort Benning, Ga. | | 1 | 2 | | |
| 205th Infantry | AR | Fort Snelling, Minn. | | 2 | 1 | | |
| 218th Infantry (M) | NG | Newberry, S.C. | | 2 | 1 | | |
| 256th Infantry (RO) | NG | Lafayette, La. | | 2 | 1 | | |

reserves continued to suffer major recruiting problems. When planning for the three new Regular Army divisions, some Army Staff members and Secretary of the Army Howard Callaway had wanted to use an Army Reserve infantry brigade as a round-out unit, but none of the component's brigades met the required manning and equipment levels. As an alternative the staff considered moving either the 157th or the 187th Infantry Brigade, or both, to the southern part of the United States and shifting the 205th Infantry Brigade to the West Coast, all areas where recruiting was thought to be better. But congressional opposition stopped these proposals, and the units remained generally in their existing areas.35

Despite these difficulties, Forces Command wished to improve the readiness of the Army Reserve brigades. At first it proposed reducing the number of units, particularly in the northeast, the First U.S. Army's area, and in February 1975 it inactivated a battalion in the 157th Infantry Brigade at Harrisburg, Pennsylvania. Then, early in 1976, Maj. Gen. Henry Mohr, Chief of the Army Reserve, submitted a brigade improvement plan that retained the units in their recruiting areas but eliminated other units from the areas to limit the competition for scarce personnel resources. As the Army Reserve staff developed the plan, Deputy Chief of Staff for Operations and Plans (DCSOPS) Lt. Gen. Donald H. Cowles selected the 41st Infantry Brigade, the only brigade with a northern Arctic mission, as the round-out unit for the 7th Infantry Division. To replace the brigade in the contingency plans, Mohr agreed to reorganize the 205th Infantry Brigade as a light unit. The brigade assumed responsibility for the contingency mission on 4 July 1976.36

As the Army National Guard and Army Reserve shouldered a more active role in the Total Army's deterrence plans, the Army Staff developed a plan in the mid-1970s to upgrade the effectiveness of brigade- and battalion-size units. Known as the Affiliation Program, the initiative had three goals: improving readiness; establishing a formal relationship between regular and reserve units; and developing a system of priorities for manpower, equipment, training, funding, and administrative resources. Within the program five categories of combined arms brigades existed: round-out units, which gave Regular Army divisions their full organizational structure; augmentation units, which increased the combat potential of standard divisions; worldwide deployable units, which needed assistance to meet deployment schedules; special mission units, which served as theater defense forces; and units to support the Army school system. Thus, each brigade in the reserves was to have a mission and train for it in a "come-as-you-are for war" mode, which was a far cry from mobilization planning that had existed before and after World War II.37

In 1970 the Army had revised the tables of organization for the administrative training division so that it could function more effectively in reserve status. The division consisted of a division base, a headquarters and headquarters company, a leadership academy, and a support battalion; a committee group; and four brigades—two brigades for basic training, one for advanced individual training, and one for combat support training (*Chart 43*). Basic combat training brigades

## CHART 43—Training Division, 1970

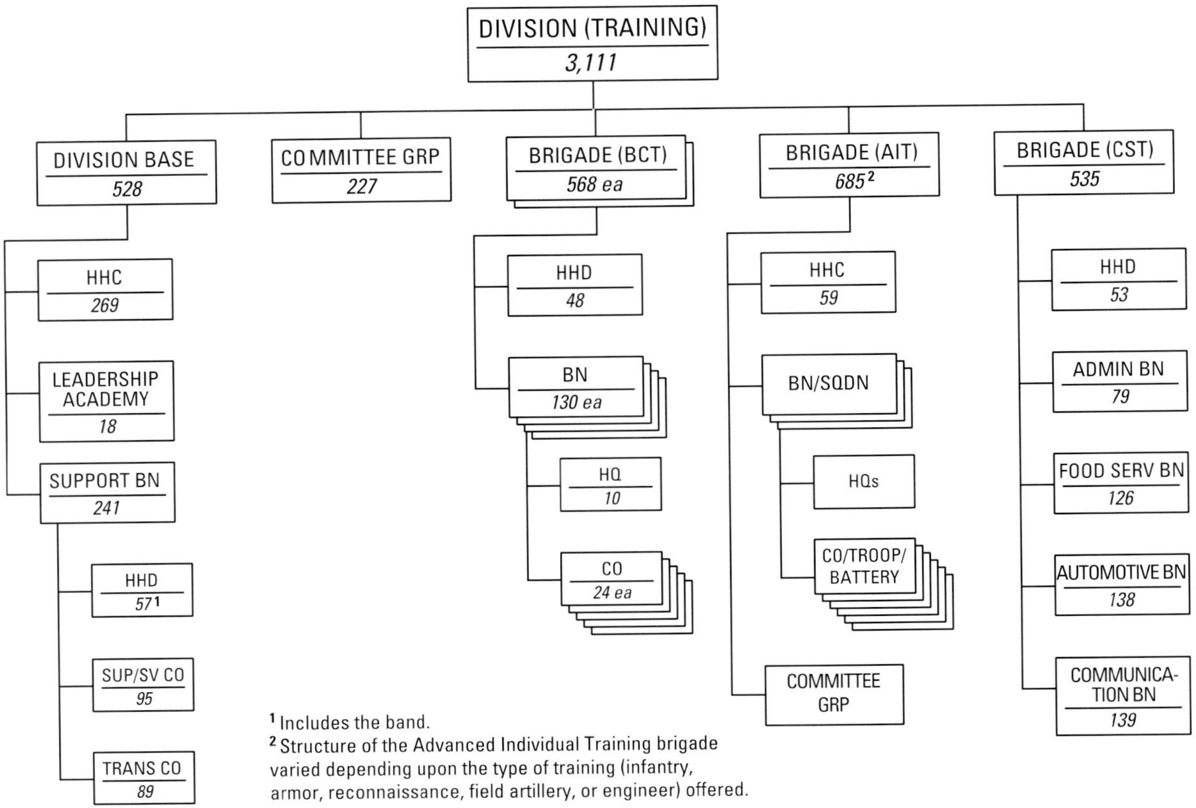

- DIVISION (TRAINING) — 3,111
  - DIVISION BASE — 528
    - HHC — 269
    - LEADERSHIP ACADEMY — 18
    - SUPPORT BN — 241
      - HHD — 57[1]
      - SUP/SV CO — 95
      - TRANS CO — 89
  - COMMITTEE GRP — 227
  - BRIGADE (BCT) — 568 ea
    - HHD — 48
    - BN — 130 ea
      - HQ — 10
      - CO — 24 ea
  - BRIGADE (AIT) — 685[2]
    - HHC — 59
    - BN/SQDN
      - HQs
      - CO/TROOP/BATTERY
    - COMMITTEE GRP
  - BRIGADE (CST) — 535
    - HHD — 53
    - ADMIN BN — 79
    - FOOD SERV BN — 126
    - AUTOMOTIVE BN — 138
    - COMMUNICATION BN — 139

[1] Includes the band.
[2] Structure of the Advanced Individual Training brigade varied depending upon the type of training (infantry, armor, reconnaissance, field artillery, or engineer) offered.

and the committee group underwent little change, but significant modifications were made in both advanced individual training and combat support training brigades. The composition of the advanced individual training brigade varied with the type of training (infantry, armor, reconnaissance, artillery, or engineer) offered, and the combat support training brigade was reorganized to consist of administrative, food service/supply, automotive, and communications battalions. Upon mobilization the division could train between 12,500 and 14,000 enlisted personnel, depending upon the type of training provided by each brigade. All thirteen training divisions had adopted the tables by the end of 1971.38

Two years later, seeking again to improve readiness of the Army Reserve units, Forces Command inactivated some training division elements. Advanced individual training brigades in the 76th, 78th, 80th, 85th, and 91st Divisions and the combat support training brigades in the 89th and 100th Divisions were inactivated and the spaces used to organize "mini" maneuver area commands. The new commands planned, prepared, conducted, and controlled company and battalion exercises for the reserves.39

As in other reserve units, recruiting difficulties caused undermanning in some training units. In 1975 Forces Command inactivated the 89th Division. The personnel formerly assigned to it were used to strengthen other Army Reserve units and to organize the 5th Brigade (Training), an armor training unit with headquarters at Lincoln, Nebraska, that consisted of one squadron and two battalions. With the saving in personnel, a nondivisional Army Reserve combat unit, the 3d Battalion, 87th Infantry, was organized at Fort Carson, Colorado, to support the 193d Infantry Brigade in the Canal Zone.40

The Army Reserve's 5th Brigade (Training) and the training divisions were reorganized once again in late 1978. To save both time and money in training, the active Army had earlier adopted the One Station Unit Training (OSUT) program, under which recruits received both basic and advanced individual training at the professional home of their arm or service. The program proved successful, and Forces Command adopted it for the Army Reserve training divisions. In addition, the revised structure allowed divisions to be tailored for specific mobilization stations. To reflect these changes, the Department of the Army published new tables of organization, which retained as the division base a leadership academy and a support battalion but broke the brigades and battalions down into cells that fitted together to meet specific training requirements. Divisional training brigades no longer conducted basic combat or advanced individual training but carried out both, the same as in the Regular Army. The former divisional committee group and the committee group from the combat support brigade evolved into a training command.41

By October 1978 the Army was fielding the 24-division, 24-brigade force that Abrams had envisaged five years earlier. But organizational developments had been eclipsed by even deeper changes in the fabric of the Army. Prior to its withdrawal from Vietnam, the Nixon administration had adopted an all-volunteer force and imposed cuts in money and personnel. To make up for these losses, Army leaders drew the Regular Army and reserve components closer together, first through the round-out and then though the affiliation programs. The Army could no longer enjoy the luxury of general-purpose forces. Every division and brigade was either forward deployed or assigned a specific mission within the current contingency and mobilization plans. The Regular Army's special mission combined arms brigades included the 193d Infantry Brigade in the Canal Zone and the 172d Infantry Brigade in Alaska. The 194th Armored and 197th Infantry Brigades served both as Strategic Army Force units and as support troops for the Infantry School at Fort Benning, Georgia, and the Armor School at Fort Knox, Kentucky, in the training base. Changes in the Total Army since the withdrawal from Vietnam stressed combat units at the expense of support units. The nation did not have the resources for both.

## Notes

1 Melvin R. Laird, *National Security Strategy of Realistic Deterrence: Annual Defense Department Report, FY 1973* (Washington, D.C.: Government Printing Office, 1972), p. 24.

2 Ibid., pp. 86–87.

3 U.S. Army Combat Developments Command (CDC), "Annual Historical Summary, FY 1970," p. 116, DAMH-HSR; DF, ACSFOR to DCSPER and other addresses, 9 Jan 70, sub: H-Series TOE, FOR OT OM TO, Division General file, DAMH-HSO.

4 U.S. Army CDC, "Historical Summary, FY 66," p. 362, FY 70, pp. 116–17; TOE 7H, Infantry Division, 1970; TOE 17H, Armored Division, 1970; TOE 37H, Mechanized Infantry Division, 1970; TOE 44–325H, Air Defense Artillery Battalion, 1970; TOE 29–1H, TOE 29–11H, and TOE 29–21H, Division Support Command, 1970; TOE 17–87H, Division Aviation Company, Armored Division, 1970; TOE 37–87H, Division Aviation Company, Mechanized Division, 1970; TOE 29–3H, Division Materiel Management Center, 1975.

5 TOE 7–15H, Infantry Battalion, 1970; TOE 17–15H, Armor Battalion, 1970; TOE 7–45H, Mechanized Infantry Battalion, 1970; James Stone, "TOW Really Works," *Infantry* 64 (Sep–Oct 1974): 12–13. The tables provided two variations of the infantry and mechanized infantry battalions: one variation authorized the unit to be equipped with TOWs, the other with 106-mm. recoilless rifles.

6 Changes 1 and 2, TOE 7H, Infantry Division, 1970; Changes 1 and 2, TOE 17H, Armored Division, 1970; Changes 1 and 2, TOE 37H, Mechanized Infantry Division, 1970; TOE 6–100H, Infantry Division Artillery, 1970; Change 1, TOE 6–300H, Armored or Infantry Division Artillery (Mechanized), 1970; TOE 29–lH, Infantry Division Support Command, 1970, and changes 1–3; TOE 29–11H, Infantry Division Support Command (Mechanized), 1970, and changes 1–3; TOE 29–21H, Armored Division Support Command, 1970; TOE 30–17H, Military Intelligence Company (Division), 30 Nov 1970; TOE 30–19T, Combat Intelligence Company, Armored Division or Infantry (Mechanized) Division, 1975; Msg, ACSFOR to CG, CONARC, DA 892178, 31 Dec 68, sub: Activation Order, 1st Bn, 59th Air Defense Artillery (ADA) file, Msg, ACSFOR to CG, CONARC, and other addresses, 201544 Apr 72, sub: DA Staff Review of H Series Conversion Schedule, and Assignment of ADA units, Reorganization of Divisional Administrative Companies as Adjutant General and Finance Companies, Activation of Divisional Materiel Management Centers and Military Intelligence Units, and Inactivation of Divisional Honest John Units, author's notes, all G/H TOEs file, DAMH-HSO.

7 U.S. Army CDC, "Historical Summary, FY 70," p. 116; Ltr, TAG to CinC, USAREUR, 17 Aug 72, sub: Approval of MTOE, DAAG-ASO-D (M) (15 Aug 72) DAFD, AG Reference files, Msg, DALO-SMS-D (Deputy CofS for Logistics, Distribution Branch) to Cdr, CONARC, 201946 Dec 72, sub: Medium Tanks M60A1 for Unit Activation, 1st Bn, 77th Armor; Msg, DA to CG, CONARC, 121215Z Apr 72, sub: Movement Directive 72–10, 6th Bn, 32d Armor; file, Historical Data Cards, 3d and 8th Infantry Divisions, all DAMH-HSO.

8 Msg, ACSFOR to CinC, USARPAC, DA 101815Z Nov 71, sub: Organization and Structure of 25th Infantry Division and Support Units, Msg, ACSFOR to CinC, USARPAC, DA 172209Z Feb 72, sub: Reorganization of 25th Inf Div and ISI (Initial Sustaining Increment) units, Msg, DCSOPS to Cdr, 25th Infantry Division, DA 101930Z Nov 72, sub: Readiness Reporting of 25th Inf Div, Msg, DSCOPS to CinC, USARPAC, DA 272141Z Nov 72, sub: Stationing and Organization of 25th Inf Div in Hawaii, and Memo of Agreement, sub: Command and Staff Relationship Between the 25th Infantry Division and the 29th Brigade (HIARNG) and the 100th Battalion, 442d Infantry Regiment (USAR), 2 Aug 73, all 25th Inf Div file, DAMH-HSO.

9 Msg, CG, CONARC, to CG, Sixth U.S. Army, 212039Z Jan 72, sub: Planning Data for CONUS/Activation, and Msg, U.S. Army Training Center, Inf and Fort Lewis, Wash., to CG, Sixth U.S. Army, 100018 Feb 72, sub: Proposed News Release Activation of the 9th Infantry Division, both 9th Inf Div file, DAMH-HSO; 9th Infantry Division, "Annual Historical Supplement," 1974, pp. 43–44, DAMH-HSR.

THE TOTAL ARMY                                                                    375

10 SS, ACSFOR to CofS, 22 Jun 72, sub: Force Structure, Fort Benning, DAFD-MFP, Msg, ACSFOR to CG, CONARC, 161845Z Oct 72, sub: Unit Designation 197th Bde, DAFD-MFP-T, Ltr, CG, CONARC, to Cdr, Third U.S. Army, 18 Oct 72, sub: Formation of a School Support Organization and Conversion of the 197th Infantry Brigade, ATFOR-FS-SR, and Msg, U.S. Army Infantry Center to Cdr, Third, U.S. Army, 221427Z Mar 73, same subject, all 197th Inf Bde file, DAMH-HSO.

11 U.S. Armor Center and Fort Knox, "Annual Historical Supplement," 1 Jan–31 Dec 74, preface, DAMH-HSR.

12 SS, ACSFOR to CofS, 28 Nov 72, sub: Reorganization of 101st Airborne Div (Ambl), DD DAPT-MFP, 101st Abn Div file, DAMH-HSO. The omission of the 155-mm. towed howitzer battalion reduced the division by 546 officers and enlisted men.

13 SS, TAG Center to CofS, 13 Sep 74, sub: Proposed Change in Nomenclature, 101st Airborne Division (Airmobile), DAAG-AMO, and Ltr, TAG to Cdr, 101st Airborne Division, 16 Oct 74, sub: Change of Parenthetical Identifier, both 101st Abn Div file, DAMH-HSO; "101st Airborne Division Historical Summary, 1974," pp. 10–12, DAMH-HSR; "Interview of LTG John Winn McEmery, 11 Apr 83, p. 16, 101st Abn Div file, DAMH-HSO; AR 672–5–1, Military Awards, 1984.

14 TOE 57H, Airborne Division, 1974; TOE 29-51H, Support Command, Airborne Division, 1973; TOE 29-45H, Supply and Service Battalion, 173; TOE 10-37F, Supply Company (Airborne Division), 1965; TOE 17-215H, Armor Battalion (Airborne), 1973, GO 600, 603, 605, 608, U.S. Army Forces Command (FORSCOM, 174, 407th Spt Bn file, DAMH-HSO; and author's note G/H Tables File, DAMH-HSO.

15 Fact Sheet, ACSFOR to SofA, 15 Jan 71, Formation of the TRICAP Division, FOR DS TRICAP, News Release, New Army Test Division Announced, 25 Mar 71, Msg, SECDEF to Supreme Allied Commander, Europe, DA 252110Z Jan 71, sub: Redesignation and Reorganization of First Armored Division; Msg, ACSFOR to CG, CONARC, DA 292217Z Jan 71, sub: Contingency Planning for TRICAP Div; Msg, OCINFO to CG, CONARC, and other addresses, 232114Z Mar 71, sub: TRICAP Division, documents located in TRICAP file, DAMH-HSO; TOE 47T, TRICAP Division, 15 February 1971; Cheng, *Air Mobility*, p. 180; John Norton, "TRICAP," *Army 21* (Jun 1971): 14-19.

16 Memo for Record, ACSFOR, undated, sub: Conference 15 June 1972 on TRICAP/ACCB Organization and Testing, DAFD, TRICAP file; TOE 17-285T, Attack Helicopter Squadron, TRICAP Division or Attack Helicopter Squadron Air Cavalry Combat Brigade, 1972.

17 U.S. Army CDC, "Reconfiguration of the TRICAP Division," Executive Summary, 15 Dec 72, CGSC Library; Msg, ACSFOR to Cdr, CONARC, DA 131807Z Mar 73, sub: Unit Designation, 1st Cav Div, DAFD-MFP-T, OPS 28, ACSFOR, 30 Sep 73, sub: Reorganization of the 1st Cavalry Division, DAFD-MPF-M, both in TRICAP file, DAMH-HSO.

18 "TRICAP Shortcomings Bared," *Army Times*, 5 Jun 1974; News Release, 1st Cavalry Division Reorganization, 10 May 1974, TRICAP file; GO 200, FORSCOM, 13 Feb 75, 6th Cav Bde file, both DAMH-HSO; TOE 17-200H, Air Cavalry Combat Brigade, 1975; Change 1, TOE 17-205H, Air Cavalry Squadron, Infantry Division, 1975.

19 *Annual Report, Chief, National Guard Bureau, 1971*, pp. 32, 38-40, *1972*, p. 32, 38-41; TOE 44-85G, Air Defense Artillery Automatic Weapons Battalion, Self-Propelled, 1966.

20 Draft ltr, Chief, National Guard Bureau, to Winfield Dunn, NGB-ZA, and Memo, NGB for SA, sub: After Action Reports, 13 Dec 73, NGB-ARO, both 30th Armd Div file, DAMH-HSO.

21 Memo, NGB for SA, 21 Nov 73, sub: After Action Reports, NGB-ARZ-A, 30 Inf Div file, DAMH-HSO; Ltr, NGB for SA, sub: After Action Report, 13 Dec 73.

22 LaVern E. Weber, "For the Minutemen of the '70s: The Guard: `A Long Way'" *Army* 24 (Oct 1974): 65-71; Milnor Robert, "Strong Reserve Boosted by Total Force Impetus," *Army* 24 (Oct 1974): 76-79.

23 Point Paper, DAMO-RQF (Deputy Chief of Staff for Operations and Plans-Requirements Directorate), sub: Why a 16-Division Active Army, 27 Sep 74, 16-Div Force file, DAMH-HSO.

24 Ibid.; Creighton W. Abrams, Jr., "The Sixteen Division Force: Anatomy of a Decision,"

thesis, Command and General Staff College, Fort Leavenworth, Kans., 1975; SS, ACSFOR to CofS, 16 Apr 74, sub: Revised FY Force Structure Actions, DAFD-MFD (ACofS for Force Development-Manpower and Forces Directorate), 16-Div Force file, DAMH-HSO.

25 Robert Sorley, *Thunderbolt: General Creighton Abrams and the Army of His Times* (New York: Simon and Schuster, 1992), pp. 362-64; Ltr, TAG to Cdrs, FORSCOM, and TRADOC, 7 May 74, sub: Revised FY 75-80 Force Structure Guidance, DAAG-AMM DAFD-MFP, 16-Div Force file, DAMH-HSO.

26 Ibid; Msg, Cdr, FORSCOM, to DSCOPS, 041800Z May 74, sub: Inactivation of Infantry Battalions (Mech) in FY 75, 2d Bn, 16th Inf file, DAMH-HSO; OPS 28 DAMO-RQD, Firepower Division, for DCSOPS, sub: ACCB, 13 Jan 75, DAMO-RQD, TRICAP file; "Army Guard AT' 75 Highlights," *National Guardsman* 29 (May 1975): 2–5; Notes Based on FORSCOM GOs, 16-Div Force file, DAMH-HSO.

27 CofS Memo 75–10 for Heads of Army Staff Agencies, 12 Feb 74, sub: Action Required to Attain a 24-Division Total Force Prior to FY 77, and Msg, DSCOPS to Cdrs, FORSCOM, and TRADOC, DA 282101Z Aug 75, sub: Activation of the 5th and 24th Infantry Division and Redesignation of the 194th and 197th Brigades, both 16-Div Force file, DAMH-HSO.

28 "Separate Brigade Plan Out," *Army Times*, 3 Dec 1975; Notes Based on FORSCOM GOs, 16-Div Force file; Robert F. Fairchild, "Training Guard and Reserve Divisions," *Armor* 86 (Mar–Apr 1977): 47–48.

29 U.S. Army FORSCOM, "Annual Historical Review, 1 July 1975–30 Sep 1976," pp. 198–05; Msg, DSCOPS to Cdrs, FORSCOM, and TRADOC, DA 282101Z Aug 75, sub: Activation of the 5th and 24th Infantry Divisions and Redesignation of the 194th and 197th Brigades; "Bde to Become Heavy," *Army Times*, 12 Nov 1975; Historical Data Card, 194th Armored Brigade, DAMH-HSO. Also see notes in 194th Armd Bde file, DAMH-HSO.

30 CofS Memo 74-5-70 for Heads of Army Staff Agencies, sub: Increased Combat Capability in Europe, 2 Aug 74, Bde-75 file, DAMH-HSO; Frank W. Pew, *The U.S. Army Forces Command and the Development of the Brigade 75/76 Concept for the Support of Europe* (Fort McPherson, Ga.: U.S. Army Forces Command, 1980), pp. 1–4.

31 "How DOD Is Improving the Combat Proportions of US Forces in Europe," *Commander Digest* 19 (20 Nov 1975): 2–3; Msg, Cdr, FORSCOM, to Cdr, III Corps and Fort Hood, Tex., 032207Z Dec 74, sub: Reorganization of Units at Fort Hood/ Selected FY Activations, Msg, DAMO-FDP-T to Cdr, FORSCOM, DA 162021Z Apr 75, sub: Involvement of lst Cavalry Division in Brigade 75, both Bde-75 file DAMH-HSO; Pew, *Brigade 75/76 Concept*, pp. 74–109. The Nunn amendment limited the additional combat units to battalion or smaller size units, therefore the Army Staff considered the headquarters and headquarters company of each brigade as one of the smaller units.

32 Msg, DAMO-ODO to Cdr, FORSCOM, and CinC, USAREUR, DA 131830Z Jul 76, sub: Movement Directive 23–76, Bde-75 file, DAMH-HSO; U.S. Army Europe and Seventh Army, *Strengthening NATO (North Atlantic Treaty Organization): Stationing of the 2d Armored Division (Forward) in Northern Germany* (n.p., 1980), p. 3; Pew, *Brigade 75/76 Concept*, pp. 184–208.

33 CofS Memo 75-570-94 for Heads of Army Staff Agencies, sub: Conversion of Rotational Brigades to PCS, 10 Dec 75, Msg, DAMO-ODO to CinC, USAREUR, DA 241942Z Sep 75, sub: Declassification of Bde 76 stationing, and Msg, DAMO-ODO to Cdr, FORSCOM, and other addresses, DA 131515Z May 76, sub: Termination of Unit Rotations, all Brigade 75/76 file, DAMH-HSO; PO 48–1 and 52–1, 1st Infantry Division and Fort Riley, 24 Sep 1976, 3d Bn, 28th Inf file, DAMH-HSO; Msg, DAMO-ODO to Cdr, FORSCOM, and other addresses, 201845Z Apr 78, sub: Movement Directive 24–78, and PO 63–2, FORSCOM, 21 Apr 1979, both 5th Bn, 7th Cav file, DAMH-HSO; USAREUR and Seventh Army, *Strengthening NATO*, pp. 2–7.

34 FM 100–5, *Operations*, p. 1–1; CofS Memo for Heads of Army Staff Agencies, 5 Feb 75, sub: Realignment of ARNG Split Divisions, Information Paper, NGB, same subject, 24 Nov 74, NGB-ARO-O, Memo, NGB to Sec of Army, undated, same subject, NGB-ARO, all National Guard Reorganization, 1975, file, DAMH-HSO; *Annual Report, Chief, National Guard Bureau, FY 1975*, p. 32; *Annual Review (formerly Report), Chief, National Guard Bureau, FY 1976 and TQ*, p.

30; Ltr, NGB to AG, Ohio, 25 Feb 77, sub: Reorganization of Ohio ARNG Units, NGB-ARO-O 207–02, Ohio National Guard file, DAMH-HSO; Reserve Components Troop Basis of the Army Annex I: Army National Guard Unit Program, 28 Feb 1977, DAMH-HSO.

35 Telephone or Verbal Conversation Record (DA Form 751), Mr. Bart, FORSCOM, and author, sub: 187th Inf Bde (Mass), 13 Jun 75, and DA Form 751, Mr. Smith, TAG, and author, 18 Jun 75, both 187th Inf Bde file, DAMH-HSO; "Callaway, Thurmond: Brigade Affiliation to Involve Politics?" *Army Times*, 3 Sep 1975. Congressional leaders traditionally have been protective of military units and installations in their districts because they are a source of jobs and income.

36 U.S. Army FORSCOM, "Annual Historical Review, 1 Jul 75–30 Sep 76," p. 226–27; Ltr, OCAR to Maj Gen Gordon J. Duquemin, 29 Jan 76, "Taking A Candid Look," *Reserve* 22 (Nov–Dec 1976): 18–19; Msg, DA 0714452 May 76, sub: 205th Infantry Brigade, Msg, DA 251520Z May, same subject, and PO 6–2, Fifth US Army, 1976, all 205th Inf Bde file, DAMH-HSO.

37 AR 11–29, Affiliation Program, 1975; Information Paper, NGB, sub: Affiliation Program, 13 Jun 78, NGB-ARO-T, Roundout/Affiliation file, DAMH-HSO; U.S. Army FORSCOM, "Annual Historical Review, 1 Oct 76–30 Sep 77," pp. 238–42.

38 TOE 97, Division (Training), 1970; Ltr, Organization and Directory Branch to TAG, subject: Change in Status of Units, AGAO-D, 18 Feb 71, AG Reference files, also see Training Division General files, 1970-71, DAMH-HSO.

39 J. Milnor Roberts, "USAR Moves into 1973," *Army Reserve Magazine* 19 (Mar 1973): 4–5.

40 GO 174, Sixth US Army, 1975, 5th Brigade (Training) file, DAMH-HSO, U.S. Army FORSCOM, "Annual Historical Review, FY 1975," p. 181, GO 64, U.S. Sixth Army, 3d Bn, 87th Inf file, DAMH-HSO.

41 *Department of the Army Historical Summary, 1974*, p. 32, 1979, p. 16; U.S. Army FORSCOM, "Annual Historical Review, 1 Oct 77–30 Sep 78," p. 166; TOE 97-500H8, Recruit Training Organization, 1978; "It's No Easy Job Retaining Trainers as the USAR's 108th Division Outdoes Itself," Reserve 25, No. 1, (1979): 20–21.

# CHAPTER 14

# A New Assessment

*The most demanding challenge confronting the US military in the decade of the 1980s is to develop and demonstrate the capability to successfully meet threats to vital US interests outside of Europe, without compromising the decisive theater in Central Europe.*

General Edward C. Meyer[1]

Following the conflict in Vietnam the Army undertook a concerted program to achieve parity with the heavy forces of the Soviet Union. Various schools, commands, and agencies devised divisional models from which they argued the need for new weapons, equipment, tactics, and doctrine, a process similar to that which had produced the pentomic and ROAD divisions. Yet even as the Army retooled for a European battlefield, its senior leaders also tried to anticipate what other contingencies would have to be faced in the future. By 1990 the effectiveness of this work in searching for organizational designs that would give the Army even greater flexibility would be put to a severe test.

## *The Division Restructuring Study*

The lightning war between the Arabs and Israelis in 1973, when the Egyptian and Syrian armies lost more tanks than the United States had in Europe at the time, caused the Army to rethink its doctrine and the structure of its divisions and brigades. An examination of the seventeen-day conflict led to new ideas about how to prepare for war and how to fight. Known as the "Active Defense," the new doctrine stressed defense as the principal mode of combat. Other factors embedded in the new approach were the speed with which decisive actions would take place and an awareness of the increased lethality of modern weapons on the battlefield. Both considerations put added pressure on the Army to improve the combat capabilities of forward-deployed active forces and the speed with which effective reserve components units could be delivered to overseas battlegrounds.[2]

Since the Army was on the threshold of adopting new equipment and weapons that increased mobility, firepower, and maneuver, the Army's schools, commands, and agencies examined such issues as military intelligence organizations; signal and aviation requirements; and chemical, biological, and nuclear defense, seeking better ways to maximize the new technology and not just providing "tag alongs" in existing organizations. Fire support teams for artillery;

*General Weyand*

bifunctional staffs (the unit commander serving as a chief of staff with two deputies, one for operations and military intelligence and the other for personnel and logistics); rearmament, refueling, and maintenance in the forward area of the battlefield; and consolidation of administration at the battalion level also came under scrutiny.[3]

In March 1975 Chief of Staff General Fred C. Weyand suggested to Deputy Chief of Staff for Operations and Plans Lt. Gen. Donald H. Cowles that the structure of divisions should be reexamined. Weyand was concerned that new technology had resulted in only "add ons" to divisions, increasing their weight and complexity and decreasing their overall flexibility. Cowles turned to General William E. DePuy, commander of the U.S. Army Training and Doctrine Command (TRADOC), established in 1973 specifically to address training and doctrine issues, for his views. DePuy assembled a group of officers from his command and the Army's schools and centers to conduct a division restructuring analysis focused on finding the optimum antiarmor capability for divisions. Among the areas considered were the employment of the new armored vehicles coming into service and the problems associated with exploiting new artillery and target acquisition systems whose range had been greatly increased.[4]

The major product of the Division Restructuring Study (DRS) was the "heavy division" (*Chart 44*), an organization designed to replace both mechanized infantry and armored divisions. Headed by Col. (later General) John Foss, from the Training and Doctrine Command, the planning group believed that the principles underlying the new organization could be applied to all divisions.

The heavy division included three brigades, each consisting of a permanent combat team of two mechanized infantry and three tank battalions. Infantry battalions consisted of one combat support, one TOW, and three small rifle companies; tank battalions, similar in structure to the mechanized infantry units, fielded three tank companies and maintenance, TOW, and combat support companies. A tank company had three tank platoons with each platoon having only three tanks. The precise location of the TOW antitank missile launchers posed the old problem of centralized versus decentralized control for the planners, much as had the introduction of other new weapons and equipment, such as the machine gun, tank, antitank gun, airplane, and helicopter. For now they remained under control of the battalion.[5]

# CHART 44—Heavy Division, Division Restructuring Study
## 1 March 1977

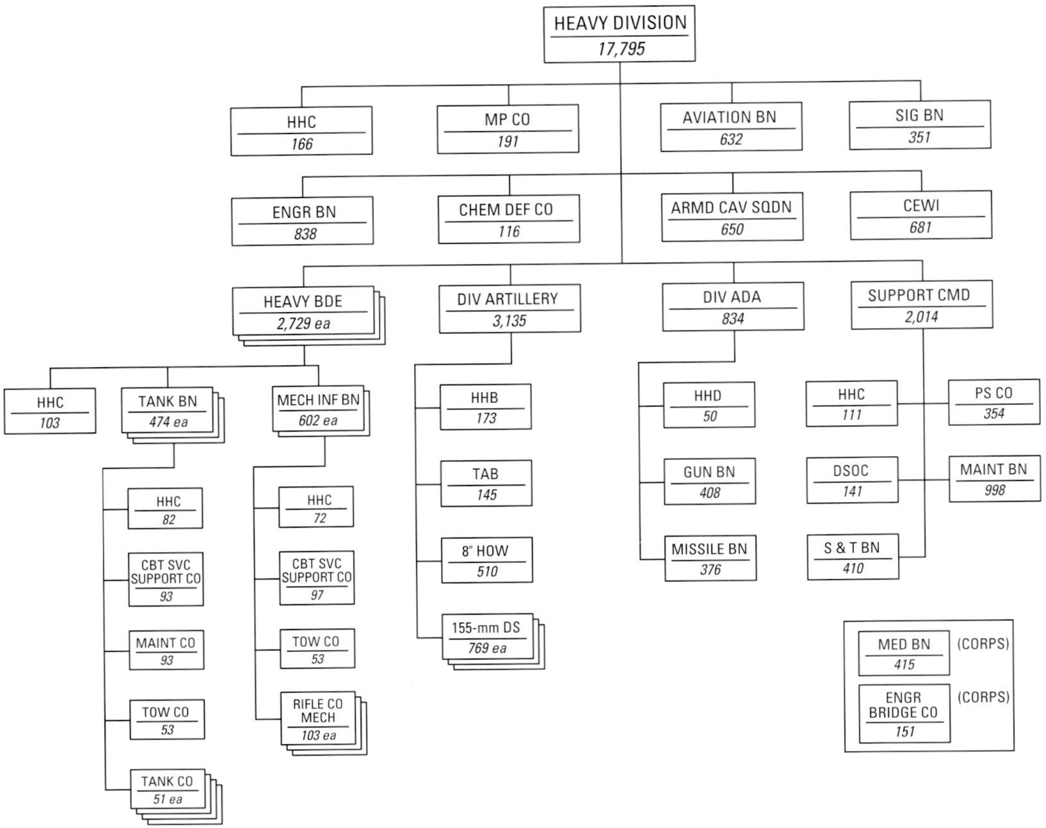

- **HEAVY DIVISION** — 17,795
  - **HHC** — 166
  - **MP CO** — 191
  - **AVIATION BN** — 632
    - **SIG BN** — 351
  - **ENGR BN** — 838
  - **CHEM DEF CO** — 116
  - **ARMD CAV SQDN** — 650
    - **CEWI** — 681
  - **HEAVY BDE** — 2,729 ea
    - **TANK BN** — 474 ea
      - **HHC** — 103
      - **HHC** — 82
      - **CBT SVC SUPPORT CO** — 93
      - **MAINT CO** — 93
      - **TOW CO** — 53
      - **TANK CO** — 51 ea
    - **MECH INF BN** — 602 ea
      - **HHC** — 72
      - **CBT SVC SUPPORT CO** — 97
      - **TOW CO** — 53
      - **RIFLE CO MECH** — 103 ea
  - **DIV ARTILLERY** — 3,135
    - **HHB** — 173
    - **TAB** — 145
    - **8" HOW** — 510
    - **155-mm DS** — 769 ea
  - **DIV ADA** — 834
    - **HHD** — 50
    - **GUN BN** — 408
    - **MISSILE BN** — 376
  - **SUPPORT CMD** — 2,014
    - **HHC** — 111
    - **PS CO** — 354
    - **DSOC** — 141
    - **MAINT BN** — 998
    - **S & T BN** — 410

- **MED BN (CORPS)** — 415
- **ENGR BRIDGE CO (CORPS)** — 151

To increase firepower, the number of 155-mm. howitzers in each direct support artillery battery was increased from six to eight, and the number of firing batteries in a battalion rose from three to four. The number of batteries in the 8-inch howitzer battalion was also increased to four. Since the group foresaw a larger divisional combat area in both width and depth, the artillery's counterfire (destroying enemy artillery) capabilities moved from the corps level to the division, with a target acquisition battery added to the division artillery to locate those targets. A smaller cavalry squadron fielded only three ground troops, with the air cavalry troop moved to a new divisional aviation battalion. For antiaircraft defense, the study gave the heavy division an air defense artillery brigade comprising two battalions, one for the forward area of the battlefield and another for the rear.[6]

With smaller divisional infantry and armor battalions, planners envisioned integrating the combat arms at the battalion rather than at the company level. Under the ROAD concept a company team had been the principal combat formation. For example, a mechanized infantry company was normally reinforced with engineers, forward artillery observers, and possibly tanks, antitank weapons, and helicopters. But the company commander who integrated these forces had no staff and probably lacked the experience to achieve the most effective use of all these resources. A change of focus therefore appeared necessary.[7]

Combat support within the new division also underwent radical changes. A combat electronic warfare intelligence (CEWI) battalion was organized from military intelligence and Army Security Agency resources. Consisting of an electronic warfare company and a ground surveillance company, along with a headquarters and operations company, the battalion greatly expanded the division's intelligence collection and analysis capabilities. As noted, the reconnaissance squadron's aviation troop was moved to a new divisional aviation battalion, which consolidated the attack helicopter company and the division's command and control aviation resources in one unit. All mess resources were grouped at battalion level, and a personnel service company merged finance and personnel services into one company, which was included in the support command. That command also fielded a supply and transport battalion, a maintenance battalion, and a support operations center. A chemical company provided the division with smoke-generating resources and the ability to assist in defense against biological, nuclear, and chemical weapons. In the past no chemical unit had existed in a division, and all units had been expected to defend against those weapons as a primary responsibility. Finally, the study moved the divisional medical battalion and the bridge company from the engineer battalion to the corps level.[8]

A field test of the new structure at Fort Hood by a brigade of the 1st Cavalry Division in 1979 produced mixed results. Lt. Gen. Marvin D. Fuller, the III Corps commander, who oversaw the test, found the division overmanned and overequipped in many areas, giving commanders resources to cover every possible deficiency or contingency. He thought the additional costs in personnel and equipment would price the division out of reach. He also found that radios had

# A NEW ASSESSMENT

proliferated to the extent that communications were hampered rather than improved, that bifunctional staffs filtered information needed by commanders, and that air defense coverage was still inadequate. However, the test validated the belief that tank and mechanized infantry battalions should be the focal point for the integration of the combined arms.[9]

During the evaluation of the division restructuring concept, the Army Staff approved selective improvements in existing divisions based on lessons learned from the 1973 Arab-Israeli War. A target acquisition battery was placed in the division artillery to identify targets up to 50 kilometers in front of the forward edge of the battle area. Chemical companies were added to divisions to provide nuclear, biological, and chemical reconnaissance and decontamination support. Because of the need to acquire and evaluate information about the enemy, divisional military intelligence battalions of the CEWI type were organized beginning in 1979. In the armored and mechanized infantry divisions, aviation resources were again pooled to form aviation battalions. The airborne division was assigned three antitank TOW companies, one for each brigade, while the infantry division in Korea was assigned only a company. When the aerial field artillery battalion was inactivated in the air assault division, antitank resources were concentrated in an aviation battalion.[10]

Along with upgrading existing divisions, the Department of Defense directed the Army to increase its mechanized forces. In September 1979 the 24th Infantry Division converted from infantry to mechanized infantry, and the following year elements were assigned to the previously unmanned 149th Armored Brigade in the Kentucky Army National Guard, raising the number of brigades in the total force to twenty-five. By 1980 the Texas Guard had eliminated its unfilled 36th Airborne Brigade, using its personnel to organize a corps-level combat engineer battalion. Planners also considered reorganizing all infantry divisions, except the airborne and the airmobile forces, as mechanized units.[11]

## *Division-86*

Before the 1st Cavalry Division completed its evaluation of the heavy division in 1979, the new commander of the Training and Doctrine Command, General Donn A. Starry, began to develop another divisional concept that built upon the Division Restructuring Study. From his experience as the V Corps commander in Europe, Starry believed that Foss' Division Restructuring Study group had worked too quickly. Units had conducted tests without proper training, and the opposing forces lacked adequate knowledge of Soviet tactics. Therefore, he judged that the test results could not be totally ascribed to deficiencies in tactics, leadership, or organization.[12]

The Division Restructuring Study had concentrated on the active defense, the lethality of the battlefield, and the need to win the first battle, but Starry stressed the offense and "central battle" where all aspects of firepower and maneuver, air

*General Starry*

and ground, would come together over a wide area to produce a decisive action. He believed that analysis of those elements in the battle area, including the range of weapons and their rates of fire, the size of the opposing forces, the terrain over which they would advance, and the speed of that advance, would permit development of more effective operational concepts. In addition, he thought consideration had to be given to "force generation," the task of concentrating the combat power of the division for the central battle. These ideas evolved into the "AirLand Battle" doctrine, which was published in 1982 in the revised Field Manual, 100–5, *Operations*.[13]

Analysis of combat within the framework of the AirLand Battle concept led to the development of "Division-86," so named because 1986 was as far out as General Meyer and his advisers could project the threat. Because of the importance of Europe to national security, Division-86, like the Division Restructuring Study, emphasized a standardized heavy division, which combined both armored and mechanized infantry divisions, and focused on maximizing the new equipment entering the inventory. In October 1979, four months after General Edward C. Meyer became Chief of Staff, Starry presented his Division-86 proposal, which Meyer approved in principle on the 18th of that month. His final decision about fielding such a division depended upon studies to be conducted for light divisions (infantry, airborne, and airmobile), corps, and echelons above the corps level.[14]

Division-86, as presented to General Meyer, retained the flexible ROAD structure. The new heavy division consisted of a headquarters and headquarters company; three brigade headquarters; a military police company; signal, air defense artillery, engineer, and military intelligence battalions; a reconnaissance squadron; division artillery; an air cavalry attack brigade; a division support command; and a number of maneuver elements to be determined, possibly four or five mechanized infantry battalions and five or six armor battalions. The division would total approximately 20,000 officers and enlisted men (*Chart 45*).[15]

Under the "come-as-you-are, fight-as-you-are" approach to war, combat service support had to be immediately available in the battle area. To meet the new

CHART 45—Heavy Division (Tank Heavy)
As Briefed to General Meyer on 18 October 1979

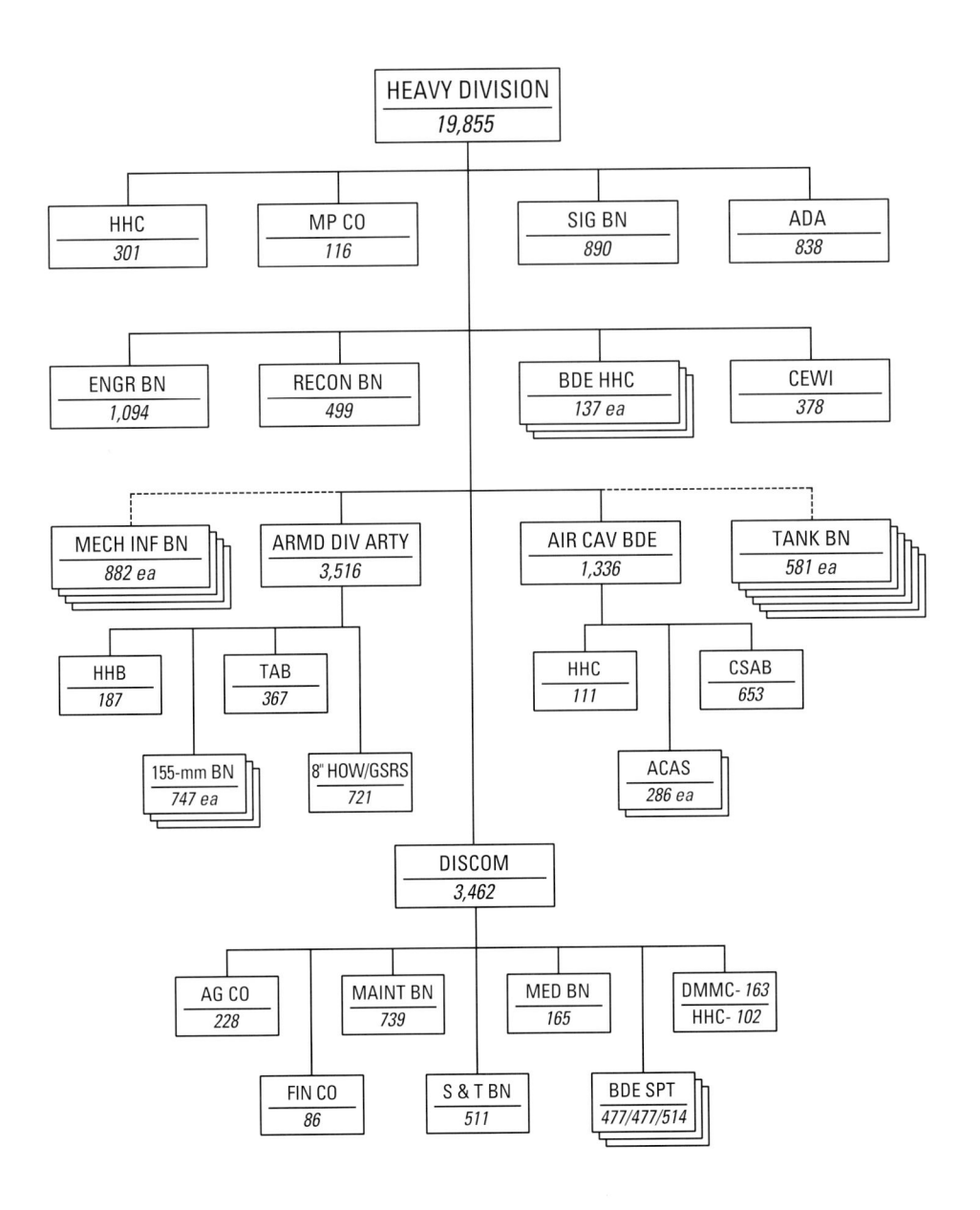

- HEAVY DIVISION — 19,855
  - HHC — 301
  - MP CO — 116
  - SIG BN — 890
  - ADA — 838
  - ENGR BN — 1,094
  - RECON BN — 499
  - BDE HHC — 137 ea
  - CEWI — 378
  - MECH INF BN — 882 ea
  - ARMD DIV ARTY — 3,516
    - HHB — 187
    - TAB — 367
    - 155-mm BN — 747 ea
    - 8" HOW/GSRS — 721
  - AIR CAV BDE — 1,336
    - HHC — 111
    - CSAB — 653
    - ACAS — 286 ea
  - TANK BN — 581 ea
  - DISCOM — 3,462
    - AG CO — 228
    - MAINT BN — 739
    - MED BN — 165
    - DMMC — 163 / HHC — 102
    - FIN CO — 86
    - S & T BN — 511
    - BDE SPT — 477/477/514

*General Meyer*

logistical requirements, the study called for a radical reorganization of the division support command, primarily to address the forward area of the battlefield. The command included a materiel management center, adjutant general and finance companies, a supply and transport battalion, a maintenance battalion, and three support battalions, one for each divisional brigade. Support battalions, which were to "arm, fuel, fix, and feed forward," included headquarters and headquarters, supply, maintenance, and medical companies. A small medical battalion supported the rest of the division. Planners had difficulty deciding whether to place a chemical company at corps, division, or division support command level, but gave it to the supply and transport battalion in the support command.[16]

Evidence of fundamental change existed within the combat arms. Each tank battalion consisted of a headquarters element and four tank companies, and each tank company fielded three platoons of four tanks each. Mechanized infantry battalions contained a headquarters element along with one TOW and four rifle companies, with the riflemen to be mounted on new Bradley infantry fighting vehicles. To counter the Soviet Union's high density of artillery and improved weapons, the Division-86 study, like its predecessor, significantly increased the division artillery. It fielded three battalions of 155-mm. self-propelled howitzers organized into three batteries, each having eight pieces; one battalion of sixteen 8-inch howitzers and nine multiple launch rocket systems (MLRS) mounted on vehicles; and a target acquisition battalion.[17]

The reconnaissance squadron called for three troops, each having two platoons equipped with cavalry fighting vehicles—similar to the Bradley fighting vehicle—and a platoon of motorcycles. A new organization, an air cavalry attack brigade (later designated as an aviation brigade), which resulted from the pioneer work of the 1st Cavalry Division and the 6th Cavalry Brigade at Fort Hood and others, appeared in the division to provide helicopters for an antitank role. Two attack battalions, each consisting of four companies with six helicopters each, and a combat support aviation battalion, which provided resources for command aviation, aircraft maintenance, and the military intelligence battalion, made up the brigade. The brigade fielded 134 aircraft.[18]

*The Bradley fighting vehicle and,* below, *multiple launch rocket systems*

# CHART 46—Heavy Division, 1 October 1982

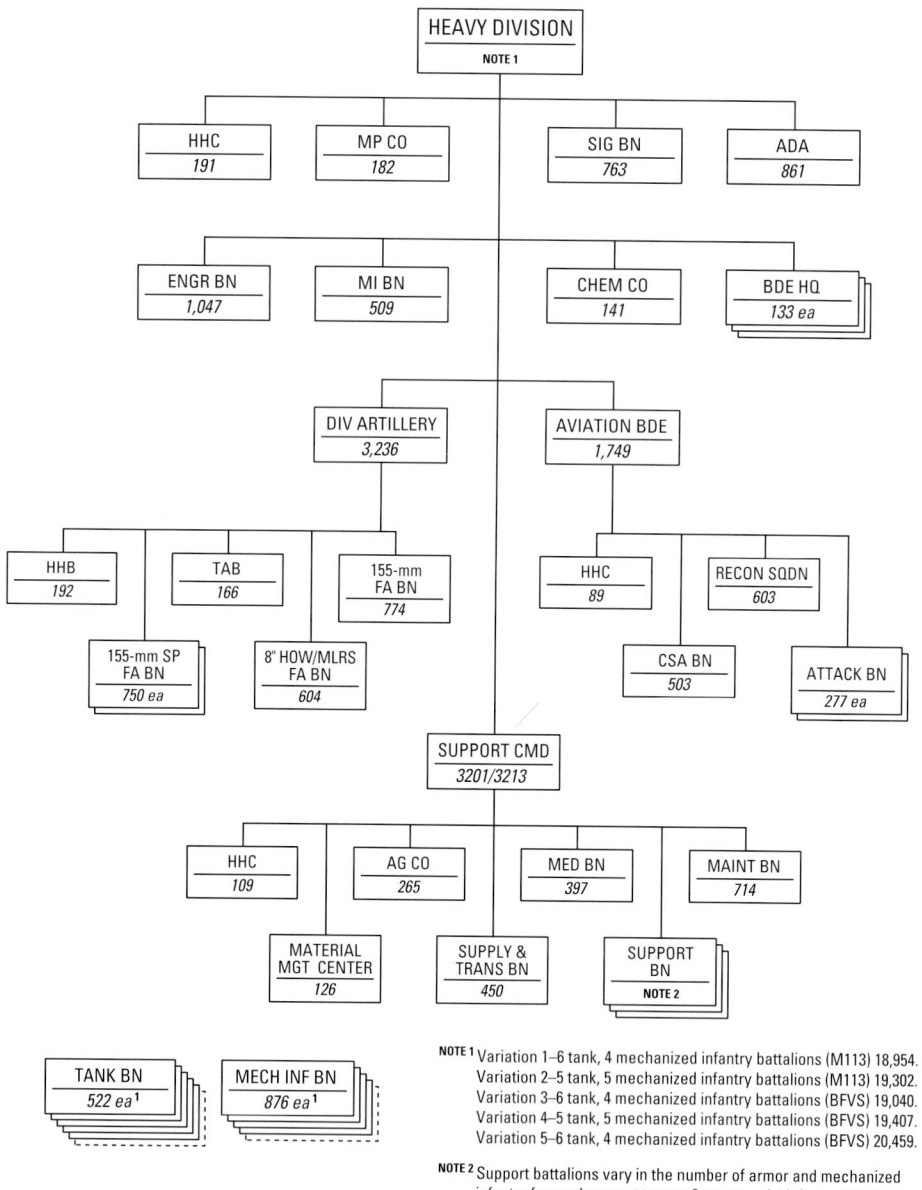

- **HEAVY DIVISION** (NOTE 1)
  - HHC — 191
  - MP CO — 182
  - SIG BN — 763
  - ADA — 861
  - ENGR BN — 1,047
  - MI BN — 509
  - CHEM CO — 141
  - BDE HQ — 133 ea
  - **DIV ARTILLERY** — 3,236
    - HHB — 192
    - TAB — 166
    - 155-mm FA BN — 774
    - 155-mm SP FA BN — 750 ea
    - 8" HOW/MLRS FA BN — 604
  - **AVIATION BDE** — 1,749
    - HHC — 89
    - RECON SQDN — 603
    - CSA BN — 503
    - ATTACK BN — 277 ea
  - **SUPPORT CMD** — 3201/3213
    - HHC — 109
    - AG CO — 265
    - MED BN — 397
    - MAINT BN — 714
    - MATERIAL MGT CENTER — 126
    - SUPPLY & TRANS BN — 450
    - SUPPORT BN (NOTE 2)

- TANK BN — 522 ea[1]
- MECH INF BN — 876 ea[1]

**NOTE 1** Variation 1–6 tank, 4 mechanized infantry battalions (M113) 18,954. Variation 2–5 tank, 5 mechanized infantry battalions (M113) 19,302. Variation 3–6 tank, 4 mechanized infantry battalions (BFVS) 19,040. Variation 4–5 tank, 5 mechanized infantry battalions (BFVS) 19,407. Variation 5–6 tank, 4 mechanized infantry battalions (BFVS) 20,459.

**NOTE 2** Support battalions vary in the number of armor and mechanized infantry forward support teams: 2 armor and 1 infantry, 377; 2 armor and 2 infantry, 402; and 1 armor and 2 infantry, 363.

The distribution of air defense weapons had haunted the planners. Because of the breadth and depth of the battlefield one commander could not easily supervise air defense in the division's forward and rear areas, with each area requiring unique weapons. An air defense artillery brigade seemed to be one solution, but personnel constraints ruled it out. Therefore, the division was authorized an air defense artillery battalion outfitted with a mix of short-range (man-portable Stingers) and mid-range (Chaparral) missiles, to be supplemented by the still experimental Sergeant York gun system.[19]

The Training and Doctrine Command published tables of organization and equipment for this second try at the heavy division concept on 1 October 1982 (*Chart 46*). One set of tables covered both the mechanized infantry division and the armored division, but with five variations. Five or six armor and four or five mechanized infantry battalions were to be assigned to an armored division, and a mechanized infantry division was to have five armor and five mechanized infantry battalions. Variations in the tables also covered different equipment, M60 tanks and M113 armored personnel carriers or the new M1 Abrams tanks and Bradley infantry fighting vehicles. Given the variations, the strength of heavy divisions ranged between 19,000 and 20,500 officers and enlisted men.[20]

The published tables differed somewhat from the proposed heavy division that Meyer had approved three years earlier. Cavalry fighting vehicles replaced tanks in the reconnaissance squadron, and the squadron, consisting of two ground and two air troops, had no motorcycles. Rather than being a divisional unit, it was a part of the aviation brigade. The finance unit moved to the corps level, and the reorganized military intelligence battalion fielded electronic warfare, surveillance, and service companies. In the support command, the medical battalion reappeared, but the chemical company was returned to divisional level, and the target acquisition element was reduced to a battery.[21]

The Army faced complex problems in fielding Division-86. Over forty major weapons or new pieces of equipment needed to be procured, and some were still in developmental stages. Doctrinal literature and training programs required revision, and budgetary limitations had to be considered. The solution approved by the Army Staff, as in the past, was to adopt the heavy division concept but with interim organizations using obsolete equipment until new weapons and equipment were available. Delivery of many new items was expected to begin in 1983. Therefore, organizational and equipment modernization was to begin in January of that year. The number of maneuver elements for a heavy armored division was set at six armor and four mechanized infantry battalions, while that for a heavy mechanized infantry division was placed at five armor and five mechanized infantry battalions.[22]

The Army also faced another problem in fielding the new heavy division, a shortfall in personnel. The Training and Doctrine Command estimated that a strength of 836,000 was required to field Army-86, but only 780,000 was authorized for the foreseeable future. Therefore to provide manpower spaces for modernizing the forces in Germany, the 4th Brigade, 4th Infantry Division, was inactivated in Europe in 1984 along with other units throughout the Army. Shortly thereafter the modernization plan went awry. Because of various problems involved in funding and procuring equipment, the Army leadership slipped the completion date for modernizing heavy divisions to the mid-1990s.[23]

Early in the planning process for modernizing divisional forces, Meyer also decided to adopt a new regimental system. It was to address one aspect of the "hollow Army" (the problem of having sufficient personnel and equipment to support and sustain the forward-deployed Army), unit cohesion.[24] Patterned after the Combat Arms Regimental System (CARS), the new United States Army Regimental System assigned each armor, air defense artillery, cavalry, field artillery, and infantry regiment—later aviation regiments and special forces[25] were added—a home base from which regimental elements would rotate between continental and overseas assignments. A soldier could affiliate with a regiment and expect to serve in it for most of his or her career. By necessity the new system broke traditional regimental associations with divisions since fewer regiments could be accommodated in the system because of the linking of elements between overseas and continental stations. Meyer believed that the benefits of unit cohesion outweighed the loss of divisional affiliation. He tied implementation of the new regimental system to modernization of the force. By 1985 implementation of the regimental system was separated from force modernization because of production delays, and unit rotation was abandoned because of personnel turbulence and its adverse effect on readiness. Nevertheless, designating regiments as part of the system continued, paced by the number of flags that the U.S. Army Support Activity, Philadelphia, could manufacture each month. The flags were needed when the battalion designations were changed.[26]

## *Elusive Light Divisions*

In 1979, when Meyer had approved the heavy division, he also had directed Starry to standardize infantry, airborne, and airmobile divisions—now called "light divisions." Meyer, who opposed the total heavy force envisioned by Department of Defense planners, wanted the Training and Doctrine Command to focus on the infantry division; airborne and airmobile divisions were to be considered later. He particularly wanted to know if the infantry division could be designed to move and fight in contingency areas, such as the Asiatic rim, and still have sufficient resources to delay and fight Soviet forces in Central Europe. This question posed the dilemma that had plagued the airborne division community since World War II—how to give a unit strategic mobility and still have it possess the firepower and the resources to sustain itself in combat. Meyer thought the answer to the problem lay in the use of new technology, which included advanced radar, intelligence, and satellite resources; containerized food and equipment; lightweight, high power communications; new lightweight vehicles; highly accurate and powerful, but lightweight, weapons; advanced helicopters; and other developments. Two international events in 1979, the widening of the conflict between the Soviets and the Afghans and Iran's seizure of American hostages, spurred the need for light, versatile units.[27]

An effective structure for the "non-heavy" infantry division, however, proved elusive. Initially Starry set restrictions on the division. Its size was not to exceed 14,000 soldiers, it was to be without organic tank or mechanized infantry units, and it was to be deployable in Air Force C–141 aircraft. After four tries and a relaxation of the strength requirement, Starry recommended a division of 17,773 officers and enlisted men, which Meyer approved for further development and testing on 18 September 1980.[28]

As planners developed various ideas for a light division, the Army Staff selected the 9th Infantry Division at Fort Lewis, Washington, to serve as a "test bed," or a field laboratory, for equipment, organization, and operations. One objective was to shorten the equipment developmental cycle—typically from five to seven years—which had frustrated Meyer and others. Although Meyer obviously wanted the division to experiment with new equipment, difficulties in funding hobbled the effort from the start. Some of these problems were overcome through the direct intervention of the Army Staff, but others were never surmounted. In 1982 Meyer thus changed the emphasis of the 9th Division's mission from testing highly technical equipment to developing innovative organizational and operational concepts. The result was the design of a motorized division of 13,000 men and capable of being airlifted anywhere in the world. Before the 9th Infantry Division completed its new assignment, however, the Army set off in a new direction for the light division.[29]

## *The Army of Excellence*

By 1983 planners had reassessed the nature and direction of world events and the types of conflicts that could be expected. As Meyer saw a need for a balance between heavy and light divisions, so did his replacement, Chief of Staff General John A. Wickham. The successful operations of the British in the Falkland Islands, the Israelis in Lebanon, and the United States in Grenada all drove home the point that credible forces did not have to be heavy forces. To have light divisions within the Army's limited resources, Wickham ordered the replacement of the 16,000-man standard infantry division with a new light infantry unit of about 10,000 men and the adaptation of light concepts to airborne and airmobile divisions. He also wanted the design applied to the motorized division under development at Fort Lewis. Furthermore, Wickham desired light divisions to have an improved "tooth-to-tail" (i.e., combat strength to logistics) ratio and to be deployable three times faster than existing infantry divisions. With these changes he anticipated that the corps would be strengthened and made the focus of the AirLand Battle doctrine.[30]

*9th Infantry Division "dune buggy" used in training*

Under Wickham's guidance the Army specified that corps were to plan and conduct major operations, while divisions were to concentrate on the tactical battlefield. The revised Field Manual 100–5, *Operations*, of 1986 defined the corps as the Army's largest tactical unit. Tailored for a particular theater and mission, the corps was to contain all combat, combat support, and combat service support required for sustained operations. In addition to various types of divisions, the corps was to have available an armored cavalry regiment; field artillery, air defense artillery, engineer, signal, aviation, and military intelligence brigades; and a military police group. Infantry and armored brigades and psychological operations, special operations forces, and civil affairs units could be attached as needed. When organized for a particular theater and mission, the corps was thus to be a relatively fixed organization with area as well as combat responsibilities. The newly defined corps was really a throwback to the beginning of the century when *Field Service Regulations* described a prototype corps.[31]

Wickham's guidance resulted in the development of units for the "Army of Excellence."[32] Within that rubric, the tables of organization and equipment called for a 10,220-man light infantry division, which comprised a headquarters and headquarters company; a military police company; signal, air defense artillery, and engineer battalions; three brigade headquarters; nine infantry battalions; division artillery; an aviation brigade; a support command; and a band. Shortly thereafter a military intelligence battalion was added and additional personnel autho-

# A NEW ASSESSMENT

*General Wickham*

rized for the support command, which raised the division's strength to 10,791 (*Chart 47*). All men and their equipment were transportable in fewer than 550 C–141 sorties in less than four days, a key feature in Wickham's guidance for the design of the light division.[33]

The light division greatly improved the ratio of combat troops to support personnel. Infantry battalions fielded three rifle companies and a headquarters company, a total of 559 officers and enlisted men. The battalion headquarters company included a "footmobile" reconnaissance platoon (no vehicles in it), an antiarmor platoon (four TOW launchers), and a heavy mortar platoon (four 4.2-inch mortars). The only vehicles in the battalions were the new "high mobility multi-purpose wheeled vehicles" (HMMWVs, or "Hummers") and motorcycles. Brigades provided mess and maintenance for battalions. The division artillery consisted of three towed 105-mm. howitzer battalions, three batteries with six howitzers each and one battery of 155-mm. howitzers fielding eight pieces. A command aviation company, an attack helicopter battalion, and the reconnaissance squadron comprised the aviation brigade. The air defense artillery battalion fielded 20-mm. multibarrel, electrically driven Vulcan guns and the Stinger missiles fired from a shoulder position, and the engineer battalion had no bridging equipment. Support elements followed the functional ideas of ROAD, with the division having a maintenance battalion, a supply and transport battalion, a medical battalion, and a transportation aircraft maintenance company, along with the command headquarters and materiel management center. Support troops totaled about 1,300 men.[34]

The light division met several needs of the Army. It cost less and was simpler to maintain and support than the heavy infantry division. It was well suited for rear area operations if provided with air and ground transport and could easily adapt to urban operations, heavily forested or rugged areas, and adverse weather conditions—all circumstances found in Western Europe. Easily deployed, the division enhanced the Army's strategic response options. The division's weaknesses included lack of organic ground and air transport and an inability to face heavy forces in open terrain because it lacked armor. Also, the division was vulnerable to heavy artillery, nuclear, and chemical attacks and had only minimal

## CHART 47—Light Division, 1 October 1985

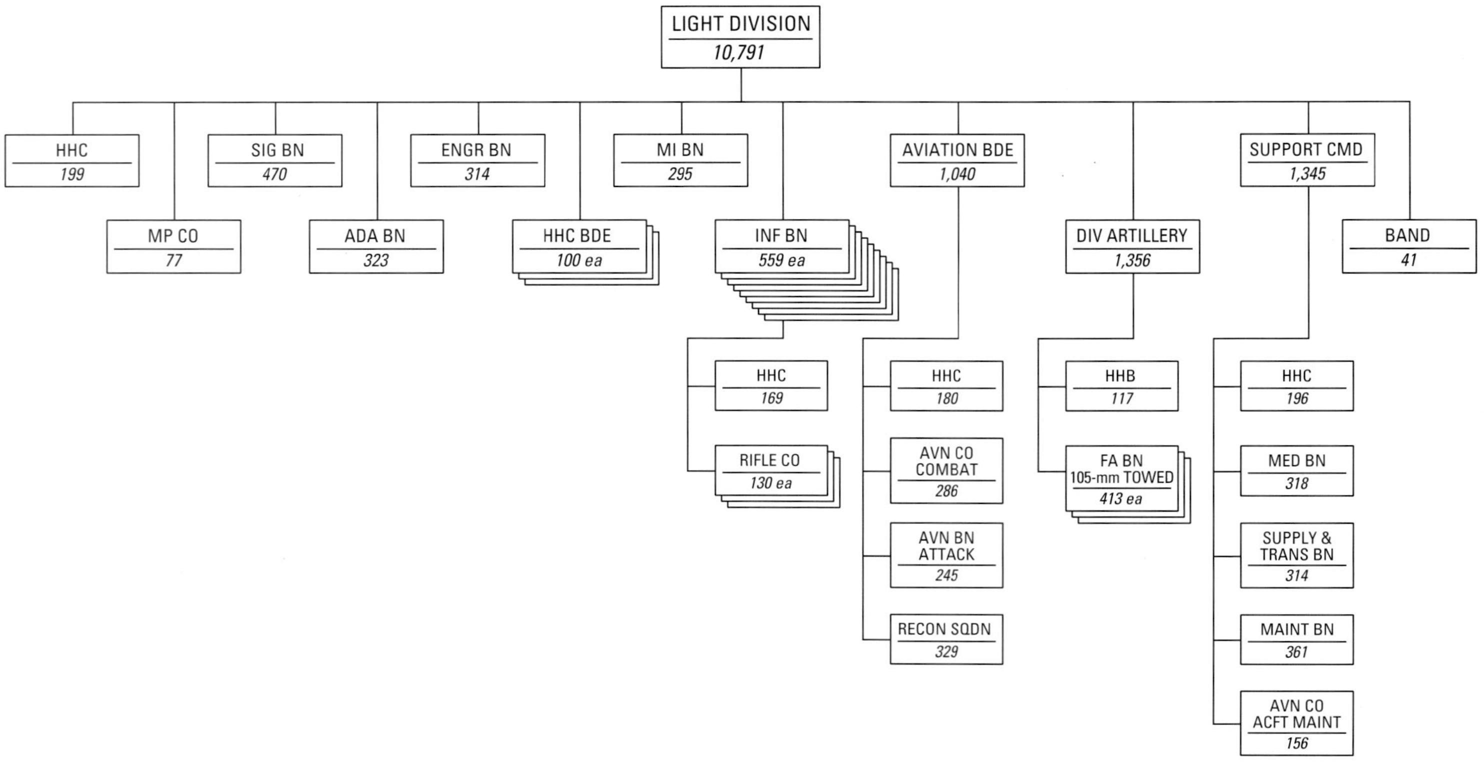

- **LIGHT DIVISION** — 10,791
  - **HHC** — 199
  - **MP CO** — 77
  - **SIG BN** — 470
  - **ADA BN** — 323
  - **ENGR BN** — 314
  - **HHC BDE** — 100 ea
  - **MI BN** — 295
  - **INF BN** — 559 ea
    - HHC — 169
    - RIFLE CO — 130 ea
  - **AVIATION BDE** — 1,040
    - HHC — 180
    - AVN CO COMBAT — 286
    - AVN BN ATTACK — 245
    - RECON SQDN — 329
  - **DIV ARTILLERY** — 1,356
    - HHB — 117
    - FA BN 105-mm TOWED — 413 ea
  - **SUPPORT CMD** — 1,345
    - BAND — 41
    - HHC — 196
    - MED BN — 318
    - SUPPLY & TRANS BN — 314
    - MAINT BN — 361
    - AVN CO ACFT MAINT — 156

indirect fire support. To compensate for those deficiencies, the division was to look to the corps for reinforcements.35

Plans to introduce light divisions sent reverberations throughout all Regular Army divisions since there was to be no increase in strength. Wickham directed reductions in the size of heavy divisions to about 17,000 officers and enlisted men, with armored divisions maintaining six armor and four mechanized battalions while mechanized divisions continued to field five armor and five mechanized infantry battalions. Cuts were therefore made in the combat support and service support elements. As noted, the motorized division was limited to 13,000 men. He ordered the reorganization of the 7th Infantry Division at Fort Ord and of the 25th Infantry Division at Schofield Barracks as light divisions without round-out brigades and the activation of the 10th Mountain Division at Fort Drum, New York, and of the 6th Infantry Division at Fort Richardson, Alaska. The 10th was to have a Guard round-out brigade, and the 6th was to draw its round-out units from both the National Guard and the Army Reserve.36

With the plans to reorganize two standard infantry divisions as untested light divisions, the Defense Department decided to add another mechanized infantry division to the National Guard force. In August 1984 the Guard's 35th Infantry Division, organized from three existing brigades, returned to the active rolls under the new tables as a mechanized division. Five states—Colorado, Kansas, Kentucky, Missouri, and Nebraska—contributed units to the division, including a mechanized infantry brigade each from Kansas and Nebraska and an armored brigade from the Kentucky National Guard. The headquarters of the new mechanized infantry division was at Fort Leavenworth, Kansas. To preclude the command and control problems that some multistate divisions experienced after their reorganizations in 1967 and 1968, the five states supporting the division agreed that a division council (the adjutant generals from the five states) was to select the division commander and key personnel, who would serve a maximum of three years.37

The 7th Infantry Division began to transition to light division structure in 1984, and it was followed by the conversion of the 25th Infantry Division and the activation of the 10th Mountain and 6th Infantry Divisions. Because Fort Drum lacked facilities to house even a small division, one Regular Army brigade of the 10th was stationed at Fort Benning, Georgia, for three years. A new brigade, the 27th Infantry Brigade from the New York Army National Guard, completed the 10th. The 172d Infantry Brigade in Alaska was inactivated, and its personnel provided the nucleus for the 6th Infantry Division. To retain an airborne capability in Alaska, one company in each of the initial three infantry battalions assigned to the 6th remained airborne qualified. Eventually all airborne assets were concentrated in one divisional battalion. Although the chief of Army Reserve agreed to have the 205th Infantry Brigade round out the 6th Infantry Division, the Regular Army still lacked all the resources to complete the division. Therefore, additional round-out units from the Alaska Army National Guard and the Army Reserve were assigned. The 6th Division, howev-

*Winter training, 205th Infantry Brigade, 1986;* below, *29th Infantry Division reactivation ceremony, 1985.*

er, never met the approved design for a light division, as one light infantry battalion was not organized because of the want of resources.38

In addition to the Regular Army divisions, the Department of Defense authorized the National Guard to organize one light division, raising the total number of such divisions to five. The 29th Infantry Division returned to the active force in the Maryland and Virginia Army National Guard as a light division in 1985. Resources from the 58th and 116th Infantry Brigades provided the nucleus for the new division, which was headquartered at Fort Belvoir, Virginia. With the activation of light infantry divisions, the number of divisions in the force rose to 28 (18 Regular Army and 10 National Guard) and the number of brigades fell to 23 (16 in the National Guard, 4 in the Regular Army, and 3 in the Army Reserve).39

As part of the Army of Excellence program, Wickham's directive included cutting and standardizing airborne, airmobile, and motorized divisions. As a result, the Training and Doctrine Command published tables for a smaller airborne division, with its strength plummeting from over 16,000 officers and enlisted men to approximately 13,000 (*Chart 48*). The new division was built on the light division base with three brigade headquarters and nine infantry battalions as its major components. However, it was stripped of both its armor battalion and its separate TOW-equipped infantry companies. Each infantry battalion consisted of a headquarters and headquarters company, three rifle companies, and an antitank company fielding five platoons, each equipped with four TOWs. The one divisional addition, an aviation brigade, contained the reconnaissance squadron, an attack helicopter battalion, and two combat aviation companies. The target acquisition battery was eliminated from the division artillery, and its three 105-mm. howitzer battalions were organized similarly to those in the light division. No 155-mm. howitzers were assigned.40

The greatest personnel economy in the airborne division took place in the support command. It embodied a headquarters and headquarters company; a materiel management center; medical, supply and transport, and maintenance battalions; and an aviation maintenance company, a total of about 1,750 soldiers rather than 2,500. Military police and chemical companies and signal, military intelligence, air defense artillery, and engineer battalions completed the airborne division. As in the light infantry division, it had to be reinforced from corps level when engaged in sustained operations. The 82d Airborne Division began adopting the new structure during fiscal year 1986 and completed it the following year when the quartermaster airdrop equipment company, which had been a nondivisional unit at Fort Bragg since 1952, was added to the supply and transport battalion, almost doubling its size.41

Along with the airborne division, the Training and Doctrine Command standardized the air assault division, which was decreased by about 25 percent (*Chart 49*). It also was similar to its old organization, but with a light division base. The division consisted of three brigades, nine airmobile infantry battalions, division artillery, a support command, and divisional troops. The one exception was the

CHART 48—Airborne Division, 1 April 1987

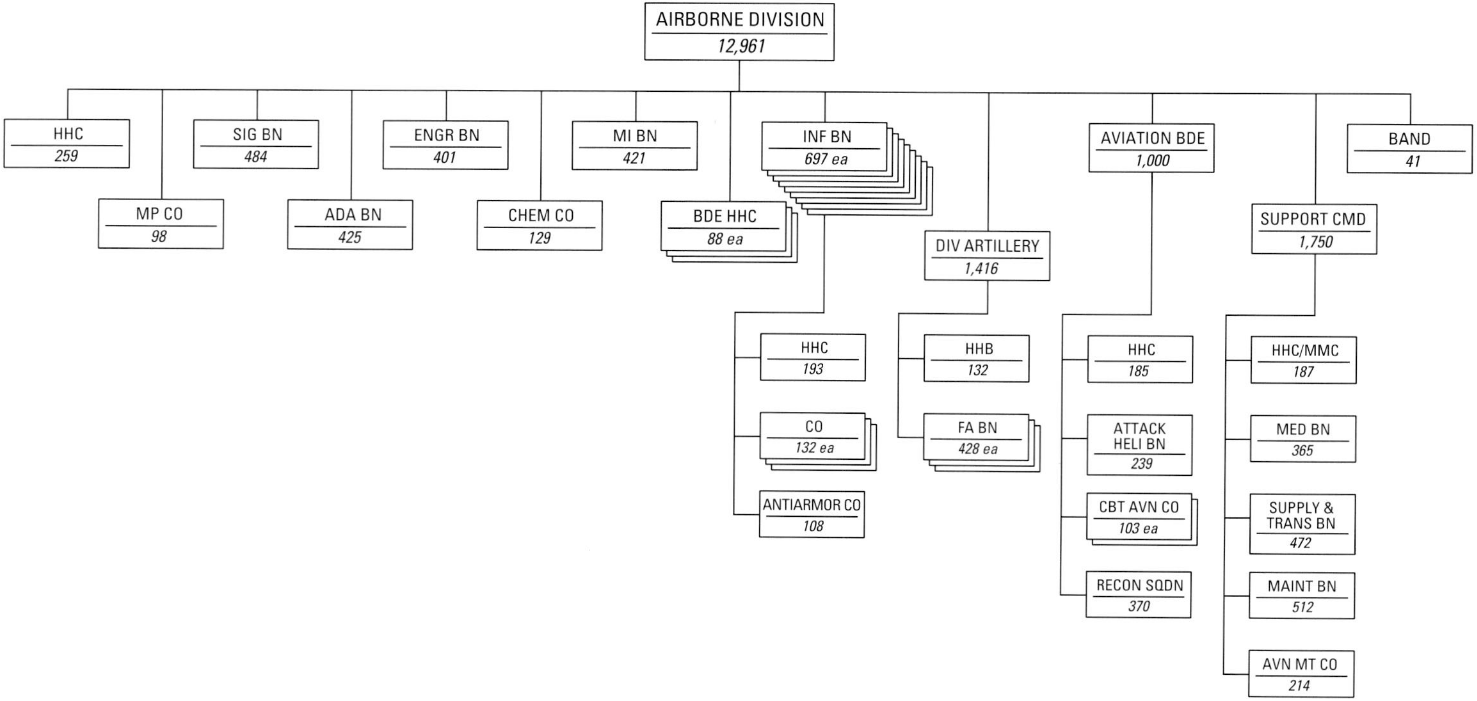

- AIRBORNE DIVISION — 12,961
  - HHC — 259
  - MP CO — 98
  - SIG BN — 484
  - ADA BN — 425
  - ENGR BN — 401
  - CHEM CO — 129
  - MI BN — 421
  - BDE HHC — 88 ea
  - INF BN — 697 ea
    - HHC — 193
    - CO — 132 ea
    - ANTIARMOR CO — 108
  - DIV ARTILLERY — 1,416
    - HHB — 132
    - FA BN — 428 ea
  - AVIATION BDE — 1,000
    - HHC — 185
    - ATTACK HELI BN — 239
    - CBT AVN CO — 103 ea
    - RECON SQDN — 370
  - SUPPORT CMD — 1,750
    - HHC/MMC — 187
    - MED BN — 365
    - SUPPLY & TRANS BN — 472
    - MAINT BN — 512
    - AVN MT CO — 214
  - BAND — 41

## CHART 49—Air Assault Division, 1 April 1987

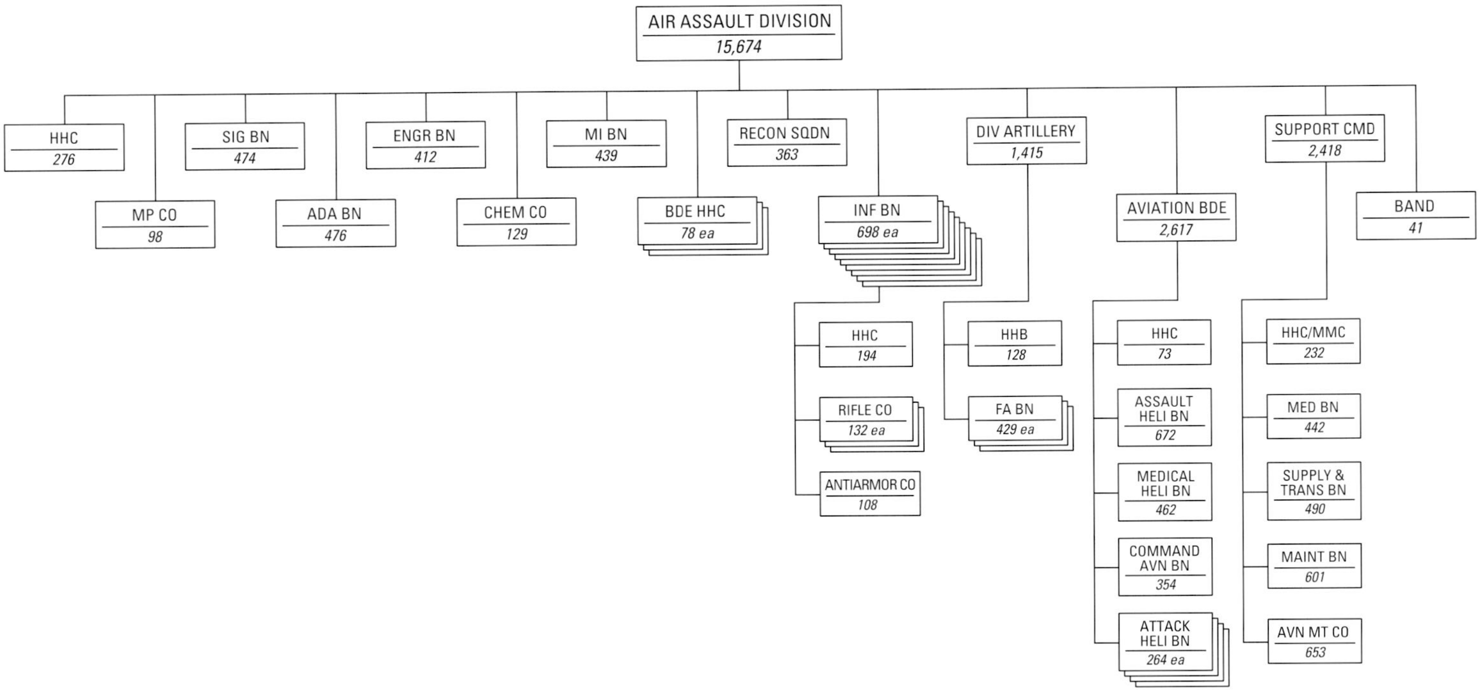

- AIR ASSAULT DIVISION — 15,674
  - HHC — 276
  - MP CO — 98
  - SIG BN — 474
  - ADA BN — 476
  - ENGR BN — 412
  - CHEM CO — 129
  - MI BN — 439
  - BDE HHC — 78 ea
  - RECON SQDN — 363
  - INF BN — 698 ea
    - HHC — 194
    - RIFLE CO — 132 ea
    - ANTIARMOR CO — 108
  - DIV ARTILLERY — 1,415
    - HHB — 128
    - FA BN — 429 ea
  - AVIATION BDE — 2,617
    - HHC — 73
    - ASSAULT HELI BN — 672
    - MEDICAL HELI BN — 462
    - COMMAND AVN BN — 354
    - ATTACK HELI BN — 264 ea
  - SUPPORT CMD — 2,418
    - HHC/MMC — 232
    - MED BN — 442
    - SUPPLY & TRANS BN — 490
    - MAINT BN — 601
    - AVN MT CO — 653
  - BAND — 41

replacement of the aviation group by an aviation brigade; the latter consisted of a command aviation battalion, a combat aviation battalion, a medium aviation battalion, and four attack aviation battalions. Artillery units were patterned after those in the airborne division, having three 105-mm. towed howitzer battalions, and the support command retained medical, supply and transport, and maintenance battalions, along with an aviation maintenance battalion. The reconnaissance squadron had a headquarters and four troops plus a long-range surveillance detachment. The latter was a military intelligence unit manned by infantrymen who were dependent on the cavalry squadron for transportation; doctrinally its location created a problem, and the planners had no easy solution for its position within the division. Each air assault infantry battalion fielded three rifle companies and an antiarmor company.[42]

In 1986 Forces Command began to phase the new structure into the 101st Airborne Division; by 1990, however, the Training and Doctrine Command changed the aviation brigade. The reconnaissance squadron, which had been a divisional element, moved to the brigade, which fielded one command, one medium, two assault, three attack battalions, along with the reconnaissance unit. A fourth attack battalion was planned for the brigade, but not active.[43]

The one type of division that failed to win a place in the Army of Excellence was the motorized infantry division (also referred to as the middleweight rather than light division). Motorized experiments conducted by the 9th Infantry Division had produced unsatisfactory results because of funding problems created by going outside normal combat development channels. The kinetic energy assault gun, the division's primary weapons system, and the fast attack vehicle never got beyond the experimental stage. In 1988 a reduction in the size of the Army forced the inactivation of the 9th Division's 2d Brigade. To maintain the integrity of the division, the 81st Infantry Brigade, from the Washington Army National Guard, was assigned as a round-out unit. Also, Forces Command transferred the 1st Battalion, 33d Armor, a Regular Army unit, from I Corps to the division. Its new maneuver element mix, including round-out units, consisted of two light attack infantry, two mechanized infantry, three armor, and four combined arms (motorized) battalions. The latter included two rifle companies and an assault gun company equipped with TOWs mounted on HMMWVs.[44]

With the reorganization of the Army into heavy and light divisions, only the 2d Infantry Division in Korea and the 26th, 28th, 38th, 42d, and 47th Infantry Divisions in the Army National Guard remained organized under the dated standard infantry division's tables of organization and equipment. Wickham exempted the 2d Infantry Division from conversion to either the heavy or light configuration because of its mission in Korea, the absence of a corps organization there, and Korean augmentation assigned to it. Working with the Training and Doctrine Command, Eighth Army devised a unique structure for the 2d that increased its firepower, especially the artillery and the antiarmor capabilities, and provided a mix of light and heavy maneuver battalions. The division was planned to field two armor, two mechanized infantry, and two air assault infantry battalions, while the other maneuver elements were to come from the Korean Army. By September 1990 the 2d Infantry Division had adopted its Army of Excellence structure.[45]

The reorganization of the National Guard divisions under the Army of Excellence concepts, except for the 29th Infantry Division, which returned to the active force in 1985 as a light division, proved to be a challenging endeavor. In 1985 the 49th and 50th Armored Divisions and 35th and 40th Infantry Divisions were reorganized as heavy divisions with the same maneuver element mix as the Regular Army divisions. Because of recruiting problems the areas that supported the Guard divisions were expanded, usually to adjacent states. One exception to the expansion was the 50th Armored Division, which was headquartered in New Jersey but had the allotment of one of its brigades moved to the Texas Army National Guard in 1988. Thus the future of the division in the force was uncertain.[46]

The Guard's five infantry divisions carried on under modified versions of the "H" series tables of organization and equipment, which were nearly twenty years old. Strengths for those divisions ranged from 14,000 to 17,000. With uncertainty about the need for more light divisions, the need for state troops, which the local authorities were unwilling to lose, and the lack of funds, which did not materialize, the reorganization of the units was held in abeyance. The National Guard divisions were, however, truly a part of the "Total Army." Because of concerns over sensitive equipment in the military intelligence battalion, the Army Reserve provided that unit for each Guard division except the 29th Infantry Division, which organized with its guardsmen.[47]

As the Army modernized its heavy divisions, it continued to revise their structure. In 1986 the 8-inch howitzers were transferred from the heavy division to corps level, but the multiple-launch rockets, organized as separate batteries, remained a part of the division artillery. The same year the division's support command was reorganized. Three forward support battalions (one for each brigade), a main support battalion, and an aviation maintenance company replaced the divisional medical, support and transport, and maintenance battalions in the support command. The functions and services provided by the displaced units were performed by mixed area support battalions. The divisional adjutant general company was inactivated, and its functions moved to the corps level where they were reorganized as a personnel service company, and the divisional materiel management center was absorbed by the headquarters company in the support command. The reorganization of the support command saved over 400 personnel spaces. In the National Guard heavy divisions, the air defense artillery battalions were eliminated because spare parts for antiquated M42 Dusters were not available. On mobilization the corps was to provide antiaircraft resources for these divisions.[48]

By the end of 1989 the only Army of Excellence structure that the Training and Doctrine Command had developed for separate brigades was for the heavy one—armored and mechanized infantry. Like the tables of organization and equipment for heavy divisions, they included variations for the types of equipment and the number of maneuver elements that the brigades fielded. Each brigade, authorized approximately 4,100 soldiers, included a headquarters and headquarters company, engineer and military intelligence companies, a cavalry reconnaissance troop, a field artillery battalion (three batteries of six self-propelled 155-mm. howitzers each), a support battalion, and a combination of armor and mechanized infantry battalions.[49]

The reorganization of reserve brigade forces, both separate and round-out units, also became an ongoing process. For the 9th Infantry Division (Motorized), the 1st Cavalry Division, and 5th and 24th Infantry Divisions the maneuver element mix of their National Guard round-out brigades was increased from three to four battalions, two armor and two mechanized infantry. The light round-out brigades for the 6th Infantry and 10th Mountain Divisions continued to field three maneuver battalions. The 27th Infantry Brigade, rounding out the 10th Mountain Division, however, did not have all of its brigade base units. Five other heavy brigades in the National Guard were also organized under Army of Excellence tables, while the eight National Guard and the two Army Reserve infantry brigades, like the National Guard infantry divisions, employed a mishmash of old and new structures. Although eight Guard infantry brigades were not modernized, each had the same number of assigned maneuver elements, except for the 92d Infantry Brigade in Puerto Rico, which had four rather than three infantry battalions. The 157th Infantry Brigade, the only mechanized infantry brigade in the Army Reserve, fielded only three maneuver elements as did the 187th Infantry Brigade.[50]

The Regular Army brigades continued to lack uniformity. In 1984 Forces Command reorganized the 194th Armored and 197th Infantry Brigades under the heavy brigade configuration. The 193d Infantry Brigade, the special mission brigade in Panama, was reorganized as a light unit consisting of two infantry battalions (one being airborne qualified), a field artillery battery, and a support battalion. The 3d Battalion, 87th Infantry, from the Army Reserve was identified as a round-out unit for the brigade. An additional table of organization brigade was added to the Regular Army in 1983 when United States Army, Europe, and Seventh Army organized the Berlin Brigade under a standard separate infantry brigade table, which provided resources for improved command and control of its assigned units. It had three infantry battalions, a field artillery battery (eight 155-mm. self-propelled howitzers), a tank company, and a newly activated support battalion.[51]

The cellular organization adopted in 1978 for the twelve training divisions and two training brigades (a new brigade, the 402d, had been organized in 1985 for field artillery training) in the Army Reserve created problems, particularly in accounting for the personnel assigned to the units. Some positions were authorized within divisional tables of organization and equipment cells and others were provided for as a part of the United States Army Reserve centers to which the divisions and brigades were assigned. Between the two documentation sources,

Forces Command found it difficult to tell which parts of the reserve centers were dedicated to support the training units. The command eventually recommended a solution, which the Army Staff approved on 11 December 1986. The training divisions and brigades were to be reduced to zero strength to keep the units active and then backfilled using tables of distribution and allowance. The change allowed Forces Command to identify specific billets for each division, brigade, and reserve center for its specific mission. The lineage, honors, and history of the divisions and brigades continued to be represented in the reserve forces. Units began adopting the system in September 1988 and completed the process September 1990.[52]

## *A New Direction*

With its light and heavy divisions and brigades, the Army of Excellence reorganization was expensive, and ultimately the high cost forced the Army to move in a new direction during the late 1980s. All elements of the military establishment, Army, Navy, Marine Corps, and Air Force, competed for modernization monies, which helped drive the national debt to unacceptable levels. In 1988, as a part of its share in reducing defense costs, the Army inactivated one brigade from the 9th Infantry Division, as already noted, and replaced it with the 81st Infantry Brigade from the Washington Army National Guard. The following year the 2d Brigade, 4th Infantry Division, was inactivated, creating a gap that was closed by the 116th Cavalry Brigade from the Idaho, Oregon, and Nevada National Guard. The Guard's 116th and 163d Armored Cavalry regiments had been reorganized by 1989 as armored brigades because no requirement existed for those regiments in the force. By the end of fiscal year 1989 the Army had twenty-eight divisions and twenty-five brigades (*Tables 37 and 38*) in the active Army and reserve components combined.[53]

During the summer of 1989 the Warsaw Pact began to disintegrate. Economic and social issues fired the changes, and nations in Eastern Europe wrenched control of their affairs from the Soviet Union. By the end of the year most Soviet client states were set on a path of self-determination. Given this change, the rationale for the North Atlantic Treaty Organization, the basis for having United States forces forward deployed in Europe, and much of the Army doctrine for fighting the AirLand Battle came under close scrutiny.

Before any reassessment of the defense establishment in light of these events was completed, in December 1989 the Army was called upon to deploy the 7th Infantry Division and the 1st Brigade, 82d Airborne Division, to Panama as a part of Operation JUST CAUSE, an effort to restore democracy to that Latin American republic. Several months later American divisions and brigades participated in Operation DESERT SHIELD/DESERT STORM, a multinational endeavor to halt Iraqi aggression in Southwest Asia and to restore the independence of Kuwait (*Table 39* lists the divisions and brigades that deployed to Southwest Asia).

TABLE 37

Divisions, 1989

| Division | Component | Location of Headquarters | Inf | Mech | Ar | Abn | AAST | LI | CAB | Round-out Unit |
|---|---|---|---|---|---|---|---|---|---|---|
| 1st Armored | RA | Ansbach, Germany | | 4 | 6 | | | | | |
| 1st Cavalry | RA | Fort Hood, Tex. | | 2 | 3 | | | | | 155th Armored Brigade |
| 1st Infantry | RA | Fort Riley, Kans. | | 4 | 6 | | | | | 2d Bn, 136th Infantry |
| 2d Armored | RA | Fort Hood, Tex. | | 4 | 5 | | | | | 2d Bn, 252d Armor |
| 2d Infantry | RA | Korea | | 2 | 2 | | 3[1] | | | |
| 3d Armored | RA | Frankfurt, Germany | | 4 | 6 | | | | | |
| 3d Infantry | RA | Wuerzburg, Germany | | 5 | 5 | | | | | |
| 4th Infantry | RA | Fort Carson, Colo. | | 4 | 5 | | | | | 2d Bn, 120th Infantry |
| 5th Infantry | RA | Fort Polk, La. | | 3 | 3 | | | | | 256th Infantry Brigade |
| 6th Infantry | RA | Fort Richardson, Alaska | 3 | | | | | | | 205th Infantry Brigade |
| 7th Infantry | RA | Fort Ord, Calif. | | | | | | 9 | | |
| 8th Infantry | RA | Bad Kreuznach, Germany | | 5 | 5 | | | | | |
| 9th Infantry | RA | Fort Lewis, Wash. | | | 1 | | | 2 | 4 | 81st Infantry Brigade |
| 10th Mountain | RA | Fort Drum, N.Y. | | | | | | 6 | | 27th Infantry Brigade |
| 24th Infantry | RA | Fort Stewart, Ga. | | 3 | 3 | | | | | 48th Infantry Brigade |
| 25th Infantry | RA | Schofield Barracks, Hawaii | | | | | 9 | | | |
| 26th Infantry | NG | Buzzards Bay, Mass. | 8 | | 2 | | | | | |
| 28th Infantry | NG | Harrisburg, Pa. | 8 | 1 | 1 | | | | | |
| 29th Infantry | NG | Fort Belvoir, Va. | | | | | | 9 | | |

TABLE 37—Continued

| Division | Component | Location of Headquarters | Maneuver Battalion ||||||| Round-out Unit |
|---|---|---|---|---|---|---|---|---|---|---|
| | | | Inf | Mech | Ar | Abn | AAST | LI | CAB | |
| 35th Infantry | NG | Fort Leavenworth, Kans. | | 5 | 5 | | | | | |
| 38th Infantry | NG | Indianapolis, Ind. | 8 | 1 | 1 | | | | | |
| 40th Infantry | NG | Los Alamitos, Calif. | | 5 | 5 | | | | | |
| 42d Infantry | NG | New York, N.Y. | 6 | 1 | 3 | | | | | |
| 47th Infantry | NG | St. Paul, Minn. | 8 | 1 | 1 | | | | | |
| 49th Armored | NG | Austin, Tex. | | 4 | 6 | | | | | |
| 50th Armored | NG | Somerset, N.Y. | | 4 | 6 | | | | | |
| 82d Airborne | RA | Fort Bragg, N.C. | | | | 9 | | | | |
| 101st Airborne | RA | Fort Campbell, Ky. | | | | | 9 | | | |

1 One air assault battalion inactivated in September 1990.

TABLE 38
Brigades, 1989

| Brigade | Component | Location of Headquarters | Inf | Maneuver Battalion Mech | Ar | Abn | Lt Inf |
|---|---|---|---|---|---|---|---|
| 27th Infantry | NG | Syracuse, N.Y. | 3[1] | | | | 3 |
| 29th Infantry | NG | Honolulu, Hawaii | | | | | |
| 30th Armored | NG | Jackson, Tenn. | | 1 | 2 | | |
| 30th Infantry | NG | Clinton, S.C. | | 2 | 1 | | |
| 31st Armored | NG | Northport, Ala | | 1 | 2 | | |
| 32d Infantry | NG | Milwaukee, Wisc. | | 2 | 1 | | |
| 33d Infantry | NG | Chicago, Ill. | 3 | | | | |
| 39th Infantry | NG | Little Rock Ark. | 3 | | | | |
| 41st Infantry | NG | Portland, Oreg. | 3 | | | | |
| 45th Infantry | NG | Edmond, Okla. | 3 | | | | |
| 48th Infantry | NG | Macon, Ga. | | 2 | 2 | | |
| 53d Infantry | NG | Tampa, Fla. | 3 | | | | |
| 73d Infantry | NG | Columbus, Ohio | 3 | | | | |
| 81st Infantry | NG | Seattle, Wash. | | 2 | 2 | | |
| 92d Infantry | NG | San Juan, Puerto Rico | 4 | | | | |
| 116th Cavalry[2] | NG | Boise, Idaho | | 1 | 2 | | |
| 155th Armored | NG | Tupelo, Miss. | | 2 | 2 | | |
| 157th Infantry | AR | Horsham, Pa. | | 2 | 1 | | |
| 163d Armored | NG | Bozeman, Mont. | | 1 | 2 | | |
| 187th Infantry | AR | Fort Devens, Mass. | 3 | | | | |
| 193d Infantry | RA | Fort Clayton, Canal Zone | | | | 1 | 2[3] |
| 194th Armored | RA | Fort Knox, Ky. | | 1 | 2 | | |
| 197th Infantry | RA | Fort Benning, Ga. | | 2 | 1 | | |
| 205th Infantry | AR | Fort Snelling, Minn. | 3 | | | | |
| 218th Infantry | NG | Newberry, S.C. | | 2 | 1 | | |
| 256th Infantry | NG | Lafayette, La. | | 2 | 2 | | |
| Berlin | RA | Berlin, Germany | 3 | | | | |

[1] One Army Reserve and two National Guard Battalions.
[2] Reorganization of the 116th Armored Cavalry as the 116th Cavalry Brigade not complete.
[3] One Army Reserve and one Regular Army battalion.

TABLE 39

Divisions and Brigades in Southwest Asia, 1990–91

| Unit | Home Station |
|---|---|
| 1st Armored Division (less 1st Brigade) | Germany |
| 1st Cavalry Division (less 256th Infantry Brigade) | Fort Hood, Texas |
| 1st Infantry Division (less 1st Infantry Division Forward) | Fort Riley, Kansas |
| 1st Brigade, 2d Armored Division | Fort Hood, Texas |
| 3d Brigade, 2d Armored Division | Germany |
| 3d Armored Division | Germany |
| 3d Brigade, 3d Infantry Division | Germany |
| 24th Infantry Division (less 48th Infantry Brigade) | Fort Stewart, Georgia |
| 82d Airborne Division | Fort Bragg, North Carolina |
| 101st Airborne Division | Fort Campbell, Kentucky |
| 197th Infantry Brigade | Fort Benning, Georgia |

The nation and the Army reached a watershed in 1990 with the disintegration of Soviet Union and the deployment of forces to Southwest Asia. Since the end of the conflict in Vietnam, national leaders had focused on the countering of the Soviet menace, and the Army's Division Restructuring Study, the Airland Battle doctrine, and the Army of Excellence heavy divisions, first and foremost, had addressed that threat. Although the need for other types of divisions and separate brigades was recognized, limited resources bridled full implementation of the Army of Excellence design. Aggression by the small Iraqi nation introduced a series of new questions about the size, type, and location of division and separate brigade forces needed. The answers to these questions are left to the future, but an ever-changing world and ongoing revolution in weapons and information technology will continue to challenge the designers of the Army force structure in years ahead.

## Notes

[1] E. C. Meyer, *General, United States Army, Chief of Staff, June 1979–June 1983* (n.p., 1983), p. 52.

[2] John P. Rose, *The Evolution of U.S. Army Nuclear Doctrine, 1945–1980* (Boulder, Colo.: Westview Press, 1980), pp. 115–16.

[3] FM 100–5, *Operations*, 1976, pp. 1–1–5; Kevin P. Sheehan, "Preparing for an Imaginary War: Examining Peacetime Functions and Changes of Army Doctrine," Ph.D. thesis, Harvard University, 1988, pp. 75–76; U.S. TRADOC, "Annual Historical Review, FY 1976," pp. 38–47; Memo, CG, TRADOC, undated, sub: Outline Concept Paper Division Restructuring Study (DRS) ATCG-R, TRADOC, Executive Summary: draft, Phase I: Division Restructuring Study (DRS), 20 Dec 76, both DRS file, DAMH-HSO; John W. Foss, Donald S. Pihl, and Thomas E. Fitzgerald, "The Division Restructuring Study: The Heavy Division," *Military Review* 57 (Mar 1977): 11–21.

[4] Ltr, DCSOPS to TRADOC, 21 Mar 75, no subject, DRS file; Foss et al., "The Heavy Division," pp. 11–21; TRADOC, Executive Summary, DRS.

[5] TRADOC, Executive Summary, DRS.

[6] Ibid.; Foss et al., "The Heavy Division," pp. 11–21.

[7] Foss et al., "The Heavy Division," pp. 11–21.

[8] TRADOC, Executive Summary, DRS; John P. Finnegan, "Military Intelligence, An Overview, 1885–1987," Ms, 1988, pp. 205–07, DAMH-HSO. Also see TRADOC, "Annual Historical Review, FY 1977," pp. 170–73 for a discussion of the new division.

[9] Ltr, CG, III Corps and Fort Hood, to FORSCOM, 16 Aug 79, sub: Letter of Transmittal-DRS Report-Phase III, and DRS, Brigade Evaluation, 2d Bde, 1st Cav Div, Phase III Final Report, vol. 1, 31 Aug 79, both DRS file.

[10] FORSCOM, "Annual Historical Review, 1 Oct 1977–30 Sep 1978," pp. 155–56, and 1 Oct 1978–30 Sep 1979, pp. 161–66; John L. Romjue, *A History of Army 86*, vol. I, *Division 86: The Development of the Heavy Division* (Fort Monroe, Va.: U.S. Army Training and Doctrine Command, 1982), pp. 42–48; Change 2, TOE 6–300H, Armored Division or Infantry Division (Mechanized) Artillery, 1976; TOE 6–307H, Target Acquisition Battery, Airborne, Armored, Infantry, and Mechanized Infantry Division, 1976; TOE 3–87H, Nuclear, Biological, Chemical Defense Company, 1977; OPS 28, Dir, Force Management, DCSOPS, to DCSOPS, 18 Apr 79, sub: CBR JA Teams, DAMO-RDP, Chemical General file, DAMH-HSO; TOE 17–85H, Combat Aviation Battalion, Armored or Mechanized Infantry Division, 1977; TOE 34–165H, Combat Electronic Warfare Intelligence Battalion, 1979; TOE 7–107H, Antiarmor Company, 1977; see author's notes for implementation date, Div Reorganization 1976–1980, DAMH-HSO.

[11] *Department of the Army Historical Summary, FY 79*, p. 13; PO 64–7, FORSCOM, 1978, 24th Inf Div file, Ltr, NGB to AG, Kentucky, 30 Sep 80, sub: Reorganization of KY ARNG Units, NGB-ARO-O 207–02, No. 195–80, Kentucky NG file, Ltr, NGB to AG, Texas, 1 Apr 80, sub: Reorganization of Texas ARNG Units, NGB-ARO-O 207–02, No. 71–80, Texas NG file, all DAMH-HSO; John L. Romjue, *A History of Army 86*, vol. II, *The Development of the Light Division, the Corps, and Echelons above Corps* (Fort Monroe, Va.: U.S. Army Training and Doctrine Command, 1982), p. 25.

[12] Romjue, *The Heavy Division*, p. 11.

[13] Ibid., pp. 11–16; *Department of the Army Historical Summary, FY 79*, p. 18; Clyde J. Tate and L. D. Holder, "New Doctrine for the Defense," *Military Review* 59 (Mar 1981): 2–9; Donn A. Starry, "Extending the Battlefield," *Military Review* 59 (Mar 1981): 31–50; FM 100–5, *Operations*, 1982, pp. 2–1–10; John L. Romjue, *From Active Defense to AirLand Battle: The Development of Army Doctrine 1973–1982* (Fort Monroe, Va.: U.S. Army Training and Doctrine Command, 1984), pp. 51–73.

[14] LuAnne K. Leven and Benjamin F. Schemmer, "AFJ Interview: 'Now everybody can shoot at me,'" *Armed Forces Journal International* (Mar 1980): 46; Romjue, *The Heavy Division*, pp. 42–46, 48–49, 111, 128. Between pages 50 and 110 of this work is a detailed discussion of the evo-

lution of Division-86.

15 Meyer, *Chief of Staff*, p. 55; Romjue, *The Heavy Division*, p. 112.

16 Romjue, *The Heavy Division*, pp. 81–85, 89; Paul A. Bigelman, "Force Designs for the Future," *Army* 31 (Jun 1981): 22–33.

17 Romjue, *The Heavy Division*, pp. 113, 116.

18 Ibid., pp. 115, 117.

19 Ibid., pp. 119–20.

20 TOE 87, Heavy Division, 1982, and associated TOEs. The M1 tank was named the "Abrams" in memory of General Creighton Abrams, Chief of Staff, who died in office in 1974.

21 TOE 87, Heavy Division, 1982, and associated TOEs.

22 John L. Romjue, *The Light Division*, pp. 17–24; U.S. Army TRADOC, "Annual Command History, 1 Oct 82–30 Sep 83," pp. 296–302; USAREUR, "Historical Review, 1 Jan 82–31 Dec 83," pp. 20–22.

23 Romjue, *The Light Division*, p. 17; John L. Romjue, *The Army of Excellence: The Development of the 1980s Army* (Fort Monroe, Va.: U.S. Army Training and Doctrine Command, 1993), pp.20–21; John A. Wickham, Jr., *Collected Works of the Thirtieth Chief of Staff, United States Army* (n.p., 1987), pp. 157–60, 217–18; PO 58–5, USAREUR and Seventh Army, 1983, 4th Bde, 4th Inf Div, file, DAMH-HSO.

24 Meyer, *Chief of Staff*, p. 174

25 The 1st Special Forces regiment under CARS was considered a part of infantry, but in 1983 they were made a separate arm.

26 AR 600–82, *The U.S. Army Regimental System 1986*; Ltr, ODCSOPS to TAG and other addresses, 8 Feb 83, sub: Regimental Implementation Plan-Initial Regiments, DAMO-ODO, and Memo for Record, DCSPER, Chief, New Manning System Division, 29 Mar 85, sub: CSA Guidance on U.S. Army Regimental System/COHORT, DAPE-PSB, USARS file, both DAMH-HSO.

27 Romjue, *The Light Division*, pp. 25–27; Joseph R. Bongiovi, "I Corps: Light Infantry Division," Ms, p. 8, DAMH-HSR.

28 Romjue, *The Light Division*, pp. 26–55.

29 Stephen L. Bowman, John M. Kendall, and James L. Saunders, *Motorized Experience of the 9th Infantry Division* (Fort Lewis, Wash.: n.p., 1989), pp. 8–13, 30–41; FORSCOM, "Annual History Review, FY 1982," pp. 175–76; Glen R. Hawkins, *U.S. Army Force Structure and Force Design Initiative, 1939–1989* (Washington, D.C.: U.S. Army Center of Military History, undated), pp. 76–78.

30 Wickham, "White Paper 1984, Light Infantry Division," *Collected Works*, pp. 311–12; TRADOC, "Historical Review, 1 Oct 83 to 31 Dec 86," p. 108; FORSCOM, "Annual Historical Review, 1 Oct 83–30 Sep 84," p. 178.

31 FM 100–5, *Operations*, 1986, p. 185.

32 The term "Army of Excellence" appears to have been an outgrowth of the Army's theme, "Excellence," for 1983. All briefing slides prepared by the U.S. Army Combined Arms Combat Development Activity at Fort Leavenworth, Kansas, had the logo "Army of Excellence," which was adopted for the new organizational initiative.

33 John L. Romjue, *The Army of Excellence*, pp. 46–47, 52; TOE 77, Infantry Division, 1984, and associated tables.

34 Velocci, "The New Light Division, Will it Work?" *Infantry* 74 (Jan–Feb 1984): 56–60; James J. Lindsey, "The Infantry Division (Light)," *Infantry* 74 (Jan–Feb 1984): 2–3 and (Mar–Apr 1984): 14–16.

35 David H. Petraeus, "Light Infantry in Europe: Strategic Flexibility and Conventional Deterrence," *Military Review* 64 (Dec 1984): 35–53.

36 *Department of the Army Historical Summary, FY 1985*, pp. 59–60; TRADOC, "Historical Review, 1 Oct 83–31 Dec 86," pp. 113–14; Wickham, "White Paper 1984, Light Infantry Divisions." Although the 10th Mountain Division was light infantry, the Secretary of Army, John O. Marsh, decided to use the designation that the unit fought under during World War II.

37 Ltr, NGB to AG, Kansas, 9 May 84, sub: Reorganization of KS ARNG Unit, 9 May 84, NGB-ARO-O 207–2, No. 13–84, Ltr, NGB to AG, Kansas, 23 Aug 85, sub: Organization of 35th Infantry Division Units in Kansas, NGB-ARO-O No. 73–85, Ltr, NGB to AG, Kentucky, 14 Sep 85, sub: Organization of units of the 35th Infantry Division (Mech) and Reorganization and Consolidation of Co B, 201st Engineer Bn in Kentucky, NGB-ARO-O No. 72–85, Ltr, NGB to AG, Missouri, 14 Jun 85, sub: Organization of 35th Infantry Division (Mechanized) units in Missouri, NGB-ARO-O No. 70–85, Ltr, NGB to AG, Nebraska, 27 Sep 85, sub: Organization of units of the 35th Infantry Division (Mech) and 105th Personnel Service Co in Nebraska, NGB-ARO-O No. 71–85, Ltr, NGB to AG, Colorado, 27 Sep 85, sub: Organization of units of the 35th Aviation Battalion and Det 1, 2113th Trans Co in Colorado, NGB-ARO-O No. 69–85, Memo of Understanding between Adjutants General of Colorado, Kansas, Kentucky, Missouri, Nebraska, and the Chief, National Guard Bureau, 6 Dec 83, sub: Command and Control 35th Infantry Division (Mechanized), all 35th Inf Div file, DAMH-HSO.

38 Wickham, "White Paper 1984, Light Infantry Divisions"; *Department of the Army Historical Summary, Fiscal Year 1986*, pp. 65–66; Romjue, *The Army of Excellence*, pp. 62–65; Activation Ceremony 10th Mountain Division (Light Infantry) 13 Feb 1985, 10th Mountain Division file, DAMH-HSO; Bulletin of the Chief, Army Reserve, *CARNOTES*, Sep–Oct 1985.

39 Ltr, NGB to AGs Maryland and Virginia, 30 Sep 85, sub: Organization of the 29th Infantry Division (Light), NGB-ARO-FD-207–02, No. 125–85, 29th Inf Div file, DAMH-HSO.

40 Combined Arms Combat Development Agency (CACDA), *Light Infantry Division: The Army of Excellence: Final Report*, 1 Oct 1984, ch. 9, pp. 1–7; FORSCOM, "Annual Historical Review, 1983–1984," p. 182; TOE 57L, Airborne Division, 1985, and associated tables, published 1 April 1987. Earlier versions of TOE omitted the chemical company and contained a smaller aviation brigade and a military intelligence battalion.

41 CACDA, *Light Infantry Division*, ch. 9, pp. 1–7; FORSCOM, "Annual Historical Review, 1983–1984," p. 182; TOE 57L, Airborne Division, 1985, and associated tables; *Department of the Army Historical Summary, Fiscal Year 1987*, p. 30; PO 88–19, FORSCOM, 1987, 407th Supt Bn file, DAMH-HSO.

42 CACDA, *Light Infantry Division*, ch. 9, pp. 1–7; TOE 67L, Airborne Division, 1986, and associated tables.

43 *Department of the Army Historical Summary, Fiscal Year 1986*, p. 66; TOE 1–200L, Division Aviation Brigade (AASLT), 1 October 1990; 1st–8th Battalions, 101st Aviation, assigned to the division in September-October 1987, see 101st Aviation file, DAMH-HSO.

44 Romjue, *The Army Of Excellence*, pp. 74–76; Bowman et al., *Motorized Experience of the 9th Infantry Division*, pp. 38–44, 285–86; TRADOC, "Historical Review, 1 Oct 83–31 Dec 86," pp. 115; FORSCOM, "Annual Historical Review, FY 88," p. 4–3; FORSCOM, "Annual Historical Review, FY 89," p. IV–27; PO 56–19, FORSCOM, 1988; The 1st Battalion, 803d Armor, which earlier had been designated as a round-out unit to the division, was made an element of the 81st Infantry Brigade at this time. Reserve Components Troop Basis of the Army, Annex I, Army National Guard Unit Program, 31 March 1989, pt. III, pp. 16–17; TOE 7–95L, Infantry Battalion (CAB-Lt), 1987.

45 TRADOC, "Historical Review, 1 Oct 83–31 Dec 86," p. 114; PO 100–2, Eighth Army, 1990, 2d Bn, 503d Inf, file, DAMH-HSO.

46 Ltr, NGB to AG, Texas, 28 May 88, sub: Reorganization of Texas ARNG Units, NGB-ARO-F 310–49e, 50th Armd Div file, DAMH-HSO; *Annual Review of the Chief, National Guard Bureau, 1985*, p. 26; Reserve Components Troops Basis of the Army, Annex 1, Army National Guard Unit Program, 30 Sep 1989, pp. III–5–15, III–61–66.

47 Romjue, *Army of Excellence*, pp. 79–80; Reserve Components Troops Basis of the Army, Annex 1, Army National Guard Unit Program, 30 Sep 1989; Memo, Central Security Service for Sec of Def, 29 Feb 88, sub: Signal Intelligence Capability for Army National Guard Units, and Memo, Office Sec of Def for Dir Central Security Service, 26 Apr 88, no subject, 629th MI file, DAMH-HSO; PO 66–5 and 66–12, First U.S. Army, 1986, 126th and 128th MI Bn files, PO 69–4 and 82–8, Fourth U.S. Army, 1986, 147th and 138th MI Bn files, and PO 24–1, First U.S. Army, 1987, 542d MI Bn file, all DAMH-HSO.

# A NEW ASSESSMENT

48 TOE 63–100L, Support Command Heavy Division, 1986, and associated tables; TOE 6–300L, Division Artillery, Heavy Division, 1986, and associated tables; The Institute of Land Warfare, AUSA, "Divisions of the United States Army," 1 Oct 1989; "Air Defense Artillery Modernization," *National Guard* 63 (Jan 1989): 101.

49 TOE 87–100L, Heavy Separate Brigade, 1986, and associated tables.

50 Ltr, NGB to AG, New York, 1 Oct 85, sub: Reorganization of 27th Inf Bde, NGB-ARO-FD, 141–85, 27th Inf Bde file, DAMH-HSO; Reserve Components Troop Basis of the Army, Annex 1, Army National Guard Unit Program, 30 Sep 1989, Annex II, US Army Reserve Unit Allocation, 1989, pp. 29–30.

51 FORSCOM, "Annual Historical Review, 1 Oct 84–30 Sep 85," p. 141; PO 132–5, FORSCOM, 1983, 197th Inf Bde file, PO 132–4, FORSCOM, 1983, 194th Armd Bde file, and Ltr, CG, Berlin Brigade to CinC, USAREUR, 4 Jan 80, sub: Concept Plan for Reorganization of the Berlin Brigade, AEBA-GA-M, PO 59–6, USAREUR and Seventh Army, 1982, Berlin Brigade file, all DAMH-HSO. From 1961 to 1983 the Berlin Brigade had been organized under a table of distribution and allowance, which did not provide adequate resources to command and control its fire support and service support units.

52 PO 73–2, Fifth U.S. Army, 1985, 402d Brigade (Training) file; Information Paper, 24 May 83, sub: Training Organization Structure, FORSCOM, DCofS Operations, Force Structure and Stationing Division, Reserve (AFOP-FSR), Ltr, FORSCOM to Ch, Army Reserve, 7 Nov 1986, sub: Reorganization of USAR Training Division, AFOP-FSR, Ltr, TAG to CG, FORSCOM, 11 Dec 86, same subject, Ch, Army Reserve, Force Mobilization and Plans (DAAR-FMP), Division General file, DAMH-HSO; September 1988 reorganization of training divisions and brigades based on POs from First, Second, Fourth, Fifth, and Sixth Armies, 1988–1990 PO file, DAMH-HSO.

53 PO 56–10, FORSCOM, 1988, 2d Bde, 9th Inf Div file, PO 78–10, FORSCOM, 1989, 2d Bde, 4th Inf Div file, Ltr, NGB to AGs, Idaho, Oregon, and Nevada, 18 Aug 88, sub: Reorganization of Idaho, Oregon, and Nevada ARNG Units, NGB-ARO-F, 310–49e, No. 183–88, 116th Cav Bde file, Ltr, AG Montana, Wyoming, 25 Aug 88, sub: Reorganization of Montana and Wyoming ARNG Units, NGB-ARO-F 310–49c, No. 189–88, 163d Cav Bde file, all DAMH-HSO. Under the fixed corps concept outlined in FM 100–5, Operations, 1986, the Army maintained the I, III, V, and VII Corps and the XVIII Airborne Corps, which required five armored cavalry regiments. The Regular Army fielded three and the Army National Guard four, for a total of seven armored cavalry regiments. With the reduced requirement, the Guard converted two of its regiments to brigades.

# CHAPTER 15

# Conclusion

*It may be taken as an axiom that the organization of units comprising armies should be adapted to the terrain . . . the probable theater of war and to the characteristics of the enemies to be encountered.*

Maj. Nathaniel F. McClure[1]

In 1912 Maj. (later Brig. Gen.) Nathaniel F. McClure, a future instructor in military art at the Service Schools at Fort Leavenworth, Kansas, listed terrain, theater of war, and the enemy as issues that planners should consider in developing military organizations. These ideas had particular application to divisions and separate combined arms brigades, and over the last eighty-odd years have been expressed in various ways. Yet other factors have also had significant impact on military organizations. The rapid evolution of military technology is perhaps the most obvious. Others include the manner in which the nation has raised its military manpower—a combination of active, reserve, and expansion components; the aptitude of that manpower to harness the new technology; and the political and economic constraints that create the environmental parameters within which military structures must operate. This study has attempted to show the influence of these broad and interrelated factors on the changing organization of the Army's large, combined arms tactical units.

Prior to the twentieth century the Army did not use one specific command level at which to organize infantry, artillery, and cavalry units into combined arms teams. Brigades and divisions often comprised a single arm, while the army corps was the combined arms unit, with its size varying greatly according to the mission and the forces available. Reflecting the Army of the eighteenth and nineteenth centuries, little specialization existed within the Army's corps, divisions, and brigades beyond the traditional combat arms. Field units for signal, medical, transportation, military police, ordnance, and other supporting branches simply did not exist. Often civilians were hired to undertake those duties, soldiers were detailed from the combat regiments to perform them, or entire regiments were reorganized for new missions, such as infantry units' service as engineers during the Civil War.

By the beginning of the twentieth century, technological developments, primarily in the range and lethality of weapons, greatly expanded the size of the bat-

---

[1] McClure, "The Infantry Division and Its Composition," p. 8

tlefield, making the coordination of fire and maneuver exceedingly complex. To simplify and regularize that coordination, the Army organized its field units into permanent combined arms teams, termed divisions, capable of independent operations. Included in such organization, in increasingly larger numbers, were combat support and combat service support units that contributed to the combat power and self-sufficiency of the division on both the battlefield and the training ground. The organization of permanent divisions, with their fixed requirements for personnel and equipment, training, and research and development, also greatly facilitated the expansion of the Army upon the outbreak of war.

From the turn of the century until American intervention in World War I, the Army defended the nation and its modest insular possessions with what was basically a constabulary force. To some limited extent the Army tested the infantry division as a basic combined arms unit in field exercises or maneuvers. The cavalry division, although not totally neglected, remained more or less a theoretical organization. In 1916 and 1917, when the Army pursued bandits along the Mexican border, a provisional division was organized. Heavy in cavalry and light in infantry, it was tailored to meet an elusive, mobile enemy.

Mobilization for the crisis on the border and observation of trends in foreign armies during the initial campaigns of World War I caused national leaders to become increasingly concerned about the need to create permanent tactical divisions. Congress approved their organization in 1916, but the Army entered World War I before any such units had been organized, and the ensuing mobilization and battlefield experiences witnessed constant changes in both their theoretical (i.e., authorized) and their actual composition.

The Army created the square infantry division during World War I in response to the German use of entrenched positions that blocked flanking movements. The division was designed to punch through the enemy's position using overwhelming manpower and tremendous firepower. Strong in staying power, the division lacked the mobility and flexibility to conduct highly mobile operations. But the nature of the war also put a premium on coordination between the combat arms and combat support organizations within the infantry division. Not infantry and not artillery but coordination of all the branches held the key to success. Infantry could not move forward without engineers and artillery; artillery could not provide adequate fire support without a constant supply of ammunition; quartermaster troops supplied food and clothing; signalmen served as the link between the arms and support units; and medical personnel cared for casualties of all types. This complex combined arms interaction, or synergy, became both necessary and possible because of advances in weapons, communications, and transportation.

World War I posed problems that military planners would face for the remainder of the century. They had to balance military requirements against those of the home front, which provided the materiel for war. Mobilization for total war theoretically demanded the maximum amount of the nation's best manpower for its military forces, but without the civilian manpower to provide the logistical base for that force, it would soon collapse of its own weight. A related question concerned the size and readiness of the peacetime active and reserve forces, which influenced the preparation for a swift industrial and manpower mobilization without bankrupting the nation. Military planners in the United States also had to confront the problem in the twentieth century of how best to deploy their military forces abroad in the face of limited means, because the number of ships available for what was termed "strategic mobility" would always constrain the speed with which the Army could bring its major combat organizations to bear on far-away battlefields.

Although memories of the Army's helter-skelter mobilization during World War I cast a long shadow over the interwar period, 1919–39, isolationist sentiment caused a certain malaise in organizational development. Nevertheless, Army leaders recognized that infantry and cavalry divisions, rather than regiments or smaller units, had become the pillars that supported a future mobilization. Officers examined the structure of various types of divisions, and the Army adopted in the post–World War I era a modified but powerful square infantry division designed for a straightforward frontal attack, and a smaller cavalry division for reconnaissance. Although the lessons of World War I influenced the structure of these divisions, the traditional nineteenth century criterion of distance or road space still dominated their design.

Once permanent divisions were established, any reorganization of them was controversial. Because no foreign threat or opponent could be identified, divisions were initially designed to fight on the North American continent, and their organizations stressed firepower over mobility. And once that organizational structure became embedded in both the Regular Army and the reserve components, it became exceedingly difficult to alter it in any substantial way. Although many Army leaders viewed the situation with increasing misgivings, major changes ultimately depended on changes in the political climate of the nation. Before any major reorganization of its divisions could be effected, the Army needed more specific guidance from its political leaders regarding future missions and the availability of commensurate resources.

From the fall of 1937 to the summer of 1943 the Army slowly fashioned the divisional designs it used to fight World War II. Not only revised infantry and cavalry divisions, but also armored, motorized divisions and airborne divisions appeared. The concept of having three regimental combat teams within the infantry and airborne divisions also solidified. Other trends included steady increases in firepower—with mobility or maneuvering capability, always trying to catch up—and the increasing standardization of division base elements. In the entire process, the horse cavalry and motorized divisions died, while the armored division, designed initially as a two-element organization, was often committed on the battlefield as small task forces.

One principle holds that military units should be organized to counter the characteristics of the enemy they expect to face on the battlefield, whether

German foot-soldiers or tanks, Philippine or Viet Cong guerrillas, or an army equipped with chemical and nuclear weapons. Such problems inevitably brought soldiers from the theoretical realm of the schoolhouse into conflict with those living in the reality of the army in the field. Doctrine, which dictated how units should be organized, fell within the domain of the service schools, while employment of the units rested with field commanders. To both, such seemingly esoteric matters as the best span of control, the number of command echelons, the composition of the staff, the balance between infantry and artillery, the location of the reconnaissance element, the role of engineers, and the organization of the supply system were recurring subjects of exploration and argument in designing divisions and separate brigades. No final determination emerged as to whether the schools or the field commands should perform organizational studies, but one aspect of the Army's experience became clear. The Army could not solve all its organizational issues in a single study. The questions were—and still are—too enormous and complex for one group of planners to address. The reorganization study of 1936, PENTANA 1955, and MOMAR 1959 all failed because the issues they addressed were too broad and varied. After the Army came to terms with its divisional echelon, as in the triangular, ROAD flexible response, and Army of Excellence studies, the remainder of the force somehow fell into place.

Ultimately nothing influenced Army planners in their search for the right combined arms units more than the desire to ensure mobility and maneuverability on the battlefield. The disappearance of operational flexibility on the Western Front in World War I convinced many officers that the resulting stalemate had caused unacceptable losses in men and equipment for both the victors and the vanquished. The square division was adopted for the peacetime Army because Army leaders relied upon their World War I experience and believed that the unit could be adapted to maneuver and mobility.

The evolution of technology eventually brought about more mobile and flexible forces, which included various types of infantry divisions (airborne, airmobile, light, and motorized), the replacement of obsolete horse cavalry divisions with armored and mechanized units, and the introduction of separate combined arms brigades. Infantry divisions dominated World War II, due primarily to the influence of such leaders as Chief of Staff General George C. Marshall and Lt. Gen. Lesley J. McNair, the chief of Army Ground Forces, who believed that it was vital to standardize, at least for the moment, the size and structure of the field army to assist in both manpower and materiel mobilization planning. However, in the postwar era the regular "foot" or "leg" infantry division was slowly replaced by various types of armored, mechanized, airborne, and airmobile organizations developed to serve special needs. Tanks stopped tanks; airborne troops intimidated and threw the enemy's rear area into disarray; and helicopters inserted and extracted units with precision on the battlefield. Given the specialization of division and brigade forces, planners had to decide how many of each type the Army needed and how many it could afford. Since each specialized unit

CONCLUSION                                                                  417

created different requirements for equipment and training, advocates of such organizations were pitted against those who favored more universal formations that performed a variety of missions. As always, permanent solutions proved elusive, and planners continued to balance the number and type of divisions and separate brigades required to meet threats, both real and perceived. By the 1990s the trend was toward two types of divisions and brigades, light and heavy, but within those two types were variations that allowed the Army to build tailored forces for specific missions with armored, infantry, mechanized infantry, light infantry, airborne, and air assault units.

New weapons often presented problems for planners of divisions and brigades. First, they had to decide the level at which a weapon belonged—army, corps, division, or brigade—and where it fit within the chosen organization. Examples of this dilemma were the tank and machine gun in World War I, the tank destroyer in World War II, the Honest John rocket in the atomic field army and pentomic divisions, and the TOW in the Army of Excellence. This recurring problem also manifested itself in the conflict between centralization and decentralization of resources. When introduced into a division, new weapons were often put under centralized control, usually in a battalion or company-size unit, and attached to the user only when needed. Since such practices violated the principle of command and control, eventually new weapons were reassigned to the primary user. Certain divisional items, however, were better used under centralized control. Aircraft, for example, which used a common airfield and required sophisticated maintenance, still require centralized organization.

As weapons evolved, dispersion within and between units on the battlefield became more necessary, especially as more lethal weapons, including those with nuclear warheads, became available. The problem within the division was how to separate divisional elements physically yet maintain effective command and control over them. Improved communication systems and the use of airplanes and helicopters aided such dispersion, but the need for the division to operate in a widely dispersed nuclear environment fortunately has never arisen.

Perhaps it is endemic to a democracy that in peacetime its army suffers from neglect. The economic and financial wherewithal for personnel, equipment, training, research, and development are often available only when a threat to the nation's security is readily apparent. The Army's divisions, separate brigades, and other units in peacetime were seldom fully manned and trained and at times were only paper organizations. This neglect manifested the American people's ingrained disdain for standing armies, which dated from the beginning of the nation. After World War II, although begrudgingly, the nation improved the Army's sustaining base, which lessened the time required for mobilization. Nevertheless, during the forty years of the Cold War many units, particularly those in the reserve components, were only marginally ready for combat.

After World Wars I and II and the Korean War, the Army's divisional forces, as well as the Army itself, were devastated by a tidal wave of turbulence caused by demobilization, or force reduction. Following each period the Army struggled to rebuild and maintain a mobilization force of standing and reserve forces before the next crisis struck. On each occasion military planners designed a mobilization force requiring more divisions and brigades than the nation needed or was willing to support. Also, political pressure, particularly from the reserve components, often influenced the size of that force more than defense requirements. The result was what many called a "hollow army," with some units deteriorating into paper organizations, some serving as training units, and others lacking so much of their personnel and equipment that they had little ability to conduct either combat or training.

Following major conflicts the poor manning and equipping levels that characterized most Army units resulted partly from a lack of resources and partly from unreasonable expectations. Obviously, funding limited the number of soldiers, both officers and enlisted personnel, in the Regular Army and the reserve components. In the Organized Reserves, between 1921 and 1948 no system was even available to recruit untrained enlisted personnel; Congress simply expected that reserve enlisted personnel would be unpaid volunteers with prior service. Few former enlisted personnel, however, volunteered to serve in the Organized Reserve, and reserve officers came into the Army through the Reserve Officer Training Corps (ROTC). Although Congress funded officers and enlisted men in both reserve components after World War II, interest in serving as reservists lagged. Between the end of World War II and the early 1970s, when conscription was eliminated, the draft served as a stimulus for serving in the reserves. With the elimination of the draft, recruitment in the reserves suffered further, and their division and separate brigade forces underwent an almost continuous series of realignments.

Time and again after the disappearance of any immediate threat Congress or the administration cut the Army's funding drastically. At times money was available only to provide skeletal units in the Regular Army. These units manned garrisons, supported limited reserve training, and provided the overhead to operate the Army. Few men were available for combat units or for occupation forces overseas. Scattered throughout the nation on small posts or serving overseas, the Army often had neither the money nor the opportunity for combined arms training. Under the "come as you are, fight as you are" philosophy adopted in the 1970s, only the Regular Army divisions in Europe were maintained at full strength. Regular Army divisions in the United States were rounded out by reserve units, and the division in Korea relied upon KATUSA, or Korean Army personnel.

During periods of scant resources for the defense establishment, the largest share of the military budget went to the other services. Both the Navy and the Air Force required sophisticated, expensive equipment whose construction also provided civilian jobs and valuable investments in advanced technology. The Army, in contrast, is the most labor-intensive of the services. To gain support from the executive and legislative branches, its leaders used divisional models to justify

# CONCLUSION

funding requests for the research, development, and production of new equipment and weapons. Looking at the division as a weapons system rather than merely as a personnel organization has in fact proved useful in conceptualizing what the Army needs and what it does for both Congress and the general public.

The end of the Cold War has prompted another examination of divisions and brigades as the Army adapts to new threats and new national missions. Whatever direction the changes may take, divisions and brigades will be organized for a particular mission, against a particular enemy, at a particular time, and in a particular place. The search for better combined arms units will continue unabated as new lessons and experiences are weighed, and the search to integrate new technology into existing organizational concepts will likewise present an ongoing challenge in the immediate future.

# A Look Forward

In 1990 the U.S. Army began deploying major units to Southwest Asia as part of a coalition effort to counter the military aggression of the Iraqi armed forces. But even before that, major changes in the Army's organization had begun. Between 1989 and 1991 the Soviet Union collapsed and with it the Communist Warsaw Pact alliance system that had posed a major threat to the United States and its West European NATO allies for nearly fifty years. In the wake of those momentous events, the national leadership began to transform the Army from a "forward-deployed" force to a "power-projection" force based in the United States, with the war in Southwest Asia the first test of that concept. But at the same time, the Army assumed a host of major humanitarian and peacekeeping missions that soon took it to new areas of the globe, many of which it had never visited previously in any major way. Although an objective assessment of these developments is premature, some brief observations about what happened during the years between 1990 and 1996 are appropriate.

Even before the successful 100-hour Persian Gulf War in February 1991, Army plans called for a significant reduction in the number of divisions and brigades. Without the threat posed by the Soviet Union, the nation no longer saw the need to field twenty-eight divisions and twenty-seven combined arms brigades. Both political pundits and national leaders expected that the American "victory" in the Cold War would result in what was termed a "peace dividend," allowing the government to shift its economic priorities from military readiness to other programs, including the pressing need to reduce the annual deficit. One of the first Army units to feel the axe was the 9th Infantry Division at Fort Lewis, Washington, with one of its two remaining brigades inactivated in September 1990, and then the entire division the following year. With what remained, the Army organized the independent 199th Infantry Brigade, but that unit would enjoy only a short existence.

As divisions and brigades returned from Southwest Asia in the summer of 1991, the force underwent further change. Readiness concerns had prevented the deployment of the National Guard round-out brigades to the Gulf region with the 24th Infantry Division and 1st Cavalry Division. Consequently, to fill, or round out, these divisions, the active duty 197th Infantry Brigade from Fort Benning, Georgia, and 1st Brigade, 2d Armored Division, at Fort Hood, Texas, had taken their place. Now these brigades were inactivated, with their personnel and equipment used to organize third maneuver brigades in the 24th Infantry and 1st Cavalry Divisions. At the same time, the failure to deploy the reserve component round-out units set off a debate over the utility of the twenty-year-old concept, which remained to be settled in 1996.

Meanwhile, U.S. Army, Europe, resumed its plans to inactivate two divisions and two brigades and to realign its two remaining divisions as a part of the expected peace dividend. In August 1991 the 1st Infantry Division Forward (a reinforced brigade) left the active force. Five months later the 8th Infantry Division was inactivated, followed by the 3d Armored Division in August 1992 and the 3d Brigade, 2d Armored Division (the forward-deployed brigade in Garlstedt, Germany), in December of that year. About the same time, the VII Corps, one of the two corps headquarters in Europe, also was inactivated, with its armored cavalry regiment, the 2d Armored Cavalry, returning to the United States. The reduction left only the V Corps headquarters in Europe, along with the 1st Armored Division, the 3d Infantry Division, and one armored cavalry regiment, the 11th Armored Cavalry.

Forces in the United States also took their share of cuts in 1992. The 2d Armored Division, the only armored division continuously active since the organization of the Armored Force in 1940, was slated for inactivation but, to keep it on the active rolls, it replaced the 5th Infantry Division, which was scheduled to move from Fort Polk, Louisiana, to Fort Hood, Texas. In the summer of 1992 the 199th Infantry Brigade was inactivated when the 2d Armored Cavalry moved to Fort Lewis, Washington. In addition, forces in Korea felt the reduction knife, with the 2d Infantry Division forced to inactivate one of its brigades. Less than two years after fighting in Southwest Asia, the Regular Army had thus lost four divisions, one divisional brigade, and two separate brigades.

The precipitous decline in the number of Regular Army divisions and brigades continued after 1992, with Congress tentatively setting the strength of the active Army at 495,000 by end of 1996. In 1994 the 6th and 7th Infantry Divisions were inactivated, with one brigade of each division remaining active at Fort Richardson, Alaska, and Fort Lewis, Washington, respectively. In Germany the 2d Brigade, 3d Infantry Division, was eliminated, and the 3d Brigade, 1st Armored Division, the only divisional unit to redeploy with its personnel and equipment, moved from Germany to Fort Lewis, Washington. These cuts reduced the Army's forward-deployed European maneuver force to the 1st Armored Division and the 3d Infantry Division, both with only two brigades each, and the 11th Armored Cavalry.

To meet the projected end strength of 495,000, political as well as economic factors had to be considered, and a series of flag and designation changes began in 1995. Three factors drove the decision of which flags would continue to fly: the desire to retain historic divisions in the active force; the decision to field all divisions with a full complement of maneuver brigades; and the advantages of maintaining a regional distribution of divisional troops in the United States. In

A LOOK FORWARD 423

April 1995 the 3d Brigade, 2d Infantry Division, replaced the 3d Brigade, 1st Armored Division, at Fort Lewis, Washington, with the latter's flag moving to Fort Riley, Kansas. Also, the flag of the 3d Brigade, 25th Infantry Division, moved to Fort Lewis from Schofield Barracks, Hawaii, to dislodge the 1st Brigade, 7th Infantry, which was inactivated. In November 1995 the 1st Brigade, 6th Infantry Division, in Alaska was associated with the 10th Mountain Division at Fort Drum, New York, but without a change in the brigade's designation. The following month the 4th Infantry Division (less its 3d Brigade, which remained at Fort Carson, Colorado) relocated to Fort Hood, Texas, where it replaced the 2d Armored Division, which was eliminated from the active force.

A significant change took place in January 1996, when the 1st Infantry Division (less its 3d Brigade) transferred its flags and colors from Fort Riley, Kansas, to Germany, where it succeeded the 3d Infantry Division; concurrently the 3d Infantry Division shifted its division and brigade flags and colors to Forts Stewart and Benning, Georgia, to replace the 24th Infantry Division, which was inactivated. In order to have three maneuver brigades in the 1st Infantry Division, its 3d Brigade, inactivated in 1991, returned to the active rolls. Upon completion of the programmed changes the Regular Army force had been pared down to 10 divisions—1 airborne, 1 air assault, 2 light, and 6 heavy divisions. Only the 1st Cavalry Division at Fort Hood, Texas; the 82d Airborne Division at Fort Bragg, North Carolina; and the 101st Airborne Division at Fort Campbell, Kentucky, were concentrated; all of the others were split between two or more installations.

The independent brigades in the active Army suffered more severe reductions. When the 199th Infantry Brigade was inactivated in 1992, only the Berlin Brigade, the 193d Infantry Brigade, and the 177th and 194th Armored Brigades remained in the force. For almost fifty years the Army had units stationed in Berlin, but with the end of the Cold War and the return of the city of Berlin to the German government, the Berlin Brigade fell from the force in the summer of 1994. Next to go was the 193d Infantry Brigade, stationed in the Panama Canal Zone. In anticipation of the Panamanian government's taking over complete control of the Canal Zone in 1999, the 193d Infantry Brigade was inactivated in 1994. That same year the 11th Armored Cavalry, which could not be supported within U.S. Army, Europe, troop strength, returned to the United States. To retain it in the force, the chief of staff approved replacing the 177th Armored Brigade at the National Training Center, Fort Irwin, California, with the armored cavalry regiment in October 1994. Reductions also required the inactivation of the 194th Armored Brigade at Fort Knox, Kentucky, in 1995, leaving the Regular Army without any separate combined arms brigades.

The reserve components also underwent turmoil caused by force reduction. In 1993 the National Guard lost two divisions, the 26th Infantry and the 50th Armored. Both had been experiencing recruitment problems over the past twenty-five years. At the same time, to maintain heavy forces in the National Guard, the 28th and 42d Infantry Divisions were reorganized as heavy divisions. The 42d, now an armored division, retained its traditional designation for historical and esprit de corps reasons. To strengthen the 28th Infantry Division, the 37th Infantry Brigade, Ohio National Guard, was reorganized as a brigade of that division, but a year later the brigade was transferred to the 38th Infantry Division. To make room for the unit in the 38th, the 76th Brigade, 38th Infantry Division, Indiana National Guard, was withdrawn from the division and reorganized as the 76th Infantry Brigade. The net result of these changes was that the National Guard fielded 8 divisions—1 light, 2 infantry, 2 armored, and 3 mechanized infantry divisions. At the same time, the Guard continued to field 20 separate combined arms brigades. Although these units provided the Army with the flexibility to tailor forces upon mobilization, planned reductions would leave only 14 enhanced and 2 theater defense brigades in the force by 1997 (with an armored cavalry regiment often counted as the National Guard's fifteenth "enhanced brigade").

Following the "Bottom-Up" review, an assessment of all military requirements by Secretary of Defense Les Aspin in 1993, the Army Reserve agreed to give up its combat arms units and focus on maintaining combat support and combat service support formations. Consequently, the Army inactivated the 157th, 187th, and 205th Infantry Brigades in 1994. To improve the readiness of the remaining reserve units prior to mobilization, the U.S. Army Forces Command developed the "exercise division," an organization designed to both conduct and assist the training of Army Reserve combat support and combat service support units. Through the use of simulations and simulators, the new organization also provided exercises to improve unit proficiency and command and staff training. In 1993 the 78th, 85th, and 91st Divisions (Training) were reorganized as exercise divisions. At the same time the 75th and 87th Maneuver Area Commands were discontinued and the 75th and 87th Infantry Divisions reactivated as the 75th and 87th Divisions (Exercise). In 1996 the functions of training divisions were expanded to include institutional as well as basic and advanced training under the Total Army Training Strategy. Although the functions of the training divisions were expanded, two unneeded training brigades and two surplus training divisions were eliminated, leaving the Army Reserve with the 80th, 84th, 95th, 98th, 100th, 104th, and 108th Divisions (Training). By the mid-1990s the Army Reserve had no combined arms units, but fielded five exercise and seven training divisions. In sum, as the Army moved toward the end of the century, the total force had been pared down to eighteen combat divisions (ten Regular Army and eight National Guard), with plans to reduce the number of National Guard independent combined arms brigades from twenty to sixteen. As noted above, the Army Reserve had five exercise and seven training divisions.

Although the number of divisions and separate brigades decreased rapidly in the 1990s, the story of the post–Cold War era encompassed more than just numbers of units. The divisions and separate brigades that remained in the force continued to be constructed from building blocks, a practice that provided the flexibility to tailor units for specific missions and for different regions of the world.

Such methods also made it easier to introduce new technologies and new capabilities into the existing force organization.

Under the Force XXI program, the Army's current effort to guide the modernization of the Army into the early twenty-first century, Army leaders wanted even more flexible divisions rather than more specialized but rigid ones. In June 1996 General William W. Hartzog, the commander of the U.S. Training and Doctrine Command, noted that the Army no longer could send only its light units, such as the 10th Mountain Division and the 82d Airborne Division, to every unconventional or low-intensity operation. Elements of the 82d Airborne Division had served in Panama (Operation JUST CAUSE) in 1989, in Southwest Asia (DESERT SHIELD/STORM) in 1990 and 1991, and in south Florida after Hurricane Andrew in 1992. Elements of the 10th Mountain Division had also served in south Florida in 1992 and deployed to Somalia (Operation RESTORE HOPE) in 1992 and 1993 and to Haiti (Operation UPHOLD DEMOCRACY) in 1994. Henceforth, like the 1st Armored Division in Bosnia (Operation JOINT ENDEAVOR) in 1995 and 1996, all divisions in the force had to be prepared to undertake humanitarian and peacekeeping missions.

To meet the need for future contingencies and still provide forces for conventional operations, the Training and Doctrine Command began taking a new look at the Army's heavy division. Previously it had set the maneuver element mix for an armored division at five tank and four mechanized infantry battalions while reversing those numbers in the mechanized infantry division. Proposals in 1996 envisioned eliminating about 3,000 soldiers from organizational tables of the heavy division while increasing the maneuver element mix to five tank and five mechanized infantry battalions. The projected change would add about 300 dismounted infantrymen to each mechanized infantry unit, eliminate the antitank company of each infantry battalion, and move support functions from each infantry battalion to the division support battalions. The engineer brigade with three engineer battalions, which was tested in Southwest Asia and added to divisions shortly thereafter, was to lose one battalion, and one of the heavy division's two attack aviation battalions would also disappear. In the latter case, planners expected that new "Long Bow" Apache and Comanche helicopters would provide greater combat power to make up for the loss. Also, a newly improved, self-propelled 155-mm. howitzer, the Paladin, was to be fielded in three batteries of six weapons each, replacing the existing battalions, which had three batteries of eight pieces each of older weapons. The divisional target acquisition and multiple-launch rocket batteries were programmed to be combined in a single artillery battalion, giving the division greater flexibility in engaging close-up and distant targets. In addition, the maneuver brigades in the division were given increased scouting capability in the form of a reconnaissance troop. Finally, the key to this smaller but more deadly division was to be a digital communication system, or what was referred to as digitalization. Using new information technology, Army leaders wanted to provide engaged commanders with immediate data regarding available resources and the enemy they faced, enabling them to bring a wide variety of forces to bear on the foe as quickly as possible and to sustain them until final victory. A test of the new division was scheduled for 1997.

Six years after the war in Southwest Asia, many questions regarding the Army's future force structure remain. The failure to implement the round-out concept during that conflict is only the first of many. How well did the Army's divisions and separate brigades perform in Southwest Asia against a confused and greatly weakened adversary? Has the Army cut too many divisions from the force too quickly; will it attain the right balance of divisions in the active and reserve forces; and how radically can the heavy and light divisions be redesigned to meet contingencies of the future within budgetary constraints that appear ever changing? How seriously has the elimination of the separate combined arms brigades hindered flexibility in designing the active force? A more basic question was also left unanswered. Is the division the best vehicle to organize the combat arms for the future or should it be the brigade, as some have argued? If history has shown us anything, it is that the future is always unpredictable and that the basic ingredient of success will continue to be a mind-set that allows the greatest speed and flexibility in adopting new technologies, new missions, and new constraints to the Army's ever-changing organizations for combat.

# Bibliographical Note

When George Washington organized the first American army in 1775, the organization of divisions and brigades almost immediately became a subject for discussion, but no comprehensive study has ever been published about their evolution in the United States military. This study, prepared from a wide range of sources, was intended to fill that gap. Many of the sources consulted are part of the archival holdings of the National Archives and Records Administration (NARA), Washington, D.C. Although many record groups in the National Archives were searched, the following groups were particularly useful: 165, records of the War Department and special staffs; 168, records of the National Guard Bureau; 177, records of the Chief of Arms; 94 and 407, records of the Adjutant General; 393 and 394, records of the U.S. Army Continental Commands; and 337, records of Headquarters, Army Ground Forces. At the Military History Institute (MHI), Carlisle Barracks, Pennsylvania, the records of the Army War College, 1920–40, were a rich source of information. Also valuable were the holdings in the Manuscript Division of the Library of Congress, Washington, D.C., which house the papers of Leonard Wood, John J. Pershing, John McAuley Palmer, George Van Horn Moseley, John L. Hinds, Charles L. Scott, and others. The George C. Marshall Foundation, Lexington, Virginia; the Command and General Staff College Library, Fort Leavenworth, Kansas; the Infantry Center and School Library, Fort Benning, Georgia; the Institute of Heraldry Library, Fort Belvoir, Virginia; and the Patton Museum, Fort Knox, Kentucky, all were helpful in locating and providing documents. Since World War II, the weekly newspaper *Army Times* has been a source of information about the Army, and routinely information about divisions and brigades has been culled from it by members of the Center of Military History.

The official publications of the War Department and the Department of the Army were essential to the study. They included the periodic *General Regulations of the United States Army; Field Service Regulations, United States Army*; and *Official Army Registers*; and War Department and Department of the Army regulations, general orders, circulars, bulletins, and field manuals. Another collection of official material that proved to be invaluable in preparing the work was the published Annual Reports of the War Department. Within those reports, the most frequently cited were the *Report of the Secretary of War, Report of the Major*

*General Commanding the Army, Report of the Chief of Staff, Report of the Adjutant General,* and *Report of the Chief of the Militia Bureau,* later the *Report of the Chief of the National Guard Bureau.* Between 1920 and 1941 the reports were basically limited to those of the Secretary of War, the Chief of Staff, and Chief of the National Guard Bureau (the last still being published annually). Between 1948 and 1968 the reports pertaining to activities of the Department of the Army were published in the *Department of Defense Reports.* After 1968 the *Department of the Army Historical Summaries* carried on the tradition of the official *Reports of the War Department.* Since 1939 reports of the Chief of Staff of the Army have been published intermittently under various titles. All of the official publications listed in the notes are in the library of the U.S. Army Center of Military History (DAMH), Washington, D.C., and when cited in the notes no location was given.

The third category of documents that proved particularly significant was the unpublished annual summaries or reviews that the major commands have prepared since World War II. They included documents prepared by the Office, Chief of Army Field Forces (OCAFF), U.S. Continental Army Command (CONARC), U.S. Army Combat Developments Command (CDC), U.S. Army Forces Command (FORSCOM), U.S. Army Training and Doctrine Command (TRADOC), U.S. Army, Europe (USAREUR), U.S. Army, Pacific (USARPAC), and others, which are a part of the holdings of the Historical Records Branch, U.S. Army Center of Military History, cited as DAMH-HSR.

Although many types of documents have been consulted, tables of organization and equipment (TOE) published in the twentieth century served as the skeleton for the study. The Army first published TOEs in 1914 as an aid to mobilization planning, and many are required to describe a division or separate combined arms brigade. To list all used in preparing this study is prohibitive, but those cited in the notes are available in the Organizational History Branch of the Center, cited as DAMH-HSO. Along with the TOEs, the subject files in the Organizational History Branch pertaining to such topics as the National Guard, Army Reserve, mobilizations, and other areas involving units; the adjutant general reference files and the unit historical data cards, both of which contain data about the changes in status of units, were indispensable. The last group of files in the Organizational History Branch without which the study could not have been prepared was the unit files. They also contain letters of instructions for changes in status of units, general orders from the commands implementing those instructions, studies prepared by staff officers concerning the organizations, newspaper articles about the units, and sundry miscellaneous papers about them.

The selective bibliography that follows has been divided into books, journals, and unpublished manuscripts.

## Books

Acheson, Dean. *Present at the Creation: My Years in the State Department*. New York: W. W. Norton and Co., 1969.

Adler, Julius O. *History of the Seventy-Seventh Division*. New York: Wynokoop Hallenbeck Crawford Co., 1919.

Alger, Russell A. *The Spanish-American War*. New York: Harper and Co., 1901.

Allen, Henry T. *The Rhineland Occupation*. Indianapolis: Robbs-Merrill Co., 1927.

*American Archives: A Collection of Authentic Records, State Papers, and Letters and Other Notices of Public Affairs*. 9 vols. Ser. 4. Washington, D.C.: M. St. Clair and Peter Force, 1839–53.

*American State Papers, Military Affairs*. 7 vols. Washington, D.C.: Gales and Seaton, 1834.

Appleman, Roy E. *South to the Naktong, North to the Yalu*. United States Army in the Korean War. Washington, D.C.: Government Printing Office, 1961.

Balck, William. *Taktik (Tactics)*, vol. 3, *Kriegsgliederung, Nachrichten, Befehle, Marschdienst (Military Organization, Communications, Orders, Marches)*. 4th ed. Berlin: R. Eisenschmidt, 1907.

Barnett, Correlli. *Britain and Her Army 1509–1970*. Warmondsworth, England: Allen Lane, Penguin Press, 1974.

Benwell, Harry *A. History of the Yankee Division*. Boston: Cornhill Co., 1919.

Birkhimer, William E. *Historical Sketch of the Organization, Administration, Materiel, and Tactics of the Artillery, United States Army*. Washington, D.C.: James J. Chapman, 1884.

Blumenson, Martin. *Salerno to Cassino*. United States Army in World War II. Washington, D.C.: Government Printing Office, 1969.

Bowman, Stephen L., John M. Kendall, and James L. Saunders. *Motorized Experience of the 9th Infantry Division*. Fort Lewis, Wash.: N.p., 1989.

Brown, Sevellon. *The Story of Ordnance in the World War*. Washington, D.C.: James William Bryan Press, 1920.

Butterfield, Julia Lorrilard, ed. *A Biographical Memorial of General Daniel Butterfield*. New York: Grafton Press, 1904.

Callan, John F., comp. *The Military Laws of the United States*. Philadelphia: G. W. Childs, 1863.

Chambers, John Whiteclay II. *To Raise an Army: The Draft Comes to Modern America*. New York: Free Press, 1987.

Cheng, Christopher C.S. *Air Mobility: The Development of a Doctrine*. Westport, Conn.: Praeger, 1994.

Chin, George M. *The Machine Gun*. 3 vols. Washington, D.C.: Government Printing Office, 1951.

Clendenen, Clarence C. *Blood on the Border: The United States Army and the Mexican Irregulars*. London: Macmillan and Co., 1969.

Clinger, Fred, Arthur Johnson, and Vincent Masel. *The History of the 71st Infantry Division*. Augsburg, Germany: E. Kieser KG, 1946.

Coakley, Robert W., and Richard M. Leighton. *Global Logistics and Strategy: 1943–1945*. United States Army in World War II. Washington, D.C.: Government Printing Office, 1968.

Coffman, Edward N. *The Hilt of the Sword, The Career of Peyton C. March*. Madison: University of Wisconsin Press, 1966.

———. *The War to End All Wars*. New York: Oxford University Press, 1966.

Coleman, J. D. *Pleiku: The Dawn of Helicopter Warfare in Vietnam*. New York: St. Martin's Press, 1988.

Conn, Stetson, Rose C. Engelman, and Byron Fairchild. *Guarding the United States and Its Outposts*. United States Army in World War II. Washington, D.C.: Government Printing Office, 1964.

*Correspondence Relating to the War with Spain*. 2 vols. Washington, D.C.: Government Printing Office, 1902. Reprinted. Washington, D.C.: Government Printing Office, 1993.

Cosmas, Graham A. *An Army for Empire, The United States in the Spanish-American War*. Columbia: University of Missouri Press, 1971.

Cronin, Francis D. *Under the Southern Cross, The Saga of the Americal Division*. Washington, D.C.: Combat Forces Press, 1951.

Crossland, Richard B., and James T Currie. *Twice the Citizen: A History of the United States Army Reserve, 1908–1983*. Washington, D.C.: Office of the Chief, Army Reserve, 1984.

Department of the Army Chief of Information, *Why Merge*. N.p., March 1965.

Dastrup, Boyd L. *King of Battle: A Branch History of the U.S. Army's Field Artillery*. Fort Monroe, Va.: U.S. Army Training and Doctrine Command, 1992.

Delaney, John P. *The Blue Devils in Italy: A History of the 88th Infantry Division in World War II*. Washington, D.C.: Infantry Journal Press, 1947.

Devlin, Gerard M. *Paratroopers: The Saga of Parachute and Glider Combat Troop, 1914 to 1945*. New York: St. Martin's Press, 1986.

Diamond, Maynard L., Willard E. Simms, Edward B. Baldinger, and Meyer Siegelbaum. *The 89th Infantry Division, 1942–1945*. Washington, D.C.: Infantry Journal Press, 1946.

Dickinson, John. *The Building of an Army*. New York: Century Co.,1922.

Dolcater, Max W. *3d Infantry Division in Korea*. Tokyo: Toppan Printing Co., 1953.

Doughty, Robert A. *The Evaluation of the US Army Tactical Doctrine, 1946–76*. Leavenworth Papers. Fort Leavenworth, Kans.: Combat Studies Institute, 1979.

Duane, William. *A Hand Book for Infantry*. Philadelphia: William Duane, 1814.

Dyer, Frederick H. *A Compendium of the War of the Rebellion*. Des Moines, Iowa: Dyer Publishing Company, 1908.

*88th Division in the World War of 1914–1918, The*. New York: Wynkoop Hallenbeck Crawford Co., 1919.

Eisenhower, John D. *So Far From God: The U.S. War With Mexico 1846–1848*. New York: Random House, 1989.

Elliott, Charles W. *Winfield Scott: The Soldier and the Man*. New York: Macmillan Co., 1937.

Fehrenback, T. R. *This Kind of War: A Study in Unpreparedness*. New York: Macmillan Co., 1963.

Finnegan, John P. *Against the Specter of a Dragon*. Westport, Conn.: Greenwood Press, 1974.

Flanagan, Edward M. *The Angels: A History of the 11th Airborne Division 1943–1946*. Washington, D.C.: Infantry Journal Press, 1948.

Ford, Worthington C., ed. *Journals of the Continental Congress, 1774–1789*. 34 vols. Washington, D.C.: Government Printing Office, 1904–37.

Fuller, J. F. C. *British Light Infantry in the Eighteenth Century*. London: Hutchinson, 1925.

Fulton, William F. *Riverine Operations, 1966–1969*. Washington, D.C.: Government Printing Office, 1973.

Gabel, Christopher R. *The U.S. Army GHQ Maneuvers of 1941*. Washington, D.C.: Government Printing Office, 1992.

Gavin, James M. *On to Berlin: Battle of an Airborne Commander, 1943–1946*. New York: Viking Press, 1978.

*Genesis of the American First Army*. Washington, D.C.: Government Printing Office, 1938.

Gillett, Mary C. *The Army Medical Department, 1818–1865*. Washington, D.C.: Government Printing Office, 1987.

Gillie, Mildred Hanson. *Forging the Thunderbolt*. Harrisburg, Pa.: Military Service Publishing Co., 1947.

Greenfield, Kent Roberts, Robert R. Palmer, and Bell I. Wiley. *The Organization of Ground Combat Troops*. United States Army in World War II. Washington, D.C.: Government Printing Office, 1949.

Guderian, Heinz. *Panzer Leader*. New York: E. P. Dutton and Co., Inc., 1952.

Gunsburg, Jeffery A. *Divided and Conquered: The French High Command and the Defeat of the West, 1940*. Westport, Conn.: Greenwood Press, 1979.

Hagood, John. *The Services of Supply, A Memoir of the Great War*. Boston: Houghton Mifflin Co., 1927.

Harbord, James G. *The American Army in France, 1917–1918*. Boston: Little, Brown and Co., 1936.

*Harper's Pictorial History of the War With Spain*. New York: Harper and Co., 1899.

Hay, John H., Jr. *Tactical and Materiel Innovations*. Washington, D.C.: Government Printing Office, 1974.

Heitman, Francis B. *Historical Register and Dictionary of the United States Army From Its Organization, September 1779 to March 2, 1903*, Washington, D.C.: Government Printing Office, 1903.

Hermes, Walter G. *Truce Tent and Fighting Front*. United States Army in the Korean War. Washington, D.C.: Government Printing Office, 1966.

Hewes, James E., Jr. *From Root to McNamara: Army Organization and Administration, 1900–1963*. Washington, D.C.: Government Printing Office, 1975.

*Historical and Pictorial Review Second Cavalry Division, United States Army*. Baton Rouge, La.: Army Navy Publishing Co., 1941.

*History and Traditions of the Corps of Engineers*. Fort Belvoir, Va.: Engineer School, 1953.

Holley, I. B. *General John M. Palmer, Citizen Soldiers, and the Army of a Democracy*. Westport, Conn.: Greenwood Press, 1983.

Howard, Michael. *War in European History*. Oxford: Oxford University Press, 1976.

Howze, Hamilton H. *A Cavalryman's Story*. Washington, D.C.: Smithsonian Institution Press, 1996.

Huidekoper, Frederic L. *Military Unpreparedness of the United States*. New York: Macmillan, 1915.

———. *The History of the 33d Division, A.E.F.* 4 vols. Springfield: Illinois State Historical Library, 1921.

Hunt, Irwin L. *American Military Government of Occupied Germany, 1918–1919*. Washington, D.C.: Government Printing Office, 1943.

Huston, James A. *Sinews of War: Army Logistics*. Washington, D.C.: Government Printing Office, 1966.

Hutnik, Joseph J., and Leonard Kobrick, eds. *We Ripened Fast, The Unofficial History of the Seventy-Sixth Infantry Division*. Frankfurt, Germany: Otto Lembeck, 1946.

Jamieson, Perry D. *Crossing the Deadly Ground: United States Army Tactics, 1865–1899*. Tuscaloosa: University of Alabama Press, 1994.

Johnson, Lyndon Baines. *The Vantage Point*. New York: Holt, Rinehard, and Winston, 1971.

Kirkpatrick, Charles E. *An Unknown Future and a Doubtful Present: Writing the Victory Plan of 1941*. Washington, D.C.: Government Printing Office, 1991.

Knox, Henry. *A Plan for the General Arrangement of the Militia of the United States*. Political Pamphlets, No. 95, 1786.

Kreidberg, Marvin A., and Merton G. Henry. *History of Military Mobilization in the United States Army, 1775–1945*. Washington, D.C.: Government Printing Office, 1955.

Laird, Melvin R. *National Security Strategy of Realistic Deterrence: Annual Defense Department Report, Fiscal Year 1973*.

Lee, Ulysses. *The Employment of Negro Troops*. United States Army in World War II. Washington, D.C.: Government Printing Office, 1966.

Lesser, Charles H. *The Sinews of Independence: Monthly Strength Report of the Continental Army*. Chicago: University of Chicago Press, 1976.

# BIBLIOGRAPHICAL NOTE

Liddell Hart, Basil Henry. *Colonel Lawrence*. New York: Halcyon House, 1937.

Liggett, Hunter. *AEF, Ten Years Ago in France*. New York: Dodd, Mead, and Co., 1928.

*Lightning: The History of the 78th Infantry Division*. Washington, D.C.: Infantry Journal Press, 1947.

Little, John G., Jr. *The Official History of the Eighty-Sixth Division*. Chicago: State Publication Society, 1921.

Lossing, Benson J. *The Pictorial Field-Book of the War of 1812*, New York: Harper and Brothers, 1869.

McClellan, George B. *McClellan's Own Story: The War of the Union*. New York: Charles L. Webster and Co., 1887.

MacGregor, Morris J., Jr. *Integration of the Armed Forces 1940–1965*. Washington, D.C.: Government Printing Office, 1981.

McKenney, Janice E. *Air Defense Artillery*. Army Lineage Series. Washington, D.C.: Government Printing Office, 1985.

Mahon, John K., and Romana Danysh. *Infantry Part I: Regular Army*. Army Lineage Series. Washington, D.C.: Government Printing Office, 1972.

Mansfield, Edward D. *The Mexican War: A History of Its Origin*. New York: A. S. Barnes and Co., 1850.

March, Peyton C. *The Nation at War*. Garden City, N.Y.: Doubleday, Dorn, and Co., Inc., 1922.

Matloff, Maurice. "The 90-Division Gamble." In *Command Decisions*. Washington, D.C.: Government Printing Office, 1960.

———, ed. *American Military History*. Washington, D.C.: Government Printing Office, 1969.

*Mexican War Correspondence*. Washington, D.C.: Wendell and van Benthuysen Printer, 1848.

Meyer, Edward C. *General, United States Army, Chief of Staff, June 1979–June 1983*. N.p., 1983.

Midgley, John J. *Deadly Illusions: Army Policy for the Nuclear Battlefield*. Boulder, Colo.: Westview Press, 1986.

Millett, Allan R. S*emper Fidelis: The History of the United States Marine Corps*. New York: Macmillan Publishing Co., 1980.

*Mission Accomplished: Third United States Army Occupation of Germany, 9 May 1945–15 February 1947*. N.p., 1947.

Moenk, Jean. *A History of Large-Scale Army Maneuvers in the United States, 1935–64*. Fort Monroe, Va.: U.S. Continental Army Command, 1969.

Morton, Louis. *The Fall of the Philippines*. United States Army in World War II. Washington, D.C.: Government Printing Office, 1953.

Mossman, Billy C. *Ebb and Flow November 1950–July 1951*. United States Army in the Korean War. Washington, D.C.: Government Printing Office, 1990.

Mrazek, James E. *The Glider War*. London: Robert Hale and Co., 1975.

Naisawald, L. van Loan. *The US Infantry Division: Changing Concepts in*

*Organization, 1900–39*. Project Shop, ORO-S 23. Baltimore: Johns Hopkins University, 1952.

Nalty, Bernard C., and Morris J. MacGregor. *Blacks in the Military: Essential Documents*. Wilmington, Del.: Scholarly Resources, Inc., 1981.

Nenninger, Timothy K. *The Leavenworth Schools and the Old Army*. Westport, Conn.: Greenwood Press, 1978.

*Operation Gyroscope in the US Army Europe, 1957*. Historical Division, U.S. Army Europe, 1957.

*Order of Battle of the United States Land Forces in the World War (1917–19): American Expeditionary Forces: General Headquarters, Armies, Army Corps, Services of Supply, Separate Forces; Directory of Troops; Divisions; Zone of the Interior*. 5 vols. Washington, D.C.: Government Printing Office, 1931–49. Reprinted. Washington, D.C.: Government Printing Office, 1988.

O'Ryan, John F. *The Story of the 27th Division*. 2 vols. New York: Wynkoop Hallenbeck Crawford Co., 1921.

Ott, David Ewing. *Field Artillery, 1964–1973*. Washington, D.C.: Government Printing Office, 1972.

Palmer, Frederick. *Bliss, The Peacemaker: The Life and Letters of General Tasker Howard Bliss*. New York: Dodd, Mead, and Co., 1934.

———. *Newton D. Baker, America at War*. 2 vols. New York: Dodd, Mead and Co., 1931.

Palmer, Robert R., Bell I. Wiley, and William R. Keast. *The Procurement and Training of Ground Combat Troops*. United States Army in World War II. Washington, D.C.: Government Printing Office, 1948.

Paxson, Frederic Logan. *The Great Demobilization and Other Essays*. Madison: University of Wisconsin Press, 1941.

*Pennsylvania in the World War: An Illustrated History of the Twenty-Eighth Division*. 2 vols. Pittsburgh, Pa.: States Publication Society, 1921.

Pershing, John J. *My Experiences in the World War*. 2 vols. New York: Frederick A. Stokes Co., 1921.

Pew, Frank W. *The US Army Forces Command and the Development of the Brigade 75/76 Concept for the Support of Europe*. Fort McPherson, Ga.: U.S. Army Forces Command, 1980.

Pogue, Forrest C. *George C. Marshall: Education of a General*. New York: Viking Press, 1963.

Prucha, Francis Paul. *The Sword of the Republic: The United States Army on the Frontier, 1783–1846*. Bloomington: Indiana University Press, 1977.

Public Affairs Division. *Big Lift, 1963*. U.S. Army, Europe, 1963.

*Public Papers of the Presidents of the United States: Dwight D. Eisenhower*. Washington, D.C.: Government Printing Office, 1960.

*Public Papers of the Presidents of the United States: Harry S. Truman*. Washington, D.C.: Government Printing Office, 1965.

*Public Papers of the Presidents of the United States: John F. Kennedy*.

Washington, D.C.: Government Printing Office, 1961.
*Public Papers of the Presidents of the United States: Lyndon B. Johnson.* Washington, D.C.: Government Printing Office, 1966 and 1969.
*Public Papers of the Presidents of the United States: Richard M. Nixon.* Washington, D.C.: Government Printing Office, 1969 and 1971.
Quartermaster General of the Army, comp. *Tabular Statements Showing the Names of Commanders of Army Corps, Divisions, and Brigades, United States Army, During the War of 1861 to 1865*. Philadelphia: Burk and McFetrigde, Printers and Lithographers, 1887.
Quimby, Robert S. *The Background of Napoleonic Warfare*. New York: AMS Press, Inc., 1957.
Ridgway, Matthew B. *Soldier: The Memoirs of Matthew B. Ridgway*. New York: Harper and Brothers, 1956.
Ripley, R. S. *The War With Mexico*. New York: Harper and Brothers, 1849.
Risch, Erna. *Quartermaster Support of the Army: A History of the Corps, 1775–1939*. Washington, D.C.: Government Printing Office, 1962.
Risch, Erna, and Chester L. Kieffer. *The Quartermaster Corps: Organization, Supply, and Services*. 2 vols. United States Army in World War II. Washington, D.C.: Government Printing Office, 1955.
Robertson, James I. *Soldiers Blue and Gray*. Columbia: University of South Carolina Press, 1988.
Romjue, John L. *A History of the Army 86. Division 86: The Development of the Heavy Division*. Fort Monroe, Va.: U.S. Army Training and Doctrine Command, 1982.
———. *A History of the Army 86. Division 86: The Development of the Light Division, the Corps, and Echelons Above Corps*. Fort Monroe, Va.: U.S. Army Training and Doctrine Command, 1982.
———. *The Army of Excellence: The Development of the 1980s Army*. Fort Monroe, Va.: U.S. Army Training and Doctrine Command, 1993.
———. *From Active Defense to AirLand Battle: The Development of Army Doctrine, 1973–1982*. Fort Monroe, Va.: U.S. Army Training and Doctrine Command, 1984.
Rose, John P. *The Evolution of U.S. Army Nuclear Doctrine, 1945–1980*. Boulder, Colo.: Westview Press, 1980.
Rostow, W. W. *The Diffusion of Power*. New York: Macmillan Co., 1972.
Saxe, Maurice de. *Reveries on the Art of War*. Translated by Thomas R. Philipps. Harrisburg, Pa.: Military Service Publishing Co., 1944.
Schellendorff, Paul Bronsart von. *The Duties of the General Staff*. 4th ed. London: Harrison and Sons, 1895.
Schnabel, James F. *Policy and Direction: The First Year*. United States Army in the Korean War. Washington, D.C.: Government Printing Office, 1972.
Scott, Hugh L. *Some Memories of a Soldier*. New York: Century Co., 1928.
*Semi-Annual Report: U.S. Army Forces Western Pacific, 1 Jan–30 Jun 1946*. N.p.,

1946?

Sharp, U. S. G., and W. C. Westmoreland. *Report on the War in Vietnam*. Washington, D.C.: Government Printing Office, 1969.

Sheridan, Philip H. *Personal Memoirs of Ph. Sheridan*. 2 vols. New York: Charles L. Webster & Co., 1888.

Shipley, Thomas. *The History of the A.E.F.* New York: George H. Dorna Co., 1920.

Sligh, Robert Bruce. *The National Guard and National Defense: The Mobilization of the Guard in World War II*. New York: Praeger, 1992.

Smith, Justin H. *The War With Mexico*. 2 vols. New York: Macmillan Co., 1919.

Smythe, Donald. *Pershing: General of the Armies*. Bloomington: Indiana University Press, 1986.

Snyder, James M. *The Establishment and Operations of the U.S. Constabulary, 3 Oct 1945–30 June 1947*. Historical Sub-Section, G–3, U.S. Constabulary, 1947.

Society of the First Division. *History of the First Division During the World War, 1917–1919*. Philadelphia: John C. Winston Co., 1922.

Sommers, Richard J. *Richmond Redeemed: The Siege at Petersburg*. Garden City, N.Y.: Doubleday and Co., Inc., 1981.

Sorley, Robert. *Thunderbolt: General Creighton Abrams and the Army of His Times*. New York: Simon and Schuster, 1992.

Sorrill, Barbara A., and Constance J. Suwalsky. *The Origins, Deliberations, and Recommendations of the U.S. Army Tactical Mobility Requirements Board (Howze Board)*. Fort Leavenworth, Kans.: U.S. Army Combat Developments Command, 1970.

Sparrow, John W. *History of Personnel Demobilization of the United States Army*. Washington, D.C.: Government Printing Office, 1952.

Spaulding, Oliver L., Hoffman Nickerson, and John W. Wright. *Warfare*. Washington, D.C.: Harcourt, Brace, and Co., 1925.

Spaulding, Oliver L., and John W. Wright. *The Second Division, American Expeditionary Forces in France 1917–1919*. New York: Hillman Press, Inc., 1937.

Starry, Donn A. *Mounted Combat in Vietnam*. Washington, D.C.: Government Printing Office, 1978.

Steuben, Frederick W. von. *A Letter on the Subject of an Established Militia, and the Military Arrangements, Addressed to the Inhabitants of the United States*. New York: J. McLean and Co., 1784.

Strobridge, William. *Golden Gate to Golden Horn*. San Mateo, Calif.: San Mateo County Historical Association, 1975.

Stubbs, Mary Lee, and Stanley R. Connor. *Armor-Cavalry*. Army Lineage Series. Washington, D.C.: Government Printing Office, 1969.

Taylor, John M. *General Maxwell Taylor: The Sword and the Pen*. New York: Doubleday, 1989.

Taylor, Maxwell D. *Swords and Plowshares*. New York: W. W. Norton and Co., 1972.
Tierney, Richard. *The Army Aviation Story*. Northport, Ala.: Colonial Press, 1963.
Tolson, John J. *Airmobility, 1961–1971*. Washington, D.C.: Government Printing Office, 1973.
U.S. Army Combined Arms Combat Development Agency. *The Light Infantry Division: The Army of Excellence: Final Report*. 1 Oct 1984.
U.S. Army, Europe, and Seventh Army. *Strengthening NATO: Stationing of the 2d Armored Division (Forward) in Northern Germany*. 1980.
*United States Army in the World War, 1918–19*. 17 vols. Washington, D.C.: Government Printing Office, 1948. Reprinted. Washington, D.C.: Government Printing Office, 1988–1992.
*United States Defense Policies in 1959*. Washington, D.C.: Government Printing Office, 1964.
*Universal Military Dictionary, An*. Reprint. Ottawa: Museum Restoration Service, 1969.
Wagner, Arthur L. *Organization and Tactics*. Kansas City, Mo.: Franklin Hudson Publishing Co., 1897.
*War of the Rebellion: A Compilation of the Official Records of the Union and Confederate Armies, The*. Ser. 1, 53 vols. Washington, D.C.: Government Printing Office, 1881–98.
Washington, George. *The Writings of George Washington from the Original Manuscript Sources*. Edited by John C. Fitzpatrick. 39 vols. Washington, D.C.: Government Printing Office, 1931–44.
Watson, Mark Skinner. *Chief of Staff: Prewar Plans and Preparation*. United States Army in World War II. Washington, D.C.: Government Printing Office, 1950.
Weigley, Russell F. *History of the United States Army*. New York: Macmillan Company, 1967.
Weinert, Richard P. *USCONARC and Redeployment of Forces From Europe (REFORGER)*. Fort Monroe, Va.: U.S. Continental Army Command, 1969.
―――. The *Role of USCONARC in the Army Buildup FY 1966*. Fort Monroe, Va.: U.S. Continental Army Command, 1967.
―――. *The Role of USCONARC in the Army Buildup FY 1967*. Fort Monroe, Va.: U.S. Continental Army Command, 1968.
Westmoreland, William C. *A Soldier Reports*. Garden City, N.Y.: Doubleday and Co., 1976.
Wickham, John A., Jr. *Collected Works of the Thirtieth Chief of Staff, United States Army*. N.p., 1987.
Williams, George W. *A History of the Negro Troops in the War of the Rebellion, 1861–1865*. New York: Harper and Brothers, 1888.
Williams, Kenneth P. *Lincoln Finds a General*. 4 vols. New York: Macmillan and Co., 1949–59.

Wilson, John B. *Armies, Corps, Divisions, and Separate Brigades*. Army Lineage Series. Washington, D.C.: Government Printing Office, 1987.

Wright, Bertram C., ed. *The 1st Cavalry Division in World War II*. Tokyo: Toppan Printing Co., 1947.

Wright, Robert K. *The Continental Army*. Army Lineage Series. Washington, D.C.: Government Printing Office, 1983.

## *Journal Articles*

"Army Guard AT'75 Highlights." *National Guardsman* 29 (May 1975): 2–5.

"Army's Month, The." *Army* 8 (April 1958): 20.

"Army's New M48 Medium Tank Ready for Distribution to Armor Troops." *Armor* 61 (May–June 1952): 30–31.

"Battalions Declared Inactive." *Infantry Journal* 30 (June 1927): 660.

Beall, John A. "Revisions of ROCAD." *Armor* 68 (March–April 1959): 48–51.

Bigelman, Paul A. "Force Designs for the Future." *Army* 31 (June 1981): 22–23.

Bonanno, Joseph. "The Helicopter in Combat." *Ordnance* 37 (March–April 1954): 868–72.

Bowen, John W. "Reorganizing the Reserve Components." *Army Information Digest* 13 (November 1959): 11–15.

"Bulletin of the Chief, Army Reserve." *CARNOTES* (September–October 1985).

Burdett, Thomas P. "Mobilizations 1911 and 1913." *Military Review* 53 (July 1974): 65–74.

Cantwell, James F. "A Salute to the `Lost' Divisions."*National Guardsman* 22 (February 1968): inside front cover.

"Cavalry Organization." *Cavalry Journal* 29 (July 1920): 116.

"Cavalry Reorganization." *Cavalry Journal* 30 (January 1921): 62–63.

"Cavalry Reorganization." *Cavalry Journal* 30 (October 1921): 422.

Chaffee, Adna R. "The Maneuvers of the First Cavalry Division, September–October, 1923." 33 *Cavalry Journal* (April 1924): 133–62.

"CONARC Report on US Army Reserve 68." *Army Reserve Magazine* 25 (March 1968): 4–5.

Crowninshield, B. W. "Cavalry in Virginia During the War of the Rebellion." *Journal of the Military Service Institute* 12 (May 1891): 527–51.

"DA Publishes Details on Reorganization of the Army Reserve." *Army Reservist* 9 (March 1963): 6–10.

Dexter, George E. "Search and Destroy in Vietnam." *Infantry* 56 (July–August 1966): 36–42.

Dillman, George. "1st Cavalry Division Maneuvers." *Cavalry Journal* 37 (January 1928): 47.

"Division Command Rotation Plan Set Aside." *National Guardsman* 22 (March 1968): 16.

"Division of Military Affairs, Circ. 19, 1914 and 'The Division Plan.'" *National*

*Guard Magazine* 10 (January 1914): 14.

"Division Replacement Company, The." *Infantry School Quarterly* 33 (October 1948): 67.

Dunlap, D. C., Jr. "The Third Armored Training Division." *Armored Cavalry Journal* 57 (July–August 1948): 26.

"Editorial Comment: Mechanization of Military Force." *Infantry Journal* 30 (May 1927): 533–35.

Epstein, Robert M. "The Creation and Evolution of the Army Corps in the American Civil War." *Journal of Military History* 55 (January 1991): 41–46.

"Extracts from the Annual Report of the Chief of Cavalry, Major General Herbert B. Crosby." *Cavalry Journal* 37 (January 1928): 108.

Fairchild, Robert F. "Training Guard and Reserve Divisions." *Armor* (March–April 1977): 47–48.

Falk, Stanley L. "Artillery for the Land Service: TheDevelopment of a System." *Military Affairs* 28 (Fall 1964): 97–110.

"First Field Army, the Initial Step in the Correlation of the Regular Army with the National Guard, The." *National Guard Magazine* (April 1910): 352–54.

"Five Battalions of Infantry To Be Made Inactive." *Infantry Journal* 32 (September 1929): 317–18.

"For Freedom Under the Southern Cross." *Americal* 1 (May 1968): 2–6.

Foss, John W., Donald S. Pihl, and Thomas E. Fitzgerald. "The Division Restructuring Study: The Heavy Division." *Military Review* 57 (March 1977): 11–21.

Fryklund, Richard. "Soldiers of the Sky." *National Guardsman* 18 (March 1964): 3–7+.

Fuller, J. F. C. "Tactics and Mechanization." *Infantry Journal* 30 (May 1927): 457–76.

"General Orders No. 9." *Infantry Journal* 9 (March–April 1913): 706–08.

"Guard Goes ROAD, The." *National Guardsman* 17 (February 1963): 2–4.

Harmon, Ernest H. "U.S. Constabulary." *Armored Cavalry Journal* 55 (September–October 1946): 16.

Henry, Guy V. "The Trend of Organization and Equipment of Cavalry in the Principal World Powers and Its Probable Role in Wars of the Near Future." *Cavalry Journal* 41 (March–April 1932): 5–9.

"How DOD Is Improving the Combat Proportions of US Forces in Europe." *Commander Digest* 18 (20 November 1975): 2–3.

Hunt, Henry J. "Our Experience in Artillery Administration." *Journal of the Military Service Institution* 12 (March 1891): 197–224.

"Infantry Division (Light)." *Infantry*. 74 (March–April 1984): 14–15.

Ingles, Harry C. "The New Division." *Signal Corps Bulletin* 108 (April–June 1940): 15–31.

———. "The New Division." *Infantry* 49 (November–December 1939): 521–29.

Institute of Land Warfare, AUSA. "The Divisions of the United States Army."

Association of the U.S. Army, 1989.

"Is Division Aviation Worthwhile?" *Infantry Journal* 36 (May 1929): 511–12.

"It's No Easy Job Retaining Trainers as the USAR's 108th Division Out Does Itself." *Army Reserve Magazine* 25 (January 1979): 20–21.

Kellett, Donald T., and William Friedman. "Airborne on Paper Wings." *Infantry Journal* 62 (May 1948): 12.

King, James I., and Melvin A. Goers. "Modern Armored Cavalry Organization." *Armored Cavalry Journal* 57 (July–August 1948): 47–50.

Kinnard, Harry W. O. "A Victory in the Ia Drang: The Triumph of a Concept." *Army* 17 (September 1967): 71–90.

Kleinman, Forrest K. "Front and Center: The Changing Army." *Army* 12 (February 1962): 16.

Kolb, Richard K. "Polar Bears vs. Bols." *VFW Magazine* (January 1991): 16–20.

Lane, Arthur L. "Tables of Organization." *Infantry Journal* 18 (May 1921): 489–91.

Lanze, Conrad H. "The Artillery Support of the Infantry in the A.E.F." *Field Artillery* 26 (January–February 1936): 67–68.

Lindsey, James J. "The Infantry Division (Light)." *Infantry* 74 (January–February 1984): 2–3 and (March–April 1984): 14–16.

Lippincott, Aubrey. "New Regimental Organization." *Cavalry Journal* 32 (January 1929): 22–24.

McClure, N. F. "The Infantry Division and Its Composition." *Journal of Military Service Institute* 50 (January–February 1912): 5–9.

McGowan, Donald. "Army National Guard Today." *Army Information Digest* 15 (March 1950): 17.

McWilliams, Keith E. "Divisions or Brigades for the National Guard." *Military Review* 51 (January 1971): 35–42.

Milnor, Robert J. "Strong Reserve Boosted by Total Force Impetus." *Army* 24 (October 1974): 76–79.

———. "USAR Moves into 1973." *Army Reserve Magazine* 19 (March 1973): 4–5.

Nenninger, Timothy. "Tactical Disfunction in the AEF, 1917–1918." *Military Affairs* 51 (October 1987): 177–81.

———. "The Experimental Mechanized Forces." *Armor* 78 (May–June 1969): 33–39.

———. "A Revised Mechanization Policy." *Armor* 78 (September–October 1969): 45–49.

"New Tables of Organization." *Infantry Journal* 21 (August 1922): 186–92.

"New T/O—Greater Firepower, Greater Strength, The." *National Guardsman* 2 (November 1948): 25.

Norman, Lloyd. "The New Look Strategy." *Combat Forces Journal* 4 (February 1954): 15–20.

Norton, John. "TRICAP." *Army* 21 (June 1971): 14–19.

"Notes from the Chief of Cavalry." *Cavalry Journal* 49 (September–October 1940): 410–11.

Oliphant, F. W. "A New Deal for the Organized Reserves." *Quartermaster Review* 27 (September–October 1947): 27–28.

O'Meara, Andrew P. "Drawdown for Vietnam: How USAREUR Makes Do." *Army* 16 (October 1966): 73–75+.

"Our Floundering Army Reserve Program." *Reserve Officer* 25 (July 1948): 4–6ff.

Perret-Gential, J. "Divisions—Three or Five Elements?" *Military Review* 41 (February 1961): 16–25.

Petraeus, David H. "Light Infantry in Europe: Strategic Flexibility and Conventional Deterrence." *Military Review* 64 (December 1984): 35–53.

"Philippine Scouts." *Military Review* 29 (July 1949): 72.

Pittman, J. M. "Reorganization of the Armored Division." *Military Review* 24 (April 1944): 44–47.

Polk, James H. "A Changing US Army Europe: Building Combat Capability for Tomorrow." *Army* 17 (October 1967): 65–66+.

"President Reports to the 89th General Conference, The." *National Guardsman* 21 (October 1967): inside front cover and 36.

"Progress of Assignment of Infantry Reserve Officers to Infantry Divisions of the Organized Reserves." *U.S. Army Recruiting News* 5 (May 1922): no pagination.

"'Rainbow Division,' The." *National Guardsman* 3 (March 1949):18–19.

Rainey, James W. "Ambivalent Warfare: The Tactical Doctrine of the AEF in World War I." *Parameters* 13 (September 1983): 34–46.

Ramsey, Walter H. "The Big Bazooka: Russian Tanks Were No Match for Our 3.5-Inch Weapon." *Ordnance* 35 (May–June 1951): 638–40.

"Reorganization of the Cavalry." *Cavalry Journal* 30 (October 1921): 422.

"Reserve Units in Selected Reserve Force." *Army Reserve Magazine* 11 (December 1965): 4–6.

"Revised Tables of Organization, Cavalry Regiment, Horse." *Cavalry Journal* 48 (March–April 1939): 58–63.

Roberts, J. Milnor. "USAR Moves into 1973." *Army Reserve Magazine* 19 (March 1973): 4–5.

"Run Down on the 101." *Army* 7 (October 1956): 51–53.

Sawitzke, Ken. "The Shoulder Patch." *Infantry* 65 (December 1985): 40–42.

Shetler, John S. "Motors for the Guard." *Quartermaster Review* 14 (March–April 1935): 47–49.

"Shifting of Infantry Units." *Infantry Journal* 31 (July 1927): 89.

Skaggs, David C. "The KATUSA Experiment: The Integration of Korean Nationals into the U.S. Army, 1950–1965." *Military Affairs* 38 (April 1974): 53–58.

Smith, Herbert E. "The Proposed Infantry 'Streamlined' Division." *Recruiting News* 20 (January 1938): 9–11 and (February 1938): 8–10.

Smith, James C. "Centralized Operations." *Army Aviation Digest* 1 (March 1955): 19–25.

Smith, John B. "Our First National Guard Cavalry Division." *Cavalry Journal* 46 (September–October 1936): 378–79.

"SRF Born 27 September 1965; Died September 1969." *National Guardsman* 23 (September 1969): 12–16.

Starry, Donn A. "Extending the Battlefield." *Military Review* 59 (March 1981): 31–50.

Stewart, Thomas F. "Aviation Personnel Notes." *US Army Aviation Digest* 30 (June 1984): 28.

Stone, James. "TOW Really Works." *Infantry* 64 (September–October 1974): 12–13.

"T43 Heavy Tank, The." *Armor* 63 (May–June 1954): 32–33.

Tat, Clyde J., and L. D. Holder. "New Doctrine for the Defense." *Military Review* 59 (March 1981): 2–9.

Tench, C. T. "The New Organization." *Infantry Journal* 59 (July 1946): 18–22.

"Things To Come: CONARC Presents Plans for the New Year." *Army Reserve Magazine* 13 (December 1967): 8–9.

Tidball, John C. "The Artillery Service in the War of the Rebellion, 1861–1865." *Journal of the Military Service Institution* 12 (July 1891): 697–733.

"Tools for the Fighting Man: Small Arms." *Armed Forces Talk* 18 (January 1952).

"Two More Cavalry Divisions Authorized." *Cavalry Journal* 48 (January–February 1939): 67.

"US, UK, and Germany Conclude Trilateral Talks." *Department of State Bulletin* 56 (22 November 1967): 788–89.

Vance, William E. "History of Army Aviation." *Aviation Digest* 3 (June 1957): 7–12.

Walsh, Ellward A. "Grab for Power." *National Guardsman* 2 (February 1944): 32.

Weber, LaVern E. "For the Minutemen of the '70s: The Guard: 'A Long Way.'" *Army* 24 (October 1974): 65–69.

Wike, John W. "The Wearing of Army Corps and Division Insignia in the Union Army." *Military Collector and Historian* 4 (June 1952): 353–58.

Wiktorin, Mauriz. "Motorized and Cavalry Divisions." *Cavalry Journal* 37 (July 1928): 421.

Wilson, John B. "Mobility Versus Firepower: The Post–World War I Infantry Division." *Parameters* 13 (September 1983): 47–52.

Wisnack, Joseph R. "'Old Ironsides' Response to the Cuban Crisis." *Army* (April 1963): 26–30.

"World-wide Unit Rotation." *Army Combat Forces Journal* 5 (November 1954): 37.

Yakshe, John S. "REDEYE Ground to Air." *Infantry* 56 (July–August 1966): 22–23.

Young, Robert N. "Operation GYROSCOPE." *Army Information Digest* (10 March 1955): 2–6.

## Unpublished Manuscripts

Abrams, Creighton W., Jr. "The Sixteen Division Force: Anatomy of a Decision." Thesis, Command and General Staff College, 1975.

Army Ground Forces Study No. 17, "History of Third Army." Historical Section, Army Ground Forces, 1946.

Army Ground Forces Study No. 23, "Training in Mountain and Winter Warfare." Historical Section, Army Ground Forces, 1946.

Army Ground Forces Study No. 25, "The Airborne Command and Center." Historical Section, Army Ground Forces, 1946.

Army Ground Forces Study No. 27, "History of the Armored Force, Command, and Center." Historical Section, Army Ground Forces, 1946.

Army Ground Forces Study No. 28, "History of the Tenth Light Division." Historical Section, Army Ground Forces, 1946.

Bongiove, Joseph R. "I Corps: Light Infantry Division." Ms, DAMH-HSR.

Bonin, John A. "Combat Copter Cavalry: A Study in Conceptual Confusion and Inter-Service Misunderstanding in the Exploitation of Armed Helicopters as Cavalry in the U.S. Army, 1950–1965." Master thesis, Duke University, 1982.

Cameron, Robert Stewart. "Americanizing the Tank: U.S. Army Administration and Mechanized Development within the Army, 1917–1943." Ph.D. dissertation, Temple University, 1994.

Cary, Norman Miller. "The Use of Motor Vehicles in the United States Army, 1899–1939." Ph.D. dissertation, University of Georgia, 1980.

Chaffee, Adna R. "Mechanized Cavalry." Lecture, Army War College (AWC), 29 September 1939. Military History Institute.

Cleaver, Charles G. "History of the Korean War." Ms, DAMH-HSR.

Coakley, Robert W., Karl E. Cocke, and Daniel P. Griffin. "Demobilization Following the Korean War." Ms, DAMH-HSR.

Coakley, Robert W., Walter G. Hermes, James F. Schnabel, and Earl F. Ziemke. "U.S. Army Expansion and Readiness, 1961–1962." Ms, DAMH-HSR.

Cocke, Karl. "The Reserve Component." Ms, DAMH-HSR.

Finnegan, John P. "Military Intelligence." Ms, DAMH-HSO.

Fletcher, Robert H., Jr. "The 35th Division in the First Phase of the Meuse Argonne Operation, September 26–October, 1918." Ms, DAMH-HSO.

Galle, Joe F. "A History of the 11th Infantry Brigade, 1 July 1966–1 May 1970." Ms, DAMH-HSO.

Grow, Robert W. "The Ten Lean Years." Ms, DAMH-HSR.

Harrison, Donald F. "A History of Army Aviation." Ms, DAMH-HSR.

Hellmich, Glenn B. "Charles de Gaulle: His Ideas on Mechanized Warfare and the Army of the Future and the Application of These Ideas." Master thesis, Xavier University, 1955.

Hermes, Walter. "The Buildup." Ms, DAMH-HD.

"History of the 65th Infantry 1899–1946." Ms, DAMH-HSO.

"History of United States Armed Forces in Korea." Ms, DAMH-HSR.
"Lineage and Honors: History, Principles, and Preparation." Ms, DAMH-HSO.
McKenney, Janice E. "Field Artillery." Ms, DAMH-HSO.
Military History Section, U.S. Army Forces Far East. "A Brief History of the 34th Infantry Regiment." Ms, DAMH-HSO.
Moseley, George Van Horn. "One Soldier's Journey." Ms, Library of Congress.
Raines, Edgar. "MG J. Franklin Bell and Military Reform: The Chief of Staff Years, 1906–1910." Ph.D. dissertation, University of Wisconsin, 1976.
"Redeployment." Occupation Forces in Europe series. Ms, DAMH-HSR.
Regnier, T. C. "History of the 91st Reconnaissance Squadron, 1st Cavalry Division." Ms, undated, DAMH-HSO.
"Replacement and Augmentation System in Europe, The." Ms, Historical Section, U.S. Army, Europe. DAMH-HSR.
Rockis, Joseph. "Reorganization of AGF During Demobilization." Demobilization Series, Study 3, DAMH-HSR.
Scott, Charles L. "Early History of Mechanization." Ms, Scott Papers, LC.
Scudieri, James C. "The Continentals: Comparative Analysis of a Late Eighteenth-Century Standing Army." Ph.D. dissertation, City University of New York, 1993.
Sheehan, Kevin P. "Preparing for an Imaginary War: Examining Peacetime Functions and Changes of Army Doctrine." Ph.D. thesis, Harvard University, 1988.
"Stability Operations, Dominican Republic." Ms, DAMH-HSR.
Stillwaugh, Elva. "Personnel Policies in the Korean Conflict." Ms, DAMH-HSR.
Thomas, Robert S., and Inez V. Allen. "The Mexican Punitive Expedition under Brig. Gen. John J. Pershing." Ms, DAMH-HSO.
Thomas, Robert S. "The United States Army 1914–1923." Ms, DAMH-HSR.
Trask, David F., ed. "Historical Survey of US Mobilization: Eight Topical Studies of the Twentieth Century." Ms, DAMH-HSR.
Van Voorhis, Daniel. "Mechanization." Lecture, AWC, 13 October 1937. MHI.
Wiley, Bell I. "AGF on the Eve of Demobilization Period." Ms, DAMH-HSR.
Wilson, Powell B. "AGF During the Demobilization Period." Demobilization Series, Study 4, DAMH-HSR.

# Index

Abrams, General Creighton: 343, 356, 359, 361, 364, 365, 367, 372–73, 409*n20*
Adjutant general companies: 354–55, 356, 357, 386, 401
Adjutants general: 12, 14, 17, 20*n2*, 24–25, 28, 55, 98, 99, 117, 284, 286, 306–07
Administration companies: 267, 270, 272, 274, 276–77, 281, 296–97, 354
Administrative sections: 338, 340
Aero squadrons: 38, 181
Affiliation Program: 370, 373
AIM project: 353–54
Air Assault Division, 11th: 316
Air assault divisions: 314, 316, 383, 397, 400
Air assault infantry battalions: 400–401
Air cavalry attack brigades: 384, 386
Air cavalry combat brigades: 314, 316, 357, 359
Air cavalry squadrons: 359
Air cavalry troops: 309, 382
Air defense artillery battalions: 354–55, 356, 357, 361, 367, 384, 389, 392–93, 397, 401
Air defense artillery brigades: 382, 389, 392
Air Defense Artillery School: 354–55
Air squadrons: 49, 53, 85, 94, 112
Air Transport Brigade, 10th: 316
Air transport brigades: 314, 316
Air units (divisional): 35, 49
Airborne battalions: 327–28, 338
Airborne brigades: 190, 196, 300, 303, 309, 356
   36th: 367, 383
   173d: 312, 323, 327–28, 334, 335, 344, 345–346
Airborne Command: 190
Airborne Corps, XVIII: 194
Airborne Division, 82d
   and Dominican Republic: 329
   elements of used to test regimental organization: 264
   and Korean War: 240, 242, 249
   and Operation JUST CAUSE: 403, 425
   organized: 167
   post–Korean War: 250
   post–World War II: 212–13, 232
   reorganized: 193–94, 276, 357, 397

Airborne Division, 82d—Continued
   and ROAD: 308
   used to test airborne division structure: 229
   in Vietnam: 332, 338, 344
   and World War II: 193, 194, 196
Airborne Division, 101st
   inactivated: 250
   organized: 167
   post–World War II: 212–13
   reactivated: 251
   reorganized: 243, 274, 276, 333–34, 356, 400
   and ROAD: 308
   used to test pentomic division: 274
   in Vietnam: 328, 330–32, 333, 344, 346
   and World War II: 194, 196, 200
Airborne divisions
   aircraft for: 248
   battle groups: 272, 274
   development of: 166–67, 169, 188, 190
   need to be air-transportable: 229, 272, 274
   and nuclear weapons: 272, 274
   in Organized Reserve Corps: 217
   reorganized for combat: 193–96
   strength: 167, 169, 196, 229, 272, 274, 397
   tables of organization: 167, 169
   tables of organization and equipment: 194–96, 223–24, 229, 272, 274, 276–77, 298, 300, 308, 356–57
   in World War II: 193
Airborne divisions, composition of
   1970s: 357
   1980s: 390–91
   ATFA–1: 265, 267
   pentomic: 276–77
   ROAD: 308
   ROTAD: 272, 274
Airborne divisions (units)
   11th: 190, 196, 232, 240, 242, 253, 274, 279, 316
   13th: 190, 196
   15th: 204*n36*, 217
   17th: 190, 196
   80th: 255

Airborne divisions (units)—Continued
   82d. *See* Airborne Division, 82d.
   84th: 217, 255
   98th: 217
   99th: 217
   100th: 217, 255
   101st. *See* Airborne Division, 101st.
   108th: 217, 255
Airborne Infantry, 187th: 240–41
Airborne infantry battalions: 307, 308, 312, 331, 332, 334–35, 357
Airborne infantry brigades
   1st: 190
   2d: 190, 196
Airborne units
   in airmobile divisions: 318, 356–57
   in infantry divisions: 279
Aircraft
   for airborne divisions: 248
   for armored divisions: 227, 248, 267, 314, 316
   for field artillery units: 181, 185, 196, 227
   for infantry divisions: 30, 181, 199, 227, 248, 267, 314, 316
   for infantry regiments: 227
   for mechanized infantry divisions: 314, 316
   role of in Army units: 314, 316, 318, 417
   used for reconnaissance: 30
Aircraft maintenance battalions: 333–34, 386
Aircraft maintenance companies: 393
Aircraft maintenance detachments: 333–34
Airfield operation: 333
AirLand Battle doctrine: 384, 386, 391, 403, 407
Airmobile brigades: 356
Airmobile companies: 309
Airmobile divisions: 333–34, 335, 356, 390–91, 397
Airmobile infantry battalions: 318, 327–28, 334–35, 359, 397, 400
Airmobility: 314, 316, 318, 333
Alabama National Guard units: 100–101, 243, 361
Alaska: 309, 326, 333, 338, 346, 356, 373, 395, 397
Alaska National Guard units: 395
Aleutian Islands: 180
Alger, Russell A.: 18
All-volunteer Army: 353, 372–73
Allen, Maj. Harvey G.: 141*n46*
Allen, Maj. Gen. Robert H.: 126
Ambulance companies: 28, 30, 94
Ambulance Company, 337th: 69
Ambulance trains: 55
Ambulance units in divisions: 52–53, 55

Ambulances: 28, 67
Americal Division: 159–60, 187, 214, 252, 331, 334. *See also* Infantry divisions, 23d.
American Expeditionary Forces: 49, 52, 55–57, 67, 68, 83–86, 87, 105*n17*
Ammunition column: 24, 25, 28
Ammunition resupply, responsibility for: 129, 131–32, 198–99
Ammunition trains: 29, 30, 33, 38, 52–53, 55, 84, 92, 115, 122, 129
Ammunition wagons: 5
Amphibious operations: 187–88
Anderson, Lt. Col. Edward D.: 74*n12*
Andrews, Maj. Gen. Frank M.: 145, 147, 149, 173*n11*
Animals
   cavalry: 147, 153, 172, 191, 213
   in light divisions: 188, 190
   numbers of: 28
   problems shipping: 55
   shortages of: 71, 121
   use of between the world wars: 90, 92, 121, 126
Antiaircraft artillery battalions: 130, 166, 167, 184–85, 194–96, 223, 224, 227, 239, 240, 267, 277, 354
Antiaircraft artillery batteries: 269
Antiaircraft artillery detachments: 122
Antiaircraft weapons: 161, 354–55
   in airborne brigades: 303
   Chaparral: 354–55, 389
   Duster: 361, 401
   machine guns: 67
   in National Guard units: 361, 401
   placement of: 185, 267, 269, 389
   Sergeant York gun system: 389
   Vulcan guns: 354
Antiarmor companies: 400
Antiarmor platoons: 393
Antitank battalions: 130, 131, 154–55, 185, 196, 198–99
Antitank companies: 130, 131, 144, 194–96, 198–99, 223, 397, 425
Antitank forces
   placement of: 154–55, 166, 172, 181, 185, 198
   weapons for. *See* Antitank weapons.
Antitank platoons: 325
Antitank troops: 147, 161
Antitank weapons: 198
   37-mm.: 55, 122–23, 144, 147, 154–55
   57-mm.: 182, 198–99
   90-mm. self-propelled: 300, 335
   ENTAC: 297, 335
   LAW (light antitank weapon): 335

INDEX 447

Antitank weapons—Continued
  M56 SPAT: 300
  numbers of: 264
  placement of: 380, 382
  TOW: 354, 374n5, 380, 382, 383, 386, 393, 397, 400
Arizona National Guard units: 36, 217, 284, 314
Arkansas National Guard units: 100–101
Armies (U.S.)
  First: 71, 217, 306, 325, 370
  Second: 71, 217
  Third: 79–80, 167, 281, 307
  Fourth: 120, 159, 252, 306
  Fifth: 184, 217, 284, 306, 325, 344
  Sixth: 254, 327
  Seventh: 217, 253, 366–67, 402
  Eighth: 241, 271–72, 400–401
Armor
  33d, 1st Battalion: 400
  40th, 8th Battalion: 365
  803d, 1st Battalion: 410n44
Armor battalions: 296, 297, 306, 307, 334–35, 336, 337, 338, 341, 344, 351n48, 354, 355, 357, 359, 366, 380, 382, 384, 389, 397, 400–402
Armor companies: 281, 335
Armor Group, 16th: 338
Armor School: 271, 338, 356, 365, 373
Armored brigades
  30th: 361
  31st: 361
  53d: 314
  86th: 314
  149th: 367, 383
  155th: 361
  177th: 423
  194th: 312, 338, 356, 364–65, 373, 402, 423
Armored brigades, composition of: 149–50, 163, 359, 366
Armored car squadrons: 115
Armored car troops: 122–23, 125, 161
Armored cavalry regiments: 392, 411n53, 424
  2d: 422
  11th: 422, 423
  116th: 403
  163d: 403
Armored cavalry units: 123, 125
Armored Division, 1st
  and ATFA–1: 267, 269
  and Bosnia: 425
  in Germany: 344, 422
  and Korean War: 243
  in the 1990s: 422–23
  organized: 150, 154

Armored Division, 1st—Continued
  post–Korean War: 279
  post–World War II: 213
  as reinforcement unit for NATO: 250
  reorganized: 187, 306, 307
  round-out units for: 357
  and U.S. Constabulary: 211
  in Vietnam: 330, 334, 336
  and World War II: 184, 200
Armored Division, 2d
  in Germany: 246–47, 305, 366–67, 422
  inactivated: 423
  organized: 150, 154
  post–World War II: 212–13, 232, 242
  in Southwest Asia: 421–22
  in Vietnam: 330, 336
  and World War II: 184, 187, 198
Armored divisions
  aircraft for: 248
  ATFA–1: 265, 267
  designations of brigades in: 307
  missions: 149–50, 184
  nuclear weapons for: 277
  number of: 170
  organized: 147, 149–50
  Organized Reserve Corps: 217
  post–World War II: 224
  reorganized: 182, 187, 196, 277, 279, 309
  strength: 149–50, 154, 185, 196, 224, 225, 267, 269, 277, 282, 284, 353–54
  tables of organization: 150, 184–85, 196, 225, 227, 277, 279, 284, 286, 298
  tanks for: 248–49
  trains: 163, 185
  in World War II: 193, 196, 198–99
Armored divisions, composition of
  AIM: 354, 355
  Army of Excellence: 395
  ATFA–1: 267, 269
  Division-86: 389
  in Europe: 336
  pentomic: 277, 281–82, 284, 286
  post–World War II: 224
  ROAD: 296–98, 308
  ROCAD: 282, 284, 286
  World War II: 163, 184–85
Armored divisions (units)
  3d: 154, 187, 198, 213, 222, 252, 279, 422
  4th: 154, 211, 213, 252, 279, 344
  5th: 154, 243, 254
  6th: 154, 170, 243, 254
  7th: 170, 243, 250
  8th: 170
  9th: 170, 172
  10th: 170

Armored divisions (units)—Continued
  11th: 170
  12th: 170
  13th: 170, 220–21, 255
  14th: 170
  16th: 190
  18th: 204*n36*
  19th: 204*n36*, 217, 220–21
  20th: 190
  21st: 204*n36*, 217, 255
  22d: 204*n36*, 217, 255
  30th: 256, 340, 361
  49th: 214, 220–21, 305, 307, 361, 401
  50th: 214–15, 340, 367, 401, 423–24
Armored Force: 150, 153, 154, 163, 170, 172
Armored groups: 198, 205*n54*, 224
Armored infantry battalions: 184–85, 227, 267
Armored infantry regiments: 224
Armored motorcar machine gun ("tank") companies: 53, 55
Armored personnel carriers: 150, 163, 182, 276–77, 282, 305
  M113: 286, 305, 308, 335, 389
Armored reconnaissance cars: 122–23, 127
Armored regiments: 149–50, 163, 224
Armored rifle battalions: 224
Armorers: 4–5
Arms chests: 5
Armstrong, John: 9
Army, U.S. Department of the: 225
Army-86: 389–90
Army Air Corps: 111
Army Air Forces: 180, 227
Army Areas: 87, 97, 101
Army Field Forces: 217, 229, 243, 263–65, 267, 269
Army Ground Forces: 170, 172, 173*n2*, 175*n38*, 180, 185, 187–88, 190–91, 198–99, 217, 224–25, 227, 229
Army Ground Forces Reduction Board: 180–82, 184–85, 187
Army group: 117
Army National Guard. *See* National Guard.
Army of Excellence: 391–403, 407, 409*n32*, 416, 417
Army of the Potomac: 12–15
Army of the United States: 190, 213
Army Reserve: 255. *See also* Organized Reserve Corps.
  combat service support units: 424
  combat support units: 424
  number of divisions and brigades: 284, 286, 309, 328–29, 338, 340–41, 353, 359, 361, 367, 370, 397, 423–24
  officer billets: 284

Army Reserve—Continued
  and pentomic structures: 284, 286
  and volunteers: 256
Army Reserve brigades. *See by type of brigade.*
Army Reserve centers: 402–03
Army Reserve divisions
  ordered to active duty: 305, 332
  reorganized: 284, 312, 341, 372, 402
  and ROAD: 309, 312
  strength: 284, 286
Army Reserve units
  readiness of: 367, 370, 372, 424
  round-out units: 395, 402–03
  training for: 424
Army School of the Line: 27–28
Army Security Agency detachments: 330, 382
Army Service Forces: 180
Army Service Schools: 33
Army Staff. *See also* War Department General Staff.
  and air mobility: 316, 318
  and Army Reserve: 309, 365
  and General Reserve: 250
  and mobilization for World War I: 55, 57–58
  and numbers of divisions: 355, 364
  Operations Division: 187–88
  organization of: 140*n32*
  and post–Korean War period: 252, 284
  and troop basis: 214
  and unit designations: 331
  and unit replacement system: 252–53, 366
Army War College: 135, 214–15, 270–71, 319*n7*
Artificers: 4–5
Artillery batteries: 12, 13–14, 16, 24, 25, 123, 307, 335
Artillery batteries, weapons for: 223, 276, 337, 382, 425
Artillery coordination centers: 284
Artillery School: 271
Aspin, Les: 424
Assault aviation battalions: 318
Assault gun companies: 400
Assault gun (tank) battalions: 308
Assault gun troops: 185
Assault support battalions: 318
Assault weapons platoons: 282
Atomic Field Army (ATFA–1). *See* Amored divisons; Infantry divisions.
Atomic weapons. *See* Nuclear weapons, tactical.
Attack helicopter battalions: 359, 382, 386, 387, 393, 397, 425
Attack helicopter squadrons: 357, 359
Aultman, Col. Dwight E.: 74*n12*

# INDEX

Australia: 191, 327–28
Austria: 208
Aviation battalions: 309, 337, 382, 383, 386, 397, 400, 425
Aviation brigades: 386, 389, 392–93, 397, 400, 410*n40*
Aviation companies: 248, 265, 267, 269–70, 272, 276–77, 282, 284, 296, 338, 354–55, 393, 397
Aviation groups: 318, 397, 400
Aviation maintenance battalions: 400
Aviation maintenance companies: 397, 401
Aviation observation squadrons: 149
Aviation sections: 112, 115
Aviation support companies: 318
Aviation units: 314, 316, 333–34, 335

Badges
  air assault personnel: 356
  Union corps (Civil War): 16
  War with Spain: 18
Bailey, Maj. Gen. Charles J.: 72
Baker, Col. Chauncey: 52, 53, 55, 74*n12*
Baker, Newton D.: 52, 57, 60, 62, 63, 64, 65, 66, 76*n32*, 86, 90, 111
Baker Board: 52–55, 74*n14*
Balloon companies: 85
Ballou, Brig. Gen. Charles C.: 63
Bands: 125, 131, 132, 133, 181, 194–96, 239, 269, 274, 277, 284, 296, 392–93
Bare, Col. Walter E.: 107*n50*
Barker, Maj. Alvin: 52
Battle groups (divisional)
  airborne: 272, 274, 305
  composition of: 272, 274, 276–77, 282, 297
  and unit morale: 281
Battlefield information coordination centers: 355
Bazookas: 167, 180–81, 182, 247–48
Beal, Thaddeus R.: 343
Bell, Maj. Gen. James Franklin: 28–29
Berlin, Germany: 303, 305–06, 309, 312
Berlin Brigade: 312, 322*n43*, 402, 411*n51*, 423
Berry, Maj. Gen. Sidney B.: 356
"Big Red One, The." *See* Infantry Division, 1st.
Black soldiers: 15, 154, 170, 182, 249–50
Black units: 62–63, 66, 97, 99, 107*n53*, 154, 170, 182, 191, 217, 220, 239, 249–50
Bliss, Maj. Gen. Tasker H.: 49, 54–55, 57, 60, 62
Bloomfield, Brig. Gen. Joseph: 7–8
"Bottom-Up" review: 424
Bradley, General Omar N.: 225, 229

Bradson, Col. Fay W.: 141*n46*
Brees, Maj. Gen. Herbert J.: 132, 133
Brigade, 1st Hawaiian: 31
Brigade-75: 366–67
Brigade-76: 366–67
Brigade inspectors: 5, 6–7, 8–9
Brigade majors: 3, 5, 6–7, 8–9
Brigade (Training)
  5th: 372
  402d: 402–03
Brigades (1913)
  2d: 34
  4th: 34
  5th: 34
  6th: 34
  8th: 34
Brigading together of Regular Army and militia units: 8, 16
British Army: 121–22, 125, 166, 184
Brown, Brig. Gen. Lytle: 83
Brown, Maj. Gen. Preston: 115
Browning, John M.: 67
Brucker, Wilber M.: 281
Bryden, Maj. William: 107*n50*
Buckley, Col. Michael: 188
Buena Vista, Battle of: 10
Bull, Brig. Gen. Harold R.: 170, 172
Burnside, Maj. Gen. Ambrose: 13

California National Guard units: 115, 221, 243, 255–56, 361
Callaway, Howard: 370
Camps. *See also* Forts.
  Beauregard, La.: 154
  Breckinridge, Ky.: 243
  Campbell, Ky.: 208
  Carson, Colo.: 188
  Chaffee, Ark.: 243
  Claiborne, La.: 166, 167
  Clark, Tex.: 191
  Eustis, Va.: 123
  Fremont, Calif.: 60, 62
  Funston, Kans.: 57, 63
  Greene, N.C.: 60, 62
  Hale, Colo.: 188
  Hood, Tex.: 232
  Henry Knox, Ky.: 123, 125
  Lockett, Calif.: 191
  Losey, P.R.: 242
  Mills, N.Y.: 60
  Roberts, Calif.: 243
Cannon companies: 160–61, 180, 182, 196, 198, 202*n8*, 223. *See also* Infantry regiments.
Caribbean Defense Command: 153
Carter, Maj. Gen. William H.: 34–35

Cavalry
  mechanized: 123
  missions of: 48–49, 64, 85, 123
  and Modernization Board: 127
  and War with Spain: 18
  and World War I: 48–49, 54, 64, 85
Cavalry Brigade (Air Combat), 6th: 359, 364, 386
Cavalry Brigade (Mechanized), 7th: 123, 125, 143–45, 147, 150
Cavalry brigades
  composition of: 25, 33–34, 35, 38, 95, 115, 123, 125, 145, 147, 161, 288n24, 359
  designations for: 57–58
Cavalry brigades (units)
  1st: 64, 98
  2d: 64, 98
  3d: 64
  4th: 172
  51st: 116
  52d: 116
  53d: 116
  54th: 116
  55th: 116
  56th: 116, 153, 191–92
  57th: 116
  58th: 116
  59th: 116
  116th: 403
  1st (1913): 34
  2d (1913): 34
  3d (1913): 34
  4th (1913): 34
Cavalry corps: 13, 117, 120, 145, 147, 149
Cavalry Division (1913): 31
Cavalry Division, 1st
  between the world wars: 112, 115, 120, 135
  elements in Germany: 366, 367
  in Japan: 211–12, 232, 239
  in Korea: 240, 245–46, 258n17, 279, 284, 308
  organized: 98
  post–World War II: 213
  reorganized: 316, 318, 344, 357, 364, 402
  in Southwest Asia: 421–22
  and training maneuvers: 112, 143–45, 147
  units of sent to North Africa: 172, 190–91
  used for organizational studies (TRICAP): 344, 357, 359, 382–83, 386
  and World War II: 172, 190–91
Cavalry Division (Airmobile), 1st: 316, 318, 323, 327–28, 333–34, 335, 344, 346
Cavalry Division (Infantry), 1st: 213
Cavalry Division, Special, 1st: 191
Cavalry divisions
  between the world wars: 86–87, 95, 97, 98,

Cavalry divisions—Continued
  101, 107n45, 116
  Civil War: 13, 16
  composition of: 25, 28, 33–34, 38, 85–86, 95, 115, 133, 135, 137, 145, 147, 161
  designations for: 28, 57
  mechanized: 172
  National Guard: 87, 97, 101, 116
  Organized Reserves: 87, 170
  road space: 38, 95
  staff for: 25, 28
  strength: 33–34, 38, 85–86, 95, 107n45, 115, 137, 147, 161
  tables of organization: 37–38, 95, 101, 115
Cavalry divisions (units)
  2d: 98, 120, 154, 172, 190–92
  3d: 117, 120
  15th: 64, 77n44
  21st: 101, 116, 153
  22d: 101, 116, 153
  23d: 101, 116, 153
  24th: 101, 116, 153
  61st: 101
  62d: 101
  63d: 101
  64th: 101
  65th: 101
  66th: 101
Cavalry fighting vehicles: 386, 389
*Cavalry Journal*: 95
Cavalry Reconnaissance Troop, 82d: 167
Cavalry Reconnaissance Troop, Mechanized, 56th: 191–92
Cavalry reconnaissance troops: 402
Cavalry regiments: 5–6, 8, 12, 24, 28
  composition of: 54, 95, 112, 115, 125, 135, 137, 145, 147, 161
Cavalry regiments (units)
  1st: 123, 125
  1st, 1st Squadron: 334
  6th: 64
  9th: 99
  10th: 99
  15th: 64
Cavalry School: 99
Cavalry squadrons: 13, 21n35, 223, 382, 400
Cavalry troops: 6–7, 366
Chaffee, Maj. Gen. Adna R.: 23–24, 25
Chaffee, Brig. Gen. Adna R. 140n35, 147, 149, 150, 154
Chaparral-Vulcan battalions. *See* Antiaircraft weapons.
Chaplains: 4–5, 8–9, 10
Chemical companies: 122, 382, 383, 386, 389, 397, 410n40

# INDEX

Chemical detachments: 330
Chemical platoons: 122, 281, 307
Chemical warfare detachments: 135, 137
Cheney, Lt. Col. Sherwood A.: 74*n12*
Chickamauga National Park, Ga.: 16
Chief of artillery, divisional: 49, 55
Chief of Staff's Advisory Group: 236*n41*
China, U.S. forces in: 99
Chippewa, Battle of: 7–8
Chynoweth, Maj. Bradford G.: 126
Civil War: 12–16
Clark, Maj. Gen. Mark W.: 172, 259*n29*
Clarke, Lt. Gen. Bruce C.: 253, 291, 293
Clifford, Clark: 338, 343
Coast Artillery Brigade, 101st: 153
Coast Artillery Corps: 29–30
Coast artillery districts: 31
Collier, Lt. Gen. John H.: 269
Collins, Maj. Gen. Harry J.: 190
Collins, General J. Lawton: 240, 247
Colorado National Guard units: 217, 395
Columbus, N. Mex.: 35
Combat Arms Regimental System (CARS): 281, 290*n49*, 390, 409*n25*
Combat car squadrons: 125
Combat command headquarters in armored divisions: 163, 185, 205*n54*, 224, 225, 227, 265, 267
Combat Developments Command: 306, 312, 338, 353–54, 359
Combat electronic warfare intelligence (CEWI) battalions. *See* Military intelligence battalions.
Combat service support system
   armored divisions: 185
   infantry divisions: 223
   Modernization Board: 127, 129, 130, 131
   World War II: 181–82
Combined arms (motorized) battalions: 400
Command and control battalions (airborne divisions): 272, 274, 277
Command and General Staff College: 265, 270, 271
Command and General Staff School: 135
Command headquarters (division): 309, 312
   34th: 312
   35th: 312
   43d: 312
   51st: 312
   55th: 312
   79th: 312, 329
   94th: 312, 329
   96th: 312, 329
   103d: 312, 329
Commissaries: 4–5, 10, 17, 24–25, 28

Commissaries of muster and subsistence: 14
Commissaries of subsistence: 12, 14
Communications, divisional: 28, 84, 94, 129, 131, 132, 198–99, 267, 270, 272, 335. *See also* Signal units.
Communications equipment: 30, 35, 84, 122–23, 267, 335, 382–83, 425–26
Conductors of military stores: 5
Confederate Army: 15–16
Connecticut National Guard units: 243, 312
Conner, Maj. Gen. Fox: 52, 90, 94, 130
Conrad, Col. Casper H.: 80
Continental Army: 3–6, 20*n2*
"Continental Army" plan: 37
Continental Congress: 6–7
Cook, Maj. Gen. Gilbert R.: 141*n46*, 236*n41*
Corps: 9, 12–13, 14, 15–17, 21*n34*, 24, 49, 54, 67–69, 71, 117, 120, 181–82, 392
   I: 68
   V: 422
   VII: 422
   X (Civil War): 15
   XVIII (Civil War): 15
   XXV (Civil War): 15
   IV (War with Spain): 17–18
   V (War with Spain): 17–18, 422
Corps area commanders: 100, 101, 109–10
Corps areas: 87, 97, 99, 100, 116
   Second: 99, 110
   Fourth: 100, 120
   Eighth: 98–99, 132, 135
   Ninth: 99
Cowles, Lt. Gen. Donald H.: 370, 380
Craig, General Malin: 109, 126, 127, 129, 130, 132, 133, 236*n41*
Crosby, Maj. Gen. Herbert B.: 112, 115
Cuba: 18, 307

Dahlquist, General John E.: 252–53, 271, 276
Danford, Maj. Gen. Robert M.: 160–61
Davidson, Maj. Gen. Garrison H.: 270
Davis, Dwight F.: 115, 122, 123
Davis, Brig. Gen. Richmond P.: 110–11
Davison, General Michael S.: 359
Davy Crocketts. *See* Nuclear weapons, tactical.
Dearborn, Maj. Gen. Henry: 7–8
Decker, General George H.: 296, 298, 300, 307–08
Defense, U.S. Department of: 305, 308, 309, 338, 340–41, 361, 364, 383, 397
Demobilization
   after the Civil War: 16
   after the Korean War: 250–51
   after the war in Vietnam: 343–44
   after the War of 1812: 9

Demobilization—Continued
  after World War I: 79, 80–81, 83, 97
  after World War II: 199–200, 207–08, 211–13
Departments
  Central: 31, 34
  Eastern: 31
  Panama Canal: 115
  Southern: 31, 34, 35, 36–37
  Western: 31
Depot brigades: 60, 76*n32*
Depot divisions: 68–69, 71, 73
DePuy, General William E.: 325, 380
Devers, General Jacob L.: 163, 184, 187, 207, 224
Dick Act of 1903: 25
Dickinson, Jacob M.: 29
Dickman, Maj. Gen. Joseph T.: 23–24, 79, 83
District of Columbia National Guard: 43*n12*
Division, 2d (Provisional): 132
Division, Hawaiian: 99, 112, 121, 155
Division, Panama Canal: 99, 111, 112, 115
Division, Philippine: 99, 111–12, 158, 212
Division-86: 383–84, 386, 389–90
Division artillery
  aircraft for: 199, 227, 337
  ATFA–1: 265, 267
  headquarters batteries for: 144, 159, 169–70, 181, 269
  in heavy divisions: 382, 383, 384, 386, 401
  in light divisions: 392–93, 397, 400
  ROAD: 296–97
  ROCID: 277
  ROTAD: 274
  World War II: 181, 194–96, 198
Division Restructuring Study (DRS): 379–80, 382–84, 407
Division trains. *See by type of division.*
Divisions (1913)
  1st: 34
  2d: 34
  3d: 34
Divisions (World War I). *See also by type of division.*
  10th: 65, 99, 213, 250, 251, 253, 279
  11th: 65, 99
  12th: 65, 99
  14th: 65
  17th: 65
  20th: 65
Divisions, base and training: 54, 65, 67, 68
Divisions, heavy: 380, 382–83, 384, 386, 389, 395, 400–403, 407, 417, 425
Divisions, light: 390–91, 392–95, 397, 400–403, 409*n36*, 417
Divisions, light (World War II): 187–88, 190,

Divisions, light (World War II)—Continued
  203*n27*
  10th: 188, 190
  71st: 188, 190
  89th: 188, 190
Divisions, National Army
  designations of: 57–58
  as sources of manpower for Regular Army: 62
Divisions, replacement and school: 65
"Doctrinal and Organizational Concepts for Atomic-Nonatomic Army During the Period of 1960–1970": 270–72, 281, 291
Dominican Republic: 323, 329
Douglas, Ariz.: 98
Doyen, Brig. Gen. Charles A.: 61
Draftees. *See also* Army of the United States; "National Army" units.
  Black: 62–63, 66, 170
  Civil War: 15
  and Korean War: 243
  Puerto Rican: 64
  reserve service requirements for: 222
  training of: 57, 60, 170, 243
  in Vietnam: 325
  World War I: 55, 57, 58, 60, 62
Dragoon regiments: 10, 11
Dragoons: 21*n23*
Dragoons, 2d: 10
Drum, Maj. Hugh A.: 52, 90, 94, 110, 111
Duane, William: 9
Dunn, Winfield: 361
"Dusters." *See* Antiaircraft weapons.

Eckhardt, Maj. Gen. George S.: 325
Eddleman, General Clyde D.: 253, 277, 293, 297, 298, 300, 303, 319*n7*
Edwards, Brig. Gen. Clarence E.: 60
Edwards, Maj. Gen. Idwal: 181–82
Eisenhower, General Dwight D.: 200, 213, 225, 229, 250
Electronic warfare companies. *See* Military intelligence battalions.
Ellison, Maj. Frederick A.: 74*n12*
Ely, Lt. Col. Hanson E.: 74*n12*
Engineer battalions (divisional)
  1990s: 425
  for armored division: 149–50, 163
  Army of Excellence: 392–93, 397
  ATFA–1: 265, 267, 269
  Division Restructuring Study: 382
  Field Service Regulations of 1905: 24
  Field Service Regulations of 1910: 28
  Modernization Board: 127, 131, 132, 133
  pentomic divisions: 276–77

# INDEX

453

Engineer battalions (divisional)—Continued
  post–World War II: 225, 227, 229
  ROAD: 296, 300, 384
  ROTAD: 272
  World War I: 49
  World War II: 181, 185, 194–96, 199
Engineer battalions (nondivisional): 383
Engineer bridge companies: 163, 185, 269, 300, 382
Engineer brigades (corps): 392, 425
Engineer companies: 25, 35, 122–23, 185, 281, 303, 307, 325, 326, 338, 340, 366, 402
Engineer officers: 24–25, 28, 55
Engineer regiments: 38, 52–53, 54, 84, 85, 92, 223
Engineer squadrons: 135, 137, 147, 172
Engineer trains: 33, 38, 84, 92
Engineer units: 54, 68
Engineers: 12, 14, 17
Engineers, 310th: 69
Enlisted Reserve Corps: 37
Equipment shortages: 8, 58, 64, 122–23, 152, 172, 309, 326, 328–29, 333, 337, 347, 354–55, 361, 366, 370
Estridge, Col. Oliver: 122
Evans, Brig. Gen. Robert K.: 29
Exercise divisions: 424
Exercises
  BLUE BOLT: 267
  FOLLOW ME: 267
  REFORGER: 337
  SAGEBRUSH: 267, 269, 270
Expeditionary Division, 1st. *See* Infantry Division, 1st.
Experimental Mechanized Force: 122

Far East Command: 211, 212, 239, 240, 242, 247–48, 249–50, 259*n*29
Farnsworth, Col. Charles S.: 90
Field armies: 27, 28–30
Field Army, First: 28–29
Field Artillery, 6th: 52
Field artillery battalions (units)
  63d: 241
  321st: 167
  907th: 167
Field artillery batteries: 225, 227, 229, 239, 274, 276
Field artillery brigades: 14, 28, 38, 49, 52–53, 54, 55, 57–58, 68, 69, 84–85, 120, 159, 392
Field artillery brigades (units)
  2d: 61
  71st: 153
Field artillery companies: 6–7, 10–11, 12
Field artillery guns
  3-inch: 38, 48, 52–53, 65

Field artillery guns—Continued
  37-mm.: 85, 131
  75-mm.: 67, 71, 85, 112, 120, 121, 130–31, 144, 161
  Civil War: 13–14, 16
  horse-drawn: 65, 85
  Mexican War: 11
  "Napoleon": 13–14
  Revolutionary War: 4, 5
  stock-trail gun carriage: 11
  truck-mounted: 65, 121
Field artillery regiments: 24, 28–29, 38, 43*n*8, 48, 52–53, 65, 71, 84–85, 115–16, 149–50
Field hospital companies: 94
Field hospital units: 52–53
Field hospitals: 24, 25, 30
  331st: 69
  337th: 69
Field Manual, 100–5, *Operations*
  1982: 384
  1986 392, 411*n*53
*Field Service Regulations, United States Army*: 121
  1905: 23–24, 25
  1910: 27–30, 31
  1914: 34
Finance companies: 354–55, 356, 357, 386
Fire direction control centers: 144, 196, 198, 277, 335
"First Team." *See* Cavalry Division, 1st.
Flags
  Civil War units: 16, 18
  divisional: 111, 215, 422–23
  National Guard units: 215
  regimental: 390
  War with Spain: 18
Florida National Guard units: 100–101, 215, 255–56, 312
Fonesca, Pfc. David: 160
Food service companies: 274
Forage masters: 4–5
Foreign garrisons, military personnel needed for: 87
Forges, traveling: 4–5
Forts. *See also* Camps.
  Amador, Panama Canal Zone: 252
  Belvoir, Va.: 397
  Benning, Ga.: 99, 126, 150, 159, 232, 243, 251, 253, 279, 281, 306–07, 316, 326, 337–38, 355–56, 361, 373, 395, 421, 423
  Bliss, Tex.: 64, 98, 147, 354–55
  Bragg, N.C.: 167, 212, 232, 344, 397, 423
  Campbell, Ky.: 208, 212, 232, 253, 274, 332, 344, 423
  Carson, Colo.: 251, 284, 305, 325, 332, 338,

Forts—Continued
  344, 355, 366, 372, 423
  Chaffee, Ark.: 254, 305, 307
  Devens, Mass.: 232, 281, 306, 324, 325
  Drum, N.Y.: 154, 395, 423
  Hood, Tex.: 212, 232, 305, 306, 307, 330, 344, 346, 357, 359, 366, 367, 382–83, 386, 421, 422, 423
  Sam Houston, Tex.: 64, 99, 112
  Huachuca, Ariz.: 170
  Irwin, Calif.: 306, 423
  Jackson, S.C.: 243
  Knox, Ky.: 123, 125, 150, 338, 356, 365, 373, 423
  Leavenworth, Kans.: 25, 27–28, 33, 395, 409*n32*
  Lewis, Wash.: 212, 232, 251, 327, 346, 355, 391, 421, 422, 423
  George G. Meade, Md.: 122
  Ord, Calif.: 180, 243, 253, 279, 312, 338, 364, 395
  Polk, La.: 305, 364, 422
  Richardson, Alaska: 252, 312, 346, 395, 422
  Riley, Kans.: 57, 99, 154, 251, 325, 337, 343, 344, 366, 423
  D.A. Russell, Wyo.: 112
  Sill, Okla.: 232
  Stewart, Ga.: 307, 364, 423
  Wainwright, Alaska: 312, 346
  Leonard Wood, Mo.: 243
Foss, General John: 380, 383
France
  army. *See* French Army.
  and weapons for U.S. units: 67, 68
French Army: 74*n4*
  and mechanization: 121–22, 125
  as model for World War I army corps: 68–69
Froehlke, Robert F.: 361
Fuller, J. F. C.: 120, 122
Fuller, Lt. Gen. Marvin D.: 382–83
Funston, Maj. Gen. Frederick: 35, 36–37

Galveston, Tex.: 29–30, 34
Garrison, Lindley M.: 37
General Board, U.S. European Theater of Operations (ETO): 222–24
General Headquarters (GHQ), United States Army: 117, 120
General Organization Project (World War I): 52–53, 53, 54–55, 65
*General Policies and Regulations for the Organized Reserves* (Special Regulations No. 46): 101
*General Regulations for the United States Army* (1821): 9

General Reserve: 212–13, 242–47, 250, 252
General Service Schools: 87, 90
General Staff College: 87, 90
Georgia National Guard units: 100–101, 215, 255–56, 361, 365
German Army: 125, 184
Germany
  equipment stockpiled in: 305
  occupation forces in: 208, 211, 232
  U.S. forces in: 99, 246–47, 249, 253, 279, 303, 305, 308, 337, 344, 355, 365, 366–67, 389–90, 422–23
  and World War I: 65
Gillem, Col. Alvan C.: 147
Glen Springs, Tex.: 36
Glider artillery battalions: 196
Glider field artillery battalions
  321st: 167
  907th: 167
Glider infantry, 327th: 167
Glider infantry regiments: 193, 194–96
Graves, Col. William A.: 74*n12*
Great Britain, and World War I: 47–49, 53, 64, 65, 68, 69
Greenlief, Maj. Gen. Francis S.: 361
Griswold, Lt. Gen. Oscar W.: 225
Ground surveillance companies. *See* Military intelligence battalions.
Guadalcanal: 187
Gulick, Lt. Col. John W.: 90, 107*n50*
Gun regiments: 52–53, 65
GYROSCOPE program: 252–53, 254, 274, 279

Haines, General Ralph E.: 330, 334
Haislip, Lt. Gen. Wade H.: 236*n41*
Hall, Brig. Gen. William E.: 236*n41*
Hammond, Col. Greed G.: 107*n50*
Harbord, Maj. Gen. James G.: 71, 99
Harmon, Maj. Gen. Ernest N.: 184
Harney, Col. William S.: 11
Hartzog, General William W.: 425
Hawaii: 31, 99, 107*n49*
  infantry regiments from: 65
  National Guard units: 65, 155, 284, 332, 340, 355
  units sent to: 159, 251, 305, 326, 332, 343, 344, 355
Hawaiian Department: 155
Headquarters, armored groups: 198, 205*n54*, 224
Headquarters, special troops: 94, 95, 135, 137, 182, 227
Headquarters defense platoons: 181, 182
Heavy weapons companies: 144. *See also* Infantry regiments.

# INDEX

Heavy weapons troops: 191. *See also* Cavalry regiments.
Heintzelman, Maj. Stuart: 90, 94
Helicopters. *See also by type of aviation unit.*
  AH–1 (Cobra): 361
  in Korean War period: 248
  in Vietnam: 335
Hersey, Col. Mark L.: 74*n12*
Hibbs, Maj. Gen. Louis E.: 212
Hickey, Lt. Gen. Thomas F.: 274, 276
High mobility multi-purpose wheeled vehicles (HMMWVs): 393, 400
Hines, Maj. Gen. John L.: 110
Hitler, Adolph: 125
Hodges, Maj. Gen. Courtney H.: 160–61
Holbrook, Maj. Gen. Willard: 64
Honest John rockets: 271, 274, 277, 282, 296–97, 298, 300, 305, 307, 308, 309, 324, 354–55
Hooker, Maj. Gen. Joseph: 13
Hospitals: 129, 132. *See also* Medical regiments.
Howitzer companies: 92. *See also* Infantry regiments.
Howitzers
  3.8-inch: 38
  4.7-inch: 54, 65
  6-inch: 48, 65
  8-inch: 277, 282, 296, 298, 300, 382, 386, 401
  75-mm.: 67, 122–23, 125, 127, 130–31, 145, 147, 167, 180, 188, 191, 196, 202*n8*
  75-mm. (horse): 95
  105-mm.: 122–23, 127, 129, 130–31, 144, 145, 147, 163, 172, 180–81, 191, 196, 198, 199, 202*n8*, 223, 224, 227, 239, 265, 267, 269, 272, 274, 276, 277, 282, 296, 298, 303, 307, 314, 337, 393, 397, 400
  155-mm.: 52–53, 54, 71, 85, 92, 112, 115–16, 120, 130–31, 144, 161, 181, 191, 199, 223, 227, 229, 269, 274, 276, 277, 282, 296, 298, 300, 307, 314, 335, 337, 356, 375*n12*, 382, 386, 393, 397, 402
  British: 54
  French: 54
  mobility of: 54, 92, 112, 196, 198
  motorized: 65, 71, 77*n45*, 84–85, 112
  self-propelled: 122–23, 125, 163, 180, 198, 202*n8*, 223, 227, 267, 282, 296, 298, 386, 402
  towed: 180–81, 191, 223, 282, 298, 300, 375*n12*, 393, 400
Howze, Lt. Gen. Hamilton H.: 314
Howze, Maj. Gen. Robert L.: 269
Howze Board: 314, 316, 318

Hughes, Maj. Gen. John H.: 126, 127, 129, 141*n46*
Hull, General John E.: 255
Humphreys, Maj. Gen. Andrew A.: 27

Idaho National Guard units: 403
Illinois National Guard units: 159–60, 214–15, 243–44, 246, 251, 255–56
Independent Cavalry Brigade (1911): 29–30
Indiana National Guard units: 367, 424
Indiantown Gap Military Reservation, Pa.: 244
Individual replacement system: 252–53
Infantry battalions: 4, 111–12, 122, 144, 265, 269, 296, 297, 298, 300, 307–08, 309, 323–24, 325, 326–27, 330, 332, 334–35, 336, 337–38, 341, 344, 346, 350*n34*, 351*n48*, 354, 355, 366, 374*n5*, 380, 382, 392–93, 397, 400
Infantry Board: 126
Infantry brigades
  composition of: 3–5, 6–7, 8–9, 10–11, 12, 16–17, 24–25, 28, 29–30, 35, 38, 47–48, 52–53, 84, 120, 281, 284, 325, 326, 355–56
  designations for: 5, 12, 14, 16, 28, 57–58
  eliminated from division structure: 127
  numbers of: 286, 309, 353–59, 361
  provisional: 24
  reinforced: 117, 120
  staffs for: 3, 4–5, 6–7, 8–9, 10, 12, 14, 17, 49, 55, 84
Infantry brigades (units)
  1st: 281, 306. *See also* Airborne infantry brigades, 1st.
  2d: 281, 306. *See also* Airborne infantry brigades, 2d.
  4th: 98, 106*n42*
  8th: 98, 109–10, 111–12
  10th: 98, 109–10, 111–12
  11th: 326, 331–32, 334
  12th: 98, 109–10, 111–12
  14th: 98, 109–10, 111–12, 117
  16th: 99, 109–10, 111–12, 117
  18th: 99, 109–10, 111–12, 117
  27th: 395, 402
  29th: 284, 312, 328, 332, 338, 343, 355
  30th: 361
  32d: 359, 361
  36th: 329
  37th: 424
  39th: 341
  40th: 341
  41st: 328, 365, 370
  48th: 361, 365
  49th: 328

Infantry brigades (units)—Continued
 51st: 159–60
 53d: 312, 314
 58th: 367, 397
 67th: 312, 314, 328
 69th: 312, 328, 332, 338, 344
 73d: 367
 76th: 424
 81st: 359, 361, 400, 403, 410n44
 86th: 312, 314
 92d: 115, 153, 284, 312, 402
 93d: 115, 153
 116th: 367, 397
 157th: 312, 340–41, 370, 402, 424
 171st: 312, 338, 346
 172d: 312, 338, 346, 356, 373, 395
 185th: 63
 186th: 63
 187th: 312, 340–41, 370, 402, 424
 191st: 312, 341
 193d: 307, 312, 338, 356, 372–73, 402, 423
 196th: 325, 329–30, 331, 334, 346
 197th: 306–07, 312, 337–38, 355–56, 361, 364–65, 373, 402, 421–22
 198th: 306–07, 330–31, 334
 199th: 326, 334, 336, 421, 422, 423
 205th: 312, 340–41, 370, 395, 424
 218th: 361
 256th: 341, 365
 258th: 284, 312, 314
Infantry Center: 307
Infantry Division, 1st
 between the world wars: 79, 81, 98, 109–10, 111, 112, 117
 in Germany: 227, 232, 246–47, 366–67, 423
 as mechanized division: 344
 reorganized (1939): 133, 143
 round-out units for: 364
 and training maneuvers, 1940: 143–45
 in Vietnam: 323–24, 335, 350n37
 and World War I: 52, 57–58, 60–61, 67, 68, 72
Infantry Division, 2d
 between the world wars: 79, 81, 98, 99, 106n42, 112, 117, 120, 126
 composition of: 61, 98
 elements of inactivated: 422
 elements moved: 423
 in Korea: 240–41, 246, 249–50, 251, 346, 400–401
 organized: 60–61
 post–Korean War: 279, 332
 post–World War II: 212–13, 232
 reorganized: 133, 143, 346
 and training maneuvers, 1940: 143–45

Infantry Division, 2d—Continued
 used for organizational studies: 126, 130–31, 132, 316
 and World War I: 67, 68
Infantry Division, 3d
 1990s: 422–23
 and ATFA–1: 267, 269
 between the world wars: 79, 81, 98, 109–11, 112, 117, 120
 in Europe: 253, 279, 303, 305, 337, 355
 and Korean War: 241–42, 246, 249–50, 251
 organized: 62
 post–World War II: 208, 212–13, 232
 reorganized: 133, 143
 and World War II: 187
Infantry Division, 4th
 1990s: 423
 between the world wars: 79, 81, 98, 117, 120, 121
 in Germany: 246–47, 305, 366–67, 389–90
 inactivated: 98
 motorization of: 121, 150, 163, 172, 182
 organized: 62
 reactivated: 147, 222
 reorganized: 182, 184, 243, 327, 344, 355, 403
 round-out units for: 364
 in Vietnam: 327, 330–31
 and World War I: 68
Infantry Division, 5th
 1990s: 422
 activation of: 133, 143, 222, 244
 between the world wars: 79, 81, 98, 117, 120
 elements of sent to Vietnam: 324, 325, 328, 332
 in Europe: 251, 253
 inactivated: 98, 250, 279
 motorization of: 121
 organized: 62
 post–World War II: 208, 212–13
 reorganized: 306–07, 364–65, 402
 and training maneuvers, 1940: 143–45
 units of activated: 344
 units attached to: 338
Infantry Division, 6th
 1990s: 423
 activated: 133, 143, 332
 between the world wars: 79, 81, 98, 117, 120
 element of activated: 326
 inactivated: 98, 232, 254, 338, 422
 in Korea: 211
 motorized: 172
 organized: 62
 reactivated: 243, 395, 397
 reorganized: 182, 402

# INDEX 457

Infantry Division, 6th—Continued
  and training maneuvers, 1940: 143–45
Infantry Division, 7th
  1990s: 423
  between the world wars: 81, 98, 117, 120
  inactivated: 98, 346, 422
  in Japan: 232, 239, 240, 241
  in Korea: 211, 241–42, 246, 251, 279, 284, 308, 346
  motorized: 172
  and Operation JUST CAUSE: 403
  organized: 62
  reactivated: 147
  reorganized: 308, 364–65, 395
  round-out units for: 370
  World War II: 180
Infantry Division, 8th
  1990s: 422
  between the world wars: 99, 117, 120
  in Europe: 279, 303, 305, 308, 337, 355
  motorized: 172
  organized: 62
  post–Korean War: 251
  reactivated: 147, 243
  reorganized: 159, 182
  and Siberian Expedition: 66
  and World War I: 73
Infantry Division, 9th
  between the world wars: 99, 117, 120
  in Europe: 251
  inactivated: 208, 284, 421
  organized: 65
  reactivated: 147, 222, 325, 355
  reorganized: 402, 403
  used for organizational tests: 391, 400
  in Vietnam: 334, 343, 350*n37*
Infantry Division, 24th. *See also* Division, Hawaiian.
  1990s: 423
  in Germany: 279, 303, 305, 308, 337, 344
  in Japan: 232, 239, 240
  in Korea: 240, 241, 245–46, 247–48, 251, 258*n17*, 279
  organized: 155
  post–World War II: 213
  reorganized: 364–65, 383, 402
  in Southwest Asia: 421–22
Infantry Division, 25th
  1990s: 423
  in Hawaii: 251, 252, 326, 361
  in Japan: 232, 239
  in Korea: 240, 246, 249–50
  organized: 155, 156
  post–World War II: 213
  readiness of: 305

Infantry Division, 25th—Continued
  reorganized: 279, 355, 395
  in Vietnam: 326–27, 330, 343, 344
Infantry Division Forward, 1st: 422
Infantry divisions
  command and control of: 83, 84, 127, 129, 130, 131, 132, 133, 144–45, 185, 198, 224, 227, 269, 282, 297
  motorized: 150, 172, 179, 180, 182, 184
  road space required for: 24, 33–34, 38, 40, 92
  stationing of: 31, 98–99, 112, 117, 120, 133, 150, 212, 243, 252, 306, 338, 340, 344, 422–23
Infantry divisions, composition of
  AIM: 355
  Army of the Potomac: 12–13, 14
  ATFA–1: 265, 267, 269
  between the world wars: 120, 135, 144–45
  Division Restructuring Study: 380, 382–84
  *Field Service Regulations* of 1905: 24–25
  *Field Service Regulations* of 1910: 27–28, 29–30
  Infantry School proposal (1950s): 264
  Korean War period: 247
  Lassiter Committee: 91–92, 94–95
  Mexican War: 10, 11–12
  Modernization Board: 127, 129–33
  pentomic: 276–77, 281–82, 284, 286
  Pershing proposal: 87, 90
  post–World War II: 223, 416–17
  Punitive Expedition: 35
  Revolutionary War: 3, 5
  ROAD: 296–98, 308, 309, 314, 335, 346–47, 353–54, 382, 384
  square: 47–48, 55, 57, 58, 60, 72–73, 83, 85–86, 87, 90, 91–92, 94–95, 125–26, 127, 414, 415, 416
  Stimson Plan: 33
  Superior Board recommendations: 84–86
  triangular: 24, 33, 90, 94, 125–26, 127, 135, 143–44, 161, 170, 247, 264, 415–16
  in Vietnam: 326–27
  War of 1812: 7–8
  War with Spain: 16–17
  World War I: 47–49, 52–53, 54, 55, 83
Infantry divisions, designations for
  air assault divisions: 356
  airmobile divisions: 334–35
  Civil War: 14, 16
  and designations for brigades: 57–58, 306–07, 322*n44*
  *Field Service Regulations* of 1910: 28
  Mexican War: 12
  post–World War II: 212–13, 217

Infantry divisions, designations for—Continued
   priorities for: 213, 422–23
   territorial: 99
   used for replacement training centers: 222
   World War I: 57–58
   World War II: 156
Infantry divisions, numbers of: 364–65, 403, 421–24
   after the war in Vietnam: 325, 332–33
   between the world wars: 86–87, 97–98, 101, 104
   post–Korean War: 252, 254, 279, 284, 286
   post-Vietnam: 346, 353–57, 361
   post–World War II: 207, 208, 212
   World War I: 55, 57–58, 64, 73
   World War II: 169, 179, 192, 193, 207
Infantry divisions, staff
   ATFA–1: 265, 267, 269
   chief of staff: 24–25, 28, 49, 55
   Civil War: 12, 14
   *Federal Service Regulations* of 1905: 24–25
   *Federal Service Regulations* of 1910: 28
   Mexican War: 12
   Modernization Board: 129, 132
   organization of: 67
   post–Revolutionary War: 6–7
   Revolutionary War: 3
   ROCID: 282
   War of 1812: 9
   War with Spain: 17
   World War I: 49, 55, 67
   World War II: 181
Infantry divisions, strength
   1917: 38
   1940: 144–45, 150, 155, 161
   1943: 180–82
   1945: 196, 199
   1946: 211–12
   1970s: 353–54
   ATFA–1: 265, 267, 269
   between the world wars: 81, 98, 106*n42*, 127, 132, 133
   *Federal Service Regulations* of 1910: 28
   and General Board (ETO): 223
   Infantry School proposal (1950s): 264
   in Japan: 239
   and Lassiter Committee: 91–92, 95
   Mexican border buildup, 1911: 30
   Modernization Board: 127, 132, 133
   motorized divisions: 166
   pentomic divisions: 276–77, 282
   Pershing proposal: 87, 90
   post–Korean War: 252
   post–World War II: 212
   Revolutionary War: 5

Infantry divisions, strength—Continued
   ROCID: 282
   Stimson Plan: 33
   Superior Board recommendations: 85
   War with Spain: 17
   World War I: 49, 52–53, 67, 71
   World War II: 180–81
Infantry divisions, tables of organization
   1917: 37–38
   1940: 169–70
   1942: 161
   1943: 180–82
   1945: 96, 198–99
   Lassiter Committee: 92, 95
   post–Korean War: 252
   post–World War II: 222–23, 225, 227, 252
   ROAD: 298
   ROCID: 276–77, 279, 282, 284, 286
   World War I: 49, 55
Infantry divisions (units)
   10th: 250, 251, 253, 279. *See also* Mountain Division, 10th.
   23d: 252, 254, 331, 332, 334, 335
   24th. *See* Infantry Division, 24th.
   25th. *See* Infantry Division, 25th.
   26th: 58, 60, 67, 68, 100, 159–60, 214, 341, 367, 400, 423–24
   27th: 68, 100, 159, 214, 255–56
   28th: 68, 100, 159, 214, 243, 246–47, 250–51, 328, 367, 400, 423–24
   29th: 214, 340, 397, 401
   30th: 68, 100, 152, 159, 214, 255–56, 361
   31st: 58, 69, 71, 100, 101, 159, 214, 243, 250–51
   32d: 58, 68, 79, 100, 159, 214, 305, 307
   33d: 58, 68, 79, 100, 159–60, 214
   34th: 58, 71, 100, 187, 214, 312
   35th: 58, 68, 100, 214, 312, 395, 401
   36th: 58, 100, 159, 214, 328
   37th: 58, 100, 159, 214, 243–44, 246, 250–51
   38th: 58, 71, 100, 214, 328, 367, 400, 424
   39th: 58, 69, 71, 100–101, 214
   40th: 58, 69, 71, 100, 115, 211, 214, 243, 244–46, 249, 255–56, 361, 401
   41st: 58, 60, 62, 67, 68, 69, 71, 100, 152, 159, 214, 328
   42d: 60, 67, 68, 79, 100, 190, 208, 214, 341, 367, 400, 423–24
   43d: 100, 159, 214, 243, 246–47, 250–51, 312
   44th: 100, 121, 152, 214–15, 243–44, 246, 250, 251, 255–56
   45th: 100, 152, 214, 215, 243, 244–46, 249, 250
   46th: 214

# INDEX

Infantry divisions (units)—Continued
  47th: 214, 243, 251, 328, 340, 367, 400
  48th: 214, 215, 255–56
  49th: 328
  51st: 214, 215, 312
  52d: 214, 220–21
  53d: 312
  55th: 312
  61st: 204*n36*
  62d: 204*n36*
  63d: 190, 255, 309, 329
  67th: 204*n36*
  68th: 204*n36*
  69th: 190, 251, 254
  70th: 190, 255
  71st: 252, 254
  72d: 204*n36*
  73d: 204*n36*
  74th: 204*n36*
  75th: 190, 255, 424
  76th: 58, 60, 69, 71, 101, 179, 217, 255, 372
  77th: 58, 60, 68, 101, 169, 217, 309, 329
  78th: 58, 60, 68, 101, 179, 255, 372, 424
  79th: 58, 60, 67, 101, 217, 309, 312, 329
  80th: 58, 60, 67, 68, 101, 217, 255, 372, 424. *See also* Airborne divisions, 80th.
  81st: 58, 60, 72, 101, 217, 309, 329
  82d: 58, 60, 68, 101, 166–67. *See also* Airborne Division, 82d.
  83d: 58, 60, 69, 71, 101, 217, 309, 329
  84th: 58, 60, 71, 101, 255, 424. *See also* Airborne divisions, 84th.
  85th: 58, 60, 69, 71, 101, 217, 255, 372, 424
  86th: 58, 60, 71, 101, 200, 208, 217
  87th: 58, 60, 71, 101, 217, 255, 424
  88th: 58, 60, 101, 211–12, 217, 232
  89th: 58, 60, 79, 101, 188, 203*n27*, 217, 255, 372
  90th: 58, 60, 79, 101, 172, 182, 217, 309, 329
  91st: 58, 60, 101, 217, 255, 372, 424
  92d: 62–63, 81, 107*n53*, 170, 220
  93d: 170, 220
  94th: 63–64, 101, 107*n53*, 217, 309, 312, 329
  95th: 66, 101, 200, 217, 255, 424
  96th: 66, 101, 217, 309, 312, 329
  97th: 66, 101, 170, 179, 190, 200, 217
  98th: 66, 101, 217, 255, 424. *See also* Airborne divisions, 98th.
  99th: 66, 101, 217, 306–07
  100th: 66, 101, 255, 305, 307, 372, 424. *See also* Airborne divisions, 100th.
  101st: 66, 101, 166–67. *See also* Airborne Division, 101st.
  102d: 66, 101, 217, 309, 329
  103d: 101, 107*n53*, 169, 217, 309, 312, 329

Infantry divisions (units)—Continued
  104th: 101, 107*n53*, 200, 217, 284, 424
  105th: 170
  106th: 190, 221
  107th: 170
  108th: 255, 424. *See also* Airborne divisions, 108th.
Infantry fighting vehicle, Bradley: 386, 389
Infantry regiments: 3–7, 14, 20*n3*, 28, 29, 33, 38, 48, 53, 54, 55, 57, 81, 92, 111–12, 127, 130–31, 160–61, 163, 180–81, 182, 198, 199, 225, 227, 247–48
Infantry regiments (units)
  5th: 188, 241
  6th: 147, 150
  9th: 61
  9th, 3d Battalion: 249–50
  14th: 188, 249–50
  15th, 3d Battalion: 249–50
  16th: 52
  16th, 1st Battalion: 350*n37*
  18th: 52
  21st, 3d Battalion: 346
  23d: 61
  24th: 99, 239, 249–50
  25th: 99
  26th: 52
  28th: 52
  28th, 3d Battalion: 367
  34th: 121, 159, 241, 249–50
  60th, 5th Battalion: 350*n37*
  65th: 242
  86th: 188
  87th: 188
  87th, 3d Battalion: 372, 402
  121st: 159
  124th: 159
  132d: 159–60
  133d, 2d Battalion: 332
  161st: 159
  182d: 159–60
  325th: 264
  327th: 167
  332d: 69
  339th: 69
  373d: 64
  374th: 64
  375th: 64
  376th: 64
  442d, 100th Battalion: 332, 355
  503d, 1st and 2d Battle Groups: 312
Infantry School: 87, 90, 126, 159
  divisional studies: 263–64
  support brigade: 281, 337–38, 355–56, 373
Influenza epidemics: 77*n59*

Ingles, Lt. Col. Harry: 133, 141*n46*
Insignia: 58, 62, 72, 111, 222
Inspectors general: 17, 24–25, 28, 30, 55
Inter-American Peace Force: 329
Iowa
   Army Reserve units: 340–41
   National Guard units: 217, 312, 332
Italy: 69, 198, 208, 211–12, 217, 232
Ives, Maj. J. Ross: 107*n50*
"Ivy Division." *See* Infantry Division, 4th.

Japan: 208, 211–12, 232, 239, 240–41, 244–46, 249, 279
Johnson, General Harold K.: 324, 326–27, 334
Johnson, Louis: 243, 332
Johnson, Lyndon B.: 323, 325, 329–30, 332
Joint Chiefs of Staff
   and airmobility of Army units: 316
   and Dominican Republic: 329
   and Korean War: 240, 243–44
Jones, Maj. Gen. Lloyd E.: 188
Joyce, Brig. Gen. Kenyon A.: 135, 145, 147
Judge advocates: 9, 25, 28, 55

Kansas National Guard units: 312, 332, 395
Kennedy, John F.: 291, 303, 318
Kentucky National Guard units: 383, 395
Kibler, Brig. Gen. A. Franklin: 222–23
Kilbourne, Brig. Gen. Charles E.: 120
King, Maj. Campbell: 90, 94
Knox, Henry: 7
Korea
   military advisory group in: 211
   occupation forces in: 208, 211, 232
   U.S. forces in: 239–56, 258*n17*, 279, 284, 286, 305, 308, 316, 318, 323, 332–33, 400–401, 422
Korean Augmentation to the United States Army (KATUSA) program: 240, 242, 284, 286, 308, 400–401, 418
Krueger, Maj. Gen. Walter: 132, 133

Laird, Melvin R.: 353
Lane, Capt. Arthur W.: 90
Lassiter, Col. William: 31, 87, 90
Lassiter Committee (1920): 90–92, 94–95
Leadership academies: 370, 372. *See also* Training divisions.
Lee, Maj. Gen. Charles: 3–4
Lee, Brig. Gen. William C.: 166
Legion of the United States: 6–7
Liddell Hart, Basil: 120, 122
Liggett, Maj. Gen. Hunter: 60
Light dragoons: 5–6
Light (Pack) Division, 89th: 188, 190. *See*

Light (Pack) Division, 89th—Continued
   *also* Infantry divisions, 89th.
Lincoln, Abraham: 12, 13
Litter battalions: 85. *See also* Medical regiments.
Little John rockets: 300, 305, 314, 316, 318
Lock, Maj. Morris E.: 74*n12*
Logan, Maj. James A.: 34
Lonning, Col. Stanley N.: 263
Louisiana National Guard units: 100–101, 361, 365
Lynch, Maj. Gen. George A.: 130
Lynch, Maj. Gen. George E.: 269

MacArthur, General Douglas: 60
   as Chief of Staff: 117, 120, 123, 126
   and Korean War: 240–42
   and World War II: 156, 158, 187, 191
McClellan, Maj. Gen. George B.: 12–13
McClure, Brig. Gen. Nathaniel F.: 33, 413
McElroy, Neil H.: 284
Machine Gun Battalion, 3d: 60
Machine Gun Battalion [Marines], 6th: 61
Machine gun battalions: 52, 55, 67, 84, 127, 145, 147
Machine gun companies: 33, 38, 48, 53, 67, 71, 84, 90, 92, 122, 130, 131
Machine gun squadrons: 95, 115, 135
Machine gun troops: 28, 112, 115, 125, 135, 137, 145, 161
Machine guns
   .30-caliber: 131, 167
   .50-caliber: 131, 144, 161
   air-cooled: 126
   antiaircraft: 67
   M60: 286, 305
McKinley, William: 16–17
McNair, Lt. Gen. Lesley J.: 130–31, 159, 160–61, 163, 166–67, 180, 181–82, 184–85, 187–88, 201, 416
McNamara, Robert S.: 303, 305–06, 307, 314, 316, 318, 325, 326, 328–29, 338, 340–41
McNarney, General Joseph T.: 169, 182, 188, 213–14
Magruder, Brig. Gen. Bruce: 147, 149, 150
Maintenance battalions: 163, 185, 223, 267, 269, 272, 296–97, 337, 382, 386, 393, 397, 400, 401
Maintenance companies: 229, 265, 338, 340, 380, 386
Maneuver area commands: 372
   75th: 255, 424
   87th: 255, 424
Maneuver Division (1911): 29–30, 34
Maneuver elements, interchangability of: 291, 296, 297–98, 303, 308, 309

# INDEX

Maneuvers, training
  1902: 25
  1904: 25
  1927: 112
  1940: 143–44
  General Headquarters (GHQ): 143–45, 147, 153, 154–55, 160, 161, 163, 173*n2*
  Louisiana: 143–45, 147, 173*n2*
  National Guard: 100–101, 361, 365
Mann, James Robert: 75*n31*
Mann, Brig. Gen. William A.: 40, 60, 75*n31*
March, General Peyton C.: 62, 80–81, 83, 86, 92, 95, 97, 98, 99
Marine Brigade, 4th: 60, 98
Marines
  5th: 60–61, 98
  6th: 61
Marsh, John O.: 409*n36*
Marshall, General George C.: 90, 94, 130, 133, 137, 143, 149, 150, 153, 154, 156, 158–59, 160–61, 166, 179, 180, 181–82, 190, 192, 194, 212, 416
Maryland National Guard units: 215, 367, 397
Massachusetts
  Army Reserve units: 312, 340–41
  National Guard units: 159–60
Materiel management centers: 354–55, 356, 357, 386, 393, 397, 401
Mechanization: 120–23, 125, 149
Mechanized Force: 123, 124
Mechanized Force Board: 122, 140*n35*
Mechanized infantry battalions: 365, 366–67, 402
  and AIM: 354, 355
  and Army of Excellence: 400–401
  in Army Reserve: 341
  and Division-86: 389
  and Division Restructuring Study: 380
  in Europe: 337
  National Guard: 309, 336, 351*n48*
  in Regular Army divisions: 344
  reorganized as infantry battalions: 324, 327
  and ROAD: 296, 297, 306, 307–08, 309, 384, 386
  and TRICAP/ACCB: 359
  in Vietnam: 325, 326–27, 332, 335, 336, 350*n37*
  weapons for: 374*n5*
Mechanized infantry divisions: 149–50, 293, 296–98, 306, 308, 336, 344, 353–55, 364, 380, 383, 389, 395
Medical battalions: 49, 129, 144, 150, 181, 185, 225, 277, 296–97, 382, 386, 389, 393, 397, 400, 401
Medical companies: 194–96, 225, 265, 269,

Medical companies—Continued
  272, 274, 281, 338, 340, 386
Medical detachments: 129, 194–96, 225, 239, 269
Medical regiments (divisional): 94, 112
Medical squadrons: 115, 135, 137, 147, 191
Medical units (early): 28, 30, 35, 115
Mediterranean theater: 190, 191
Meuse-Argonne campaign: 71, 72–73
Mexican Revolution: 29–30
Mexican War: 10–12
Mexico: 10–12, 29–30, 34–37, 64, 99
Meyer, General Edward C.: 379, 384, 389, 390, 391
Michigan National Guard units: 367
Miles, Maj. Gen. Nelson A.: 17
Military districts: 27
Military history detachments: 330
Military intelligence battalions: 384, 386, 389, 392–93, 397, 401, 410*n40*
Military intelligence brigades: 392
Military intelligence companies: 355, 402
Military intelligence detachments: 276, 330
Military personnel, shortages of
  for Army-86: 389–90
  between the world wars: 81, 111–12, 120, 147
  post–Korean War: 252, 256, 308
  post-Vietnam period: 361, 366
  post–World War II: 212, 221–22
  reserve units: 221–22, 367, 370, 372
  Revolutionary War: 3, 5
  in Vietnam: 326, 328–29, 347
  World War I: 71
  World War II: 172, 180, 182, 192, 198, 199
Military police
  ATFA–1: 267
  sources for: 33, 350*n34*
  World War I: 52–53, 84
Military police companies (divisional): 159
  Army of Excellence: 392–93, 397
  ATFA–1: 267, 269
  in brigades: 326
  General Board (ETO): 223
  in Japan: 239
  Lassiter Committee: 94
  Modernization Board: 131, 132
  motorized divisions: 163, 166
  post–World War II: 227, 239
  ROAD divisions: 296, 384
  World War II: 198–99
Military police groups: 392
Military police platoons: 161, 167, 181, 182, 194–96, 330
Militia brigades: 6–8, 10, 12, 16. *See also* National Guard.

Militia Bureau: 40, 57, 115, 116
Millikin, Maj. Gen. John: 188
Minnesota
   Army Reserve units: 312, 340–41
   National Guard units: 115, 153, 217, 243
Missiles
   Chaparral: 354–55, 389
   ENTAC: 297
   Lance: 354–55
   Redeye: 337
   Stinger: 389, 393
   TOW: 354, 374n5, 380, 382, 383, 386, 393, 397, 400
Mississippi National Guard units: 100–101, 243, 361
Missouri National Guard units: 312, 314, 395
Mitchell, Col. William (Billy): 91
Mobile, Ala.: 16
Mobile Afloat (Riverine) Force: 325
Mobility Requirements Board: 314
Mobilization planning: 414–15
   1970s: 370, 371–72
   after the War with Spain: 23–24
   between the world wars: 87, 98, 99, 101, 104, 115, 117, 120, 143–44,
   "come-as-you-are for war" mode: 370, 384, 386
   Korean War: 243–45, 254
   lack of: 30
   pre–World War I: 34–35, 38
   post–World War II: 214
   Stimson Plan: 31–34
Modernization Board: 127, 129–33, 135, 137, 141n46
Mohr, Maj. Gen. Henry: 370
MOMAR–1 (Modern Mobile Army 1965): 291, 293
Montana Army Reserve units: 312
Monterrey, Mexico: 10
Moore, Maj. Dan T.: 48, 52
Moore, Lt. Gen. James E.: 282
Mortar batteries: 272, 276, 277. *See also* Battle groups.
Mortar platoons: 282, 325, 335, 393
Mortars
   4.2-inch: 247–48, 265, 272, 282, 286, 335, 393
   60-mm.: 167
   81-mm.: 127, 131, 144, 147, 167, 247–48, 335
   Stokes: 54, 55, 67, 84–85
Moseley, Capt. George Van Horn: 31, 32
Motor repair sections: 112, 122
Motor vehicles
   armored: 122–23, 127, 150, 161, 163, 198

Motor vehicles—Continued
   armored personnel carriers. *See* Armored personnel carriers.
   half-track: 150
   HMMWVs: 393
   maintenance of: 129, 132
   numbers of: 95, 121, 150, 161, 182, 184, 277, 314, 318, 325
   repair of: 161, 163
   scout cars: 150
   variety of: 184, 185
Motorcycles: 95, 121, 161, 184, 185, 386, 389, 393
Motorization: 120–23, 126, 133, 172, 182, 184
Motorized divisions
   1940s: 163, 166
   1980s: 395, 397, 400
   4th: 172, 182, 184
   6th: 182
   8th: 182
   9th: 391
   90th: 182
Mountain Division, 10th: 190, 193, 200, 213, 395, 402, 409n36, 423, 425. *See also* Infantry divisions, 10th.
Murmansk Expedition: 69
Muster officers: 24–25, 28

Naco, Ariz.: 34
"National Army" units: 55, 80, 81
National Defense Act of 1916: 37, 55, 57, 65, 83
National Defense Act of 1920: 86–87, 95, 97, 99–100, 107n49, 109, 213–14, 234n16
National Guard
   allotment of units: 99–101, 214–15, 309
   command headquarters maintained: 312
   and Congress: 43n12, 213–14
   districts: 32, 36
   federalization of: 36, 37, 55, 58, 65, 152–53, 243–44, 246, 249, 250–51, 305, 332
   officer billets: 153, 214
   and pentomic divisions: 284, 286
   post–World War II reorganization of: 213–17
   round-out units. *See* Round-out units.
   Selected Reserve Force: 328–29, 341
   state units. *See by individual state*.
   troop basis: 214, 255–56
National Guard Association: 213–14, 215–16
National Guard Bureau: 100, 116, 153, 214, 215, 367
National Guard divisions
   between the world wars: 87, 97, 99–100, 101, 104, 115–16
   geographic bases for: 57

INDEX 463

National Guard divisions—Continued
  multistate: 215, 312, 338, 361, 367, 395
  numbers of divisions and brigades: 32, 37, 40, 57, 97, 152–53, 214, 246, 254, 284, 286, 309, 338, 340–41, 353, 359, 361, 367, 397, 423–24
  state. *See by individual state.*
National Guard of the United States: 214, 246, 251
National Guard units
  command arrangements: 215, 312, 338, 361, 395
  designations of: 57–58, 246
  draftees assigned to: 152–53
  federal recognition of: 115, 215
  and *Field Service Regulations* of 1905: 25
  missions of: 25, 32, 97, 214
  mobilization of (1940): 152–53
  preservation of historical continuity in: 214–15
  reorganized: 115–16, 158–60, 215, 220–22, 284, 309, 312, 314, 338, 340–41, 359, 361, 367, 395, 401–02
  replacements for federalized units: 246
  state. *See by individual state.*
"National" regiments: 29
National Security Act of 1947: 227
Nebraska National Guard units: 312, 395
Nevada National Guard units: 403
New Caledonia: 159
New Guinea: 187–88, 191
New Jersey National Guard units: 214–15, 367, 401
New Mexico National Guard units: 36, 217
New Orleans, La.: 16
New York National Guard units: 27, 32, 36, 115, 153, 214, 255–56, 367, 395
New York Times: 130
Nixon, Richard M.: 341, 344, 346
Nixon Doctrine: 346, 353
North African theater: 172, 179, 181–82, 184, 187–88, 190–91
North Atlantic Treaty Organization (NATO): 207, 246–47, 250, 307, 337, 344, 347, 359, 403
North Carolina National Guard units: 255–56, 361
North Dakota National Guard units: 217, 243
Nuclear battlefield: 263, 267, 270–71, 281–82, 286, 291, 293, 297, 298
Nuclear weapons, tactical: 207, 263, 270
  Davy Crockett: 297, 298, 308, 324, 337
  doctrine for the use of: 272, 298
  Honest John: 271, 274, 277, 282, 296–97, 298, 300, 305, 307, 308, 309, 324, 354–55

Nuclear weapons, tactical—Continued
  Little John: 300, 305, 314, 316, 318
  placement in military organizations: 263, 267, 271, 272, 274, 276–77, 279, 282, 293, 296–97, 308, 316, 318, 417
Nunn amendment: 366–67, 376*n31*

Observation squadrons: 125, 135, 137
Occupation forces: 207–08
  Austria: 208
  Germany: 208, 211
  Italy: 208
  Japan: 208
  Korea: 208, 211, 232
  Philippine Islands: 208
Officer billets
  Army Reserve: 284, 309, 312
  brigades: 281, 312
  divisions: 91, 129, 132, 133, 144–45, 185, 223, 224, 227
  General Board (ETO): 224–25
  Modernization Board: 129, 132, 133
  National Guard: 153, 214
  post–World War II: 224–25, 227
  ROAD: 296–97, 309, 312
  ROCID: 282
  ROTAD: 276
  shortages of: 17, 58
  training of: 58
Officers, lack of: 54–55
Ohio National Guard units: 243–44, 367, 424
Okinawa: 305, 309, 312, 323, 344
Oklahoma National Guard units: 215, 243
"Old Ironsides." *See* Armored Division, 1st.
"Old Reliables." *See* Infantry Division, 9th.
Oliver, Robert Shaw: 27
One Station Unit Training program: 372
Operations
  BIG LIFT: 305
  DESERT SHIELD/DESERT STORM: 403, 407, 421, 425
  JUST CAUSE: 403, 425
  TORCH: 179
Ordnance battalions: 150, 247, 277
Ordnance companies: 94, 125, 131, 132, 150, 163, 166, 167, 181, 182, 194–96, 281
Ordnance light maintenance company: 161
Ordnance maintenance companies: 94, 95
Ordnance maintenance platoon: 122
Ordnance officers: 12, 14, 17, 24–25, 28, 55, 92, 94
Ordnance troops: 135, 137
Oregon National Guard units: 403
Organized Reserve Corps: 37, 234*n16*
  cavalry divisions: 97–98, 101, 120, 170

Organized Reserve Corps—Continued
  infantry divisions: 97–98, 169–70, 217, 254
  missions: 97, 214
  organization of units: 101, 116–17, 169–70
  post–World War II reorganization of: 213–17
  strength: 87, 97–98, 109
  troop basis: 215, 217
  units: 166, 169–70, 215–17, 220–22, 229, 232
    use of designations for independent brigades: 306–07

Pack trains: 24, 25, 28, 33
Page, Maj. J. Watt: 107*n50*
Paladin: 425. *See also* Howitzers, 155-mm.
Palmer, General Bruce, Jr.: 338, 357, 359
Palmer, Lt. Col. John McAuley: 31, 48, 52
Panama Canal Zone: 99, 107*n49*
  infantry regiments from: 65
  U.S. forces in: 252, 307, 309, 333, 338, 356, 372–73, 402, 403, 423
Panzer divisions (German): 147, 149–50
Paper organizations
  field armies: 28–29
  infantry divisions: 98, 101, 104, 109–12, 120, 208, 344, 347, 356, 417–18
Parachute field artillery battalions: 193
Parachute Infantry Brigade, 1st: 169
Parachute infantry regiments: 166–67, 193, 194–96
  502d: 167
  504th: 167
Parachute maintenance companies: 194–96, 229
Parker, Maj. Gen. Frank: 122, 125–26
Parson, Maj. Gen. James K.: 130
Patch, Maj. Gen. Alexander M.: 159–60
Pathfinder teams: 193, 229
Patterson, Robert P.: 199
Paxon, Frederic L.: 81
Paymasters: 20*n2*
Pennsylvania
  Army Reserve units: 312, 340–41
  National Guard units: 32, 36, 243, 367
PENTANA. *See* "Doctrinal and Organizational Concepts for Atomic-Nonatomic Army During the Period of 1960–1970."
Pentomic divisions: 270–77, 279, 281–82, 284, 286, 288*n24*, *n27*, 291, 297, 303, 307–08, 318
Pershing, General John J.: 35, 36–37, 105*n17*
  as chief of staff: 94–95, 111
  and Lassiter Committee: 90, 91, 92, 94, 95
  and Superior Board: 83, 85–86, 87, 90, 105*n12*

Pershing, General John J.—Continued
  and World War I: 49, 52, 53, 54–55, 58, 60–61, 64, 65, 67–69, 71–72, 76*n32*, 79, 81
Personnel service companies: 265, 267, 382, 401
Peyton, Col. Philip B.: 141*n46*
Philippine Islands: 18, 99, 107*n49*
  militia in: 66
  occupation forces in: 208
  and Philippine Scouts: 99, 158, 212
  and World War I: 65–66
  and World War II: 152, 156, 158, 159
Photographic sections: 85, 112
Pioneer infantry: 27, 54, 66
Porter, Maj. Gen. Ray E.: 216
Powell, General Herbert B.: 293, 296, 298, 300, 303, 306
Preparedness movement: 32
Provisional Infantry Division (PID): 130
Provisional Tank Brigade: 147, 149, 150
Provost marshals: 24–25, 28, 33, 129, 131
Public information detachments: 330
Public Works Administration: 121
Puerto Rican Mobile Force: 153
Puerto Ricans, segregation of: 63–64, 242
Puerto Rico: 18, 99
  infantry regiment from: 57, 242
  National Guard units: 153, 221, 284, 402
  U.S. forces in: 252
Punitive Expedition: 35–37

Quakemeyer, Capt. John J.: 74*n12*
Quartermaster airdrop equipment companies: 397
Quartermaster battalions: 131–32, 133, 150, 161, 223, 227
Quartermaster companies: 125, 161, 181, 182, 194–96, 229, 277, 281
Quartermaster Corps: 33, 57, 150
Quartermaster light maintenance companies: 129, 132
Quartermaster service companies: 127, 129, 131
Quartermaster squadrons: 135, 137, 147
Quartermaster trains: 92, 112
Quartermasters: 4–5, 8–9, 10, 12, 14, 17, 20*n2*, 24–25, 28, 55

Racial integration of the Army: 249–50
Radar sections: 281
Radio intelligence platoons: 181. *See also* Signal companies.
Radiological centers: 284
Radios: 30, 84, 335
  excess of: 382–83
  FM: 267

# INDEX

Radios—Continued
  two-way: 122–23
"Rainbow Division": 60. *See also* Infantry divisions, 42d.
Ready Reserve: 255
Receiving companies: 284
Reckord, Maj. Gen. Milton A.: 107*n50*, 215–16
Reconnaissance
  air squadrons used for: 38, 85, 94
  aircraft used for: 30
  as cavalry mission: 48–49, 123, 127
Reconnaissance airborne assault vehicles: 300, 357
Reconnaissance and surveillance platoons: 277, 282, 284
Reconnaissance battalions: 149, 163, 227, 267, 269, 277
Reconnaissance companies: 163, 225, 229, 239, 265
Reconnaissance platoons: 194–96, 282, 297, 325, 393
Reconnaissance squadrons: 127, 131, 135, 137, 161, 172, 185, 248–49, 276–77, 282, 284, 288*n24*, 296–97, 298, 300, 309, 324, 335, 337, 382, 384, 386, 389, 393, 397, 400
Reconnaissance Troop, 99th: 306
Reconnaissance troops, brigades: 281, 303, 325, 326, 346
Reconnaissance troops, divisional: 144, 159, 161, 169–70, 182, 185, 191, 198–99, 272, 276, 425
Reed, Maj. Gen. George W.: 64
Regimental combat teams
  as basis of divisions: 252, 415
  eliminated: 281, 284
  Modernization Board: 129, 131
  World War II: 144–45, 172
Regimental combat teams (units)
  4th: 281
  5th: 241
  65th: 242
  187th: 274
  508th: 274
*Register of the Army, The* (1813): 8–9
Reinforcement battalions: 223
"Reorganization Objective Army Divisions (1961–1965)" (ROAD). *See by type of division.*
Replacement and school divisions: 54, 67, 68
Replacement companies: 225, 227, 229, 239
Replacement personnel
  post–World War II: 223, 270
  World War I: 62, 63, 68, 69, 71, 73, 76*n32*
  World War II: 179, 198

Replacement systems: 240, 241, 252–53. *See also* GYROSCOPE program.
Replacement training centers: 222, 249, 254–55, 284, 286
*Report on the Organization of Land Forces of the United States* (Stimson Plan): 31
Republic of Korea Army: 240, 250, 251, 271–72
Reserve command (armored divisions): 185, 227
Reserve Officer Training Corps (ROTC): 222, 418
Reservists, individual: 87, 97, 243
Resor, Stanley: 341
Return of Forces to Europe (REFORGER): 337. *See also* Exercises.
Revolutionary War: 3–7
Rhode Island National Guard units: 243
Rich, Lt. Gen. Charles W. G.: 316
Richards, Col. George C.: 107*n50*
Ridgway, General Matthew B.: 166, 193–94, 249–50, 252, 264–65, 270–71
Rifles
  automatic: 53, 67, 74*n14*, 180–81, 247–48, 305, 318, 325, 335
  Browning (BAR): 67, 74*n14*
  Garand: 129
  M14: 286, 305, 318, 325
  M16 (MX16E1): 318, 335
  recoilless: 198, 205*n57*, 247–48, 286, 300, 335, 354, 374*n5*
  semiautomatic: 122–23, 126, 129
Riverine operations: 325
ROAD divisions. *See by type of division.*
ROCAD (Reorganization of the Current Armored Division). *See* Armored divisions.
Rochenback, Brig. Gen. Samuel D.: 91
ROCID (Reorganization of the Current Infantry Division). *See* Infantry divisions.
Rockets
  air-to-ground: 314
  Honest John: 271, 274, 277, 282, 296–97, 298, 300, 305, 307, 308, 309, 324, 354–55
  Little John: 300, 305, 314, 316, 318
  multiple-launch: 401, 425
  surface-to-surface: 271
Roosevelt, Franklin D.: 154, 169
Root, Elihu: 23, 25
Rosson, Maj. Gen. William E.: 349*n20*
ROTAD (Reorganization of the Airborne Division). *See* Airborne divisions.
Round-out units: 337, 355, 357, 359, 361, 364–65, 370, 373, 395, 400, 402, 403, 410*n44*, 418, 421–22, 426
Rumbold, Col. Frank M.: 107*n50*

Russia: 65, 69, 74*n7*
Russian Army: 125

San Antonio, Tex.: 29–30
San Diego, Calif.: 29–30
Sanitary (collecting) battalions: 94. *See also* Medical regiments.
Sanitary trains: 38, 67, 85, 94
Saxe, Marshal Maurice de: 7
Schofield Barracks, Hawaii: 99, 112, 252, 326, 332, 338, 355, 361, 395, 423
Scott, Brig. Gen. Charles L.: 150
Scott, Maj. Gen. Hugh L.: 47–48, 49, 52, 62, 74*n7*
Scott, Maj. Gen. Winfield: 7–8, 9, 10–11
"Screaming Eagles." *See* Airborne Division, 101st.
Seaman, Maj. Gen. Jonathan O.: 324
Section V committee: 99–100, 107*n50*, 213–14, 254–55, 260*n42*
Segregation, racial
 blacks: 62–63, 66, 154, 170
 Civil War: 15
 Korean War: 242, 249–50
 Puerto Ricans: 63–64
Selected Reserve Force: 328–29, 341
Service batteries: 181, 182
Service companies: 131–32, 163, 184–85
Service troops, cavalry regiments: 95, 125
Service troops command, divisional: 129, 130, 131, 132
Services of Supply: 68, 69, 71
Sheridan, M551 armored reconnaissance vehicle: 300, 335, 361
Sheridan, Maj. Gen. Philip H.: 13
Ships, shortages of
 World War I: 55, 68
 World War II: 180, 182, 187–88, 191, 193
Short, Lt. Gen. Walter C.: 155
Siberian Expedition (1918): 66
Sibert, Brig. Gen. William L.: 52
Sicilian campaign: 193
Signal battalions: 28, 38, 49, 52–53, 198–99, 265, 267, 269, 272, 276–77, 296, 384, 392–93, 397
Signal brigades: 392
Signal companies: 24, 25, 28, 94, 127, 131, 132, 149–50, 181, 182, 359
Signal detachments: 127, 130
Signal officers (division staff): 24–25, 28, 55, 67
Signal platoons: 281, 326, 330
Signal troops: 95, 115, 135, 137
Signal units: 35, 68, 84, 335
Simonds, Maj. George S.: 74*n12*
Snow, Maj. Gen. William J.: 64

Snyder, Maj. Gen. Howard M.: 236*n41*
Solomon Islands: 187–88
South Carolina National Guard units: 215, 312
South Dakota National Guard units: 217
South Vietnamese Army: 323
Southwest Asia: 403, 407, 421
Southwest Pacific Area Command: 188, 190, 191
Sparks, Lt. Col. Leonard C.: 141*n46*
Special Forces Regiment, 1st: 409*n25*
Special weapons troops: 135, 137, 145, 161
Spragin, Brig. Gen. Robert L.: 188
Starry, General Donn A.: 383–84, 390–91
*Statement of Proper Military Policy* (1915): 37, 38
Steuben, Maj. Gen. Frederick Wilhelm von: 7
Stimson, Henry L.: 31, 32, 172, 190–91
Stimson Plan: 31–34, 36, 40
Stoneman, Brig. Gen. George: 13
Strategic Army Force (STRAF): 305–06, 307, 319*n21*, 325, 332, 338, 355–56, 357, 373
Strategic reserve units: 365
Strategic Striking Force: 212
Strength. *See by type of division and brigade.*
Sturgis, Lt. Gen. Samuel D., Jr.: 271
Summerall, Maj. Gen. Charles P.: 54, 74*n12*, 110, 112, 117, 122, 123, 126
Superior Board (AEF): 83–86, 87, 90, 94
Supply and service battalions: 357
Supply and transport battalions: 267, 269, 296–97, 337, 382, 386, 393, 397, 400, 401
Supply and transport companies: 265, 267, 269, 272
Supply battalions: 163, 185, 227
Supply columns: 24, 25, 28, 29, 30, 33
Supply companies: 33, 38, 48, 53, 92, 386. *See also* Infantry regiments.
Supply system, Modernization Board: 127, 129, 131–32
Supply trains: 38, 55, 121. *See also* Supply columns.
Support battalions: 303, 325, 326, 359, 370, 372, 386, 401–02, 425
Support command (divisional): 265, 267, 269–70, 296–97, 298, 354, 382, 384, 386, 389, 392–93, 397, 400
Support groups, divisional: 272, 274, 276
Surgeons: 10, 12, 17, 20*n2*, 24–25, 28
Surles, Maj. Gen. Alexander D.: 236*n41*
Swing, Maj. Gen. Joseph: 196

Tables of distribution and allowances: 312, 322*n43*
Tables of organization. *See also* Airborne divisions; Armored divisions; Cavalry

# INDEX

Tables of organization—Continued
    divisions; Cavalry regiments; Infantry divisions; Infantry regiments.
  creation of: 32–34
  motorized divisions: 150, 163
Tables of organization and equipment: 202*n14*. *See also* Air assault divisions; Airborne divisions; Armored divisions; Atomic Field Army; Infantry divisions; Training divisions.
Taft, William Howard: 25, 34
Tank battalions
  ATFA–1: 265, 267, 269
  Division-86: 386
  and Division Restructuring Study: 380
  General Board (ETO): 224
  heavy: 227, 229, 248–49, 267, 269
  light: 122, 163, 184–85
  medium: 163, 166, 227, 267, 269
  post–World War II: 225, 227, 239
  ROAD: 296, 297, 300, 306, 308, 309, 365
  ROCAD: 277
  ROCID: 276–77
  as round-out units: 355
  in Vietnam: 324, 327, 336
  World War II: 196, 199
Tank companies: 92, 94, 115, 121–23, 184–85, 191, 198–99, 239, 240, 303, 380, 382, 386, 402
Tank destroyer battalions: 154–55, 161, 166, 184, 196, 224
Tank guns
  75-mm.: 277
  90-mm.: 248, 252, 277
  120-mm.: 248
Tank units: 85
Tanks: 55, 122–23, 150, 184, 185, 277
  M1 Abrams: 389, 409*n20*
  M24: 239
  M41: 248–49
  M47: 248
  M48: 252
  M48A3: 324, 327, 335
  M60: 286, 305, 361, 389
  M103: 248
  T43: 248
Target acquisition batteries: 382, 383, 386, 389, 397, 425
Target acquisition systems: 380
Task forces
  6814: 159–60
  "A": 179
  Oregon: 330–31, 349*n20*
  Smith: 240, 252
Taylor, General Maxwell D.: 194, 270, 271–72,

Taylor, General Maxwell D.—Continued
  274, 276–77, 279, 286, 288n27, 291, 303
Taylor, Brig. Gen. Zachary: 10, 11
Tennessee National Guard units: 255–56, 361
Texas: 10, 34
  as division test site: 130, 135, 143–44
  National Guard: 36, 153, 361, 383, 401
Texas City, Tex.: 34
Tompkins, Maj. Gen. William F.: 199
Total Army Training Strategy: 424
TOW battalions: 380
TOW companies: 383, 386
Toyahvale, Tex.: 135
"Train and retain" programs: 325
Training
  advanced individual: 253, 254, 341, 370, 372
  air assault: 356
  airborne: 166, 167, 169, 190
  amphibious: 180, 187–88
  armored divisions: 150, 372
  Army Reserve units: 424
  artillery units: 68, 69
  artillerymen: 13, 52, 115
  basic: 152, 253, 254, 256, 286, 305, 325, 341, 370, 372
  combat support: 370, 372
  combined arms: 25, 86, 117
  conducted by divisions: 253, 254
  corps area responsibility for: 87
  draftees: 57, 60, 325
  in France, World War I: 52, 60, 68
  at garrison schools: 25
  lack of facilities for: 217
  lack of funding for: 212
  light divisions: 187–88
  machine gun units: 68, 84
  National Guard units: 25, 27, 87, 152–53
  officers: 24, 58, 222, 418
  One Station Unit Training (OSUT) program: 372
  Organized Reserves: 116–17, 170, 217, 222
  recruits: 52, 372
  of Regular and National Guard units together: 27
  for reservists: 116–17, 170, 217, 222, 256
  Scott's Regular Army brigade: 8
  and stationing of divisions: 117, 133
  use of Regular Army personnel for: 57, 87, 97
  War with Spain: 17–18
Training areas, World War I: 57, 58, 62
Training brigades: 372, 402–03
Training centers: 243, 250, 254, 305, 307, 327
Training divisions: 243, 244, 249, 254, 255, 256, 284, 286, 290*n49*, 305, 307, 309, 341, 370, 372, 402–03, 424

Training regiments: 284, 286, 290*n49*
Transportation
　animals used for. *See* Animals.
　assets: 28, 35, 95, 167, 169, 180, 298
　shortages of: 11, 30, 71, 180, 182
Transportation aircraft maintenance companies: 393
Transportation battalions: 276–77, 282
Transportation companies: 281
Trench mortar batteries: 52–53, 54, 84–85
Trench mortars: 48
TRICAP. *See* Cavalry Division, 1st.
Troop basis: 169, 170, 176*n55*, 190–92, 200
　Army Reserve: 255, 328–29
　National Guard: 214–15, 255–56, 309
Truck battalions (divisional): 127, 129
Truck companies, divisional: 131–32, 182, 282
Trucks: 121, 161, 163, 181, 188
Truman, Harry S.: 212, 215, 239, 240, 241–42, 243, 246–47, 249
Twaddle, Brig. Gen. Harry L.: 154, 158–59, 163, 169, 172

Union Army: 12–16
Union of Soviet Socialist Republics
　and Cold War: 207, 242–43, 303, 305
　and Cuba: 307
　and Europe: 246–47, 248, 353–54, 359, 386, 403, 407
Unit replacement system. *See* GYROSCOPE program.
United Nations forces in Korea: 240–41, 242
U.S. Air Force: 316, 318
U.S. Army, Alaska: 312, 346
U.S. Army, Caribbean: 254
U.S. Army, Europe: 253, 279, 336, 359, 366–67, 402, 422, 423
U.S. Army, Pacific: 312, 332, 343
U.S. Army, Vietnam: 324, 333, 334–35, 343
U.S. Army Airborne Command: 166–67, 169
U.S. Army Combined Arms Combat Development Activity: 409*n32*
U.S. Army Forces, Far East: 250, 259*n29*
U.S. Army Forces Command: 356, 364–65, 366, 370, 372, 400, 402–03, 424
U. S. Army Regimental System (USARS): 390
U.S. Army Training and Doctrine Command (TRADOC): 380, 383, 389–90, 397, 400–402, 425
U.S. Army Training Center, Field Artillery: 254
U.S. Congress
　and Army Reserve: 256
　and artillery regiments: 43*n8*
　and the Civil War: 12, 21*n34*

U.S. Congress—Continued
　and Korean War: 244–45, 246
　and Mexican War: 10
　and National Guard: 43*n12*, 152–53
　and Organized Reserve Corps: 222
　and post–Revolutionary War military establishment: 6–7
　and Stimson Plan: 31
　and universal military training: 221–22
　and War of 1812: 7–8
U.S. Constabulary: 211, 213
U.S. Continental Army Command (CONARC): 253, 269–70, 272, 274, 276–77, 279, 281–82, 284, 286, 291, 293, 298, 300, 303, 314, 316, 328, 341, 355–56
U.S. European Command: 196, 200, 211
U.S. European Theater of Operations, General Board: 222–24
U.S. Marine Corps: 60–61, 332
U.S. Navy, joint operations with: 325
Universal military training: 86, 87, 221–22

Van Voorhis, Col. Daniel: 123, 124
Vance, Cyrus R.: 307, 308, 309
Vera Cruz, Mexico: 34
Vermont National Guard units: 243, 312, 367
Veterinary companies: 94, 95
Veterinary troops: 33, 94, 191
Vietnam: 323–47
　redeployment from: 343–44, 346, 352*n57*
　U.S. forces in: 323–35, 337–38, 346–47, 350*n34*, *n37*, 357
Vietnam, Republic of: 323, 341
Virginia National Guard units: 314, 397
Volunteers: 7–8, 10–11, 12, 17–18, 20*n13*, 325
　divisions: 10–11
　and Korean War: 243
　and National Guard: 256
　as source for reserves: 222, 256

Wagner, Col. Arthur L.: 27
Wagon companies: 112, 121
Wagon drivers: 33
Wagon masters: 4–5, 8–9
Walker, Lt. Col. Kirby: 74*n12*
Walker, Lt. Gen. Walton H.: 225, 241, 248–49
"Walker Bulldog." *See* Tanks, M41.
Wallace, Brig. Gen. Fred C.: 163
Waller, William L.: 361
Walsh, Maj. Gen. Ellard A.: 213–14, 215–16
War, Col. Franklin W.: 107*n50*
War Department
　and black divisions: 220
　Circulars: 185, 187
　and Organized Reserve Corps reorganization,

# INDEX

War Department—Continued
    1946: 215–17
    and post–World War II policy: 213–14
War Department General Staff (WDGS)
    creation of: 23
    Operations Division (OPD): 159–60, 175*n38*
    Organization and Training Division: 229
    and reorganization of 1910: 27–28
    reorganization of 1942: 175*n38*, *n40*
    Special Plans Division: 199
    War College Division: 47–48, 49, 55, 57, 58, 63–64, 76*n32*
    War Plans Division: 63–64, 65, 80, 87, 95, 97, 99, 120
War of 1812: 7–9
War with Spain: 16–18
Washington, George: 3–5, 6, 20*n2*
Washington National Guard units: 355, 359, 361, 365, 400, 403
Weapons. *See* by specific type.
Weeks, John W.: 98, 101
Weibir, Lt. Gen. Walter L.: 254

Wells, Col. Briant H.: 48, 52, 90, 107*n50*
West German Army: 293, 296
Western hemisphere, defense of: 143–44
Westmoreland, General William C.: 323, 324, 325, 326, 327–28, 329–30, 331, 332, 334, 344, 346, 357
Weyand, General Frederick C.: 326–27, 367, 380
Wickham, General John A.: 391–93, 395, 397, 400–401
"Wildcat." *See* Infantry divisions, 81st.
Wilson, Lt. Col. Chalmer R.: 107*n50*
Wilson, Charles E.: 250–51, 252, 279
Wilson, Lt. Col. Guy M.: 107*n50*
Wilson, Woodrow: 34, 36, 52, 65, 66
"Wilson Divisions": 252
Wisconsin National Guard units: 359, 361
Wood, Maj. Gen. Leonard: 29, 30
Woodring, Harry W.: 117

Young, Maj. Gen. Robert N.: 252–53, 264